Fodor's

SCOTLAND

19TH EDITION

Where to Stay and Eat
for All Budgets

Must-See Sights
and Local Secrets

Ratings You Can Trust

Fodor's Travel Publications New York, Toronto, London, Sydney, Auckland
www.fodors.com

FODOR'S SCOTLAND

Editor: Emmanuelle Morgen

Editorial Production: Ira-Neil Dittersdorf
Editorial Contributors: Nick Bruno, James Gracie, Satu Hummasti, Beth Ingpen, Shona Main, Chris Townsend, and William Wallace
Maps: David Lindroth *cartographer;* Bob Blake and Rebecca Baer, *map editors*
Design: Fabrizio La Rocca, *creative director;* Guido Caroti, *art director;* Melanie Marin, *senior picture editor*
Production/Manufacturing: Angela L. McLean
Cover Photo (Glencoe): Giovanni Simeone/DIAF

COPYRIGHT

Nineteenth Edition

ISBN 1-4000-1273-2

ISSN 0743-0973

SPECIAL SALES

Fodor's Travel Publications are available at special discounts for bulk purchases for sales promotions or premiums. Special editions, including personalized covers, excerpts of existing guides, and corporate imprints, can be created in large quantities for special needs. For more information, contact your local bookseller or write to Special Markets, Fodor's Travel Publications, 1745 Broadway, New York, NY 10019. Inquiries from Canada should be directed to your local Canadian bookseller or sent to Random House of Canada, Ltd., Marketing Department, 2775 Matheson Boulevard East, Mississauga, Ontario L4W 4P7. Inquiries from the United Kingdom should be sent to Fodor's Travel Publications, 20 Vauxhall Bridge Road, London SW1V 2SA, England.

AN IMPORTANT TIP & AN INVITATION

Although all prices, opening times, and other details in this book are based on information supplied to us at press time, changes occur all the time in the travel world, and Fodor's cannot accept responsibility for facts that become outdated or for inadvertent errors or omissions. So **always confirm information when it matters,** especially if you're making a detour to visit a specific place. Your experiences—positive and negative—matter to us. If we have missed or misstated something, **please write to us.** We follow up on all suggestions. Contact the Scotland editor at editors@fodors.com or c/o Fodor's at 1745 Broadway, New York, New York 10019.

PRINTED IN THE UNITED STATES OF AMERICA

10 9 8 7 6 5 4 3 2 1

DESTINATION SCOTLAND

Many travel destinations, including the most visited and famous, merely impress you. Scotland is different; it sweeps you off your feet. Then it imprints itself on your heart. North Sea to Irish Sea, Highlands to Lowlands to islands, the landscapes of Scotland—wooded glens, windswept moors, rocky beaches, lochs as deep as the imagination—take your breath away, whether resplendent in sunlight or mysterious under the nation's storied, brooding skies. Urban travelers can spend days wandering about Edinburgh's medieval Old Town and stately Georgian New Town. And in Glasgow, the glorious Victorian architecture vies with lively arts and nightlife scenes for your attention. Mere minutes from both cities lies open land scattered with gardens and distilleries and rich with castles and grand country hotels such as golden, battlemented Inverlochy. Amid the antiques, crafts, fine woolens, and tartans for which Scotland is famous, shoppers rejoice. Tipplers toast the nation's many distilleries. And to anglers and golfers, heaven may be better than Scotland, but they'd need to see it to believe it. You're going to have a fabulous trip!

Karen Cure

Karen Cure, Editorial Director

CONTENTS

Maps

CloseUps

ON THE ROAD WITH FODOR'S

A trip takes you out of yourself. Concerns of life at home completely disappear, driven away by more immediate thoughts—about, say, what marvels will beguile the next day, or where you'll have dinner. That's where Fodor's comes in. We make sure that you know all your options, so that you don't miss something that's around the next bend just because you didn't know it was there. Because the best memories of your trip might well have nothing to do with what you came to Scotland to see, we guide you to sights large and small all over the country. You might set out to tour castles and medieval ruins, but back at home you find yourself unable to forget strolling across a windswept moor or peering into a deep, dark loch. With Fodor's at your side, serendipitous discoveries are never far away.

Our success in showing you every corner of Scotland is a credit to our extraordinary writers. Although there's no substitute for travel advice from a good friend who knows your style, our contributors are the next best thing—the kind of people you would poll for travel advice if you knew them.

Our Fife & Angus updater, **Nick Bruno,** is a freelance writer, photographer, and English-Italian translator living in Dundee. He contributes to many online and print publications, including wcities.com, the Dundee *Evening Telegraph,* and Moon Metro guides.

James Gracie, who updated the Borders and Edinburgh chapters, has worked as a travel writer for 11 years. His articles have appeared in the *Sunday Herald,* the *Daily Record,* and the *Highlander,* and in the Scottish magazines, *The Lady* and *The Herald.* He is the author of two guidebooks on Scotland and one on the Northumberland and Durham area of northern England. His most recent work is a travel/history book about the Granton area of Edinburgh.

The information in these pages is largely the work of **Beth Ingpen.** A longtime editorial contributor to *Fodor's Scotland,* Beth works as a freelance editor and writer. She was previously publishing manager with the Royal Society of Edinburgh, Scotland's premier learned society, and spent lunchtimes soaking up that city's culture, particularly in its art galleries and concert halls. Close to the sea, Beth's countryside house is set in the barley fields in the rural northeast.

Shona Main, the Glasgow updater, gave up law to be a journalist and now writes about travel, culture, social affairs, and politics for such publications as the *Press and Journal,* the *Scottish Sunday Express,* and the *Sunday Post Magazine.* When she's not keeping tabs on Glasgow's busy arts, music, shopping, and dining scenes, she travels to Italy, enjoying the contrasts and similarities between southern Italy and her native country.

Chris Townsend, the Northern Highlands updater, spends much of his time exploring the walking paths and seeking out the quiet corners around his home in the Highlands. He is the author of two Ramblers' Guides, one about the Isle of Skye, the other about Ben Nevis and Glen Coe.

Willie Wallace has visited nearly 40 countries and lived in seven of them, but he always returns to his beloved native Scotland, where he has a home on the Isle of Arran. He applied his knowledge of Western Scotland to the Argyll & the Isles chapter. Wallace created and maintains several travel Web sites about Scotland, and he occasionally writes travel articles for Scottish and Irish publications.

ABOUT THIS BOOK

	There's no doubt that the best source for travel advice is a like-minded friend who's just been where you're headed. But with or without that friend, you'll have a better trip with a Fodor's guide in hand. Once you've learned to find your way around its pages, you'll be in great shape to find your way around your destination.
SELECTION	Our goal is to cover the best properties, sights, and activities in their category, as well as the most interesting communities to visit. We make a point of including local food-lovers' hot spots as well as neighborhood options, and we avoid what's touristy unless it's really worth your time. You can go on the assumption that everything you read about in this book is recommended wholeheartedly by our writers and editors. Flip to On the Road with Fodor's to learn more about who they are. It goes without saying that no property mentioned in the book has paid to be included.
RATINGS	Orange stars ★ denote sights and properties that our editors and writers consider the very best in the area covered by the entire book. These, the best of the best, are listed in the Fodor's Choice section in the front of the book. Black stars ★ highlight the sights and properties we deem Highly Recommended, the don't-miss sights within any region. Fodor's Choice and Highly Recommended options in each region are usually listed on the title page of the chapter covering that region. Use the index to find complete descriptions. In cities, sights pinpointed with numbered map bullets ❶ in the margins tend to be more important than those without bullets.
SPECIAL SPOTS	Pleasures & Pastimes focuses on types of experiences that reveal the spirit of the destination. Watch for Off the Beaten Path sights. Some are out of the way, some are quirky, and all are worth your while. If the munchies hit while you're exploring, look for Need a Break? suggestions.
TIME IT RIGHT	Wondering when to go? Check On the Calendar up front and chapters' Timing sections for weather and crowd overviews and best days and times to visit.
SEE IT ALL	Use Fodor's exclusive Great Itineraries as a model for your trip. (For a good overview of the entire destination, follow those that begin the book, or mix regional itineraries from several chapters.) In cities, Good Walks guide you to important sights in each neighborhood; ⚑ indicates the starting points of walks and itineraries in the text and on the map.
BUDGET WELL	Hotel and restaurant price categories from £ to £££££ are defined in the opening pages of each chapter—expect to find a balanced selection for every budget. For attractions, we always give standard adult admission fees; reductions are usually available for children, students, and senior citizens. Look in Discounts & Deals in Smart Travel Tips for information on destination-wide ticket schemes.
BASIC INFO	Smart Travel Tips lists travel essentials for the entire area covered by the book; city- and region-specific basics end each chapter. To find the best way to get around, see the transportation section; see individual modes of travel ("By Car," "By Train") for details. We assume you'll check Web sites or call for particulars.

ON THE MAPS	Maps throughout the book show you what's where and help you find your way around. Black and orange numbered bullets ❶ ❶ in the text correlate to bullets on maps.
BACKGROUND	In general, we give background information within the chapters in the course of explaining sights as well as in CloseUp boxes and in Understanding Scotland at the end of the book. To get in the mood, review the suggestions in Books & Movies.
FIND IT FAST	Within the book, chapters are arranged in a roughly south to north direction after the first two chapters, which cover Edinburgh and Glasgow. Except for these two, chapters are divided into small regions, within which towns are covered in logical geographical order. Attractive routes and interesting places between towns are flagged as En Route. Headings at the top of each page help you find what you need within a chapter.
DON'T FORGET	Restaurants are open for lunch and dinner daily unless we state otherwise; we mention dress only when there's a specific requirement and reservations only when they're essential or not accepted—it's always best to book ahead. Hotels have air-conditioning, private baths, phones, and TVs, unless noted otherwise. We always list facilities but not whether you'll be charged extra to use them, so when pricing accommodations, find out what's included.

SYMBOLS

Many Listings

- ★ Fodor's Choice
- ★ Highly recommended
- ⊠ Physical address
- ✣ Directions
- 📫 Mailing address
- ☎ Telephone
- 📠 Fax
- 🌐 On the Web
- ✉ E-mail
- 🎟 Admission fee
- ⏲ Open/closed times
- ▶ Start of walk/itinerary
- 💳 Credit cards

Outdoors

- ⛳ Golf
- ⛺ Camping

Hotels & Restaurants

- 🏨 Hotel
- Number of rooms
- Facilities
- Meal plans
- ✕ Restaurant
- Reservations
- Dress code
- BYOB
- Hotel with restaurant that warrants a visit

Other

- Family-friendly
- Contact information
- ⇨ See also
- Branch address
- ☞ Take note

Scotland
Mainland
Kirkwall
Hoy
South Ronaldsay
Pentland Firth
ORKNEY ISLANDS
The North Sound
Westray
Sanday
Rousay
Birsay
Whitehall
Stronsay
Gurness Broch
Mainland
Shapinsay
Finstown
Kirkwall
Stromness
Rackwick
St. Mary's
Hoy
South Ronaldsay
Pentland Firth
Old Head
John o' Groats
Thurso
Port of Ness
OUTER HEBRIDES
Isle of Lewis
Stornoway
The Minch
Harris
Tarbert
Rodel
North Uist
Lochmaddy
The Little Minch
South Uist
Daliburgh
Barra
North Channel
HEBRIDES
Rhum
Cape Wrath
Durness
Kinlochbervie
Scourie
Lochinver
Ledmore Junction
Tongue
Golval
Thurso
John o' Groats
Wick
Latheron
Lairg
Bonar Bridge
Dornoch
Dornoch Firth
Tain
Ullapool
Laide
Poolewe
Kinlochewe
Shieldaig
Lochcarron
Inner Sound
Uig
Dunvegan
Portree
Isle of Skye
Broadford
Kyle of Lochalsh
Ardvasar
Mallaig
Glenfinnan
Achnasheen
Dingwall
Cromarty
Moray Firth
Tore
Nairn
Inverness
Cannich
Invermoriston
Loch Ness
Invergarry
Spean Bridge
Laggan
Kingussie
Aviemore
HIGHLANDS
GRAMPIAN MOUNTAINS
Braemar
Elgin
Forres
Banff
Macduff
Buckie
Keith
Huntly
Fraserburgh
Peterhead
Ellon
Aberdeen
Banchory
Stonehaven
A857
A868
A859
A865
A855
A838
A836
A837
A835
A832
A897
A882
A9
A839
B9176
A896
A890
A831
A82
A87
A851
A830
A86
A96
A98
A95
A938
A920
A97
A90
A944
A93
A92

INNER
Tiree
Coll
Tobermory
Lochaline
Mull
Iona
Bunessan
ATLANTIC OCEAN
Colonsay
Port Askaig
Jura
Islay
0 20 miles
0 30 km
Duror
Loch Linnhe
Oban
Firth of Lorn
Arduaine
Lochgilphead
Tarbert
Kintyre
Campbeltown
Crianlarich
Inveraray
Tarbet
Helensburgh
Gourock
Greenock
Rothesay
Largs
Ardrossan
Brodick
Arran
Irvine
Firth of Clyde
Ayr
Prestwick
Kilmarnock
Girvan
Stranraer
Portpatrick
Luce Bay
Drummore
North Channel
NORTHERN IRELAND
SHETLAND ISLANDS
Herma Ness
Baltasound
Unst
Yell
Fetlar
Ulsta
Hillswick
Toft
Hamnavoe
Brae
St. Magnus Bay
Voe
Whalsay
Mainland
Walls
Scalloway
Lerwick
Levenwick
Sumburgh
Sumburgh Roost
Pitlochry
Blairgowrie
Perth
Crieff
Stirling
Kinross
Dunfermline
Falkirk
Glasgow
Paisley
Airdrie
Hamilton
Motherwell
East Kilbride
Kirkconnel
SOUTHERN UPLANDS
Newton Stewart
Castle Douglas
Dumfries
Solway Firth
Annan
Lockerbie
Moffat
Biggar
Peebles
Livingston
EDINBURGH
Dalkeith
Firth of Forth
Kirkcaldy
Glenrothes
Cupar
St. Andrews
Firth of Tay
Dundee
Forfar
Brechin
Montrose
Arbroath
North Sea
North Berwick
Dunbar
Duns
Berwick
Coldstream
Kelso
Jedburgh
Hawick
The Cheviot Hills
Alnwick
Newcastle
Carlisle
ENGLAND

Great Britain

REPUBLIC OF IRELAND
ENGLAND
WALES
FRANCE
LONDON
Belfast
Portadown
Armagh
Dublin
Keswick
Kendal
Isle of Man
Lancaster
Blackpool
Irish Sea
Middlesbrough
Whitby
Scarborough
York
Kingston-upon-Hull
Bradford
Leeds
Grimsby
Bolton
Manchester
Liverpool
Birkenhead
Doncaster
Holyhead
Llandudno
Sheffield
Skegness
Lincoln
Boston
The Wash
Cromer
Stoke-on-Trent
Nottingham
Derby
Norwich
Great Yarmouth
Stamford
Shrewsbury
Leicester
Peterborough
Wolverhampton
Lowestoft
Aberystwyth
Birmingham
Coventry
Cambridge
Bury St. Edmunds
St. George's Channel
Stratford
Northampton
Ipswich
Fishguard
Banbury
Harwich
Colchester
Gloucester
Oxford
Swansea
Newport
Pembroke
Bristol
Windsor
Cardiff
Reading
Canterbury
Bath
Maidstone
Bristol Channel
Dover
Tunbridge Wells
Folkestone
Barnstaple
Winchester
Reigate
Taunton
Salisbury
Southampton
Brighton
Strait of Dover
Yeovil
Bude
Dorchester
Portsmouth
Exeter
Bournemouth
Isle of Wight
Bodmin
Torquay
English Channel
Plymouth
Penzance
Falmouth
Scilly Isles
Land's End
0
50 miles
100 miles
0
50 km
100 km
150 km

World Time Zones

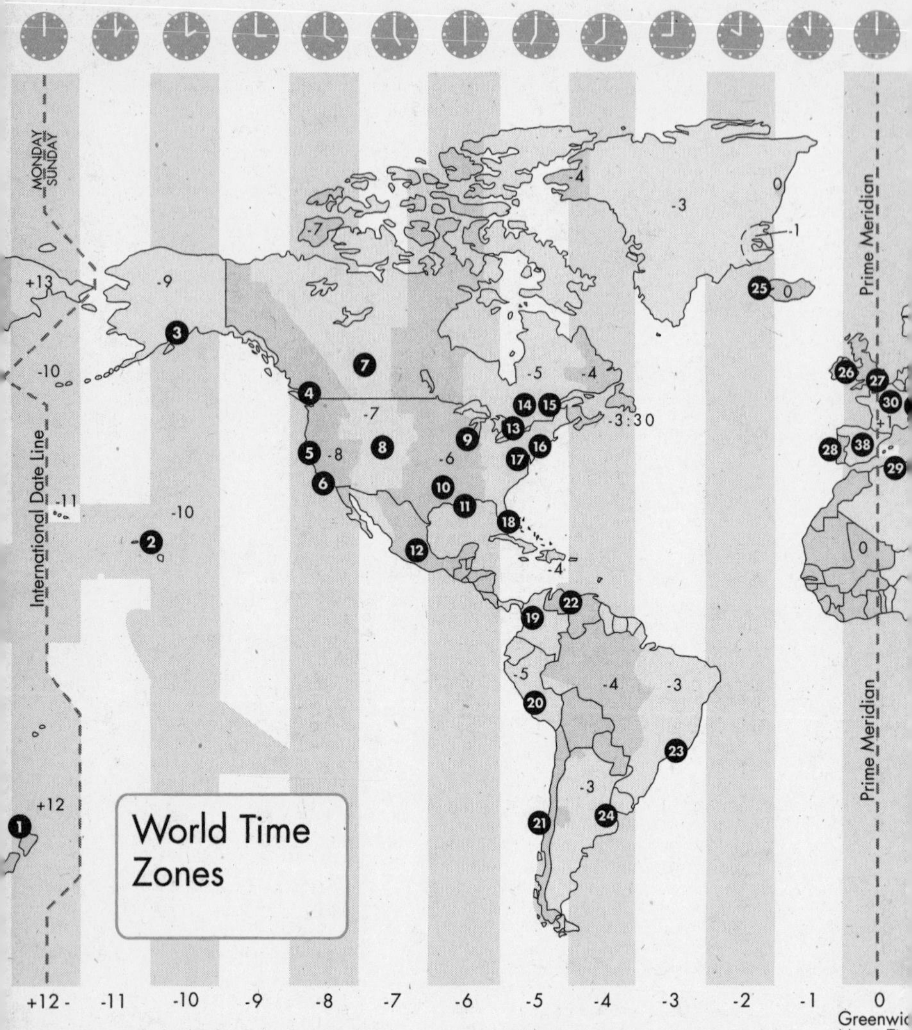

Numbers below vertical bands relate each zone to Greenwich Mean Time (0 hrs.). Local times frequently differ from these general indications, as indicated by light-face numbers on map.

Algiers **29**
Anchorage **3**
Athens **41**
Auckland **1**
Baghdad **46**
Bangkok **50**
Beijing **54**
Berlin **34**
Bogotá **19**
Budapest **37**
Buenos Aires **24**
Caracas **22**
Chicago **9**
Copenhagen **33**
Dallas **10**
Delhi **48**
Denver **8**
Dublin **26**
Edmonton **7**
Hong Kong **56**
Honolulu **2**
Istanbul **40**
Jakarta **53**
Jerusalem **42**
Johannesburg **44**
Lima **20**
Lisbon **28**
London (Greenwich) **27**
Los Angeles **6**
Madrid **38**

MONDAY
SUNDAY
International Date Line
+1
+2
+3
+4
+5
+6
+7
+8
+9
+10
+11
+12 -
-11

WHAT'S WHERE

Scotland's regions vary greatly in landscape and climate, from the Southwest's radiant gardens to the wind-beaten moors and cliffs of the Northern Isles. The paragraphs below mirror the organization of the chapters in this book, arranged in a roughly south to north direction, beginning with Scotland's two largest cities.

1 Edinburgh & the Lothians

Scotland's capital, on the south coast of the Firth of Forth, makes a strong first impression—Edinburgh Castle looming from the crags of an ancient volcano, the Royal Mile stretching from the castle to the Palace of Holyroodhouse, and Arthur's Seat, a small mountain with steep slopes and spectacular vistas over the city. Like Rome, Edinburgh is built on seven hills, and it has an Old Town district that retains striking evidence of a colorful history. The medieval Old Town, with its winding closes (narrow, stone-arched walkways) contrasts sharply with the Georgian New Town and its planned squares and streets. The Lothians—West Lothian, East Lothian, and Midlothian—spread out from Edinburgh, beckoning urbanites with getaways to pretty coastal towns, beaches, green hills, and castles.

2 Glasgow

Warm as a pint with friends but also bold and exuberant, Glasgow used to call itself the Second City—not of Scotland but of the British Empire. Commerce hummed and prosperity ruled through Victorian times, just before a long depression humbled the city's pride. These days the mood is upbeat again. Glasgow crackles with the energy of urban renaissance, complete with a thriving cultural life, and trendy stores and restaurants. And it's very proud of its buildings by two great homegrown architects, Charles Rennie Mackintosh and Alexander Thomson. With Glasgow less than an hour from Loch Lomond, Burns Country, and great golf on the Clyde Coast, it's easy to crown a trip into the country with a sophisticated dinner in the city.

3 The Borders & the Southwest

The Borders area comprises the great rolling fields, moors, wooded river valleys, and farmland that stretch south from Lothian to England. The Dumfries and Galloway region, south of Glasgow, is a hilly and sparsely populated area, divided from England by the Solway Firth. The county seat is Dumfries, associated with Robert Burns—he spent the last years of his life here—in much the same way that the Borders is tied to Sir Walter Scott.

4 Fife & Angus

Fife, northwest of Edinburgh, has the distinction of being the sunniest and driest part of Scotland. This area is one of sandy beaches, fishing villages, and windswept cliffs. Some 30 golf courses grace Fife, many of them seaside links with few if any windbreaks. The ultimate golf experience is a round on the Old Course at the Royal & Ancient Golf Club of St. Andrews. North of Fife is Angus, with the industrial port and main city of Dundee. Angus is renowned for its long glens and seacoast views, perfect for scenic hikes.

5 The Central Highlands

The main towns of Perth and Stirling are gateways to the Central Highlands, the rugged and spectacular terrain stretching north from Glasgow. This may not be the famed Highlands of the north, but there's plenty of wild country to be experienced, especially in the new Loch Lomond and the Trossachs National Park, Scotland's first. Here you'll find lush green woodlands and deep, shimmering lochs (*loch* is Scots for lake). Sir Walter Scott's poems about the area, including *The Lady of the Lake,* have ensured its popularity as a tourist destination.

6 Aberdeen & the Northeast

Aberdeen is a sophisticated port city built largely of glittering granite. To the west, the Grampian Mountains and the Cairngorms, beautiful regions of heather and forest, granite peaks, and deep glens, are ideal terrain for hill walking in warm weather and skiing in cold weather. Here, too, is that wonderland of castles called Royal Deeside, seat of Her Majesty's Balmoral Castle, plus a wealth of distilleries that make up the famous Malt Whisky Trail.

7 Argyll & the Isles

The Argyll area is a remote, sparsely populated group of islands in western Scotland. Oban, the hub of transportation for Argyll, is the main sea gateway for the Isle of Mull and the Southern Islands. Iona, near Mull, is Scotland's most important Christian site, with an abbey and a royal graveyard. The Isle of Islay is synonymous with whisky—it produces several malts. Jura is covered with wild mountains. Arran is more developed than most southern isles, with mist-shrouded mountains in the north and farmland in the south.

8 Around the Great Glen

The Great Glen is an enormous valley laced with rivers and streams, ringed by Scotland's tallest mountains and containing Scotland's greatest lochs, including the watery home of the fabled Loch Ness monster. Inverness, on the Moray Firth, is a major shipping port and the last substantial outpost as you head north. East of Fort William, Glen Nevis has Ben Nevis, Britain's highest peak. Serious climbers come from far and wide to scale it.

9 The Northern Highlands

The lore of the clans, the big skies, the immensity of the rolling moors—Scotland seems more intense here, in the remote and wild Northern Highlands. The great surprises are the changing terrain and the stunning effects of light and shade, cloud and sunshine, as well as the occasional rainbow. Sea inlets are deep and fjordlike, and the black shapes of the isles cluster like basking whales on the skyline. Gaelic-speaking natives on the Isle of Skye live in villages along the coast. The Outer Hebrides, also known as the Western Isles, arc outward to the Atlantic; this is possibly the most rugged part of Scotland, with frequent wind and rain, and an often inhospitable landscape where anything that grows seems a gift.

10 The Northern Isles

The nearly unceasing wind in the Northern Isles contributes to the feeling you've reached the end of the world. Orkney, a grouping of almost 70 islands, 20 of them inhabited, has the greatest concentration of prehistoric sites in Scotland, including phenomenally well-preserved standing circles, *brochs* (circular towers), and tombs. Shetland's islands have barren moors and dramatic vertical cliffs crowded with seabirds. Winter days are sometimes no more than five hours long, and beautiful summer days last almost 20 hours, with a persistent twilight known as the *simmer* (summer) dim.

GREAT ITINERARIES

A Heritage in Stone

7 to 10 days

Stone is a distinctive element of the Scottish landscape. On this tour you see it in many forms, on 18th-century Edinburgh streetscapes and in Aberdeen castles, in rural Angus and in Orkney's prehistoric monuments. Distilleries flourish, too: the stony soil makes for clear, mineral-rich water that is the basis for the nation's distinctive whiskies.

SOUTH OF ABERDEEN

2 or 3 days. Head toward Dundee to spectacular 17th-century Glamis Castle, the Queen Mother's childhood home. Heading north you'll see the remarkable Aberlemno sculptured stones on your way to Brechin, a market town whose cathedral is filled with antiquities. Crathes Castle, inland, has a classic tower and a garden of clipped yews. The south Deeside road, the B976 west of Banchory, is a much quieter alternative to the busier A93 heading west toward Balmoral Castle, a Victorian fantasy designed by Prince Albert and now a beloved retreat of Queen Elizabeth II. From there go north at Dinnet and drive west through Strathdon. Nearby are the ruined 13th-century Kildrummy Castle and its gardens, and to the northeast, across rich farmland, Oyne and the fascinating Archaeolink Prehistory Park. ⇨ Dundee & Angus *in* Chapter 4 and Royal Deeside & Castle Country *in* Chapter 6.

ORKNEY

3 or 4 days. From Aberdeen, take the eight-hour ferry ride north to Kirkwall on Mainland Orkney. Northwest of town are reminders of the area's long history, including the huge Maes Howe burial mound (circa 2500 BC) and Ring of Brogar, with three dozen immense standing stones. Nearby Skara Brae is a Neolithic village of stone houses first occupied three millennia ago; they're complete with stone beds, cupboards, and fireplaces. The Brough of Birsay, the ruined Earl's Palace, and the Gurness Broch, an Iron Age tower, are on your way as you circle back to Kirkwall. To the south, causeways link Orkney to the island of South Ronaldsay, site of the Italian Chapel, created by prisoners of war during World War II. From Stromness, ferry back to the mainland town of Scrabster, past the magnificent cliffs of Hoy. ⇨ Around Orkney *in* Chapter 10.

SOUTH TO EDINBURGH

2 or 3 days. From Scrabster drive south toward Wick, but follow signs for the Grey Cairns of Camster, two Neolithic chambered burial cairns. Proceed south to the behemoth Dunrobin Castle just south of unassuming Golspie, then on to Inverness. East of town, not far from the infamous battlefield at Culloden Moor, are the well-preserved early Bronze Age Clava Cairns, a burial complex, and Cawdor Castle, associated with Shakespeare's Macbeth. Travel south via Grantown-on-Spey over wild moorland to the main Deeside route close to the holiday resort of Ballater, where the buildings are all silver-gray stone. To the west, beyond 19th-century Balmoral Castle, is walled 17th-century Braemar Castle. Drive south from Braemar over the highest main road in Britain and down to Blairgowrie. Continue to Perth and Scone Palace, where early Scottish kings were crowned. Then head back to Edinburgh. ⇨ The Northern Landscapes in Chapter 9, Speyside & Loch Ness *in* Chapter 8, Royal Deeside & Castle Country *in* Chapter 6, Perthshire *in* Chapter 5.

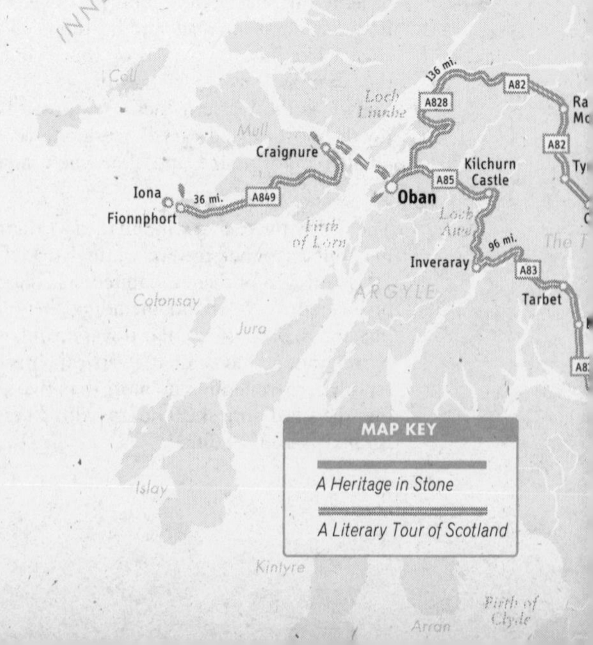

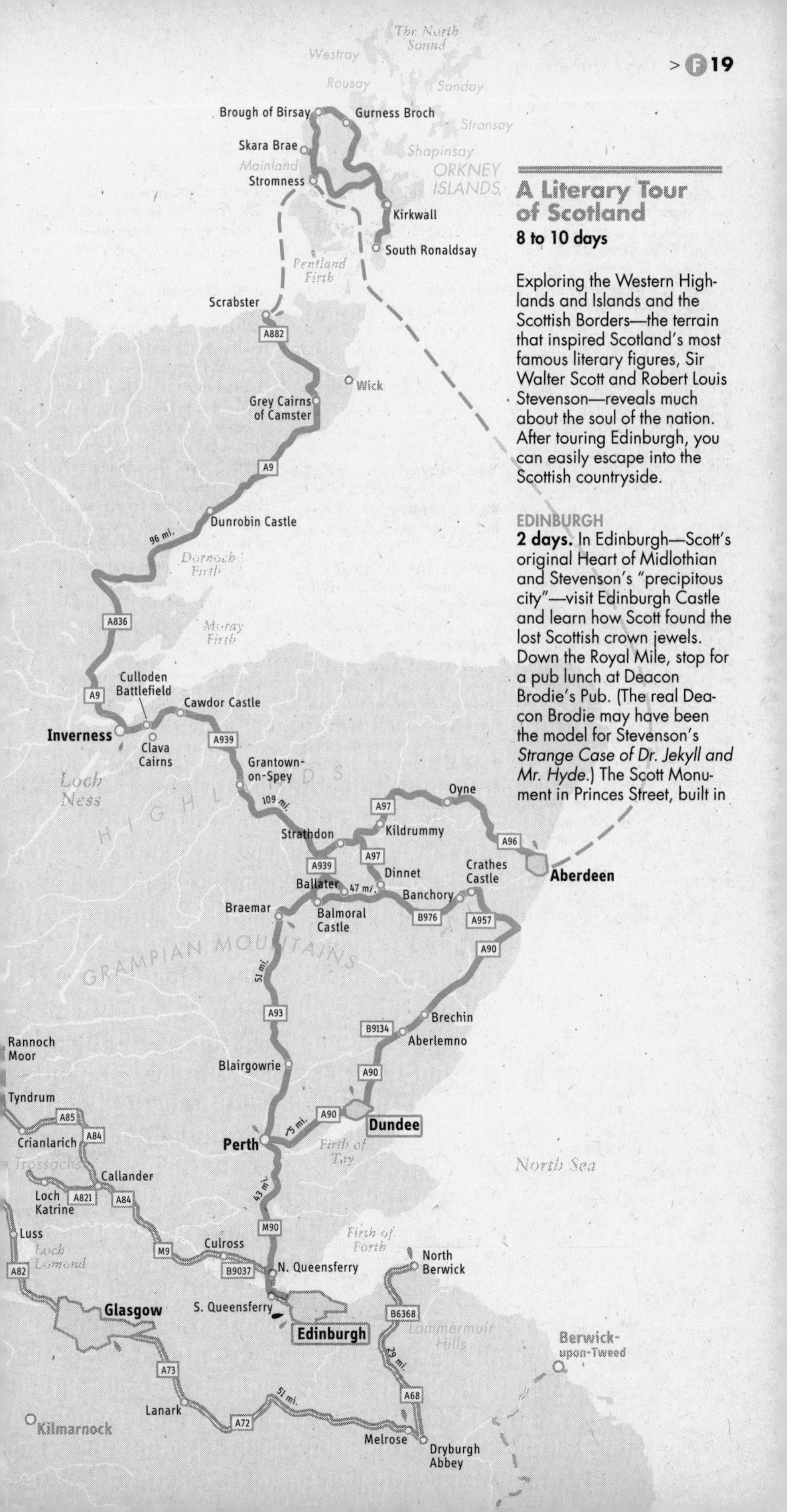

A Literary Tour of Scotland

8 to 10 days

Exploring the Western Highlands and Islands and the Scottish Borders—the terrain that inspired Scotland's most famous literary figures, Sir Walter Scott and Robert Louis Stevenson—reveals much about the soul of the nation. After touring Edinburgh, you can easily escape into the Scottish countryside.

EDINBURGH

2 days. In Edinburgh—Scott's original Heart of Midlothian and Stevenson's "precipitous city"—visit Edinburgh Castle and learn how Scott found the lost Scottish crown jewels. Down the Royal Mile, stop for a pub lunch at Deacon Brodie's Pub. (The real Deacon Brodie may have been the model for Stevenson's *Strange Case of Dr. Jekyll and Mr. Hyde*.) The Scott Monument in Princes Street, built in

1844 to commemorate the author, is an Edinburgh landmark. Take a morning to tour the Palace of Holyroodhouse, the queen's official residence in Scotland and scene of the triumphant visit by George IV in 1822, with Sir Walter Scott in charge of the publicity. Then take a bus to the pretty waterside village of Cramond, where you can visit the Cramond Inn, once the haunt of Stevenson. ⇨ Exploring Edinburgh & the Lothians and Side Trips from Edinburgh *in* Chapter 1.

INTO THE TROSSACHS

2 days. Drive to South Queensferry for magnificent views of the bridge over the Firth of Forth, and visit the 16th-century Hawes Inn, which put in an appearance in Stevenson's *Kidnapped.* Over the Forth Road Bridge and to the west is 18th-century Culross, another setting from *Kidnapped.* At Callander you are near the Trossachs. Scott's popular *Lady of the Lake,* published in 1810, put the place firmly on the map. *Rob Roy,* on the other hand, was set in countryside you can identify from cruises aboard the steam-powered SS *Sir Walter Scott,* which has sailed from the Trossachs Pier on Loch Katrine for a century. To the north, past Crianlarich and Tyndrum, you cross Rannoch Moor. In Stevenson's *Kidnapped,* redcoats pursued David Balfour and Alan Breck here, amid dramatic highland scenery. ⇨ Side Trips from Edinburgh *in* Chapter 1 and the Trossachs & Loch Lomond *in* Chapter 5.

AROUND ARGYLL

2 to 3 days. From Oban, the busy ferry port, cross over to the Isle of Mull. Near Fionnphort, to the southwest, is an area of Mull described in *Kidnapped.* The tiny Isle of Iona, accessible via ferry, was the burial place of Scottish kings in ancient times. Back on the mainland, en route to the head of Loch Awe, you'll pass ruined Kilchurn Castle. The drive south passes through beautiful countryside en route to the 18th-century planned town of Inveraray. ⇨ Around Argyll and Iona and the Isle of Mull *in* Chapter 7.

MELROSE & EAST LOTHIAN

2 to 3 days. Passing through Glasgow and Lanark, visit the market town of Melrose, epicenter of Scott Country. Here you will find the famous ruined abbey that was the setting for Scott's *Lay of the Last Minstrel,* and the poet's country home, Abbotsford House. Nearby Scott's View offers a panorama of the River Tweed and Eildon Hills. Dryburgh Abbey is also a must; the author is buried in this atmospheric ruin. The Lammermuir Hills extend north, into East Lothian, and the countryside east of Edinburgh is sometimes known as the Garden of Scotland. Stevenson set his novel *Catriona* along the coast here, around the small

MAP KEY

A Literary Tour of Scotland

Island-Hopping on the Western Seaboard

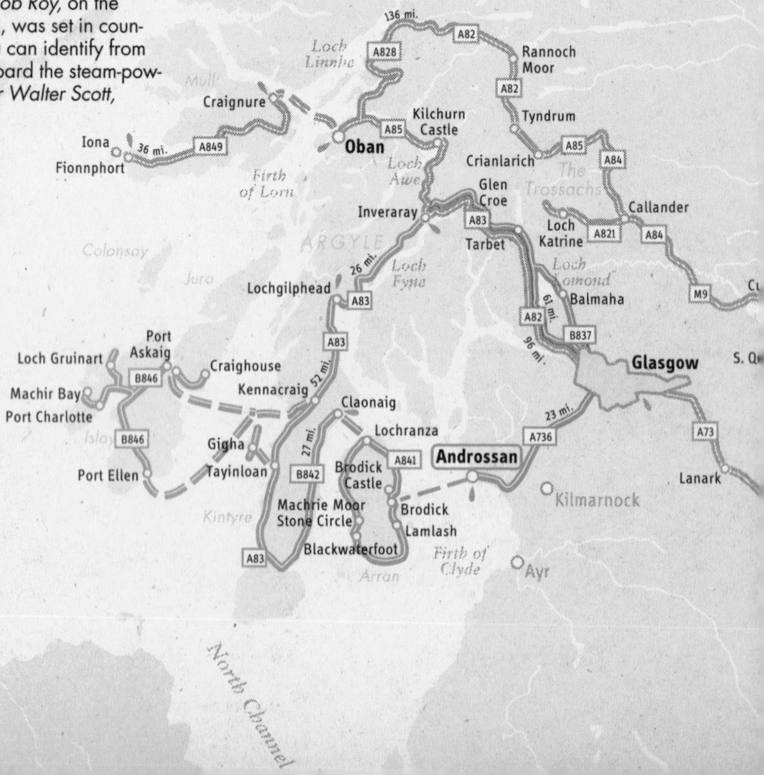

resort of North Berwick. ⇨ Side Trips from Glasgow: Robert Burns Country *in* Chapter 2, the Borders *in* Chapter 3, and Side Trips from Edinburgh *in* Chapter 1.

Island-Hopping on the Western Seaboard

7 to 9 days

This island-hopping tour takes in landfalls that are accessible even if you start your trip in Glasgow and don't have time to go farther north. Here distilleries and beaches are set amid mountain scenery, and you can experience the rhythm of island life.

ARRAN

2 or 3 days. In the port of Ardrossan catch the car ferry to Brodick. A mile north of the ferry pier is red-sandstone Brodick Castle, with beautiful interiors and gardens that are astonishingly yellow when rhododendrons bloom, in late spring and early summer. The road that circles the island leads south to a beach and palm trees at the holiday resort of Lamlash—the climate is that mild—and on to Blackwaterfoot and the Machrie Moor Stone Circle, where there are mysterious red monoliths. The area is full of hut circles, chambered cairns, and other prehistoric sites. On Arran's northern tip is Lochranza, site of Lochranza Castle. Also on the island is Goat Fell, which at 2,866 feet is the highest mountain on Arran. Allow five hours to climb it. ⇨ Arran *in* Chapter 7.

KINTYRE PENINSULA, ISLAY, JURA

3 or 4 days. From Lochranza take the ferry to Claonaig on the Kintyre Peninsula. The narrow B842 down the eastern shore of the peninsula is a lovely scenic drive past mountains and sea views. The main A83 heads back to Tayinloan. Take a 20-minute ferry ride from here to the balmy Isle of Gigha. The quiet roads make for great biking, and rentals are available. There are lovely beaches, and tender shrubs flourish in the gardens at Achamore. Back in Tayinloan head north to Kennacraig, where you can catch a ferry to Port Ellen on the unspoiled Isle of Islay. Beaches here are deserted, especially at Machir Bay on the west coast; and distilleries here make a famous peaty malt whisky. A short ferry crossing at Port Askaig takes you to mountainous Jura, a good place for experienced walkers. Novelist George Orwell wrote *1984* while he lived on this island, in the late 1940s. The single good road takes you north past the impressive Jura House gardens and on to Craighouse, the main village, where there is a hotel and a distillery. You can catch a ferry back to Kennacraig from Port Askaig or Port Ellen. ⇨ Around Argyll and Islay & Jura *in* Chapter 7.

INVERARAY & LOCH LOMOND

2 days. From Kennacraig return to Glasgow via Lochgilphead and Inveraray, an 18th-century town on the shores of Loch Fyne. Here you can eat your fill of Loch Fyne oysters. A drive through Glen Croe reveals the magnificent mountains near Tarbet at the head of Loch Lomond, the largest lake in Scotland in terms of surface area. There are great views of the loch from the A82 south, and even better views from the B837 eastern-shore road, where the village of Balmaha makes a pleasant stop before the last hour's drive to Glasgow. ⇨ Around Argyll *in* Chapter 7 and the Trossachs & Loch Lomond *in* Chapter 5.

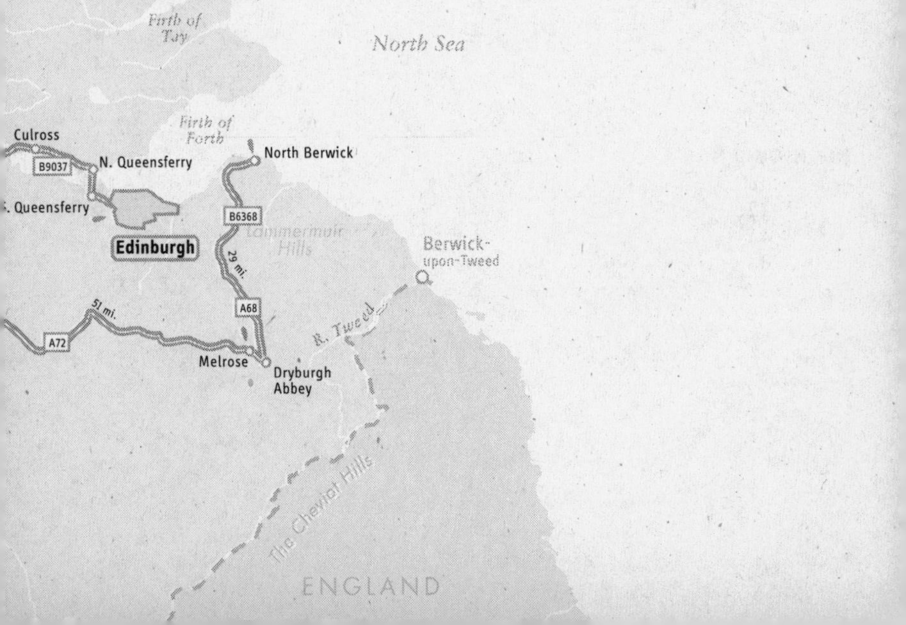

WHEN TO GO

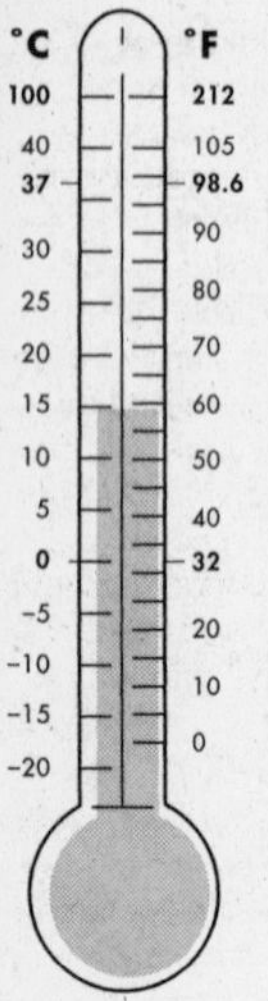

The best months for a visit to Scotland are May, June, September, and October, when all visitor attractions are open and less crowded, lodging is easy to find, and the weather is often dry, sunny, and warm (for Scotland, that is). Try to avoid July and August, when British schools are on holiday and everything is much more crowded. That said, Edinburgh festival time in August is absolutely thrilling.

Climate

The Scottish climate has been much maligned, sometimes with justification. You can be unlucky and spend a summer week under low clouds and drizzle. But on the other hand, you may enjoy calm Mediterranean-like weather even in early spring and late fall. Generally Scotland is three or four degrees cooler than southern England, and the east is drier and colder than the west. Dawn in Orkney and Shetland in June is around 1 AM, no more than an hour or so after sunset. Winter days are very short. Scotland has few thunderstorms and little fog, except for local mists near the coasts. But there are often variable winds that reach gale force even in summer. They blow away the hordes of gnats and midges, the curse of the western Highlands.

Forecasts **Weather Channel Connection** ☎ 900/932–8437, 95¢ per minute from a Touch-Tone phone 🌐 www.weather.com.

ABERDEEN

Jan.	43F	6C	May	54F	12C	Sept.	59F	15C
	36	2		43	6		49	9
Feb.	43F	6C	June	61F	16C	Oct.	54F	12C
	36	2		49	9		43	6
Mar.	47F	8C	July	63F	17C	Nov.	47F	8C
	49	9		37	3		48	9
Apr.	49F	9C	Aug.	63F	17C	Dec.	45F	7C
	40	4		52	11		36	2

EDINBURGH

Jan.	43F	6C	May	58F	14C	Sept.	61F	16C
	34	1		43	6		49	9
Feb.	43F	6C	June	63F	17C	Oct.	54F	12C
	34	1		49	9		45	7
Mar.	47F	8C	July	65F	18C	Nov.	49F	9C
	36	2		52	11		40	4
Apr.	52F	11C	Aug.	65F	18C	Dec.	45F	7C
	40	4		52	11		36	2

THE HIGHLANDS

Jan.	43F	6C	May	58F	14C	Sept.	61F	16C
	32	0		43	6		49	9
Feb.	45F	7C	June	63F	17C	Oct.	56F	13C
	34	1		49	9		45	6
Mar.	49F	9C	July	65F	18C	Nov.	49F	9C
	36	2		52	11		38	3
Apr.	52F	11C	Aug.	65F	18C	Dec.	45F	7C
	40	4		52	11		34	1

ON THE CALENDAR

WINTER	
Dec. 30–Jan. 1	**Hogmanay** is Scotland's ancient, still-thriving New Year's celebration.
Jan. 25	**Burns Night** dinners and other events are held in memory of Robert Burns on his birthday.
Mid-Jan.–Early Feb.	**Celtic Connections** (✉ Glasgow Royal Concert Hall, 2 Sauchiehall St., Glasgow ☎ 0141/353–8000), an annual homage to Celtic music, hosts hands-on workshops and musicians from all over the world.
Last Tues. in Jan.	During **Up Helly Aa** (☎ 01595/693434), Shetlanders celebrate their Viking heritage and torch a replica Viking long ship.
SPRING	
Early Apr.	**Edinburgh International Science Festival** (☎ 0131/473–2070 🌐 www.sciencefestival.co.uk) aims to make science accessible, interesting, and, above all, fun, especially—but not exclusively—for children.
April	**Shetland Folk Festival** (☎ 01595/693434) is one of the biggest folk gatherings in Scotland, set in the home of fiddle playing.
Mid-May	The **Perth Festival of the Arts** (☎ 01738/475295) offers orchestral and choral concerts, drama, opera, and ballet throughout Perth.
Late May	**Orkney Folk Festival** (☎ 01856/851331) brings the folkies back up to the remote far north by the hundreds.
SUMMER	
June–Aug.	**Highland Games**, held annually in many Highland towns, include athletic and cultural events such as hammer throwing, caber tossing, Highland dancing, and pipe-band performances.
Third week in June	**St. Magnus Festival** (☎ 01856/871445 🌐 www.stmagnusfestival.com) is a feast of classical and modern music, often showcasing new vocal or orchestral compositions.
Early Aug.–Early Sept.	The **Edinburgh International Festival** (☎ 0131/473–2099 or 0131/473–2000 🌐 www.eif.co.uk) is the world's largest festival of the arts. The **Edinburgh Festival Fringe** (☎ 0131/226–5257 🌐 www.edfringe.com) is the rowdy, unofficial escort of the Edinburgh International Festival. The **Edinburgh International Film Festival** (☎ 0131/228–4051 🌐 www.edfilmfest.org.uk) concentrates on the best new films from all over the world. The **Edinburgh Military Tattoo** (✉ 32 Market St., Edinburgh EH1 1QB ☎ 0131/225–1188 🌐 www.edintattoo.co.uk) is a show of marching bands and military regiments.
Early Sept.	The **Braemar Royal Highland Gathering** (☎ 013397/55377 🌐 www.braemargathering.org) hosts kilted clansmen from all over Scotland.
FALL	
October	**Shetland Accordion and Fiddle Festival** (☎ 01595/693434) concentrates on two of the most popular instruments of folk musicians in Scotland.

PLEASURES & PASTIMES

Biking

Scotland's many backcountry and forestry roads meander through bright-green glens, beside deep-blue lochs, and over steel-gray moors. Many cyclists head straight for the national parks in the interior or the mild weather and forested hills of the Southwest. The islands of Arran and Islay, dotted with bike rental shops, are also popular. Many of the safest and prettiest routes are along dedicated cycle paths. The Glasgow-Loch Lomond-Killin Cycleway runs partly along a former railway. Edinburgh's Innocent Railway path also makes use of a former track bed. Although some terrain may be flat, strong winds and thick mists can make conditions hazardous. It's a good idea to find out the weather forecast before setting out on a long ride. And even in the remote North, you are sure to cross the occasional truck or bus, so wear bright, colorful to make yourself more visible.

Castles

If you love castles, you've come to the right place. Scotland has just about every type of castle imaginable, from medieval ruins, complete with gory tales, such as Kildrummy, to magnificent Georgian piles like Culzean, full of antiques and paintings and surrounded by parkland. The northeast of Scotland inland from Aberdeen, in particular, has a great number of castles, strung together along a series of roadways that the local tourist board has helpfully labeled as the Castle Trail. Whether just a jumble of stones atop a hill, or still in private ownership, or under the care of a preservation society—such as Historic Scotland (a government agency) or the National Trust for Scotland (a private, charitable organization)—Scotland's castles and forts vividly demonstrate the country's unsettled past and its historically uneasy relationship with its southern neighbor.

Cultural Festivals

The Edinburgh International Festival is the spectacular flagship of mainstream cultural events, from orchestral music to comedy skits. In fact, the capital suffers from Festival overkill in late August, partly because of the size of the Fringe, the less formal and rowdier offshoot of the official festival. This huge grab bag of performances spreads out of halls and theaters onto the streets of the city. Adding to the throng are the Edinburgh Military Tattoo, International Film Festival, and Jazz Festival. Folk festivals are also held at various times of the year all over the country. One of the most popular festivals is Up Helly Aa, held in Shetland at the end of January, when Viking ceremonies culminate in the burning of a replica Viking long ship.

Restaurants

Traditional recipes and fresh ingredients, notably seafood, continue to define Scottish cuisine, although the trend toward culinary innovation has taken over in some restaurants, particularly in the cities. Excellent red meats and game, wild salmon and brook trout, oatmeal and wild berries, are staples in the kitchens of up-and-coming chefs as well as in rural guesthouses, where the owner may also be the cook. Some restaurants have a "Taste of Scotland" menu, which means they belong to an organization dedicated to high standards of traditional cooking using fresh local produce. Initiated by the Scottish Tourist Board but now run independently, the Taste of Scotland program has even done its part to help preserve some of the Scots language, at least on menus. Most smaller towns and many villages have at least one restaurant where—certainly if a local is in charge—the service is a reminder of a Highland tradition that ensured that no stranger could travel through the country without receiving a welcome.

The Malt Whisky Trail

No tour of Speyside, in the Northeast, or Islay, in western Scotland, is complete without a visit to at least one distillery, and signs along the major roads in both regions indicate stops on the Malt Whisky Trail. The British government closely monitors the process of producing whisky (and, in Scotland, the product is most definitely spelled *whisky,* without an *e*). Distilling of Scotch whisky is strictly commercially licensed and takes place only in Scotland's distilleries. Many distilleries have installed excellent visitor facilities and attempt to inject some drama and excitement into a process that is visually undramatic but nevertheless requires skill, method, and large-scale investment. A typical visit includes some kind of audiovisual presentation and a tour, and then a dram is usually offered, sometimes accompanied by a lesson in nosing.

Gardens

Somewhat surprisingly perhaps, Scotland's lowland climate is very favorable to a wide variety of plants, and a highlight of a Scottish visit for any gardening enthusiast is discovering the nation's gardens. In the southwest there are Castle Kennedy Gardens, dotted with ponds and rhododendrons; Logan Botanic Gardens, with palm trees and warm-weather flowers; and Threave Gardens, with an extraordinary show of daffodils each spring. On the east coast, in addition to the impressive Royal Botanic Gardens in Edinburgh, beautifully tended gardens and parkland surround many of the stately homes, in private ownership and under the care of the National Trust for Scotland. Even in the far northwestern Highlands, Inverewe defies the elements to display luxuriant rhododendrons and South American shrubs. And these are just a few of the major gardens; in addition, many private gardens open for one or two days each summer for charity under Scotland's Gardens Scheme; look for the yellow posters and you may well discover some normally hidden delights.

Golf

Scotland is often called the home of golf, although some historians have argued that the game originated in the Low Countries. What is certain is that Scotland has a number of very old established courses, often close to town centers, where, had it not been for the early laws protecting the rights of golfers, the land would have been swallowed up by developments long ago. Golf in Scotland has also long been known as a virtually classless game; anybody can play. Although a few clubs are exclusive, most are affordable and accessible, even to beginners. There are some 500 golf courses in Scotland, including some of the most famous on earth. St. Andrews is so popular that reservations for summer play are sometimes required a year in advance. Courses are also in the major urban centers; there are 30 in or close to Edinburgh and seven courses in Glasgow.

Hiking

People who have hiked in Scotland return again and again to explore the country's rural and varied landscape of loch-dotted glens and forested hills. From Edinburgh's Arthur's Seat to Ben Nevis, Britain's tallest peak, Scotland holds unlimited walking and hiking possibilities. Plus, there are two national parks, Loch Lomond and the Trossachs National Park, in the Central Highlands, and Cairngorms National Park, in the Northeast. Trails are often unmarked, however, so it is important to know how to use a map and compass and to be properly equipped at all times; weather conditions can change very rapidly in Scotland's hills, even at low altitude, and people have been known to die of exposure even in high summer.

Pubs

Whether you join in a lively political discussion in a bar in Glasgow or enjoy folk music and dancing in a rural pub in the Highlands, you'll find that a public house is the perfect site to experience the Scottish spirit and, of course, to enjoy a pint or a wee dram. Most bars sell two kinds of beer—lager and ale. Lager, most familiar to American drinkers, is light in color, heavily carbonated, and served cold; try Tennent's or McEwan's. Ale is dark, semicarbonated, and served just below room temperature; try McEwan 80 Shilling and Caledonian 80. An increasing number of pubs, especially in major cities, also serve a small selection of "real ales"—hand-drawn beers produced by smaller breweries, whose range of flavors is a revelation compared to the usual pub beers. All pubs carry any number of single-malt and blended whiskies as well.

Shopping

The best buys in Britain in general are antiques, craft items, woolen goods, china, men's shoes, books, confectionery, and toys. In Scotland, many people buy tweeds, designer knitwear, Shetland and Fair Isle woolens, tartan rugs and fabrics, Edinburgh crystal, Caithness glass, malt whisky, Celtic silver, and pebble jewelry. The Scottish Highlands bristle with old *bothies* (farm buildings) that have been turned into small crafts workshops where you are welcome—but not pressured—to buy attractive handmade items of bone, silver, wood, pottery, leather, and glass. Handmade chocolates, often with whisky or Drambuie fillings, and the traditional petticoat-tail shortbread in tin boxes are popular; so, too, at a more mundane level, are boiled sweets (hard candies) in jars from particular localities—Berwick cockles, Jethart snails, Edinburgh rock, and the like. Dundee cake, a rich fruit mixture with almonds on top, and Dundee marmalades and heather honeys are among the other prize edibles.

FODOR'S CHOICE

Fodor's Choice ★

The sights, restaurants, hotels, and other travel experiences on these pages are our writers' and editors' top picks—our Fodor's Choices. They're the best of their type in Scotland—not to be missed and always worth your time. In the destination chapters that follow, you will find all the details.

LODGING

£££££ **Balmoral Hotel**, Edinburgh. A 1902 railway hotel in the center of town, the Balmoral has lovely rooms with deep armchairs, books on Scotland, and prints depicting the Highlands.

£££££ **Cameron House**, Loch Lomond, the Central Highlands. The grand stone-castle look of this mansion, perched on the edge of beautiful Loch Lomond, belies the contemporary comforts inside, including a state-of-the-art health club.

£££££ **Gleneagles Hotel**, Auchterarder, the Central Highlands. Scotland's most famous resort hotel, Gleneagles is a destination unto itself, with four golf courses, miles of riding trails, and luxurious accommodations.

£££££ **Peebles Hydro**, Peebles, the Borders. Every type of leisure activity, from horseback riding to tennis is offered at this enormous 1907 countryside resort.

£££££ **The Scotsman**, Edinburgh. This majestic Edwardian hotel, fitted with contemporary, elegant "Editors" rooms and "Publishers" suites, used to house the offices of the *Scotsman* newspaper.

££££–£££££ **Roman Camp**, Callander, the Central Highlands. You can hear the river from your cozy, flowery room in this welcoming country home flanking Loch Lomond and the Trossachs National Park.

££££ **Marcliffe at Pitfodels**, near Aberdeen. The spacious, individually decorated rooms at this small manor hotel have just the right mix of antique and contemporary furnishings. Ask about fishing for wild salmon on the hotel's private River Dee beat.

£££–££££ **Ceilidh Place**, Ullapool, the Northern Highlands. This pretty inn overlooking Loch Broom is an Ullapool hotspot, and in summer it hosts frequent *ceilidhs* (folk music with dancing).

£££ **Radisson SAS**, Glasgow. With its sleek, minimalist look both outside and in, this hotel's design falls squarely within the Glaswegian tradition of architectural elegance.

BUDGET LODGING

££ **Ambassador Hotel**, Glasgow. Sophisticated rooms and attentive, faultless service are the trademarks of this superior hotel in a terraced town house across from the Botanic Gardens.

££ **Creel Inn**, Orkney, the Northern Isles. For an unforgettable island stay, reserve for both dinner and a room at this pretty waterfront inn at St. Margaret's Hope. After a fine meal of local specialties, you can bask in the last rays of the sun as it drops slowly into the sea.

££ **The George Hotel**, Inverary, Argyll. This whitewashed, three-story coaching inn has large bedrooms decorated with rich, dark fabrics,

	and warm common areas, including a restaurant with stone walls, wood beams, and a fireplace.
££	**The Lodge at Daviot Mains,** near Inverness. In this large country house surrounded by lush gardens, rooms are large, facilities modern, and furnishings sweetly upholstered. Speyside distilleries, quaint Moray Firth villages, and Loch Ness boat rides are within a half-hour's drive.
££	**22 Murrayfield Gardens,** Edinburgh. Rooms have fluffy duvets and Victorian flourishes in this stately stone manor in an affluent suburb, and the friendly hosts will help you get the most out of your visit to the capital.
£–££	**Manor Park Hotel,** Glasgow. You can practice your Gaelic with the amicable owners of this neat little hotel in the West End.
£	**Osprey Hotel,** Kingussie, Around the Great Glen. Nature lovers, cyclists, and other outdoor lovers appreciate the proximity of wild and protected forestland to this stone house in a quiet glen about an hour's drive from Inverness.

RESTAURANTS

£££££	**Three Chimneys Restaurant with Rooms,** near Glendale on Skye, the Northern Highlands. The kitchen turns out prime Isle of Skye lamb and seafood in this beautifully restored shoreside cottage.
££££–£££££	**The Peat Inn,** Ceres, Fife. The restaurant in this inn is one of the finest in Scotland, serving such delicacies as lobster-and-monkfish medallions and "little pots of chocolate and rosemary."
£££–£££££	**Rogano,** Glasgow. As you dine on the catch of the day here, you might imagine yourself at the captain's table of an elegant cruise ship in the 1930s.
££££	**Silver Darling,** Aberdeen. Seafood here is creatively prepared and served in a lovely room with a view of the harbor.
£££–££££	**Witchery by the Castle,** Edinburgh. Candlelight flickers in this cavernous haunt festooned with cauldrons and broomsticks—but there's nothing spooky about the Scottish-accented French food.
£££	**Creel Inn,** Orkney, the Northern Isles. Meals have big-city sophistication in this island inn's restaurant. The ingredients are local and superbly fresh—and you're likely to encounter fish you've never tasted before.
£££	**Ostlers Close Restaurant,** Cupar, Fife. The cuisine is unexpectedly imaginative at this simple cottage-style restaurant, and the seafood is excellent.

BUDGET RESTAURANTS

£–£££	**Mussel Inn,** Glasgow. For the freshest of oysters, scallops, and mussels in Glasgow's city center, you can't do better than this restaurant owned by shellfish farmers.
£–££	**Het Theatercafe,** Dundee, Fife & Angus. From *steak frites* to fish cakes to pizza, the artsy Rep Theatre restaurant has it all at unbeatable prices.

££ **Hoebridge Inn,** near Melrose, the Borders. This small country inn has a creative chef and a menu of such dishes as spicy prawns and duck roasted with figs that reflects British, Mediterranean, and Asian influences.

£–££ **Fratelli Sarti,** Glasgow. This loud, unpretentious Italian restaurant in Glasgow's city center serves authentic, delectable pastas, seafood, salads, desserts, and anything else you could possibly want, from a seemingly unending menu.

£–££ **Kalpna,** in Edinburgh. Behind the plain facade of this South Side eatery, an eager crowd tucks into extraordinary vegetarian Indian fare. After one bite of the exquisite sweet-and-spicy combinations, you will not miss the meat.

£–££ **The Mountain Restaurant and Lodge,** Gairloch, the Northern Highlands. After browsing among walls of books, you can lunch on fresh pot pie and soup before a view of the sea.

ARCHAEOLOGY

Maes Howe, Orkney, the Northern Isles. Beneath a 115-ft-wide mound lies one of Britain's largest and best-preserved megalithic chambered tombs.

Jarslhof, Shetland, the Northern Isles. The ruins of this village show that it was inhabited from the Iron Age until the 17th century.

Old Scatness, Shetland, the Northern Isles. Continuing excavation at this site, discovered in the mid-1990s, reveals an Iron Age broch, house, and wheelhouse, as well as Pictish artifacts.

Ring of Brogar, Orkney, the Northern Isles. These 36 mysterious Neolithic standing stones leave most visitors perplexed.

Skara Brae, Orkney, the Northern Isles. This Neolithic village is so well preserved, with individual stone houses and "furniture," that you can well imagine someone living there in 3000 BC.

ARCHITECTURE

City Chambers, Glasgow. A grand monument to Glasgow's power and influence in the late 19th century, this imposing structure houses the city's government offices.

Fort George, Ardersier, near Nairn. Built by the English for protection against Highland uprisings, this perfectly preserved 18th-century military installation sits on a promontory reaching into the Moray Firth.

King's College, Aberdeen. One of few surviving pre-Reformation chapels, with gorgeous interior wood carvings, can be found on this 15th-century college campus.

CASTLES & STATELY HOMES

Abbotsford House, near Melrose, the Borders. Sir Walter Scott's former home, this somewhat architecturally eclectic mansion is more than meets the eye. Inside, you can inspect hundreds of historical artifacts and oddities plus Scott's 9,000-book library.

Blair Castle, near Pitlochry, the Central Highlands. As you approach this pretty white castle in a wooded glen, the first thing you see is its 13th-century tower. Later, Victorian turrets and castellations were added. Inside, canopied beds, intricate tapestries, and 19th-century paintings abound.

Caerlaverock Castle, Ruthwell, Dumfriesshire. Britain's only triangular castle, this 13th-century stone stronghold, surrounded by two moats, was built to defend the Maxwell family from attacks by the English.

Cawdor Castle, near Nairn, Great Glen. Shakespeare's Macbeth, the Thane of Cawdor, was fictional. But the 600 years of history revealed by this 14th-century castle is completely real.

Edinburgh Castle, Edinburgh. Standing proud on a hill in the Old Town, despite damage sustained in seven centuries' worth of wars fought on its battlements, Edinburgh Castle remains the expression of Scotland's fortitude and nationalism.

Eilean Donan Castle, Dornie, the Northern Highlands. Occupying its own island where three lochs meet, Eileen Dornan Castle is an impressive sight, and you can explore almost every inch of it.

Floors Castle, Kelso, the Borders. This sprawling 18th-century castle has been the home of the Roxburghe family since it was built. Today you can wander through the sitting, dining, drawing, needle, and billiard rooms, among others.

Glamis Castle, Glamis, Angus. The setting of Shakespeare's *Macbeth* and the birthplace of royal Princess Margaret in 1930, this many-turreted castle rises from a flat plain and captures the imagination.

Scone Palace, Perth, the Central Highlands. Scottish kings of long ago were crowned here; today, you can explore the Mansfield earls' collection of decorative arts. Two castellated towers anchor the lovely, vine-covered facade.

Stirling Castle, Stirling. This stalwart fortress on a hill above the Forth Valley resisted English attacks for five centuries. Views from the ramparts are extraordinary.

Traquair House, near Innerleithen, Borders. A bed used by Mary, Queen of Scots, secret stairs, and a maze, are just a few of the discoveries inside Traquair House, which is said to be the oldest continually occupied house in Scotland.

GOLF

Nairn, on the Moray Coast. Gorse, beach hazards, and high winds conspire against you on this par-72 course dating from 1887, but the biggest challenge by far is to ignore the gorgeous view over the Moray Firth.

Royal Dornoch, in Dornoch Firth. One of Scotland's best-kept secrets, Royal Dornoch is a tough championship course on the coast in the north of Scotland. It has a top-notch reputation, although it adheres to a policy of informality.

MUSEUMS

Burrell Collection, Glasgow. This small museum has one of Scotland's finest art collections, with exhibits ranging from Egyptian, Greek, and Roman artifacts to stained glass and French impressionist paintings.

National Gallery of Scotland, Edinburgh. The museum's small but exquisite collection of paintings from the Renaissance to the postimpressionist period includes works by Dutch, Spanish, and French masters.

The Royal Museum and the Museum of Scotland, Edinburgh. If you like history, don't miss these side-by-side museums. The Royal Museum displays natural and ethnological artifacts from around the world, while the Museum of Scotland focuses on Scottish history from prehistoric to modern times.

NATURE

Loch Maree, near Gairloch, the Northern Highlands. Lovely Loch Maree may be Scotland's prettiest lake. You can walk alongside it, or go fishing in its calm waters.

SACRED PLACES

Iona, Argyll and the Isles. Medieval Scotland's most important Christian site, St. Columba's monastery on the isle of Iona is the burial place of more than 50 Scottish, Pictish, and Celtic kings.

Rosslyn Chapel, Roslin, Midlothian. This beautiful 15th-century stone chapel is carved from top to bottom with intricate figures, animals, and plants, many depicting biblical scenes.

TOWNS & VILLAGES

Crail, in Fife. Full of pretty stone cottages and centered on a 15th-century tollbooth, Crail is the oldest and most-photographed of Fife's fishing villages.

Doune, the Central Highlands. With a forbidding medieval castle and a heritage of pistol-making in the 18th century, the hilly town of Doune transports your imagination to a bygone time.

Falkland, in Fife. A gorgeous 16th-century palace, charming stone church, and narrow, winding streets make Falkland one of Scotland's most picturesque towns.

SMART TRAVEL TIPS

Finding out about your destination before you leave home means you won't squander time organizing everyday minutiae once you've arrived. You'll be more streetwise when you hit the ground as well, better prepared to explore the aspects of Scotland that drew you here in the first place. The organizations in this section can provide information to supplement this guide; contact them for up-to-the-minute details, and consult the A to Z sections that end each chapter for facts on the various topics as they relate to Scotland's many regions. Happy landings!

AIR TRAVEL

BOOKING

When you book, **look for nonstop flights** and **remember that "direct" flights stop at least once.** Try to avoid connecting flights, which require a change of plane. Two airlines may operate a connecting flight jointly, so ask whether your airline operates every segment of the trip; you may find that the carrier you prefer flies you only part of the way. To find more booking tips and to check prices and make on-line flight reservations, log on to www.fodors.com.

CARRIERS

Although a small country, Scotland has a significant air network. Contact British Airways or British Airways Express for details on flights from London's Heathrow Airport or from Glasgow, Edinburgh, Aberdeen, and Inverness to the farthest corners of the Scottish mainland and to the islands. Ryanair flies from London Stansted to Prestwick, south of Glasgow; British Midland has service from Heathrow; and easyJet and GO fly from London Luton/Gatwick/Stansted to and between Glasgow, Edinburgh, Aberdeen, and Inverness, plus to and from Belfast.

To & From Scotland **American Airlines** ☎ 800/433–7300 www.aa.com. **British Airways** ☎ 800/247–9297 www.britishairways.com. **Continental** ☎ 800/525–0280 www.continental.com. **Delta** ☎ 800/221–1212 www.delta.com. **Northwest Airlines** ☎ 800/447–4747 www.nwa.com. **United** ☎ 800/241–6522 www.ual.com. **Virgin Atlantic** ☎ 800/862–8621 www.virgin-atlantic.com.

From London to Edinburgh & Glasgow **BMI Baby** ☎ 0870/264–2229 in London www.bmibaby.com. **British Airways** ☎ 08457/733377 www.britishairways.com. **easyJet/GO** ☎ 0870/600–0000. **Ryanair** ☎ 01292/678000 www.ryanair.com.

Around Scotland **British Airways Express** ☎ 08457/733377 🌐 www.britishairways.com. **easyJet/GO** ☎ 0870/600–0000 🌐 www.easyjet.com.

CHECK-IN & BOARDING

Always **find out your carrier's check-in policy.** Plan to arrive at the airport about two hours before your scheduled departure time for domestic flights and 2½ to 3 hours before international flights. You may need to arrive earlier if you're flying from one of the busier airports or during peak air-traffic times. To avoid delays at airport-security checkpoints, try not to wear any metal. Jewelry, belt and other buckles, steel-toe shoes, barrettes, and underwire bras are among the items that can set off detectors.

Assuming that not everyone with a ticket will show up, airlines routinely overbook planes. When everyone does, airlines ask for volunteers to give up their seats. In return, these volunteers usually get a several-hundred-dollar flight voucher, which can be used toward the purchase of another ticket, and are rebooked on the next flight out. If there are not enough volunteers, the airline must choose who will be denied boarding. The first to get bumped are passengers who checked in late and those flying on discounted tickets, so **get to the gate and check in as early as possible,** especially during peak periods.

Always **bring a government-issued photo I.D. to the airport;** even when it's not required, a passport is best.

CUTTING COSTS

The least expensive airfares to Scotland are priced for round-trip travel and must usually be purchased in advance. Airlines generally allow you to change your return date for a fee; most low-fare tickets, however, are nonrefundable. It's smart to **call a number of airlines and check the Internet;** when you are quoted a good price, **book it on the spot**—the same fare may not be available the next day, or even the next hour. Always **check different routings** and look into using alternate airports. Also, price off-peak flights, which may be significantly less expensive than others. Travel agents, especially low-fare specialists (⇨ Discounts and Deals), are helpful.

Many airlines, singly or in collaboration, offer discount air passes that allow foreigners to travel economically in a particular country or region. These visitor passes usually must be reserved and purchased before you leave home. Information about passes often can be found on most airlines' international Web pages, which tend to be aimed at travelers from outside the carrier's home country. Also, try typing the name of the pass into a search engine, or search for "pass" within the carrier's Web site.

The Discover Europe Airpass from British Midland is available on the airline's British and European flights. The pass is valid for up to 90 days and starts at $109 for shorter routes and $159 for longer flights. The Europe Pass from British Airways offers travelers a way to choose from the airline's and its partners' networks in Great Britain and Europe; prices vary.

Consolidators are another good source. They buy tickets for scheduled flights at reduced rates from the airlines, then sell them at prices that beat the best fare available directly from the airlines. Sometimes you can even get your money back if you need to return the ticket. Carefully read the fine print detailing penalties for changes and cancellations, purchase the ticket with a credit card, and **confirm your consolidator reservation with the airline.**

In Britain, the best place to **search for consolidator, or so-called bucket shop, tickets** is through Cheap Flights, a Web site that pools all flights available and then directs you to a phone number or site to purchase tickets.

When you **fly as a courier,** you trade your checked-luggage space for a ticket deeply subsidized by a courier service. There are restrictions on when you can book and how long you can stay. Some courier companies list with membership organizations, such as the Air Courier Association and the International Association of Air Travel Couriers; these require you to become a member before you can book a flight.

If you intend to fly to Scotland from London, **take advantage of the current fare wars** on internal routes—notably between London's four airports and Glasgow–Edinburgh. Among the cheapest are Ryanair between London Stansted (with its excellent rail links from London's Liverpool Street Station) and Glasgow Prestwick; and easyJet and GO, offering bargain fares from London Luton (with good rail links from central London) to Glasgow, Edinburgh, Aberdeen, and Inverness. Even

British Airways now offers competitive fares on some flights.

Consolidators **AirlineConsolidator.com** ☎ 888/468-5385 🌐 www.airlineconsolidator.com; for international tickets. **Best Fares** ☎ 800/576-8255 or 800/576-1600 🌐 www.bestfares.com; $59.90 annual membership. **Cheap Tickets** ☎ 800/377-1000 or 888/922-8849 🌐 www.cheaptickets.com. **Expedia** ☎ 800/397-3342 or 404/728-8787 🌐 www.expedia.com. **Hotwire** ☎ 866/468-9473 or 920/330-9418 🌐 www.hotwire.com. **Now Voyager Travel** ✉ 45 W. 21st St., 5th floor, New York, NY 10010 ☎ 212/459-1616 📠 212/243-2711 🌐 www.nowvoyagertravel.com. **Onetravel.com** 🌐 www.onetravel.com. **Orbitz** ☎ 888/656-4546 🌐 www.orbitz.com. **Priceline.com** 🌐 www.priceline.com. **Travelocity** ☎ 888/709-5983, 877/282-2925 in Canada, 0870/111-7060 in the U.K. 🌐 www.travelocity.com.

Courier Resources **Air Courier Association/Cheaptrips.com** ☎ 800/282-1202 🌐 www.aircourier.org or www.cheaptrips.com; $29 annual membership. **International Association of Air Travel Couriers** ☎ 308/632-3273 🌐 www.courier.org; $45 annual membership.

Discount Passes **British Airways** ☎ 800/247-9297, 0845/773-3377 in London, 1300/767-177 in Australia, 09/356-8690 in New Zealand 🌐 www.britishairways.com. **British Midland** ☎ 800/788-0555, 020/8745-7321 in London 🌐 www.flybmi.com. **DER Travel Services** ✉ 9501 W. Devon Ave., Rosemont, IL 60018 ☎ 800/782-2424 📠 800/282-7474 for information, 800/860-9944 for brochures 🌐 www.der.com.EuropebyAir **FlightPass**, ☎ 888/387-2479 🌐 www.europebyair.com.

ENJOYING THE FLIGHT

State your seat preference when purchasing your ticket, and then repeat it when you confirm and when you check in. For more legroom, you can request one of the few emergency-aisle seats at check-in, if you are capable of lifting at least 50 pounds—a Federal Aviation Administration requirement of passengers in these seats. Seats behind a bulkhead also offer more legroom, but they don't have under-seat storage. Don't sit in the row in front of the emergency aisle or in front of a bulkhead, where seats may not recline.

Ask the airline whether a snack or meal is served on the flight. If you have dietary concerns, **request special meals when booking.** These can be vegetarian, low-cholesterol, or kosher, for example. It's a good idea to pack some healthful snacks and a small (plastic) bottle of water in your carry-on bag. On long flights, try to maintain a normal routine, to help fight jet lag. At night, **get some sleep.** By day, **eat light meals, drink water** (not alcohol), and **move around the cabin** to stretch your legs. For additional jet-lag tips consult *Fodor's FYI: Travel Fit & Healthy* (available at bookstores everywhere).

Smoking policies vary from carrier to carrier. Many airlines prohibit smoking on all of their flights; others allow smoking only on certain routes or certain departures. Ask your carrier about its policy.

FLYING TIMES

Flying time to Glasgow is 6½ hours from New York, 7½ hours from Chicago, 9½ hours from Dallas, 10 hours from Los Angeles, and 21½ hours from Sydney.

HOW TO COMPLAIN

If your baggage goes astray or your flight goes awry, complain right away. Most carriers require that you **file a claim immediately.** The Aviation Consumer Protection Division of the Department of Transportation publishes *Fly-Rights,* which discusses airlines and consumer issues and is available on-line. You can also find articles and information on mytravelrights.com, the Web site of the nonprofit Consumer Travel Rights Center.

Airline Complaints **Aviation Consumer Protection Division** ✉ U.S. Department of Transportation, C-75, Room 4107, 400 7th St. SW, Washington, DC 20590 ☎ 202/366-2220 🌐 airconsumer.ost.dot.gov. **Federal Aviation Administration Consumer Hotline** ✉ for inquiries: FAA, 800 Independence Ave. SW, Washington, DC 20591 ☎ 800/322-7873 🌐 www.faa.gov.

RECONFIRMING

Check the status of your flight before you leave for the airport. You can do this on your carrier's Web site, by linking to a flight-status checker (many Web booking services offer these), or by calling your carrier or travel agent. Always confirm international flights at least 72 hours ahead of the scheduled departure time.

AIRPORTS

The major gateway to Scotland is Glasgow Airport, about 7 mi outside Glasgow. Edinburgh Airport, 7 mi from the city, doesn't serve transatlantic flights, but does offer connections for dozens of European cities and hourly flights to London's Gatwick and Heathrow airports. It's also possible to fly into Glasgow and then take bus or train service to Edinburgh in less than two hours. Aberdeen Airport has direct flights from Amsterdam. Refer to chapter A to Z sections for information on airport transfers.

Airport Information **Aberdeen Airport** ☎ 01224/722331. **Edinburgh Airport** ☎ 0131/333-1000. **Glasgow Airport** ☎ 0141/887-1111 🌐 www.baa.co.uk (for all airports).

BIKE TRAVEL

The best months for cycling in Scotland are May, June, and September, when the roads are often quieter and the weather is usually better. Winds are predominantly from the southwest, so plan your route accordingly.

Because Scotland's main roads are continually being upgraded, bicyclists can easily reach the network of quieter rural roads in southern and much of eastern Scotland, especially Grampian. Still, care must be taken in getting from some town centers to rural riding areas, so if in doubt, ask a local. In a few areas of the Highlands, notably in northwestern Scotland, the rugged terrain and limited population have resulted in the lack of side roads, making it more difficult—sometimes impossible—to plan a minor-road route in these areas.

Several agencies now promote "safe routes" for recreational cyclists. These routes are signposted, and the agencies have produced maps or leaflets showing where they run. Perhaps best known is the Glasgow–Loch Lomond–Killin Cycleway, which makes use of former railway track beds, forest trails, quiet rural side roads, and some main roads. The Glasgow–Irvine Cycle Route runs south and west of Glasgow and links with the Johnstone and Greenock Railway Path. In Edinburgh there's the Innocent Railway Path from Holyrood Path to St. Leonards. Contact the relevant tourist board for more information.

VisitScotland's (⇨ Visitor Information) free brochure "Cycling in Scotland" has some suggested routes and practical advice. The Ordnance Survey Landranger series of maps, which shows gradients, is available in many city bookstores and invaluable for cyclists.

BIKES ON BUSES

Although some rural bus services will transport cycles if space is available, **don't count on getting your bike on a bus.** Be sure to check well in advance with the appropriate bus company.

BIKES ON FERRIES

You can take bicycles on car and passenger ferries in Scotland, and it's not generally necessary to book in advance. The three main ferry service operators (⇨ Boat & Ferry Travel) are Caledonian MacBrayne, which charges £1–£4 per journey for accompanied bicycles on some routes (on many routes, bicycles are carried free), and Western Ferries and Northlink Ferries, both of which carry accompanied bicycles free. **Check cycles on car ferries early** so that they can be loaded through the car entrance.

BIKES IN FLIGHT

Most airlines accommodate bikes as luggage, provided they are dismantled and boxed; check with individual airlines about packing requirements. Some airlines sell bike boxes, which are often free at bike shops, for about $15 (bike bags can be considerably more expensive). International travelers often can substitute a bike for a piece of checked luggage at no charge; otherwise, the cost is about $100. U.S. and Canadian airlines charge $40–$80 each way.

BIKES ON TRAINS

ScotRail strongly advises that you **make a train reservation for you and your bike at least one month in advance.** On several trains reservations are compulsory. A leaflet containing the latest information is available through ScotRail and can be picked up at most manned train stations within Scotland.

BIKING OFF-ROAD

Scotland's legal position on off-road cycling is complex. Cycling is covered by road traffic laws because a bike is classified as a vehicle. In a strict legal sense, cycling off-road is possible only on specifically designated cycle tracks, routes that have a common-law right-of-way for cycles, or routes that have the consent of the landowner. Legally, cyclists aren't allowed on pedestrian rights-of-way, but many landowners don't mind if cyclists use them. It's best to seek local advice when planning off-road routes.

BIKING ORGANIZATIONS

The Cyclists' Touring Club actively campaigns for better cyclist facilities throughout the United Kingdom. It publishes a members' magazine, route maps, and guides. Sustrans Ltd. is a nonprofit organization dedicated to providing environmentally friendly routes for cyclists, notably in and around cities.

Bike Maps & Information **Cyclists' Touring Club** ✉ National Headquarters, Cotterell House, 69 Meadrow, Godalming, Surrey GU7 3HS, England ☎ 0870/8730060 📠 01483/426994 🌐 www.ctc.org.uk. **Sustrans Ltd.** ✉ 162 Fountainbridge, Edinburgh EH3 9RX ☎ 0131/624-7660 📠 0131/624-7664 🌐 www.sustrans.org.uk.

BIKING TOURS

Bikesport runs guided mountain-bike tours and can customize tours to individual requirements. Bike hire is also available, complete with all safety equipment. Wildcat Bike Tours also runs bike tours throughout Scotland for novices and experts.

Bike Tour Operators **Bikesport** ✉ Peebles Rd., Innerleithen EH44 6QX ☎ 01896/830880 📠 01896/831857 ✉ bike.sport@virgin.net. **Wildcat Bike Tours** ✉ Unit 111, John Player Bldg., Stirling Enterprise Park, Stirling FK7 7RP ☎📠 01786/464333 🌐 www.wildcat-bike-tours.co.uk.

BOAT & FERRY TRAVEL

With so many islands, plus the great Firth of Clyde waterway, ferry services in Scotland are of paramount importance. Most ferries transport vehicles as well as foot passengers, although a few of the smaller ones are still for passengers only.

The main operator is Caledonian MacBrayne Ltd., known generally as CalMac. Services extend from the Firth of Clyde, where there's an extremely extensive network, right up to the northwest of Scotland and all of the Hebrides. CalMac sells an Island Rover runabout ticket, which is ideal for touring holidays in the islands, as well as an island-hopping scheme called Island Hopscotch.

The Dunoon–Gourock route on the Clyde is served by Western Ferries; the Islay–Jura service is operated by Serco Denholm.

The Falkirk Wheel in Tamfourhill, about halfway between Glasgow and Edinburgh, is an attraction as much as a form of transportation. The only rotating boat lift in the world, it carries private and tour boats from the Forth and Clyde Canal over to the Union Canal, and back again.

Northlink Ferries operates a car ferry for Orkney between Scrabster, near Thurso, and Stromness, on the main island of Orkney; and between Aberdeen and Kirkwall, which is also on Mainland, Orkney. Northlink also runs ferries for Shetland between Aberdeen and Lerwick.

FARES & SCHEDULES

For fares and schedules, contact ferry companies directly. Travelers checks (in pounds), cash, and major credit cards are accepted for payment.

Boat & Ferry Information **Caledonian MacBrayne** ✉ The Ferry Terminal, Gourock PA19 1QP ☎ 01475/650100; 08705/650000 reservations; 01475/650288 brochure hotline 📠 01475/637607 🌐 www.calmac.co.uk. **The Falkirk Wheel** ✉ Lime Rd., Tamfourhill ☎ 01324/619888; reservations 08700/500208 🌐 www.thefalkirkwheel.co.uk. **Northlink Ferries** ✉ New Harbour Bldg., Ferry Rd., Stromness, Orkney, KW16 3BH ☎ 01856/851144 📠 01856/851155 🌐 www.northlinkferries.co.uk. **Serco Denholm** ☎ 01475/731540. **Western Ferries** ☎ 01369/704452 📠 01369/706020 🌐 www.western-ferries.co.uk.

BUSINESS HOURS

BANKS

Banks are open weekdays 9:30 to 3:30, some days to 4:45. Some banks have extended hours on Thursday evening, and a few are open on Saturday morning. Some also close for an hour at lunchtime. The major airports operate 24-hour banking services seven days a week.

GAS STATIONS

Service stations are at regular intervals on motorways and are usually open 24 hours a day, though stations elsewhere usually close from 9 PM to 7 AM; in rural areas many close at 6 PM and all day on Sunday.

MUSEUMS & SIGHTS

Most museums in cities and larger towns are open daily, although some may be closed on Sunday morning. In smaller villages museums are often open when there are visitors around—even late on summer evenings—but closed in poor weather, when visitors are unlikely; there's often a contact phone number on the door.

PHARMACIES

Pharmacies (often called "chemists" in Scotland) usually open 9 to 5 or 5:30 Monday through Saturday, though most large towns and cities have either a large supermarket open extended hours, with a pharmacy on the premises, or have a rotation system for pharmacists on call (there will be a note displayed in the pharmacy's window with the number to call). In rural areas doctors often dispense medicines themselves. In an emergency the police should be able to locate a pharmacist.

SHOPS

Usual business hours are Monday through Saturday 9 to 5 or 5:30. Outside the main centers, most shops observe an early closing day (they close at 1 PM) once a week, often Wednesday or Thursday. In small villages many shops also close for lunch. Department stores in large cities and many supermarkets even in smaller towns stay open for late-night shopping (usually until 7:30 or 8) one or more days a week. Apart from some newsstands and small food stores, many shops are closed on Sunday except in larger towns and cities, where main shopping malls may be open.

BUS TRAVEL

The country's bus network is extensive. Bus service is comprehensive in cities, less so in country districts. Express service links main cities and towns, connecting, for example, Glasgow and Edinburgh to Inverness, Aberdeen, Perth, Skye, Ayr, Dumfries, and Carlisle; or Inverness with Aberdeen, Wick, Thurso, and Fort William. These express services are very fast, and fares are reasonable.

CUTTING COSTS

On bus routes, Explorer Pass offers complete freedom of travel on any National Express or Scottish Citylink services throughout the mainland United Kingdom. Four permutations give up to 8 days of travel in a 16-day period. It's available from Scottish Citylink offices, most bus stations, and any National Express appointed agent.

Discount Passes **National Express** ☎ 08705/808080 ⊕ www.nationalexpress.co.uk. **Scottish Citylink** ☎ 08705/505050 ⊕ www.citylink.co.uk.

FARES & SCHEDULES

Contact Traveline Scotland for information on all public transportation and timetables.

Bus Information **Traveline Scotland** ☎ 0870/608-2608.

PAYING

For town, suburban, or short-distance journeys, you normally buy your ticket on the bus, from a pay box, or from the driver. Sometimes you need exact change. For longer journeys—for example, Glasgow–Inverness—it's usual to reserve a seat and pay at the bus station booking office. Credit cards and traveler's checks are accepted at most bus stations.

FROM ENGLAND

Coaches usually provide the cheapest way to travel between England and Scotland; fares may be as little as a third of the rail fares for comparable trips. About 20 companies operate service between major cities, including National Express (single class only). Journey time between London and Glasgow or Edinburgh is 8–8¼ hours. The main London terminal is Victoria Coach Station, but some Scottish companies use Gloucester Road Coach Station in west London. Many people travel to Scotland by coach; in summer a reservation three or four days ahead is advisable. Fares are about £32 round-trip, and credit cards are accepted.

Bus Lines **National Express** ✉ Buchanan Street Bus Station, Killermont St., Glasgow G2 3NP ☎ 08705/808080 ⊕ www.nationalexpress.co.uk.

CAMERAS & PHOTOGRAPHY

The *Kodak Guide to Shooting Great Travel Pictures* (available at bookstores everywhere) is loaded with tips.

Photo Help **Kodak Information Center** ☎ 800/242-2424 ⊕ www.kodak.com.

EQUIPMENT PRECAUTIONS

Don't pack film and equipment in checked luggage, where it is much more susceptible to damage. X-ray machines used to view checked luggage are extremely powerful and therefore are likely to ruin your film. Try to **ask for hand inspection of film,** which becomes clouded after repeated exposure to airport X-ray machines, and **keep videotapes and computer disks away from metal detectors.** Always **keep film, tape, and com-**

puter disks out of the sun. Carry an extra supply of batteries, and **be prepared to turn on your camera, camcorder, or laptop** to prove to airport security personnel that the device is real.

FILM & DEVELOPING

Film is available at pharmacies, newsstands, and supermarkets, as well as photography stores. Kodak, followed by Agfa and Fuji, are the most common brands, and prices range from £2 to £4 for a roll of 36-exposure color print film. Chain drugstores and supermarkets run cost-cutting deals and offer one-hour photo developing.

VIDEOS

Remember that most video cartridges sold in Britain (marked PAL) do not interface with American video players (NTSC). The top tourist attractions that have videos also market versions specially made for the American and overseas markets. If you're bringing your own video camcorder, bring a supply of cassettes as well.

CAR RENTAL

If you're traveling to more than one country, make sure your rental contract permits you to take the car across borders and that the insurance policy covers you in every country you visit. British cars have the steering wheel on the right, so you may want to leave your rented car in Britain and pick up a left-side drive when you cross the Channel.

Rates in Glasgow begin at £35 a day and £170 a week for an economy car with a manual transmission and unlimited mileage. This does not include tax on car rentals, which is 17.5%.

Major Agencies **Alamo** ☎ 800/522-9696 🌐 www.alamo.com. **Avis** ☎ 800/331-1084, 800/879-2847 in Canada, 0870/606-0100 in the U.K., 02/9353-9000 in Australia, 09/526-2847 in New Zealand 🌐 www.avis.com. **Budget** ☎ 800/527-0700, 0870/156-5656 in the U.K. 🌐 www.budget.com. **Dollar** ☎ 800/800-6000, 0124/622-0111 in the U.K., where it's affiliated with Sixt, 02/9223-1444 in Australia 🌐 www.dollar.com. **Hertz** ☎ 800/654-3001, 800/263-0600 in Canada, 0870/844-8844 in the U.K., 02/9669-2444 in Australia, 09/256-8690 in New Zealand 🌐 www.hertz.com. **National Car Rental** ☎ 800/227-7368, 0870/600-6666 in the U.K., where it is affiliated with Alamo 🌐 www.nationalcar.com.

CUTTING COSTS

For a good deal, **book through a travel agent who will shop around.** Do **look into wholesalers,** companies that do not own fleets but rent in bulk from those that do and often offer better rates than traditional car-rental operations. Prices are best during off-peak periods. Rentals booked through wholesalers often must be paid for before you leave home.

Wholesalers **Auto Europe** ☎ 207/842-2000 or 800/223-5555 📠 207/842-2222 🌐 www.autoeurope.com. **Europe by Car** ☎ 212/581-3040 or 800/223-1516 📠 212/246-1458 🌐 www.europebycar.com. **Destination Europe Resources** (DER) ✉ 9501 W. Devon Ave., Rosemont, IL 60018 ☎ 800/782-2424 🌐 www.der.com. **Kemwel** ☎ 800/678-0678 📠 207/842-2124 🌐 www.kemwel.com.

INSURANCE

When driving a rented car you are generally responsible for any damage to or loss of the vehicle. Collision policies that car-rental companies sell for European rentals typically do not cover stolen vehicles. Before you rent—and purchase collision or theft coverage—see what coverage you already have under the terms of your personal auto-insurance policy and credit cards.

REQUIREMENTS & RESTRICTIONS

Companies frequently restrict rentals to people over age 23 and under age 75.

SURCHARGES

Before you pick up a car in one city and leave it in another, **ask about drop-off charges or one-way service fees,** which can be substantial. Note, too, that some rental agencies charge extra if you return the car before the time specified in your contract. To avoid a hefty refueling fee, **fill the tank just before you turn in the car,** but be aware that gas stations near the rental outlet may overcharge. It's almost never a deal to buy the tank of gas that's in the car when you rent it; the understanding is that you'll return it empty, but some fuel usually remains. Car seats usually cost about £20 extra. Adding one extra driver is usually included in the original rental price.

CAR TRAVEL

One of the best ways to see Scotland is to rent a car and drive (on the left side of the road, of course). A car allows you to set your own pace and visit several off-the-beaten-path towns and sights.

In Scotland your own driver's license is acceptable. An International Driver's Permit is a good idea; it's available from the American or Canadian automobile associations and, in the United Kingdom, from the Automobile Association or Royal Automobile Club. These international permits, valid only in conjunction with your regular driver's license, are universally recognized; having one may save you a problem with local authorities.

EMERGENCY SERVICES

For aid if your car breaks down, contact the 24-hour rescue numbers of either the Automobile Association or the Royal Automobile Club. If you are a member of the AAA (American Automobile Association) or another association, check your membership details before you travel; reciprocal agreements may give you free roadside aid.

In Australia **Australian Automobile Association** ☎ 02/6247-7311 🌐 www.aaa.asn.au.

In Canada **Canadian Automobile Association** (CAA) ☎ 613/247-0117 🌐 www.caa.ca.

In New Zealand **New Zealand Automobile Association** ☎ 09/377-4660 🌐 www.aa.co.nz.

In the U.K. **Automobile Association AA** ☎ 08705/500600 🌐 www.theaa.co.uk. **Royal Automobile Club** (RAC) ☎ 08705/722-722 🌐 www.rac.co.uk.

In the U.S. **American Automobile Association** (AAA) ☎ 800/564-6222 🌐 www.aaa.com.

GASOLINE

Expect to pay a lot more for gasoline, about £3.50 a gallon (77p a liter) for unleaded—up to 10p a gallon higher in remote rural locations. The British imperial gallon is about 20% more in volume than the U.S. gallon—approximately 4.5 liters. Pumps dispense in liters, not gallons. Most gas stations stock unleaded, super unleaded, and LRP (replacing 4-star) plus diesel; most also accept major credit cards.

ROAD CONDITIONS

A good network of superhighways, known as motorways, and divided highways, known as dual carriageways, extends throughout Britain, though in the remoter areas of Scotland where the motorway hasn't penetrated, travel is noticeably slower. Motorways shown with the prefix M are mainly two or three lanes in each direction, without any right-hand turns. These are the roads to use to cover long distances, though inevitably you'll see less of the countryside. Service areas are at most about an hour apart. Dual carriageways, usually shown on a map as a thick red line (often with a black line in the center) and the prefix A followed by a number perhaps with a bracketed T (for example, A304[T]), are similar to motorways, except that right turns are sometimes permitted, and you'll find both traffic lights and traffic circles on them.

The vast network of other main roads, which typical maps show as either single red "A" roads, or narrower brown "B" roads, also numbered, are for the most part the old coach and turnpike roads built originally for horses and carriages. Travel along these roads is slower than on motorways because passing is more difficult. On the other hand, you'll see much more of Scotland.

Minor roads (shown as yellow or white on most maps, unlettered and unnumbered) are the ancient lanes and byways of Britain, roads that are not only living history but a superb way of discovering hidden parts of Scotland. You have to drive along them slowly and carefully. On single-track roads, found in the north and west of Scotland, there isn't room for two vehicles to pass, and you must use a passing place if you meet an oncoming car or tractor, or if a car behind wishes to overtake you. Never hold up traffic on single-track roads.

ROAD MAPS

The best general purpose touring map is the Scottish Tourist Board's Touring Map of Scotland (5 mi to the inch), widely available in bookshops, tourist information centers, and from the Scottish Tourist Board (⇨ Visitor Information). Any bookshop in the main cities will usually sell good maps. For walking or getting to know a smaller area, the readily available Ordnance Survey Landranger series (1:50,000 scale) can't be beaten.

RULES OF THE ROAD

The most noticeable difference for most visitors is that when in Britain, you drive on the left and steer the car on the right. **Give yourself time to adjust to driving on the left**—especially if you pick up your car at the airport and are still suffering from jet lag.

One of the most complicated questions facing visitors to Britain is that of speed limits. In urban areas, except for certain freeways, it's generally 30 mph, but it is 40 mph on some main roads, as indicated by circular red-rimmed signs. In rural areas the official limit is 60 mph on ordinary roads and 70 mph on divided highways and motorways—and traffic police can be hard on speeders, especially in urban areas. Driving while using a cell phone is legal but not recommended.

CHILDREN IN SCOTLAND

On the whole, Scotland caters reasonably well to children. If you are renting a car, don't forget to **arrange for a car seat** when you reserve. For general advice about traveling with children, consult *Fodor's FYI: Travel with Your Baby* (available in bookstores everywhere).

FLYING

If your children are two or older, **ask about children's airfares.** As a general rule, infants under two not occupying a seat fly at greatly reduced fares or even for free. But if you want to guarantee a seat for an infant, you have to pay full fare. Consider flying during off-peak days and times; most airlines will grant an infant a seat without a ticket if there are available seats. When booking, **confirm carry-on allowances** if you're traveling with infants. In general, for babies charged 10% to 50% of the adult fare you are allowed one carry-on bag and a collapsible stroller; if the flight is full, the stroller may have to be checked or you may be limited to less.

Experts agree that it's a good idea to use safety seats aloft for children weighing less than 40 pounds. Airlines set their own policies: if you use a safety seat, U.S. carriers usually require that the child be ticketed, even if he or she is young enough to ride free, because the seats must be strapped into regular seats. And even if you pay the full adult fare for the seat, it may be worth it, especially on longer trips. Do **check your airline's policy about using safety seats during takeoff and landing.** Safety seats are not allowed everywhere in the plane, so get your seat assignments as early as possible.

When reserving, **request children's meals or a freestanding bassinet** (not available at all airlines) if you need them. But note that bulkhead seats, where you must sit to use the bassinet, may lack an overhead bin or storage space on the floor.

FOOD

Many (generally the cheaper) restaurants have a children's menu, but it's worth asking for the children's meal to be served first, so kids don't get bored waiting for more elaborate adult dishes to be prepared.

LODGING

The Scottish Tourist Board's two *Where to Stay* accommodation guides, *Hotels & Guest Houses* and *Bed & Breakfast,* indicate establishments that welcome children and have facilities for them, such as cots and high chairs. When booking, **confirm that the equipment you need will be available.** Also, **mention the age of your children when booking**—some of the more upscale country house hotels, in particular, don't allow children under a certain age (e.g., 12) to stay.

Some outstanding child-friendly lodgings are Polmaily House, at Drumnadrochit, and the Isles of Glencoe Hotel, at Ballachulish (⇨ Chapter 8 for both hotels), where families definitely come first.

Although there's no general policy regarding hotel rates for children in Scotland, many hotels allow children under 14 to stay for free in their parents' room: inquire when booking. Many also have adjoining family rooms.

Best Choices **Isles of Glencoe Hotel** ✉ Ballachulish PA39 4HL ☎ 01855/821582 📠 01855/821463 🌐 www.freedomglen.co.uk. **Polmaily House** ✉ Drumnadrochit IV63 6XT ☎ 01456/450343 📠 01456/450813 🌐 www.polmaily.co.uk.

SIGHTS & ATTRACTIONS

Places that are especially appealing to children are indicated by a rubber-duckie icon (🐤) in the margin. Major cities, as well as many larger towns, have plenty of the usual attractions for children—zoos and aquariums, hands-on science centers, swimming pools and sports centers—as well as museums, art galleries, and historic buildings (all of which often offer activity sheets for children). Farther afield, say in the far northwest Highlands and on the remoter islands, opportunities for outdoor and cultural activities abound—walking, riding, beachcombing, exploring prehistoric cairns, scrambling over castle ramparts. Local tourist information centers can fill you in on what's best in the area for kids.

SUPPLIES & EQUIPMENT

You'll find everything you need for babies and children in supermarkets and pharmacies. American brands are widely available.

COMPUTERS ON THE ROAD

Make sure your laptop is dual-voltage; most, but not all, laptops operate equally well on 110 and 220 volts and so require only an adapter. **Never plug your computer into any socket without first asking about surge protection**: although Scotland is computer-friendly, few hotels and B&Bs outside the major cities have built-in current stabilizers. Electrical fluctuations and surges can short your adapter or even destroy your computer, so it is worthwhile to purchase a surge protector in the United Kingdom that plugs into the socket. Also, the high winds, which can blow at any time of year (though more usually between October and March), especially in northern Scotland, often damage overhead power lines and cause power cuts: if it's a really windy day, you may want to turn off your computer.

Many hotels and some B&Bs have facilities for computer users, such as in-room data ports or even a dedicated PC room. For Internet access you need a BT-style telephone adapter, purchasable in the United Kingdom.

CONSUMER PROTECTION

Whether you're shopping for gifts or purchasing travel services, **pay with a major credit card** whenever possible, so you can cancel payment or get reimbursed if there's a problem (and you can provide documentation). If you're doing business with a particular company for the first time, **contact your local Better Business Bureau and the attorney general's offices** in your state and (for U.S. businesses) the company's home state as well. Have any complaints been filed? Finally, if you're buying a package or tour, always **consider travel insurance** that includes default coverage (⇨ Insurance).

BBBs **Council of Better Business Bureaus** ✉ 4200 Wilson Blvd., Suite 800, Arlington, VA 22203 ☎ 703/276-0100 🖷 703/525-8277 🌐 www.bbb.org.

CRUISE TRAVEL

Many of the crossings from North America to Europe are repositioning sailings for ships that cruise the Caribbean in winter and European waters in summer. Sometimes rates are reduced, and fly-cruise packages are usually available. Check the travel pages of your Sunday newspaper or contact a travel agent for lines and sailing dates. To get the best deal on a cruise, **consult a cruise-only travel agency.**

The Scottish Tourist Board's free brochure "Sail Scotland" includes details of many charter firms operating among the islands. The National Trust for Scotland runs a regular cruise program with lectures on natural history. The destination changes each year but may well include the west coast or Northern Isles the year you wish to visit. Hebridean Island Cruises offers 4-, 6-, 7-, and 14-night luxury cruises aboard the MV *Hebridean Princess* around the Scottish islands, including all the Western Isles.

To learn how to plan, choose, and book a cruise-ship voyage, consult *Fodor's FYI: Plan & Enjoy Your Cruise* (available in bookstores everywhere).

Cruise Information **Hebridean Island Cruises Ltd.** ✉ Griffin House, Broughton Hall, Skipton, North Yorkshire BD23 3AN ☎ 01756/701338 🖷 01756/704794 🌐 www.hebridean.co.uk. **National Trust for Scotland** ✉ National Trust for Scotland, Holiday Department, 28 Charlotte Sq., Edinburgh EH2 4ET ☎ 0131/243-9334 🌐 www.nts.org.uk.

CUSTOMS & DUTIES

When shopping abroad, **keep receipts** for all purchases. Upon reentering the country, **be ready to show customs officials what you've bought.** Pack purchases together in an easily accessible place. If you think a duty is incorrect, appeal the assessment. If you object to the way your clearance was handled, note the inspector's badge number. In either case, first ask to see a supervisor. If the problem isn't resolved, write to the appropriate authorities, beginning with the port director at your point of entry.

IN AUSTRALIA

Australian residents who are 18 or older may bring home A$400 worth of souvenirs and gifts (including jewelry), 250 cigarettes or 250 grams of cigars or other tobacco products, and 1,125 ml of alcohol (including wine, beer, and spirits). Residents under 18 may bring back A$200 worth of goods. Members of the same family traveling together may pool their allowances. Prohibited items include meat products. Seeds, plants, and fruits need to be declared upon arrival.

Australian Customs Service Regional Director, Box 8, Sydney, NSW 2001 02/9213-2000 or 1300/363263, 02/9364-7222 or 1800/803-006 quarantine-inquiry line 02/9213-4043 www.customs.gov.au.

IN CANADA

Canadian residents who have been out of Canada for at least seven days may bring in C$750 worth of goods duty-free. If you've been away fewer than seven days but more than 48 hours, the duty-free allowance drops to C$200. If your trip lasts 24 to 48 hours, the allowance is C$50. You may not pool allowances with family members. Goods claimed under the C$750 exemption may follow you by mail; those claimed under the lesser exemptions must accompany you. Alcohol and tobacco products may be included in the seven-day and 48-hour exemptions but not in the 24-hour exemption. If you meet the age requirements of the province or territory through which you reenter Canada, you may bring in, duty-free, 1.5 liters of wine *or* 1.14 liters (40 imperial ounces) of liquor *or* 24 12-ounce cans or bottles of beer or ale. Also, if you meet the local age requirement for tobacco products, you may bring in, duty-free, 200 cigarettes and 50 cigars. Check ahead of time with the Canada Customs and Revenue Agency or the Department of Agriculture for policies regarding meat products, seeds, plants, and fruits.

You may send an unlimited number of gifts (only one gift per recipient, however) worth up to C$60 each duty-free to Canada. Label the package UNSOLICITED GIFT—VALUE UNDER $60. Alcohol and tobacco are excluded.

Canada Customs and Revenue Agency 2265 St. Laurent Blvd., Ottawa, Ontario K1G 4K3 800/461-9999, 204/983-3500, 506/636-5064 www.ccra.gc.ca.

IN NEW ZEALAND

All homeward-bound residents may bring back NZ$700 worth of souvenirs and gifts; passengers may not pool their allowances, and children can claim only the concession on goods intended for their own use. For those 17 or older, the duty-free allowance also includes 4.5 liters of wine or beer; one 1,125-ml bottle of spirits; and either 200 cigarettes, 250 grams of tobacco, 50 cigars, *or* a combination of the three up to 250 grams. Meat products, seeds, plants, and fruits must be declared upon arrival to the Agricultural Services Department.

New Zealand Customs Head office: The Customhouse, 17–21 Whitmore St., Box 2218, Wellington 09/300-5399 or 0800/428-786 www.customs.govt.nz.

IN SCOTLAND

Entering the United Kingdom from outside Europe, a traveler 17 or older can take in (a) 200 cigarettes or 100 cigarillos or 50 cigars or 250 grams of tobacco; (b) 1 liter of spirits or strong liqueur more than 22% volume or 2 liters of fortified wine, sparkling wine, or other liqueurs; (c) 2 liters of still table wine; (d) 60 ml of perfume and 250 ml of toilet water; (e) other goods to a value of £145 (no pooling of exemptions is allowed).

HM Customs and Excise Portcullis House, 21 Cowbridge Rd. E, Cardiff CF11 9SS National Advice Line 0845/0109000 www.hmce.gov.uk.

IN THE U.S.

U.S. residents who have been out of the country for at least 48 hours may bring home, for personal use, $800 worth of foreign goods duty-free, as long as they haven't used the $800 allowance or any part of it in the past 30 days. This exemption may include 1 liter of alcohol (for travelers 21 and older), 200 cigarettes, and 100 non-Cuban cigars. Family members from the same household who are traveling together may pool their $800 personal exemptions. For fewer than 48 hours, the duty-free allowance drops to $200, which may include 50 cigarettes, 10 non-Cuban cigars, and 150 ml of alcohol (or 150 ml of perfume containing alcohol). The $200 allowance cannot be combined with other individuals' exemptions, and if you exceed it, the full value of all the goods will be taxed. Antiques, which the U.S. Bureau of Customs and Border Protection defines as objects more than 100 years old, enter duty-free, as do original works of art done entirely by hand, including paintings, drawings, and sculptures. This doesn't apply to folk art or handicrafts, which are in general dutiable.

You may also send packages home duty-free, with a limit of one parcel per addressee per day (except alcohol or tobacco products or perfume worth more than $5). You can mail up to $200 worth of goods for personal use; label the package PERSONAL USE and attach a list of its contents and their retail value. If the package contains your used personal belongings, mark it AMERICAN GOODS RETURNED to avoid paying duties. You may send up to $100 worth of goods as a gift; mark the package UNSOLICITED GIFT. Mailed items do not affect your duty-free allowance on your return.

To avoid paying duty on foreign-made high-ticket items you already own and will take on your trip, register them with Customs before you leave the country. Consider filing a Certificate of Registration for laptops, cameras, watches, and other digital devices identified with serial numbers or other permanent markings; you can keep the certificate for other trips. Otherwise, bring a sales receipt or insurance form to show that you owned the item before you left the United States.

U.S. Bureau of Customs and Border Protection ✉ for inquiries and equipment registration, 1300 Pennsylvania Ave. NW, Washington, DC 20229 🌐 www.customs.gov ☎ 877/287-8667, 202/354-1000 ✉ for complaints, Customer Satisfaction Unit, 1300 Pennsylvania Ave. NW, Room 5.5D, Washington, DC 20229.

DISABILITIES & ACCESSIBILITY

In Scotland many hotels provide facilities for people using wheelchairs, and special carriages are available on some intercity and long-distance trains. However, since much of Scotland's beauty is found in hidden hills and corners "off the beaten track," renting a car is probably a better option.

The Royal Association for Disability and Rehabilitation (RADAR) is command central for travel information and advice on accommodations through the British Isles and Europe. Its annual publication, *Holidays in Britain and Ireland,* is a good resource.

Local Resources **RADAR** ✉ 12 City Forum, 250 City Rd., London EC1V 8AF ☎ 020/7250-3222 🌐 www.radar.org.uk.

LODGING

Though many hotels, especially the newer ones, have facilities for travelers with disabilities, this is not usually the case in B&Bs and small guest houses in Scotland.

RESERVATIONS

When discussing accessibility with an operator or reservations agent, **ask hard questions.** Are there any stairs, inside *or* out? Are there grab bars next to the toilet *and* in the shower/tub? How wide is the doorway to the room? To the bathroom? For the most extensive facilities meeting the latest legal specifications, **opt for newer accommodations.** If you reserve through a toll-free number, consider also calling the hotel's local number to confirm the information from the central reservations office. Get confirmation in writing when you can.

SIGHTS & ATTRACTIONS

Many of the older castles may not be accessible to people who use wheelchairs. However, many of the recently built visitor centers must by law be accessible to people with mobility problems, and castles often have lovely gardens that may also be accessible. Most museums and galleries are wheelchair-accessible.

TRANSPORTATION

Hertz (⇨ Car Rental) can provide hand controls for its cars at its rental offices in Glasgow and Edinburgh. With advance notice, ScotRail staff will assist passengers with disabilities; inquire at any ScotRail area office.

Complaints **Aviation Consumer Protection Division** (⇨ Air Travel) for airline-related problems. **Departmental Office of Civil Rights** ✉ for general inquiries, U.S. Department of Transportation, S-30, 400 7th St. SW, Room 10215, Washington, DC 20590 ☎ 202/366-4648 🖷 202/366-9371 🌐 www.dot.gov/ost/docr/index.htm. **Disability Rights Section** ✉ NYAV, U.S. Department of Justice, Civil Rights Division, 950 Pennsylvania Ave. NW, Washington, DC 20530 ☎ ADA information line 202/514-0301, 800/514-0301, 202/514-0383 TTY, 800/514-0383 TTY 🌐 www.ada.gov. **U.S. Department of Transportation Hotline** ☎ for disability-related air-travel problems, 800/778-4838 or 800/455-9880 TTY.

TRAVEL AGENCIES

In the United States, the Americans with Disabilities Act requires that travel firms serve the needs of all travelers. Some agencies specialize in working with people with disabilities.

Travelers with Mobility Problems **Access Adventures/B. Roberts Travel** ✉ 206 Chestnut Ridge

Rd., Scottsville, NY 14624 ☎ 585/889-9096 🌐 www.brobertstravel.com ✉ dltravel@prodigy.net, run by a former physical-rehabilitation counselor. **CareVacations** ✉ No. 5, 5110-50 Ave., Leduc, Alberta, Canada, T9E 6V4 ☎ 780/986-6404 or 877/478-7827 📠 780/986-8332 🌐 www.carevacations.com, for group tours and cruise vacations. **Flying Wheels Travel** ✉ 143 W. Bridge St., Box 382, Owatonna, MN 55060 ☎ 507/451-5005 📠 507/451-1685 🌐 www.flyingwheelstravel.com.

DISCOUNTS & DEALS

Be a smart shopper and **compare all your options** before making decisions. A plane ticket bought with a promotional coupon from travel clubs, coupon books, and direct-mail offers or purchased on the Internet may not be cheaper than the least expensive fare from a discount ticket agency. And always keep in mind that what you get is just as important as what you save.

The Scottish Explorer Ticket, available from any staffed Historic Scotland (HS) property and from many tourist information centers, allows visits to HS properties for 3 days in a 5-day period (£15), 7 days in a 10-day period (£20), or 10 days in a 21-day period (£23). The Trust Discovery Pass, issued by the National Trust for Scotland, is available for 3 days (£12), 7 days (£17), or 14 days (£22) and allows access to all National Trust for Scotland properties. It's available to overseas visitors only and can be purchased from the National Trust for Scotland or some of the main tourist information centers.

The Great British Heritage Pass grants you access to sights administered by National Trust for Scotland and Historic Scotland as well as numerous other sights throughout Great Britain. A 7-day pass costs £35; 15-day and 30-day passes are also available. Contact the British Tourist Authority for more information.

The Royal Oak Foundation is the American affiliate of the British National Trust and the National Trust for Scotland. A $50 membership grants you free admission to National Trust for Scotland–administered sights for a year. Family memberships are also available.

i Discount Passes **British Tourist Authority** BTA; in the U.S. ✉ 551 5th Ave., 7th floor, New York, NY 10176 ☎ 212/986-2200 or 800/462-2748 ✉ [drop-in visits only] ✉ 625 N. Michigan Ave., Suite 1510, Chicago, IL 60611 ✉ in Canada ✉ 5915 Airport Rd., Suite 120, Mississauga, Ontario L4V 1T1 ☎ 905/405-1840 or 800/847-4885 🌐 www.travelbritain.com. **Royal Oak Society** ✉ 26 Broadway, Suite 950, New York, NY, 10004 ☎ 212/480-2889 or 800/913-6565 🌐 www.royal-oak.org. **Trust Touring Pass** ☎ 0131/243-9300.

DISCOUNT RESERVATIONS

To save money, **look into discount reservations services** with Web sites and toll-free numbers, which use their buying power to get a better price on hotels, airline tickets (⇨ Air Travel), even car rentals. When booking a room, always **call the hotel's local toll-free number** (if one is available) rather than the central reservations number—you'll often get a better price. Always ask about special packages or corporate rates.

When shopping for the best deal on hotels and car rentals, **look for guaranteed exchange rates,** which protect you against a falling dollar. With your rate locked in, you won't pay more, even if the price goes up in the local currency.

i Airline Tickets **Air 4 Less** ☎ 800/AIR4LESS; low-fare specialist.

i Hotel Rooms **Accommodations Express** ☎ 800/444-7666 or 800/277-1064 🌐 www.accommodationsexpress.com. **Hotels.com** ☎ 800/246-8357 or 214/369-1246 🌐 www.hotels.com. **Travel Interlink** ☎ 800/888-5898 🌐 www.travelinterlink.com. **Turbotrip.com** ☎ 800/473-7829 🌐 www.turbotrip.com.

PACKAGE DEALS

Don't confuse packages and guided tours. When you buy a package, you travel on your own, just as though you had planned the trip yourself. Fly/drive packages, which combine airfare and car rental, are often a good deal. If you **buy a rail/drive pass,** you may save on train tickets and car rentals. All Eurail- and Europass holders get a discount on Eurostar fares through the Channel Tunnel.

In cities, ask the local visitor's bureau about hotel packages that include tickets to major museum exhibits or other special events.

EATING & DRINKING

The restaurants we review in this book are the cream of the crop in each price category. City Scots usually take their midday meals in a pub, wine bar, bistro, or department-store restaurant (which might not serve alcohol and which might ban smoking). When traveling, Scots generally eat inexpensively and quickly at a country pub or village tearoom. Places like Glasgow, Edinburgh, and Aberdeen have restaurants of cosmopolitan character and various price levels; of these, the more notable tend to open only in the evening.

CATEGORY	COST
££££££	over £22
££££	£18–£22
£££	£13–£17
££	£7–£12
£	under £7

Prices are for a main course at dinner and are given in pounds.

MEALS & SPECIALTIES

Some restaurants have a Taste of Scotland menu, which allows you to try traditional Scottish cuisine.

To start the day with a full stomach, try a traditional Scottish breakfast of bacon and fried eggs served with sausage, fried mushrooms and tomatoes, and usually fried bread or potato scones. Most places also serve kippers (smoked herring). All this is in addition to juice, porridge, cereal, and toast and other bread products.

MEALTIMES

In a country so involved in the tourism industry, "all-day" meal places are becoming widespread. The normal lunch period, however, is 12:30–2:30. A few places serve "high tea"—one hot dish and masses of cakes, bread and butter, and jam, served with tea only, around 5:30–6:30.

Unless otherwise noted, the restaurants listed in this guide are open daily for lunch and dinner.

PAYING

Many restaurants exclude service charges from the printed menu (which the law obliges them to display outside), then add 10%–15% to the check, or else stamp SERVICE NOT INCLUDED along the bottom, in which case you should add the 10%–15% yourself. Just **don't pay twice for service**—unscrupulous restaurateurs have been known to add service but leave the total on the credit-card slip blank.

Credit cards are widely accepted at most types of restaurants.

RESERVATIONS & DRESS

Reservations are always a good idea; we mention them only when they're essential or not accepted. Book as far ahead as you can, and reconfirm as soon as you arrive. (Large parties should always call ahead to check the reservations policy.) We mention dress only when men are required to wear a jacket or a jacket and tie.

SERVICE

Note that most pubs do not have any waitstaff, and you're expected to go to the bar and order a beverage and your meal—this can be particularly disconcerting when you are seated in a "restaurant" upstairs but are still expected to go downstairs and get your own drinks and food. You are not expected to tip the bartender, but you are expected to tip restaurant waitstaff, by leaving 10%–15% of the tab on the table, *only* if SERVICE NOT INCLUDED is stamped on your bill.

WINE, BEER & SPIRITS

Bars typically sell two kinds of beer: lager is light in color, very carbonated, and served cold, and ale is dark, semicarbonated, and served just below room temperature. You may also come across a pub serving "real ales," which are hand-drawn, very flavorful beers from smaller breweries.

You can order Scotland's most famous beverage—whisky (here, most definitely spelled without an *e*)—at any local pub. All pubs serve any number of single-malt and blended whiskies. It's also possible to tour numerous distilleries, where you can sample a dram and purchase a bottle for the trip home. Most distilleries are concentrated in Speyside (on the Malt Whisky Trail) and Islay.

ELECTRICITY

To use electric-powered equipment purchased in the U.S. or Canada, **bring a converter and adapter.** The electrical current in Scotland is 220 volts, 50 cycles alternating current (AC); wall outlets take plugs with two round oversize prongs and plugs with three prongs.

If your appliances are dual-voltage, you'll need only an adapter. Don't use 110-volt outlets marked FOR SHAVERS ONLY for high-wattage appliances such as blow-dryers. Most laptops operate equally well on 110 and 220 volts and so require only an adapter. **Inquire at your hotel about surge protection,** however, as many properties do not have built-in current stabilizers.

EMBASSIES

Australia **Australia House** ✉ Strand, London, WC2 ☎ 020/7379–4334 🌐 www.australia.org.uk.

Canada **MacDonald House** ✉ 1 Grosvenor Sq., London, W1 ☎ 020/7258–6600 🌐 www.travelcanada.ca.

New Zealand **New Zealand House** ✉ 80 Haymarket, London, SW1Y 4TQ ☎ 020/7930–8422 🌐 www.newzealandhc.org.uk.

United States **American Consulate General** ✉ 3 Regent Terr., Calton, Edinburgh ☎ 0131/556–8315. **U.S. Embassy** ✉ 24 Grosvenor Sq., London, W1A 1AE ☎ 020/7499–9000; for passports go to the **U.S. Passport Unit** ✉ 55 Upper Brook St., London, W1A 2LQ ☎ 020/7499–9000 🌐 www.usembassy.org.uk.

EMERGENCIES

To contact the police, fire brigade, ambulance service, or coast guard, dial 999 from any phone. No coins are needed for emergency calls from public phone boxes.

ETIQUETTE & BEHAVIOR

If you're visiting a family home, a simple bouquet of flowers is a welcome gift. If you're invited for a meal, bringing a bottle of wine is appropriate, if you wish, as is some candy for the children. Kissing on greeting is still too Continental for most Brits; a warm handshake is just fine. The British can never say please or thank you too often, and to thank a host for hospitality, either a phone call or thank-you card is always appreciated.

BUSINESS ETIQUETTE

Punctuality is of prime importance, so **call ahead if you anticipate a late arrival.** Spouses do not generally attend business dinners, unless specifically invited. If you invite someone to dine, it is usually assumed that you will pick up the tab. However, if you are the visitor, your host may insist on paying.

GAY & LESBIAN TRAVEL

Outside the main cities, at least a sector of Scottish society is not given to much in the way of open expression of heterosexuality, let alone anything else. In short, Scotland isn't San Francisco. However, most Scots also have an attitude of live and let live, so it's unlikely you'll encounter problems or any real hostility.

The British Tourist Authority has a helpful Web site (🌐 www.gaybritain.org) for gay and lesbian travelers in Great Britain, including Edinburgh and Glasgow. You'll find recommendations for gay-friendly accommodations as well as great tips on restaurants, nightlife, festivals, and general travel information in these two cities.

Gay- & Lesbian-Friendly Travel Agencies **Different Roads Travel** ✉ 8383 Wilshire Blvd., Suite 520, Beverly Hills, CA 90211 ☎ 323/651–5557 or 800/429–8747 (Ext. 14 for both) 📠 323/651–3678 ✉ lgernert@tzell.com. **Kennedy Travel** ✉ 130 W. 42nd St., Suite 401, New York, NY 10036 ☎ 212/840–8659 or 800/237–7433 📠 212/730–2269 🌐 www.kennedytravel.com. **Now, Voyager** ✉ 4406 18th St., San Francisco, CA 94114 ☎ 415/626–1169 or 800/255–6951 📠 415/626–8626 🌐 www.nowvoyager.com. **Skylink Travel and Tour** ✉ 1455 N. Dutton Ave., Suite A, Santa Rosa, CA 95401 ☎ 707/546–9888 or 800/225–5759 📠 707/636–0951; serving lesbian travelers.

GUIDEBOOKS

Plan well and you won't be sorry. Guidebooks are excellent tools—and you can take them with you. You may want to check out color-photo-illustrated *Fodor's Exploring Scotland,* which is thorough on culture and history and is available at online retailers and bookstores everywhere.

HEALTH

No particular shots are necessary for visiting Scotland from the United States. If you are traveling in the Highlands and islands in summer, **pack some midge repellent and antihistamine cream** to reduce swelling: the Highland midge is a force to be reckoned with.

HOLIDAYS

The following dates are for public holidays in Scotland; note that the dates for England and Wales are slightly different. January 1–2 (Ne'er Day—and a day to recover), April 9 (Good Friday), May 3 (May Day), May 31, August 2 (Summer Bank Holiday), December 25–26. Note also that Scottish towns and villages set their own local holidays, on five or six Mondays in spring and summer, varying from town to town.

INSURANCE

The most useful travel-insurance plan is a comprehensive policy that includes coverage for trip cancellation and interruption, default, trip delay, and medical expenses (with a waiver for preexisting conditions).

Without insurance you'll lose all or most of your money if you cancel your trip, regardless of the reason. Default insurance covers you if your tour operator, airline, or cruise line goes out of business. Trip-delay covers expenses that arise because of bad weather or mechanical delays. Study the fine print when comparing policies.

If you're traveling internationally, a key component of travel insurance is coverage for medical bills incurred if you get sick on the road. Such expenses aren't generally covered by Medicare or private policies. Always **buy travel policies directly from the insurance company**; if you buy them from a cruise line, airline, or tour operator that goes out of business you probably won't be covered for the agency or operator's default, a major risk. Before making any purchase, **review your existing health and home-owner's policies** to find what they cover away from home.

Travel Insurers In the U.S.: **Access America** ✉ 6600 W. Broad St., Richmond, VA 23230 ☎ 800/284-8300 🖷 804/673-1491 or 800/346-9265 🌐 www.accessamerica.com. **Travel Guard International** ✉ 1145 Clark St., Stevens Point, WI 54481 ☎ 715/345-0505 or 800/826-1300 🖷 800/955-8785 🌐 www.travelguard.com.

In the U.K.: **Association of British Insurers** ✉ 51 Gresham St., London EC2V 7HQ ☎ 020/7600-3333 🖷 020/7696-8999 🌐 www.abi.org.uk. In Canada: **RBC Insurance** ✉ 6880 Financial Dr., Mississauga, Ontario L5N 7Y5 ☎ 800/565-3129 🖷 905/813-4704 🌐 www.rbcinsurance.com. In Australia: **Insurance Council of Australia** ✉ Insurance Enquiries and Complaints, Level 3, 56 Pitt St., Sydney, NSW 2000 ☎ 1300/363683 or 02/9251-4456 🖷 02/9251-4453 🌐 www.iecltd.com.au. In New Zealand: **Insurance Council of New Zealand** ✉ Level 7, 111-115 Customhouse Quay, Box 474, Wellington ☎ 04/472-5230 🖷 04/473-3011 🌐 www.icnz.org.nz.

LANGUAGE

The Lowland Scots language, which borrows from Scandinavian, Dutch, French, and Gaelic, survives in various forms but is virtually an underground language, spoken at home among ordinary folk, especially in its heartland, in northeast Scotland. Gaelic, too, hangs on in spite of the Highlands depopulation. Otherwise, Scots speak English with only an accent and virtually all will "modulate" either unconsciously or out of politeness into understandable English when conversing with a non-Scots speaker.

LODGING

The Scottish Tourist Board publishes two annually updated *Where to Stay* guides, *Hotels & Guest Houses* (£8.99) and *Bed & Breakfast* (£5.99), which give detailed information on facilities provided and classify and grade the accommodation using a simple star system (⇨ Hotels). These publications also indicate if an establishment participates in the Green Tourism Business Scheme, a program that encourages properties to undertake environmentally friendly business practices. The various area tourist boards also annually publish separate accommodation listings for their areas, which can be obtained either from the Scottish Tourist Board or from the individual area tourist authority.

The lodgings we list are the cream of the crop in each price category. Properties are assigned price categories based on the range from their least-expensive standard double room at high season (excluding holidays) to the most expensive. Properties marked ✕🏨 are lodging establishments whose restaurants warrant a special trip. Unless otherwise noted, all lodgings listed have a private bathroom, air-conditioning, a room phone, and a television.

We always list the facilities that are available, but we don't specify whether they cost extra; when pricing accommodations, always ask what's included and what costs extra. Many hotels and most guest houses and B&Bs include a breakfast within the basic room rate. Assume that hotels operate on the **European Plan** (EP, with no meals) unless we specify that they use the **Continental Plan** (CP, with a Continental breakfast), **Breakfast Plan** (BP, with a full breakfast), or the**Modified American Plan** (MAP, with breakfast and dinner). Meal plan symbols appear at the end of a review.

CATEGORY	MAIN CITIES	ELSEWHERE
££££££	over £175	over £150
££££	£135-£175	£110-£150
£££	£95-£135	£80-£110
££	£55-£95	£50-£80
£	under £55	under £50

Prices are for two people in a standard double room in high season, including the 17.5% VAT, and are given in pounds. Main cities include Edinburgh and Glasgow.

APARTMENT & VILLA RENTALS

If you want a home base that's roomy enough for a family and comes with cooking facilities, **consider a furnished rental.** These can save you money, especially if you're traveling with a group. Home-exchange directories sometimes list rentals as well as exchanges.

International Agents **At Home Abroad** ✉ 405 E. 56th St., Suite 6H, New York, NY 10022 ☎ 212/421-9165 📠 212/752-1591 🌐 www.athomeabroadinc.com. **Hideaways International** ✉ 767 Islington St., Portsmouth, NH 03801 ☎ 603/430-4433 or 800/843-4433 📠 603/430-4444 🌐 www.hideaways.com, membership $145. **Hometours International** ✉ 1108 Scottie La., Knoxville, TN 37919 ☎ 865/690-8484 or 866/367-4668 🌐 http://thor.he.net/~hometour/. **Interhome** ✉ 1990 N.E. 163rd St., Suite 110, North Miami Beach, FL 33162 ☎ 305/940-2299 or 800/882-6864 📠 305/940-2911 🌐 www.interhome.us. **Villas and Apartments Abroad** ✉ 370 Lexington Ave., Suite 1401, New York, NY 10017 ☎ 212/897-5045 or 800/433-3020 📠 212/897-5039 🌐 www.ideal-villas.com.**Villas International** ✉ 4340 Redwood Hwy., Suite D309, San Rafael, CA 94903fm8 ☎ 415/499-9490 or 800/221-2260 📠 415/499-9491 🌐 www.villasintl.com.

BED-AND-BREAKFASTS

B&Bs, common throughout Scotland, are a special British tradition and the backbone of budget travel. They are usually in a family home, don't often have private bathrooms, and usually offer only breakfast. Guest houses are a slightly larger, somewhat more luxurious version. More upscale B&Bs, along the line of American B&Bs, can be found in Edinburgh and Glasgow especially, but in other parts of Scotland as well. All provide a glimpse of everyday British life.

Reservation Services **Bed & Breakfast (GB)** ☎ 800/454-8704, 01491/578803 in the U.K. 📠 01491/410806 🌐 www.bedbreak.com.

CAMPING

Camping is an economical option for budget travelers. Consult *Forestry Commission Camping and Caravan Sites* and *Cabin Sites* (both free from the Forestry Commission), or the Scottish Tourist Board publication, *Caravan & Camping Parks* (£3.99). For assistance planning a bicycle-camping trip, contact the Camping and Caravanning Club.

Camping and Caravanning Club ✉ Greenfields House, Westwood Way, Coventry, England CV4 8JH ☎ 024/7669-4995 🌐 www.campingandcaravanningclub.co.uk. **Forestry Commission** ✉ 231 Corstorphine Rd., Edinburgh, Scotland EH12 7AT ☎ 0131/334-0303 🌐 www.forestry.gov.uk.

FARMHOUSE & CROFTING HOLIDAYS

A popular option for families with children is a farmhouse holiday, combining the freedom of B&B accommodations with the hospitality of Scottish family life. Information is available from the British Tourist Authority or the Scottish Tourist Board (⇨ Visitor Information), from Scottish Farmhouse Holidays, and from the Farm Stay UK.

Farm Stay UK ✉ National Agricultural Centre, Stoneleigh, Warwickshire, England CV8 2LG ☎ 024/7669-6909 🌐 www.farmstayuk.co.uk. **Scottish Farmhouse Holidays** ✉ 1 Renton Terr., Eyemouth, Berwickshire, Scotland TD14 5DF ☎ 01890/751830 📠 01890/751831 🌐 www.scotfarmhols.co.uk.

HOME EXCHANGES

If you would like to exchange your home for someone else's, **join a home-exchange organization,** which will send you its updated listings of available exchanges for a year and will include your own listing in at least one of them. It's up to you to make specific arrangements.

Exchange Clubs **HomeLink International** 📫 Box 47747, Tampa, FL 33647 ☎ 813/975-9825 or 800/638-3841 📠 813/910-8144 🌐 www.homelink.org; $110 yearly for a listing, on-line access, and catalog; $40 without catalog. **Intervac U.S.** ✉ 30 Corte San Fernando, Tiburon, CA 94920 ☎ 800/756-4663 📠 415/435-7440 🌐 www.intervacus.com; $105 yearly for a listing, on-line access, and a catalog; $50 without catalog.

HOSTELS

No matter what your age, you can **save on lodging costs by staying at hostels.** In some 4,500 locations in more than 70 countries around the world, Hostelling International (HI), the umbrella group for a number of national youth-hostel associations, offers single-sex, dorm-style beds and sometimes rooms for couples and families. Most hostels in Scotland are very basic, but some are quite funky. Hostels in rural areas tend to fill up with older people, hill walkers, and nature lovers (a quieter bunch). Hostels are not good for people who want privacy or don't want to sit around a communal table to eat meals and talk to fellow travelers. Most hostels have very few rooms with double or triple accommodation, so book well in advance. Membership in any HI national hostel association, open to travelers of all ages, allows you to stay in HI-affiliated hostels at member rates; one-year membership is about $28 for adults (C$35 for a two-year minimum membership in Canada, £13.50 in the U.K., A$52 in Australia, and NZ$40 in New Zealand); hostels charge about $10–$30 per night. Members have priority if the hostel is full; they're also eligible for discounts around the world, even on rail and bus travel in some countries.

Organizations **Hostelling International–USA** ✉ 8401 Colesville Rd., Suite 600, Silver Spring, MD 20910 ☎ 301/495-1240 📠 301/495-6697 🌐 www.hiayh.org. **Hostelling International–Canada** ✉ 205 Catherine St., Suite 400, Ottawa, Ontario K2P 1C3 ☎ 613/237-7884 or 800/663-5777 📠 613/237-7868 🌐 www.hihostels.ca. **YHA England and Wales** ✉ Trevelyan House, Dimple Rd., Matlock, Derbyshire DE4 3YH, U.K. ☎ 0870/870-8808, 0870/770-8868, 0162/959-2700 📠 0870/770-6127 🌐 www.yha.org.uk.**YHA Australia** ✉ 422 Kent St., Sydney, NSW 2001 ☎ 02/9261-1111 📠 02/9261-1969 🌐 www.yha.com.au.**YHA New Zealand** ✉ Level 4, Torrens House, 195 Hereford St., Box 436, Christchurch ☎ 03/379-9970 or 0800/278-299 📠 03/365-4476 🌐 www.yha.org.nz.

HOTELS

Hotels in the larger cities are generally of good quality. Glasgow and Edinburgh have good hotels in all price categories, including a number of superior establishment.

If you are touring around, you are not likely to be stranded: in recent years, even in the height of the season—July and August—hotel occupancy has run at about 80%. On the other hand, if you arrive in Edinburgh at festival time or some place where a big Highland Gathering or golf tournament is in progress, you'll have an extremely limited choice of accommodations, and your best bet will be to try for a room in a nearby village. To secure your first choice, **reserve in advance**, either through a travel agent at home, directly with the facility, or through local information centers (⇨ individual city or regional chapters), making use of their "Book-a-Bed-Ahead" services. Telephone bookings made from home should be confirmed by letter. Country hotels expect you to turn up by about 6 PM.

Scotland, like the rest of the United Kingdom, runs a national star (1–5 stars) grading scheme to take some of the guesswork out of booking accommodations. When you're considering a hotel, guest house, or B&B, make sure that you pay close attention to its grading. The awards are part of the accommodations listing in the *Where to Stay* guides distributed at most tourist information centers. Not all establishments participate, but the scheme is becoming popular.

All hotels listed have private bath unless otherwise noted.

Recommended Hotels **Scotland's Hotels of Distinction** ✆ Central Reservations Office, Box 14610, Leven, Fife, KY8 6ZA ☎ 01333/360888 📠 01333/360809 🌐 www.hotels-of-distinction.com.

Toll-Free Numbers **Best Western** ☎ 800/528-1234 🌐 www.bestwestern.com. **Choice** ☎ 800/424-6423 🌐 www.choicehotels.com. **Comfort Inn** ☎ 800/424-6423 🌐 www.choicehotels.com.**Days Inn** ☎ 800/325-2525 🌐 www.daysinn.com. **Hilton** ☎ 800/445-8667 🌐 www.hilton.com. **Holiday Inn** ☎ 800/465-4329 🌐 www.sixcontinentshotels.com. **Inter-Continental** ☎ 800/327-0200 🌐 www.intercontinental.com. **Marriott** ☎ 800/228-9290 🌐 www.marriott.com. **Le Meridien** ☎ 800/543-4300 🌐 www.lemeridien-hotels.com. **Quality Inn** ☎ 800/424-6423 🌐 www.choicehotels.com. **Radisson** ☎ 800/333-3333 🌐 www.radisson.com. **Ramada** ☎ 800/228-2828, 800/854-7854 international reservations 🌐 www.ramada.com or www.ramadahotels.com. **Sheraton** ☎ 800/325-3535 🌐 www.starwood.com/sheraton. **Westin Hotels & Resorts** ☎ 800/228-3000 🌐 www.starwood.com/westin.

MAIL & SHIPPING

Allow at least four days for a letter or postcard to reach the United States by air mail. Surface mail service can take up to four or five weeks.

OVERNIGHT SERVICES

To find the nearest branch providing overnight mail services, contact the following agencies.

Major Services **DHL** ☎ 08701/100300. **FedEx** ☎ 0870/2400555 for Omega, agent for FedEx. **TNT** ☎ 0800/100600.

POSTAL RATES

Airmail letters and aerograms to the United States, Canada, Australia, and New Zealand cost 45p (under 10 grams) or 65p (under 20 grams); postcards cost 40p. Letters and postcards to Europe under 20 grams cost 37p. Within the United Kingdom first-class letters cost 28p, second-class letters and postcards 20p.

RECEIVING MAIL

If you're uncertain where you'll be staying, you can **arrange to have your mail sent to American Express.** The service is free to cardholders; all others pay a small fee. You can also collect letters at any post office by addressing them to "poste restante" at the post office you nominate. In Edinburgh a convenient central office is St. James Centre Post Office, St. James Centre, Edinburgh, EH1 3SR, Scotland.

SHIPPING PARCELS

Most department stores and retail outlets can arrange to ship your goods home. You should check your insurance for coverage of possible damage. If you want to ship goods yourself, use one of the overnight postal services, such as Federal Express, DHL, or Parcelforce. Shipping to North America, New Zealand, or Australia can take anywhere from overnight to a month, depending on how much you pay.

MEDIA

NEWSPAPERS & MAGAZINES

Scotland's major newspapers include the *Scotsman*—a conservative sheet that also self-styles itself as the journal of record—and the moderate *Glasgow Herald,* along with the tabloid *Daily Record.* The leader in terms of circulation, if not downright regional Scottish style, is the Aberdeen-based *Press and Journal*; an apocryphal tale relates that the *P&J* headlined the *Titanic* sinking as "North-East Man Drowns at Sea." The *Sunday Post,* conservative in bent, is the country's leading Sunday paper; *Scotland on Sunday* competes directly with London's *Sunday Times* for clout north of the border; and the *Sunday Herald,* an offshoot of the *Glasgow Herald,* is another major title. There are also many regional publications in Scotland; the *List,* a twice-monthly magazine with listings comparable to London's *Time Out,* covers the Glasgow and Edinburgh scenes. Many Scottish newsstands also feature editions of the leading London newspapers, such as the *London Times,* the *Evening Standard,* the *Independent,* and the *Guardian;* the *Sunday Telegraph* usually has the biggest Scotland coverage.

For magazines the selection is smaller and its purview is less sophisticated. *Heritage Scotland,* a publication of the National Trust, covers the historic preservation beat. *Scottish Homes and Interiors* is devoted to home design and style, and the *Scottish Field* covers matters dealing with the countryside. More regional in focus are the *People's Friend,* a Dundee-based publication that can be likened to a down-market *Readers' Digest,* and the *Leopard,* which covers the northeast regions around Aberdeen. For more regional coverage check out the glossy *Scottish Life.*

RADIO & TELEVISION

The Scotland offshoot of the British Broadcasting Corporation, BBC Scotland, is based in Glasgow and has a wide variety of Scotland-based TV programming. BBC Scotland usually feeds its programs into the various BBC channels, including BBC1 and BBC2, the latter considered the more eclectic and artsy, with a higher proportion of alternative humor, drama, and documentaries. Channel 3 is used by independent channels, which can change from region to region in Scotland: Grampian, the Borders, and Scottish are three channels that are regional in focus, with Grampian beamed into the north and west of Scotland and Scottish into the southern regions. Scottish TV ranges from popular weekly shows such as *The Bill,* a detective drama, to enormous coverage of Scottish soccer and rugby matches. Originating in England, Channel 4 is a mixture of mainstream and off-the-wall programming, whereas Channel 5 has more sports and films. Satellite TV has brought dozens more channels to Britain.

Radio has seen a similar explosion for every taste, from 24-hour classics on Classic FM (100–102 MHz) to rock (Richard Branson's Virgin at 105.8 MHz). BBC Radio Scotland is a leading radio station, tops for local news and useful as it provides Scottish (rather than English) weather information. Originating from England—and therefore not always received in regions throughout Scotland—the BBC channels include Channel 1 (FM 97.6) for the young and hip; 2 (FM 88) for middle-of-the-roadsters; 3 (FM 90.2) for classics, jazz, and arts; 4 (FM 92.4) for news, current affairs, drama, and documentaries; and 5 Live (MW 693 kHz) for sports and news coverage, with listener phone-ins.

MONEY MATTERS

A local newspaper will cost you about 40p and a national daily, 50p. A pint of beer costs around £1.80 and a serving of whisky about the same. A cup of coffee will run from 90p to £1.50, depending on where you drink it; a ham sandwich, £2; lunch in a pub, £4 and up (plus your drink).

A man's haircut costs £4 and up; a woman's anywhere from £10 to £30. It costs about £1.50 to have a shirt laundered, from £6 to dry-clean a dress, and from £9 to dry-clean a man's suit.

A theater seat will cost from £5 to £30 in Edinburgh and Glasgow, less elsewhere.

Prices throughout this guide are given for adults. Substantially reduced fees are almost always available for children, students, and senior citizens. For information on taxes, *see* Taxes.

ATMS

ATMs are available throughout Scotland at banks and numerous other locations such as railway stations, gas stations, and department stores.

ATM Locations **Cirrus** ☎ 800/424-7787 🌐 www.mastercard.com. **Plus** ☎ 800/843-7587 🌐 www.visa.com.

CREDIT CARDS

MasterCard and Visa are the most widely accepted credit cards. American Express is accepted at larger department stores and hotels, but Diners Club is not widely accepted in Scotland.

Throughout this guide, the following abbreviations are used: **AE,** American Express; **DC,** Diners Club; **MC,** MasterCard; and **V,** Visa.

Reporting Lost Cards **American Express** ☎ 312/935-3600, 910/668-5309 in U.S. collect. **Diners Club** ☎ 303/779-1504 in U.S. collect, 0800/460800 in Scotland. **MasterCard** ☎ 800/964-767 toll free, 314/542-7111 in U.S. collect. **Visa** ☎ 800/985082 toll free, 410/581-3836 in U.S. collect.

CURRENCY

Britain's currency is the pound sterling, which is divided into 100 pence (100p). Notes are issued in the values of £50, £20, £10, and £5. Coins are issued in the values of £2, £1, 50p, 20p, 10p, 5p, 2p, and 1p. Scottish coins are the same as English ones, but Scottish notes are issued by three banks: the Bank of Scotland, the Royal Bank of Scotland, and the Clydesdale Bank. They have the same face values as English notes, and English notes are interchangeable with them in Scotland.

CURRENCY EXCHANGE

At press time, the exchange rate was about Australian $2.50, Canadian $2.25, New Zealand $2.77, and U.S. $1.60 to the pound. Britain's entry into the European Union's currency—the euro—continues to be debated.

For the most favorable rates, **change money through banks.** Although ATM transaction fees may be higher abroad than at home, ATM rates are excellent because they're based on wholesale rates offered only by major banks. You won't do as well at exchange booths in airports or rail and bus stations, in hotels, in restaurants, or in stores. To avoid lines at airport exchange booths, **get a bit of local currency before you leave home.**

Exchange Services **International Currency Express** ✉ 427 N. Camden Dr., Suite F, Beverly Hills, CA 90210 ☎ 888/278-6628 orders 📠 310/278-6410 🌐 www.foreignmoney.com. **Thomas Cook International Money Services** ☎ 800/287-7362 orders and retail locations 🌐 www.us.thomascook.com.

TRAVELER'S CHECKS

Do you need traveler's checks? It depends on where you're headed. If you're going to rural areas and small towns, go with cash; traveler's checks are best used in cities. Lost or stolen checks can usually be replaced within 24 hours. To ensure a speedy refund, buy your own traveler's checks—don't let someone else pay for them: irregularities like this can cause delays. The person who bought the checks should make the call to request a refund. If you plan to use traveler's checks, buy them in pounds.

PACKING

Travel light. Porters are more or less wholly extinct these days (and very expensive where you can find them).

In Scotland casual clothes are de rigueur, and very few hotels or restaurants insist on jackets and ties for men in the evening. For summer, lightweight clothing is usually adequate, except in the evenings, when you'll need a jacket or sweater. A waterproof coat or parka is essential. Drip-dry and wrinkle-resistant fabrics are a good bet since only the most prestigious hotels have speedy laundering or dry-cleaning service.

Many visitors to Scotland appear to think it necessary to adopt a Scottish costume. It's not. Scots themselves do not wear tartan ties or Balmoral "bunnets" (caps), and only an enthusiastic minority prefers the kilt for everyday wear.

In your carry-on luggage, **pack an extra pair of eyeglasses or contact lenses and enough of any medication** you take to last a few days longer than the entire trip. You may also ask your doctor to write a spare prescription using the drug's generic name, as brand names may vary from country to country. In luggage to be checked, **never pack prescription drugs, valuables, or undeveloped film.** And don't forget to carry with you the addresses of offices that handle refunds of lost traveler's checks. Check *Fodor's How to Pack* (available at on-line retailers and bookstores everywhere) for more tips.

To avoid customs and security delays, carry medications in their original packaging. Don't pack any sharp objects in your carry-on luggage, including knives of any size or material, scissors, and corkscrews, or anything else that might arouse suspicion.

To avoid having your checked luggage chosen for hand inspection, don't cram bags full. The U.S. Transportation Security Administration suggests packing shoes on top and placing personal items you don't want touched in clear plastic bags.

CHECKING LUGGAGE

You're allowed to carry aboard one bag and one personal article, such as a purse or a laptop computer. Make sure what you carry on fits under your seat or in the overhead bin. Get to the gate early, so you can board as soon as possible, before the overhead bins fill up.

Baggage allowances vary by carrier, destination, and ticket class. On international flights, you're usually allowed to check two bags weighing up to 70 pounds (32 kilograms) each, although a few airlines allow checked bags of up to 88 pounds (40 kilograms) in first class. Some international carriers don't allow more than 66 pounds (30 kilograms) per bag in business class and 44 pounds (20 kilograms) in economy. On domestic flights, the limit is usually 50 to 70 pounds (23 to 32 kilograms) per bag. In general, carry-on bags shouldn't exceed 40 pounds (18 kilograms). Most airlines won't accept bags that weigh more than 100 pounds (45 kilograms) on domestic or international flights. Check baggage restrictions with your carrier before you pack.

Airline liability for baggage is limited to $2,500 per person on flights within the United States. On international flights it amounts to $9.07 per pound or $20 per kilogram for checked baggage (roughly $640 per 70-pound bag), with a maximum of $634.90 per piece, and $400 per passenger for unchecked baggage. You can buy additional coverage at check-in for about $10 per $1,000 of coverage, but it often excludes a rather extensive list of items, shown on your airline ticket.

Before departure, **itemize your bags' contents** and their worth, and label the bags with your name, address, and phone number. (If you use your home address, cover it so potential thieves can't see it readily.) Include a label inside each bag and **pack a copy of your itinerary.** At check-in, **make sure each bag is correctly tagged** with the destination airport's three-letter code. Because some checked bags will be opened for hand inspection, the U.S. Transportation Security Administration recommends that you leave luggage unlocked or use the plastic locks offered at check-in. TSA screeners place an inspection notice inside searched bags, which are re-sealed with a special lock.

If your bag has been searched and contents are missing or damaged, file a claim with the TSA Consumer Response Center as soon as possible. If your bags arrive damaged or fail to arrive at all, file a written report with the airline before leaving the airport.

Complaints **U.S. Transportation Security Administration Consumer Response Center** ☎ 866/289-9673 🌐 www.tsa.gov.

PASSPORTS & VISAS

When traveling internationally, **carry your passport** even if you don't need one (it's always the best form of I.D.) and **make two photocopies of the data page** (one for someone at home and another for you, carried separately from your passport). If you lose your passport, promptly call the nearest embassy or consulate and the local police.

U.S. passport applications for children under age 14 require consent from both parents or legal guardians; both parents must appear together to sign the application. If only one parent appears, he or she must submit a written statement from the other parent authorizing passport issuance for the child. A parent with sole authority must present evidence of it when applying; acceptable documentation includes the child's certified birth certificate listing only the applying parent, a court order specifically permitting this parent's travel with the child, or a death certificate for the non-applying parent. Application forms and instructions are available on the Web site of the U.S. State Department's Bureau of Consular Affairs (www.travel.state.gov).

ENTERING SCOTLAND

U.S. and Canadian citizens need only a valid passport to enter Great Britain for stays of up to six months. Australian citizens need a passport with at least six months' validity and can stay in Britain for up to six months without a visa when on vacation. New Zealand citizens need a valid passport and can stay up to six months on vacation. Travelers should be prepared to show sufficient funds to support and accommodate themselves while in Britain and to show a return or onward ticket. Health certificates are not required. The best time to apply for, or renew, a passport is in fall and winter. Before any trip, check your passport's expiration date, and, if necessary, renew it as soon as possible.

Australian Citizens **Passports Australia** 131-232 www.passports.gov.au.

Canadian Citizens **Passport Office** to mail in applications: 200 Promenade du Portage, Hull, Québec J8X 4B7 819/994-3500, 800/567-6868, 866/255-7655 TTY www.ppt.gc.ca.

New Zealand Citizens **New Zealand Passports Office** 0800/22-5050 or 04/474-8100 www.passports.govt.nz.

U.S. Citizens **National Passport Information Center** 900/225-5674 or 900/225-7778 TTY (calls are 55¢ per minute for automated service or $1.50 per minute for operator service), 888/362-8668 or 888/498-3648 TTY (calls are $5.50 each) www.travel.state.gov.

REST ROOMS

Most cities, towns, and villages have public rest rooms, indicated by signposts to WC, TOILETS, or PUBLIC CONVENIENCES. They vary hugely in cleanliness. You'll often have to pay a small amount (usually 20p) to enter public conveniences; a request for payment usually indicates a high standard of cleanliness. Gas stations, called petrol stations, also usually have rest rooms (to which the above comments also apply). In towns and cities, department stores, hotels and restaurants, and pubs are usually your best bets for at least reasonable standards of hygiene.

SAFETY

Don't wear a money belt or a waist pack, both of which peg you as a tourist. Distribute your cash and any valuables (including your credit cards and passport) between a deep front pocket, an inside jacket or vest pocket, and a hidden money pouch. Do not reach for the money pouch once you're in public.

WOMEN IN SCOTLAND

Scotland in general is a safe country for travel, but normal rules of common sense apply. Don't walk on your own late at night in major cities. If you carry a purse, choose one with a zipper and a thick strap that you can drape across your body; adjust the length so that the purse sits in front of you at or above hip level. Note that single rooms may be hard to find in hotels and guest houses, and proprietors may not be willing to rent a double room at the single rate if it's early enough in the day to hope for a couple to book it. Booking accommodations in advance is a good idea, especially if you're traveling in rural areas.

SENIOR-CITIZEN TRAVEL

Scotland has a wide variety of discounts and travel bargains for anyone over 60. Look into the Senior Citizen Railcard; it's available in all major railway stations and offers one-third off most rail fares. The cost is £18. Travelers age 50 and older are eligible for the Vantage 50 Coach Card (£7), available at all bus stations. It provides up to 20% off all long-distance National Express or Scottish Citylink coach fares in Britain.

Many hotels advertise off-season discounts for senior citizens, and some offer year-round savings. Budget-minded seniors may also **consider overnight accommodations at a university or college residence hall** (⇨ Students in Scotland).

For discounted admission to hundreds of museums, historic buildings, and attractions throughout Britain, senior citizens need show only a passport as proof of age. Reduced-rate tickets to the theater and ballet are also available.

To qualify for age-related discounts, **mention your senior-citizen status up front** when booking hotel reservations (not when checking out) and before you're seated in restaurants (not when paying the bill). Be sure to have identification on hand. When renting a car, ask about promotional car-rental discounts, which can be cheaper than senior-citizen rates.

Educational Programs **Elderhostel** ✉ 11 Ave. de Lafayette, Boston, MA 02111-1746 ☎ 877/426-8056, 978/323-4141 international callers, 877/426-2167 TTY 📠 877/426-2166 🌐 www.elderhostel.org. **Interhostel** ✉ University of New Hampshire, 6 Garrison Ave., Durham, NH 03824 ☎ 603/862-1147 or 800/733-9753 📠 603/862-1113 🌐 www.learn.unh.edu.

SHOPPING

Tartans, tweeds, and woolens may be a Scottish cliché, but nevertheless the selection, quality, and generally reasonable prices of these goods make them a must-have for many visitors, whether a complete made-to-measure traditional kilt outfit or a classy designer sweater from Skye. Particular bargains can be found in Scottish cashmere sweaters; look for Johnstons of Elgin, and Ballantyne, two high-quality labels.

Food items are another popular purchase: whether shortbread, smoked salmon, boiled sweets, *tablet* (a type of hard fudge), marmalade and raspberry jams, Dundee cake, or black bun, it's far too easy to eat your way around Scotland.

Unique jewelry is available all over Scotland but especially in some of the remote regions where get-away-from-it-all craftspeople have set up shop amid the idyllic scenery.

Scottish antique pottery and table silver make unusual, if sometimes pricey, souvenirs: a Wemyss-ware pig for the mantelpiece, perhaps, or Edinburgh silver candelabra for the dining table. Antiques shops and one- or two-day antiques fairs held in hotels abound all over Scotland. In general, goods are reasonably priced: shops in small communities must deal fairly if they hope for repeat business. Most dealers will drop the price a little if asked, "What's your best price?"

KEY DESTINATIONS

For designer clothing Glasgow is the place to start; the Princes Square mall is an especially rich hunting ground. However, if you're coming from the United States you may find clothing rather expensive compared with the prices back home for similar items, such as designer jeans.

For jewelry, Skye Silver, of Glendale on Skye (⇨ Chapter 9), and Ola Gorrie at the Longship, of Kirkwall, Orkney (⇨ Chapter 10), sell particularly attractive and unusual designs. Antique Scottish pebble jewelry is another unique style of jewelry; several specialist antique jewelry shops can be found in Edinburgh and Glasgow.

SMART SOUVENIRS

Shops in museums, galleries, and stately homes around the country are often good choices for interesting merchandise, such as high-quality art reproductions, stationery, and beautifully packaged foods such as jam, toffee, and tea. Bookshops and antiques stores stock a plethora of unique and interesting souvenirs.

WATCH OUT

For art or antiques more than 100 years old, get a Certificate of Age and Origin for customs from the Association of Art and Antique Dealers (LAPADA) or from the dealer selling the piece. Anything more than 50 years old and valued at £39,600 or more needs a certificate, too. Beware of antique items that contain anything from an endangered species, such as tortoiseshell or ivory. You need a permit from the Department of Environment, Food and Rural Affairs to take such items out of Britain.

Association of Art and Antiques Dealers ✉ 535 Kings Rd. London SW10 0SZ ☎ 020/7823-3511 🌐 www.lapada.co.uk. **Department of Environment, Food and Rural Affairs** ✉ Global Wildlife Division, 2 The Square, Temple Quay Bristol BS1 6EH ☎ 0117/372-8433.

SIGHTSEEING GUIDES

The Scottish Tourist Guides Association has members throughout Scotland who are fully qualified professional guides able to conduct walking tours in the major cities, half- or full-day tours or extended tours throughout Scotland, driving tours, and special study tours. Many guides speak at least one language in addition to English. Fees are negotiable with individual guides, a list of whom can be obtained from the address below.

Tourist Guides Association **Scottish Tourist Guides Association** ✉ Bookings Service, STGA, Old Town Jail, St. John's St., Stirling FK8 1EA ☎ 01786/451953 🌐 www.stga.co.uk.

SPORTS & OUTDOORS

A drive of an hour or two outside Edinburgh and Glasgow brings you to the sort of landscape you'd have to travel hours to reach in other countries. And within this landscape you can play on some 500 golf courses; walk and hike, whether on a long-distance path or up a 3,000-ft mountain; fish in glistening lochs and rivers; and bike on dedicated cycleways. You may also find some surprises, such as surfing: the waves off the beaches of Harris and Tiree, in the west, and off Fraserburgh Beach, in the far northeast, attract aficionados from the whole of Britain. Diving is also a possibility; the wrecks of the German navy scuttled in 1919 in Scapa Flow, Orkney, draw divers from far and wide.

With sports and the outdoors being such a large part of Scottish life and a big attraction for visitors, VisitScotland (the Scottish Tourist Board) is well prepared, with numerous books and leaflets covering each activity. Contact VisitScotland's Central Information Department, which can provide all the advice you'll need in advance, whatever your interest. If you're interested in hiking through the mountains of the north and west Highlands, visit 🌐 www.walkingwild.com, run by VisitScotland.

Once you arrive in Scotland, check out the tourist information centers wherever you're staying for local information and fishing permits.

VisitScotland, Central Information Department ✉ 23 Ravelston Terr., Edinburgh EH4 3EU ☎ 0131/332-2433 🌐 www.visitscotland.com.

STUDENTS IN SCOTLAND

A student I.D. card can get you discounted admissions at some sights.

A Student Coach Card from National Express, available in two versions to full-time students age 17 and older, provides 20% or 30% off all long-distance coach fares in Britain; contact any National Express agent in Britain. Those 16–25 are eligible for the same reductions via the National Express Young Person's Coach Card. The 20%-off passes are free; the 30%-off passes cost £7.

A Young Person's rail card costs £18, is available to people 16–25, and provides discounts of up to one-third off the regular train ticket price. The card is available through most train stations; you'll need to show proof of student status and provide a passport photo. Contact ScotRail for more information.

I.D.s & Services **STA Travel** ✉ 10 Downing St., New York, NY 10014 ☎ 212/627-3111, 800/777-0112 24-hour service center 📠 212/627-3387 🌐 www.sta.com. **Travel Cuts** ✉ 187 College St., Toronto, Ontario M5T 1P7, Canada ☎ 800/592-2887 in the U.S., 416/979-2406 or 866/246-9762 in Canada 📠 416/979-8167 🌐 www.travelcuts.com.

UNIVERSITY HOUSING

Many universities and colleges throughout Britain open their halls of residence to visitors during vacation periods—that is, from mid-March to mid-April, from July to September, and during the Christmas holidays. Campus accommodations—usually single rooms with access to lounges, libraries, and sports facilities—include breakfast and generally cost about £30 per night. Locations vary, from city centers to bucolic lakeside parks.

University of Strathclyde ☎ 0141/553-4148 📠 0141/553-4149 🌐 www.rescat.strath.ac.uk. **University of Glasgow** ☎ 0141/330-3123 📠 0141/330-2036 🌐 www.cvso.co.uk. **University of Stirling** ☎ 01786/466066 🌐 www.external.stir.ac.uk. **Venuemasters Scotland** ☎ 01786/466066 🌐 www.venuemasters.co.uk.

TAXES

An airport departure tax of £20 (£10 for within U.K. and EU countries) per person is payable, and may be subject to more government increases, although it is included in the price of your ticket.

VALUE-ADDED TAX

The British sales tax, V.A.T. (Value-Added Tax), is 17.5%. The tax is almost always included in quoted prices in shops, hotels, and restaurants. The most common exception is at high-end hotels, where prices often exclude V.A.T. Be sure to verify whether the quoted room price includes V.A.T.

When making a purchase, **ask for a V.A.T. refund form** and find out whether the merchant gives refunds—not all stores do, nor are they required to. Have the form stamped like any customs form by customs officials when you leave the country or, if you're visiting several European Union countries, when you leave the EU. Be ready to show customs officials what you've bought (pack purchases together, in your carry-on luggage); budget extra time for this. After you're through passport control, take the form to a refund-service counter for an on-the-spot refund, or mail it back to the store or a refund service after you arrive home.

A refund service can save you some hassle, for a fee. Global Refund is a Europe-wide service with 190,000 affiliated stores and more than 700 refund counters—located at every major airport and border crossing. Its refund form is called a Tax Free Check. The service issues refunds in the form of cash, check, or credit-card adjustment, minus a processing fee. If you don't have time to wait at the refund counter, you can mail in the form instead.

Further details on how to get a VAT refund and a list of stores offering tax-free shopping are available from the British Tourist Authority (⇨ Visitor Information).

V.A.T. Refunds **Global Refund** ✉ 99 Main St., Suite 307, Nyack, NY 10960 ☎ 800/566-9828 📠 845/348-1549 🌐 www.globalrefund.com.

TAXIS

In Edinburgh, Glasgow, and the larger cities, taxis with their TAXI sign illuminated can be hailed on the street, or booked by phone (expect a charge). Elsewhere, most communities of any size at all have a taxi service; your hotel will be able to supply telephone numbers. Very often you will find an advertisement for the local taxi service in public phone booths.

TELEPHONES

Bear in mind that hotels usually levy a hefty (up to 300%) surcharge on calls; it's better to **use pay phones or calling cards.**

AREA & COUNTRY CODES

The country code for Great Britain is 44. When dialing a Scottish or British number from abroad, drop the initial 0 from the local area code. For instance, if you are calling Edinburgh Castle from New York City to ask about opening hours, you first dial 011 (the international code), 44 (the Great Britain country code), 131 (the Edinburgh city code), then 225–9846 (the number proper). In Scotland cellular phone numbers, the 0800 toll-free code, and local-rate 0345 numbers do not have a 1 after the initial 0, nor do many premium-rate numbers, for example 0891, and special-rate numbers, for example 08705.

DIRECTORY & OPERATOR ASSISTANCE

To call the operator, dial 100; directory inquiries (information), 192; international directory inquiries, 153.

INTERNATIONAL CALLS

To make international calls *from* Scotland, dial 00 + the country code + area code + number. For the international operator, credit card, or collect calls, dial 155. The country code is 1 for the United States and Canada, 61 for Australia, and 64 for New Zealand.

LOCAL CALLS

To call a number with the same area code as the number from which you are dialing, omit the area-code digits when you dial. A local call before 6 PM costs 15p, 30p from a pay phone.

LONG-DISTANCE CALLS

For long-distance calls within Britain, dial the area code (which usually begins with 01), followed by the telephone number. The area code prefix is used only when you are dialing from outside the city. In provincial areas the dialing codes for nearby towns are often posted in the booth.

LONG-DISTANCE SERVICES

AT&T, MCI, and Sprint access codes make calling long-distance relatively convenient, but you may find the local access number blocked in many hotel rooms. First ask the hotel operator to connect you. If the hotel operator balks, ask for an international operator, or dial the international operator yourself. One way to improve your odds of getting connected to your long-distance carrier is to travel with more than one company's calling card (a hotel may block Sprint, for example, but not MCI). If all else fails, call from a pay phone. Note that when dialing access numbers in the United Kingdom for AT&T and Sprint, there are different numbers for each phone type—cable, wireless, and British Telecom phones.

Access Codes **AT&T Direct** ☎ 0500/890011 for cable and wireless, 0800/890011 for British Telecom, 0800/0130011 for AT&T, 800/435-0812 for other areas. **MCI WorldPhone** in the U.K. ☎ 0800/890222 to call the U.S. via MCI, 800/444-4141 for other areas. **Sprint International Access** ☎ 0500/890877 cable and wireless, 0800/890877 British Telecom, 800/877-4646 for other areas.

PHONE CARDS

You can purchase BT (British Telecom) phone cards for use on public phones from shops, post offices, and newsstands. They are ideal for longer calls, are composed of units of 20p, and come in values of £2, £5, £10, and £20. An indicator panel on the phone shows the number of units you've used; at the end of your call the card is returned. Where credit cards are taken, slide the card through, as indicated. Beware of buying cards that require you to dial a free phone number; some of these are not legitimate. It's better to get a BT card.

PUBLIC PHONES

There are three types of public pay phones: those that accept only coins, those that accept only phone cards, and those that take British Telecom (BT) phone cards and credit cards. For coin-only phones, insert coins *before* dialing (minimum charge is 10p). Sometimes phones have a "press on answer" (POA) button, which you press when the caller answers.

All calls are charged according to the time of day. Standard rate is weekdays 8 AM–6 PM; cheap rate is weekdays 6 PM–8 AM and all day on weekends, when it's even cheaper. A local call from a pay phone before 6 PM costs 30p for three minutes. A daytime call to the United States will cost 24p a minute on a regular phone (weekends are cheaper), 80p on a pay phone.

TIME

Great Britain sets its clocks by Greenwich Mean Time, five hours ahead of the U.S. East Coast. British summer time (GMT plus one hour) requires an additional adjustment from about the end of March to the end of October.

TIPPING

Some restaurants and most hotels add a service charge of 10%–15% to the bill. In this case you aren't expected to tip. If no service charge is indicated, add 10%–15% to your total bill, but always check first. Taxi drivers, hairdressers, and barbers should also get 10%–15%. If you get help from a hotel concierge, a tip of £1–£2 is appropriate. You are not expected to tip theater or movie theater ushers, elevator operators, or bartenders in pubs.

TOURS & PACKAGES

Because everything is prearranged on a prepackaged tour or independent vacation, you spend less time planning—and often get it all at a good price.

BOOKING WITH AN AGENT

Travel agents are excellent resources. But it's a good idea to collect brochures from several agencies, as some agents' suggestions may be influenced by relationships with tour and package firms that reward them for volume sales. If you have a special interest, **find an agent with expertise in that area**; the American Society of Travel Agents (ASTA; ⇨ Travel Agencies) has a database of specialists worldwide. You can log on to the group's Web site to find an ASTA travel agent in your area.

Make sure your travel agent knows the accommodations and other services of the place being recommended. Ask about the hotel's location, room size, beds, and whether it has a pool, room service, or programs for children, if you care about these. Has your agent been there in person or sent others whom you can contact?

Do some homework on your own, too: local tourism boards can provide information about lesser-known and small-niche operators, some of which may sell only direct.

BUYER BEWARE

Each year consumers are stranded or lose their money when tour operators—even large ones with excellent reputations—go out of business. So **check out the operator.** Ask several travel agents about its reputation, and try to **book with a company that has a consumer-protection program.** (Look for information in the company's brochure.) In the United States, members of the National Tour Association and the United States Tour Operators Association are required to set aside funds to cover payments and travel arrangements in the event that the company defaults. It's also a good idea to choose a company that participates in the American Society of Travel Agents' Tour Operator Program; ASTA will act as mediator in any disputes between you and your tour operator.

Remember that the more your package or tour includes, the better you can predict the ultimate cost of your vacation. Make sure you know exactly what is covered, and **beware of hidden costs.** Are taxes, tips, and transfers included? Entertainment and excursions? These can add up.

Tour-Operator Recommendations **American Society of Travel Agents** (⇨ Travel Agencies). **National Tour Association** (NTA) ✉ 546 E. Main St., Lexington, KY 40508 ☎ 859/226-4444 or 800/682-8886 📠 859/226-4404 🌐 www.ntaonline.com. **United States Tour Operators Association** (USTOA) ✉ 275 Madison Ave., Suite 2014, New York, NY 10016 ☎ 212/599-6599 📠 212/599-6744 🌐 www.ustoa.com.

TRAIN TRAVEL

Train service within Scotland is generally run by ScotRail, one of the most efficient of Britain's service providers. Trains are modern, clean, and comfortable. Scotland's rail network extends all the way to Thurso and Wick, the most northerly stations in the British Isles. Lowland services, most of which originate in Glasgow or Edinburgh, are generally fast and reliable. A shuttle makes the 50-minute trip between the cities every half hour. Long-distance services carry buffet and refreshment cars. One word of caution: there are very few trains in the Highlands on Sunday.

For train information, prices, and schedules throughout Britain contact the National Rail Enquiries line.

CLASSES

Most trains have first-class and standard-class coaches. First-class coaches are always less crowded; they have wider seats and are often cleaner and less well-worn than standard-class cars, and they're a lot more expensive. However, on weekends you can often upgrade from standard to first class for a small fee (often £5)—ask at the time of booking.

CUTTING COSTS

To save money, **look into rail passes.** But be aware that if you don't plan to cover many miles, you may come out ahead by buying individual tickets. If you plan to travel by train in Scotland, **consider purchasing a BritRail Pass,** which also allows travel in England and Wales. Remember that EurailPasses aren't honored in Great Britain. The cost of an unlimited BritRail adult pass for 4 days is $189 standard and $285 first class; for 8 days, $269 standard and $405 first class; for 15 days, $405 standard and $609 first class; for 22 days, $515 and $769; and for a month, $609 and $915. The Youth Pass, for those ages 16–25, provides unlimited second-class travel and costs $155 for 4 days, $219 for 8 days, $285 for 15 days, $359 for 22 days, and $429 for one month. The Senior Pass, for passengers over 60, is first class only and costs $245 for 4 days, $345 for 8 days, $519 for 15 days, $659 for 22 days, and $779 for one month. (These are U.S. dollar figures.)

If you want the flexibility of a car combined with the speed and comfort of the train, try BritRail/Drive (from $259 for two adults, with a $205 supplement for additional adults and $99.50 for children 5–15); this gives you a three-day BritRail Flexipass and two vouchers valid for Avis car rental from more than 100 locations throughout Great Britain. Additional car days start at $49. Prices listed are for compact, manual transmission cars, with standard-class rail seats; automatic transmission and first-class rail seats cost more.

The Freedom of Scotland Pass allows transportation on all Caledonian MacBrayne and Strathclyde ferries. You can travel any 4 days in an 8-day period ($139); 8 days in a 15-day period ($179); and 12 days in a 20-day period ($229).

Although some passes may be purchased in Scotland, most must be purchased in your home country; they're sold by travel agents as well as BritRail or Rail Europe. Rail passes do not guarantee seats on the trains, so be sure to reserve ahead.

FARES

Train fares vary according to class of ticket purchased and distance traveled, and you can pay with credit cards. Before you buy your ticket, stop at the Information Office/Travel Centre and request the lowest fare to your destination and information about any special offers. There's often little difference between the cost of a one-way and round-trip ticket. So if you're planning on departing from and returning to the same destination, buy a round-trip fare upon your departure, rather than purchasing two separate one-way tickets. Your ticket does *not* guarantee you a seat, so make a seat reservation at the same time you buy the ticket or at least before you board the train.

FROM ENGLAND

There are two main rail routes to Scotland from the south of England. The first, the west-coast main line, runs from London Euston to Glasgow Central; it takes 5½ hours to make the 400-mi trip to central Scotland, and service is frequent and reliable. Useful for daytime travel to the Scottish Highlands is the direct train to Stirling and Aviemore, terminating at Inverness. For a restful route to the Scottish Highlands, take the overnight sleeper service, with soundproof sleeping carriages. It runs from London Euston, departing in late evening, to Perth, Stirling, Aviemore, and Inverness, where it arrives the following morning.

The second route is the east-coast main line from London King's Cross to Edinburgh; it provides the quickest trip to the Scottish capital, and between 8 AM and 6 PM there are 16 trains to Edinburgh, three of them through to Aberdeen. Limited-stop expresses like the *Flying Scotsman* make the 393-mi London-to-Edinburgh journey in around four hours. Connecting services to most parts of Scotland—particularly the Western Highlands—are often better from Edinburgh than from Glasgow.

Trains from elsewhere in England are good: regular service connects Birmingham, Manchester, Liverpool, and Bristol with Glasgow and Edinburgh. From Harwich (the port of call for ships from Holland, Germany, and Denmark), you can travel to Glasgow via Manchester. But it's faster to change at Peterborough for the east-coast main line to Edinburgh.

SCENIC ROUTES

Although many routes in Scotland run through extremely attractive countryside, several stand out: from Glasgow to Oban via Loch Lomond; to Fort William and Mallaig via Rannoch (ferry connection to Skye); from Edinburgh to Inverness via the Forth Bridge and Perth; from Inverness to Kyle of Lochalsh and to Wick; and from Inverness to Aberdeen.

A private train, the *Royal Scotsman*, does scenic tours, partly under steam power, with banquets en route. This is a luxury experience: some evenings require formal wear. For trips within Scotland there's a choice of a one-night (£550), two-night (£1,390) or four-night (£2,590) tour. Contact Abercrombie & Kent for more information on these tours.

PAYING

All major credit cards and cash are accepted for train fares paid both in person and by phone.

RESERVATIONS

Tickets and rail passes do not guarantee seats on the trains. For that you need a seat reservation, which if made at the time of ticket purchase is usually included in the ticket price, or if booked separately, must be paid for at a cost of £1 *per train* on your itinerary. Seat reservations are required on some European trains, particularly high-speed trains, and are a good idea on trains that may be crowded—particularly in summer on popular routes. You also need a reservation if you purchase overnight sleeping accommodations.

Train Information **BritRail Travel** ✉ 226 Westchester Ave., White Plains, NY 10604 ☎ 888/274-8724 or 800/677-8585 🌐 www.britrail.com. **National Rail Enquiries** ☎ 08457/484950, 01332/387601 outside U.K. **Rail Europe** ✉ 226 Westchester Ave., White Plains, NY 10604 ☎ 800/848-7245 🌐 www.raileurope.com. **ScotRail** ☎ 08457/550033 🌐 www.scotrail.co.uk.

Train Tours **Abercrombie & Kent** ✉ Sloane Square House, Holbein Pl., London, England SW1W 8NS ☎ 0845/0700606 ⎙ 020/7730-9376 ✉ 1420 Kensington Rd., Oak Brook, IL, United States 60523 ☎ 312/954-2944 or 800/323-7308 ✉ Berkeley Hall, 1 Princes St., Box 327, St. Kilda, Melbourne, Victoria, Australia 3182 ☎ 03/9536-1800 🌐 www.abercrombiekent.com.

TRANSPORTATION AROUND SCOTLAND

If you plan to stick mostly to the cities, you will not need a car. All cities here are either so compact that all attractions are within easy walking distance of each other (Aberdeen, Dundee, Edinburgh, Inverness, and Stirling) or have an excellent local public transport system (Glasgow). And there is often good train and/or bus service from major cities to nearby day-trip destinations. Bus tours are also a good option for a day trip out of town; from Inverness, you can even catch a (quick) glance at the isles of Orkney this way. The scenic train trips mentioned under Train Travel will also let you glimpse some of the more rural parts of Scotland.

Once you leave Edinburgh, Glasgow and the Central Belt, and the other major cities, a car will make journeys faster and much more enjoyable than trying to work out public transport connections to the farther-flung reaches of Scotland (though it is possible to see much of the country by public transportation).

TRAVEL AGENCIES

A good travel agent puts your needs first. Look for an agency that has been in business at least five years, emphasizes customer service, and has someone on staff who specializes in your destination. In addition, **make sure the agency belongs to a professional trade organization.** The American Society of Travel Agents (ASTA)—the largest and most influential in the field with more than 20,000 members in some 140 countries—maintains and enforces a strict code of ethics and will step in to help mediate any agent-client disputes involving ASTA members if necessary. ASTA (whose motto is "Without a travel agent, you're on your own") also maintains a Web site that includes a directory of agents. (If a travel agency is also acting as your tour operator, *see* Buyer Beware *in* Tours and Packages.)

Local Agent Referrals **American Society of Travel Agents** (ASTA) ✉ 1101 King St., Suite 200, Alexandria, VA 22314 ☎ 703/739-2782 or 800/965-2782 24-hr hot line 📠 703/739-3268 🌐 www.astanet.com. **Association of British Travel Agents** ✉ 68-71 Newman St., London W1T 3AH ☎ 020/7637-2444 📠 020/7637-0713 🌐 www.abta.com. **Association of Canadian Travel Agencies** ✉ 130 Albert St., Suite 1705, Ottawa, Ontario K1P 5G4 ☎ 613/237-3657 📠 613/237-7052 🌐 www.acta.ca. **Australian Federation of Travel Agents** ✉ Level 3, 309 Pitt St., Sydney, NSW 2000 ☎ 02/9264-3299 📠 02/9264-1085 🌐 www.afta.com.au. **Travel Agents' Association of New Zealand** ✉ Level 5, Tourism and Travel House, 79 Boulcott St., Box 1888, Wellington 6001 ☎ 04/499-0104 📠 04/499-0786 🌐 www.taanz.org.nz.

VISITOR INFORMATION

For general information about Scotland contact the British and Scottish tourism offices.

VisitScotland ✉ 23 Ravelston Terr., Edinburgh EH4 3EU ☎ 0131/332-2433 📠 0131/343-1513 🌐 www.visitscotland.com ✉ [drop-in visits only] ✉ 19 Cockspur St., London SW1Y 5BL.

British Tourist Authority in the U.S. (BTA) ✉ 551 5th Ave., 7th floor, New York, NY 10176 ☎ 212/986-2200 or 800/462-2748 ✉ [drop-in visits only] ✉ 625 N. Michigan Ave., Suite 1510, Chicago, IL 60611 ✉ in Canada: ✉ 5915 Airport Rd., Suite 120, Mississauga, Ontario L4V 1T1 ☎ 905/405-1840 or 800/847-4885 🌐 www.visitbritain.com. **The Scotland Desk, British Visitor Centre** [drop-in visits] ✉ 1 Piccadilly Circus, London ✉ [mail inquiries only] ✉ Thames Tower, Black's Rd., London W6 9EL.

Government Advisories **U.S. Department of State** ✉ Overseas Citizens Services Office, Room 4811, 2201 C St. NW, Washington, DC 20520 ☎ 202/647-5225 interactive hot line or 888/407-4747 🌐 www.travel.state.gov; enclose a cover letter with your request and a business-size SASE. **Consular Affairs Bureau of Canada** ☎ 800/267-6788 or 613/944-6788 🌐 www.voyage.gc.ca. **Australian Department of Foreign Affairs and Trade** ☎ 02/6261-1299 Consular Travel Advice Faxback Service 🌐 www.dfat.gov.au. **New Zealand Ministry of Foreign Affairs and Trade** ☎ 04/439-8000 🌐 www.mft.govt.nz.

WEB SITES

Do check out the World Wide Web when planning your trip. You'll find everything from weather forecasts to virtual tours of famous cities. Be sure to **visit Fodors.com** (🌐 www.fodors.com), a complete travel-planning site. You can research prices and book plane tickets, hotel rooms, rental cars, vacation packages, and more. In addition, you can post your pressing questions in the Travel Talk section. Other planning tools include a currency converter and weather reports, and there are loads of links to travel resources.

For more specific information on Scotland, go to 🌐 www.visitscotland.com the Scottish Tourism Board's Web site. For stately homes and castles, try the National Trust for Scotland's site 🌐 www.nts.org.uk or the Historic Scotland site 🌐 www.historic-scotland.gov.uk.

EDINBURGH & THE LOTHIANS

1

FODOR'S CHOICE

Balmoral Hotel, *in the New Town*
Edinburgh Castle, *in the Old Town*
Kalpna, *in the South Side*
National Gallery of Scotland, *in the Old Town*
Rosslyn Chapel, *in Roslin*
Royal Museum and Museum of Scotland, *in the Old Town*
The Scotsman Hotel, *in the Old Town*
22 Murrayfield Gardens, *in Murrayfield*
Witchery by the Castle Restaurant, *in the Old Town*

HIGHLY RECOMMENDED

RESTAURANTS
Bouzy Rouge, *in the West End*
Martins, *in the New Town*
Martin Wishart, *in Leith*
Pompadour, *in the New Town*

HOTELS
Caledonian Hilton Hotel, *in the New Town*
Channings, *in the West End*
The Glasshouse, *in the New Town*
Greywalls, *in Gullane*
Hilton Edinburgh Grosvenor, *in the Haymarket area*
The Howard, *in the New Town*
Kew House and Apartments, *in the New Town*
17 Abercromby Place, *in the New Town*

SIGHTS
Falkirk Wheel, *near Falkirk*
Forth Bridges, *in South Queensferry*
Georgian House, *in the New Town*
Palace of Holyroodhouse, *in the Old Town*
Scottish National Portrait Gallery, *in the New Town*

By Gilbert Summers
Updated by James Gracie

EDINBURGH IS TO LONDON AS POETRY IS TO PROSE, as Charlotte Brontë once wrote. One of the world's stateliest cities and proudest capitals, it is built—like Rome—on seven hills, making it the perfect backdrop for the ancient pageant of history. In a skyline of sheer drama, Edinburgh Castle watches over the capital city, frowning down on Princes Street as if disapproving of its modern razzmatazz. Its ramparts still echo with gunfire each day when the traditional one-o'clock gun booms out over the city, startling unwary shoppers.

Nearly everywhere in Edinburgh (the *burgh* is always pronounced *burra* in Scotland) there are spectacular buildings, whose Doric, Ionic, and Corinthian pillars add touches of neoclassical grandeur to the largely Presbyterian backdrop. The most notable examples perch amid the greenery of Calton Hill, which overlooks the city center from the east. Large gardens and greenery are a strong feature of central Edinburgh, where the city council is one of the most stridently conservationist in Europe. Conspicuous from Princes Street is Arthur's Seat, a mountain of bright green and yellow furze rearing up behind the spires of the Old Town. This child-size mountain jutting 822 feet above its surroundings has steep slopes and little crags, like a miniature Highlands set down in the middle of the busy city. Appropriately, these theatrical elements match Edinburgh's character—after all, the city has been a stage that has seen its fair share of romance, violence, tragedy, and triumph.

Nearly 300 years after the Union of Parliaments, Edinburgh is once again the seat of a Scottish parliament. A new parliament building, designed by the late Spanish architect Enric Miralles, is under construction adjacent to the Palace of Holyroodhouse, at the foot of the Royal Mile. The first-time visitor to Scotland may be surprised that the country still has a capital city at all, perhaps believing the seat of government was drained of its resources and power after the union with England in 1707, but far from it. The Union of Parliaments brought with it a set of political partnerships—such as separate legal, ecclesiastical, and educational systems—that Edinburgh assimilated and integrated with its own surviving institutions.

Scotland now has significantly more control over its own affairs than at any time since 1707, and the 129 Members of the Scottish Parliament (MSPs) have extensive powers in Scotland over education, health, housing, transport, training, economic development, the environment, and agriculture. Foreign policy, defense, and economic policy, however, remain under the jurisdiction of the U.K. government in London.

Towering over the city, Edinburgh Castle was actually built over the plug of an ancient volcano. Many thousands of years ago, an eastward-grinding glacier encountered the tough basalt core of the volcano and swept around it, scouring steep cliffs and leaving a trail of matter, like the tail of a comet. This material formed a ramp gently leading down from the rocky summit. On this *crag* and *tail* would grow the city of Edinburgh and its castle.

The lands that rolled down to the sea were for centuries open country, sitting between Castle Rock and the tiny community clustered by the shore that grew into Leith, Edinburgh's seaport. By the 12th century Edinburgh had become a walled town, still perched on the hill. Its shape was becoming clearer: like a fish with its head at the castle, its backbone running down the ridge, and its ribs leading briefly off on either side. The backbone gradually became the continuous thoroughfare now known as the Royal Mile, and the ribs became the closes (alleyways), some still surviving, that were the scene of many historic incidents.

Edinburgh's spectacular setting makes a good first impression. You can be here for a day and think you know the place, as even a cursory open-top bus tour will enable you to grasp the layout of the castle, Royal Mile, Old Town, New Town, and so on. If your taste is more for leisurely strolling through the nooks and crannies of the Old Town closes, however, then allow three or four days for exploring.

If you have 2 days

To start off, make your way to Edinburgh Castle—not just the battlements—and spend some time here, if only to revel in its sense of history. Take a city bus tour for an overview of Edinburgh, and while you ride, consider your must-sees: the National Gallery, the Royal Museum, and, unless it's January or February, the Georgian House for an idea of life in the New Town.

If you have 5 days

Five days allow plenty of time for Old Town exploration, including the important museums of Huntly House and the People's Story (in the Canongate Tolbooth), and for a walk around the New Town, including a visit to the Scottish National Portrait Gallery and the Scottish National Gallery of Modern Art. You'll also have time for shopping, not only in areas close to the city center, such as Rose Street and Victoria Street, but also in some of the less touristy areas, such as Bruntsfield. Head to Leith to visit the former royal yacht *Britannia* and to have a meal on the waterfront. You could also get out of town: hop on a bus out to Midlothian to see Rosslyn Chapel, at Roslin, and visit the Edinburgh Crystal Visitor Centre at Penicuik. Consider spending another half day traveling out to South Queensferry to admire the Forth road and rail bridges; then visit palatial Hopetoun House, with its wealth of portraits and fine furniture.

If you have 8 days

In eight days, in addition to a thorough exploration of Edinburgh's Old Town and New Town, including a few museums and a shopping trip or two, you will not only have time to explore Leith, Roslin, and South Queensferry but you may also be able to take a couple of side trips from the city. Allow at least a day for each trip so you have time to enjoy stately homes, historic ruins, beaches, and museums. If it's festival time, however, you might want to take in shows, concerts, and exhibitions for eight solid days and hardly stray from the city center.

By the early 15th century Edinburgh had become the undisputed capital of Scotland. The bitter defeat of Scotland at Flodden in 1513, when Scotland aligned itself with France against England, caused a new defensive city wall to be built. Though the castle escaped destruction, the city was burned by the English earl of Hertford under orders from King Henry VIII (1491–1547) of England. This was during a time known as the "Rough Wooing," when Henry was trying to coerce the Scots into allowing the young Mary, Queen of Scots (1542–1587) to marry his son Edward. The plan failed and Mary married Francis, the Dauphin of France. By 1561, when Mary returned from France already widowed, the guest house of the Abbey of Holyrood had grown to become the Palace of Holyroodhouse, replacing Edinburgh castle as the main royal residence. Mary's legacy to the city included the destruction of most of the earliest buildings of Edinburgh Castle, held by her supporters after she was forced to flee to England, where she was eventually executed by Elizabeth I.

In the trying decades after the union with England in 1707, many influential Scots, both in Edinburgh and elsewhere, went through an identity crisis, characterized by people like James Boswell (1740–1795), who, though he lived with his family in Edinburgh, preferred to spend most of his time in London. Out of the 18th-century difficulties, however, grew the Scottish Enlightenment, during which educated Scots made great strides in medicine, economics, and science.

Changes came to the cityscape, too. By the mid-18th century it had become the custom for wealthy Scottish landowners to spend the winter in the Old Town of Edinburgh, in town houses huddled between the high Castle Rock and the Royal Palace below. Cross-fertilized in coffeehouses and taverns, intellectual notions flourished among a people determined to remain Scottish despite their parliament's having voted to dissolve itself. One result was a campaign to expand and beautify the city, to give it a look worthy of its future nickname, the Athens of the North. Thus was the New Town of Edinburgh built, whose broad streets and gracious buildings created a harmony that even today's throbbing traffic cannot obscure.

Today's Edinburgh is the second-most important financial center in the United Kingdom, and the fifth most important in Europe. This is one of the many reasons that people from all over Britain come to live here. Not the least of the other reasons is that the city regularly is ranked near the top in "quality of life" surveys. Accordingly, New Town apartments on fashionable streets sell for considerable sums. In some senses the city is showy and materialistic, but Edinburgh still supports learned societies, some of which have their roots in the Scottish Enlightenment: the Royal Society of Edinburgh, for example, established in 1783 "for the advancement of learning and useful knowledge," is still an important forum for interdisciplinary activities, both in Edinburgh and in Scotland as a whole. Hand in hand with the city's academic and scientific life is a rich cultural force, with the Edinburgh International Festival attracting lovers of all the arts to the city in August and September.

But even as Edinburgh moves through the 21st century, its tall guardian castle remains the focal point of the city and its venerable history. Take time to explore its streets—peopled by the spirits of Mary, Queen of Scots, Sir Walter Scott, and Robert Louis Stevenson—and don't forget to pay your respects to the world's best-loved terrier, Greyfriars Bobby. In the evenings, you can enjoy candlelit restaurants or a folk *ceilidh*, though you should remember that you haven't earned your porridge until you've climbed Arthur's Seat. Should you wander around a corner, say, on George Street, you might see not an endless cityscape, but blue sea and a patchwork of fields. This is the county of Fife, beyond the inlet of the North Sea called the Firth of Forth—a reminder, like the mountains to the northwest, which can be glimpsed from Edinburgh's highest points, that the rest of Scotland lies within easy reach.

Culinary Delights As befits one of the richest cities in Britain, Edinburgh has many diverse, sophisticated restaurants representing cuisines from around the world. Perhaps the most exotic, however, is genuine Scottish cuisine. On restaurant menus, look for the traditional and nouvelle versions of classic Scottish foods, including salmon, venison, *partan bree* (a rich crab soup), Loch Fyne herring, and, of course, spicy haggis, usually served with *neeps and tatties* (mashed turnips and potatoes). Scotland is also known as the "land o' cakes," with delicious buns, pancakes, scones, and biscuits served for breakfast or high tea. Not so long ago the standards of cooking and service too often betrayed that puritanical Scottish conviction that enjoying yourself is a sin. Today Scottish game and seafood are often presented with great flair. After the feast, other delicacies await: handmade chocolates, often with whisky or Drambuie fillings, and the "petticoat tail" shortbread are good choices. Oatmeal, local cheeses, and malt whisky (turning up in any course) amplify the Scottish dimension. And speaking of whisky, be sure to try a "wee dram" of a single malt when you visit Scotland's capital.

Hotels & Guest Houses From grand hotel suites done up in tartan fabrics to bed-and-breakfasts decorated with a personal touch, Edinburgh is splendidly served by lodging properties of all kinds. You'll find many lovely traditional Georgian and Victorian properties in the city center, plus homey and less expensive B&Bs in the outer villages, most of which are well-connected to the city center by bus. If you're planning to stay in Edinburgh during festival time, be sure to reserve several months in advance.

Nightlife & the Arts At night, Edinburgh comes alive with jazz and folk music performances, dinner dances, nightclubs, and *ceilidhs* (a mix of country dancing, music, and song; pronounced *kay*-lees). As for the arts, the city is world renowned for the Edinburgh International Festival, which takes place mid-August through early September. The festival attracts all sorts of international performers, from first-tier orchestras to leading theater performers. Even more obvious to the casual stroller during this time is the refreshingly irreverent Edinburgh Festival Fringe, which spills out of halls and theaters and onto the streets all over town. Film and book festivals are also regulars on the calendar. At other times throughout the year, professional and amateur groups offer diverse cultural performances.

Shopping Edinburgh's downtown has the usual chain stores, but within a few yards, along some of the side streets, you'll find shops carrying more exclusive wares, such as designer clothing, craft items, 18th-century silverware, and wild-caught, smoked Scottish salmon. Venture into Edinburgh's "villages"—perhaps Stockbridge, Bruntsfield, Morningside, or even the Old Town itself—and you'll notice stores specializing in single items, such as antique clocks or designer knitwear using the finest Scottish wool or cashmere. Scotland has a strong tradition of distinctive furniture makers, silversmiths, and artists; and Edinburgh is a fruitful hunting ground for antiques.

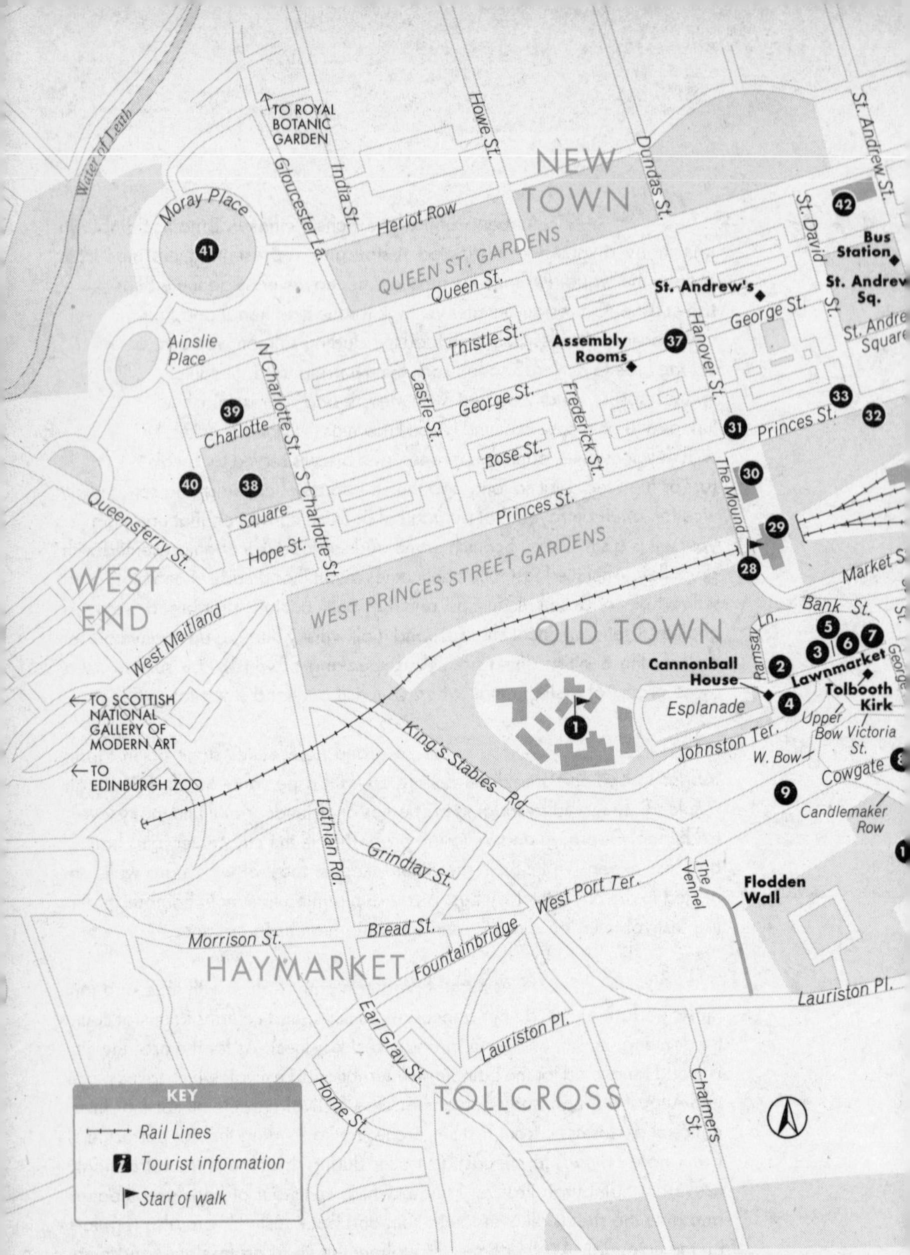

KEY
- Rail Lines
- Tourist information
- Start of walk

Brass Rubbing Centre18
Calton Hill36
Canongate21
Canongate Kirk24
Canongate Tolbooth22
Castlehill2

Charlotte Square38
Edinburgh Castle1
George IV Bridge8
George Street37
Georgian House39
Gladstone's Land5
Grassmarket9

High Kirk of St. Giles15
High Street13
Huntly House23
Jenners33
John Knox House19
Kirk of the Greyfriars11

Lawnmarket7
Moray Place41
The Mound28
Museum of Childhood17
National Gallery of Scotland29
National Library of Scotland10

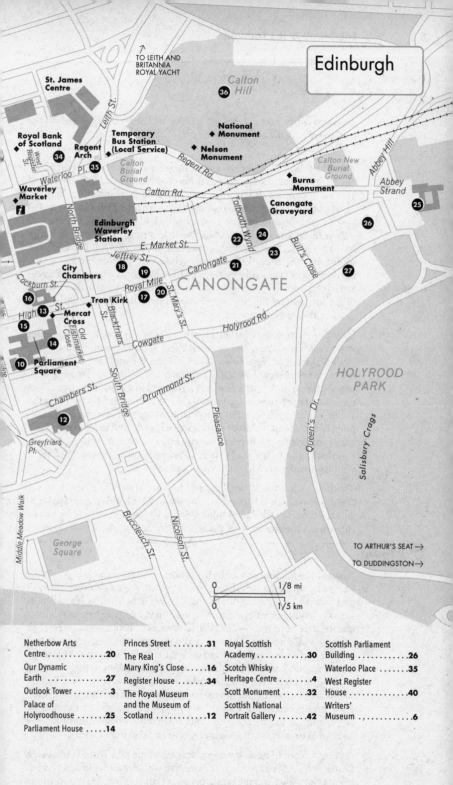

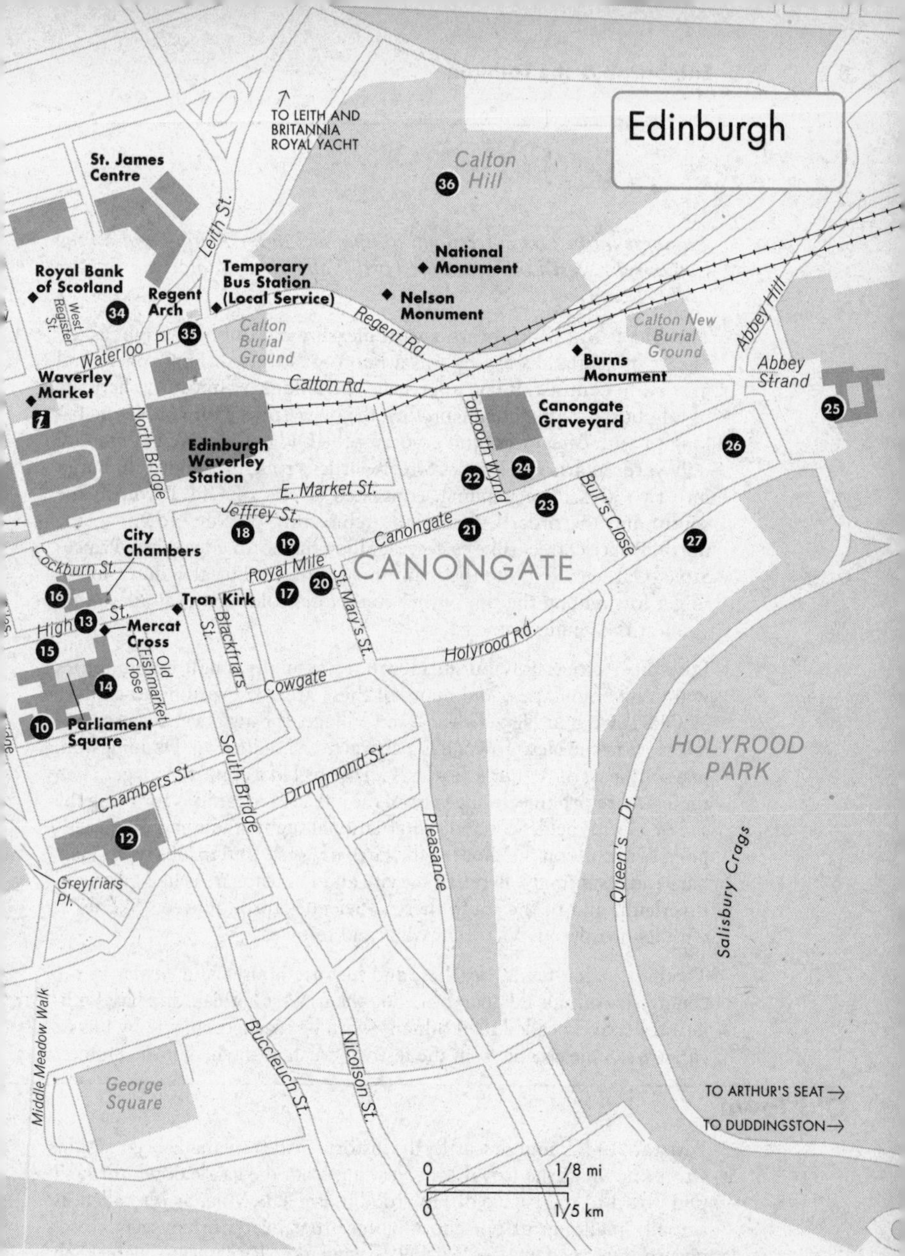

Netherbow Arts Centre 20
Our Dynamic Earth 27
Outlook Tower 3
Palace of Holyroodhouse 25
Parliament House 14
Princes Street 31
The Real Mary King's Close 16
Register House 34
The Royal Museum and the Museum of Scotland 12
Royal Scottish Academy 30
Scotch Whisky Heritage Centre 4
Scott Monument 32
Scottish National Portrait Gallery 42
Scottish Parliament Building 26
Waterloo Place 35
West Register House 40
Writers' Museum 6

EXPLORING EDINBURGH & THE LOTHIANS

Numbers in the text correspond to numbers in the margin and on the Edinburgh, West Lothian & the Forth Valley, and Midlothian & East Lothian maps.

The Old Town, which bears a great measure of symbolic weight as the "heart of Scotland's capital," is a boon for lovers of atmosphere and history. In contrast, if you appreciate the unique architectural heritage of Edinburgh's Enlightenment, then the New Town's for you. If you belong to both categories, don't worry—the Old and the New towns are only yards apart. The Princes Street Gardens roughly divide Edinburgh into two areas: the winding, congested streets of Old Town, to the south, and the orderly, Georgian architecture of New Town, to the north. Princes Street runs east–west along the north edge of the Princes Street Gardens. Explore the main thoroughfares but also don't forget to get lost among the tiny *wynds* and *closes*: old medieval alleys that connect the winding streets.

Like most cities, Edinburgh incorporates many small communities within its boundaries, and many of these are as rewarding to explore as Old Town and New Town. Dean Village, for instance, even though it is close to the New Town, has a character all of its own. Duddingston, just southeast of Arthur's Seat, has all the feel of a country village. Then there's Corstorphine, to the west of the city center, famous for being the site of Murrayfield, Scotland's international rugby stadium. Edinburgh's port, Leith, sits on the shore of the Firth of Forth, and throbs with smart bars and restaurants. Between the city and Leith are areas like Pilrig and Inverleith, and to the south there is Sciennes (pronounced "Skeens"), with its prosperous Victorian villas and terraces.

The hills, green fields, beaches, and historic houses and castles in the countryside outside Edinburgh—Midlothian, West Lothian, and East Lothian, collectively called the Lothians—can be reached quickly by bus or car, a welcome escape from the festival crush at the height of summer.

Old Town

Eastward of Edinburgh Castle, the historic castle esplanade becomes the street known as the Royal Mile, leading from the castle down through Old Town to the Palace of Holyroodhouse. The Mile, as it's called, is actually made up of one thoroughfare that bears, in consecutive sequence, different names—Castlehill, Lawnmarket, Parliament Square, High Street, and Canongate. The streets and passages winding into their tenements, or "lands," and crammed onto the ridge in back of the Mile really *were* Edinburgh until the 18th century saw expansions to the south and north. Everybody lived here, the richer folk on the lower floors of houses, with less well-to-do families on the middle floors—the higher up, the poorer. Time and progress (of a sort) have swept away some of the narrow closes and tall tenements of the Old Town, but enough survive for you to be able to imagine the original profile of Scotland's capital.

a good walk

A perfect place to begin your exploration of the Old Town is **Edinburgh Castle** 1 ⚑. After exploring its extensive complex of buildings and admiring the view from the battlements, set off down the first part of the Royal Mile, stopping en route at your choice of museums and other interesting ports of call. To the left of **Castlehill** 2, the **Outlook Tower** 3 affords more splendid views of the city from its camera obscura. Opposite, the **Scotch Whisky Heritage Centre** ❹ provides an unusual opportunity to discover Scotland's liquid gold—stop off for a sample. The six-story tenement known as **Gladstone's Land** ❺, a survivor of 16th-century domestic life, is on the left as you head east. Near Gladstone's Land, down another close, stands the **Writers' Museum** ❻, housed in a fine example of 17th-century urban architecture called Lady Stair's House. Farther down on the right are the Tolbooth Kirk (a *tolbooth* was a town hall or prison, and *kirk* means "church") and Upper Bow.

From the **Lawnmarket** ❼ you can start your discovery of the Old Town closes. For a worthwhile shopping diversion, turn right down **George IV Bridge** ❽, then to the right down Victoria Street, a 19th-century addition to the Old Town. Its shops carry antiques, old prints, and Scottish clothing. Down in the historic **Grassmarket** ❾, parts of the old city walls still stand and there are more shops. Retrace your steps to George IV Bridge, then detour again southward to see the **National Library of Scotland** ❿, the **Kirk of the Greyfriars** ⓫, and the little statue of faithful Greyfriars Bobby at the corner of Candlemaker's Row. On Chambers Street, at the foot of George IV Bridge, are the impressive galleries of the **Royal Museum and the Museum of Scotland** ⓬, the former housed in a lavish Victorian building, the latter in an attached late-20th century structure.

Returning to the junction of George IV Bridge with the Royal Mile, turn right (eastward) down **High Street** ⓭ to visit the old **Parliament House** ⓮; the **High Kirk of St. Giles** ⓯; the Mercat Cross; and the elegant City Chambers, bringing a flavor of the New Town's neoclassicism to the Old Town's severity. Beneath the chambers is the eerie **Real Mary King's Close** ⓰, a lane that was closed off in the 17th century when the bubonic plague struck the city. Farther down on the right stands the Tron Kirk, with the **Museum of Childhood** ⓱ and **Brass Rubbing Centre** ⓲ beyond. **John Knox House** ⓳, associated with Scotland's severe 16th-century religious reformer, and the **Netherbow Arts Centre** ⓴ are on this section of the Royal Mile, which immediately afterward becomes **Canongate** ㉑.

A short distance down Canongate on the left is **Canongate Tolbooth** ㉒. **Huntly House** ㉓ stands opposite, and the **Canongate Kirk** ㉔ and Acheson House are nearby. This walk draws to a close, as it started, on a high note: the **Palace of Holyroodhouse** ㉕, full of historic and architectural interest and some fine paintings, tapestries, and furnishings to admire, in Holyrood Park. Being erected nearby is the new **Scottish Parliament Building** ㉖. And **Our Dynamic Earth** ㉗, on Holyrood Road, which uses state-of-the-art technology to educate and entertain, makes a nice stop for those interested in science.

TIMING This walk could be accomplished in a day, but to give the major sights—the castle, Palace of Holyroodhouse, and Royal Museum—the time they deserve and also to see at least some of the other attractions properly, you should allow two days. Consider ending the first day with an afternoon in the Royal Museum and devoting the second afternoon to Holyroodhouse.

What to See

⓲ **Brass Rubbing Centre.** No experience is necessary for you to make your own souvenirs of Scotland at this center. You can explore the past by creating do-it-yourself replicas from original Pictish stones and markers, rare Scottish brasses, and medieval church brasses. All the materials are here, and children find the pastime quite absorbing. It's down a close opposite the Museum of Childhood. ✉ *Trinity Apse, Chalmers Close, Old Town* ☎ *0131/556–4364* *Free, rubbings £1.20–£15 each* ⏲ *Apr.–Oct., Mon.–Sat. 10–5, Sun. during festival noon–5.*

21 **Canongate.** This section of the Royal Mile takes its name from the canons who once ran the abbey at Holyrood. Canongate—in Scots, *gate* means "street"—was originally an independent town, or *burgh*, another Scottish term used to refer to a community with trading rights granted by the monarch. Here you'll find the ⇨ **Canongate Kirk** and Graveyard, ⇨ **Canongate Tolbooth,** and ⇨ **Huntly House.** ✉ *Section of Royal Mile from end of High St. to Abbey Strand at entrance to Palace of Holyroodhouse, Old Town.*

24 **Canongate Kirk.** The graveyard of the Canongate Kirk, built in 1688, is the burial place of some notable Scots, including economist Adam Smith (1723–90), author of *The Wealth of Nations* (1776), who once lived in the nearby 17th-century Panmure House. Also buried here is Dugald Stewart (1753–1828), the leading European philosopher of his time, and the undervalued Scots poet Robert Fergusson (1750–74). That Fergusson's grave is even marked is the result of efforts by the much more famous Robert Burns (1759–96). On a visit to the city Burns was dismayed to find the grave had no headstone, so he commissioned an architect—by the name of Robert Burn—to design one. (Burn reportedly took two years to complete the commission, so Burns, in turn, took two years to pay). Burn also designed the Nelson Monument, the tall column on Calton Hill to the north, which you can see from the graveyard.

Against the eastern wall of the graveyard is a bronze sculpture of the head of Mrs. Agnes McLehose, the "Clarinda" of the copious correspondence in which Robert Burns engaged while confined to his lodgings with an injured leg in 1788. Burns and McLehose—a high born, talented woman who had been abandoned by her husband—exchanged passionate letters for some six weeks that year, Burns signing his name "Sylvander," Mrs. McLehose "Clarinda." The missives were dispatched across town by a postal service that delivered them within the hour for one penny. The curiously literary affair ended when Burns left Edinburgh in 1788 to take up a farm tenancy and to marry Jean Armour. ✉ *Canongate, Old Town,* ☎ *0131/556–3515* *Free* *Daily.*

22 **Canongate Tolbooth.** Nearly every city and town in Scotland once had a tolbooth. Originally a customhouse where tolls were gathered, a tolbooth came to mean "town hall" and later "prison" because detention cells were housed in the basement. The building where Canongate's town council once met now houses a museum, the **People's Story,** which focuses on the lives of "ordinary" people from the 18th century to today. Exhibits describe how Canongate, in some ways a rather sterile street, once bustled with the activities of the various tradesmen needed to supply life's essentials in the days before superstores. Special displays include a reconstruction of a cooper's workshop and a 1940s kitchen. ✉ *Canongate, Old Town* ☎ *0131/529–4057* *Free* *Mon.–Sat. 10–5, Sun. during festival 2–5.*

need a break?

You can get a good cup of tea and a scone, a quintessentially Scottish indulgence, at **Clarinda's** (✉ 69 Canongate, Old Town ☎ 0131/557–1888). Like most tearooms, Clarinda's doesn't accept reservations. You may have to wait a short while for a table, but the experience is well worth it.

2 **Castlehill.** In the late 16th century witches were brought to what is now a street in the Royal Mile to be burned at the stake, as a bronze plaque here recalls. The cannonball embedded in the west gable of Castlehill's **Cannonball House** was, according to legend, fired from the castle during the Jacobite Rebellion of 1745, led by Charles Edward Stuart (also

known as Bonnie Prince Charlie, 1720–88), the most romantic of the Stuart pretenders to the British throne. Most authorities agree on a more prosaic explanation, however; they say it was a height marker for Edinburgh's first piped-water supply system, installed in 1681. Atop the Gothic **Tolbooth Kirk,** built in 1842–44 for the General Assembly of the Church of Scotland, is, at 240 ft, the tallest spire in the city. The church houses the Edinburgh Festival offices, the **Festival Centre.**

The **Upper Bow,** running from Lawnmarket to Victoria Street, was once the main route westward from the town and castle. Before Victoria Street was built in the late 19th century, the Upper Bow led down into a narrow dark thoroughfare coursing between a canyon of tenements. All traffic struggled up and down this steep slope from the Grassmarket, which joins the now-truncated West Bow at its lower end. ✉ *East of the Esplanade and west of Lawnmarket, Old Town.*

off the beaten path

DUDDINGSTON – Tucked behind Arthur's Seat, and about a one-hour walk from Princes Street via Holyrood Park, this little community, formerly of brewers and weavers, still seems like a country village. The Duddingston Kirk has a Norman doorway and a watchtower that was built to keep body snatchers out of the graveyard. The church overlooks Duddingston Loch, popular with bird-watchers, and moments away is an old-style pub called the Sheep's Heid Inn, which serves a wide selection of beers and has the oldest skittle (bowling) alley in Scotland. ✉ *Take Lothian Bus 42, Duddingston.*

Fodor's Choice ★

1 Edinburgh Castle. The crowning glory of the Scottish capital, Edinburgh Castle is popular not only because it is the symbolic heart of Scotland but also because of the views from its battlements: on a clear day the vistas—stretching to the "kingdom" of Fife—are breathtaking.

The castle opens the chronicle of Scottish history. Archaeological investigations have established that the rock on which the castle stands was inhabited as far back as 1000 BC, in the latter part of the Bronze Age. There have been fortifications here since the mysterious people called the Picts first used it as a stronghold in the 3rd and 4th centuries AD. The Picts were dislodged by Anglian invaders from northern England in AD 452, and for the next 1,300 years the site saw countless battles and skirmishes. You'll hear the story of how Randolph, earl of Moray, nephew of freedom-fighter Robert the Bruce, scaled the heights one dark night in 1313, surprised the English guard, and recaptured the castle for the Scots. At the same time he destroyed every one of its buildings except for St. Margaret's Chapel, dating from around 1076, so that successive Stewart kings had to rebuild the castle bit by bit.

The castle has been held over time by Scots and Englishmen, Catholics and Protestants, soldiers and royalty. In the 16th century Mary, Queen of Scots, gave birth here to the future James VI of Scotland (1566–1625), who was also to rule England as James I. In 1573 it was the last fortress to support Mary's claim as the rightful Catholic queen of Britain, causing the castle to be virtually destroyed by English artillery fire.

You enter across the **Esplanade,** the huge forecourt, which was built in the 18th century as a parade ground and now serves as the castle parking lot. It comes alive with color and music each August when it is used for the Military Tattoo, a festival of magnificently outfitted marching bands and regiments. Heading over the drawbridge and through the gatehouse, past the guards, you'll find the rough stone walls of the **Half-Moon Battery,** where the one-o'clock gun is fired every day in an impressively anachronistic ceremony; these curving ramparts give Edinburgh Castle its distinctive appearance from miles away. Climb up through a second gateway and you come to the oldest surviving building in the complex, the tiny 11th-century **St. Margaret's Chapel,** named in honor of Saxon queen Margaret (1046–93), who had persuaded her husband, King Malcolm III (circa 1031–93), to move his court from Dunfermline to Edinburgh. Edinburgh's environs—the Lothians—were occupied by Anglian settlers with whom the queen felt more at home, or so the story goes (Dunfermline was surrounded by Celts). The **Crown Room** contains the "Honours of Scotland"—the crown, scepter, and sword that once graced the Scottish monarch. Upon the **Stone of Scone,** also in the Crown Room, Scottish monarchs once sat to be crowned. In the section now called **Queen Mary's Apartments,** Mary, Queen of Scots, gave birth to James VI of Scotland. The **Great Hall** displays arms and armor under an impressive vaulted, beamed ceiling. Scottish parliament meetings were conducted here until 1840. During the Napoleonic Wars in the early 19th century, the castle held French prisoners of war, whose carvings can still be seen on the vaults under the Great Hall.

Military features of interest include the **Scottish National War Memorial,** the **Scottish United Services Museum,** and the famous 15th-century Belgian-made cannon ***Mons Meg.*** This enormous piece of artillery has been silent since 1682, when it exploded while firing a salute for the duke of York; it now stands in an ancient hall behind the Half-Moon Battery. Contrary to what you may hear from locals, it is not *Mons Meg* but the battery's time gun that goes off with a bang every weekday at 1 PM, frightening visitors and reminding Edinburghers to check their watches. ☎ *0131/225–9846 for Edinburgh Castle, 0131/226–7393 for War Memorial* 🌐 *www.historic-scotland.gov.uk* 🎫 *£8* ⏲ *Apr.–Sept., daily 9:30–6; Oct.–Mar., daily 9:30–5.*

need a break?

You can have lunch or afternoon tea overlooking panoramic views of the city at the **Edinburgh Castle Café** (✉ Edinburgh Castle, Old Town ☎ 0131/225–9746). You'll find baked sweets, sandwiches, soup, tea, and Starbucks coffee, all available at reasonable prices.

8 **George IV Bridge.** It's not immediately obvious that this is in fact a bridge, as buildings are closely packed most of the way along both sides. At the corner of the bridge stands one of the most photographed sculptures in Scotland, ***Greyfriars Bobby.*** This statue pays tribute to the famous Skye terrier who kept vigil beside John Grey's grave in the Greyfriar's churchyard for 14 years after he died in 1858. Bobby left only for a short time each day to be fed at a nearby coffee house. The 1961 Walt Disney film *Greyfriars Bobby* tells the story, though liberties were taken with the historical details. ✉ *Between Bank St. and intersection with Candlemaker Row, Old Town.*

5 **Gladstone's Land.** This narrow, six-story tenement, next to the Assembly Hall on Lawnmarket, is a survivor from the 17th century. Typical Scottish architectural features are on show here on two floors, including an arcaded ground floor (believe it or not, even here—in the city center—livestock sometimes inhabited the ground floor). The house has magnificent painted ceilings and is furnished in the style of a 17th-century merchant's home. ✉ *477B Lawnmarket, Old Town* ☎ *0131/226–5856* 🌐 *www.nts.org.uk/gladstone.html* 🎫 *£3.50* ⏲ *Apr.–Oct., Mon.–Sat. 10–5, Sun. 2–5; last admission at 4:30.*

9 **Grassmarket.** For centuries an agricultural marketplace, Grassmarket now hosts numerous shops, bars, and restaurants, making it a hive of activ-

ity at night. Sections of the Old Town wall can be traced on the north (castle) side by a series of steps that run steeply up from Grassmarket to Johnston Terrace above. The best-preserved section of the wall can be found by crossing to the south side and climbing the steps of the lane called the Vennel. Here, the 16th-century **Flodden Wall** comes in from the east and turns southward at Telfer's Wall, a 17th-century extension. Grassmarket's history is long and fabulous. Nineteenth-century body snatchers Burke and Hare lived close to here, and the **cobbled cross** at the east end marks the site of the town gallows. Among those hanged here were many 17th-century Covenanters. Judges were known to issue the death sentence for these religious reformers with the words, "Let them glorify God in the Grassmarket."

From the northeast corner of the Grassmarket, **Victoria Street,** a 19th-century addition to the Old Town, leads up to George IV Bridge. Shops here sell antiques, designer clothing, and high-quality gifts.

15 **High Kirk of St. Giles.** Sometimes called St. Giles's Cathedral, this is one of the city's principal churches. However, anyone expecting a rival to Paris's Notre Dame or London's Westminster Abbey will be disappointed: St. Giles is more like a large parish church than a great European cathedral. There has been a church here since AD 854, although most of the present structure dates from either 1120 or 1829, when the church was restored. The tower, with its stone crown towering 161 feet above the ground, was completed between 1495 and 1500. The most elaborate feature is the **Chapel of the Order of the Thistle,** built onto the southeast corner of the church in 1911 for the exclusive use of Scotland's only chivalric order, the Most Ancient and Noble Order of the Thistle. It bears the belligerent national motto NEMO ME IMPUNE LACESSIT ("No one provokes me with impunity"). Outside the west end of the church stands a life-size bronze statue of the Scot whose spirit still dominates the place—the great religious reformer and preacher John Knox, before whose zeal all of Scotland once trembled. The church lies about one-third of the way along the Royal Mile from Edinburgh Castle. ✉ *High St., Old Town* ☎ *0131/225–9442* 🌐 *www.stgiles.net* 🎫 *£1 suggested donation* ⏲ *May–Sept., weekdays 9–7, Sat. 9–5, Sun 1–5; Oct.–April, Mon.–Sat. 9–5, Sun. 1–5.*

13 **High Street.** Some of Old Town's most impressive buildings and sights can be found on High Street, one of the five streets making up the Royal Mile. There are also other, less obvious historic relics to be seen. Near Parliament Square, look on the west side for a **heart** set in cobbles. This marks the site of the vanished Tolbooth, the center of city life from the 15th century until the building's demolition in 1817. The ancient civic edifice housed the Scottish parliament and was used as a prison—it also inspired Sir Walter Scott's novel *The Heart of Midlothian.*

Just outside Parliament House is the **Mercat Cross** (*mercat* means "market"), a great landmark of Old Town life. It was an old mercantile center, where in the early days executions were held, and where royal proclamations were—and are still—read. Most of the present cross is comparatively modern, dating from the time of William Ewart Gladstone (1809–98), the great Victorian prime minister and rival of Benjamin Disraeli (1804–81). Across High Street from St. Giles's Cathedral stands the **City Chambers,** now the seat of local government. Built by John Fergus, who adapted a design of John Adam in 1753, the chambers were originally known as the Royal Exchange and intended to be where merchants and lawyers could conduct business. Note how the building drops 11 stories to Cockburn Street on its north side.

A *tron* is a weigh beam used in public weigh houses, and the **Tron Kirk** was named after a salt tron that used to stand nearby. The kirk itself was built after 1633, when St. Giles's became an Episcopal cathedral for a brief time. In this church in 1693, a minister offered an often-quoted prayer for the local government: "Lord, hae mercy on a' [all] fools and idiots, and particularly on the Magistrates of Edinburgh."

You would once have passed out of the safety of the town walls through a gate called the **Netherbow Port.** Look for the brass studs in the street cobbles that mark its location. A plaque outside the Netherbow Arts Centre depicts the gate. ✉ *Between Lawnmarket and Canongate, Old Town.*

23 **Huntly House.** A must-see if you're interested in the details of Old Town life, this former home, dating from 1570, houses a fascinating museum of local history, displaying Scottish pottery and Edinburgh silver and glassware. ✉ *142 Canongate, Old Town* ☎ *0131/529–4143* 🌐 *www.cac.org.uk* 🎫 *Free* ⏲ *Mon.–Sat. 10–5, Sun. during festival 2–5.*

19 **John Knox House.** It's not certain that Scotland's severe religious reformer John Knox ever lived here, but there is evidence to show that he died here in 1572. Mementos of his life are on view inside, and the distinctive dwelling gives you a glimpse of what Old Town life was like in the 16th century. The projecting upper stories were once commonplace along the Royal Mile, darkening and further closing in the already narrow passage. Look for the initials of former owner James Mossman and his wife, carved into the stonework on the "marriage lintel." Mossman was goldsmith to Mary, Queen of Scots, and was hanged in 1573 for his allegiance to her. ✉ *45 High St., Old Town* ☎ *0131/556–2647* 🌐 *www.johnknoxhouse.org.uk* 🎫 *£2.25* ⏲ *July, Mon.–Sat. 10–5, Sun. noon–4; Aug., Mon.–Sat. 10–7, Sun. noon–4; Sept.–June, Mon.–Sat. 10–5 (last admission ½ hr before closing).*

11 **Kirk of the Greyfriars.** Greyfriars Church, built circa 1620 on the site of a medieval monastery, was where the National Covenant, declaring that the Presbyterian Church in Scotland was independent of the monarch and not Episcopalian in government, was signed in 1638. The covenant plunged Scotland into decades of civil war. Informative panels tell the story, and there's a visitor center on-site. Be sure to search out the graveyard—one of the most evocative in Europe. Its old, tottering, elaborate tombstones mark the graves of some of Scotland's most respected heroes and despised villains. Nearby, at the corner of George IV Bridge and Candlemaker Row, stands one of the most photographed sites in Scotland, the Greyfriars Bobby statue. ✉ *Greyfriars Pl., Old Town* ☎ *0131/225–1900* 🌐 *www.greyfriarskirk.com* 🎫 *Free* ⏲ *Easter–Oct., weekdays 10:30–4:30, Sat. 10:30–2:30; Nov.–Easter, Thurs. 1:30–3:30; groups by appointment.*

7 **Lawnmarket.** The name "Lawnmarket" is a corruption of "land market", and is the second of the streets that make up the Royal Mile. It was formerly the site of the produce market for the city, with a once-a-week special sale of wool and linen. Now it's home to ⇨ **Gladstone's Land** and the ⇨ **Writers' Museum.** At different times the Lawnmarket Courts housed James Boswell, David Hume, and Robert Burns. In nearby Brodie's Close in the 1770s lived the infamous Deacon Brodie, pillar of society by day and a murdering gang leader by night. Robert Louis Stevenson (1850–94) may well have used Brodie as the inspiration for his *Strange Case of Dr. Jekyll and Mr. Hyde,* though the book isn't set in Edinburgh. ✉ *Between Castlehill and High St., Old Town.*

need a break?

Several atmospheric pubs and restaurants bustle on this section of the Royal Mile. Try the friendly **Jolly Judge** (✉ 7 James Ct., Old Town ☎ 0131/225–2669), where firelight brightens the dark-wood beams and a mixed crowd of university professors and students, and people who work in the Scottish Parliament, sip ale and eat light lunches of soup, pasta, quiche, or baked potatoes.

17 **Museum of Childhood.** Even adults tend to enjoy this cheerfully noisy museum—a cacophony of childhood memorabilia, vintage toys, and dolls, as well as a reconstructed schoolroom, street scene, fancy-dress party, and nursery. The museum claims to be the first in the world to be devoted solely to the history of childhood. It's two blocks past the North Bridge–South Bridge junction on High Street. ✉ *42 High St., Old Town* ☎ *0131/529–4142* 📠 *0131/558–3103* 🌐 *www.cac.org.uk* *Free* ⏲ *Mon.–Sat. 10–5, Sun. during festival 2–5.*

10 **National Library of Scotland.** Founded in 1689, the National Library houses a superb collection of books and manuscripts on the history and culture of Scotland, and also mounts regular exhibitions. Genealogists investigating family trees come here, and amateur family sleuths will find the staff helpful in their research. ✉ *George IV Bridge, Old Town* ☎ *0131/226–4531* 🌐 *www.nls.uk* *Free* ⏲ *Mon., Tues., Thurs., Fri. 9:30–8:30; Wed. 10–8:30; Sat. 9:30–1; exhibitions Mon.–Sat. 10–5; festival hrs weekdays 10–8, Sat. 10–5, Sun. 2–5.*

20 **Netherbow Arts Centre.** The gallery hosts painting and photography exhibitions, and the theater produces contemporary dramas and children's shows. A café serves lunch and tea. ✉ *43 High St., Old Town* ☎ *0131/556–9579* *Gallery, free; performances, £3–£7* ⏲ *Mon.–Sat. 10–5; call for performance times.*

27 **Our Dynamic Earth.** Using state-of-the-art technology, Our Dynamic Earth educates and entertains as it brings to life the wonders of the planet. From the big bang to the unknown future, you'll travel through every environment on Earth and encounter creatures you probably never even knew existed—and that's just in the parking lot. ✉ *Holyrood Rd., Holyrood* ☎ *0131/550–7800* 🌐 *www.dynamicearth.co.uk* *£7.95* ⏲ *Apr.–Nov., daily 10–6; Nov.–Mar., Wed.–Sun. 10–5; last admission 1 hr before closing.*

3 **Outlook Tower.** Want to view Edinburgh as Victorian travelers once did? Then head for the 17th-century Outlook Tower's **camera obscura,** where you'll find an optical instrument—a sort of projecting telescope—that affords bird's-eye views of the whole city (on a clear day, that is) illuminated onto a concave table. The structure was significantly altered in the 1840s and 1850s with the installation of the telescopic "magic lantern." ✉ *Castlehill, Old Town* ☎ *0131/226–3709* 🌐 *www.explore-edinburgh.com/camera* *£4.50* ⏲ *Apr.–Oct., weekdays 9:30–6, weekends 10–6; Nov.–Mar., daily 10–5.*

★ 25 **Palace of Holyroodhouse.** Once the haunt of Mary, Queen of Scots, and the setting for high drama—including at least one notorious murder, several major fires, and centuries of the colorful lifestyles of larger-than-life, power-hungry personalities—this is now Queen Elizabeth's official residence in Scotland. A doughty and impressive palace standing at the foot of the Royal Mile in a hilly public park, it is built around a graceful, lawned central court at the end of Canongate. When the queen or royal family is not in residence, you can take a guided tour. Many monarchs, including Charles II, Queen Victoria, and George V, have left their mark on its rooms, but it is Mary, Queen of Scots, whose spirit looms largest. For some visitors the most memorable room here is the little chamber in which David Rizzio, secretary to Mary, Queen of Scots, met an unhappy end in 1566. In part because Rizzio was hated at court for his social-climbing ways, Mary's second husband, Lord Darnley (Henry Stewart, 1545–65), burst into the queen's rooms with his henchmen, dragged Rizzio into an antechamber, and stabbed him more than 50 times; a bronze plaque marks the spot. Darnley himself was murdered the next year to make way for the queen's marriage to her lover, Bothwell.

The **King James Tower** is the oldest surviving section, containing the rooms of Mary, Queen of Scots, on the second floor, and Lord Darnley's rooms below. Though much has been altered, there are fine fireplaces, paneling, plasterwork, tapestries, and 18th- and 19th-century furnishings throughout. At the south end of the palace front you'll find the **Royal Dining Room,** and along the south side are the **Throne Room** and other drawing rooms now used for social and ceremonial occasions.

At the back of the palace is the **King's Bedchamber.** The 150-foot-long **Great Picture Gallery,** on the north side, displays the portraits of 110 Scottish monarchs. These were commissioned by Charles II, who was eager to demonstrate his Scottish ancestry—some of the royal figures here are fictional and the likenesses of others imaginary. All the portraits were painted by a Dutch artist, Jacob De Witt, who signed a contract in 1684 with the queen's cash keeper, Hugh Wallace, that bound him to deliver 110 pictures within two years, for which he received an annual stipend of £120. Surely one of the most desperate scenes in the palace's history is that of the artist feverishly turning out potboiler portraits at the rate of one a week for two years.

Holyroodhouse has its origins in an Augustinian monastery founded by David I (1084–1153) in 1128. In the 15th and 16th centuries, Scottish royalty, preferring the comforts of the abbey to the drafty rooms of Edinburgh Castle, settled into Holyroodhouse, expanding and altering the buildings until the palace eventually eclipsed the monastery. Look for the brass letters SSS set into the road at the beginning of Abbey Strand (the continuation of the Royal Mile beyond the traffic circle). The letters stand for "sanctuary" and recall the days when the abbey served as a retreat for debtors, which it was until 1880, when the government stopped imprisoning people for debt. Curiously, the area of sanctuary extended across what is now Holyrood Park, so debtors could get some fresh air without fear of being caught by their creditors. Oddest of all, however, was the agreement that after debtors checked in at Holyrood they were able to go anywhere in the city on Sunday. This made for great entertainment on Sunday evening as midnight approached: the debtors raced back to Holyrood before the stroke of 12, often hotly pursued by their creditors. The poet Thomas de Quincey (1785–1859) and the comte d'Artois (known as Charles X, 1757–1836), brother of the deposed king of France, Louis XVIII (1755–1824), were two of the more famous of Holyrood's denizens.

After the Union of the Crowns in 1603, when the Scottish royal court packed its bags and decamped for England, the building fell into decline. Oliver Cromwell (1599–1658), the Protestant Lord Protector of England who had conquered Scotland, ordered the palace rebuilt after a fire in 1650, but the work was poorly carried out. When the monarchy was restored with the ascension of Charles II (1630–1685) to the British throne in 1660, Holyrood was rebuilt in the architectural style of Louis XIV (1638–1715), and this is the style you see today.

In 1688 an anti-Catholic faction ran riot within the palace, and in 1745, during the last Jacobite campaign, Charles Edward Stuart occupied the palace, followed a short while later by the duke of Cumberland, who defeated Charles at Culloden. After the 1822 visit of King George IV (1762–1830), at a more peaceable time, the palace sank into decline once again. But Queen Victoria (1819–1901) and her grandson King George V (1865–1936) renewed interest in the palace: the buildings were once more refurbished and made suitable for royal residence. Behind the palace lie the open grounds and looming crags of Holyrood Park, the hunting ground of early Scottish kings.

Queen's Gallery, in a former church and school at the entrance to the palace, holds rotating exhibits from the Royal Collection. From the top of Edinburgh's minimountain, **Arthur's Seat** (822 feet), views are breathtaking. ✉ *Abbey Strand, Holyrood, Old Town* ☎ *0131/556–7371, 0131/556–1096 for recorded information* 📠 *0131/557–5256* 🌐 *www.royal.gov.uk* 🎟 *£6.50* ⏲ *Apr.–Oct., daily 9:30–5:15; Nov.–Mar., daily 9:30–3:45. Closed during royal visits.*

14 **Parliament House.** The seat of Scottish government until 1707, when the governments of Scotland and England were united, Parliament House now contains the Supreme Law Courts of Scotland. The structure is partially hidden by the bulk of St. Giles's. Inside, it is remarkable for its hammer-beam roof and its display of portraits by major Scottish artists. ✉ *Parliament Sq., Old Town* ☎ *0131/225–2595* 🌐 *www.scotcourts.gov.uk* 🎟 *Free* ⏲ *Weekdays 10–4.*

16 **The Real Mary King's Close.** Hidden beneath the City Chambers, this narrow, cobbled *close,* or lane, named after a former landowner, is said to be one of Edinburgh's most haunted sites. The close was sealed off in 1645 to quarantine residents who became sick when the bubonic plague swept through the city, and many victims were herded there to die. After the plague passed, the bodies were removed and buried, and the street was reopened. A few people returned, but they soon reported ghostly goings-on and departed, leaving the close empty for decades afterward. In 1753, city authorities built the Royal Exchange (later the City Chambers) directly over the close, sealing it off and, unwittingly, ensuring it remain intact, except for the buildings' upper stories, which were destroyed. Today, you can walk among the remains of the shops and houses. People still report so-called cold spots in some of the rooms, ghostly visions, and eerie sounds, such as the crying of a young girl. Over the years, visitors have left small offerings for her, such as dolls, pieces of ribbon, or candy. Children under 5 are not admitted. ✉ *Writers' Court, Old Town* ☎ *0870/243–0160 for inquiries, 0870/411415 for group reservations* 🌐 *www.realmarykingsclose.com* 🎟 *£7* ⏲ *Apr.–Oct., daily 10–9; Nov.–Mar., daily 10–4.*

12 **The Royal Museum and the Museum of Scotland.** In an imposing Victorian building on Chambers Street, the Royal Museum houses an internationally renowned collection of art and artifacts relating to natural, scientific, and industrial history. Its treasures include the Lewis Chessmen, 11 intricately carved ivory chessmen found on one of the Western Isles in the 19th century. The museum's main hall, with its soaring roof and "birdcage" design, is architecturally interesting in its own right. The striking, contemporary building next door houses the **Museum of Scotland,** with displays concentrating on Scotland's own heritage. This state-of-the-art, no-expense-spared museum is full of playful models, complex reconstructions, and paraphernalia stretching from the Bronze Age to the latest Scottish pop stars. The preserved body of Dolly the sheep, the first mammal cloned from adult cells, is on display in the passageway

Fodor's Choice ★

connecting the two museum buildings. ✉ *Chambers St., Old Town* ☎ *0131/225–7534* 🌐 *www.nms.ac.uk* 🎫 *Free* ⏲ *Mon. and Wed.–Sat. 10–5, Tues. 10–8, Sun. noon–5.*

need a break?

Café Delos (☎ 0131/225–7534) in the Royal Museum's main hall serves tea, coffee, cookies, cakes, and savory snacks from 10 to 4. The **Soupson Tearoom** (☎ 0131/225–7534), also in the museum, adds soup and salad to its offerings.

4 **Scotch Whisky Heritage Centre.** The mysterious process that turns malted barley and spring water into one of Scotland's most important exports is revealed in this museum. Although whisky-making is not in itself packed with drama, the center manages an imaginative presentation using models and tableaux viewed while riding in low-speed barrel-cars. At one point you'll find yourself inside a huge vat surrounded by bubbling sounds and malty smells. ✉ *354 Castlehill, Old Town* ☎ *0131/220–0441* 🌐 *www.whisky-heritage.co.uk* 🎫 *£7.50* ⏲ *May–Sept., daily 9:30–6:30 (last tour 5:30); Oct.–Apr., daily 10–5 (last tour 4).*

26 **Scottish Parliament Building.** After four years of construction and a cost of many millions of pounds, no date has been set yet for the opening of this building at the foot of the Royal Mile. When completed, it will house offices, committee rooms, and a parliament chamber for the 129 members of the Scottish Parliament (MSPs) and its civil servants. The structure was designed by Barcelona architect Enric Miralles, in association with Edinburgh's RMJM Architects. Donald Dewar, Scotland's first and highly respected first minister, chose the site. Both Dewar and Miralles died in 2000, before witnessing the completion of the structure. **The Parliament Visitor Centre,** open Monday through Saturday from 9:30 to 5 (times may vary), provides general information about the role of parliament. ✉ *Scottish Parliament EH99 1SP* ☎ *0131/348–5411* 🌐 *www.scottish.parliament.uk.*

6 **Writers' Museum.** Down a close off Lawnmarket is Lady Stair's House, built in 1622 and a good example of 17th-century urban architecture. Inside, the Writer's Museum evokes Scotland's literary past with such exhibits as the letters, possessions, and original manuscripts of Sir Walter Scott, Robert Louis Stevenson, and Robert Burns. ✉ *Off Lawnmarket, Old Town* ☎ *0131/529–4901* 🌐 *www.cac.org.uk* 🎫 *Free* ⏲ *Mon.–Sat. 10–5 (last admission 4:45), Sun. during festival 2–5.*

New Town

It was not until the Scottish Enlightenment, a civilizing time of expansion in the 1700s, that the city fathers decided to break away from the Royal Mile's rocky slope and create a new Edinburgh below the castle, a little to the north. This was to become the New Town, with elegant squares, classical facades, wide streets, and harmonious proportions. Clearly, change had to come. For at the dawn of the 18th century, Edinburgh's unsanitary environment—primarily a result of over-crowded conditions—was becoming notorious. The well-known Scots fiddle tune "The Flooers (flowers) of Edinburgh" was only one of many ironic references to the capital's unpleasant environment, which greatly embarrassed the Scot James Boswell (1740–95), biographer and companion of the English lexicographer Dr. Samuel Johnson (1709–84). In his *Journal of a Tour of the Hebrides,* Boswell recalled that on retrieving the newly arrived Johnson from his grubby inn in the Canongate, "I could not prevent his being assailed by the evening effluvia of Edinburgh. . . .Walking the streets at night was pretty perilous and a good deal odoriferous."

To help remedy this sorry state of affairs, in 1767 James Drummond, the city's lord provost (the Scots term for mayor), urged the town council to hold a competition to design a new district for Edinburgh. The winner was an unknown young architect named James Craig (1744–95). His plan called for a grid of three main east–west streets, balanced at either end by two grand squares. These streets survive today, though some of the buildings that line them have been altered by later development. Princes Street is the southernmost, with Queen Street to the north and George Street as the axis, punctuated by St. Andrew and Charlotte squares. A look at the map will reveal a geometric symmetry unusual in Britain. Even the Princes Street Gardens are balanced by the Queen Street Gardens, to the north. Princes Street was conceived as an exclusive residential address, with an open vista facing the castle. It has since been altered by the demands of business and shopping, but the vista remains.

The New Town was expanded several times after Craig's death and now covers an area about three times larger than Craig envisioned. Indeed, some of the most elegant facades came later and can be found by strolling north of the Queen Street Gardens.

a good walk

Start your walk on **the Mound** 28 ⚑, the sloping street that joins the Old and New towns. Two galleries immediately east of this great linking ramp, the **National Gallery of Scotland** 29 and the **Royal Scottish Academy** 30, are the work of William Playfair (1789–1857), an architect whose neoclassical buildings contributed greatly to Edinburgh's title: the Athens of the North.

At the foot of the Mound is the city's most famous thoroughfare, **Princes Street** 31, the humming center of modern-day Edinburgh. A ceaseless promenade of natives and visitors patter along its mile or so of retail establishments. Residents lament the disappearance of the dignified old shops that once lined this street; now a long sequence of chain stores has replaced them, although there is still a grand vista of the castle to the south. Walk east until you reach the soaring Gothic spire of the **Scott Monument** 32. Opposite is that most Edinburgh of institutions, **Jenners** 33 department store. **Register House** 34, an elegant neoclassical treasure designed by Robert Adam (1728–92), marks the east end of Princes Street. Immediately west of Register House is the Café Royal, one of the city's most colorful pubs, with ornate tiles, stained glass, and great beer.

The monuments on Calton Hill, growing ever more noticeable ahead as you walk east along Princes Street, can be reached by first continuing along **Waterloo Place** 35, the eastern extension of Princes Street, from which you can get to the Regent Bridge. Waterloo Place continues in a single sweep through the Calton Burial Ground to the screen walling at the base of **Calton Hill** 36. On the left you'll see steps that lead to the hilltop. If you're walking and don't feel up to the steep climb, take the road farther on to the left, which loops up the hill at a more leisurely pace.

Leaving Calton Hill, you may wish to continue east along Regent Road, perhaps as far as the Burns Monument, to admire the views westward of the castle and of the facade of the former Royal High School directly above you. Then retrace your steps to the Waterloo Place traffic lights and make your way to St. Andrew Square by cutting through the St. James Centre shopping mall, taking in the upscale Harvey Nichols store. After admiring the lavish interior of the Royal Bank of Scotland, on the east side of the square—the building was originally the town house of the immensely rich Sir Lawrence Dundas, one of Chippendale's most lavish patrons—walk west along **George Street** 37, with its variety of shops.

The essence of the New Town spirit survives in **Charlotte Square** 38, at the west end of George Street, and especially in the beautiful **Georgian**

House 39 and **West Register House** 40. To explore further, choose your own route northward, down to the wide and elegant streets centering on **Moray Place** 41, a fine example of an 1820s development. Then make your way back eastward along Queen Street to visit the **Scottish National Portrait Gallery** 42, which has exceptional paintings and a fine restaurant. Also within reach of the New Town via taxi or a 20 minute walk is the 70-acre **Royal Botanic Garden** on the northwest side of Edinburgh's small-scale river, the Water of Leith.

TIMING This walk could be done in a morning if you start early, but if you want to get the most out of the National Gallery of Scotland and the Scottish National Portrait Gallery, take the whole day and allow at least an hour for each museum. The Portrait Gallery has a good restaurant, so one option is to arrive in time for lunch, then spend the afternoon there. Save time by riding the free galleries bus, which connects the National Gallery of Scotland, Scottish National Portrait Gallery, Scottish National Gallery of Modern Art, and Dean Gallery daily from 11 to 5. You can board or leave the bus at any of the galleries.

What to See

36 **Calton Hill.** Robert Louis Stevenson's favorite view of his beloved city was from the top of this hill. The architectural styles represented by the extraordinary collection of monuments here include mock Gothic—the Old Observatory, for example—and neoclassical. Under the latter category falls William Playfair's (1789–1857) monument to his talented uncle, the geologist and mathematician John Playfair (1748–1819), as well as his cruciform **New Observatory.** The piece that commands the most attention, however, is the so-called **National Monument,** often referred to as "Edinburgh's [or Scotland's] Disgrace." Intended to mimic Athens's Parthenon, this monument for the dead of the Napoleonic Wars was started in 1822 to the specifications of a design by Playfair. But in 1830, only 12 columns later, money ran out, and the columned facade became a monument to high aspirations and poor fund-raising. The tallest monument on Calton Hill is the 100-foot-high **Nelson Monument,** completed in 1815 in honor of Britain's naval hero Horatio Nelson (1758–1805). The **Burns Monument** is the circular Corinthian temple below Regent Road. Devotees of Robert Burns may want to visit one other grave—that of Mrs. Agnes McLehose, or "Clarinda," in the Canongate Graveyard. ✉ *Bounded by Leith St. to the west and Regent Rd. to the south, Calton* ☎ *0131/556–2716* 🌐 *www.cac.org.uk* 💷 *£2.50 (Nelson Monument)* ⏲ *Apr.–Sept., Mon. 1–6, Tues.–Sat. 10–6; Oct.–Mar., Mon.–Sat. 10–3.*

38 **Charlotte Square.** At the west end of George Street is the New Town's centerpiece—an 18th-century square that is home to one of the proudest achievements of Robert Adam, Scotland's noted neoclassical architect. On the north side, Adam designed a palatial facade to unite three separate town houses of such sublime simplicity and perfect proportions that architects come from all over the world to study it. Happily, the Age of Enlightenment grace notes continue within, as the center town house is now occupied by the **Georgian House** museum, and to the west stands **West Register House.** ✉ *West end of George St., New Town.*

off the beaten path

EDINBURGH ZOO – Children love to visit the some 1,000 animals that live in Edinburgh Zoo. You can even handle some of the animals from April to September. The ever-popular Penguin Parade is scheduled for 2:15 in summer and 12:45 in winter, but since penguin participation is totally voluntary, the event is rather unpredictable. The zoo spreads out over an 80-acre site on the slopes of Corstorphine

Hill. Take buses 12, 26, or 31. ✉ *Corstorphine Rd., next to Holiday Inn Edinburgh, Corstorphine, 3 mi west of the city center* ☎ *0131/334–9171* 🌐 *www.edinburghzoo.org.uk* 🎫 *£7.50* 🕒 *Apr.–Sept., daily 9–6; Oct. and Mar., daily 9–5; Nov.–Feb., daily 9–4:30.*

37 **George Street.** With its upscale shops and handsome Georgian frontages, this is a more pleasant, less crowded street for wandering than Princes Street. The **statue of King George IV,** at the intersection of George and Hanover streets, recalls the visit of George IV to Scotland in 1822. He was the first British monarch to do so since King Charles II, in the 17th century. By the 19th century, enough time had passed since the Jacobite Uprising of 1745 for Scotland to be perceived at Westminster as being safe enough for a monarch to visit.

The ubiquitous Sir Walter Scott turns up farther down the street. It was at a grand dinner in the **Assembly Rooms,** between Hanover and Frederick streets, that Scott acknowledged having written the *Waverley* novels (the name of the author had hitherto been a secret, albeit a badly kept one). You can meet Scott once again, in the form of a plaque just downhill, at 39 Castle Street, his Edinburgh address before he moved to Abbotsford, in the Borders region, where he died in 1832. ✉ *Between Charlotte and St. Andrew sqs., New Town.*

★ 39 **Georgian House.** The National Trust for Scotland has furnished this house in period style to show the elegant domestic arrangements of an affluent family of the late 18th century. The hallway was designed to accommodate sedan chairs, in which 18th-century grandees were carried through the streets. ✉ *7 Charlotte Sq., New Town* ☎ *0131/225–2160* 🌐 *www.nts.org.uk* 🎫 *£5* 🕒 *Late Mar.–late Oct., daily 10–6; late Oct.–late Dec. and late Jan.–late Mar., daily 11–4 (last admission ½ hr before closing).*

33 **Jenners.** Edinburgh's equivalent of London's Harrods department store, Jenners is noteworthy not only for its high-quality wares and good restaurants, but also because of the building's interesting architectural detail—baroque on the outside, with a mock-Jacobean central well inside. It was one of the earliest department stores ever to be established, in 1838. The caryatids decorating the exterior were said to have been placed in honor of the store's predominantly female customers. ✉ *48 Princes St., New Town* ☎ *0131/225–2442* 🌐 *www.jenners.com* 🕒 *Mon., Wed., Fri., Sat. 9–5:30, Tues. 9:30–5:30, Thurs. 9–7:30.*

off the beaten path

LEITH – Edinburgh's ancient seaport has been revitalized with the restoration of those fine commercial buildings that survived an earlier, and insensitive, redevelopment phase. It's worth exploring the lowest reaches of the Water of Leith, an area where pubs and restaurants now proliferate. The major attraction for visitors here, however, is the former royal yacht ***Britannia*** (☎ 0131/555–5566 🌐 www.royalyachtbritannia.co.uk 🎫 £8) moored outside the huge Ocean Terminal shopping mall, where you can wander around the ship that Queen Elizabeth called "the one place where I can truly relax," then check in at the shore-based visitor center, which tells the ship's sometimes fabled story. Reach Leith by walking down Leith Street and Leith Walk, from the east end of Princes Street (20–30 minutes); or take Lothian Bus 22. ✉ *Britannia Ocean Dr., Leith.*

41 **Moray Place.** Moray Place—with its "pendants" of Ainslie Place and Randolph Crescent—was laid out in 1822 by the earl of Moray. From the start the homes were planned to be of particularly high quality, with lovely

curving facades, imposing porticos, and a central secluded garden (for residents only). ✉ *Between Charlotte Sq. and the Water of Leith, New Town.*

28 **The Mound.** This rising street originated from the need for a dry-shod crossing of the muddy quagmire left behind when Nor' Loch, the body of water below the castle, was drained (the railway now cuts through this area). The work is said to have been started by a local tailor, George Boyd, who tired of struggling through the mud en route from his New Town house to his Old Town shop. The building of a ramp was under way by 1781, and by the time of its completion, in 1830, "Geordie Boyd's mud brig [bridge]," as the street was first known, had been built up with an estimated 2 million cartloads of earth dug from the foundations of the New Town.

29 **National Gallery of Scotland.** Opened to the public in 1859, the National Gallery presents a wide selection of paintings from the Renaissance to the postimpressionist period within a grand neoclassical building designed by William Playfair. Most famous are the old-master paintings bequeathed by the duke of Sutherland, including Titian's *Three Ages of Man.* All the great names are here; works by Velázquez, El Greco, Rembrandt, Goya, Poussin, Clouet, Turner, Degas, Monet, and van Gogh, among others, complement a fine collection of Scottish art, including Sir Henry Raeburn's *Reverend Robert Walker Skating on Duddingston Loch* and other masterworks by Ramsay, Raeburn, and Wilkie. The free galleries bus stops here daily on the hour from 11 to 4. ✉ *The Mound, Old Town* ☎ *0131/624–6200 (general inquiries), 0131/332–2266 (recorded information)* 🌐 *www.nationalgalleries.org* 🎫 *Free* 🕑 *Thurs. 10–7, Fri.–Wed. 10–5; extended hrs during the festival. Print Room, weekdays 10–12:30 and 2–4:30 by appointment.*

Fodor's Choice ★

31 **Princes Street.** The south side of this well-planned street is occupied by the well-kept Princes Street Gardens, which act as a wide green moat to the castle on its rock. Unfortunately, the north side is now one long sequence of chain stores with unappealing modern fronts that can be seen in almost any large British town. ✉ *Running east–west from Waterloo Pl. to Lothian Rd., East End to West End.*

need a break?

Café Royal (✉ 17 W. Register St., New Town ☎ 0131/557–4792), immediately west of Register House, serves good Scottish lagers and ales, and simple lunch items like nachos and macaroni and cheese. The 18th-century building has plenty of character, with ornate tiles and stained-glass windows. Local musicians sometimes play gigs in a separate suite.

34 **Register House.** Scotland's first custom-built archives depository, Register House, designed by the great Robert Adam, was partly funded by the sale of estates forfeited by Jacobite landowners after their last rebellion in Britain (1745–46). Work on the Regency-style building, which marks the end of Princes Street, started in 1774. The statue in front is of the first duke of Wellington (1769–1852). It's possible to conduct genealogical research here; call ahead for more information. ✉ *Princes St., New Town* ☎ *0131/535–1314* 🌐 *www.nas.gov.uk* 🎫 *Free* 🕑 *Weekdays 9–4:45.*

off the beaten path

ROYAL BOTANIC GARDEN – Britain's largest rhododendron and azalea gardens are part of the varied and comprehensive collection of plant and flower species in Scotland's 70-acre Royal Botanic Garden, just north of the city center. An impressive Chinese garden has the largest collection of wild-origin Chinese plants outside China. There is a cafeteria, plus a gift shop that sells plants and books. Take a taxi to the garden; or ride Bus 27 from Princes Street or Bus 23 from Hanover Street. To walk to the garden from the New Town, take Dundas Street, the continuation of Hanover Street, and turn left at the clock tower onto Inverleith Row (about 20 minutes). ✉ *Inverleith Row, Inverleith* ☎ *0131/552–7171* 🌐 *www.rbge.org.uk* 🎫 *Free; donations accepted* ⏲ *Nov.–Feb., daily 10–4; Mar. and Oct., daily, 10–6; Apr.–Sept., daily, 10–7. Guided tours, Apr.–Sept., daily at 11 and 2.*

30 **Royal Scottish Academy.** The William Playfair–designed Academy, slated to reopen in late 2003 after a renovation, hosts temporary art exhibitions (Monet paintings, for example), but is also worth visiting for a look at the imposing, neoclassic architecture. ✉ *Princes St., Old Town* ☎ *0131/558–7097* 🌐 *www.royalscottishacademy.org* 🎫 *£6–£8* ⏲ *Mon.–Sat. 10–5, Sun. 12–5.*

32 **Scott Monument.** What appears to be a Gothic cathedral spire chopped off and planted in the east end of the Princes Street Gardens is the nation's tribute to Sir Walter—a 200-foot-high monument looming over Princes Street. Built in 1844 in honor of Scotland's most famous author, Sir Walter Scott, the author of *Ivanhoe, Waverley,* and many other novels and poems, it's centered on a marble statue of Scott and his favorite dog, Maida. It's worth taking the time to explore the immediate area, Princes Street Gardens, one of the prettiest city parks in Britain. In the open-air theater, amid the park's trim flower beds, stately trees, and carefully tended lawns, brass bands occasionally play. Here, too, is the famous **monument to David Livingstone,** whose African meeting with H. M. Stanley is part of Scot-American history. ✉ *Princes St., New Town* ☎ *0131/529–4068* 🌐 *www.cac.org.uk* 🎫 *£2.50* ⏲ *April–Sept., Mon.–Sat. 9–6, Sun. 10–6; Oct.–Mar., Mon.–Sat. 9–3, Sun. 10–3.*

off the beaten path

SCOTTISH NATIONAL GALLERY OF MODERN ART – This handsome former school building on Belford Road, close to the New Town, displays paintings and sculpture, including works by Pablo Picasso, Georges Braque, Henri Matisse, and André Derain. The gallery also has an excellent restaurant in the basement. The free galleries bus is scheduled to stop here on the half hour. ✉ *Belford Rd., Dean Village* ☎ *0131/556–8921* 🎫 *Free* ⏲ *Thurs. 10–7, Fri.–Wed. 10–5; extended hrs during the festival.*

★ 42 **Scottish National Portrait Gallery.** A magnificent red-sandstone Gothic building dating from 1889 on Queen Street houses this must-visit institution. The gallery contains a superb Thomas Gainsborough painting and portraits by the Scottish artists Allan Ramsay (1713–84) and Sir Henry Raeburn (1756–1823), among many others. You can see portraits of classic literary figures such as Robert Burns and Sir Walter Scott, and modern portraits depict actors, sports stars, and living members of the royal family. The building's beautiful William Hole murals representing Scots from the Stone Age to the 19th century are themselves worthy of study. The free galleries bus is scheduled to stop here every day from 11:15 to 4:15. ✉ *Queen St., New Town* ☎ *0131/624–6200* 🌐 *www.natgalscot.ac.uk* 🎫 *Free; charge for special exhibitions* ⏲ *Thurs. 10–7, Fri.–Wed. 10–5; extended hrs during the festival.*

35 **Waterloo Place.** The fine neoclassically inspired architecture on this street was designed as a piece by Archibald Elliot (d. 1823) in 1815. Waterloo Place extends over Regent Bridge, bounded by the 1815 **Regent Arch,**

a simple, triumphal Corinthian-column war memorial at the center of Ionic screens bordering the bridge. ✉ *Eastern extension of Princes St., East End.*

40 **West Register House.** The former St. George's Church, in the middle of the west side of Charlotte Square, today fulfills a different role, as an extension of the original Register House on Princes Street. You may view modern records, but call ahead if you wish to carry out extensive genealogical research. ✉ *Charlotte Sq., New Town* ☎ *0131/535–1400* 🌐 *www.nas.gov.uk* 💷 *Free* ⏲ *Weekdays 9–4:30.*

WHERE TO EAT

Edinburgh has a huge number of restaurants in a cosmopolitan range, but you may also notice a strong emphasis on traditional style. This tends to mean the Scottish-French style that harks back to the historical "Auld Alliance," founded in the 13th century against the English. The Scots element is the preference for plain and fresh foodstuffs; the French supply the sauces, often to be poured on after cooking. Restaurants tend to be small, so it's best to make reservations at the more popular ones, even on weekdays and definitely at festival time. As Edinburgh is an unusually small capital, most of the good restaurants are within easy walking distance of the main streets, Princes Street and the Royal Mile.

Prices

It's possible to eat well in Edinburgh without spending a fortune. Prix-fixe, multicourse options are common and almost always less expensive than ordering à la carte. Even at restaurants in the ££££ price category, you can spend under £40 for two if you order prudently. A service charge of 10% or more may be added to your bill, though this practice is not adhered to uniformly. If no charge has been added and you are satisfied with the service, a 10% tip is appropriate. People tend to eat later in Scotland than in England, or rather they finish eating and then drink on in leisurely Scottish fashion.

WHAT IT COSTS In pounds

	£££££	££££	£££	££	£
AT DINNER	over £22	£18–£22	£13–£17	£7–£12	under £7

Prices are per person for a main course. The final tab will include a 17.5% VAT.

Old Town

French

££££–£££££ ✕ **Merchants.** This is a bustling, cheery cavern of bright scarlet walls, mirrors, plants, and a nonstop jazz sound track, all set beneath the dramatic arch of George IV Bridge. The menu ranges from simple haggis and beef to a mille-feuille of scallops and lamb chops with raspberry-and-mint sauce. Its ambitious dishes are reminiscent of nouvelle cuisine, but Merchants really does the basics best. Prix-fixe lunches run from £10.50 to £12.50, dinners from £19.50 to £23.50. ✉ *17 Merchant St., Old Town* ☎ *0131/225–4009* 💳 *AE, DC, MC, V.*

£££–££££ Fodor's Choice ★ ✕ **Witchery by the Castle.** The hundreds of "witches" who were executed on Castlehill, just yards from where you will be seated, are the inspiration for this atmospheric restaurant. The cavernous interior, complete with flickering candlelight, is festooned with cabalistic insignia and tarot-card characters. Gilded and painted ceilings reflect the close links between France and Scotland, as does the menu, which includes venison, duck, lamb, salmon, and steak. Pre- and post-theater (5:30–6:30 and 10:30–11:30) £9.95 two-course specials are an inexpensive way to sample the exceptional cuisine. (The restaurant also offers lodging in six sumptuous suites.) ✉ *352 Castlehill, Royal Mile, Old Town* ☎ *0131/225–5613* 🌐 *www.thewitchery.com* ✍ *Reservations essential* ▭ *AE, DC, MC, V.*

£–£££ ✕ **Le Sept.** Down a little cobbled lane off the Royal Mile, this low-arched restaurant in the city center is a refined gem and an understated local institution. It's friendly, lively, unfussy, and famed for its crepes with adventurous fillings. The daily changing menu also lists simple staples such as delicately cooked salmon fillets and succulent lamb stew. The wine list is similarly select, and the service is always delightful. Set lunches offer an unbeatable value, with three courses costing £8. ✉ *7 Old Fishmarket Close, Old Town* ☎ *0131/225–5428* ▭ *AE, DC, MC, V.*

Scottish

££–££££ ✕ **Howie's.** This chain consists of four lively neighborhood bistros, each with its own character. The steaks are tender Aberdeen beef, and the Loch Fyne herring is sweet-cured to Howie's own recipe. ✉ *10–14 Victoria Street, Old Town* ☎ *0131/225–1721* ✉ *29 Waterloo Pl., East End* ☎ *0131/556–5766* ✉ *208 Bruntsfield Pl., South Side* ☎ *0131/221–1777* ✉ *4–6 Glanville Pl., New Town* ☎ *0131/313–3334* ▭ *AE, MC, V.*

£££ ✕ **The Tower.** On the rooftop of the Museum of Scotland, this restaurant serves up a feast of contemporary aesthetics and pleasant distractions before you even get to the menu. The modern architecture affords one of the finest vistas in Edinburgh. The Tower has a high-powered ambience and an intelligible menu with an exquisite oyster and shellfish selection, Aberdeen Angus beef, roast saddle of wild red venison, and more. The two-course pre-theater (5–6:30) supper is an especially good value, but be careful not to let the lovely Edinburgh skyline work its ancient charm to the point of making you miss curtain time. ✉ *Museum of Scotland, Chambers St., Old Town* ☎ *0131/225–3003* ✍ *Reservations essential* ▭ *AE, DC, MC, V.*

££ ✕ **Beehive Inn.** Some 400 years ago the Beehive was a coaching inn, and outside the pub's doors once stood the main city gallows. Bar suppers and snacks are served throughout the day, downstairs or in the beer garden. Upstairs, Rafters Restaurant opens at 6 with a dinner menu. Try the grilled salmon steaks. Don't be put off by the noisy bar; there's usually a quieter spot to be found. You can book literary lunch and supper packages downstairs in conjunction with the McEwan's Edinburgh Literary Pub Tour, which departs from here. ✉ *18–20 Grassmarket, Old Town* ☎ *0131/225–7171* ▭ *AE, DC, MC, V.*

££ ✕ **Doric Tavern.** Beyond the bar's grand entrance staircase, there is a languid, bistro environment marked by a stripped wood floor, plain wood tables, and a color scheme in subdued orange and terra-cotta. The menu lists a selection of fresh fish, meat, and vegetarian dishes, plus a daily special such as roast-pigeon salad with raspberry-vinegar dressing. The prix-fixe lunch and dinner options are an excellent value. ✉ *15/16 Market St., Old Town* ☎ *0131/225–1084* ✍ *Reservations essential* ▭ *AE, MC, V.*

Vegetarian

£–£££ ✕ **Bann UK.** Just off the Royal Mile, in the heart of the Old Town, is Bann UK, where you can sip a cup of coffee or dine on vegetarian fare in a light and airy room with sturdy wood furniture. Try the enchiladas or a phyllo basket of cream cheese, herbs, and vegetables. ✉ *5 Hunter Sq., Old Town* ☎ *0131/226–1112* ▭ *AE, DC, MC, V.*

New Town

Chinese

££–£££ ✕ **Kweilin.** This pleasant family-run restaurant serves such favorites as aromatic crispy duck, and bean curd with vegetables. The lunch menu is a pricey-sounding £13 but worth it, and the special four-course dinner menus are an even better value, starting at £19 per person. Amid the traditional Chinese decor are several large paintings depicting scenes from the Kwangsi Province, of which Kweilin is the capital. ✉ *19–21 Dundas St., New Town* ☎ *0131/557–1875* ▭ *AE, MC, V* ⊗ *Closed Mon. Jan.–Nov.*

Eclectic

££–££££ ✕ **The Dome.** The splendid interior of this former bank, with painted plasterwork and a central dome provides an elegant backdrop for relaxed dining. Or you could just opt for a drink at the bar, a hotspot where sophisticates wind down after work. The toasted BLT sandwiches are almost big enough for two, but if you're ravenous the eclectic menu offers many other options: try the tortellini in a broccoli-and-blue-cheese sauce or the char-grilled chicken salad with nan bread. ✉ *14 George St., New Town* ☎ *0131/624–8624* ▭ *AE, MC, V.*

£££ ✕ **Oloroso.** In the heart of the New Town, Oloroso makes the perfect spot for a revitalizing lunch or dinner after exploring the city. You'll find well-prepared and -presented contemporary international cooking, efficient and friendly service, and a bar that serves some of the best cocktails in Britain. Try the roasted duck breast with braised red cabbage, apples, and tarragon jus, or the aubergine *galette* (eggplant tart) with a tomato-and-cinnamon sauce. There are about 150 different types of wine and champagne on the international wine list. The dining room and roof terrace afford stunning views across the Firth of Forth to the hills of Fife on one side, and the castle and city rooftops on the other. ✉ *33 Castle St., New Town* ☎ *0131/226–7614* ▭ *AE, DC, MC, V.*

££–£££ ✕ **Rick's.** There's no *Casablanca* theme, and Sam doesn't play it even once, but the local office crowd makes things lively after 5 at this restaurant-bar within a hotel. The minimalist design is Manhattan-esque and ultrachic. The imaginative contemporary menu includes pan-fried duck with spiced red cabbage in plum-and-ginger sauce; pan-fried salmon with polenta-tomato dressing and crème fraîche; fresh tuna with coriander mashed potatoes; and chocolate "honeycomb" mousse. The bright lobby bar serves cocktails amid brash music and chrome-and-stone decor. ✉ *55 Fredrick St., New Town* ☎ *0131/622–7800* ▭ *AE, MC, V.*

French

★ **££££** ✕ **Pompadour.** As might be expected of a restaurant named after the king's mistress, Madame de Pompadour, the dining room here is inspired by the court of Louis XV, with subtle plasterwork and rich murals. The cuisine is also classic French, with top-quality Scottish produce completing the happiest of alliances. The extensive, well-chosen wine list complements such dishes as sea bass with crispy leeks and caviar-butter sauce, whole lobster with mustard and cheese, and loin of venison with potato pancakes. This is the place to go if you want a festive night out, and it's ideal for the formal lunch that needs lightening up. ✉ *Caledonian Hilton Hotel, Princes St., New Town* ☎ *0131/222–8777* ✍ *Reservations essential* ▭ *AE, DC, MC, V* ⊗ *No lunch weekends.*

£££–££££ ✕ **Le Café St. Honoré.** Quintessentially Parisian in style, this restaurant smacks of all that is charming about French dining. From the moment you enter the beautifully lit room you are transported into a decadently stylish belle epoque. A concise menu leaves more time for chat. You might start off with a warm salad of scallops, monkfish, chorizo, and pine nuts, followed by lamb confit or panfried turbot cooked with cider, green peppercorns, and prawns. ✉ *34 N.W. Thistle Street La., New Town* ☎ *0131/226–2211* ▭ *AE, DC, MC, V* ⊗ *Closed Sun.*

Italian

£–£££ ✕ **La Rusticana.** Hanover Street exists to delight lovers of Italian food; some of the best pasta and pizza restaurants compete here, but La Rusticana usually wins the day. Stronger on pasta than pizza, this cellar restaurant does the taste-bud trick best, while being only marginally above average in price. Along with its sister restaurant in the Old Town, it is a fundamental part of Edinburgh's food culture, a favorite for business meetings, and a generous patron of charity events. ✉ *90 Hanover St., New Town* ☎ *0131/225–2227* ✉ *25 Cockburn St., Old Town* ☎ *0131/225–2832* ▭ *AE, DC, MC, V.*

Scottish

★ ££££–£££££ ✕ **Martins.** Don't be put off by the hard-to-find location of this spot, tucked away in a little back alley between Frederick and Castle Streets, for it's well worth the effort of getting there. The menu emphasizes organically grown local produce and wild-caught fish and game. Typical modern Scottish dishes include fillet of turbot panfried with fennel and green peppercorn sauce; and roasted loin of venison with queen potato, braised red cabbage, roasted root vegetables, and a juniper berry sauce. The cheese board, famed far and wide, has a sampling of unpasteurized Scottish and Irish cheeses. The wine list includes an excellent choice of half bottles. There is no smoking section. ✉ *70 Rose St. North La., New Town* ☎ *0131/225–3106* ⚠ *Reservations essential* ▭ *AE, DC, MC, V* ⊗ *Closed Sun. and Mon. No lunch Sat.*

££££–£££££ ✕ **Number One.** Within the Edwardian splendor of the Balmoral Hotel, this restaurant matches its grand surroundings with a menu that highlights the best of Scottish seafood and game. Try the roulade of organic salmon with langoustine tortellini or the loin of Perthshire venison with herb crust and beetroot-and-chive *jus*. The wine list is extensive, the service impeccable. All in all, this is the kind of stylish yet unstuffy restaurant that is perfect for an intimate dinner. ✉ *Princes St., New Town* ☎ *0131/557–26722* ⚠ *Reservations essential* ▭ *AE, DC, MC, V.*

££–£££ ✕ **A Room in the Town.** At this relaxed and friendly bistro serving Scots-French fare, there's a strong emphasis on local fresh meat, with the Scottish touch accounting for slightly sweeter-than-usual sauces. You may bring your own bottle of wine—there's an excellent wine shop a block away—to offset the somewhat high prices, although the restaurant serves wine, too, along with very nice brandy. Scottishly plain but Continentally cheerful, it's perfect for a sociable night out with friends. Note that it can get a bit smoky when full. ✉ *18 Howe St., New Town* ☎ *0131/225–8204* ⚠ *Reservations essential* ▭ *MC, V.*

Vegetarian

£ ✕ **Hendersons.** This was Edinburgh's original vegetarian restaurant long before it was fashionable to serve healthful, meatless creations. Tasty options include eggplant, tomato, and chickpea curry; and leek-and-Stilton pie. If you haven't summoned the courage to try an authentic haggis while in Scotland, come here to sample a vegetarian version. Around the corner on Thistle Street is the Bistro Bar, owned by the same proprietors. ✉ *94 Hanover St., New Town* ☎ *0131/225–2131* ▭ *AE, DC, MC, V* ⊗ *Closed Sun. except during festival.*

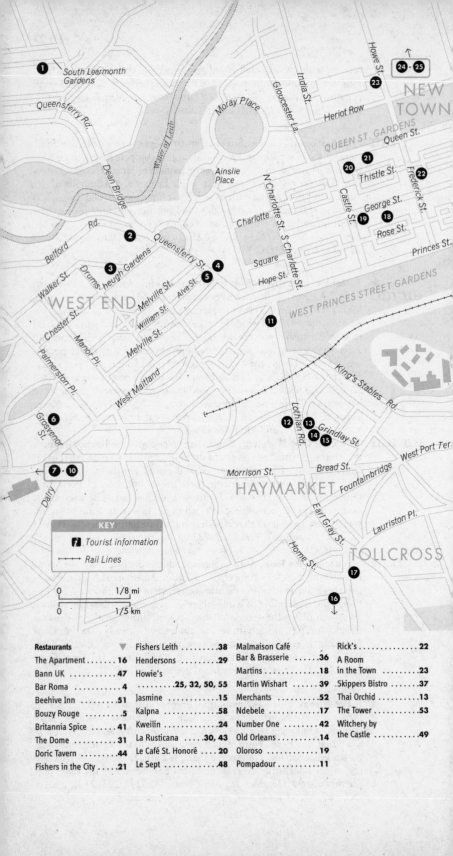

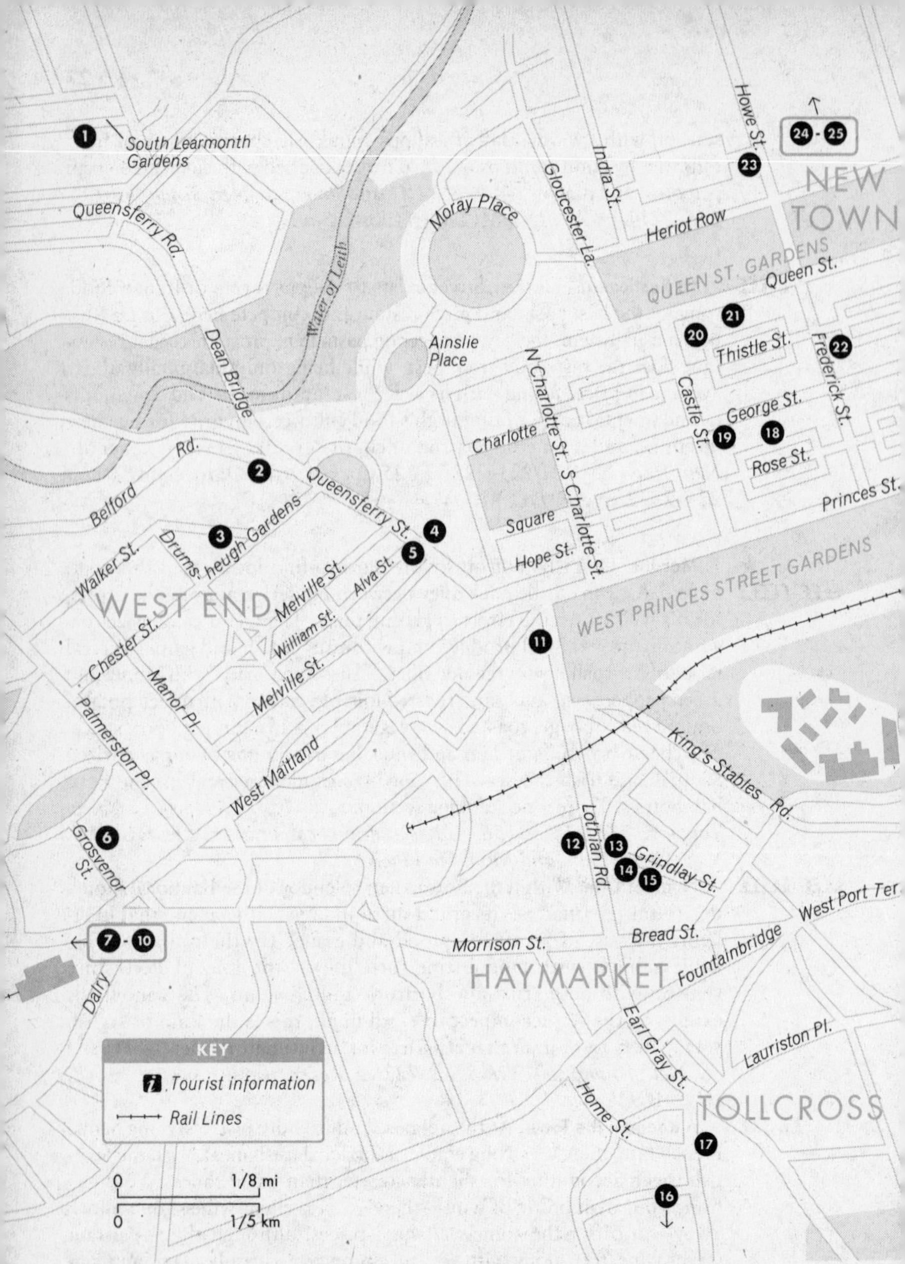

Restaurants ▼

- The Apartment **16**
- Bann UK **47**
- Bar Roma **4**
- Beehive Inn **51**
- Bouzy Rouge **5**
- Britannia Spice **41**
- The Dome **31**
- Doric Tavern **44**
- Fishers in the City **21**
- Fishers Leith **38**
- Hendersons **29**
- Howie's **25, 32, 50, 55**
- Jasmine **15**
- Kalpna **58**
- Kweilin **24**
- La Rusticana **30, 43**
- Le Café St. Honoré **20**
- Le Sept **48**
- Malmaison Café Bar & Brasserie **36**
- Martins **18**
- Martin Wishart **39**
- Merchants **52**
- Ndebele **17**
- Number One **42**
- Old Orleans **14**
- Oloroso **19**
- Pompadour **11**
- Rick's **22**
- A Room in the Town **23**
- Skippers Bistro **37**
- Thai Orchid **13**
- The Tower **53**
- Witchery by the Castle **49**

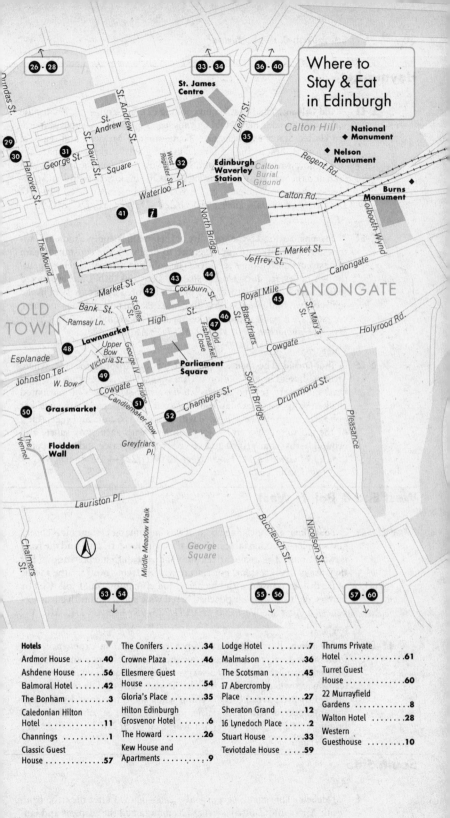

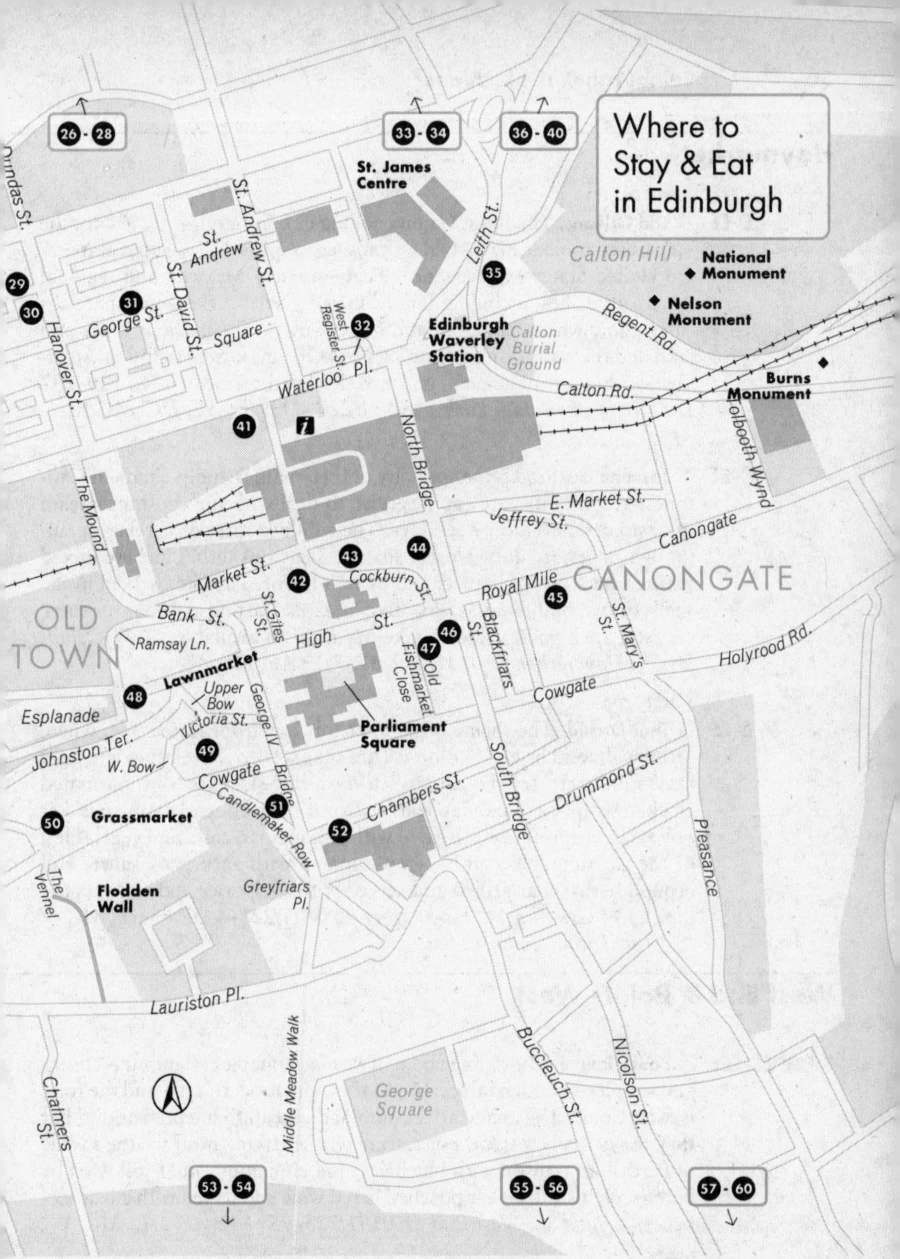

Hotels

Ardmor House 40
Ashdene House 56
Balmoral Hotel 42
The Bonham 3
Caledonian Hilton Hotel 11
Channings 1
Classic Guest House 57
The Conifers 34
Crowne Plaza 46
Ellesmere Guest House 54
Gloria's Place 35
Hilton Edinburgh Grosvenor Hotel 6
The Howard 26
Kew House and Apartments 9
Lodge Hotel 7
Malmaison 36
The Scotsman 45
17 Abercromby Place 27
Sheraton Grand 12
16 Lynedoch Place 2
Stuart House 33
Teviotdale House 59
Thrums Private Hotel 61
Turret Guest House 60
22 Murrayfield Gardens 8
Walton Hotel 28
Western Guesthouse 10

Haymarket

Cajun

£–££ ✕ **Old Orleans.** The finest Cajun cooking in Edinburgh—no, it's not the *only* Cajun cooking here—Old Orleans serves up its dishes with real southern United States extravagance. There are also Mexican and regional American dishes, including fajitas, maple-glazed turkey, and spareribs (they come with a large bib and finger bowl). The music is blues and jazz, and the walls display amusing New Orleans kitsch: trellis- and metalwork, brass instruments, and travel-related mementos. ✉ *130–137 Dundee St., Fountain Park* ☎ *0131/228–8339* 💳 *AE, DC, MC, V.*

Chinese

£–££ ✕ **Jasmine.** Seafood is the specialty of this small, friendly, candlelit Cantonese restaurant, with rapid service to deal with the constant stream of customers, even on weekdays. The subdued interior is relaxing, although tables are quite closely spaced. Delicious dishes include mixed seafood on a bed of lettuce, and mango-flavored chicken served in the shells of two half mangos. Prix-fixe lunches, starting at £6.80 for three courses, are a good value. A take-out menu is available. ✉ *32 Grindlay St., Haymarket* ☎ *0131/229–5757* 💳 *AE, MC, V.*

Thai

£–££ ✕ **Thai Orchid.** The theme is green at this bowfront restaurant, where green walls and brightly colored Thai silks set off Thai statues and gold masks. To start, try the *gaihan bai thoy,* bite-size pieces of marinated chicken wrapped in pandan leaf. For your main course, try the *pad kee hoa nella,* strips of beef stir-fried with lemongrass, chili, and vegetables; or the *gai yang,* chicken breast marinated with garlic, soy sauce, and ground herbs, char-grilled and served with sticky rice and chili-pepper dip. ✉ *44 Grindlay St., Haymarket* ☎ *0131/228–4438* 💳 *AE, MC, V* ⏲ *Closed Sun. No lunch Sat.*

West End & Points West

Eclectic

★ ££–£££ ✕ **Bouzy Rouge.** The dining room of this fashionable restaurant is cheery and simple—wooden tables, bright tiles, and modern art—and the food is exceptional. The imaginative combinations can sound pretentious, but they are actually a treat. For a strangely satisfying meal try the saddle of Perthshire venison with blueberry-and-cinnamon coulis followed by butterscotch-stuffed pear poached in red wine and served with citrus sorbet. ✉ *1 Alva St., West End* ☎ *0131/225–9594* 💳 *AE, DC, MC, V.*

Italian

££–££££ ✕ **Bar Roma.** Bar Roma serves up a genuine Italian experience. The food tastes great, the place is noisy and fun, the chatty waiters are full of energy, and the hosts are always willing to squeeze you in, no matter how crowded the place may be. If you want to dine in peace and quiet, however, avoid early evening when the office crowd warms up for a night on the town. Specialties include bumper calzone and seafood linguine. ✉ *39a Queensferry St., West End* ☎ *0131/226–2977* 💳 *AE, DC, MC, V.*

South Side

African

£ ✕ **Ndebele.** This small, very friendly café—named after the tribe from South Africa and Zimbabwe that has maintained the customs and language of its Zulu ancestors—is ideally placed for a snack before a trip to the Cameo cinema opposite. The tasty *boerewors* (South African sausage), smoked ostrich, and the large selection of interesting sandwiches on a choice of breads can be eaten on the spot or ordered out. Deli products, including *biltong* (strips of cured, air-dried meat), are also for sale. African art hangs on the wood-panel, geometric-pattern walls in bright shades of purple and orange. There is a separate dining room for nonsmokers. ✉ *57 Home St., Tollcross* ☎ *0131/221–1141* ▭ *AE, MC, V.*

Eclectic

££££ ✕ **The Apartment.** A wacky, whirlwind affair, the Apartment is a popular restaurant with a varied, innovative menu that materializes into huge portions. Choose from one of four menu categories: CHL (Chunky Healthy Lines), Fish Things, Other Things, and The Slab. Dishes include fabulous mussels in a creamy sauce, North African spicy marinated lamb patties, *merguez* (spicy sausage) and grilled basil-wrapped goat cheese, and huge salads like *tiede* piquant (spicy olives, potatoes, roasted peppers, and chorizo, topped with a poached egg). ✉ *7–13 Barclay Pl., near King's Theatre, Tollcross* ☎ *0131/228–6456* ▭ *MC, V.*

Indian

£–££ Fodor'sChoice ★ ✕ **Kalpna.** The unremarkable facade of this vegetarian Indian restaurant, amid an ordinary row of shops, and the low-key interior, enlivened by Indian prints and fabric pictures, belie the food—unlike anything you are likely to encounter elsewhere in the city. *Dam aloo Kashmiri* is a medium-spicy potato dish with a sauce made from honey, pistachios, and almonds. *Bangan mirch masala* is spicier, with eggplant and red chili peppers. For the unsure palate, a lunchtime buffet allows you to pick and mix for only £5 and to do it again on Wednesday evening for £9.95. ✉ *2–3 St. Patricks Sq., South Side* ☎ *0131/667–9890* ▭ *MC, V* ⊙ *No lunch Sun.*

Leith

French

★ ££££ ✕ **Martin Wishart.** Slightly out of town but worth every penny of the taxi fare, this rising culinary star woos diners with an impeccable and varied menu of French-influenced and beautifully presented dishes. Terrine of foie gras, compote of Agen prunes, and sole Murat (glazed fillet of sole with baby onions, artichoke, parsley, and lemon) with *pommes en cocotte* (potatoes cooked in a casserole) typify the cuisine served here. Reservations are essential on weekends. ✉ *54 The Shore, Leith* ☎ *0131/553–3557* ▭ *AE, MC, V* ⊙ *Closed Sun.–Mon. No lunch Sat.*

££–£££ ✕ **Malmaison Café Bar and Brasserie.** Freshly made soups, crunchy salads, inventive sandwiches (try the roasted red pepper and pesto), and gooey pastries are the choices in the café at the stylish Malmaison Hotel, in Edinburgh's rejuvenated dockside area. If you fancy something more substantial (and more expensive), try the Brasserie, which serves traditional French and modern British cuisine. The fish cakes with chips, buttered spinach, and parsley sauce are especially popular. ✉ *1 Tower Pl., Leith* ☎ *0131/468–5000* ✍ *Reservations essential* ▭ *AE, DC, MC, V.*

Pan-Asian

££ ✕ **Britannia Spice.** A few hundred yards from the former Royal Yacht from which it gets its name, this restaurant is a good place to recover from the Ocean Terminal shopping experience. Britannia Spice serves dishes from India, Bangladesh, Thailand, and Nepal. Try the Thai beef or the Nepalese trout with vegetables and green chilies. The waitstaff is friendly and attentive. ✉ *150 Commercial St., Leith* ☎ *0131/555–2255* ▭ *AE, DC, MC, V.*

Seafood

££–££££ ✕ **Fishers Leith.** Locals and visitors alike flock to this laid-back pub-cum-bistro down on the waterfront, and to its sister restaurant, **Fishers in the City**, in the New Town. Both have the same menu, but Fishers Leith opened first and is still the one with the better reputation and vibe. Bar meals are served, but for more comfort and elegance sit in the cozy blue-walled dining room. Seafood is the specialty—the Loch Fyne oysters are wonderful. Watch the blackboard for the daily specials, perhaps a seafood or vegetarian soup followed by North African gamba prawns as big as your hand. It's a good idea to reserve ahead for the bistro. ✉ *1 The Shore, Leith* ☎ *0131/554–5666.* ✉ *58 Thistle St., New Town* ☎ *0131/225–5109* ▭ *AE, DC, MC, V.*

££–££££ ✕ **Skippers Bistro.** This superb seafood restaurant has a traditional, snug, cluttered interior, with dark wood, shining brass, and lots of pictures and seafaring ephemera. For a starter, try the creamy fish soup. Main dishes change daily but might include halibut, salmon, monkfish, or sea bass in delicious sauces. Reservations are essential on weekends. ✉ *1A Dock Pl., Leith* ☎ *0131/554–1018* ▭ *AE, MC, V.*

WHERE TO STAY

It used to be that Scottish hotels were considered either rather better or much worse than their English counterparts; the good ones were very good, and the bad ones horrid. Today these distinctions no longer exist, and Scotland's capital has a large selection of delightful hotel accommodations. The inexpensive Scottish hotel, once reviled, is now at least the equal of anything that might be found in England.

Rooms are harder to find in August and September, when the Edinburgh International Festival and the Fringe Festival take place, so reserve at least three months in advance. Bed-and-breakfast accommodations may be harder to find in December, January, and February, when some proprietors close for a few weeks. Scots are trusting people—many B&Bs proprietors provide front-door keys and few impose curfews.

Prices

Weekend rates in the larger hotels are always much cheaper than mid-week rates, so if you want to stay in a plush hotel, come on the weekend. To save money and see how local residents live, stay in a B&B in one of the areas away from the city center, such as Pilrig to the north, Murrayfield to the west, or Sciennes to the south. Public buses can whisk you to the city center in 10–15 minutes.

WHAT IT COSTS In pounds

	£££££	££££	£££	££	£
FOR 2 PEOPLE	over £175	£135–£175	£95–£135	£55–£95	under £55

Price categories are assigned based on the range between the least and most expensive standard double rooms in high season. The final bill usually includes a 17.5% VAT (value-added tax).

Old Town

££££ Fodor's Choice ★ **The Scotsman.** This magnificent turn-of-the-20th-century, gray-sandstone building, with a marble staircase and a fascinating history—it was once the headquarters of the *Scotsman* newspaper—now houses a modern, luxurious hotel. Dark wood, earthy colors, tweeds, and contemporary furnishings decorate the rooms and public spaces. North Bridge, the casual-chic brasserie, serves shellfish and grill food, while formal Vermilion concocts beautiful presentations of Scottish-French dishes. ✉ *20 N. Bridge, Old Town, EH1 1YT ☎ 0131/556–5565 📠 0131/652–3652 🌐 www.thescotsmanhotel.co.uk ↪ 56 rooms, 12 suites ♁ 2 restaurants, in-room data ports, cable TV, indoor pool, health club, spa, bar, Internet, business services, meeting rooms ▭ AE, DC, MC, V 🍽 BP.*

££££–£££££ **Crowne Plaza.** Although it was built in the late 1980s, this city center hotel was designed to blend into its surroundings among the 16th-, 17th-, and 18th-century buildings on the Royal Mile. Rooms are spacious and contemporary—practical rather than luxurious. The hotel restaurant serves cuisine that relies on local produce. ✉ *80 High St., Royal Mile, Old Town, EH1 1TH ☎ 0131/557–9797 📠 0131/557–9789 🌐 www.crowneplazaed.co.uk ↪ 228 rooms, 10 suites ♁ Restaurant, in-room data ports, minibars, cable TV, indoor pool, health club, bar, lobby lounge, meeting rooms, parking (fee); no-smoking floors ▭ AE, DC, MC, V 🍽 BP.*

New Town

£££££ Fodor'sChoice ★ **Balmoral Hotel.** The attention to detail in the elegant, green-tinged rooms and the sheer élan of a re-created Edwardian heyday contribute to the popularity of this grand former railroad hotel. Staying here, below the impressive clock tower marking the east end of Princes Street, gives you a strong sense of being at the center of Edinburgh life. The hotel's main restaurant is the plush and stylish Number One, serving excellent Scottish seafood and game. ✉ *1 Princes St., on the border between the New Town and the Old Town, EH2 2EQ ☎ 0131/556–2414 📠 0131/557–3747 🌐 www.roccofortehotels.com ↪ 188 rooms, 2 suites ♁ 2 restaurants, in-room data ports, indoor pool, health club, bar, meeting rooms, parking (fee) ▭ AE, DC, MC, V.*

★ **£££££** **The Howard.** The Howard, close to Drummond Place, is a classic New Town building, elegant and superbly proportioned. Antique furniture and original art throughout the hotel give it a swank, private-club feel, and you can expect the most up-to-date facilities, including Web-equipped TVs. Some of the best rooms overlook the garden. ✉ *34 Great King St., New Town, EH3 6QH ☎ 0131/557–3500 📠 0131/557–6515 🌐 www.thehoward.com ↪ 18 rooms ♁ Restaurant, room service, in-room data ports, cable TV, laundry services, dry cleaning, meeting rooms, free parking; no a/c. ▭ AE, DC, MC, V 🍽 BP.*

★ **£££–£££££** **Caledonian Hilton Hotel.** "The Caley," a conspicuous block of red sandstone beyond the west end of West Princes Street Gardens, was built between 1898 and 1902 as the flagship hotel of the Caledonian Railway, and its imposing Victorian decor has been faithfully preserved. The public area has marbled green columns and an ornate stairwell with a burnished-metalwork balustrade. Rooms and corridors are exceptionally large and well appointed. ✉ *Princes St., New Town, EH1 2AB ☎ 0131/222–8888 📠 0131/222–8889 🌐 www.hilton.com ↪ 249 rooms ♁ 3 restaurants, cable TV, meeting rooms, parking (fee) ▭ AE, DC, MC, V 🍽 BP.*

£££ **Ardmor House.** This low-key guest house combines the original features of a Victorian home with tasteful contemporary furnishings. Rooms are fresh and modern, with an occasional carefully chosen antique. The friendly owners, Robin and Colin, extend a warm welcome to gay and straight travelers, and they will try to indulge your every whim. They offer a thoroughly efficient concierge service with a twist—lots of personal opinions and recommendations thrown in—and their gay guide (a listing of gay-friendly venues) will help you find bars, cafés, and even saunas. ✉ *74 Pilrig St., Pilrig, EH6 5AS ☎📠 0131/554–4944* *www.ardmorhouse.com* *5 rooms* *Dining room; no a/c* MC, V *BP.*

★ £££ **Kew House and Apartments.** The Kew's rooms and apartments are as sumptuous as a guest house can be without being classified a full-service hotel. Inside the elegant 1860 terrace house are six tastefully modernized rooms with conveniences like hair dryers, coffee makers, and pants presses, plus welcome luxuries including fresh flowers, chocolates, shortbread, and a decanter of sherry on arrival. There is also a bar and a restaurant for guests only. It's a 15-minute stroll to the center of town. *1 Kew Terr., New Town, EH12 5JE* *0131/313–0700* *0131/313–0747* *www.kewhouse.com* *6 rooms, 2 apartments* *Dining room, cable TV, lounge, free parking; no a/c, no smoking* AE, DC, MC, V *BP.*

★ ££–£££ **The Glasshouse.** Glass walls extend incongruously from the 19th-century facade of a former church, foreshadowing the daring, unique interior of Edinburgh's chicest boutique hotel, opened in mid-2003. Rooms are decorated in a minimalist style, with soft browns and beige, wood and marble. The bathrooms were built in Denmark and shipped as intact "pods" to Britain, then fitted into the hotel's architecture. A bedside control panel lets you draw the drapes or close them, and the flat-screen TV swivels to face the bed or the sitting area. Floor-to-ceiling windows face either the New Town or the rooftop garden in back. The hotel's halls and rooms serve as gallery space for a collection of 200 female nude photographs, some rather explicit, by Scottish photographers Trevor and Faye Yerbury. *2 Greenside Pl., New Town EH1 3AA* *0131/525–8200* *0131/525–8205* *www.theetoncollection.com* *65 rooms* *Dining room, room service, a/c, in-room safes, in-room data ports, minibars, cable TV, business services, meeting rooms* AE, MC, V.

★ ££–£££ **17 Abercromby Place.** Shuttered windows, antique furniture, and rugs (some used as wall hangings) characterize this Georgian terraced house, which has stunning views from the top-floor rooms. This B&B sets a high standard, with a host who enjoys meeting guests and can be a very helpful guide. Dinner can be provided by prior arrangement. *17 Abercromby Pl., New Town, EH3 6LB* *0131/557–8036* *0131/558–3453* *www.abercrombyhouse.com* *9 rooms* *Dining room, in-room data ports, refrigerators, cable TV, free parking; no a/c* MC, V *BP.*

££–£££ **Stuart House.** A Victorian terraced house with some fine plasterwork houses this B&B, just a 15-minute walk from the city center. Bold colors, floral fabrics, and billowing curtains combine with antique and traditional-style furniture to create an opulent interior. *12 E. Claremont St., Canonmills, EH7 4JP* *0131/557–9030* *0131/557–0563* *www.stuartguesthouse.co.uk* *7 rooms, 2 apartments* *Some pets allowed; no a/c, no smoking* AE, DC, MC, V *BP.*

££–£££ **Walton Hotel.** This B&B in a Georgian town house is a 10-minute walk from the city center. High-ceiling, elegant rooms are furnished in an unfussy, traditional style, and there is a choice of breakfasts—traditional Scottish, Continental, or American. Four of the rooms are on the ground floor, and six are in the basement (all have windows). *79 Dundas St., New Town, EH3 6SD* *0131/556–1137* *0131/557–8367* *www.waltonhotel.com* *10 rooms* *Free parking; no a/c, no room phones, no smoking* MC V *BP.*

£–££ **The Conifers.** This trim B&B in a red-sandstone town house north of the New Town offers simple, traditionally decorated rooms. Framed prints of old Edinburgh adorn the walls. The owner, Liz Fulton, has a wealth of knowledge about what to see and do in Edinburgh. *56 Pilrig St., Pilrig EH6 5AS* *0131/554–5162* *www.conifersguesthouse.com*

4 rooms (3 with bath) No a/c, no smoking. No credit cards BP.

Haymarket

★ **££££–£££££** **Hilton Edinburgh Grosvenor Hotel.** Several converted terrace houses make up this attractive, comfortable hotel, distinguished by an elegant Victorian facade. From the moment you enter the large reception area, furnished with ample Chesterfield armchairs, you'll be pampered. The rooms are small but well decorated with bright peach curtains, floral bedspreads, and dark-wood furniture. First- and second-floor bedrooms have high ceilings with attractive plaster cornices. The hotel is a short walk from the West End's shopping district. *Grosvenor St., Haymarket, EH12 5EF 0131/226–6001 0131/220–2387 www.hilton.com 189 rooms Restaurant, cable TV, bar, business services, meeting room; no a/c. AE, DC, MC, V BP.*

£££ **Lodge Hotel.** Spacious rooms at this detached Georgian stone house are furnished in period style, with canopy beds and swag curtains. A decanter of sherry awaits in your room. Downstairs, you can relax at the cocktail bar and in the peaceful gold-and-blue sitting room. The dining room has well-spaced tables covered with crisp white cloths and a menu heavy on fresh Scottish produce. The hotel, a 15-minute walk from Princes Street, is easy to find on the main A8 Edinburgh–Glasgow road. *6 Hampton Terr., West Coates, Haymarket, EH12 5JD 0131/337–3682 0131/313–1700 www.thelodgehotel.co.uk 11 rooms Dining room; no a/c, no smoking MC, V BP.*

West End & Points West

£££££ **Sheraton Grand.** Beyond the reception area and sweeping grand staircase, you'll find guest rooms well above average size. Many are traditionally decorated, with tartan furnishings and prints of old Edinburgh. The grandest rooms face Edinburgh Castle. Three fine restaurants include the brasserie-style Terrace, overlooking the castle and Festival Square; the intimate Grill Room, serving fine fish, game, and Scottish beef; and the Santini, serving Italian cuisine. The hotel bar is popular with locals, especially after work and in the evening before and after concerts at the Usher Hall. *1 Festival Sq., Lothian Rd., West End, EH3 9SR 0131/229–9131 0131/228–4510 www.sheraton.com 260 rooms 3 restaurants, cable TV, indoor pool, gym, spa, bar, meeting rooms, parking (fee) AE, DC, MC, V BP.*

££££–£££££ **The Bonham.** This contemporary hotel boldly mixes a sleek design and state-of-the-art facilities into its traditional town house space. Beyond unassuming white hallways, each room is decorated in a unique minimalist style, with modern pieces from local artists, geometric furnishings, and attractive lighting. The chic, unadorned restaurant has oversize mirrors and a central catwalk of light, and serves fresh Scottish cuisine with French influences. The service at the hotel is thorough, yet unobtrusive. *35 Drumsheugh Gardens, West End, EH3 7RN 0131/226–6050, 0131/623–6060 reservations 0131/226–6080 www.thebonham.com 48 rooms Restaurant, in-room data ports, cable TV, business services, meeting rooms AE, DC, MC, V BP.*

★ **££££–£££££** **Channings.** Five Edwardian terraced town houses make up this intimate, elegant hotel in an upscale West End neighborhood just minutes from Princes Street. Beyond the clubby, oak-paneled lobby lounge are the quiet guest rooms, with restrained colors, antiques, and marble baths. North-facing rooms have great views of Fife. The Brasserie offers excellent value in traditional Scottish and Continental cooking, while the Ochrevita offers Mediterranean-inspired cuisine. *12–16 S.*

Learmonth Gardens, West End, EH4 IEZ ☎ 0131/315–2226 or 0131/332–3232 📠 0131/332–9631 🌐 www.channings.co.uk 46 rooms 2 restaurants, lobby lounge, meeting rooms ▭ AE, DC, MC, V BP.

££ **16 Lynedoch Place.** You'll find considerate hosts in Andrew and Susie Hamilton (and Gertrude, the lovable dog), who have opened up their beautiful Georgian terraced house as a B&B, a five-minute walk from the center of town. Rosy pinks, cool yellows, terra-cotta oranges, and floral patterns decorate the tasteful rooms. Susie goes all out for breakfast, which is served in a magnificent hunter-green dining room filled with antiques and family pictures. In a pinch, they will connect two of the guest rooms upstairs for a family. ✉ *16 Lynedoch Pl., West End, EH3 7PY ☎ 0131/225–5507 📠 0131/226–4185 🌐 www.16lynedochplace.co.uk 3 rooms Dining room, in-room data ports, some in-room hot tubs, cable TV, library, free parking; no a/c, no room phones, no smoking ▭ MC, V BP.*

££ **22 Murrayfield Gardens.** A handsome stone house in an upscale residential area, this is an impressive B&B on all counts, with particularly friendly owners. Warm yellows decorate the elegant first-floor lounge, the sunny dining room, and the bedrooms. With prior notice, dinner will be provided. There's easy parking in this neighborhood, and it's only a 10-minute bus ride from downtown. ✉ *22 Murrayfield Gardens, Murrayfield, EH12 6DF ☎ 0131/337–3569 📠 0131/337–3803 🌐 www.number22.co.uk 3 rooms (2 with bath) Dining room, free parking; no a/c, no room TVs ▭ MC, V Closed 2 wks in Feb. BP.*

Fodor's Choice ★

££ **Western Guesthouse.** This simple guest house, detached from the main house and with a separate entrance, has a cowboys-and-Indians theme to match its name. It sits right on a bus route to the city center, and is a short stroll away from Edinburgh Zoo. The rooms are decorated with oak furnishings and soft shades of ochre. ✉ *92 Corstorphine Rd., Corstorphine, EH12 6JG ☎📠 0131/538–7490 🌐 www.westernguesthouse.co.uk 6 rooms Cable TV, free parking; no a/c, no smoking ▭ MC, V BP.*

South Side

££ **Ashdene House.** On a quiet residential street, only 10 minutes from the city center by bus, sits this Edwardian house, a first-class B&B. Country-style reproduction pine furniture and vividly colored fabrics decorate the guest rooms and common areas. The owners are particularly helpful in arranging tours and evening theater entertainment, and they will recommend local restaurants. There's ample parking on the street. ✉ *23 Fountainhall Rd., Sciennes, EH9 2LN ☎ 0131/667–6026 🌐 www.ashdenehouse.com 5 rooms No a/c, no smoking ▭ MC, V BP.*

££ **Ellesmere Guest House.** Rooms in this Victorian terraced house have antique reproduction and modern furniture with floral bedspreads and curtains; one room has a four-poster bed. You can relax in leather wingbacks in the comfortable sitting room or take a 20 minute stroll to the Old Town. Ellesmere sits close to the King's Theatre and several good restaurants. ✉ *11 Glengyle Terr., Tollcross, EH3 9LN ☎ 0131/229–4823 📠 0131/229–5285 🌐 www.edinburghbandb.co.uk 6 rooms No a/c ▭ No credit cards BP.*

££ **Teviotdale House.** The lavish Victorian interiors of this 1848 town house include canopy beds and miles of colorful, patterned fabrics. As you enter, you will be greeted by the friendly Thiebauds, your hosts. The house is a warm retreat on a tree-lined street away from but within reach of city-center bustle via a 10-minute bus ride. The hearty egg-and-sausage breakfasts are a pleasure. Note that six of the rooms have showers, but no bathtubs. ✉ *53 Grange Loan, Sciennes, EH9 2ER ☎ 0131/667–4376*

☎ *0131/667–4763* ☞ *7 rooms* ⚐ *Dining room; no a/c, no smoking* 🖃 *AE, MC, V* ❙◎❙ *BP.*

££ 🏨 **Thrums Private Hotel.** Inside this detached Georgian house are small, cozy rooms decorated with antique reproductions. Breakfast is served in a large, glass-enclosed conservatory. The family that runs the hotel is very welcoming and more than willing to advise you on what to see and do in and around Edinburgh. ✉ *14–15 Minto St., Newington, EH9 1RQ* ☎*0131/667–5545* 🖷*0131/667–8707* ☞*15 rooms* ⚐*Restaurant, bar, free parking, some pets allowed; no a/c* 🖃 *MC, V* ❙◎❙ *BP.*

£–££ 🏨 **Turret Guest House.** Modern furnishings in rooms with Victorian cornices, paneled doors, and high ceilings make this B&B, in a baronial town house, a nice combination of old-fashioned charm and contemporary comfort. One of the rooms has a four-poster bed. The inn is on a quiet residential street on the South Side, close to bus routes, the Commonwealth Pool, and Holyrood Park. In the morning, choose between several breakfast options, including omelets, sausage, haggis, waffles, and French toast. ✉ *8 Kilmaurs Terr., Prestonfield, EH16 5DR* ☎*0131/ 667–6704* 🖷 *0131/668–1368* ⊕ *www.turretguesthouse.co.uk* ☞ *8 rooms, 5 with bath* ⚐ *Dining room; no a/c, no smoking* 🖃 *MC, V* ❙◎❙ *BP.*

Leith

£££–££££ 🏨 **Malmaison.** Once a seamen's hostel, the Malmaison, in the heart of Leith, now has stylish digs only 10 minutes by bus from the city center. A dramatic black, cream, and taupe color scheme prevails in the public areas. King-size beds, CD players, and satellite TV are standard in all bedrooms, which are decorated in a bold, modern style. The French theme of the hotel, sister to the Malmaison in Glasgow, is emphasized in the Café Bar and Brasserie, which serves food all day. ✉ *1 Tower Pl., Leith, EH6 7DB* ☎ *0131/468–5000* 🖷 *0131/468–5002* ⊕ *www. malmaison.com* ☞ *60 rooms* ⚐ *Restaurant, café, cable TV, bar, free parking* 🖃 *AE, DC, MC, V* ❙◎❙ *BP.*

NIGHTLIFE & THE ARTS

The Arts

To those who think Edinburgh's arts scene consists of just the elegiac wail of a bagpipe and the twang of a fiddle or two, hundreds of performing arts options will prove them wrong. The jewel in the crown, of course, is the famed Edinburgh International Festival, which now attracts the best in music, dance, theater, painting, and sculpture from all over the globe during three weeks from mid-August to early September. The *Scotsman* and *Herald,* Scotland's leading daily newspapers, carry listings and reviews in their arts pages every day, with special editions during the festival. Tickets are generally available from box offices in advance; in some cases they are also available from certain designated travel agents or at the door, although concerts by national orchestras often sell out long before the day of the performance. The *List* and the *Day by Day Guide,* available at the **Edinburgh and Scotland Information Centre** (✉ 3 Princes St., East End ☎ 0131/473–3800 ⊕ www.edinburgh. org), carry the most up-to-date details about cultural events. The *List* is also available at newsstands throughout the city.

Dance

The Scottish Ballet performs at the **Festival Theatre** (✉ 13–29 Nicolson St., Old Town ☎ 0131/529–6000) when in Edinburgh. Visiting contemporary dance companies perform in the **Royal Lyceum** (✉ Grindlay St., West End ☎ 0131/248–4848).

EDINBURGH ARTS FESTIVALS

W**ALKING AROUND EDINBURGH IN LATE JULY,** *you'll likely feel the first vibrations of the earthquake that is festival time, which shakes the city throughout August and into September. You may hear reference to an "Edinburgh Festival," but this is really an umbrella term for six separate festivals all taking place around the same time.*

The best-known and oldest of these is the Edinburgh International Festival. The festival was founded in 1947, when Europe was recovering from World War II. Festival founders, including Austrian Rudolph Bing, who founded the Glyndebourne Festival in England and managed the Metropolitan Opera in New York City, believed that some event was needed to draw the continent together and, as Bing put it, "provide a platform for the flowering of the human spirit." As the story goes, Bing was walking along Princes Street with a friend, a soprano, and both remarked that Edinburgh was very much like Salzburg, having a castle on a hill, and would be a perfect setting for an international arts festival such as the one in Salzburg. Bing rounded up support from the British Council (an organization that promotes British culture abroad) and a program was written. The first festival, presenting the Vienna Philharmonic Orchestra conducted by Bruno Walter, was a gigantic success.

In recent years the festival has drawn as many as 400,000 people to Edinburgh, with more than 80 acts by world renowned music, opera, theater, and dance performers, filling all the major venues in the city. Tickets for the festival go on sale in April, and many sell out within the month. However, you may still be able to purchase tickets, which range from £6 to £60, during the course of the festival. You can see the program and buy tickets online at www.eif.co.uk or at Hub Tickets (Castlehill, EH1 2NE, ☎ 0131/ 443–2000).

If the Edinburgh International Festival is the grand old mother of British festivals, then the Edinburgh Festival Fringe is its unruly child. The Festival Fringe started in 1947 at the same time as the International Festival, when eight companies who were not invited to perform in the latter decided to attend anyway. Knowing there would be an audience, these companies found small, local theaters to host them. Since then, the Festival Fringe has grown at at least the same rate as its counterpart. In 2002, more than 600 companies took part in the Fringe, making it the largest festival of its kind in the world. Its events range from the brilliant to the impossibly mundane, badly-performed, and downright tacky. No one censors the material, so anything goes. It was at the Fringe in 1971 that Robin Williams was discovered when he performed in The Taming of the Shrew. *Billy Connolly, Emma Thompson, and Dudley Moore also put in appearances early in their careers.*

While the Fringe is going on, most of the city center becomes one huge performance area, with fire eaters, sword swallowers, unicyclists, jugglers, string quartets, jazz groups, stand-up comics, and magicians all thronging into High Street and Princes Street. Every available theater and pseudo-performance space is utilized—church halls, community centers, parks, sports fields, putting greens, and night clubs. In 1954, the Edinburgh Festival Fringe Society was formed, and it oversees everything from ticket sales to publicity. Purchase tickets online at www. edfringe.com or by phoning ☎ 0131/ 226–0026.

Edinburgh festival time can fill almost any artistic need. Besides the International Festival and Festival Fringe, look for the Edinburgh International Film Festival; the International Jazz & Blues Festival, the International Book Festival, and the Military Tattoo, which includes re-enactments of historic events, military marching bands, Highland dancing, and more. Edinburgh in August is an experience you are unlikely to forget!

Festivals

The **Edinburgh International Festival** (✉ The Hub, Edinburgh Festival Centre, Castlehill, Old Town, EH1 2NE ☎ information, 0131/473–2020; tickets, 0131/473–2000 📠 0131/473–2003 🌐 www.eif.co.uk), the premier arts event of the year has, since 1947, attracted performing artists of international caliber to a celebration of music, dance, drama, and artwork. The festival runs from mid-August through early September.

The **Edinburgh Festival Fringe** (✉ Edinburgh Festival Fringe Office, 180 High St., Old Town, EH1 1QS ☎ 0131/226–0026 📠 0131/226–0016 🌐 www.edfringe.com) presents many theatrical and musical events, some by amateur groups (you have been warned), and is more of a grab bag than the official festival. During festival time—roughly the same as the International Festival—it's possible to arrange your own entertainment program from morning to midnight and beyond, if you don't feel overwhelmed by the variety available.

The **Edinburgh International Film Festival** (✉ Edinburgh Film Festival Office, at the Filmhouse, 88 Lothian Rd., West End, EH3 9BZ ☎ 0131/228–4051 📠 0131/229–5501 🌐 www.edfilmfest.org.uk) is yet another aspect of the busy summer festival logjam in Edinburgh.

The **Edinburgh Military Tattoo** (✉ Edinburgh Military Tattoo Office, 32 Market St., Old Town, EH1 1QB ☎ 0131/225–1188 or 08707/555–1188 📠 0131/225–8627 🌐 www.edintattoo.co.uk) may not be art, but it is certainly Scottish culture. It's sometimes confused with the festival itself, partly because both events take place in August (though the Tattoo starts and finishes a week earlier). This celebration of martial music and skills with bands, gymnastics, and stunt motorcycle teams is set on the castle esplanade, and the dramatic backdrop augments the spectacle. Dress warmly for late-evening performances. Even if it rains, the show most definitely goes on.

Jazz enthusiasts delight in the August **International Jazz Festival** (✉ 29 St. Stephen St., Stockbridge, EH3 5AN ☎ 0131/467–5200), which attracts international top performers and brings local enthusiasts out of their living rooms and into the pubs and clubs to listen and play.

The **Edinburgh International Science Festival** (information: ✉ Roxburgh's Court, off 323 High St., Edinburgh EH1 1PW ☎ 0131/220–1882 🌐 www.sciencefestival.co.uk; tickets: ✉ The Hub, Castlehill, Edinburgh EH1 2NE), held around Easter each year, aims to make science accessible, interesting, but above all fun. Children's events turn science into entertainment and are especially popular.

Film

Apart from cinema chains, Edinburgh has the excellent three-screen **Filmhouse** (✉ 88 Lothian Rd., West End ☎ 0131/228–2688 box office), the best venue for modern, foreign-language, offbeat, or simply less-commercial films.

Music

The **Festival Theatre** (✉ 13–29 Nicolson St., Old Town ☎ 0131/529–6000) hosts performances by the Scottish Ballet and the Scottish Opera. The **Playhouse** (✉ Greenside Pl., East End ☎ 0870/606–3424) leans toward popular artists and musicals. The intimate **Queen's Hall** (✉ Clerk St., Old Town ☎ 0131/668–2019) hosts small recitals. **Usher Hall** (✉ Lothian Rd., West End ☎ 0131/228–1155) is Edinburgh's grandest venue, and international performers and orchestras, including the Royal Scottish National Orchestra, perform here.

Theater

MODERN The **Netherbow Arts Centre** (✉ 43 High St., Old Town ☎ 0131/556–9579) includes modern plays in its program of music, drama, and cabaret. The **Theatre Workshop** (✉ 34 Hamilton Pl., Stockbridge ☎ 0131/226–5425) hosts fringe events during the Edinburgh Festival and modern, community-based theater year-round. It is wheelchair accessible. The **Traverse Theatre** (✉ 10 Cambridge St., West End ☎ 0131/228–1404) has developed a solid reputation for new, stimulating Scottish plays, performed in a specially designed flexible space.

TRADITIONAL Edinburgh has three main theaters. The **Festival Theatre** (✉ 13–29 Nicolson St., Old Town ☎ 0131/529–6000) presents opera and ballet, along with the occasional excellent tour. The **King's** (✉ 2 Leven St., Tollcross ☎ 0131/529–6000) has a program of contemporary and traditional dramatic works. The **Royal Lyceum** (✉ Grindlay St., West End ☎ 0131/248–4848) shows traditional plays and contemporary works, often transferred from or prior to their London West End showings.

On the eastern outskirts of Edinburgh, the **Brunton Theatre** (✉ Ladywell Way, Musselburgh ☎ 0131/665–2240) presents a regular program of repertory, touring, and amateur performances. The **Church Hill Theatre** (✉ Morningside Rd., Morningside ☎ 0131/447–7597) hosts productions by local dramatic societies mount productions of a high standard. The **Playhouse** (✉ Greenside Pl., East End ☎ 0870/606–3424) hosts mostly popular artists and musicals.

Nightlife

The **Edinburgh and Scotland Information Centre** (✉ 3 Princes St., East End ☎ 0845/225512 🌐 www.edinburgh.org), above Maverley Market, can supply information on various types of nightlife, especially on spots hosting dinner dances. The *List,* available from newsstands throughout the city, provides information on the music scene.

Bars & Pubs

Edinburgh's 400-odd pubs are a study in themselves. In the eastern and northern districts of the city you'll find some grim, inhospitable-looking places that proclaim that drinking is no laughing matter. But throughout Edinburgh many pubs have deliberately traded in their old spit-and-sawdust images for atmospheric revivals of the warm, oak-paneled, leather-chaired *howffs* of a more leisurely age. Most pubs and bars are open weekdays and Saturday from 11 AM to midnight, and from 12:30 to midnight on Sunday.

OLD TOWN Stop in at **Deacon Brodie's Pub** (✉ 435 Lawnmarket, Old Town ☎ 0131/225–6531), named for the infamous criminal who may have inspired Robert Louis Stevenson's *Strange Case of Dr. Jekyll and Mr. Hyde,* for a traditional pub meal or a pint.

NEW TOWN **Abbotsford** (✉ 3 Rose St., New Town ☎ 0131/225–5276) has an ever-changing selection of five real ales, bar lunches, and lots of Victorian atmosphere. **Cask and Barrel** (✉ 115 Broughton St., New Town, ☎ 0131/556–3132) is a spacious, busy pub in which to sample hand-pulled ales at the horseshoe bar, reflected in a collection of brewery mirrors. **Cumberland Bar** (✉ 1–3 Cumberland St., New Town ☎ 0131/558–3134) has 11 ales on tap, wood trim, typical pub mirrors, and a comfy sitting room. **80 Queen Street** (✉ New Town, ☎ 0131/538–8111), with cozy dark-wood booths, is just the place for lunch with a pint of draft beer. There is live jazz and soul on Friday and Saturday evenings.

Guildford Arms (✉ 1 W. Register St., east end of Princes St., New Town ☎ 0131/556–4312) is worth a visit for its interior alone: ornate plasterwork, cornices, friezes, and wood paneling form the backdrop for some excellent draft ales, including Orkney Dark Island. **Harry's Bar** (✉ 7B Randolph Pl., New Town ☎ 0131/539–8100), an Americana-decorated basement bar with disco music, is hugely popular with locals. **Kay's Bar** (✉ 39 Jamaica St., New Town ☎ 0131/225–1858), a friendly, comfortable New Town spot, is a good place for a bar lunch. Don't miss the selection of 50 single-malt whiskies in addition to the real ales on draft. **Milne's Bar** (✉ 35 Hanover St., New Town ☎ 0131/225–6738) is known as the poets' pub because of its popularity with the Edinburgh literati. Pies and baked potatoes go well with seven real ales and varying guest beers (beers not of the house brewery). Victorian advertisements and photos of old Edinburgh give the place an old-time feel.

Standing Order (✉ 62– 66 George St., New Town ☎ 0131/225–4460), in a former banking hall with a magnificent painted-plasterwork ceiling, is one of the popular and expanding J. D. Wetherspoon chain of pubs, priding itself on friendly, music-free watering holes with cheap beer and ample nonsmoking areas—you can even lounge on leather sofas. Children are welcome. **Tiles** (✉ 1 St. Andrew Sq., New Town, ☎ 0131/558–1507), in a converted banking hall, gets its name from the wealth of tiles covering the walls, which are topped by elaborate plasterwork. The large selection of real ales complements a choice of bar meals or a table d'hôte menu specializing in fresh Scottish poultry, game, and fish. Sip a martini or cosmopolitan at **Tonic** (✉ 34A Castle St., New Town ☎ 0131/225–6431), one of Edinburgh's reliable cocktail bars. This is a stylish basement bar with bouncy stools and comfy sofas, pale wood, and chrome.

SOUTH SIDE **Cloisters** (✉ 26 Brougham St., Tollcross ☎ 0131/221–9997) prides itself on the absence of music, gaming machines, and any other modern pub gimmicks; it specializes instead in real ales, malt whiskies, and good food, all at reasonable prices. **Leslie's Bar** (✉ 45 Ratcliffe Terr., South Side ☎ 0131/667–7205) is a an unspoiled Victorian bar near the hotels and guest houses of Newington, with a good range of traditional Scottish ales and whiskies. **Southsider** (✉ 3–7 W. Richmond St., South Side ☎ 0131/667–2003), near the antiques and junk shops of Causewayside, is a busy, sometimes smoky bar popular with locals and students.

LEITH The 260-year-old **Malt and Hops** (✉ 45 The Shore, Leith ☎ 0131/555–0083), with its own ghost and ales, overlooks the waterfront.

Ceilidhs & Scottish Evenings

For those who feel a trip to Scotland is not complete without hearing the "Braes of Yarrow" or "Auld Robin Gray," several hotels present traditional Scottish-music evenings in the summer season. Head for the **Edinburgh Thistle Hotel** (✉ Leith St., New Town ☎ 0131/556–0111) to see *Jamie's Scottish Evening,* an extravaganza of Scottish song, tartan, plaid, and bagpipes that takes place nightly. The cost is £43.50, including a four-course dinner. You can also try the **Caledonian Brewery** (✉ 42 Slateford Rd., Dalry ☎ 0131/623–8066) for foot-stomping fun. The brewery organizes about three *ceilidhs* per month, with loads of space and plenty of beer.

Folk Clubs

You can usually find folk musicians performing in various pubs throughout Edinburgh, although of late there's been a decline in the live music scene because of dwindling profits and the predominance of popular theme bars.

The **Ensign Ewart** (✉ 521 Lawnmarket, Old Town ☎ 0131/226–1928), by the castle, is a cozy, intimate pub with live folk music most nights. The **Tron** (✉ Hunter Sq., Old Town ☎ 0131/220–1591) is well known for its performances of folk music. For a bit of *wellie* (volume, energy) put your head round the door of **Whistle Binkies Pub** (✉ South Bridge, Old Town ☎ 0131/557–5114), a friendly basement bar with great rock and folk music.

Gay & Lesbian Clubs

There is a burgeoning gay and lesbian scene in Edinburgh, and the city has many dedicated clubs, bars, and cafés. However, don't expect the scene to be as extrovert or open as it is in London, New York, or even Glasgow. The *List* has a section that focuses on the gay and lesbian scene.

CC Blooms (✉ 23–24 Greenside Pl., East End ☎ 0131/556–9331), modern, colorful, and open nightly, plays a mix of musical styles. Once a month there is an "icebreaker" evening for those new to the gay scene. **Flashback** (✉ 9 Hope St. New Town ☎ 0131/226–0901) plays pop and disco nightly. The **Honeycomb** (✉ Niddry St., off High St., Old Town ☎ 0131/556–2442), a hot spot with a live DJ, gets a mixed gay and straight crowd; it's open Friday through Sunday. **Blue Moon Café** (✉ 1 Barony St. New Town ☎ 0131/557–0911) is Edinburgh's longest running gay café, and is still the best.

Nightclubs

For the young and footloose, many Edinburgh dance clubs offer reduced admission and/or less expensive drinks for early revelers. Consult the *List* for special events.

L'Attaché Nightclub (✉ Beneath the Rutland Hotel, 3 Rutland St., West End ☎ 0131/229–3402), which is open Friday and Saturday, has DJs spinning mainstream sounds from the 70s to the present day. The well-liked **Club Massa** (✉ 36–39 Market St., Old Town ☎ 0131/226–4224) has theme nights covering the full spectrum of musical sounds; it's open Wednesday through Sunday. The **Opal Lounge** (✉ 51a George St., New Town ☎ 0131/226–2275), a casual but stylish nightspot, evolves by a subtle change of mood and lighting from a restaurant to a club for drinks and dancing to soul or funk. **Po Na Na Souk Bar** (✉ 43B Frederick St., New Town ☎ 0131/226–2224) has a cool but cozy atmosphere, and a distinctly North African feel, with its secluded booths and Bedouin furnishings. The music is a mix of funk, hip hop, R&B, house, and disco. The **Venue** (✉ 15–21 Calton Rd., Old Town ☎ 0131/557–3073) blares all forms of live and DJ-ed music.

SPORTS & THE OUTDOORS

Biking

Rates in summer are about £65 per week for a 21-speed or mountain bike. Daily rates (24 hours) are about £15, with half days costing £10. You can rent bicycles through **Bike Trax** (✉ 11-13 Lochrin Pl., Tollcross ☎ 0131/228–6333). **Recycling** (✉ 276 Leith Walk, Leith ☎ 0131/553–1130) runs a sell-and-buy-back scheme for extended periods (say, more than two weeks), which can save you money, and also has especially good deals on weekly rentals.

Golf

For the courses listed below, *SSS* indicates the "standard scratch score," or average score. VisitScotland (formerly the Scottish Tourist Board) provides a free leaflet on golf in Scotland, available from the **Edinburgh and Scotland Information Centre** (✉ 3 Princes St., East End ☎ 0845/225512 🌐 www.edinburgh.org).

Braids. The 18-hole course here was founded in 1897 and laid out over several small hills 3 mi south of Edinburgh. The nine-hole course opened in early 2003. ✉ *Braids Hill Rd., Braidburn* ☎ *0131/447–6666* ⛳ *Course 1: 18 holes, 5,865 yards, SSS 67. Course 2: 9 holes.*

Bruntsfield Links. Several tournaments are held each year at this championship course, opened in 1898 a couple miles northwest of the city. ✉ *32 Barnton Ave., Davidson's Mains* ☎ *0131/336–4050* 📠 *0131/336–5538* ⛳ *18 holes, 6,407 yards, SSS 71.*

Duddingston. You'll find this public parkland course, founded in 1895, 2 mi east of the city. ✉ *Duddingston Rd. W, Duddingston* ☎ *0131/661–7688* ⛳ *18 holes, 6,420 yards, SSS 72.*

Liberton. This public parkland course was built in 1920, 4 mi south of the city. ✉ *Kingston Grange, 297 Gilmerton Rd., Liberton* ☎ *0131/664–8580* 📠 *0131/666–0853* ⛳ *18 holes, 5,412 yards, SSS 69.*

Lothianburn. You can see good views of the Midlothian countryside from this hillside course, founded in 1893, 6 mi south of the city. ✉ *Biggar Rd., Fairmilehead* ☎ *0131/445–5067* ⛳ *18 holes, 5,662 yards, SSS 68.*

Portobello. Short and sweet, Portobello has welcomed amateur golfers since 1826. ✉ *Stanley St., Portobello, 2 mi east of the city* ☎ *0131/669–4361* ⛳ *9 holes, 2,449 yards, SSS 32.*

Rugby

At Murrayfield Stadium, home of the **Scottish Rugby Union** (☎ 0131/346–5000), Scotland's international rugby matches are played in early spring and fall. During that time of year, crowds of good-humored rugby fans from all over the world add greatly to the sense of excitement in the streets of Edinburgh.

Running

At **Holyrood Park,** at almost any time of day or night, joggers run the circuit around Arthur's Seat.

Skiing

Midlothian Ski Centre at Hillend (✉ Fairmilehead, ☎ 0131/445–4433), on the southern edge of the city, is the longest artificial ski slope in the United Kingdom—go either to ski (equipment can be rented on the spot) or to ride the chairlift, which costs £1.30, for fine city views. It's open year-round Monday through Saturday from 9:30 to 9 and on Sunday from 9:30 to 7.

Soccer

Like Glasgow, Edinburgh is soccer-mad, and there's an intense rivalry between the city's two professional teams. Remember, the game is called football in Britain. The **Heart of Midlothian Football Club ("Hearts")** (☎ 0131/200–7200) plays in maroon and white and is based at Tynecastle. The green-bedecked **Hibernian ("Hibs") Club** (☎ 0131/661–2159) plays its home matches at Easter Road.

Swimming

The **Royal Commonwealth Pool** (✉ Dalkeith Rd., Prestonfield ☎ 0131/667–7211), the largest swimming pool in the city, is part of a complex that includes a fitness center. It costs £2.40–£5.80 to use the pool, and it's open weekdays 6 to 9:30 PM and weekends 10 to 4:30.

SHOPPING

Arcades & Shopping Centers

Like most large towns, Edinburgh has succumbed to the fashion for under-one-roof shopping. **Cameron Toll** (✉ Bottom of Dalkeith Rd., Mayfield), in the city's South Side, caters to local residents, with food stores and High Street brand names. If you don't want to be distracted by wonderful views between shops—or if it's raining—try the upscale **Princes Mall** (✉ East end of Princes St., East End), with a fast-food area, designer-label boutiques, and shops that sell Scottish woolens and tweeds, whisky, and confections. The **Ocean Terminal** (✉ Ocean Dr., Leith) houses a large collection of shops as well as bars and eateries. Here you can also visit the former royal yacht *Britannia.* The **St. James Centre** (✉ Princes St., East End) has Dorothy Perkins, HMV, and numerous other chain stores. **South Gyle** (✉ off A720, near airport, Gyle) is like a typical U.S.-style shopping mall. Here you'll find the usual High Street brand names, including a huge Marks & Spencer.

Department Stores

In contrast to other major cities, Edinburgh has few true department stores. If you plan on a morning or a whole day of wandering from department to department, trying on beautiful clothes, buying crystal or china, or stocking up on Scottish food specialties, with a break for lunch at an in-store restaurant, then Jenners is your best bet.

Aitken and Niven (✉ 77–79 George St., New Town ☎ 0131/225–1461) is an Edinburgh institution: a small department store where the well-heeled come to buy upscale clothing, shoes, and accessories. **British Home Stores** (✉ 64 Princes St., East End ☎ 0131/226–2621), also known as Bhs, carries typical department-store goods: clothes, household gadgets, linens, and foodstuffs. **Frasers** (✉ Princes St., West End ☎ 0131/225–2472) is a part of Britain's largest chain of department stores. In the city center is **Jenners** (✉ 48 Princes St., New Town ☎ 0131/225–2442), which specializes in traditional china and glassware, and Scottish clothing (upscale tweeds and tartans). Its justly famous food hall sells shortbreads and Dundee cakes (a light fruit cake with a distinctive pattern of split almonds arranged in circles on the top), honeys, and marmalades, as well as high-quality groceries. **John Lewis** (✉ 69 St. James Centre, East End ☎ 0131/556–9121), part of a United Kingdom–wide chain, specializes in furniture and household goods, and pledges it is "never knowingly undersold." **Marks & Spencer** (✉ 54 and 91 Princes St., New Town ☎ 0131/225–2301) sells well-priced, stylish everyday clothes and accessories. You can also buy food items and household goods here.

Shopping Districts

Despite its renown as a shopping street, **Princes Street** in the New Town may disappoint some visitors with its dull, anonymous modern architecture, average chain stores, and fast-food outlets. It is, however, one of the best spots to shop for tartans, tweeds, and knitwear, especially if your time is limited. One block north of Princes Street, **Rose Street** has many smaller specialty shops; part of the street is a pedestrian zone, so it's a pleasant place to browse. The shops on **George Street** tend to be fairly upscale. London names, such as Laura Ashley and Waterstones bookstore, are prominent, though some of the older independent stores continue to do good business.

The streets crossing George Street—Hanover, Frederick, and Castle—are also worth exploring. **Dundas Street,** the northern extension of Hanover Street, beyond Queen Street Gardens, has several antiques shops. **Thistle Street,** originally George Street's "back lane," or service area, has several boutiques and more antiques shops. As may be expected, many shops along the **Royal Mile** sell what may be politely or euphemistically described as tourist-ware—whiskies, tartans, and tweeds.

Careful exploration, however, will reveal some worthwhile establishments. Shops here also cater to highly specialized interests and hobbies.

Close to the castle end of the Royal Mile, just off George IV Bridge, is **Victoria Street,** with specialty shops grouped in a small area. Follow the tiny West Bow to **Grassmarket** for more specialty stores. North of Princes Street, on the way to the Royal Botanic Garden, is **Stockbridge,** an oddball shopping area of some charm, particularly on St. Stephen Street. To get here, walk north down Frederick Street and Howe Street, away from Princes Street, then turn left onto North West Circus Place. **Stafford and William streets** form a small, upscale shopping area in a Georgian setting. Walk to the west end of Princes Street and then along its continuation, Shandwick Place, then turn right onto Stafford Street. William Street crosses Stafford halfway down.

Specialty Shops

Antiques

Antiques dealers tend to cluster together, so it may be easiest to concentrate on one area—St. Stephen Street, Bruntsfield Place, Causewayside, or Dundas Street, for example—if you are short on time.

Try the **Courtyard Antiques** (✉ 108A Causewayside, Sciennes ☎ 0131/662–9008) for a mixture of high-quality antiques, toys, and militaria.

Books, Paper, Maps & Games

As a university city and cultural center, Edinburgh is endowed with excellent bookstores.

Waterstone's (✉ 83 George St., New Town ☎ 0131/225–3436 ✉ 13–14 Princes St., East End ☎ 0131/556–3034 ✉ 128 Princes St., West End ☎ 0131/226–2666) is a large chain based in London with a good selection of mainstream and more obscure books, as well as a consistently helpful staff. **Carson Clark Gallery** (✉ 181–183 Canongate, Old Town ☎ 0131/556–4710) specializes in antique maps, sea charts, and prints. Try **George Waterston** (✉ 52 George St., New Town ☎ 0131/225–5690) for stationery and an excellent selection of small gift items.

Clothing Boutiques

Edinburgh is home to several top-quality designers—although, it must be said, probably not as many as are found in Glasgow, Scotland's fashion center—some of whom make a point of using Scottish materials in their creations.

Bill Baber (✉ 66 Grassmarket, Old Town ☎ 0131/225–3249) is one of the most imaginative of the many Scottish knitwear designers, and a long way from the conservative pastel "woolies" sold at some of the large mill shops. If you're shopping for children, try **Baggins** (✉ 12 Deanhaugh St., Stockbridge ☎ 0131/315–2011). The clothing is designed exclusively for this store and created in the workshop in back. Toys are also on sale. The **Extra Inch** (✉ 12 William St., West End ☎ 0131/226–3303) stocks a full selection of clothes in European sizes 16 (U.S. size 14) and up.

Jewelry

Clarksons (✉ 87 West Bow, Old Town ☎ 0131/225–8141), a family firm, handcrafts a unique collection of jewelry, including Celtic styles. The jewelry here is made with silver, gold, platinum, and precious gems, with a particular emphasis on diamonds. The jeweler **Hamilton and Inches** (✉ 87 George St., New Town ☎ 0131/225–4898), established in 1866, is a silver- and goldsmith worth visiting not only for its modern and antique gift possibilities, but also for its late-Georgian interior, designed by David Bryce in 1834—all columns and elaborate plasterwork. **Joseph**

Bonnar (✉ 72 Thistle St., New Town ☎ 0131/226–2811), tucked behind George Street, has Scotland's the largest collection of antique jewelry, including 19th-century agate jewels.

Linens, Textiles & Home Furnishings

And So To Bed (✉ 30 Dundas St., New Town ☎ 0131/652–3700) has a wonderful selection of embroidered and embellished bed linens, cushion covers, and the like. **In House** (✉ 28 Howe St., New Town ☎ 0131/225–2888) sells designer furnishings and collectibles at the forefront of modern design for the home. **Studio One** (✉ 10–16 Stafford St., New Town ☎ 0131/226–5812) has a well-established and comprehensive inventory of gift articles.

Outdoor Sports Gear

If you plan to do a lot of hiking or camping in the Highlands or the Islands, you may want to look over the selection of outdoor clothing, boots, and jackets at **Tiso** (✉ 123– 125 Rose St., New Town ☎ 0131/225–9486 ✉ 41 Commercial St., Leith ☎ 0131/554–0804).

Scottish Specialties

If you want to identify a particular tartan, several shops on Princes Street will be pleased to assist. The **Clan Tartan Centre** (✉ 70–74 Bangor Rd., Leith ☎ 0131/553–55161) has a database containing details of all known tartans, plus information on clan histories. At the **Edinburgh Old Town Weaving Company** (✉ 555 Castlehill, Old Town ☎ 0131/226–1555), you can watch and even talk to the cloth and tapestry weavers as they work, then buy the products. The company can also provide information on clan histories, and, if your name is a relatively common English or Scottish one, tell you which tartan you are entitled to wear. **Geoffrey (Tailor) Highland Crafts** (✉ 57–59 High St., Old Town ☎ 0131/557–0256) can clothe you in full Highland dress, with kilts made in its own workshops. The affiliated **21st Century Kilts** crafts contemporary kilts in leather, denim, and even camouflage. **Edinburgh Crystal** (✉ Eastfield, Penicuik ☎ 01968/675128), 10 mi south of the city center, is renowned the world over for its fine glass and crystal ware. Many large stores and gift shops in the city stock pieces from Edinburgh Crystal, but you'll find the largest selection at its main premises. You can browse discontinued lines for real bargains, and even have a go at blowing glass yourself.

SIDE TRIPS FROM EDINBURGH

If you stand on an Edinburgh eminence—the castle ramparts, Arthur's Seat, Corstorphine Hill—you can plan a few Lothian excursions without even the aid of a map. The Lothians is the collective name given to the swath of countryside south of the Firth of Forth and surrounding Edinburgh. Many courtly and aristocratic families lived here, and the region still has the castles and mansions to prove it. The rich arrived and with them, deer parks, gardens in the French style, and Lothian's fame as a seed plot for Lowland gentility. Although the region has always provided rich pickings for historians, it also used to offer even richer pickings for coal miners—for a century after the industrial revolution, gentle streams in fairy glens (so the old writings describe them) steamed and stank with pollution. Although some black spots still remain, most of the rural countryside is now once again a fitting setting for excursions. When the coal miners left, admirals came here to retire, and today the area happily affords many delights. The 70-mi round-trip exploration of the historic houses and castles of West Lothian and the Forth Valley, and territory north of the River Forth, can be accomplished in a full day with select stops. Stretching east to the sea and south to the Lowlands from Edinburgh, Midlothian and East Lothian are no more than one hour from Edinburgh. The inland river valleys, hills, and castles of Midlothian and East Lothian's delightful waterfronts, dunes, and golf links offer a taste of Scotland close to the capital.

West Lothian & the Forth Valley

West Lothian comprises a good bit of Scotland's central belt. The River Forth snakes across a widening floodplain on its descent from the Highlands, and by the time it reaches the western extremities of Edinburgh, it has already passed below the mighty Forth bridges and become a broad estuary. Castles and stately homes sprout thickly on both sides of the Forth.

Cramond

43 *4 mi west of Edinburgh.*

At this compact coastal settlement, you can watch summer sunsets upriver of where the Almond joins the Firth of Forth. The river's banks, once the site of mills and industrial works, now have pleasant, leafy walks.

WHERE TO EAT £–£££ ✕ **Cramond Inn.** In this dark 17th-century village inn—once the haunt of Robert Louis Stevenson—you can stop for a pint at the bar or a selection from the small but varied pub menu, with such dishes as grilled halibut and new potatoes, sole and salmon rolls, chicken with mango chutney and rice, and steak. ✉ *Cramond Glebe Rd., Cramond Village* ☎ *0131/336–2035* ▭ *MC, V.*

Dalmeny House

44 *6 mi west of Edinburgh.*

Dalmeny House, the first of the stately houses clustered on the western edge of Edinburgh, is the home of the earl and countess of Rosebery. This 1815 Tudor Gothic mansion displays among its sumptuous contents the best of the family's famous collection of 18th-century French furniture. Highlights include the library, the Napoléon Room, the Vincennes and Sevres porcelain collections, and the drawing room, with its tapestries and intricately wrought French furniture. ✉ *B924, by South Queensferry* ☎ *0131/331–1888* 🌐 *www.dalmeny.co.uk* 🎫 *£4* ⏲ *July–Aug., Sun.–Tues. 2–5:30; last admission at 4:30.*

South Queensferry

7 mi west of Edinburgh.

★ 45 This pleasant little waterside community, a former ferry port, is completely dominated by the **Forth Bridges**, dramatic structures of contrasting architecture that span the Firth of Forth at this historic crossing point. The **Forth Rail Bridge** was opened in 1890 and at the time hailed as the eighth wonder of the world, at 2,765 yards long, except on a hot summer's day when it expands by about another yard! Its neighbor is the 1,993-yard-long **Forth Road Bridge**, in operation since 1964.

WHERE TO EAT £–££ ✕ **The Hawes Inn.** In his novel *Kidnapped,* Robert Louis Stevenson describes a room at this inn as "a small room, with a bed in it, and heated like an oven by a great fire of coal." The dramatic setting and history alone are well worth the trip to the inn, which is 10 mi from the city center of Edinburgh and 1 mi from Dalmeny Railway station. The open fireplaces at this 1638 pub create a sense of comfort and coziness. You'll find traditional pub fare here, such as steak pie and fish-and-chips. ✉ *Newhalls Rd.* ☎ *0131/331–1990* ▭ *AE, MC, V.*

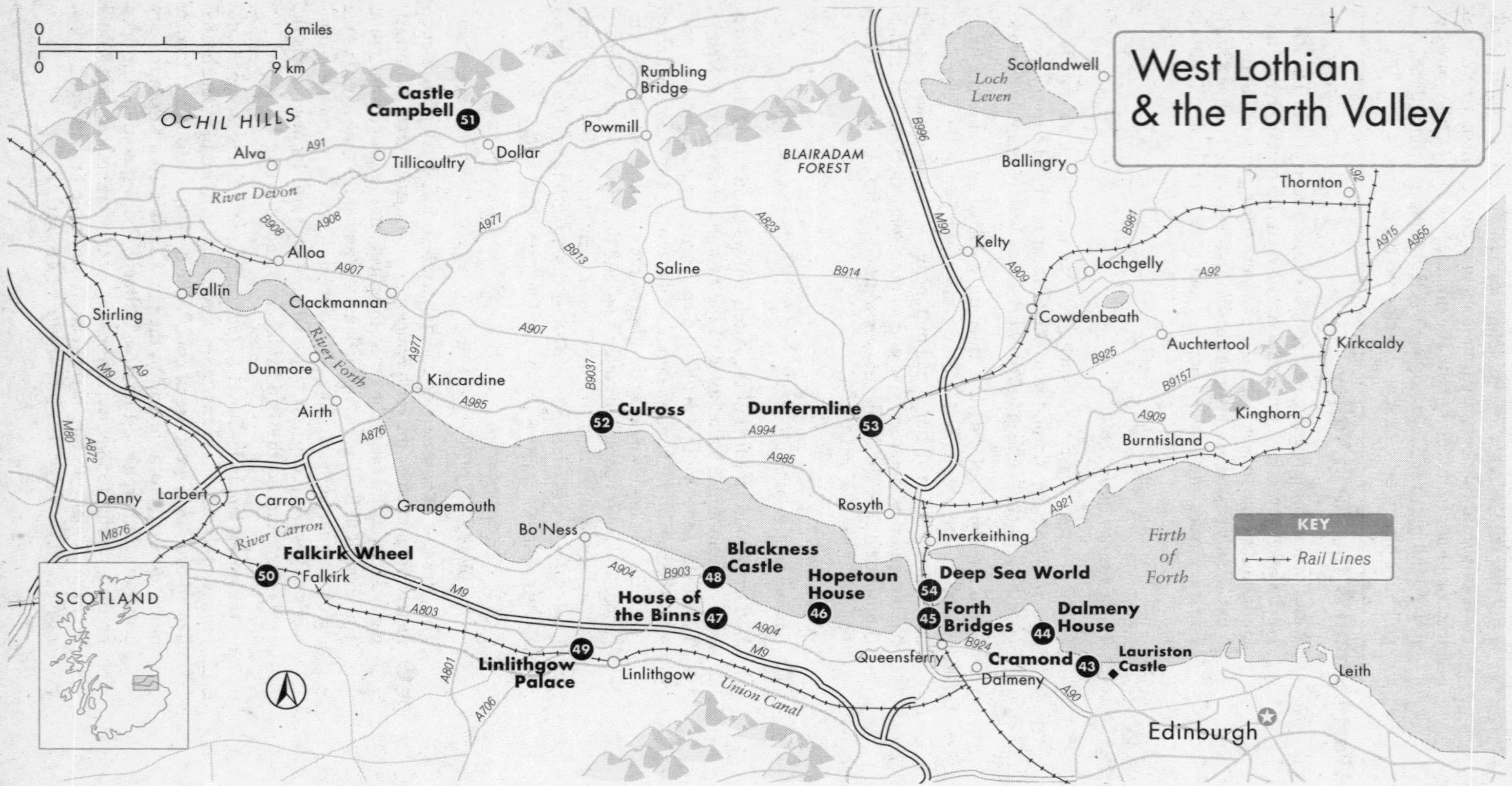
West Lothian
& the Forth Valley
KEY
Rail Lines
0
6 miles
0
9 km
OCHIL HILLS
Castle
Campbell
51
Alva
A91
Tillicoultry
Dollar
Rumbling
Bridge
Powmill
BLAIRADAM
FOREST
Loch
Leven
Scotlandwell
Ballingry
Thornton
River Devon
B908
A908
A977
B913
A823
M90
B996
Kelty
B981
A915
A955
Alloa
A907
Saline
B914
A909
Lochgelly
A92
Fallin
Clackmannan
Cowdenbeath
Stirling
A907
Auchtertool
Kirkcaldy
M9
A9
River Forth
Dunmore
A977
Kincardine
B9037
B925
B9157
A985
Airth
52
Culross
Dunfermline
53
A909
Kinghorn
M80
A872
A876
A994
Burntisland
A985
Denny
Larbert
Carron
Grangemouth
Rosyth
A921
M876
River Carron
Bo'Ness
Inverkeithing
Firth
of
Forth
Falkirk Wheel
Blackness
Castle
50
Falkirk
A904
B903
48
Hopetoun
House
Deep Sea World
54
SCOTLAND
M9
House of
the Binns
47
46
45
Forth
Bridges
Dalmeny
House
44
A803
A904
B924
49
M9
Queensferry
Cramond
43
Lauriston
Castle
Linlithgow
Palace
Linlithgow
Dalmeny
Leith
A801
Union Canal
A90
A706
Edinburgh

Hopetoun House

46 *10 mi west of Edinburgh.*

The palatial premises of Hopetoun House, probably Scotland's grandest courtly seat and home of the marquesses of Linlithgow, are considered to be among the Adam family's finest designs. The enormous house was started in 1699 to the original plans of Sir William Bruce (1630–1710), then enlarged between 1721 and 1754 by William Adam (1689–1748) and his sons Robert and John. There's a notable painting collection, and the house has decorative work of the highest order, plus all the trappings to keep you entertained: a nature trail, a restaurant in the former stables, and a museum. Much of the wealth that created this sumptuous building came from the family's mining interests in the surrounding regions. ✉ *6 mi west of South Queensferry, off A904* ☎ *0131/331–2451* 🌐 *www.hopetounhouse.com* 🎫 *£5.30* ⏲ *Apr.–Sept., daily 10–5:30, last admission at 4:30; Oct., daily 11–4, last admission at 3:30.*

House of the Binns

47 *12 mi west of Edinburgh.*

The 17th-century general "Bloody Tam" Dalyell (circa 1599–1685) transformed a fortified stronghold into a gracious mansion, the House of the Binns (the name derives from *bynn* the old Scottish word for *hill*). The present exterior dates from around 1810 and shows a remodeling into a kind of mock fort with crenellated battlements and turrets. Inside, there are magnificent plaster ceilings done in the Elizabethan style. The house is cared for by the National Trust for Scotland. ✉ *Off A904, 4 mi east of Linlithgow* ☎ *01506/834255* 🌐 *www.nts.org.uk/binns.html* 🎫 *£5* ⏲ *House May–Sept., Sat.–Thurs. and Sun. 1–5. Parkland late Mar.–late Oct., daily 10–7; Jan.–late Mar. and late Oct.–Dec., daily 10–4.*

Blackness Castle

48 *12 mi west of Edinburgh.*

The castle of Blackness stands like a grounded ship on the very edge of the Forth. A curious 15th-century structure, it has had a varied career as a strategic fortress, state prison, powder magazine, and youth hostel. The countryside is gently green and cultivated, and open views extend across the blue Forth to the distant ramparts of the Ochil Hills. The castle is run by Historic Scotland, a government organization that looks after many historic properties in Scotland. ✉ *B903, 4 mi northeast of Linlithgow* ☎ *01506/834807* 🌐 *www.historic-scotland.gov.uk* 🎫 *£2.20* ⏲ *Apr.–Sept., daily 9:30–6:30; Oct.–Mar., Mon.–Wed. and Sat. 9:30–4, Thurs. 9:30–noon, Sun. 2–4.*

Linlithgow Palace

49 *12 mi west of Edinburgh.*

On the edge of Linlithgow Loch stands the splendid ruin of Linlithgow Palace, the birthplace of Mary, Queen of Scots in 1542. Burned, perhaps accidentally, by Hanoverian troops during the last Jacobite rebellion in 1746, this impressive shell stands on a site of great antiquity, though nothing for certain survived an earlier fire in 1424. The palace gatehouse was built in the early 16th century, and the central courtyard's elaborate fountain dates from around 1535. The halls and great rooms are cold, echoing stone husks now in Historic Scotland's care. ✉ *A706, south shore of Linlithgow Loch* ☎ *01506/842896* 🌐 *www.historic-scotland.gov.uk* 🎫 *£3* ⏲ *Apr.–Sept., daily 9:30–6:30; Oct.–Mar., Mon.–Sat. 9:30–4:30, Sun. 2–4:30.*

en route

From the M9 you'll begin to gain tempting glimpses of the Highland hills to the northwest and the long, humped wall of the **Ochil Hills,** across the river plain to the north. The **River Carron,** which flows under the M9, gave its name to the *carronade,* a kind of cannon manufactured in Falkirk, a few minutes to the southwest. You'll also pass the apocalyptic complex of **Grangemouth Refinery** (impressive by night), which you may also smell if the wind is right—or wrong! The refinery processes North Sea crude oil but was originally sited here because of the now-extinct oil-shale extraction industry of West Lothian, pioneered by a Scot, James "Paraffin" Young. This landscape may not be the most scenic in Scotland, but it has certainly played its role in the nation's industrial history.

Falkirk Wheel

★ 50 *25 mi west of Edinburgh.*

In 2002, British Waterways opened the only rotating boatlift in the world to link two major waterways, the Forth and Clyde Canal and the Union Canal, between Edinburgh and Glasgow. Considered an engineering marvel, the Wheel transports eight or more boats at a time overland from one canal to the other in about 45 minutes. The boats float into a cradle-like compartment full of water, then as the Wheel turns, they are transported up or down to meet the destination canal. You can board tour boats at Falkirk to ride the Wheel, or you can take a multi-day barge cruise between Edinburgh and Glasgow. At Falkirk, allow 30 minutes before your scheduled departure time to pick up your tickets and choose your boat. ✉ *Lime Rd., Tamfourhill* ☎ *01324/619888; reservations 08700/500208* 🌐 *www.thefalkirkwheel.co.uk* 🎫 *Boat trips, £8; visitor center, free* ⏲ *Boat trips, Apr.–Oct., daily 9:30–5; Nov.–Mar., daily 10–3. Visitor center, Apr.–Oct., daily 9–6:30; Nov.–Mar. 10–5.*

Ochil Hills

24 mi northwest of Edinburgh.

The scarp face of the Ochil Hills looms unmistakably. It is an old fault line that yields up hard volcanic rocks and contrasts with the quantities of softer coal immediately around the River Forth. The steep Ochils provided grazing land and water power for Scotland's second-largest textile area. Some mills still survive in the so-called Hillfoots towns, on the scarp edge east of Stirling. Several hikers' routes run into the narrow chinks of glens here. Behind Alva sits **Alva Glen,** a park near the converted Strude Mill, at the top and eastern end of the little town. East of Alva Glen is the **Ochil Hills Woodland Park,** which provides access to Silver Glen. The **Mill Glen,** behind Tillicoultry (pronounced tilly-*coot*-ree), with its giant quarry, fine waterfalls, and interesting plants, is a good hiking option for energetic explorers.

Dollar

30 mi northwest of Edinburgh.

This *douce* (Scots for well-mannered or gentle) and tidy town below the Ochil Hills lies at the mouth of Dollar Glen. With green woods below, bracken hills above, and a view that on a clear day stretches right across
51 the Forth Valley to the tip of Tinto Hill near Lanark, **Castle Campbell** is certainly the most atmospheric fortress within easy reach of Edinburgh. Formerly known as Castle Gloom, Castle Campbell stands out among Scottish castles for the sheer drama of its setting. The sturdy square of the tower house survives from the 15th century, when the site was fortified by the first earl of Argyll (died 1493). Other buildings and enclosures were subsequently added, but the sheer lack of space on this rocky em-

inence ensured that there would never be any drastic changes. John Knox, the fiery religious reformer, once preached here. And in 1654 the castle was captured by Oliver Cromwell and garrisoned with English troops. It is now cared for by Historic Scotland. To get here you'll have to follow a road off the A91 that angles sharply up the east side of the wooded defile. ✉ *Off the A91, Dollar Glen, 1 mi north of Dollar* ☎ *0131/668–8800* 🌐 *www.historic-scotland.gov.uk* 🎟 *£3.00* ⏲ *Apr.–Sept., daily 9:30–6:30; Oct.–Mar., Mon.–Wed. 9:30–4:30, Thurs. noon–4:30, Sat. 9:30–noon, Sun. 2–4:30.*

Culross

52 *17 mi northwest of Edinburgh.*

With its Mercat Cross, cobbled streets, tolbooth, and narrow wynds, Culross, on the muddy shores of the Forth, is now a living museum of a 17th-century town and one of the most remarkable little towns in all of Scotland. It once had a thriving industry and export trade in coal and salt (the coal was used in the salt-panning process). It also had, curiously, a trade monopoly in the manufacture of baking *girdles* (griddles). But as local coal became exhausted, the impetus of the industrial revolution passed Culross by, and other parts of the Forth Valley prospered. Culross became a backwater town, and the merchants' houses of the 17th and 18th centuries were never replaced by Victorian developments or modern architecture. In the 1930s the then-new and also very poor National Trust for Scotland started to buy up the decaying properties. With the help of several other agencies, these buildings were conserved and brought to life. Today ordinary citizens live in many of the National Trust properties. A few—the Palace, Study, and Town House—are open to the public. ✉ *Off A985, 8 mi south of Dollar* ☎ *01383/880359* 🌐 *www.nts.org.uk* 🎟 *Palace, Study, and Town House £5* ⏲ *Palace, Study, and Town House July–Aug., daily 10–6; late Mar.–late June and Sept.–late Oct., daily noon–5; last admission 1 hr before closing.*

Dunfermline

53 *16 mi northwest of Edinburgh.*

Dunfermline was once the world center for the production of damask linen, but the town is better known today as the birthplace of millionaire philanthropist Andrew Carnegie (1835–1919). Undoubtedly Dunfermline's most famous son, Carnegie endowed the town with a park, library, health and fitness center, and, naturally, a Carnegie Hall, still the focus of culture and entertainment. The 18th-century weaver's cottage where Carnegie was born in 1835 is now the **Andrew Carnegie Birthplace Museum.** Don't be misled by the cottage's exterior. Inside it opens into a larger hall, where documents, photographs, and artifacts relate Carnegie's fascinating life story. You'll learn such obscure details as the claim that Carnegie was one of only three men in the United States then able to translate Morse code by ear as it came down the wire. ✉ *Moodie St.* ☎ *01383/724302* 🎟 *£2* ⏲ *Apr.–Oct., Mon.–Sat. 11–5, Sun. 2–5.*

The **Pittencrieff House Museum** tells the story of the town's damask linen industry. ✉ *Pittencrieff Park* ☎ *01383/313838 or 01383/722935* 🎟 *Free* ⏲ *Apr.– Sept., daily 11–5; Oct.–Mar., daily 11–4.*

The **Dunfermline Abbey and Palace** complex was founded in the 11th century by Queen Margaret, the English wife of the Scots king Malcolm III. Some Norman work can be seen in the present church, where Robert the Bruce (1274–1329) lies buried. The palace grew from the abbey guest house and was the birthplace of Charles I (1600–1649). Dunfermline was the seat of the royal court of Scotland until the end of the 11th century, and its central role in Scottish affairs is explored by means of display panels dotted around the drafty but hallowed buildings. ✉ *Monastery St.* ☎ *01383/739026* 💷 *£2.20* ⏲ *Apr.–Sept., daily 9:30–6:30; Oct.–Mar., Mon.–Wed. and Sat. 9:30–4:30, Thurs. 9:30–noon, Fri. and Sun. 2–4:30; last admission ½ hr before closing.*

Deep Sea World

54 *9 mi northwest of Edinburgh.*

The former ferry port in North Queensferry dropped almost into oblivion after the Forth Road Bridge opened but was dragged abruptly back into the limelight when the hugely popular Deep Sea World arrived in 1993. This sophisticated "aquarium"—for want of a better word—on the Firth of Forth offers a fascinating view of underwater life. Go down a clear acrylic tunnel for a diver's-eye look at more than 5,000 fish, including 250 sharks (some over 9 feet long); and visit the exhibition hall, which has an Amazon jungle display and an audiovisual presentation on local marine life. Ichthyophobes will feel more at ease in the adjacent café and gift shop. ✉ *North Queensferry* ☎ *01383/411880* 🌐 *www.deepseaworld.com* 💷 *£7.50* ⏲ *Apr.–Oct., daily 10–6; Nov.–Mar., weekdays 11–5, weekends 10–6; last admission 1 hr before closing.*

West Lothian & the Forth Valley A to Z

BUS TRAVEL

First Midland Bluebird bus services link most of this area, but working out a detailed itinerary by bus is best left to your travel agent or guide.
i First Midland Bluebird ☎ 01324/613777.

CAR TRAVEL

Leave Edinburgh by Queensferry Road—the A90—and follow signs for the Forth Bridge. Beyond the city boundary at Cramond take the slip road, B924, for South Queensferry, watching for signs to Dalmeny House. From Dalmeny follow the B924 for the descent to South Queensferry. The B924 continues westward under the approaches to the suspension bridge and then meets the A904. On turning right onto A904, follow signs for Hopetoun House, House of the Binns, and Blackness Castle. From Blackness take the B903 to its junction with the A904. Turn left for Linlithgow on the A803. At this point it's best to join the M9, which will speed you westward. Look for signs leading to the Falkirk Wheel, southwest of the motorway. Then return to the M9, follow signs to Kincardine Bridge, and cross the Forth, taking the A977 north from Kincardine. Take the A907 to Alloa, get on the A908 (marked TILLICOULTRY) for a short stretch, and then pick up the B908 (marked ALVA).

At this point you'll be leaving the industrial northern shore of the Forth behind and entering the Ochil Hills, which you can explore by following the A91 eastward at Alva; squeezed between the gentle River Devon and the steep slopes above, the road continues to Dollar, where you should follow signs to Castle Campbell. From the castle, retrace your route to A91 and turn left. A few minutes outside Dollar, turn right onto a minor road (signposted RUMBLING BRIDGE). Then turn right onto the A823. Follow A823 through Powmill (follow the signs for Dunfermline); turn right off A823, following the signs for Saline, and take an unclassified road due south to join the A907. Turn right, and then within a mile go left on the B9037, which leads down to Culross. Take the B9037 east to join the A994, which leads to Dunfermline. From here follow the Edinburgh signs to the A823 and return via North Queensferry and the Forth Road Bridge (toll 80p traveling north into Fife only).

TRAIN TRAVEL

Dalmeny, Linlithgow, and Dunfermline all have rail stations and can be reached from Edinburgh Waverley station.

National Train ☎ 08457/484950.

VISITOR INFORMATION

The Mill Trail Visitor Centre, at Alva, can provide information on the region's textile establishments as well as a *Mill Trail* brochure, which directs you to mill shops selling bargain woolen and tweed goods.

Mill Trail Visitor Centre ✉ W. Stirling St., Alva ☎ 01259/769696.

Midlothian & East Lothian

In spite of the finest stone carving in Scotland at Rosslyn Chapel, associations with Sir Walter Scott, outstanding castles, and miles of varied rolling countryside, Midlothian, the area immediately south of Edinburgh, for years remained off the beaten tourist path. Perhaps a little in awe of sophisticated Edinburgh to the north and the well-manicured charm of the stockbroker belt of nearby upmarket East Lothian, Midlothian was quietly preoccupied with its own workaday little towns and dormitory suburbs.

As for East Lothian, it started with the advantage of golf courses of world rank, most notably Muirfield, plus a scattering of stately homes and interesting hotels. Red-pantiled and decidedly middle class, it is an area of glowing grain fields in summer and quite a few discreetly polite STRICTLY PRIVATE signs at the end of driveways. Still, it has plenty of interest, including photogenic villages, active fishing harbors, and vistas of pastoral Lowland Scotland, seemingly a world away (but much less than an hour by car) from bustling Edinburgh.

Roslin

7 mi south of Edinburgh.

This pretty little U-shape miners' village, with its rows of stone-built terraced cottages, is famous for the extraordinary **Rosslyn Chapel.** Conceived by Sir William Sinclair (circa 1404–80) and dedicated to St. Matthew in 1446, the chapel is outstanding for the quality and variety of the stone carving inside. Covering almost every square inch of stonework are human figures, animals, and plants. The chapel's design called for a cruciform structure, but only the choir and parts of the east transept walls were completed. Some believe the Rosslyn Chapel is where the Holy Grail is buried. ✉ *Roslin, off A703* ☎ *0131/440–2159* 🌐 *www.rosslyn-chapel.com* 💷 *£4* ⏲ *Mon.–Sat. 10–5, Sun. 11:45–4:45.*

55

Fodor'sChoice ★

Edinburgh Crystal Visitor Centre

56 *8 mi south of Edinburgh.*

There are fine views of the Pentland Hills beyond the town of Penicuik, but its chief attraction is the Edinburgh Crystal Visitor Centre. Here you can learn the history of glassmaking, see craftsmen at work and learn about the skills required to transform molten glass into exquisite pieces. Sign up for the "hands-on" tour and you can even blow a bubble of glass yourself, and cut a pattern onto a crystal tumbler. Your name is then engraved on the glass, and you can take it home as a souvenir. Reservations are recommended for the tours. There are also shops and a restaurant. ✉ *Eastfield, Penicuik* ☎ *01968/675128* 🌐 *www.edinburgh-crystal.com* 💷 *Center free, tours £3.50–£10* ⏲ *Mon.–Sat. 10–5, Sun. 11–5; last tour at 4.*

Midlothian & East Lothian

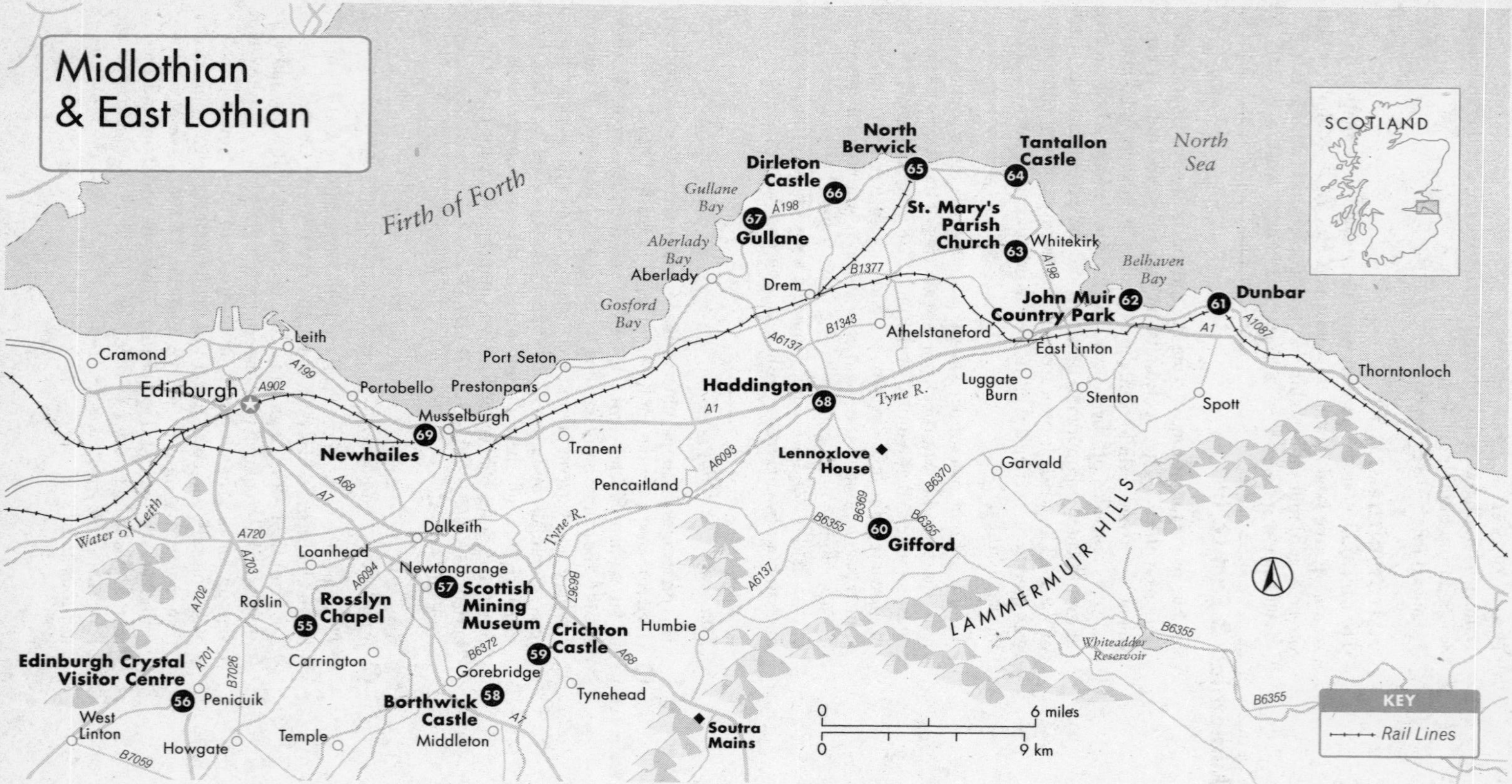

The Pentlands

2 mi south of Edinburgh

This unmistakable range of hills, which begins almost in the suburbs of the city, has the longest artificial ski slope in Europe, the **Midlothian Ski Centre at Hillend** (✉ Fairmilehead, ☎ 0131/445–443) with an all-year chairlift (£1.30) that provides magnificent views, even for nonskiers. It operates Monday through Saturday from 9:30 AM to 9 PM, and on Sunday from 9:30 to 7. There are several other access points along the A702 running parallel to the hills—the best is Flotterstone, where you'll find a parking lot, pub, and quiet roads for walking.

WHERE TO EAT
££–£££ ✕ **The Old Bakehouse.** Here you'll find home-cooked fare, made with fresh local produce, in quaint, wood-beamed rooms. Danish open sandwiches are the specialty, but homemade soups and hot main courses are also available. ✉ *West Linton, southwest of Penicuik on A702* ☎ *01968/660830* ▭ *MC, V* ⊙ *Closed Mon. and Tues. No dinner Sun.*

Scottish Mining Museum

57 *9 mi southeast of Edinburgh.*

The Scottish Mining Museum, in the former mining community of Newtongrange, provides a good introduction to the history of Scotland's mining industry. Go on shift as a coal miner and experience life at the (virtual reality) coal face. There are also interactive displays and "magic helmets" that bring the tour to life and relate the power that the mining company had over the lives of the individual workers in a frighteningly autocratic system that survived well into the 1930s—the mining company owned the houses, shops, and even the pub. Newtongrange was in fact the largest planned mining village in Scotland. The scenery is no more attractive than you would expect, though the green Pentland Hills hover in the distance. ✉ *A7, Newtongrange* ☎ *0131/663–7519* 🌐 *www.scottishminingmuseum.com* 🎫 *£4* ⊙ *Mar.–Oct., daily 10–5; Nov.–Feb., daily 10–4; last admission 1½ hrs before closing.*

Borthwick Castle

58 *12 mi southeast of Edinburgh.*

Set in green countryside with scattered woods and lush hedgerows, the village of Borthwick is dominated by Borthwick Castle, which dates from the 15th century and is still occupied. Mary, Queen of Scots, came to this stark, tall, twin-towered fortress on a kind of honeymoon with her ill-starred third husband, the earl of Bothwell. Their already-dubious bliss was interrupted by Mary's political opponents, often referred to as the Lords of the Congregation, a confederacy of powerful nobles who were against the queen's latest liaison and who instead favored the crowning of her young son, James. Rather insensitively, they laid siege to the castle while the newlyweds were there. Mary subsequently escaped disguised as a man. She was not free for long, however. It was only a short time before she was defeated in battle and imprisoned. She languished in prison for 21 years before Queen Elizabeth I of England (1558–1603) signed her death warrant in 1587. Bothwell's fate was equally gloomy: he died insane in a Danish prison. ✉ *Borthwick, 1 mi south of Gorebridge* ☎ *01875/820514* 🎫 *Free* ⊙ *Tour hrs. vary.*

WHERE TO STAY
££££–£££££ 🏨 **Borthwick Castle.** There are hotels with castle names, and hotels inside what once were castles, and then there is Borthwick, which is first a castle and only second a place where you can stay. This 15th-century fortress was taking guests half a century before Columbus sailed to the Americas. Nowhere else in Scotland offers the extraordinary experience of living a part of history. Your "bedchamber" is warm and comfort-

able, equipped with bath or shower. You dine not in a restaurant but in the Great Hall, lit by candles and the gleam of a log fire. ✉ *North Middleton, Midlothian EH23 4QY* ☎ *01875/820514* 📠 *01875/821702* *10 rooms* *Fishing, horseback riding; no a/c, no room TVs* 💳 *AE, DC, MC, V* ⏲ *Closed Jan.–mid-Mar.* 🍽 *BP.*

Crichton Castle

59 *11 mi southeast of Edinburgh.*

Crichton Castle, a Historic Scotland property, stands amid attractive, rolling Lowland scenery, interrupted here and there by patches of woodland. Crichton was a Bothwell family castle; Mary, Queen of Scots, attended the wedding here of Bothwell's sister, Lady Janet Hepburn, to Mary's brother, Lord John Stewart. The curious arcaded range reveals diamond-faceted stonework; this particular geometric pattern is unique in Scotland and is thought to have been inspired by Renaissance styles on the Continent, particularly Italy. The oldest part of the work is the 14th-century keep (square tower). You can reach this castle from Borthwick Castle by taking a peaceful walk through the woods (there are signposts along the way). ✉ *B6367, near Pathhead, 7 mi southeast of Dalkeith* ☎ *01875/320017* 🌐 *www.historic-scotland.gov.uk* 🎫 *£2* ⏲ *Apr.–Sept., daily 9:30–6.30.*

en route

If you follow the A68 5 mi south from Pathhead, you reach the very edge of the Lammermuir Hills. Just beyond the junction with the A6368 is a spot called **Soutra Mains** (16 mi southeast of the city center). From the small parking lot here, you can enjoy glorious unobstructed views extending northward over the whole of the Lothian plain.

Gifford

60 *25 mi southeast of Edinburgh.*

With its 18th-century kirk and Mercat Cross, Gifford is a good example of a tweedily respectable, well-scrubbed, red-pantile-roofed East Lothian village. John Witherspoon (1723–1794), a signatory of the U.S. Declaration of Independence, was born here. A narrow road from Gifford leads up into the Lammermuir Hills and down into Berwickshire, passing the Whiteadder Reservoir.

Dunbar

61 *25 mi east of Edinburgh.*

In the days before tour companies started offering package deals to the Mediterranean, Dunbar was a popular holiday beach resort. Now a bit faded, the town is still lovely for its spacious Georgian-style properties, characterized by the astragals, or fan-shape windows, above the doors; the symmetry of the house fronts; and the parapeted roof lines. Though not the popular seaside playground it once was, Dunbar has an attractive beach and a picturesque harbor.

John Muir Country Park

62 *23 mi east of Edinburgh.*

Taking in the estuary of the River Tyne winding down from the Moorfoot Hills, the John Muir Country Park holds varied coastal scenery: rocky shoreline, golden sands, and the mixed woodlands of Tyninghame, teeming with wildlife. Dunbar-born conservationist John Muir (1838–1914), whose family emigrated to the United States when he was a child, helped found Yosemite and Sequoia national parks in California. ✉ *Off the A1087, 2 mi west of Dunbar.*

St. Mary's Parish Church

63 *22 mi northeast of Edinburgh.*

The unmistakable red-sandstone St. Mary's Parish Church, with its Norman tower, stands on a site occupied since the 6th century. It was a place of pilgrimage in medieval times because of its healing well. Behind the kirk, in a field, stands a tithe barn. Tithe barns originated with the practice of giving to the church a portion of local produce, which then required storage space. In the 15th century, the church was visited by a young Italian nobleman, Aeneas Sylvius Piccolomini, after he was shipwrecked off the East Lothian coast. Twenty years later, Piccolomini became Pope Pius II. At one end of the barn stands a 16th-century tower house, which at one point in its history accommodated visiting pilgrims. The large three-story barn was added to the tower house in the 17th century. ✉ *A198, Whitekirk* 🎫 *Free* ⏲ *Daily 9 AM–dusk.*

Tantallon Castle

64 *23 mi northeast of Edinburgh.*

Rising on a cliff beyond the flat fields east of North Berwick, Tantallon Castle is a substantial ruin defending a headland with the sea on three sides. The red sandstone is pitted and eaten by time and sea spray, with the earliest surviving stonework dating from the late 14th century. The fortress was besieged in 1529 by the cannons of King James V (1512–42). Rather inconveniently, the besieging forces ran out of gunpowder. Cannons were used again, to deadlier effect, in a later siege during the Civil War in 1651. Twelve days of battering with the heavy guns of Cromwell's General Monk greatly damaged the flanking towers. Fortunately, much of the curtain wall of this former Douglas stronghold, now cared for by Historic Scotland, survives. ✉ *A198, 3 mi east of North Berwick* ☎ *01620/892727* 🌐 *www.historic-scotland.gov.uk* 🎫 *£3* ⏲ *Apr.–Sept., daily 9:30–6:30; Oct.–Mar., Mon.–Wed. and Sat. 9:30–4:30, Thurs. 9:30–noon, Sun. 2–4:30; last admission ½ hr before closing.*

North Berwick

65 *20 mi northeast of Edinburgh.*

The pleasant little seaside resort of North Berwick manages to retain a small-town personality even when it's thronged with city visitors on warm summer Sunday afternoons. Munching on ice cream, the city folk stroll on the beach and in the narrow streets or gaze at the sailing craft in the small harbor. An observation deck, exhibits, and films at the **Scottish Seabird Centre** provide a good introduction to the world of the gannets and puffins that nest on nearby Bass Rock. Live interactive cameras let you take an even closer look at the bird. ✉ *The Harbour* ☎ *01620/890202* 🌐 *www.seabird.org* 🎫 *£4.95* ⏲ *Apr.–Sept., daily 10–6; Oct.–Mar., weekdays 10–4, weekends 10–5:30.*

WHERE TO STAY

££ **Glebe House.** This 18th-century former manse sits amid its own secluded grounds, yet it's in the heart of town, a 10-minute walk east of the station. It's also close to the beach and 18 golf courses, including nearby Muirfield. The elegant bedrooms, one of which has a four-poster bed, are in keeping with the Georgian style of the house. Grand period furniture, paintings, and ornaments fill the sitting and dining rooms. ✉ *Law Rd., EH39 4PL* ☎ *01620/892608* 🌐 *www.aboutscotland.com/glebe/house.html* *4 rooms* *No-smoking rooms; no a/c, no room TVs* *No credit cards* *BP.*

Dirleton

22 mi northeast of Edinburgh.

66 In the center of this small village sits the 12th-century **Dirleton Castle,** surrounded by a high outer wall. Within the wall you'll find a 17th-century bowling green, set in the shade of yew trees and surrounded by a herbaceous flower border that blazes with color in high summer. Dirleton Castle, now in Historic Scotland's care, was occupied in 1298 by King Edward I of England as part of his campaign for the continued subjugation of the unruly Scots. ✉ *On the A198, 2 mi west of North Berwick* ☎ *01620/850330* 🌐 *www.historic-scotland.gov.uk* 🎫 *£2.80* ⏲ *Apr.–Sept., daily 9:30–6; Oct.–Mar., Mon.–Sat. 9:30–4, Sun. 2–4.*

Gullane

67 *15 mi northeast of Edinburgh.*

Very noticeable along this coastline are the golf courses of East Lothian, laid out wherever there is available links space. Ultrarespectable Gullane is surrounded by them, and its inhabitants are typically clad in expensive golfing sweaters. **Muirfield,** a course that hosts the Open Championship, is to the north of the village. Greywalls, now a hotel, was originally a private house, designed by Sir Edwin Lutyens (1869–1944). Apart from golf, you can enjoy restful summer evening strolls at **Gullane's beach,** well within driving distance of the village.

WHERE TO STAY

★ ££££££ **Greywalls.** This is the ideal hotel for a golfing vacation: comfortable, with attentive service and fine modern British cuisine that makes the most of local produce. The turn-of-the-20th-century house, designed by Sir Edwin Lutyens in the shape of a crescent and with a walled garden, is an architectural treasure. Edward VII used to stay here, as have Nicklaus, Trevino, Palmer, and a host of other golfing greats. Shades of restful green predominate in the stylish fabrics from the likes of Nina Campbell, Colefax and Fowler, and Osborne and Little. A separate lodge house can accommodate up to eight people. ✉ *Muirfield, Gullane EH31 2EG* ☎ *01620/842144* 📠 *01620/842241* 🌐 *www.greywalls.co.uk* *23 rooms, 1 lodge* *Restaurant, cable TV, putting green, tennis court* 💳 *AE, DC, MC, V* ⏲ *Closed mid-Oct.–mid-Apr.*

Haddington

68 *15 mi east of Edinburgh.*

One of the best-preserved medieval street plans in the country can be explored in Haddington. Among the many buildings of architectural or historical interest is the Town House, designed by William Adam in 1748 and enlarged in 1830. A wall plaque at the Sidegate recalls the great heights of floods from the River Tyne. Beyond is the medieval Nungate footbridge, with the Church of St. Mary a little way upstream.

Just to the south of Haddington stands **Lennoxlove House,** the grand ancestral home of the very grand dukes of Hamilton since 1947 and the the Baird family before them. A turreted country house, part of it dating from the 15th century, Lennoxlove is a cheerful mix of family life and Scottish history. The beautifully decorated rooms house portraits, furniture, porcelain, and items associated with Mary, Queen of Scots, including her supposed death mask. ✉ *B6369, 1 mi south of Haddington* ☎ *01620/823720* 🌐 *www.lennoxlove.com* 🎫 *£4.25* ⏲ *Tours Easter–Oct., Wed., Thurs., and Sun. 2–4:30.*

Newhailes

69 *5 mi east of Edinburgh.*

This fine late-17th century house (with 18th-century additions), owned and run by the National Trust for Scotland, was designed by Scottish architect James Smith (c. 1645–1731) in 1686 as his own home. He later sold it to Lord Bellendon, and in 1707 it was bought by Sir David Dalrymple (?–1721), first baronet of Hailes, who improved and extended the house, adding one of the finest rococo interiors in Scotland. The library played host to many famous figures from the Scottish Enlightenment, including inveterate Scot-basher Dr. Samuel Johnson, who dubbed the library "the most learned room in Europe." Most of the original interiors and furnishings remain intact. ✉ *Newhailes Road, Musselburgh EH21 6RY.* ☎ *0131 665 1546.* 🌐 *www.nts.org.uk* *House £7, grounds £2* ⏲ *House June–Oct., Thurs.–Mon. 12–5; Grounds daily 10–6.*

Midlothian & East Lothian A to Z

BUS TRAVEL

City buses travel as far as Swanston and the Pentland Hills. First Lowland buses run to towns and villages throughout Midlothian and East Lothian. For details of all services, inquire at the St. Andrew Square bus station in Edinburgh.

First Lowland ☎ 0131/663–9233.

CAR TRAVEL

Leave Edinburgh via the A701 (Liberton Road). At the former mining community of Bilston, turn left to Roslin on the B7006. From Roslin return to the A701 for Penicuik and the Edinburgh Crystal Visitor Centre. From Penicuik take the A766 to A702, which runs beneath the Pentland Hills to West Linton. Then follow the B7059 and the A701 to Leadburn, and turn right onto the A6094 for Howgate. Beyond Howgate turn right onto the B6372, and continue past Temple, an attractive village on the edge of the Moorfoot Hills, toward Gorebridge.

At the junction of B6372 with A7, just before Gorebridge, you have a choice. If your interests tend toward social history, turn left and drive 2 mi to reach Newtongrange and the Scottish Mining Museum. If your interests lie elsewhere, turn right instead, and after a few moments' travel south you will see a sign for Borthwick. Take a left onto an unclassified road off A7, and a few minutes later Borthwick Castle appears. From Borthwick take the B6372 and turn right onto the A68. Just beyond the village of Pathhead you'll see signs to Crichton Castle, to the right. Having detoured to the castle, follow the A68 south, away from Edinburgh, to the very edge of the Lammermuir Hills. Just beyond the junction with the B6368, at Soutra Mains, there's a small parking lot from which to enjoy the view. Make your way back to the A68 and turn left onto it, then turn right onto a continuation of the B6368; when you reach its junction with the B6355, turn right and continue until you reach Gifford. Go through the village, and head east for the junction with the B6370, which leads to Dunbar.

West of Dunbar, on the way back to Edinburgh, the A1087 leads to the sandy reaches of Belhaven Bay, signposted from the main road, and to the John Muir Country Park. Beyond the park turn right onto the A1, then turn right onto the A198 to reach St. Mary's Parish Church at Whitekirk, Tantallon Castle, North Berwick, Dirleton, and Gullane. A198 eventually leads to Aberlady, from which you can take the A6137 south to the former county town of Haddington and, by way of the B6369, to Lennoxlove House. Return to the A1 at Haddington and head west towards Edinburgh. At the junction of the A1 and the A6095 (a complicated arrangement of underpasses and roundabouts) turn right and head along Newgrangehall Road towards Musselburgh. Beyond the railway line the street name changes to Newhailes Road. Turn left at the first roundabout into a short driveway that takes you to Newhailes mansion. Retrace your steps back to the A1, and continue west to Edinburgh.

TRAIN TRAVEL

There is no train service in Midlothian. In East Lothian, the towns of North Berwick, Drem, and Dunbar have train stations with regular service from Edinburgh.

EDINBURGH & THE LOTHIANS A TO Z

To research prices, get advice from other travelers, and book travel arrangements, visit www.fodors.com.

AIR TRAVEL

Airlines serving Edinburgh include Aer Arann, Aer Lingus, British Airways, British Midland, Eastern Airways, easyJet, flybe, KLMuk, Lufthansa Ryanair, and ScotAirways. No transatlantic flights come through Edinburgh; you must instead fly into Glasgow, 50 mi away. Ryanair and easyJet have sparked a major price war on the Anglo-Scottish routes. They offer unbeatable, no-frills airfares on routes connecting Edinburgh Airport, Glasgow International, Prestwick Airport (30 mi south of Glasgow), and London's major airports.

Aer Arann ☎ 0800/585-2324 🌐 www.aerarann.ie **Aer Lingus** ☎ 0845/084-4444 🌐 www.aerlingus.com **British Airways** ☎ 0845/773-3377 🌐 www.britishairways.com **British Midland** ☎ 0870/607-0500 🌐 www.flybmi.com **easyJet** ☎ 0870/600-0000 🌐 www.easyjet.com **flybe** ☎ 0870/567-6676 🌐 www.flybe.com **KLMuk** ☎ 0870/507-4074 🌐 www.klm.com **Lufthansa** ☎ 0845/773-7747 🌐 www.lufthansa.com **Ryanair** ☎ 08701/56956 🌐 www.ryanair.com **ScotAirways** ☎ 0870/606-0707 🌐 www.scotairways.co.uk

AIRPORTS

At present, Edinburgh Airport, 7 mi west of the city center, offers no transatlantic flights. It does, however, have air connections throughout the United Kingdom—London (Heathrow, Gatwick, Stansted, Luton, and City), Birmingham, Bristol, East Midlands, Humberside, Jersey, Kirkwall (Orkney), Inverness, Leeds–Bradford, Manchester, Norwich, Sumburgh (Shetlands), Southampton, Wick, and Belfast (in Northern Ireland)—as well as with a number of European cities, including Amsterdam, Brussels, Copenhagen, Cork, Dublin, Frankfurt, Paris, and Zurich. Flights take off for Edinburgh Airport virtually every hour from London's Gatwick and Heathrow airports; it's usually faster and less complicated to fly through Gatwick, which has excellent rail service from London's Victoria Station.

Glasgow Airport, 50 mi west of Edinburgh, serves as the major point of entry into Scotland for transatlantic flights. Prestwick Airport, 30 mi southwest of Glasgow, after some years of eclipse by Glasgow Airport, has grown in importance, not least because of the activities of Ryanair.

Edinburgh Airport ☎ 0131/333-1000. **Glasgow Airport** ☎ 0141/887-1111 🌐 www.baa.co.uk (for both airports). **Prestwick Airport** ☎ 01292/511006 🌐 www.gpia.co.uk.

TRANSFERS FROM EDINBURGH AIRPORT There are no rail links to the city center, despite the fact that the airport sits between two main lines. By bus or car you can usually make it to Edinburgh in a comfortable half hour, unless you hit the morning (7:30 to 9) or evening (4 to 6) rush hours. Lothian Buses run between Edinburgh Airport and the city center every 15 minutes daily from 9 to 5 and less frequently (roughly every hour) during off-peak hours. The trip takes about 30 minutes, or about 45 minutes during rush hour. A single-fare ticket costs £3.30.

You can arrange for a chauffeur-driven limousine to meet your flight at Edinburgh Airport through David Grieve Chauffeur Drive for about £45 plus VAT; Little's Chauffeur Drive, £46 plus VAT; and Sleigh Ltd., £50 plus VAT.

Taxis are readily available outside the terminal. The trip takes 20–30 minutes to the city center, 15 minutes longer rush hour. The fare is roughly £17. Note that airport taxis picking up fares from the terminal are any color, not the typical black cabs.

David Grieve Chauffeur Drive ✉ 5b Polworth Gardens, Tollcross ☎ 0131/229-8666. **Little's Chauffeur Drive** ✉ 5 St. Ninian's Dr., Corstorphine ☎ 0131/334-2177. **Lothian Buses** ☎ 0131/555-6363. **Sleigh Ltd.** ✉ 6 Devon Pl., West End ☎ 0131/337-3171.

TRANSFERS FROM GLASGOW AIRPORT

Scottish Citylink buses leave Glasgow Airport every 15 minutes to travel to Glasgow's Buchanan Street (journey time is 25 minutes), where you can transfer to an Edinburgh bus (leaving every 20 minutes). The trip to Edinburgh takes 70 minutes and costs £7 round-trip and £4.50 one-way. A somewhat more pleasant option is to take a cab from Glasgow Airport to Glasgow's Queen Street train station (lasts 20 minutes and costs about £15) and then take the train to Waverley Station in Edinburgh. Trains leave about every 30 minutes; the trip takes 50 minutes and costs £7.30. Check times on weekends. Another, less expensive alternative—best for those with little luggage—is to take the bus from Glasgow Airport to Glasgow's Buchanan bus station, walk five minutes to the Queen Street train station, and catch the train to Edinburgh. Taxis from Glasgow Airport to downtown Edinburgh take about 70 minutes and cost around £90.

Scottish Citylink ☎ 08705/505050 🌐 www.citylink.co.uk. **Taxis** ☎ 0141/848-4900.

BUS TRAVEL

National Express provides bus service to and from London and other major towns and cities. The main terminal, St. Andrew Square bus station, is only a couple of minutes (on foot) north of Waverley station, immediately east of St. Andrew Square. Long-distance coaches must be booked in advance from the booking office in the terminal. Edinburgh is approximately eight hours by bus from London.

First Lowland provides much of the service between Edinburgh and the Lothians and conducts day tours around and beyond the city. First Bus Company also runs buses out of Edinburgh into the surrounding area.

First Bus Company ☎ 0131/663-1945. **First Lowland** ☎ 08706/082608. **National Express** ☎ 08705/808080 🌐 www.nationalexpress.co.uk.

BUS TRAVEL WITHIN EDINBURGH

Lothian Buses is the main operator within Edinburgh. You can buy tickets on the bus. The Bargain Day Ticket (£2.50), allowing unlimited one-day travel on the city's buses, can be purchased in advance or from the driver on any Lothian bus (exact fare is required when purchasing on a bus). The Rider Card (for which you will need a photo) is valid on all buses for seven days (Sunday through Saturday night) and costs £11; the four-week Rider costs £33.

Lothian Buses ✉ Waverley Bridge, Old Town ☎ 0131/555-6363 or 0131/554-4494 🌐 www.lothian-buses.co.uk.

CAR RENTAL

Major companies have booths at the airport. Rates start at about £48 per day. If you choose to plunge yourself into Edinburgh's traffic system, take care on the first couple of traffic circles (called roundabouts) you encounter on the way into town from the airport—even the most experienced drivers find them challenging. By car the airport is about

7 mi west of Princes Street downtown and is clearly marked from A8. The usual route to downtown is via the suburb of Corstorphine.

Agencies **Avis** ☎ 0131/333-1866. **Europcar** ☎ 0131/333-32588. **Hertz** ☎ 0131/333-1019. **National Car Rentals** ☎ 0131/333-1922.

CAR TRAVEL

Downtown Edinburgh centers on Princes Street, which runs east–west and is closed to all but taxis and buses for most of its length. If you're driving from the east coast you'll come in on A1, with Meadowbank Stadium serving as a landmark. The highway bypasses the suburbs of Musselburgh and Tranent; therefore, any bottlenecks will occur close to downtown. From the Borders the approach to Princes Street is by A7/A68 through Newington. From Newington the east end of Princes Street is reached by North Bridge and South Bridge. Approaching from the southwest, you'll join the west end of Princes Street (Lothian Road) via A701 and A702; if you're coming west from Glasgow or Stirling you'll meet Princes Street from M8 or M9, respectively. A slightly more complicated approach is via M90—from Forth Road Bridge/Perth/east coast; the key road for getting downtown is Queensferry Road, which joins Charlotte Square close to the west end of Princes Street.

Driving in Edinburgh has its quirks and pitfalls, but competent drivers should not be intimidated. Metered parking in the city center is scarce and expensive, and the local traffic wardens are a feisty, alert bunch. Note that illegally parked cars are routinely towed away, and getting your car back will be expensive. After 6 PM the parking situation improves considerably, and you may manage to find a space quite near your hotel, even downtown. If you park on a yellow line or in a resident's parking bay, be prepared to move your car by 8 the following morning, when the rush hour gets under way. Parking lots are clearly signposted; overnight parking is expensive and not permitted in all lots.

CONSULATES

The London office of the Canadian High Commission can provide local information for visitors.

Canada **Canadian High Commission** ☎ 0207/258-6600.

United States **American Consulate General** ✉ 3 Regent Terr., Calton ☎ 0131/556-8315.

EMERGENCIES

In an emergency dial **999** for an ambulance or for the police or fire departments (no coins are needed for emergency calls made from pay phones). The accident and emergency department of Edinburgh Royal Infirmary is at Lauriston Place in the city center, though the main buildings are 6 mi to the southeast in an area known as Little France.

You can find out which pharmacy is open late on a given night by looking at the notice posted on every pharmacy door. A pharmacy—or dispensing chemist, as it is called here—is easily identified by its sign, showing a green cross on a white background. Boots is open weekdays from 8 AM to 9 PM, Saturday form 8 to 6, and Sunday from 10:30 to 4:30.

To retrieve lost property, try the Lothian and Borders police headquarters, open weekdays from 9 to 5. If you lose something on a public bus, contact Lothian Buses, open weekdays from 10 to 1:30.

Hospital **Edinburgh Royal Infirmary** ✉ Dalkeith Rd., Little France ✉ Accident and Emergency, Lauriston Place, Old Town ☎ 0131/536-1000.

Late-Night Pharmacy **Boots** ✉ 48 Shandwick Pl., west end of Princes St., West End ☎ 0131/225-6757.

Lost & Found **Lothian and Borders police headquarters** ✉ Fettes Ave., Inverleith. ☎ 0131/311-3131.**Lothian Buses** ✉ 55 Annandale St., New Town ☎ 0131/558-8858.

MAIL & SHIPPING

The post office in St. James Centre is the most central and is open Monday from 9 to 5:30, Tuesday through Friday from 8:30 to 5:30, and Saturday from 8:30 to 6. There are two other main post offices in the city center. Many newsagents also sell stamps.

Post Offices **City Center post offices** ✉ 40 Frederick St., New Town ☎ 0845/722-3344 ✉ 7 Hope St., West End ☎ 0131/226-6823 **St. James Centre** ✉ St. Andrew Sq., East End ☎ 0845/722-3344.

MONEY MATTERS

Most city-center banks have a bureau de change (usual banking hours are weekdays from 9:30 to 4:45). The bureau de change at the Tourist Centre, Princes Mall, is open daily. There are also bureaux de change at Waverley Station, Edinburgh Airport, and Frasers department store, at the west end of Princes Street.

SIGHTSEEING TOURS

ORIENTATION TOURS

The best way to get oriented in Edinburgh is to take a bus tour, most of which are operated by Lothian Buses. City Sightseeing open-top bus tours (£7.50) include multi-lingual commentary; MacTours (£8) are conducted in vintage open-top buses. All tours take you to the main attractions, including Edinburgh Castle, the Royal Mile, Palace of Holyroodhouse, city museums and galleries, and the Old and New towns. They depart from Waverley Bridge, and are hop on/hop off services, with tickets lasting 24 hours. The 80-minute Britannia Tour (£8) operates with a professional guide, and takes you from Waverly Bridge to the New Town, past Charlotte Square, art galleries, the Royal Botanic Garden, and Newhaven Heritage Museum, until it reaches the Royal Yacht Britannia moored at Leith. Tickets for all tours are available from ticket sellers on Waverley Bridge or on the buses themselves.

Lothian Buses ☎ 0131/555-6363 🌐 www.edinburghtour.com.

PERSONAL GUIDES

Scottish Tourist Guides can supply guides (in 19 languages) who are fully qualified and will meet clients at any point of entry into the United Kingdom or Scotland. They can also tailor tours to your interests.

Scottish Tourist Guides contact Doreen Boyle ✉ Old Jail, St. John St., Stirling FK8 1EA ☎ 01786/451953.

WALKING TOURS

Cadies and Witchery Tours, a fully qualified member of the Scottish Tourist Guides Association, has built a reputation for combining entertainment and historical accuracy in its lively and enthusiastic Ghosts & Gore Tour and Murder & Mystery Tour (£7 each), which take you through the narrow Old Town alleyways and closes, with costumed guides and other theatrical characters showing up en route.

Cadies and Witchery Tours ✉ 537 Castlehill, Old Town ☎ 0131/225-6745 🌐 www.witcherytours.com.

TAXIS

Taxi stands can be found throughout the downtown area. The following are the most convenient: the west end of Princes Street; South St. David Street, and North St. Andrew Street (both just off St. Andrew Square); Princes Mall; Waterloo Place; and Lauriston Place. Alternatively, hail any taxi displaying an illuminated FOR HIRE sign.

TRAIN TRAVEL

Edinburgh's main train hub, Waverley Station, is downtown, below Waverley Bridge and around the corner from the unmistakable spire of the

Scott Monument. Travel time from Edinburgh to London by train is as little as 4½ hours for the fastest service.

Edinburgh's other main station is Haymarket, about four minutes (by rail) west of Waverley. Most Glasgow and other western and northern services stop here. Haymarket can be more convenient if you're staying in hotels beyond the west end of Princes Street.

National Train ☎ 08457/484950.

TRAVEL AGENTS

Local Agent Referrals **American Express** ✉ 139 Princes St., West End ☎ 0131/718-2505.

VISITOR INFORMATION

Several excellent city maps are available at bookstores. Particularly recommended is the *Bartholomew Edinburgh Plan,* with a scale of approximately 4 inches to 1 mi, by the long-established Edinburgh cartographic company John Bartholomew and Sons, Ltd.

The Edinburgh and Scotland Information Centre, adjacent to Waverley Station (follow the TIC signs in the station and throughout the city), offers an accommodations service (Book-A-Bed-Ahead) in addition to the more typical services. It's open May though June and September, from Monday to Saturday 9 to 7, Sunday 10 to 7; July and August, from Monday to Saturday 9 to 8, Sunday 10 to 8; October and April, from Monday to Saturday 9 to 6, Sunday 10 to 6; November through March, from Monday to Wednesday 9 to 5, from Thursday to Saturday 9 to 6, Sunday 10 to 5.

Complete information is also available at the information desk at the Edinburgh Airport.

The *List,* a publication available from city-center bookstores and newsstands, and the *Day by Day Guide* and *Events 2004,* from the Edinburgh and Scotland Information Centre, list information about all types of events, from movies and theater to sports. The *Herald* and *Scotsman* newspapers are good for reviews and notices of upcoming events throughout Scotland.

Edinburgh and Scotland Information Centre ✉ 3 Princes St., East End ☎ 0131/473-3800 📠 0131/473-3881 🌐 www.edinburgh.org.

GLASGOW

2

FODOR'S CHOICE

Ambassador Hotel, *in the West End*
Burrell Collection, *on the South Side*
City Chambers, *in the City Center*
Fratelli Sarti Restaurant, *in the City Center*
Manor Park Hotel, *in the West End*
Mussel Inn Restaurant, *in the City Center*
Radisson SAS, *in the City Center*
Rogano Restaurant, *in the City Center*

HIGHLY RECOMMENDED

RESTAURANTS

Amaryllis, *in the West End*
Café Cossachok, *in the Glasgow Cross area*
Café Gandolfi, *in Merchant City*
Fouter's Bistro, *in Ayr*
Fratelli Sarti, *in the City Center*
Gordon Yuill and Company, *in the City Center*
MacCallums Oyster Bar, *in Troon*

HOTELS

ArtHouse Hotel, *in the City Center*
Langs Hotel, *in the City Center*
Makerston Guest House, *in Paisley*
One Devonshire Gardens, *in the West End*

SIGHTS

Culzean Castle & Country Park, *in Ayrshire*
Glasgow Cathedral, *in the City Center*
Glasgow School of Art, *in the City Center*
Hunterian Art Gallery, *in the West End*
McLellan Galleries, *in the City Center*
Paisley Museum & Art Gallery, *in Paisley*
St. Mungo Museum of Religious Life and Art, *in the City Center*
Burrell Museum

SHOPPING

De Courcys, *in the West End*

ARTS

Citizens' Theatre, *on the South Side*

NIGHTLIFE

Uisge Beatha, *in the West End*

By John Hutchinson
Updated by Shona Main

IN THE DAYS WHEN BRITAIN still ruled over an empire, Glasgow pronounced itself the Second City of the Empire. Its people were justifiably proud of Glasgow, as it was here that Britain's great steamships, including the 80,000-ton *Queen Elizabeth,* were built. The term "Clyde-built" (from Glasgow's River Clyde) became synonymous with good workmanship and lasting quality. Scots engineers were to be found wherever there were engines—Glaswegians built the railway locomotives that opened up the Canadian prairies, the South African veldt, the Australian plains, and the Indian subcontinent. The world's greatest industrial and scientific thinkers, such as Lord Kelvin and James Watt, tested their groundbreaking theories and discoveries as young men in Glasgow.

A 16th-century traveler described Glasgow as "a flourishing cathedral city reminiscent of the beautiful fabrics and florid fields of England." Daniel Defoe in 1727 described it as "one of the cleanliest and most beautiful and best-built of cities." Massive industrialization in the 19th century, however, was soon to create a Glasgow less clean and less beautiful.

Stretching along the heavily industrialized banks of the River Clyde, Glasgow had fallen into a severely depressed state by the early 20th century. By the middle of the century its dockland slums were notorious seedbeds of inner-city decay. "All Glasgow needs," said an architecture pundit then, "is a bath and a little loving care." During the last two decades of the 20th century, happily, the city received both. Modern Glasgow has undergone an urban renaissance: trendy downtown stores, a booming and diverse cultural life, stylish restaurants, and an air of confidence make it Scotland's most exciting city.

The city's development has been unashamedly commercial, tied up with the wealth of its manufacturers and merchants, who constructed a vast number of civic buildings throughout the 19th century. Among those who helped shape Glasgow's unique Victorian cityscape during that great period of civic expansion was the local-born architect Alexander "Greek" Thomson (1817–75). Side by side with the overly Victorian, Glasgow had an architectural vision of the future in the work of Charles Rennie Mackintosh (1868–1928). The Glasgow School of Art, the Willow Tearoom, the *Glasgow Herald* building (now home to the Lighthouse architecture and design center), and the churches and schools he designed point clearly to the clarity and simplicity of the best of 20th-century design.

Glasgow first came into prominence in Scottish history somewhere around 1,400 years ago, and typically for this rambunctious city it all had to do with an argument between a husband and wife. When the king of Strathclyde gave his wife a ring, she was rash enough to present it to an admirer. The king, having surreptitiously repossessed it, threw it into the Clyde before quizzing his wife about its disappearance. In her distress, the queen turned to her confessor, St. Mungo, for advice. He instructed her to fish in the river and—surprise—the first salmon she landed had the ring in its jaws. Glasgow's coat of arms is dominated by three salmon, one with a ring in its mouth. Not surprisingly, Mungo became the city's patron saint. His tomb lies in the mighty medieval cathedral that bears his name.

Glasgow flourished quietly during the Middle Ages. Its cathedral was the center of religious life, its university a center of serious academia. Although the city was made a burgh (i.e., granted trading rights) in 1175 by King William the Lion, its population never numbered more than a few thousand people. What changed Glasgow irrevocably was the Treaty of Union between Scotland and England, in 1707, which allowed Scotland to trade with the essentially English colonies in America. Glasgow,

To take advantage of Glasgow's wealth of cultural sites and shopping, you could easily spend four or five days here, but it is possible to see the city's greatest hits in only two days.

If you have 2 days On the first day explore the core of historic Glasgow—the medieval area, dominated by Glasgow's cathedral, and Merchant City. Shoppers should head for Buchanan Street, including the Princes Square development and the Buchanan Galleries. Art lovers should make a bee-line to the Burrell Collection in Pollock Country Park on the South Side. On the second day, see the West End, including the artwork and Charles Rennie Mackintosh furniture at the Hunterian Art Gallery. If you haven't yet seen the city-center parks, venture to Glasgow Green, the art collections at Pollok Country Park, or the House for an Art Lover, at Bellahouston Park. Remember that Glasgow's pubs and clubs serve up entertainment until late in the evening.

If you have 5 days Five days will allow enough time to enjoy more of Glasgow's key museums and cultural attractions: the Glasgow Gallery of Modern Art, the Centre for Contemporary Arts, and the McLellan Galleries, in the city center; or the St. Mungo Museum of Religious Life and Art, to the east. You could easily take a full day to see the cluster of West End museums by Kelvingrove Park (Hunterian Art Gallery and Hunterian Museum, and the Museum of Transport). For a good day trip take the hour-long train ride to Wemyss Bay, and from there take the ferry to the Isle of Bute, where you can visit Mount Stuart, a spectacular, stately Victorian home.

If you have 10 days In 10 days you can thoroughly explore all the museums (you may want to visit the Burrell Collection more than once), and do some shopping in Princes Square and on Buchanan Street, Sauchiehall Street, and Argyle Street. Forego one or two museums and a day of shopping, however, for at least one side trip. You need two or three days to see everything in Ayrshire and on the Clyde Coast, including Mount Stuart House, on the Isle of Bute; Ayr and Alloway, which will delight Robert Burns enthusiasts; and the cliff-top Culzean Castle, whose Georgian elegance provides sharp contrast to the Victorian Gothic spirit of Mount Stuart. Travel up the Clyde Valley for a morning spent at New Lanark and for a walk along the waterfall-dotted River Clyde. Biggar will fill an afternoon or more with its fascinating museums, including Moat Park, which has a fine embroidery collection.

---

with its advantageous position on Scotland's west coast, prospered. In came cotton, tobacco, and rum; out went various Scottish manufactured goods and clothing. The key to it all was tobacco. The prosperous merchants known as tobacco lords ran the city, and their wealth laid the foundation for the manufacturing industries of the 19th century.

As Glasgow prospered, its population grew. The "dear green place" (the literal meaning of the Gaelic *Glas Cu,* from which the name "Glasgow" purportedly derives) expanded beyond recognition, extending westward and to the south of the original medieval city, which centered around the cathedral and High Street. The 18th-century Merchant City, now largely rejuvenated, lies just to the south and east of George Square, where all but a few of the original merchants' houses remain in their original condition. As the merchants moved to quieter areas in the west of the city, the beaux arts elegance of their mansions and quiet streets gave way to larger municipal buildings and commercial warehouses. During the 19th century the population grew from 80,000 to more than 1 million, and along with this enormous growth there developed a sense of exuberance and confidence that's still reflected in the city's public buildings. The City Chambers, built in 1888, are a proud statement in marble and gold sandstone, a clear symbol of the wealthy and powerful Victorian industrialists' hopes for the future.

Today, as always, Glasgow's eye is trained on the future. The city is Scotland's major business destination, with the Scottish Exhibition and Conference Centre serving as the hub of activity. It is also is a nexus of rail routes and motorways that can deliver you in less than an hour to Edinburgh, Stirling, Loch Lomond, the Burns Country, and the Clyde coast golfing resorts. Still, Glasgow has learned to take the best of its past and adapt it for the needs of the present day. The dear green places still remain in the city-center parks; the medieval cathedral stands proud, as it has done for 800 years; the Merchant City is revived and thriving; the Victorian splendor has been cleansed of its grime; and the cultural legacy of museums and performing arts is stronger than ever.

EXPLORING GLASGOW

Glasgow's layout is hard to read in a single glance. The city center is the area roughly defined by the M8 motorway to the north and west, the River Clyde to the south, and Glasgow Cathedral and High Street to the east. The center is relatively flat and compact, making it easy to walk around Glasgow Cathedral and Provand's Lordship, High Street, and the Merchant City. In fact, Glaswegians tend to walk a good deal, and the streets, most of which follow a grid plan, are designed for pedestrians. Good street maps are available from bookstores and the helpful Greater Glasgow and Clyde Valley Tourist Board. If you do get lost, though, just ask a local for help. Most people will be more than happy to help you find your way. The streets are also relatively safe, even at night.

The River Clyde, on which Glasgow's trade across the Atlantic developed, runs through the center of the city—literally cutting it in two and offering intriguing views of South Side buildings. In Glasgow always look up: your reward is much ornate detailing visible above eye level.

In the quieter, slightly hillier western part of the city is Glasgow University and the often forgotten bohemian side of Glasgow. Some form of transportation is required to go to either the West End or the South Side, and you should have no qualms in using Glasgow's well-planned, integrated transport network of buses, subways, and trains. Information about all options is available from Strathclyde Passenger Transport (SPT) Travel Centre.

Numbers in the text correspond to numbers in the margin and on the Glasgow and Glasgow Excursions: Ayrshire and the Clyde Valley maps.

Medieval Glasgow & the Merchant City

In this central part of the city, alongside the relatively few surviving medieval buildings, are some of the best examples of the architectural confidence and exuberance that so characterized the burgeoning Glasgow of the turn of the 20th century.

Architecture

The aspiring Victorians, including Alexander "Greek" Thomson, bequeathed Glasgow a solid legacy of striking buildings with artistic appeal, and architectural innovation continued into the 20th century with the erection of such buildings as Charles Rennie Mackintosh's Glasgow School of Art and Norman Foster's Clyde Auditorium. Glasgow's buildings manifest the city's enduring love of grand artistic statements.

Cafés & Tearooms

In the Victorian tradition, while men went to pubs, Glasgow women's social interaction would take place in the city's many tearooms and cafés. Today *everyone* goes to the café. Glaswegians have succumbed to the world-wide love for Italian-style, espresso-based coffees, but they'll never give up the comfort of a nice cup of tea, so you'll find both at most tearooms, along with scones, Scottish pancakes, other pastries, and light lunch fare like sandwiches and soup.

Shopping

Glaswegians love to dress up, and you'll find the mark of the fashion industry on the city center's hottest shopping streets, Buchanan and Sauchiehall, as well as in Princes Square. Glasgow is the biggest and most popular U.K. retail center outside of London. Besides straight-off-the-runway couture, Glasgow has an impressive number of antiques stores, and Scottish specialty shops selling woolen, cashmere, and tartan dress.

---

a good walk

George Square (1), the focal point of Glasgow's business district, is the natural starting point. It's in the very heart of the city and is convenient to the Buchanan Street bus and underground stations and parking lot, as well as the two main railway stations, Queen Street and Glasgow Central. After viewing the **City Chambers** (2), on the square's east side, leave by the northeast corner and head east through a not particularly pretty part of the city along George Street, past Strathclyde University. Turn left at High Street, then go up the hill to **Glasgow Cathedral** (3), the **St. Mungo Museum of Religious Life and Art** (4), and the fascinating if macabre **Necropolis** (5), just off Cathedral Square.

Opposite the cathedral, across Castle Street, stands **Provand's Lordship** (6), Glasgow's oldest house. Retrace your steps down Castle Street and walk south down High Street. Look for the Greek goddess Pallas atop the imposing gray-sandstone building on the right, the former Bank of Scotland, before reaching the Tolbooth Steeple at **Glasgow Cross** (7). Continue southeast along London Road (under the bridge) about a quarter of a mile, and you'll come to the **Barras** (8), Scotland's largest indoor market. Turn right down Greendyke Street from London Road to reach **Glasgow Green** (9) by the River Clyde, with the **People's Palace** (10) museum of social history as its centerpiece.

Take the walkway west through Glasgow Green to the prominent McLennan Arch, and then head northeast via Saltmarket toward Tolbooth Steeple. Continue westward along Trongate. On the right is Candleriggs, which leads through to the ancient Ramshorn Church cemetery, where, among the opulent tombstones, are those of Glasgow's rich merchants. On the left, jutting out into Trongate, is the Tron Steeple, all that remains of a church burned down in 1793 when a joke by the

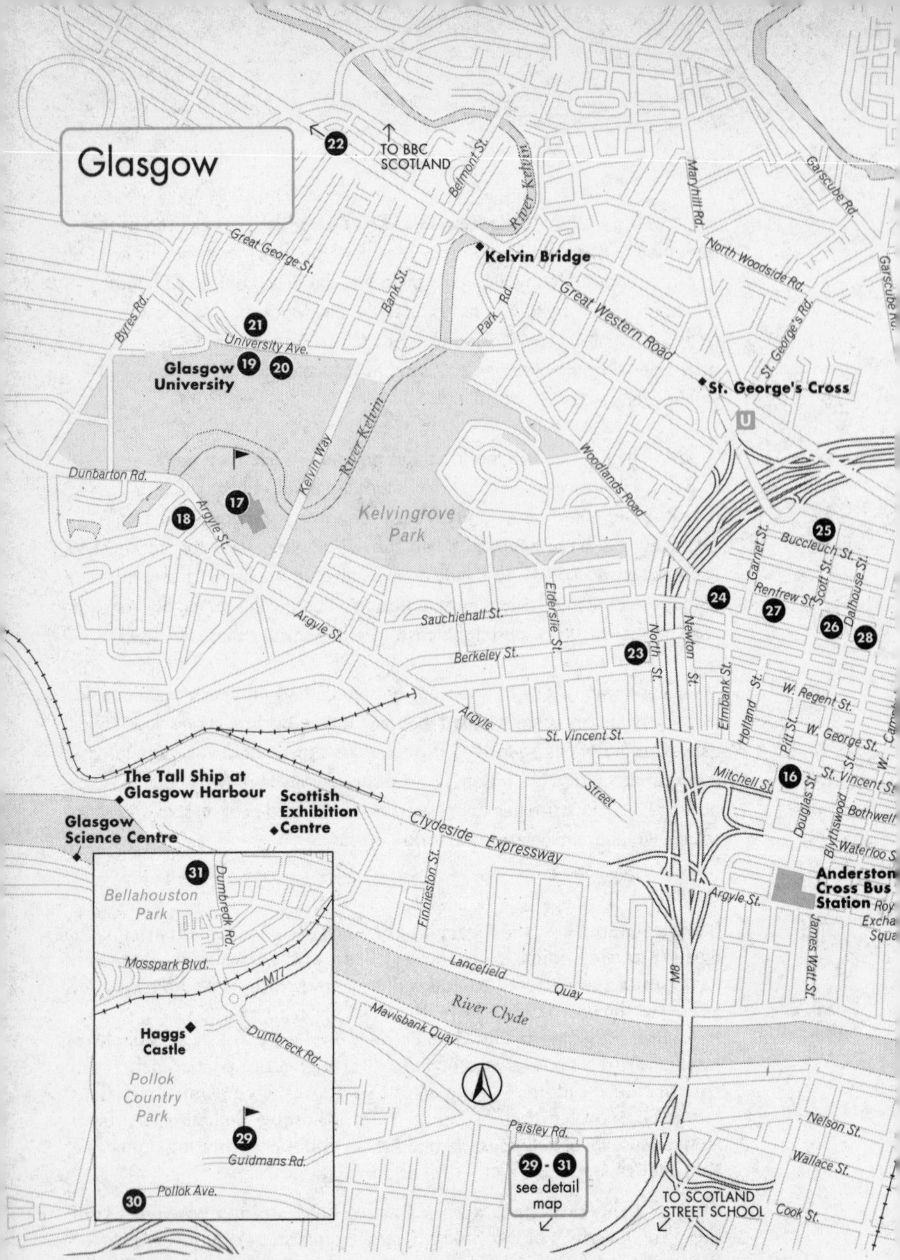

Barras 8
Botanic Gardens 22
Burrell Collection 29
Central Station 15
Center for Contemporary Arts 27
City Chambers 2
George Square 1
Glasgow Art Gallery and Museum, Kelvingrove 17
Glasgow Cathedral 3
Glasgow Cross 7
Glasgow Gallery of Modern Art 13
Glasgow Green 9
Glasgow School of Art 26
Glasgow University 19
House for an Art Lover 31
Hunterian Art Gallery 21

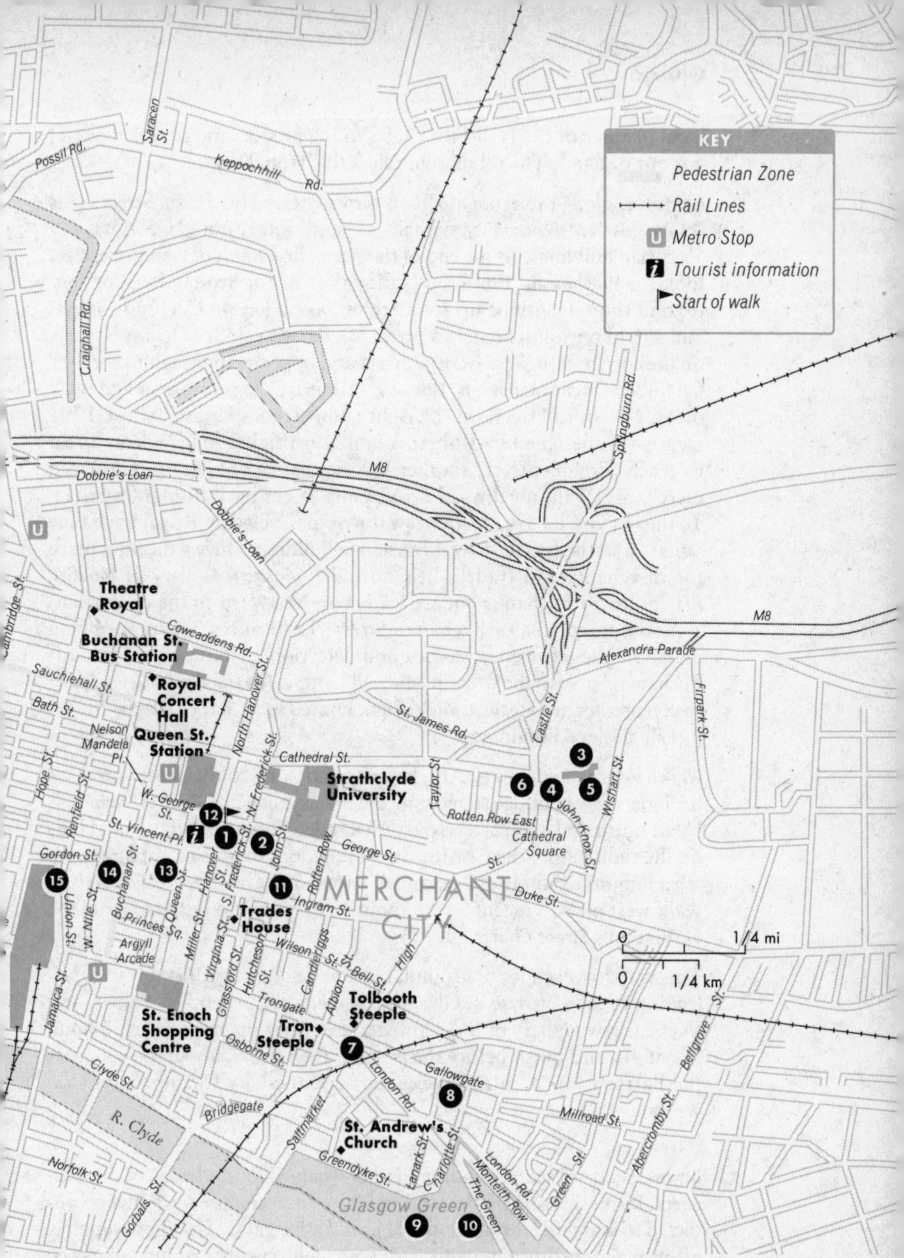
KEY
Pedestrian Zone
Rail Lines
Metro Stop
Tourist information
Start of walk
Possil Rd.
Saracen St.
Keppochhill Rd.
Craighall Rd.
Springburn Rd.
M8
Dobbie's Loan
Theatre Royal
Buchanan St. Bus Station
Cowcaddens Rd.
Royal Concert Hall
Queen St. Station
Nelson Mandela Pl.
Sauchiehall St.
Bath St.
Cambridge St.
North Hanover St.
N. Frederick St.
Cathedral St.
Strathclyde University
St. James Rd.
Castle St.
Alexandra Parade
Firpark St.
Wishart St.
Taylor St.
Rotten Row East
John Knox St.
Cathedral Square
W. George St.
St. Vincent Pl.
Hope St.
Renfield St.
Gordon St.
George St.
Duke St.
MERCHANT CITY
Ingram St.
Trades House
Wilson St.
Bell St.
Union St.
W. Nile St.
Buchanan St.
Queen St.
Princes Sq.
Argyll Arcade
Miller St.
Virginia St.
Glassford St.
Hutcheson St.
Candleriggs
Albion St.
High St.
Rotten Row
John St.
Frederick St.
Hanover St.
Tolbooth Steeple
Tron Steeple
Trongate
St. Enoch Shopping Centre
Jamaica St.
Osborne St.
Clyde St.
R. Clyde
Bridgegate
Saltmarket
London Rd.
Gallowgate
Millroad St.
St. Andrew's Church
Greendyke St.
Lanark St.
Charlotte St.
Monteith Row
The Green
Glasgow Green
Norfolk St.
Gorbals St.
Green St.
Abercromby St.
Bellgrove St.
1/4 mi
1/4 km
1
2
3
4
5
6
7
8
9
10
11
12
13
14
15

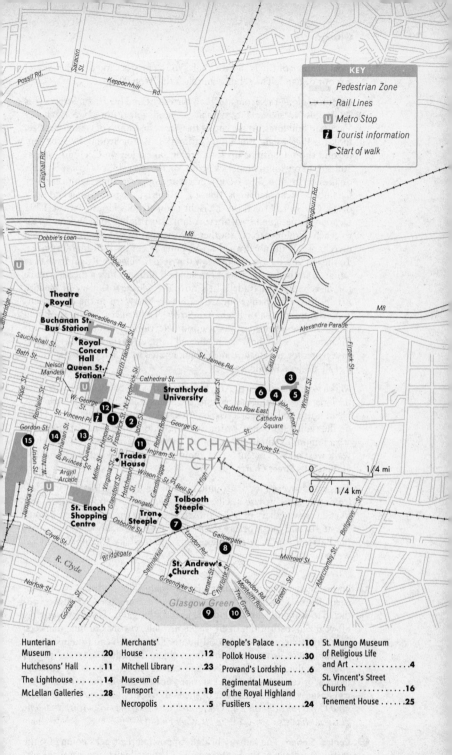

local chapter of the Hell-Fire Club (young aristocratic troublemakers) got out of hand. The rebuilt church is the Tron Theatre.

Continue along the Trongate, then turn right on Hutcheson Street. This is Glasgow's **Merchant City,** with many handsome restored Georgian and Victorian buildings. At the end of the street, just south of George Square, look for **Hutchesons' Hall** 11, a National Trust for Scotland visitor center and shop. Continue up John Street, take a left on Cochrane Street, and a right on South Frederick Street; on the west side of George Square, on the corner with West George Street and opposite the magnificent City Chambers, is the **Merchants' House** 12. Return to Ingram Street and walk down Glassford Street; on the right is the Trades House, whose 1791 facade was designed by Robert Adam. Turn right along Wilson Street to reach Virginia Street, another favorite haunt of Glasgow's tobacco merchants. Walk northward up Virginia Street back to Ingram Street. To the left you'll have a good view down to the elegant Royal Exchange Square and the former Royal Exchange building. Once a meeting place for merchants and traders, it's now the **Glasgow Gallery of Modern Art** 13. Royal Exchange Square leads you westward to the pedestrian-zone shopping area of Buchanan Street. The Princes Square shopping mall, on the east side, has a good selection of boutiques. Just off Buchanan Street to the west, in Mitchell Lane, is **The Lighthouse** 14, a showcase center for architecture and design, housed in a Charles Rennie Mackintosh–designed building.

Make your way down to Argyle Street. Looking to the west, you'll see the large railway bridge supporting the tracks going into **Central Station** 15. Head north up Union Street, past Alexander Thomson's Egyptian Halls on the right before the Gordon Street junction, to St. Vincent Street. To see a famous example of Alexander Thomson's Greek revival churches, walk west on St. Vincent Street about eight blocks to Pitt Street and the **St. Vincent's Street Church** 16.

TIMING This walk covers a lot of ground, but can be done comfortably in a day, leaving time to browse in Glasgow Cathedral, the People's Palace, and the Glasgow Gallery of Modern Art. Start after the morning rush hour, say at 10, and finish before the evening rush starts, about 4. Note that the Barras is open only on weekends and the City Chambers only on weekdays.

What to See

8 **Barras.** Scotland's largest indoor market—named for the barrows, or push-carts, formerly used by the stall holders—is a must-see for anyone addicted to searching through piles of junk for bargains. The approximately 80-year-old institution, open weekends only, consists of nine markets. The atmosphere is always good-humored, and you can find just about anything here, in any condition, from old model railroads to quality jewelry. Haggling is compulsory! You can reach the Barras by walking from ScotRail's Argyle Street station, or take any of the various buses to Glasgow Cross at the foot of the Gallowgate. ✉ *¼ mi east of Glasgow Cross on London Rd., Glasgow Cross* ☎ *0141/552–4601* 🌐 *www.glasgow-barras.com* *Free* ⏲ *Weekends 10–5.*

15 **Central Station.** The railway bridge supporting the tracks going into the station is known as the Highlandman's Umbrella because it was the traditional gathering place for immigrant Highlanders looking for work in Glasgow in the early 20th century. The depot is the main station for trains to England and the Ayrshire coast and has interesting shops. ✉ *Bounded by Gordon, Union, Argyle, Jamaica, Clyde, Oswald, and Hope Sts., City Center.*

Fodor's Choice ★

2 **City Chambers.** Dominating the east side of George Square, this exuberant expression of Victorian confidence, built by William Young in Italian Renaissance style, was opened by Queen Victoria (1819–1901) in 1888. Among the interior's outstanding features are the entrance hall's vaulted ceiling, the marble-and-alabaster staircases, the banqueting hall, and Venetian mosaics. The debating chamber has gleaming oak panels and fixtures. Free guided tours depart weekdays at 10:30 and 2:30. Note that the building is closed to visitors, and the tours canceled, during occasional civic functions. ✉ *George Sq., City Center* ☎ *0141/287–2000* 🌐 *www.glasgow.gov.uk* 🎫 *Free* ⏱ *Weekdays 9–4:30.*

1 **George Square.** The focal point of Glasgow's business district is lined with an impressive collection of statues of worthies: Queen Victoria; Scotland's national poet, Robert Burns (1759–96); the inventor and developer of the steam engine, James Watt (1736–1819); Prime Minister William Gladstone (1809–98); and towering above them all, Scotland's great historical novelist, Sir Walter Scott (1771–1832). The column was intended for George III (1738–1820), after whom the square is named, but when he was found to be insane toward the end of his reign, his statue was never erected. On the square's east side stands the magnificent Italian Renaissance–style ⇨ **City Chambers**; the handsome ⇨ **Merchants' House** fills the corner with West George Street.

Off and around George Square, several streets—Virginia Street, Miller Street, Glassford Street—recall the yesterdays of mercantile wealth. The French-style palaces, with their steep mansard roofs and cupolas, were once tobacco warehouses. Inside them are shops and offices; here and there you may trace the elaborately carved mahogany galleries where auctions once took place. ✉ *Between St. Vincent and Argyle Sts., City Center.*

★ 3 **Glasgow Cathedral.** The most complete of Scotland's cathedrals (it would have been more complete had 19th-century vandals not pulled down its two rugged towers), this is an unusual double church, one above the other, dedicated to Glasgow's patron saint, St. Mungo. Begun in the 12th century, consecrated in 1136, and completed about 300 years later, it was spared the ravages of the Reformation—which destroyed so many of Scotland's medieval churches—mainly because Glasgow's trade guilds defended it. In the lower church is the splendid crypt of St. Mungo, who was originally known as St. Kentigern (*kentigern* means "chief word,") but who was nicknamed St. Mungo (meaning "dear one") by his early followers in Glasgow. The site of the tomb has been revered since the 6th century, when St. Mungo founded a church here. Mungo features prominently in local legends; one such legend is about a pet bird that he nursed back to life, and another tells of a bush or tree, the branches of which he used to miraculously relight a fire. Tree, bird, and the salmon with a ring in its mouth (from the famous tale related in the introduction) are all to be found on the city of Glasgow's coat of arms, together with a bell that Mungo brought from Rome. ✉ *Cathedral St., City Center* ☎ *0141/552–6891* 🌐 *www.glasgowcathedral.org.uk* 🎫 *Free* ⏱ *Apr.–Sept., Mon.–Sat. 9:30–6, Sun. 1–5; Oct.–Mar., Mon.–Sat. 9:30–4, Sun. 1–4 and for services.*

7 **Glasgow Cross.** This crossroads was the center of the medieval city. The Mercat Cross (*mercat* means "market"), topped by a unicorn, marks the spot where merchants met, where the market was held, and where criminals were executed. Here, too, was the *tron,* or weigh beam, installed in 1491 and used by merchants to check weights. The Tolbooth Steeple dates from 1626 and served as the civic center and the place where travelers paid tolls. ✉ *Intersection of Saltmarket, Trongate, Gallowgate, and London Rd., Glasgow Cross.*

need a break?

Café Cossachok (✉ 10 King St., Glasgow Cross ☎ 0141/553–0733) is a colorful Russian café serving excellent borscht and about 25 kinds of heartwarming of vodka. The deep-red walls are peppered with artworks and the low buzz of conversation keeps the place lively.

13 **Glasgow Gallery of Modern Art.** One of Glasgow's boldest galleries occupies the former Royal Exchange building. The Exchange, designed by David Hamilton (1768–1843) and finished in 1829, was a meeting place for merchants and traders; later it became Stirling's Library. It incorporates the mansion built in 1780 by William Cunninghame, one of the wealthiest tobacco lords. The modern art, craft, and design collections contained within this handsome building include works by Scottish conceptual artists such as David Mach, and also paintings and sculpture from around the world, including Papua New Guinea, Ethiopia, and Mexico. The display scheme is designed for each floor to reflect the elements—air, fire, and water—which creates some unexpected juxtapositions and also allows for various interactive exhibits. ✉ *Queen St., City Center* ☎ *0141/229–1996* 🎫 *Free* ⏲ *Mon.–Thurs. and Sat. 10–5, Fri. and Sun. 11–5.*

9 **Glasgow Green.** Glasgow's oldest park, on the northeast side of the River Clyde, has a long history as a favorite spot for public recreation and political demonstrations. Note the Nelson Column, erected long before London's; the McLennan Arch, originally part of the facade of the old Assembly Halls in Ingram Street; and the Templeton Business Centre, a former carpet factory built in the late 19th century in the style of the Doge's Palace in Venice. The most significant building in the park is the **People's Palace.** ✉ *Between Greendyke St. to the north and the River Clyde to the south, and between the Green to the east and Saltmarket to the west, Glasgow Cross.*

11 **Hutchesons' Hall.** Now a visitor center and shop for the National Trust for Scotland, this elegant neoclassical building was designed by David Hamilton in 1802. The hall was originally a hospice founded by two brothers, George and Thomas Hutcheson; you can see their statues in niches in the facade. ✉ *158 Ingram St., Merchant City* ☎ *0141/552–8591* 🌐 *www.nts.org.uk* 🎫 *£2* ⏲ *Mon.–Sat. 10–5.*

14 **The Lighthouse.** Charles Rennie Mackintosh designed these former offices of the *Glasgow Herald* newspaper in 1893. Mackintosh's building now serves as a fitting setting for Scotland's **Centre for Architecture, Design and the City,** which celebrates all facets of the architectural profession. The **Mackintosh Interpretation Centre** is a great starting point for discovering more about his other buildings in the city. Inside the building, the helical staircase provides an interesting view of an external gallery below. ✉ *11 Mitchell La., City Center* ☎ *0141/225–8414* 🌐 *www.thelighthouse.co.uk* 🎫 *£2.50 for Mackintosh Interpretation Centre; £1 for temporary exhibitions* ⏲ *Mon. and Wed.–Sat. 10:30–5; Tues. 11–5; Sun. noon–5.*

Merchant City. Among the preserved Georgian and Victorian buildings of this city-center neighborhood are many elegant designer boutiques. The **City and County buildings,** on Ingram Street, were built in 1842 to house civil servants; note the impressive arrangement of bays and Corinthian columns. To see more interesting architecture, explore the roads off of Ingram Street—including Candleriggs, Wilson, and Glassford. ✉ *Between George St. to the north and Argyle St. to the south, and between Buchanan St. to the west and High St. to the east.*

⓬ **Merchants' House.** A golden sailing ship, a reminder of the importance of sea trade to Glasgow's prosperity, tops this handsome 1874 Victorian building, home to Glasgow's chamber of commerce. Inside is the fine **Merchants' Hall,** embellished with stained-glass windows and many portraits. ✉ *West side of George Sq., Merchant City* ☎ *0141/221–8272* *Free* ⏱ *Hall and anterooms, weekdays 10–noon, and 2–5 unless closed for meetings, or by appointment.*

❺ **Necropolis.** A burial ground since the beginning of recorded history, the Necropolis, modeled on the famous Père-Lachaise Cemetery in Paris, contains some extraordinarily elaborate Victorian tombs. A statue of John Knox (circa 1514–72), leader of the Scottish Reformation, watches over the cemetery, which includes the tomb of 19th-century Glasgow merchant William Miller (1810–72), author of the "Wee Willie Winkie" nursery rhyme. ✉ *Behind Glasgow Cathedral, City Center.*

❿ **People's Palace.** An impressive Victorian red-sandstone building dating from 1894 houses an intriguing museum dedicated to the city's social history. Included among the exhibits is one devoted to the ordinary folk of Glasgow, called the *People's Story.* Also on display are the writing desk of John McLean (1879–1923), the "Red Clydeside" political activist who came to Lenin's notice, and the famous "banana boots" worn on stage by Glasgow-born comedian Billy Connolly. Behind the museum are the well-restored Winter Gardens, a relatively sheltered spot where you can escape the often chilly winds whistling across the green. ✉ *Glasgow Green, Glasgow Cross* ☎ *0141/554–0223* *www.glasgow.gov.uk* *Free* ⏱ *Mon.–Thurs. and Sat. 10–5, Fri. and Sun. 11–5.*

❻ **Provand's Lordship.** Glasgow's oldest house was built in 1471 by Bishop Andrew Muirhead as a residence for churchmen. Mary, Queen of Scots (1542–87) is said to have stayed here. After her day, however, the house fell into decline and was used as a sweets shop, a soft-drink factory, the home of the city hangman, and a junk shop. The city finally rescued it and turned it into a museum. Exhibits show the house as it might have looked in its heyday, with period rooms and a spooky re-creation of the old hangman's room. ✉ *3 Castle St., City Center* ☎ *0141/553–2557* *Free* ⏱ *Mon.–Thurs. and Sat. 10–5, Fri. and Sun. 11–5.*

★ ❹ **St. Mungo Museum of Religious Life and Art.** An outstanding collection of artifacts, including Celtic crosses and statuettes of Hindu gods, reflects the many religious groups that have settled throughout the centuries in Glasgow and the west of Scotland. A Zen Garden creates a peaceful setting for rest and contemplation, and elsewhere stained-glass windows include a depiction of St. Mungo himself. The centerpiece is surrealist Salvador Dalí's (1904–89) magnificent painting *Christ of St. John of the Cross.* ✉ *2 Castle St., City Center* ☎ *0141/553–2557* *Free* ⏱ *Mon.–Thurs. and Sat. 10–5, Fri. and Sun. 11–5.*

⓰ **St. Vincent's Street Church.** Dating from 1859, this church, the work of Alexander Thomson, exemplifies his Greek revival style, replete with Ionic temple, sphinx-esque heads, Greek ornamentation, and rich interior color. ✉ *Pitt and St. Vincent Sts., City Center.*

The West End

Glasgow's West End has a stellar mix of education, culture, art, and parkland. The neighborhood is dominated by Glasgow University, founded in 1451, making it the third-oldest in Scotland, after St. Andrews and Aberdeen, and at least 130 years ahead of the University of Edinburgh. It has thrived as a center of educational excellence, particularly in the sciences. The university buildings sit amid parkland, reminding you that Glasgow is a city with more green space per citizen than any other in Europe. You'll also be reminded in the West End that Glasgow is a city of museums and art galleries, having benefited from the generosity of industrial and commercial philanthropists and from the deep-seated desire of the city founders to place Glasgow at the forefront of British cities.

a good walk

Start in **Kelvingrove Park**, at the junction of Sauchiehall (pronounced *socky*-hall) and Argyle streets, where the city's main art museum, **Glasgow Art Gallery and Museum** 17 stands. The gallery and museum are closed for renovation until 2006, but the impressive red sandstone building and its leafy surroundings are still worth a visit. Next, cross Argyle Street to the **Museum of Transport** 18, next to the Kelvin Hall Sports Arena.

After a visit to the Museum of Transport, stroll up tree-lined Kelvin Way. The skyline to your left is dominated by the Gilbert Scott Building, **Glasgow University's** 19 main edifice. Turn left onto University Avenue and walk past the Memorial Gates, which were erected in 1951 to celebrate the university's 500th birthday. On either side of the road are two important galleries, both maintained by the university. On the south side of University Avenue, in the Victorian part of the university, is the **Hunterian Museum** 20. Across University Avenue, in an unremarkable building from the 1970s, is the even more interesting **Hunterian Art Gallery** 21.

The walk from the university to the **Botanic Gardens** 22 isn't very exciting, but the 12 Victorian conservatories and their fragrant collections are worth the effort. Continue west along University Avenue, turn right at Byres Road, and walk as far as Great Western Road and the Hilton Glasgow Grosvenor Hotel. The 40 acres of gardens are across the busy Great Western Road.

After leaving the gardens, cross the River Kelvin on Queen Margaret Drive and walk past the BBC Scotland building, just after Hamilton Drive. Turn right, then right again down the steps to the Kelvin Walkway, on the north bank of the river. (Farther upstream the Kelvin Walkway connects with the West Highland Way, an official long-distance footpath leading to Fort William, approximately 100 mi away.) The walkway that heads downstream toward the city center first crosses a footbridge, then passes old mill buildings, and then goes under Belmont Street and the Great Western Road at Kelvinbridge. Here it passes the Kelvinbridge underground station and goes under the Gibson Street Bridge, then back into Kelvingrove Park. The entire loop, from the park to the gardens to Kelvinbridge and back to the park, takes about 20 minutes.

At this point, you can choose to take one of the paths up the hill and explore the stately Victorian crescents and streets of the park area, or you can take the lower road past the fountain and head directly back to Sauchiehall Street. Whichever way you choose, you should end up, having walked eastward, at the point where Sauchiehall Street crosses the M8 motorway. Down North Street to your right (southward) you'll see the front of the **Mitchell Library** 23. Cross the M8 motorway and continue down Sauchiehall Street to the **Regimental Museum of the Royal Highland Fusiliers** 24. Turn left onto Garnet Street and walk to the top. The streets are dense here, but you ultimately turn left on Buccleuch (pronounced buck-*loo*) Street to reach the **Tenement House** 25. Coming out of the Tenement House, head east on Buccleuch Street to Scott Street. As you turn south on Scott Street, notice the mural that reflects the name of the area, Garnethill, then turn left onto Renfrew Street and walk to Charles Rennie Mackintosh's masterpiece, the **Glasgow School of Art** 26. The next street down is Sauchiehall Street where you'll find the new and vibrant **Centre for Contemporary Arts** 27 and the **McLellan Galleries** 28, which, while Glasgow Art Gallery and Museum is closed, houses many of its finest pieces. Further down Sauchiehall Street is Charles Rennie Mackintosh's celebrated Willow Tearoom, where you can rest your feet and enjoy a cup of Earl Grey. To return to the city center, either continue on Sauchiehall Street, or turn south down Blythswood Street, noting the elegant Blythswood Square, constructed between 1823 and 1829.

TIMING You need at least a day for this walk, and even then you won't manage to do justice to more than two or three museums—perhaps the Hunterian Art Gallery, the Hunterian Museum, and Glasgow School of Art. If you anticipate lingering, plan at least two days.

What to See

22 **Botanic Gardens.** The Royal Botanical Institute of Glasgow began to display plants here in 1842, and today the gardens include herbs, tropical plants, and a world-famous collection of orchids. The most spectacular building in the complex is the **Kibble Palace**, built in 1873 and originally the conservatory of a Victorian eccentric named John Kibble. Its domed, interlinked greenhouses contain tree ferns, palm trees, temperate plants, and the Tropicarium, where you can experience the lushness of a tropical rain forest. Elsewhere on the grounds are more conventional greenhouses, as well as well-maintained lawns and colorful flower beds. ✉ *Great Western Rd., West End* ☎ *0141/334–2422* *Free* *Gardens Mar.–mid-Oct., daily 7–dusk; mid-Oct.–Feb., daily 7–4:15. Kibble Palace and other greenhouses Mar.–mid-Oct., daily 10–4:45; mid-Oct.–Feb., daily 10–4:15.*

27 **Centre for Contemporary Arts.** This arts, cinema, and performance venue is in a post-industrial-revolution Alexander Thomson building. It has a reputation for unusual visual arts exhibitions, from paintings and sculpture to new media, and has championed a number of emerging artists, including Toby Paterson, winner of the Beck's Future's award in 2001. Simon Starling, the Scottish representative at the Venice Bienalle in 2003, has also exhibited work here. The vibrant Tempus Bar Café is designed by Los Angeles-based artist, Jorge Pardo. ✉ *350 Sauchiehall St., City Center* ☎ *0141/352–4900* *www.cca-glasgow.com* *Free* *Tues.–Wed. 11–6, Thurs. 11–8, Fri.–Sun. 11–6.*

17 **Glasgow Art Gallery and Museum.** Following Glasgow's successful 1888 International Exhibition of Science, Art, and Industry, city officials resolved to build a museum and gallery worthy of a world-class art collection and future international exhibitions. The Glasgow Art Gallery and Museum, looking like a combination of cathedral and castle, was designed in the Renaissance style and built between 1891 and 1901. J. W. Simpson and E.J. Milner Allen were the main architects; Sir George Frampton designed the central porch; and James Harrison Mackinnon designed the decorative carving on the exterior. The magnificently ornamented red-sandstone edifice is an appropriate home for Glasgow's superior art collection, which includes paintings by Botticelli, Rembrandt, and Monet. While the building is under renovation, however, much of the collection is displayed in the ⇨ **McLellan Galleries** on Sauchiehall Street and the ⇨ **Burrell Collection** on the South Side. The museum is due to reopen in 2006 with renovated, expanded, and more accessible gallery space. ✉ *Kelvingrove Park, West End* ☎ *0141/287–2699* *www.glasgow.gov.uk.*

need a break?

The **Willow Tearoom** (✉ 217 Sauchiehall St., City Center ☎ 0141/332–0521) has been restored to its original Charles Rennie Mackintosh art nouveau design, right down to the decorated tables and chairs. The building was designed by Mackintosh in 1903 for Kate Cranston, who ran a chain of tearooms. The tree motifs reflect the street address—*sauchie* is an old Scots word for willow.

★ 26 **Glasgow School of Art.** The exterior and interior, structure, furnishings, and decoration of this art nouveau building, built between 1897 and 1909, form a unified whole, reflecting the inventive genius of Charles Rennie Mackintosh, who was only 28 years old when he won the competition for its design. Architects and designers from all over the world come to admire it, but because it's a working school of art, general access is sometimes limited. Guided tours are available; it's best to make reservations. The art-school shop sells a good selection of Mackintosh prints, postcards, and books, plus a selection of contemporary art by the school's students and graduates. A block away is Mackintosh's Willow Tearoom. ✉ *167 Renfrew St., City Center* ☎ *0141/353–4526* 🌐 *www.gsa.ac.uk* 🎫 *£5* ⏲ *Tours weekdays at 11 and 2, Sat. at 10:30 and 11:30.*

off the beaten path

GLASGOW SCIENCE CENTRE – Families with children love this center, which has an IMAX theater, a fun-packed Science Mall, and the troubled, 417-foot Glasgow Tower. The tower was designed as a unique viewing point for the whole city, but structural problems have plagued it since day one, and no one is allowed in it. In the Science Mall, state-of-the-art displays educate kids and adults about exploration, discovery, and the environment. Set aside half a day to make the most of it. ✉ *50 Pacific Quay, South Side* ☎ *0141/420–5000* 🌐 *www.gsc.org.uk* 🎫 *IMAX films £5.50, Science Mall £6.50* ⏲ *Daily 10–6.*

19 **Glasgow University.** The architecture, grounds, and great views of Glasgow all warrant a visit to the university. The Gilbert Scott Building, the university's main edifice, was built more than a century ago and is a good example of the Gothic Revival style. **Glasgow University Visitor Centre** has exhibits on the university, a coffee bar, and a gift shop and is the starting point for one-hour guided walking tours of the campus. A self-guided tour should start at the Visitor Centre and take in the East and West quadrangles, the cloisters, Professor's Square, Pearce Lodge, and the not-to-be-missed the University Chapel. ✉ *University Ave., West End* ☎ *0141/330–5511* 🌐 *www.glasgow.ac.uk* 🎫 *Free; guided tour £2* ⏲ *May–Sept., Mon.–Sat. 9:30–5, Sun. 2–5; Oct.–Apr., Mon.–Sat. 9:30–5. Tours: May–Sept., Mon.–Sat. at 2; Oct.–Apr., Wed. at 2.*

★ 21 **Hunterian Art Gallery.** This Glasgow University gallery houses Glasgow-doctor William Hunter's (1718–83) collection of paintings (his antiquarian collection is housed in the nearby Hunterian Museum), together with prints and drawings by Tintoretto, Rembrandt, Sir Joshua Reynolds, and Auguste Rodin, as well as a major collection of paintings by James McNeill Whistler, who had a great affection for the city that bought one of his earliest paintings. Also in the gallery is a replica of **Charles Rennie Mackintosh's town house,** which used to stand nearby. The rooms contain Mackintosh's distinctive art nouveau chairs, tables, beds, and cupboards, and the walls are decorated in the equally distinctive style devised by him and his artist wife, Margaret. ✉ *Glasgow University, Hillhead St., West End* ☎ *0141/330–5431* 🌐 *www.hunterian.gla.ac.uk* 🎫 *Free* ⏲ *Mon.–Sat. 9:30–5* ⏲ *Mackintosh house closed for lunch 12:30–1:30.*

20 **Hunterian Museum.** The city's oldest museum (1807) and part of Glasgow University, the Hunterian showcases part of the collections of William Hunter, an 18th-century Glasgow doctor who assembled a staggering quantity of valuable material. (The doctor's art treasures are housed in the nearby Hunterian Art Gallery.) The museum displays Hunter's hoards of coins, manuscripts, scientific instruments, and archaeological artifacts in a striking Gothic building. ✉ *Glasgow University, West End* ☎ *0141/330–4221* 🌐 *www.hunterian.gla.ac.uk* 💵 *Free* 🕑 *Mon.–Sat. 9:30–5.*

Kelvingrove Park. A peaceful retreat, the park was purchased by the city in 1852 and takes its name from the River Kelvin, which flows through it. Among the numerous statues of prominent Glaswegians is one of Lord Kelvin (1824–1907), the Scottish mathematician and physicist who pioneered a great deal of work in electricity. The park also has a massive fountain commemorating a lord provost of Glasgow from the 1850s, a duck pond, a play area, a small open-air theater, and lots of exotic trees. ✉ *Northwest of city center, bounded roughly by Sauchiehall St., Woodlands Rd., and Kelvin Way, West End.*

★ 28 **McLellan Galleries.** In an understated Victorian building designed by James Smith (1808–1863), you'll find a superior collection of 16th- and 17th-century paintings by Dutch and Italian masters, as well as contemporary work by both Scottish and international artists, such as David Hockney and David Mach. The galleries also display a portion of the Glasgow Art Gallery and Museum's collection, including paintings by Rembrandt, Monet, and Van Gogh, while the museum is closed for renovation. ✉ *270 Sauchiehall St., City Center* ☎ *0141/331–1854* 💵 *Free* 🕑 *Mon.–Thurs. and Sat. 10–5, Fri. and Sun. 11–5.*

23 **Mitchell Library.** The largest public reference library in Europe houses more than a million volumes, including what's claimed to be the world's largest collection on Robert Burns. A bust in the entrance hall commemorates the library's founder, Stephen Mitchell, who died in 1874, the same year the library was founded. Minerva, goddess of wisdom, looks down from the library's dome, encouraging the library's users and frowning at the drivers thundering along the motorway just in front of her. The western facade (at the back), with its sculpted figures of Mozart, Beethoven, Michelangelo, and other artistic figures, is particularly beautiful. ✉ *North St., City Center* ☎ *0141/287–2999* 💵 *Free* 🕑 *Mon.–Thurs. 9–8, Fri.–Sat. 9–5.*

18 **Museum of Transport.** Here Glasgow's history of locomotive building is dramatically displayed with full-size exhibits. The collection of Clyde-built ship models is world famous. Anyone who knows what Britain was like in the 1930s will wax nostalgic at the re-created street scene from that era. ✉ *Kelvin Hall, 1 Bunhouse Rd., West End* ☎ *0141/287–2720* 💵 *Free* 🕑 *Mon.–Thurs. and Sat. 10–5, Fri. and Sun. 11–5.*

off the beaten path

QUEEN'S CROSS CHURCH – Head for the Charles Rennie Mackintosh Society Headquarters, in the only church Mackintosh designed, to learn more about the famous Glasgow-born architect and designer. Although one of the leading lights in the turn-of-the-20th-century art nouveau movement, Mackintosh died in 1928 with his name scarcely known. Today he's widely accepted as a brilliant innovator. The church has beautiful stained-glass windows and a light-enhancing, carved-wood interior. The center's library and shop provide further insight into Glasgow's other Mackintosh-designed buildings, which include Scotland Street School, the Martyrs Public School, and the Glasgow School of Art. The church sits on the corner of Springbank Street at the junction of Garscube Road with Maryhill Road; a cab ride can get you here, or take a bus toward Queen's Cross from stops along Hope Street. ✉ *870 Garscube Rd., West End* ☎ *0141/946–6600* 🌐 *www.crmsociety.com* 🎫 *£2* 🕓 *Weekdays 10–5, Sun. 2–5, or by appointment.*

24 **Regimental Museum of the Royal Highland Fusiliers.** Exhibits of medals, badges, and uniforms relate the history of a famous, much-honored regiment and the men who served in it. ✉ *518 Sauchiehall St., City Center* ☎ *0141/332–0961* 🎫 *Free* 🕓 *Mon.–Thurs. 9–4:30, Fri. 9–4, weekends by appointment only.*

off the beaten path

THE TALL SHIP AT GLASGOW HARBOR – This maritime attraction centers around the restored tall ship the *Glenlee,* a former cargo ship originally built in Glasgow in 1896, purchased by the Spanish navy, and bought back by the Clyde Maritime Trust in 1993. The ship itself is fascinating, but take time to explore the Pumphouse Exhibition and Gallery, which has films of the restoration process and interactive exhibits. A bus (No. 100) runs every half hour from the Buchanan Street bus station. ✉ *100 Stobcross Rd., West End* ☎ *0141/222–2513* 🌐 *www.thetallship.com* 🎫 *£4.50* 🕓 *Mar.–Oct., daily 10–5; Nov.–Feb., daily 11–4.*

25 **Tenement House.** An ordinary, simple city-center apartment is anything but ordinary inside: it was occupied from 1911 to 1965 by Agnes Toward, who seems never to have thrown anything away. Her legacy is a fascinating time capsule, painstakingly preserved with her everyday furniture and belongings. The red-sandstone building dates from 1892 and can be found in the Garnethill area north of Charing Cross station. ✉ *145 Buccleuch St., City Center* ☎ *0141/333–0183* 🌐 *www.nts.org.uk* 🎫 *£3.50* 🕓 *Mar.–Oct., daily 1–5 (last admission at 4:30).*

The South Side: Art-Filled Parks West

Just southwest of the city center in the South Side are two of Glasgow's dear green places—Bellahouston Park and Pollok Country Park—which have important art collections: Charles Rennie Mackintosh's House for an Art Lover, the Burrell Collection, and Pollok House. A respite from the buzz of the city can also be found in the parks, where you can have a picnic or ramble through greenery and gardens. Both parks are off Paisley Road, about 3 mi southwest of the city center. You can take a taxi or car, city bus, or a train from Glasgow Central Station to Pollokshaws West Station or Dumbreck.

a good tour

Start your art exploration at the **Burrell Collection** 29 ▶, with its diverse works displayed in a supermodern structure. Repair to the museum's good café-restaurant for a bite, or plan to pack a picnic lunch to enjoy in one of the parks. **Pollok House** 30, with the Stirling Maxwell Collection of painting and fine art, is just a walk of a few hundred yards beyond the Burrell. Head north on Haggs Road and Dumbreck Road to Bellahouston Park and the fascinating **House for an Art Lover** 31, built based on Charles Rennie Mackintosh's art nouveau design entry for a 1901 competition.

TIMING Allow the good part of a day for seeing the three collections, strolls through the parks, and a picnic or lunch. Note that the House for an Art Lover is usually open only on weekends (and some weekdays).

What to See

29 **Burrell Collection.** A custom-built, ultramodern (1983), elegant building of pink sandstone and stainless steel houses thousands of items of all descriptions, from ancient Egyptian, Greek, and Roman artifacts to Chinese ceramics, bronzes, and jade. You'll also find medieval tapestries, stained glass, Rodin sculptures, and exquisite French impressionist paintings—Degas's *The Rehearsal* and Sir Henry Raeburn's *Miss Macartney*, to name a few. Eccentric millionaire Sir William Burrell (1861–1958) donated the magpie collection to the city in 1944. The exterior and interior were designed with large glass walls so that the items on display could relate to their surroundings in Pollok Country Park: art and nature, supposedly in perfect harmony. The Burrell is hosting major exhibitions of works from the Glasgow Art Gallery and Museum while the latter is closed for renovations. You can get there via buses 45, 48, and 57 from Union Street. ✉ *2060 Pollokshaws Rd., South Side* ☎ *0141/287–2550* *Free* ⏲ *Mon.–Thurs. and Sat. 10–5, Fri. and Sun. 11–5.*

Fodor's Choice ★

off the beaten path

HOLMWOOD HOUSE – The National Trust for Scotland has undertaken the restoration of this large mansion house, designed by Alexander "Greek" Thomson for the wealthy owner of a paper mill. Its classical Greek architecture and stunningly ornamented wood and marble features are among Thomson's finest. You can witness the ongoing restoration process one or two days a week. ✉ *61–63 Netherlee Rd., South Side* ☎ *0141/637–2129* 🌐 *www.nts.org.uk* *£3.50* ⏲ *Apr.–Oct., daily noon–5:30 (last admission at 5).*

31 **House for an Art Lover.** Within Bellahouston Park is a "new" Mackintosh house: based on a competition entry Charles Rennie Mackintosh submitted to a German magazine in 1901, but which was never built in his lifetime. The building houses Glasgow School of Art's postgraduate study center and exhibits of designs for the various rooms and decorative pieces Mackintosh and his wife, Margaret, created. Buses 9, 53, and 54 from Union Street will get you here. ✉ *Bellahouston Park, Dumbreck Rd., South Side* ☎ *0141/353–4770* *£3.50* ⏲ *Apr.–Sept., Sat.–Thurs. 10–4; Oct.–Mar., weekends 10–4.*

30 **Pollok House.** The classic Georgian Pollok House, dating from the mid-1700s, contains the Stirling Maxwell Collection of paintings, including works by El Greco, Murillo, Goya, Signorelli, and William Blake. Fine 18th- and early 19th-century furniture, silver, glass, and porcelain are also on display. The house has lovely gardens and looks over the White Cart River and Pollok Country Park, where, amid mature trees and abundant wildlife, the city of Glasgow's own cattle peacefully graze. Take buses 45, 47 or 57 to the Gate of Pollok County Park. ✉ *2060 Pollokshaws Rd., South Side* ☎ *0141/616–6410* 🌐 *www.nts.org.uk* *Apr.–Oct., £5; Nov.–Mar., free* ⏲ *Apr.–Oct., daily 10–5; Nov.–Mar., daily 11–4.*

off the beaten path

SCOTLAND STREET SCHOOL – A former school designed by Charles Rennie Mackintosh, this building houses a fascinating museum of education. Classrooms re-create school life in Scotland during Victorian times and World War II, and a cookery room recounts a time when education for young Scottish girls consisted of little more than learning how to become a housewife. An exhibition space and café are also here. The building sits opposite Shields Road underground station. ✉ *225 Scotland St., South Side* ☎ *0141/287–0500* 🌐 *www.glasgow.gov.uk* *Free* ⏲ *Mon.–Thurs. and Sat. 10–5, Fri. and Sun. 11–5.*

CHARLES RENNIE MACKINTOSH

NOT SO LONG AGO, *the furniture of Glasgow-born architect Charles Rennie Mackintosh (1868–1928) was broken up for firewood. Today his major bookcases and chairs go for hundreds of thousands of pounds at auction, art books are devoted to his astonishingly elegant Arts and Crafts interiors, and artisans around the world look to his theory that "decoration should not be constructed, rather construction should be decorated" as holy law. Mackintosh's stripped-down designs slammed the door on Victorian antimacassars and floral chintz, ushering in the modern age with their deceptively stark style. Ironically, Scotland's most innovative designer had an extensive influence on European design, but failed to receive recognition as a true original in his native country until well after his death.*

Mackintosh trained in architecture at the Glasgow School of Art and was apprenticed to the Glasgow firm of John Hutchison at the age of 16. During his training, he was awarded several prizes in recognition of his exceptional talent. In 1889 he joined the Glasgow firm Honeyman and Keppie. Early influences on his work included the Pre-Raphaelites, James McNeill Whistler (1834–1903), Aubrey Beardsley (1872–98), and Japanese art, but by the 1890s a distinct Glasgow style had been developed by Mackintosh and others. The building for the Glasgow Herald newspaper, which he designed in 1893 and which is now the Lighthouse Centre for Architecture, Design and the City, was soon followed by other major Glasgow buildings: Queen Margaret's Medical College; the Martyrs Public School; tearooms for Catherine Cranston, including the famous Willow Tearoom that can still be seen today; the Hill House, Helensburgh, now owned by the National Trust for Scotland; and Queen's Cross Church, completed in 1899 and now the headquarters of the Charles Rennie Mackintosh Society. In 1897 Mackintosh began work on a new home for the Glasgow School of Art, now recognized as one of his major achievements; it still retains original fittings, furnishings, ornamentation, and documents.

Mackintosh married Margaret Macdonald in 1900, and in later years her decorative work enhanced the interiors of his buildings. Over the next few years he worked abroad as well as in Scotland, being especially successful in Germany and Austria. In 1904 he became a partner in Honeyman and Keppie and designed Scotland Street School, now the Museum of Education, in the same year. Until 1913, when he left Honeyman and Keppie and moved to England, Mackintosh's various projects included work on buildings and/or interiors over much of Scotland, but especially in the Central Belt: Comrie, Bridge of Allan, Kilmacolm, and many other places. He preferred whenever possible to include interiors—furniture and fittings—as part of his overall design (a talent demonstrated clearly at the Hill House). He believed that building design should be "a total work of art, to the wholeness of which each contrived detail contributes."

Commissions in England after 1913 included a variety of design challenges not confined to buildings, including fabrics, furniture, and even bookbindings for the publishers Blackie and Sons. In 1923 Mackintosh settled in France, but he returned to London in 1927 and died there in 1928.

Glasgow must be the best place in the world to admire Mackintosh's work: in addition to the buildings mentioned above, most of which can be visited, the Hunterian Art Gallery contains magnificent reconstructions of the principal rooms at 78 Southpark Avenue, Mackintosh's Glasgow home, and original drawings, documents, and records, plus the re-creation of a room at 78 Derngate, Northampton.

WHERE TO EAT

The key to Glaswegian cuisine is not Glasgow. It's the flurry of foreign restaurants that abound—from late-night crepe stalls and *pakora* (Indian fried chickpea cakes) bars to elegant restaurants with worldly menus. Glasgow restaurants tend to be larger than their Edinburgh counterparts, so getting a table at the establishment of your choice shouldn't be a problem, though making reservations for a Friday or Saturday night is still advisable.

Prices

Eating in Glasgow can be casual or lavish, with much the same prices and variety as you'll find in Edinburgh. For inexpensive dining, consider the benefit of pre-theater menus. Wine is relatively expensive in restaurants, but beer and spirits cost much the same as they would in a bar.

WHAT IT COSTS In pounds

	£££££	££££	£££	££	£
AT DINNER	over £22	£18–£22	£13–£17	£7–£12	under £7

Prices are per person for a main course. The final tab will include a 17.5% VAT.

Medieval Glasgow & Merchant City

Chinese

£££ ✕ **Amber Regent.** This may not be the cheapest Chinese restaurant in town, but it's certainly one of the finest and most formal. For a start, the meticulously sculpted vegetables that accompany the hors d'oeuvres seem almost too artful to eat. Succulent Szechuan king prawns, and duck with mashed prawns in an oyster sauce readily attest to Amber Regent's longstanding reputation for serving excellent Cantonese and Szechuan cuisine. But this reputation also means that the restaurant can get very busy. For top value, arrive before 6:45 PM, when the main courses are half price. ✉ *50 West Regent St., City Center* ☎ *0141/331–1655* 💳 *AE, DC, MC, V* ⊗ *Closed Sun.*

££–£££ ✕ **Loon Fung.** The pleasant, efficient staff at this popular Cantonese restaurant guides you enthusiastically through the house specials, including the famed dim sum. If you like seafood, try the deep-fried wonton with prawns, crispy stuffed crab claws, or lobster in garlic-and-cheese sauce. The three-course business lunch is first class and only £7.90. ✉ *417 Sauchiehall St., City Center* ☎ *0141/332–1240* 💳 *AE, MC, V.*

Contemporary

££–££££ ✕ **Groucho Saint Jude's.** You don't have to be young and "with it" to dine here, but it helps. With glitzy, modern appeal, Groucho's is the fashionable spot for the young Glasgow executive set after office hours. Even if this is not your crowd, don't let that stop you from tackling the extensive cocktail selection and equally diverse menu. Away from the bar, the quieter, more traditional dining room serves a daunting selection of dishes, but everything from the wild-mushroom risotto to the chargrilled sirloin of Aberdeen Angus is beautifully prepared and swiftly served. ✉ *190 Bath St., City Center* ☎ *0141/352–8800* ✍ *Reservations essential* 💳 *AE, DC, MC, V.*

££–£££ ✕ **ArtHouse Grill.** Many of Glasgow's greatest treasures lie hidden in basements. This elusive mix of grill restaurant and oyster bar is no exception. Take the trouble to find it and you'll discover that underground doesn't necessarily mean understated. The slick and upbeat interior—with oak, stained glass, and burgundy and bright blue fabrics—is bold but tasteful, and never over the top. So is an eclectic menu that includes everything from marinated tuna to quality burgers and steak dishes. ✉ Art-House Hotel *129 Bath St., City Center* ☎ *0141/572–6002* ▭ *AE, DC, MC, V.*

££–£££ ✕ **City Café.** This bright, contemporary restaurant is on the edge of the city center, with one of the best riverside locations in Glasgow. It's adjacent to the Scottish Exhibition and Conference Centre and the Glasgow Science Centre. The menu dresses up traditional dishes with modern touches: roast salmon wrapped in prosciutto and served with a fennel compote, for example, or fillet of lamb with caramelized onions, broad beans, and a morel sauce. In good weather you can dine outside by the banks of the Clyde, and in the shadow of the mighty Finnieston Crane, the 195-foot-high hammerhead crane formerly used to load heavy cargo onto freighters. ✉ *Finnieston Quay, City Center* ☎ *0141/227–1010* ▭ *AE, DC, MC, V.*

Continental

££–£££ ✕ **Brasserie.** A hotel basement fitted with wooden booths provides a quiet, relaxed environment in which to appreciate a varied modern European menu. The fish cakes are a traditional favorite here, but also good are the spaghetti with mussels and clams, and the char-grilled rib-eye steak. Be sure to leave room for desserts such as the pineapple mille-feuille and homemade coconut sorbet. ✉ *Malmaison Hotel, 278 W. George St., City Center* ☎ *0141/572–1001* ✍ *Reservations essential* ▭ *AE, DC, MC, V* ⏲ *No lunch Sat.*

££–£££ ✕ **Drum and Monkey.** A glorious Victorian former bank houses this busy and friendly bar-restaurant. The food ranges from acceptable-enough pub fodder to some Scottish-French delights, served up in an adjacent bistro. Try the excellent fish cakes, the smoked salmon with spinach and lemon-butter sauce, or the chicken stuffed with smoked cheese and rosemary. ✉ *93–95 St. Vincent St., City Center* ☎ *0141/221–6636* ▭ *AE, DC, MC, V.*

Eclectic

££–££££ ✕ **78 St. Vincent.** Originally a bank, with slender interior Doric columns and strikingly carved griffins on the outside, this is now a stylish restaurant where you can enjoy contemporary French-influenced Scottish cuisine. As your eyes feast on the wall-length modern mural by Glasgow artist Donald McLean, your palate can relish the Highland venison with gin-scented *jus,* or smoked duck salad with egg, scallops, prawns, and soy-sauce dressing. ✉ *78 St. Vincent St., City Center* ☎ *0141/248–7878* ▭ *AE, DC, MC, V.*

Indian

££–£££ ✕ **Mr. Singh's India.** One of Glasgow's most popular eateries serves superb Indian and international cuisine backed by three generations of family experience. The restaurant is a restful haven in creams and blues with plenty of beech wood, rather quirkily combined with Indian waiters in kilts and a menu including haggis *pakora* (deep-fried haggis parcels). Meats and vegetables can be cooked in a number of different delicious sauces; try the lamb Mazadar—hot and spicy, with Rémy Martin—or the pistachio *korma* (curried meat with onions and vegetables). ✉ *149 Elderslie St., City Center* ☎ *0141/204–0186 or 0141/221–1452* ▭ *AE, DC, MC, V.*

Italian

£–£££ ✕ **Pavarotti Trattoria.** Despite the somewhat silly name, no doubt arising from the restaurant's proximity to Scottish Opera's Theatre Royal, this is not a kitsch affair but a sincerely Italian restaurant run by the Scala family. The menu changes regularly because chef-owner Federico will purchase only the freshest ingredients. Consequently, the standard meat and fish dishes are unusually succulent. The lunch and pretheater set menus—£7.90 and £10.50 respectively—are exceptionally good value. ✉ *91 Cambridge St., City Center* ☎ *0141/332–9713* ▭ *AE, DC, MC, V* ⊙ *No lunch Sun.*

£–££ ✕ **Fazzi Café Bar.** With its red tablecloths, tile floor, and bentwood chairs, this inexpensive Italian café-bar is a cheerful place for a quick plateful of gnocchi *alla Emiliana* (with tomato, basil, and cheese sauce) or spinach-and-ricotta ravioli. The delicatessen here sells takeout. ✉ *65–67 Cambridge St., City Center* ☎ *0141/332–0941* ▭ *AE, DC, MC, V.*

£–££ Fodor'sChoice ★ ✕ **Fratelli Sarti.** Glasgow's large Italian immigrant population is never more visible—or audible—than here. The cavernous surroundings are cluttered and the tables close together, so this is not really the place for an intimate dinner, but the food is authentic, with all of the classic dishes on an extensive menu. If you like seafood, try the wonderfully fresh and piquant pasta *vongole* (with small clams). Finish off with the light, creamy tiramisu. Note that the service can be a bit leisurely. ✉ *121 Bath St., City Center* ☎ *0141/204–0440* ▭ *AE, DC, MC, V* ⊙ *No lunch Sun.*

Japanese

£–££ ✕ **OKO.** Sit by the conveyor belt and pick off the dishes that take your fancy: tempura, sushi, and teriyaki preparations are among the classic minidishes that are both filling and reasonably priced. The interior has a metallic avant-garde design. ✉ *68 Ingram St., Merchant City* ☎ *0141/572–1500* ▭ *AE, MC, V* ⊙ *Closed Mon. No lunch Sun.*

Pan-Asian

£–£££ ✕ **Ruby.** The menu at this friendly restaurant starts with a Chinese base and layers on Thai and Indonesian specialties. It then mixes the three together, and the resulting tastes attract a cultlike clientele. The menu has something for everyone. You can even get local fish-and-chips, but far more tempting is the *ho mok talag* (mixed seafood in herbs and a coconut sauce) or *dading rendang* (Spice Islands beef). The menu prices can be deceptive, for although most main courses are under £10, adding side dishes, starters, and dessert means you're likely to spend more than £20 a head. ✉ *377 Sauchiehall St., City Center* ☎ *0141/331–1277* ▭ *AE, DC, MC, V.*

£££ ✕ **Khublai Khan Barbecue.** This sincerely Mongolian effort is about as exotic as you can get in this city. Wild boar and things you probably haven't heard of feature strongly, as you'll discover when you order the only option available, the Mongolian Feast (£15.50), which includes an unlimited barbecue main course. The massive space is festooned with handwoven rugs and a huge mural of Mongolian warriors advancing threateningly. Don't worry: the service is friendly. You may be too full for dessert, but don't pass up the unique *ristretto*—a miniature coffee that packs a giant punch. ✉ *26 Candleriggs St., Merchant City* ☎ *0141/552–5646* ▭ *AE, DC, MC, V* ⊙ *No lunch.*

Russian

★ £–£££ ✕ **Café Cossachok.** Near the Tron Theatre, this is a willfully arty place: the tables are hand-carved, the lighting is courtesy of candles, and the decor is a sea of shawls. The Russian owner pays further homage to his homeland with live music, at 8:30 Sunday, and a nicely chilled selection of vodkas. The menu includes delicious Petrushka blintzes and trout à la Pushkin (in a thirst-rousing salty sauce). This fun venue is fashionable among the fashionable, from actors to politicians, so it's best to book ahead. ✉ *10 King St., Merchant City* ☎ *0141/553–0733* ▭ *AE, MC, V* ⊙ *Closed Mon. No lunch Sun.*

Scottish

££–£££££ ✕ **City Merchant.** In Glasgow a purely Scottish restaurant is almost a novelty, and few can compare with this venue. The cooking is plain and sim-

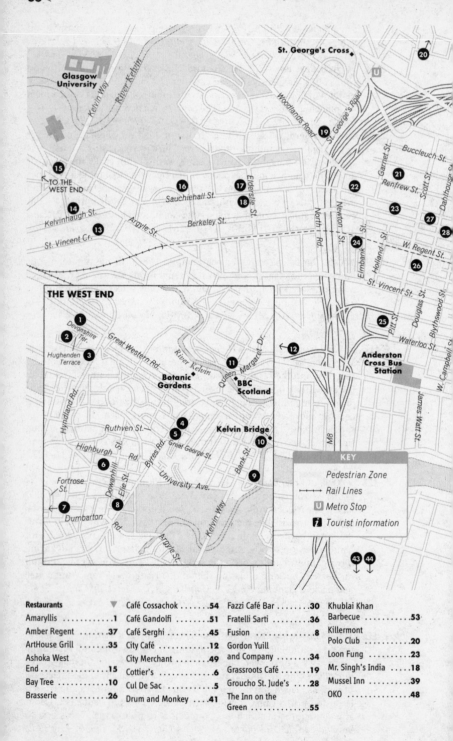

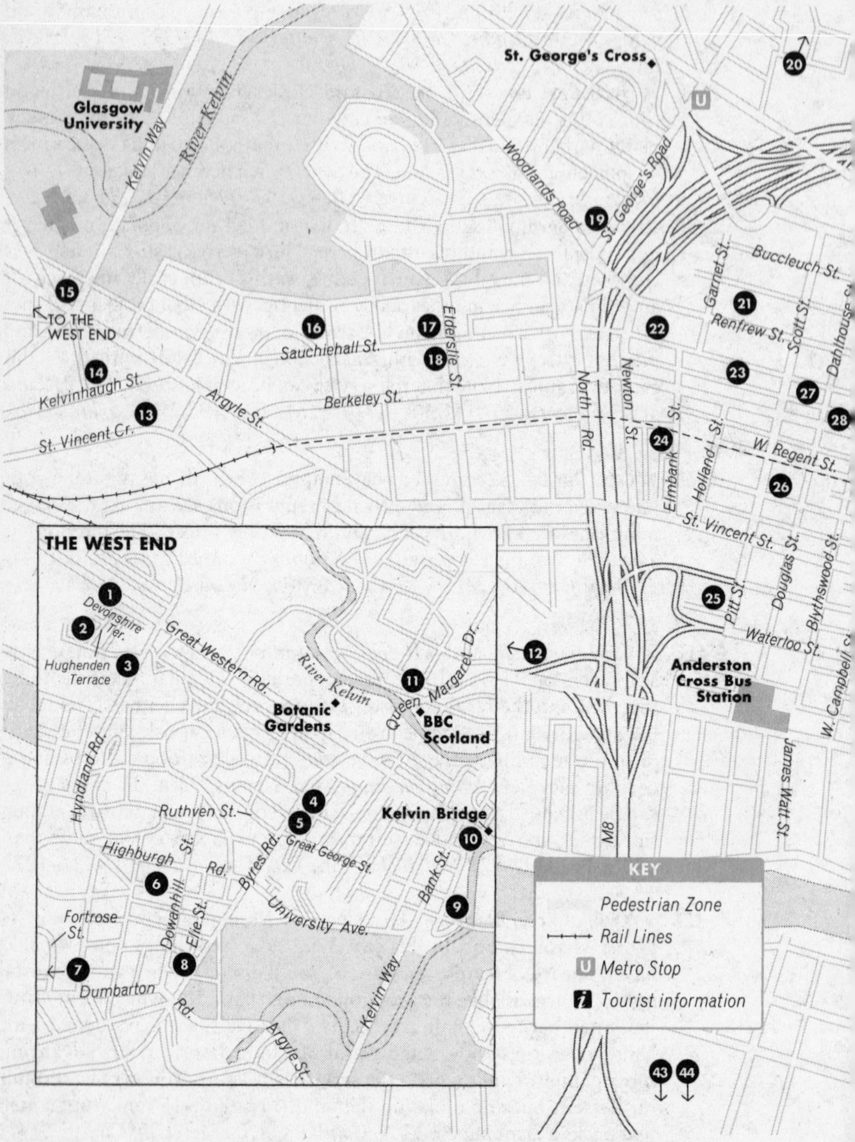

Restaurants			
Amaryllis 1	Café Cossachok 54	Fazzi Café Bar 30	Khublai Khan Barbecue 53
Amber Regent 37	Café Gandolfi 51	Fratelli Sarti 36	Killermont Polo Club 20
ArtHouse Grill 35	Café Serghi 45	Fusion 8	Loon Fung 23
Ashoka West End 15	City Café 12	Gordon Yuill and Company 34	Mr. Singh's India 18
Bay Tree 10	City Merchant 49	Grassroots Café 19	Mussel Inn 39
Brasserie 26	Cottier's 6	Groucho St. Jude's 28	OKO 48
	Cul De Sac 5	The Inn on the Green 55	
	Drum and Monkey 41		

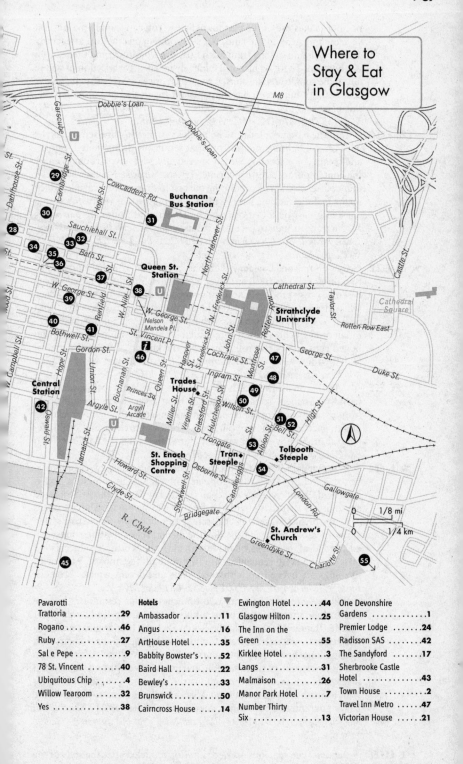

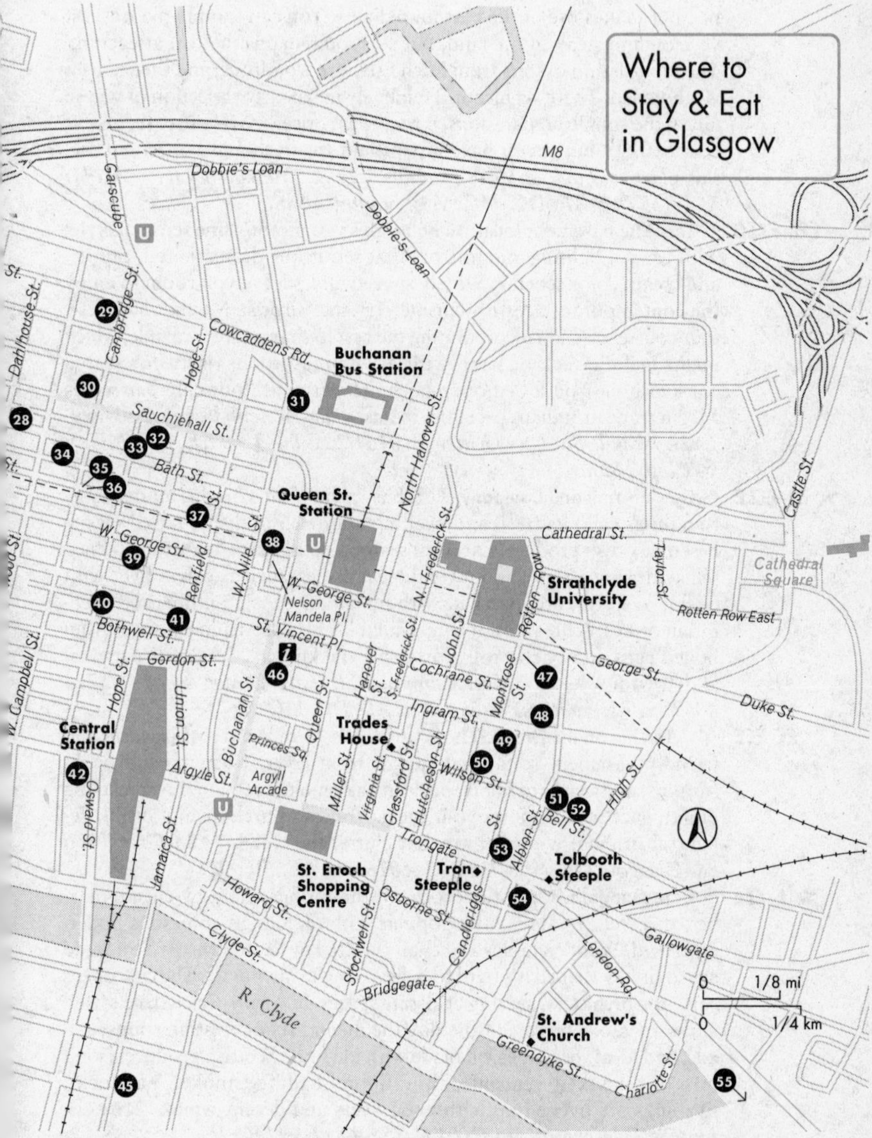

Pavarotti Trattoria **29**
Rogano **46**
Ruby **27**
Sal e Pepe **9**
78 St. Vincent **40**
Ubiquitous Chip **4**
Willow Tearoom **32**
Yes **38**

Hotels ▼
Ambassador **11**
Angus **16**
ArtHouse Hotel **35**
Babbity Bowster's **52**
Baird Hall **22**
Bewley's **33**
Brunswick **50**
Cairncross House **14**
Ewington Hotel **44**
Glasgow Hilton **25**
The Inn on the Green **55**
Kirklee Hotel **3**
Langs **31**
Malmaison **26**
Manor Park Hotel **7**
Number Thirty Six **13**
One Devonshire Gardens **1**
Premier Lodge **24**
Radisson SAS **42**
The Sandyford **17**
Sherbrooke Castle Hotel **43**
Town House **2**
Travel Inn Metro **47**
Victorian House **21**

ple, but makes use of the best ingredients. You can sample the freshest venison and steak in the land, but seafood remains the real attraction. The mussels and oysters from Loch Etive are wondrous, and the sea bass is renowned. There's a nice and relatively inexpensive selection of wines. Given the simple preparations, it may seem pricey (two-course set menus cost £10.50) but if you have a penchant for fresh and honest cuisine, this place is a joy. ✉ *97–99 Candleriggs St., Merchant City* ☎ *0141/553–1577* ▭ *AE, DC, MC, V* ⊗ *No lunch Sun.*

£££–££££ ✕ **Yes.** The basement location belies this restaurant's fine sense of style, with careful lighting and mirrors that set off the dramatic red, purple, and cream color scheme. Widely spaced tables leave you room to enjoy the contemporary Scottish cuisine. Try the Surprise Menu, an eclectic four-course selection incorporating the best fresh produce available, which might include rack of lamb with a wild-mushroom risotto or seared chicken breast on a bed of spinach. The ground-floor café-bar serves Mediterranean-Italian specialties in flashy digs. Reservations are advised. ✉ *22 W. Nile St., City Center* ☎ *0141/221–8044* ▭ *AE, DC, MC, V* ⊗ *Closed Sun.*

★ **££–££££** ✕ **Gordon Yuill and Company.** This busy restaurant's bright, modern surroundings echo its fresh and exciting approach to dishes based on the best of Scottish produce. Excellent seafood options, such as steamed mussels with lemongrass, and several meat dishes, such as calves liver with crispy pancetta, are matched with imaginative Asian-influenced vegetarian dishes. A breakfast menu, available every day from 8, ranges from boiled eggs and bacon rolls to Loch Fyne kippers. Service is personal and friendly. ✉ *257 West Campbell St., City Center* ☎ *0141/572–4052* ✍ *Reservations essential* ▭ *AE, DC, MC, V.*

££–£££ ✕🏨 **The Inn on the Green.** The Scottish à la carte menu at this warm and friendly basement restaurant ranges from layered haggis, and neeps (turnips) and mash, to hot Hebridean oak-smoked salmon. Live, relaxing nightly jazz accompanies your meal. You can purchase any of the delightful original works of art that clutter the walls. ✉ *25 Greenhead St., Glasgow Cross* ☎ *0141/554–0165* ▭ *AE, MC, V.*

★ **£–£££** ✕ **Café Gandolfi.** Once the offices of the former Glasgow cheese market, this trendy café is now popular with the design-conscious under-30 crowd. Wooden tables and chairs crafted by Scottish artist Tim Stead are so fluidly shaped it's hard to believe they're inanimate. The café opens early for breakfast, serving croissants, eggs *en cocotte* (casserole style), and espresso. The rest of the day the menu lists interesting soups, salads, and local specialties, all made with the finest Scottish produce. Don't miss the smoked venison or the finnan haddie (smoked haddock). Evenings are livened up with good beers and decent wines. ✉ *64 Albion St., Merchant City* ☎ *0141/552–6813* ▭ *MC, V.*

£ ✕ **Willow Tearoom.** There are two branches of this restaurant, but the Sauchiehall Street location is the authentic one. Conceived by the great Charles Rennie Mackintosh, the Room De Luxe (the original tearoom) is kitted out with his trademark furniture, including high-back chairs with elegant long lines and subtle curves. The St. Andrew's Platter is an exquisite selection of trout, salmon, and prawns. Scottish and Continental breakfasts are available throughout the day, and the scrambled eggs with Scottish salmon is traditional Scots food at its finest. The in-house baker guarantees fresh scones, cakes, and pastries. ✉ *217 Sauchiehall St., City Center* ☎ *0141/332–0521* ▭ *MC, V* ⊗ *No dinner.*

Seafood

£££–£££££ Fodor'sChoice ★ ✕ **Rogano.** The spacious art deco interior, modeled after the style of the *Queen Mary* ocean liner—maple paneling, chrome trim, and dramatic ocean murals—is enough to recommend this restaurant. Portions are generous in the main dining area, where impeccably prepared specialties include roast rack of lamb and classic seafood dishes like seared scallops. Downstairs in the Café Rogano (£–££), the brasserie-style food is more modern and imaginative. The theater menu provides early evening and late-night bargains, and the fixed-price lunch menu is popular upstairs. There's also an oyster bar. ✉ *11 Exchange Pl., City Center* ☎ *0141/248–4055* ▭ *AE, DC, MC, V.*

£–£££ Fodor'sChoice ★ ✕ **Mussel Inn.** West Coast shellfish farmers own this restaurant and feed their customers incredibly fresh, succulent oysters, scallops, and mussels. The kilo pots of mussels, beautifully steamed to order in any of a number of sauces, are revelatory. The surroundings and staff are unpretentious yet stylish. ✉ *61–65 Hope St., City Center* ☎ *0141/572–1405* ⊕ *www.mussel-inn.com* ▭ *AE, MC, V* ⊗ *No lunch Sun.*

West End & Environs

Eclectic

£–£££ ✕ **Cul De Sac.** At the end of a quiet cobbled lane, this is one of the most relaxing of Glasgow's trendy West End eateries, right on the edge of the Glasgow University campus. It's a nice alternative to the more formal restaurants in the area, and large French windows add to the friendly street-café atmosphere. The menu includes everything from affordable pastas to red snapper to seared medallion of pork. ✉ *44–46 Ashton La., West End* ☎ *0141/334–6688* ▭ *AE, DC, MC, V.*

Indian

£–£££ ✕ **Killermont Polo Club.** Though not the most likely setting for an Indian restaurant, this former Victorian church manse on the outskirts of Glasgow's West End has the restful and romanticized atmosphere of colonial India. It specializes in the rather unique *Dum Puhkt* cooking tradition, which for a time was held secret by the Mughal royal family. The appetizer *shammi kebab badami* consists of firm patties of minced lamb shot through with cinnamon, coriander, and almonds. The gently prepared *chandi kaliyan* main course mixes lamb with a gravy of poppy seeds, cashews, and saffron. Finish off with the gorgeous sponge dessert, *gulab jamin.* ✉ *2022 Maryhill Rd., West End* ☎ *0141/946–5412* ▭ *AE, DC, MC, V.*

£–££ ✕ **Ashoka West End.** This Punjabi restaurant consistently outperforms its many competitors in quality, range, and taste. All portions are large enough to please the ravenous, but there's nothing heavy-handed about the cooking here: vegetable *samosas* (stuffed savory deep-fried pastries) are crisp and light, the selection of breads is superb, and the spicing for the lamb, chicken, and prawn dishes is fragrant. The eclectic decor—involving a bizarre mixture of plants, murals, rugs, and brass lamps—and inappropriate Western music simply emphasize Ashoka's idiosyncrasy. Reservations are advised on weekends. ✉ *1284 Argyle St., West End* ☎ *0141/339–3371* ▭ *AE, MC, V* ⊗ *No lunch Sat.–Tues.*

Italian

£–£££ ✕ **Sal e Pepe.** Behind the inconsequential facade here are three floors of homey atmosphere and homey cooking, making it all seem like a very effortless Little Italy. Seafood is a specialty, but the half-price pizza and pasta dishes are perfect for value-conscious diners; they're available weekdays from 3 to 6, when everyone else is at work. There's also a supremely filling three-course pretheater special in the evening for only £8.95. ✉ *18 Gibson St., West End* ☎ *0141/341–0999* ▭ *MC, V.*

Japanese

£–££££ ✕ **Fusion.** This Japanese sushi bar overlooking busy Byres Road serves a refreshing mix of creative sushi and sashimi platters. The restaurant can feel a little cramped, but you'll likely be too distracted by the chefs' theatrical creations to notice. Try the sushi *kombis* or salmon, beef, or chicken teriyaki. The prawn-and-vegetable tempura is delicious. ✉ *41 Byres Rd., West End* ☎ *0141/339–3666* ▭ *MC, V.*

Latin

££–£££ ✕ **Cottier's.** A converted Victorian church decorated by Glasgow artist Daniel Cottier is the unusual setting for this theater-bar-restaurant (the Arts Theatre is attached). Red walls and beamed ceilings warm the downstairs bar, where the pub grub has Tex-Mex flavors. In the restaurant try the spicy lamb cooked with coconut, lime, cilantro, and beans, or the tuna and snapper fillets with anchovy, chili, and citrus butter—two excellent choices from the South American dishes on the menu. Reservations are advised on weekends. ✉ *93 Hyndland St., West End* ☎ *0141/357–5825* ▭ *AE, MC, V.*

Middle Eastern

£ ✕ **Bay Tree.** A small café in the university area, this eatery serves wonderful Middle Eastern vegetarian dishes. Egyptian *phool* (broad beans dressed with spices and herbs), Turkish *mulukia* (fried, sliced eggplant with a tomato-and-herb sauce), and *kurma* (stew with spinach, herbs, and beans) are among its delights. ✉ *403 Great Western Rd., West End* ☎ *0141/334–5898* ▭ *No credit cards.*

Scottish

★ ££££–£££££ ✕ **Amaryllis.** Within the plush One Devonshire Gardens hotel is one of Glasgow's most stylish restaurants. Amaryllis thrives on the reputation of its owner and celebrity chef Gordon Ramsay, and on a concise menu that contrasts sautéed sea bream and *pomme boulangère* (sliced potatoes cooked in broth) with poached pigeon from Bresse. The spacious Victorian dining rooms, in bright creams and blues, match the splendor of the original town house. ✉ *1 Devonshire Gardens, West End* ☎ *0141/337–3434* ✍ *Reservations essential* ▭ *AE, MC, V* ⊙ *Closed Mon. and Tues. No lunch Sat.*

£££–££££ ✕ **Ubiquitous Chip.** In a converted mews stable behind the Hillhead underground station is a restaurant that is an institution among members of Glasgow's media and thespian communities. The service is friendly, and the interior very outdoorsy, with a glass roof, much greenery, and a fishpond. The menu specializes in game; smoked salmon in Darjeeling tea is typical of the chef's clever blending of Scots fare with unusual elements. For the a more casual and inexpensive Ubiquitous experience, try **Upstairs at the Chip** (£–£££). ✉ *12 Ashton La., West End* ☎ *0141/334–5007* ▭ *AE, DC, MC, V.*

Vegetarian

£ ✕ **Grassroots Café.** One of Glasgow's most relaxing eateries, Grassroots provides vegetarian cooking that is wholesome, fresh, and above all, interesting. Unlike the food, which includes its specialty Thai potatoes and vegetarian chili, the interior is simple and plain. The list of fruit juices is exhaustive, and organic ingredients are guaranteed, including the wine. Set aside plenty of time, though, as nothing is hurried, especially for the popular weekend breakfasts. ✉ *97 St. George's Rd., West End* ☎ *0141/333–0534* ▭ *AE, MC, V.*

South Side

Greek

£–£££ ✕ **Café Serghi.** The dome and columns of this former bank make Café Serghi feel rather austere in the early evening. It soon livens up, however, especially on Friday nights when the ouzo starts to flow and crockery is sometimes smashed. The lamb *kleftiko* and the pork *souvlaki* are particularly recommended. ✉ *67 Bridge St., South Side* ☎ *0141/429–1547* ▭ *AE,MC,V* ⊗ *No lunch Sun.*

WHERE TO STAY

Central Glasgow never really goes to sleep, so downtown hotels will be noisier than those in the leafy and genteel West End, convenient for museums and art galleries, or southern suburbs, convenient for the Burrell Collection. The flip side is that most downtown hotels are within walking distance of all the main sights, whereas you will need to make use of the (excellent) bus service if you stay in the suburbs.

Prices

Most smaller hotels and all guest houses include breakfast in the room rate. Larger hotels usually charge extra for breakfast.

WHAT IT COSTS In pounds

	£££££	££££	£££	££	£
FOR 2 PEOPLE	over £175	£135–£175	£95–£135	£55–£95	under £55

Price categories are assigned based on the range between the least and most expensive standard double rooms in high season. The final bill usually includes a 17.5% VAT.

Medieval Glasgow & Merchant City

£££–£££££ **Glasgow Hilton.** This is a typical, very professional international hotel on first impression, but Glasgow friendliness permeates its upscale image. The rooms are spacious, and while they lack individuality, the quality fittings and furniture make them attractive and stylish. There are two restaurants: Cameron's is designed to resemble a Highland shooting lodge, and Minsky's is a New York–style deli. Raffles bar, with its colonial Singapore theme, is a popular hangout for local and visiting celebrities. ✉ *1 William St., City Center, G3 8HT* ☎ *0141/204–5555* 🖷 *0141/204–5004* 🌐 *www.hilton.com* *319 rooms* *2 restaurants, cable TV, indoor pool, health club, hair salon, bar, shop meeting room, free parking* ▭ *AE, DC, MC, V* *BP.*

★ **£££–££££** **ArtHouse Hotel.** This owners of this 1911 terrace building have retained and embellished its best original features, like the elevator and gold-leaf lions, while modernizing the rooms and facilities to meet today's high standards. Rooms have dramatic velvet-covered walls, leaded windows, and contemporary artwork. The ArtHouse Grill has a modish, international menu and the bar is one of Glasgow's hot spots. ✉ *129 Bath St., City Center G2 2SY* ☎ *0141/221–6789* 🖷 *0142/221–6777* 🌐 *www.arthousehotel.com* *44 rooms, 21 suites* *2 restaurants, minibars, cable TV, bar; no a/c* ▭ *AE, DC, MC, V* *CP.*

£££–££££ **Malmaison.** The small, modern Malmaison, housed in a converted church, prides itself on personal service and outstanding amenities: each room has puffy down comforters and CD players. The art deco interior employs bold colors in playful prints and geometric shapes all balanced out by traditional fabrics and furniture. The lobby's splendid staircase has a wrought-iron balustrade illustrating Napoléon's exploits (the hotel takes its name from his home). The warm Brasserie offers British-French cooking. Café Mal serves savory pizzas and pasta in an airy terracotta-hued room with iron fixtures and a spiral staircase. ✉ *278 W. George St., City Center, G2 4LL* ☎ *0141/572–1000* 🖷 *0141/572–1002* 🌐 *www.malmaison.com* *72 rooms, 8 suites* *2 restaurants, minibars, cable TV, gym, bar, meeting room* ▭ *AE, DC, MC, V* *CP.*

★ £££ 　🏨 **Langs.** Langs's sophisticated and ultramodern character fits perfectly with its proximity to Glasgow Royal Concert Hall and the Buchanan Galleries shopping mall. It has a Japanese minimalist look that extends from the wood reception desk to the platform beds in the bright bedrooms. Mediterranean cuisine is the specialty of the Las Brisas restaurant. The Oshi restaurant serves excellent Japanese three-course pre- and post-theater menus for around £10. Japanese body treatments are available in the Oshi Spa. ⊠ *2 Port Dundas St., City Center, G2 3LD* ☎ *0141/333–1500* 🖷 *0141/333–5700* ⊕ *www.langshotels.co.uk* ⇨ *70 rooms, 30 suites* ♢ *2 restaurants, cable TV, gym, spa, bar, meeting room; no a/c* ⊟ *AE, DC, MC, V* ⏐◎⏐ *CP.*

££–£££ 　🏨 **Brunswick.** In a contemporary six-story town house, this hotel showcases quintessential Glasgow style and ambition. The rooms are done in a mostly minimalist style, but squared-off wall fixtures and occasional splashes of color make bold statements. The three-bedroom penthouse suite has a separate kitchen and a sauna. Diablo, the downstairs bar, doesn't let its trendiness get in the way of a friendly welcome. ⊠ *106–108 Brunswick St., Merchant City, G1 1TF* ☎ *0141/552–0001* 🖷 *0141/552–1551* ⊕ *www.brunswickhotel.info* ⇨ *18 rooms, 1 suite* ♢ *Cable TV, bar; no a/c* ⊟ *AE, MC, V* ⏐◎⏐ *CP.*

££ 　🏨 **Babbity Bowster's.** The popular on-site restaurant and bar make this restored 18th-century Robert Adam town house a lively place to stay. The rooms have modern furniture and beds with starched, white linens. A first-floor gallery displays many works by Glaswegian artists. ⊠ *16–18 Blackfriars St., Merchant City, G1 1PE* ☎ *0141/552–5055* 🖷 *0141/552–7774* ⇨ *6 rooms* ♢ *Restaurant, café, bar; no a/c* ⊟ *AE, MC, V* ⏐◎⏐ *BP.*

££ 　🏨 **Bewley's.** With an emphasis on city-center convenience and practical budgets, Bewley's has simple, modern appeal: no frills, just clean-cut comfort and rich fabrics. And it's all just a stone's throw away from busy Sauchiehall Street. If the hotel doesn't have the facilities you need, the staff can often still help you out: the hotel has an affiliation, for example, with a neighboring fitness center that charges hotel guests a reduced fee of £8 per session. Loop restaurant serves breakfast, lunch, and dinner, with specialties such as Thai chicken with mint couscous. ⊠ *110 Bath St., City Center, G2 2EN* ☎ *0141/353–0800* 🖷 *0141/353–0900* ⊕ *www.bewleyshotels.com* ⇨ *103 rooms* ♢ *Restaurant, cable TV, bar; no a/c* ⊟ *AE, DC, MC, V* ⏐◎⏐ *CP.*

££ 　🏨 **The Inn on the Green.** Each spacious and bright room at this small, highly individual hotel has specially designed furniture—solid wood and metal creations, described by the owner as "designer rustic." Request one of the rooms with open views over Glasgow Green, Glasgow's oldest public park. There's a lively restaurant that dishes up Scottish fare along with live jazz music, and the whole package is but a short cab ride from downtown. ⊠ *25 Greenhead St., Glasgow Cross G40 1ES* ☎ *0141/554–0165* 🖷 *0141/556–4678* ⊕ *www.theinnonthegreen.co.uk* ⇨ *18 rooms* ♢ *Restaurant, in-room safes, cable TV, bar, no-smoking rooms; no a/c* ⊟ *AE, MC, V* ⏐◎⏐ *BP.*

££ 　🏨 **Radisson SAS.** You can't miss this eye-catching edifice behind Central Station in Glasgow's up-and-coming financial quarter. Its glass front makes the interior, particularly the lounge, seem as though it were part of the street. Your room might be in Italian, Scandinavian, or Japanese style. Both restaurants—the pop-art-inspired Collage, serving Continental cuisine, and Tapaell'Ya, the tapas bar—are popular with business and artist types, as is the sleek street-level bar. ⊠ *301 Argyle St., City Center G2 8DL* ☎ *0141/203–3333* 🖷 *0141/204–3344* ⊕ *www.radissonsas.com* ⇨ *200 rooms, 4 suites* ♢ *2 restaurants, cable TV, indoor pool, gym, bar, business services, parking (fee)* ⊟ *AE, DC, V* ⏐◎⏐ *CP.*

FodorsChoice
★

£ **Baird Hall.** Several rooms in this University of Strathclyde's residence hall are let to visitors. The building has pretty art deco features, bay windows, and wood panelling. There are rooms with one, two, or three single-person beds, and basic, respectable furnishings, plus several common rooms. The reception area is open 24 hours. ✉ *Sauchiehall St., City Center* ☎ *0141/553–4148* 🖷 *0141/553–4149* 🌐 *www.rescat.strath.ac.uk* *11 rooms with shared bath* *Dining room, lounge, laundry facilities; no a/c* *AE, MC, V.*

£ **Premier Lodge.** This converted office block offers excellent views over the city. The rooms are in standard chain-hotel style, but you can be assured that they're spotless and comfortable, with modern facilities. The hotel is between the city center and the West End, convenient to both. ✉ *10 Elmbank Gardens, City Center G2 4PP* ☎ *0870/700–1394* 🖷 *0870/700–1395* 🌐 *www.premierlodge.co.uk* *278 rooms* *Restaurant, cable TV, bar, no-smoking rooms; no a/c* *AE, MC, V.*

£ **Travel Inn Metro.** This may be one of a chain of budget hotels, but its bright, metropolitan design and low prices appeals to savvy visitors. The rooms are larger than most in a 1,400-year-old city, with coffeemakers and up-to-date bathrooms. Rooms facing the street can be noisy at night, so ask for one that looks out onto the graveyard, where noisemakers are highly unlikely to be found. ✉ *187 George St., Merchant City G1 1YU* ☎ *0870/238–3320* 🖷 *0141/553–2719* 🌐 *www.travelinn.co.uk* *239 rooms* *Restaurant, bar, parking (fee), no-smoking rooms; no a/c* *AE, MC, V.*

£ **Victorian House.** Compared with its dramatic, bright-yellow entrance hall and reception area, the rooms in this B&B are rather plain. But its location—on a quiet residential street only a block from the Charles Rennie Mackintosh–designed Glasgow School of Art—is prime. There are plenty of restaurants on nearby Sauchiehall Street, and the friendly staff is more than happy to help you choose one. ✉ *212 Renfrew St., City Center, G3 6TX* ☎ *0141/332–0129* 🖷 *0141/353–3155* 🌐 *www.thevictorian.co.uk* *57 rooms* *Dining room; no a/c* *MC, V* *BP.*

West End & Environs

★ £££–£££££ **One Devonshire Gardens.** Celebrities such as Luciano Pavarotti and Elizabeth Taylor name this hotel, which comprises a group of Victorian houses on a sloping tree-lined street, their favorite. Elegance is the theme, from the sophisticated drawing room to the sumptuous guest rooms with rich drapery and traditional mahogany furnishings; 10 of the rooms have four-poster beds. The hotel restaurant is equally stylish, with a different menu each month. Specialties include paupiette of sole filled with organic salmon and served with champagne sauce. Another restaurant, the privately-run Amaryllis, is also on site. ✉ *1 Devonshire Gardens, West End, G12 0UX* ☎ *0141/339–2001* 🖷 *0141/337–1663* 🌐 *www.onedevonshiregardens.com* *40 rooms* *2 restaurants, room service, cable TV, lounge, free parking, meeting room; no a/c* *AE, DC, MC, V* *BP.*

££ Fodor's Choice ★ **Ambassador Hotel.** Opposite the West End's peaceful Botanic Gardens, and convenient for cab, bus, and underground travel to the city center, the Ambassador forms part of an elegant terrace of town houses on the banks of the River Kelvin. The interior echoes the peacefulness of the location and the traditional Victorian ethos of the spacious former family home. Though largely traditional, the rooms have a contemporary edge, with rich red and gold fabrics and beech furniture. ✉ *7 Kelvin Dr., West End, G20 8QG* ☎ *0141/946–1018* 🖷 *0141/945–5377* 🌐 *www.glasgowhotelsandapartments.co.uk* *17 rooms* *In-room* *data ports, in-room safes, refrigerators, bar, laundry facilities, business services, no-smoking rooms, free parking; no a/c* ▭ *MC, V* 🍴 *BP.*

££ **Angus.** The biggest plus at this small, cozy hotel is the friendly staff with a knack for detail. All the rooms are spacious with tasteful, Victorian-inspired, contemporary furniture. The breakfast room overlooks Kelvingrove Park, and you are welcome to have dinner at the restaurant in the Angus's sister hotel, the Argyll, across the street. ✉ *966–970 Sauchiehall St., West End, G3 7TH* ☎ *0141/357–5155* 📠 *0141/339–9469* 🌐 *www.angushotelglasgow.co.uk* *19 rooms* *Dining room, cable TV, bar, laundry service, baby-sitting; no a/c* ▭ *AE, MC, V* 🍴 *BP.*

££ **Kirklee Hotel.** This West End B&B near the university is in a small and cozy Edwardian town house replete with home-away-from-home comforts. A bay window in the lounge overlooks a garden, and the Victorian morning room is adorned with embroidered settees and silk-wash wallpapers. Engravings and a large library offer decorative touches that any university don would appreciate. The owners are friendly and helpful. ✉ *11 Kensington Gate, West End G12 9LG* ☎ *0141/334–5555* 📠 *0141/339–3828* *kirklee@clara.net* *9 rooms* *Library; no a/c, no smoking* ▭ *AE, DC, MC, V* 🍴 *BP.*

££ **Number Thirty Six.** This Victorian terrace house in the West End is a 10-minute walk from the Hunterian museums and Kelvingrove Park. Each room is individually decorated, with antique furniture and paintings or prints. ✉ *36 St. Vincent Crescent, West End, G3 8NG* ☎ *0141/248–2086* 📠 *0141/221–1477* 🌐 *www.no36.co.uk* *5 rooms* *TV in some rooms, lounge; no a/c, no smoking* ▭ *MC, V* 🍴 *CP.*

££ **Town House.** A handsome old terraced house in a quiet cul-de-sac serves as a B&B. The owners are welcoming, and the Town House thrives on repeat business. Restrained cream-and-pastel-stripe decor, stripped pine doors, and plain fabrics complement the high ceilings, plasterwork, and other original architectural features of the house. There's a comfortable sitting room with books, a coal-burning fireplace, and informative leaflets. ✉ *4 Hughenden Ter., West End, G12 9XR* ☎ *0141/357–0862* 📠 *0141/339–9605* 🌐 *www.thetownhouseglasgow.com* *10 rooms* *Lounge, Internet, free parking; no a/c* ▭ *MC, V* 🍴 *BP.*

£ **Cairncross House.** On Glasgow University's West End campus, this modern dormitory provides affordable accommodation for visitors during summer vacation (June through mid-October). Small rooms with one or two single-person beds, and inexpensive modern furniture, are available. The hall is a few minutes' walk from the Botanic Gardens and Kelvingrove Park. ✉ *20 Kelvinhaugh Pl., West End* ☎ *0141/330–3123* 📠 *0141/330–2036* 🌐 *www.cvso.co.uk* *155 rooms with shared bath* *Kitchen, laundry facilities, free parking; no a/c* ⏲ *Closed Oct.–June* ▭ *AE, MC, V* 🍴 *CP.*

£ **Manor Park Hotel.** On a quiet street close to Victoria Park, one of Glasgow's most idyllic West End parks, this hotel combines urban spaciousness with proximity to city action. Each of the neat and airy bedrooms, even the bright attic ones, in this stately terraced town house bears the name in Gaelic of a Scottish island. The friendly owners themselves are Gaelic speakers, and tartan plays its part subtly in the homey interior. ✉ *28 Balshagray Dr., West End, G11 7DD* ☎ *0141/339–2143* 📠 *0141/339–5842* 🌐 *www.manorparkhotel.com* *10 rooms* *Lounge, business services, free parking; no a/c* ▭ *AE, MC, V* 🍴 *BP.*

Fodor's Choice ★

£ **The Sandyford.** The red-trimmed Victorian exterior of this simple B&B foretells the colorful rooms decorated with basic pine furnishings. On the west end of famous Sauchiehall Street, the hotel is convenient to all city-center sights, including the Scottish Exhibition Centre and many art galleries. ✉ *904 Sauchiehall St., West End, G3 7TF* ☎ *0141/334–0000*

0141/337–1812 www.sandyfordhotelglasgow.com 55 rooms Lounge, free parking; no a/c MC, V BP.

South Side

£££–££££ **Sherbrooke Castle Hotel.** Come to the Sherbrooke for a flight of Gothic fantasy. Its cavernous rooms hark back to grander times when the South Side of Glasgow was home to the immensely wealthy tobacco barons, whose homes boasted turrets and towers. The spacious grounds are far from the noise and bustle of the city yet only a 10-minute drive from the city center. Like the tobacco barons, the hotel's proprietor insists on tasteful interior styling and good traditional cooking. The restaurant serves fine food made with fresh ingredients prepared on the premises, including the breads. Locals flock to the busy bar. *11 Sherbrooke Ave., Pollokshields, South Side, G41 4PG 0141/427–4227 0141/427–5685 www.sherbrooke.co.uk 25 rooms Restaurant, cable TV, bar; no a/c AE, DC, MC, V BP.*

££–£££ **Ewington Hotel.** This quiet row of Victorian town houses opposite Queen's Park has an open and traditional look. Victorian-style furniture, ornately decorated bedrooms with heavy and elaborate pink-and-green floral fabrics, and an open fire in the spacious lobby all add to the relaxed, elegant character. The hotel has its own bar and restaurant. Downtown Glasgow is only a short bus or train ride away. *132 Queen's Dr., South Side, G42 8QW 0141/423–1152 0141/422–2030 www.bestwestern.co.uk 43 rooms Restaurant, bar, meeting room, free parking; no a/c AE, DC, MC, V BP.*

NIGHTLIFE & THE ARTS

Home to Scotland's national orchestra, and opera and dance companies, Glasgow is truly the artistic hub of the country. As for nightlife, Glasgow's mix of university students, artists, and professionals maintains a spirited pub-and-club scene.

The Arts

Concerts

Glasgow's **Royal Concert Hall** (2 Sauchiehall St., City Center 0141/353–8000 www.grch.com) has 2,500 seats and is the main venue of the Royal Scottish National Orchestra (RSNO), which performs winter and spring. The **Royal Scottish Academy of Music and Drama** (100 Renfrew St., City Center 0141/332–5057 www.rsamd.ac.uk) is one of the main small venues for concerts, recitals, and theater productions. The **Scottish Exhibition and Conference Centre** (Finnieston, West End 0141/248–3000 www.secc.co.uk) regularly hosts pop concerts.

Dance & Opera

Glasgow is home to the Scottish Opera and Scottish Ballet, both of which perform at the the **Theatre Royal** (282 Hope St., City Center 0141/332–9000 www.theatreroyalglasgow.com). Visiting dance companies from many countries appear here as well.

Festivals

Celtic Connections (Glasgow Royal Concert Hall, 2 Sauchiehall St., City Center, G2 3NY 0141/353–8000 www.celticconnections.co.uk) is an ever-expanding Celtic music festival held in the second half of January. Musicians from Africa, France, Canada, Ireland, and Scotland perform and conduct hands-on workshops on topics such as harp-making and -playing. **Glasgay**(0141/334–7126 www.glasgay.co.uk), held in the first half of November, is the United Kingdom's largest multi-arts festival focusing on gay and lesbian issues. The international and Scottish line-up is always impressive and draws a huge audience.

Film

The **Glasgow Film Theatre** (✉ 12 Rose St., City Center ☎ 0141/332–8128 🌐 www.gft.org.uk), an independent public cinema, screens the best new-release films from all over the world. The **Center for Contemporary Arts** (✉ 350 Sauchiehall St., City Center ☎ 0141/352–4900 🌐 www.cca-glasgow.com) screens classic, independent, and children's films.The **Grosvenor** (✉ Ashton La., West End ☎ 0141/339–4298 🌐 www.grosvenorcinema.co.uk) is a popular, compact cinema in Glasgow's West End. The **Odeon Film Centre** (✉ Renfield St., City Center ☎ 0870/505–0007), an intimate movie theater, screens all the latest releases. **UGC Cinemas** (✉ 145-159 West Nile St., City Center ☎ 0870/907–0789), an 18-screen multilevel facility, is Glasgow's busiest movie complex and the world's tallest cinema building, at 170 feet.

Theater

Tickets for theatrical performances can be purchased at theater box offices or by telephone through the booking line: **Ticket Center** (☎ 0141/287–5511).

The **Arches** (✉ 253 Argyle St., City Center ☎ 0901/022–0300 🌐 www.thearches.co.uk) stages challenging yet accessible drama from around the world. Some of the most exciting theatrical performances take place ★ at the internationally renowned **Citizens' Theatre** (✉ 119 Gorbals St., South Side ☎ 0141/429–0022 🌐 www.citz.co.uk), where productions, and their sets, are often of hair-raising originality. Behind the theater's striking contemporary glass facade is a glorious Victorian red-and-gilded auditorium. Contemporary works are staged at **Cottier's Arts Theatre** (✉ 93 Hyndland St., West End ☎ 0141/357–3868), in a converted church. The **King's Theatre** (✉ 297 Bath St., City Center ☎ 0141/240–1111 🌐 www.kings-glasgow.co.uk) puts on drama, light entertainment, variety shows, and musicals. The **Pavilion** (✉ 121 Renfield St., City Center ☎ 0141/332–1846 🌐 www.paviliontheatre.co.uk) hosts family variety entertainment along with rock and pop concerts.

The **Royal Scottish Academy of Music and Drama** (✉ 100 Renfrew St., City Center ☎ 0141/332–5057) stages international and student performances. The **Theatre Royal** (✉ 282 Hope St., City Center ☎ 0141/332–9000) hosts performances of major dramas, including an occasional season of plays by international touring companies, as well as opera and ballet. The **Tron Theatre** (✉ 63 Trongate, Merchant City ☎ 0141/552–4267 🌐 www.tron.co.uk) puts on Scottish and international contemporary theater.

Nightlife

Consult the biweekly magazine the *List,* available at newsstands and bookstores, and the *Scotsman*, *Herald*, and *Evening Times* newspapers for up-to-date performance and event listings.

Bars & Pubs

Glasgow's pubs were once known for serious drinkers who demanded few comforts. Times have changed, and many pubs have been turned into smart wine bars. Most pubs are open daily from 11 AM to 11 PM.

The **Horseshoe Bar** (✉ 17–21 Drury St., City Center ☎ 0141/229–5711) offers a sentimental, sepia-tinted glimpse of all the friendlier Glasgow myths and serves that cheerful distillation over what is purported to be the world's longest bar. Refurbishment would be a curse on its original tiling, stained glass, and deeply polished woodwork. Almost as intriguing is the clientele—a complete cross section of the city's populace. The upstairs lounge, with a bargain three-course lunch for £3, serves the steak pie for which Britain is famous.

Babbity Bowster's (✉ 16–18 Blackfriars St., Merchant City ☎ 0141/552–5055), a busy, friendly spot, serves interesting beers and good food. **Rogano** (✉ 11 Exchange Place, City Center ☎ 0141/248–4055) is famous for its champagne cocktails and general air of 1920's decadence. Despite its former austere existence as a Victorian church, the always-busy **Cottiers** (✉ Hyndland St., West End ☎ 0141/357–5825) is a famous haunt of the young. The best seat is outside in the popular beer garden. The classic Victorian **Drum and Monkey** (✉ 93 St. Vincent St., City Center ☎ 0141/221–6636) attracts an after-work crowd of young professionals.

There's good live music in the **Halt** (✉ 160 Woodlands Rd., West End ☎ 0141/564–1527), which attracts a mixed-age clientele. **King Tut's Wah Wah Hut** (✉ 227a St. Vincent St., City Center ☎ 0141/221–5279), which hosts live music most nights, claims to have been the venue that discovered the U.K. pop band Oasis. It's a favorite with students, but the cozy and traditional pub setting draws people of all ages. **Nico's** (✉ 375 Sauchiehall St., City Center ☎ 0141/332–5736), designed along the lines of a Paris café, is a favorite with art students and young Glaswegian professionals. The **Riverside Club** (✉ 33 Fox St., off Clyde St., City Center ☎ 0141/248–3144) hosts traditional *ceilidh* (a mix of country dancing, music, and song; pronounced *kay*-lee) bands on Friday and Saturday evenings; get there early, as it's very popular.

The **Scotia Bar** (✉ 112 Stockwell St., Merchant City ☎ 0141/552–8681) serves up a taste of an authentic Glasgow pub, with some traditional folk music occasionally thrown in. **Tennants** (✉ 191 Byres Rd., West End ☎ 0141/341–1021), a spacious street-corner bar, prides itself on a comprehensive selection of beers, lively conversation, and a refreshing lack of loud music. The best Gaelic pub is **Uisge Beatha** (✉ 232–246 Woodlands Rd., West End ☎ 0141/564–1596), pronounced *oos*-ki *bee*-ha, which means "water of life" and is the origin of the word *whisky* (the term is a phonetic transliteration of the Gaelic word *uisge*). It serves *fraoch* (heather beer) in season and has live music on Wednesday and Sunday.

Nightclubs

As elsewhere in Britain, electronic music—from house to techno to drum and bass—is par for the course in Glasgow's dance clubs. **Archaos** (✉ 25 Queen St., City Center ☎ 0141/204–3189), Glasgow's biggest club, has three dance floors blasting house, garage, indie, R&B, soul, and hip-hop music. It's open Wednesday through Sunday from 11 PM to 4 AM. The **Arches** (✉ 253 Argyle St., City Center ☎ 0901/022–0300) is one of the city's largest arts venues, for both its own and touring theater groups, but on Friday (from 11 PM to 3 AM) and Saturday (from 10:30 PM to 4 AM) it thumps with house and techno and welcomes big music names. The **Polo Lounge** (✉ 84 Wilson St., Merchant City ☎ 0141/553–1221) is Glasgow's largest gay club, with three bars and two dance floors for '70s, '80s, '90s, and '00s sounds—something for everyone. The festivities run Monday through Thursday from 5 PM to 1 AM, Friday from 5 PM to 3 AM, and weekends from noon to 3 AM.

SPORTS & THE OUTDOORS

The **Greater Glasgow and Clyde Valley Tourist Board** (✉ 11 George Sq., near Queen Street station, City Center ☎ 0141/204–4400) can provide information on numerous outdoor activities.

Biking & Running

The tourist board can provide a list of parks and cycle paths where you can jog or pedal.

Golf

Several municipal courses are operated within Glasgow proper by the local authorities. Bookings are relatively inexpensive and should be made directly to the course 24 hours in advance to ensure prime tee times (courses open at 7 AM). A comprehensive list of contacts, facilities, and greens fees of the 30 or so other courses near the city is available from the tourist board.

Lethamhill. The fairways of this city-owned parkland course overlook Hogganfield Loch. To get there, take the M8 north to Junction 12, and drive up the A80 about a quarter mile. ✉ *1240 Cumbernauld Rd., North City* ☎ *0141/770–6220* 🏌 *18 holes, 5,836 yards, SSS 68.*

Linn Park. This short public course is about 5 mi southwest of Glasgow's city center via the M74 and B766. ✉ *Simshill Rd., South Side* ☎ *0141/633–0337* 🏌 *18 holes, 5,132 yards, SSS 65.*

Littlehill. Level fairways and greens make this municipal course not too difficult to play. It's on the A803 about 4 mi north of the city center. ✉ *Auchinairn Rd., North City* ☎ *0141/772–1916* 🏌 *18 holes, 6,240 yards, SSS 70.*

Sailing & Water Sports

The Firth of Clyde and Loch Lomond, about a 30-minute drive southwest and north of Glasgow, respectively, have water-sports facilities for sailing, canoeing, windsurfing, and rowing, with full equipment rental. Details are available from the tourist board.

Soccer

The city has been sports mad, especially for football (soccer), for more than 100 years, and the rivalry between its two main clubs, the Rangers and the Celtic, is legendary. Matches are held usually on Saturday in winter, and Glasgow has in total four teams playing in the Scottish Leagues. Admission prices start at about £17. Don't go looking for the family-day-out atmosphere of many American football games; soccer remains a fiercely contested game attended mainly by males, though the stadiums at Ibrox and Celtic Park are fast becoming family-friendly. Rangers wear blue and play at **Ibrox** (✉ Edmiston Dr., South Side ☎ 08706/001993 🌐 www.rangers.co.uk), pronounced *eye*-brox, to the west of the city. The Celtic wear white and green hoops and play in the east at **Celtic Park** (✉ 95 Kerrydale St., East End ☎ 0141/551–8653 🌐 www.celticfc.net).But the glorious game in Glasgow isn't just blue or green, nor is it dominated by international players and big money. Partick Thistle (the Jags) wear red and yellow and their ground is **Firhill Park** (✉ 80 Firhill, West End ☎ 0141/579–1971 🌐 www.ptfc.co.uk).

SHOPPING

Glasgow has long been famous for its clothes shopping, and you can cover its main shopping centers and streets at small expense by bus, *provided* you don't get off. No one has yet discovered any way of keeping shopoholics on the buses, however, and considering the range, value, and attractiveness of the goods in the city's boutiques, no one can blame them.

Arcades & Shopping Centers

The **Buchanan Galleries** (✉ 220 Buchanan St., City Center ☎ 0141/333–9898 🌐 www.buchanangalleries.co.uk), at the top end of Buchanan Street next to the Royal Conçert Hall, is packed with high-quality shops; its magnet attraction is the John Lewis department store. By far the best complex is **Princes Square** (✉ 48 Buchanan St., City Center ☎ 0141/204–1685), with high-quality shops in an art-nouveau setting, along with cafés and restaurants. Look particularly for the Scottish Craft Centre, which carries an outstanding collection of work created by some of the nation's best craftspeople. **St. Enoch's Shopping Centre** (✉ 55 St. Enoch Sq., City Center ☎ 0141/204–3900) is eye-catching if not especially pleasing—it's a modern glass building that resembles an overgrown greenhouse. It houses various stores, but most could be found elsewhere.

Department Stores

British Home Stores (✉ 67– 81 Sauchiehall St., City Center ☎ 0141/332–0401) carries typical department-store goods: clothes, household gadgets, linens, and foodstuffs. **Debenham's** (✉ 97 Argyle St., also accessed from St. Enoch Centre, City Center ☎ 0141/221–0088) is one of Glasgow's principal department stores, with china and crystal as well as women's and men's clothing. **Frasers** (✉ 21– 45 Buchanan St., City Center ☎ 0141/221–3880), a Glasgow institution, stocks wares that reflect Glasgow's material aspirations—leading European designer clothes and fabrics combined with home-produced articles, such as tweeds, tartans, glass, and ceramics. The magnificent interior, set off by the grand staircase rising to various floors and balconies, is itself worth a visit.

Marks & Spencer (✉ 2– 12 Argyle St., City Center ☎ 0141/552–4546 ✉ 172 Sauchiehall St., City Center ☎ 0141/332–6097) sells sturdy, practical clothes and basic accessories at moderate prices; you can also buy food items and household goods here. **John Lewis** (✉ Buchanan Galleries, 220 Buchanan St., City Center ☎ 0141/353–6677) is a favorite for its good-value mix of clothing and household items.

Shopping Districts

On the main, often-crowded pedestrian area of **Argyle Street,** you'll find chain stores such as Debenham's. An interesting diversion off Argyle Street is the covered **Argyll Arcade,** which has the largest collection of jewelers under one roof in Scotland. The L-shape arcade, built in 1904, houses several locally based jewelers and a few shops specializing in antique jewelry. **Buchanan Street,** off the Argyll Arcade, is Glasgow's premier shopping street and almost totally a pedestrian area. The usual suspects are here: Laura Ashley, Burberry's, Jaeger, and other household names, some with premises in Buchanan Galleries, at the top end of the street. **St. Enoch Square,** which is also the main underground station, houses the St. Enoch Shopping Centre.

The huge **Barras** indoor market, on London Road in the Glasgow Cross neighborhood, prides itself on selling everything "from a needle to an anchor." Stalls hawk antique (and not-so-antique) furniture, bric-a-brac, good and not-so-good jewelry, and textiles—you name it, it's here. Many of Glasgow's young and upwardly mobile make their home in **Merchant City,** on the edge of the city center. Shopping here is expensive, but the area is worth visiting if you're seeking the young Glasgow style. The university dominates the area around **West End**, and the shops cater to local and student needs. The easiest way to get here is by the underground system to Hillhead. If you're an antiques connoisseur and art lover, a walk along **West Regent Street**, particularly its **Victorian Village**, is highly recommended, as there are various galleries and shops, some specializing in Scottish antiques and paintings.

Specialty Shops

Antiques & Fine Art

The **Compass Gallery** (✉ 178 W. Regent St., City Center ☎ 0141/221–6370) hosts exhibitions focusing on abstract and expressionist art. **Cyril Gerber Fine Art** (✉ 148 W. Regent St., City Center ☎ 0141/221–3095 or 0141/204–0276) specializes in British paintings from 1880 to the present; they will export, as will most galleries. ★ **De Courcys** (✉ 5–21 Cresswell La., West End), an antiques and crafts arcade, has quite a few shops to visit, and lots of goods, including paintings and jewelry, are regularly auctioned here. It's on one of the cobblestone lanes to the rear of Byres Road.

Books & Paper

Borders Books, Music and Café (✉ 98 Buchanan St., City Center ☎ 0141/222–7700), set in a former bank building, has a particularly friendly Glasgow air and carries a wide selection of Scottish books. The **Glasgow School of Art** (✉ 167 Renfrew St., City Center ☎ 0141/353–4526) has the Mackintosh Shop, selling books, cards, jewelry, and ceramics. Students often sell their work during the degree shows in June. **Papyrus** (✉ 374 Byres Rd., West End ☎ 0141/334–6514 ✉ 296–298 Sauchiehall St., City Center ☎ 0141/353–2182) carries designer cards and small gifts, as well as a good selection of books.

Clothing Boutiques

Male and female fashionista must not miss **Cruise** (✉ 180 Ingram St., City Center ☎ 0141/572–3280), which stocks the coolest labels at cool prices. **Strawberry Fields** (✉ 517 Great Western Rd., West End ☎ 0141/339–1121) sells colorful children's wear.

Food

Peckham's Delicatessen (✉ 100 Byres Rd., West End ☎ 0141/357–1454 ✉ 43 Clarence Dr., West End ☎ 0141/357–2909 ✉ Central Station, City Center ☎ 0141/248–4012 ✉ Glassford St., Merchant City ☎ 0141/553–0666) is *the* place for Continental sausages, cheeses, and anything else you'd need for a delicious picnic. **Iain Mellis Cheesemonger** (✉ 492 Great Western Rd., West End ☎ 0141/339–8998) has a comprehensive selection of fine Scottish cheeses.

Home Furnishings & Textiles

Casa Fina (✉ 1 Wilson St., Merchant City ☎ 0141/552–6791) stocks stylish modern furniture and giftware. **In House** (✉ 24–26 Wilson St., Merchant City ☎ 0141/552–5902) has top-quality, contemporary designer furniture as well as glassware, china, and textiles. **Linens Fine** (✉ The Courtyard, Princes Sq., City Center ☎ 0141/248–7082) carries wonderful embroidered and embellished bed linens and other textiles. At the shop for the **National Trust for Scotland** (✉ Hutchesons' Hall, 158 Ingram St., Merchant City ☎ 0141/552–8391) many of the items for sale, such as china, giftware, textiles, toiletries, and housewares, are designed exclusively for trust properties and are often handmade. Wander around **Stockwell Bazaar** (✉ 67–77 Glassford St., Merchant City ☎ 0141/552–5781) to view a huge selection of fine china and earthenware, glass, and ornaments. Items can be packed and sent overseas.

Scottish Specialties

For high-quality giftware in Charles Rennie Mackintosh style, head to **Catherine Shaw** (✉ 24 Gordon St., City Center ☎ 0141/204–4762 ✉ 32 Argyll Arcade, City Center ☎ 0141/221–9038). **Hector Russell Kiltmakers** (✉ 110 Buchanan St., City Center ☎ 0141/221–0217) specializes in Highland outfitting, Scottish gifts, woolens, cashmere, and women's fashions. **MacDonald MacKay Ltd.** (✉ 161 Hope St., City Center ☎ 0141/204–3930) makes, sells, and exports Highland dress and accessories.

Sports Gear

You'll find good-quality outerwear at **Tiso Sports** (✉ 129 Buchanan St., City Center 🌐 www.tiso.com ☎ 0141/248–4877), handy if you're planning some Highland walks.

Tobacco

Robert Graham (✉ 71 St. Vincent St., City Center ☎ 0141/221–6588) carries a tremendous variety of tobaccos and pipes. Much of Glasgow's wealth was generated by the tobacco lords during the 17th and 18th centuries; at Graham's you'll experience a little of that colorful history.

SIDE TRIPS FROM GLASGOW: ROBERT BURNS COUNTRY

The jigsaw puzzle of firths and straits and interlocking islands that you see as you fly into Glasgow Airport harbors numerous tempting one-day excursion destinations. You can travel south to visit the fertile farmlands of Ayrshire—Robert Burns country—or west to the Firth of Clyde, or southeast to the Clyde Valley, all by car or by public transportation. You may want to begin with the town of Paisley. Once a distinct burgh but now part of the Glasgow suburban area, it has plenty of gritty character, largely from vestiges of its industrial heritage. It was once famous for its paisley shawl manufacturing, and its museum displays a fine collection of these garments. Palatial treasures are also en route—the Hamilton Mausoleum, the Marquess of Bute's Mount Stuart House on the Isle of Bute, and Culzean Castle, a favored retreat for Eisenhower and Churchill that is famous for its Robert Adam (1728–92) design and spectacular seaside setting.

The highlight of this region is Robert Burns country. English children learn that Burns (1759–96) is a good minor poet. But Scottish children know that he's Shakespeare, Dante, Rabelais, Mozart, and Karl Marx rolled into one. As time goes by, it seems that the Scots have it more nearly right. As poet and humanist, Burns increases in stature. When you plunge into Burns country, don't forget that he's held in extreme reverence by Scots of all backgrounds. They may argue about Sir Walter Scott and Bonnie Prince Charlie, but there's no disputing the merits of the poet of "Bonnie Doon."

Paisley

32 *7 mi south of Glasgow.*

The industrial prosperity of Paisley came from textiles and, in particular, from the woolen paisley shawl. The internationally recognized paisley pattern is based on the shape of a palm shoot, an ancient Babylonian fertility symbol brought to Britain by way of Kashmir. The full story of the pattern and of the innovative weaving techniques introduced in ★ Paisley is told in the **Paisley Museum & Art Gallery,** which has a world-famous shawl collection. ✉ *High St.* ☎ *0141/889–3151* 💰 *Free* ⏲ *Tues.–Sat. 10–5, Sun. 2–5.*

To get an idea of the life led by textile industry workers, visit the **Sma' Shot Cottages.** These re-creations of mill workers' houses contain displays of linen, lace, and paisley shawls. An 18th-century weaver's cottage is also open to visitors. ✉ *11–17 George Pl.* ☎ *0141/889–1708* 🌐 *www.smashot.com* *Free* ⏲ *Apr.–Sept., Wed. and Sat. 12–4; Oct.–Mar. by appointment only.*

Paisley's 12th-century Cluniac **Abbey** dominates the town center. Almost completely destroyed by the English in 1307, the abbey was not totally restored until the early 20th century. It is associated with Walter Fitzallan, the high steward of Scotland, who gave his name to the Stewart monarchs of Scotland (Stewart is a corruption of "steward"). Outstanding features include the vaulted stone roof and stained glass of the choir. Paisley Abbey is today a busy parish church; if you're visiting with a large group you should call ahead. ☎ *0141/889–7654* *Free* ⏲ *Mon.–Sat. 10–3:30, Sun. services 11, 12:15, and 6:30.*

WHERE TO STAY & EAT

££–£££ **Glynhill Hotel.** This converted, expanded mansion combines elegant living with modern hotel convenience. Stylish and bright contemporary furnishings make the bedrooms cheerful and comfortable. The buffet-style Palm Court Carverie serves a three-course dinner for £17.95. Le Gourmet, with its table d'hôte and à la carte menus, is a favorite with locals. The hotel is just off the M8 motorway (Junction 27) and close to Glasgow Airport and Paisley town center. ✉ *169 Paisley Rd., Renfrew, PA4 8XB* ☎ *0141/886–5555* *0141/885–2838* 🌐 *www.glynhill.co.uk* *125 rooms* *Restaurant, cable TV, indoor pool, bar, meeting room, free parking; no a/c* *AE, DC, MC, V* *BP.*

★ **£–££** **Makerston Guest House.** Mary and Jim McCue run this popular guest house and take great delight in looking after their guests. The rooms are immaculately presented, with Edwardian fireplaces and ceiling roses, and many overlook lovingly cared-for gardens. The inn is close to the M8 motorway at Junction 27 and a short taxi ride from Paisley's Gilmour Street train station. ✉ *19 Park Rd. PA2 6JP* ☎ *0141/884–2520* *0141/884–2520* 🌐 *www.makerston.co.uk* *11 rooms (8 with bath)* *Restaurant; no a/c* *MC, V* *BP.*

Paisley A to Z

BUS TRAVEL

Buses to Paisley depart from the Buchanan Street bus station in Glasgow. Traveline Scotland provides information on schedules and fares.

Buchanan Street bus station ☎ 0141/333-3708. **Traveline Scotland** ☎ 0870/608-2608 🌐 www.travelinescotland.com.

CAR TRAVEL

Take the M8 westbound and turn off at Junction 27, which is clearly signposted to Paisley.

TRAIN TRAVEL

Trains to Paisley depart daily every 5–10 minutes from Glasgow Central Station.

Glasgow Central Station ☎ 0845/748-4950.

VISITOR INFORMATION

The tourist information center, which is open daily from 10 to 5, except on Sundays from October through March, is near Paisley Gilmour Street railway station.

Paisley Tourist Information Center ✉ 9A Gilmour St. ☎ 0141/889-0711.

Ayrshire & the Clyde Coast

Robert Burns is Scotland's national and best-loved poet. His birthday is celebrated with speeches and dinners, feasting, and singing (Burns Suppers) on January 25, in a way in which few other countries celebrate a poet. He was born in Alloway, beside Ayr, just an hour or so south of Glasgow, and the towns and villages where he lived and loved make for an interesting day out.

On your way here you'll travel beside the estuary and firth of the great River Clyde and will be able to look across to Dumbarton and its Rock, a nostalgic farewell point for emigrants leaving Glasgow. The river is surprisingly narrow here, considering that the *Queen Elizabeth II* and the other great ocean liners sailed these waters from the place of their birth. Farther along the coast, the views north and west to Loch Long, Holy Loch, and the Argyll Forest Park are outstanding on a clear day. Two high points of the trip, in addition to the Burns connections, are Mount Stuart House, on the Isle of Bute, and south of Ayr, Culzean Castle, flagship of the National Trust for Scotland.

Wemyss Bay

33 *31 mi west of Glasgow.*

From the old Victorian village of Wemyss Bay there's ferry service to the Isle of Bute, a favorite holiday spot for Glaswegians before air travel made it easier to go farther. The many handsome buildings, especially the station and its covered walkway between the platform and steamer pier, are a reminder of the Victorian era's grandeur and style and of the generations of visitors who used trains and ferries for their summer holidays. South of Wemyss Bay, you can look across to the Isle of Arran, another Victorian holiday favorite, and then to the island of Great Cumbrae, a weighty name for a tiny island.

Isle of Bute

34 *75 mi west of Glasgow.*

The Isle of Bute affords a host of relaxing walks and scenic vistas. **Rothesay,** a faded but appealing resort, is the main town. Bute's biggest draw is spectacular **Mount Stuart,** ancestral home of the marquesses of Bute, about 5 mi south of Rothesay. The massive Victorian Gothic palace, built in red sandstone, has ornate interiors, including the Marble Hall, with a star-studded vault, stained glass, arcaded galleries, and magnificent tapestries woven in Edinburgh in the early 20th century. The paintings and furniture throughout the house are equally outstanding. ✉ *Isle of Bute* ☎ *01700/503877* 🌐 *www.mountstuart.com* 🎫 *Joint ticket for house and gardens, £7; gardens only, £3.50* ⏲ *Gardens May–Sept., Mon., Wed., and Fri.–Sun. 10–6; house May–Sept., Mon., Wed., Fri.–Sun. 11–5.*

WHERE TO STAY & EAT

££ ✕🏨 **Ardmory House Hotel.** This garden-surrounded hotel in a peaceful residential area evokes a modern home away from home, with Bute fabric (woven on the island) covering the chairs and a cozy bar with an open fire downstairs. Muted colors decorate the plainly furnished but comfortable bedrooms. The staff is exceptionally friendly and attentive. Standard bar meals such as homemade soup, lasagna, and chili are on offer, and the restaurant serves more elaborate creations—breast of duck with spiced mandarin orange and cherry mulled-wine sauce, and salmon on a nest of fettuccine and vegetables with saffron-butter sauce. ✉ *Ardmory Rd., Ardbeg, Isle of Bute PA20 0PG* ☎ *01700/502346* 📠 *01700/505596* *5 rooms* *Restaurant, TV in some rooms, bar; no a/c* 💳 *MC, V* *BP.*

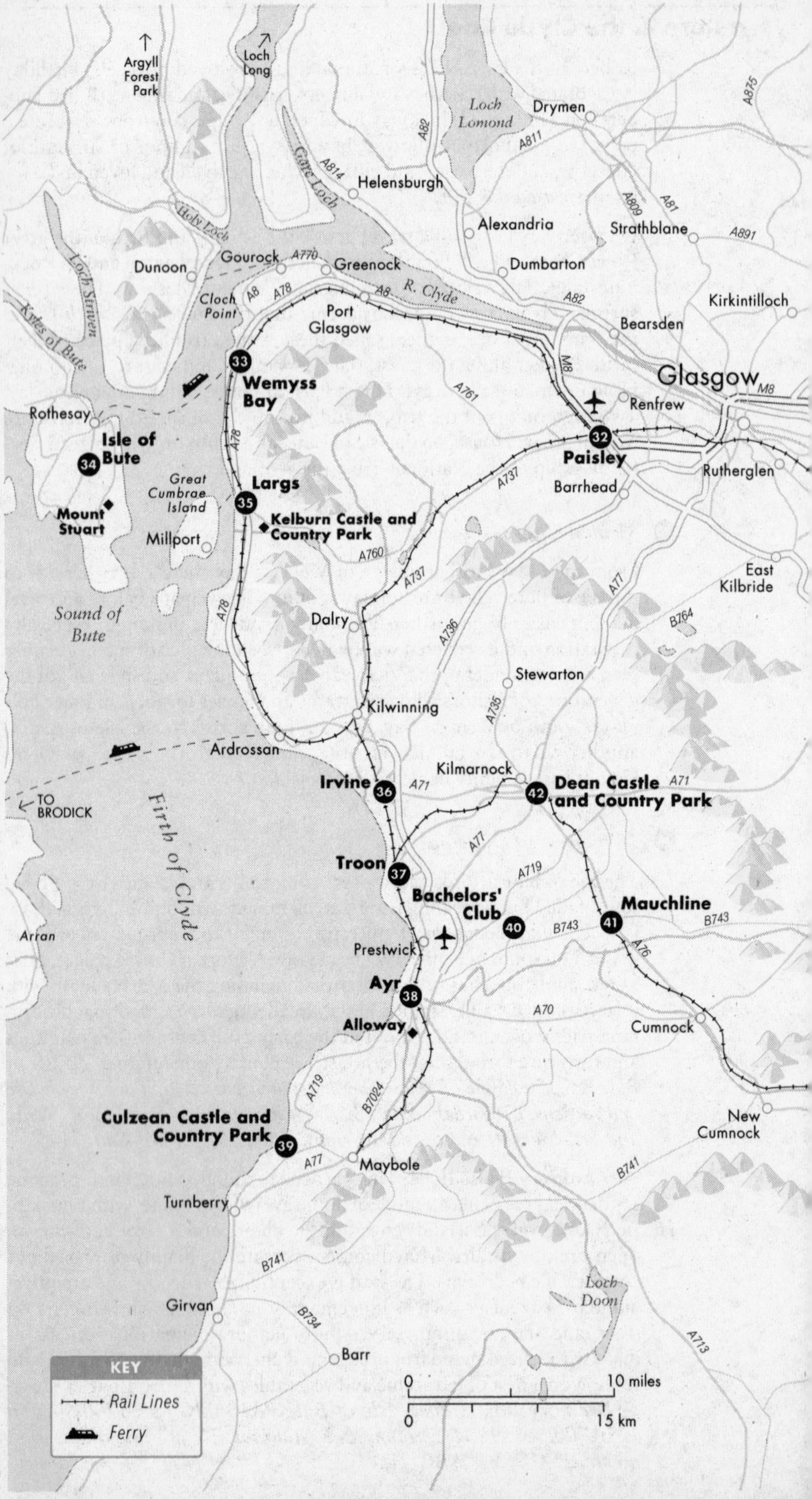
Argyll
Forest
Park
Loch
Long
Loch
Lomond
Drymen
A875
A82
A811
Gare Loch
A814
Helensburgh
A809
A81
Holy Loch
Alexandria
Strathblane
A891
Loch Striven
Dunoon
Gourock
A770
Greenock
Dumbarton
R. Clyde
A82
Kirkintilloch
Kyles of Bute
Cloch
Point
A8
A78
A8
Port
Glasgow
Bearsden
M8
33
Wemyss
Bay
A761
Glasgow
M8
Renfrew
Rothesay
32
Paisley
Isle of
Bute
34
A78
Rutherglen
Great
Cumbrae
Island
Largs
35
A737
Barrhead
Mount
Stuart
Kelburn Castle and
Country Park
Millport
A760
East
Kilbride
A737
A77
Sound of
Bute
A78
Dalry
A736
B764
Stewarton
A735
Kilwinning
Ardrossan
TO
BRODICK
Kilmarnock
Irvine
36
A71
42
Dean Castle
and Country Park
A71
Firth of Clyde
A77
Troon
37
A719
Bachelors'
Club
Mauchline
41
B743
40
B743
Arran
Prestwick
A76
Ayr
38
A70
Cumnock
Alloway
A719
B7024
New
Cumnock
Culzean Castle and
Country Park
39
A77
Maybole
B741
Turnberry
B741
Loch
Doon
Girvan
B734
A713
Barr
KEY
Rail Lines
Ferry
0
10 miles
0
15 km

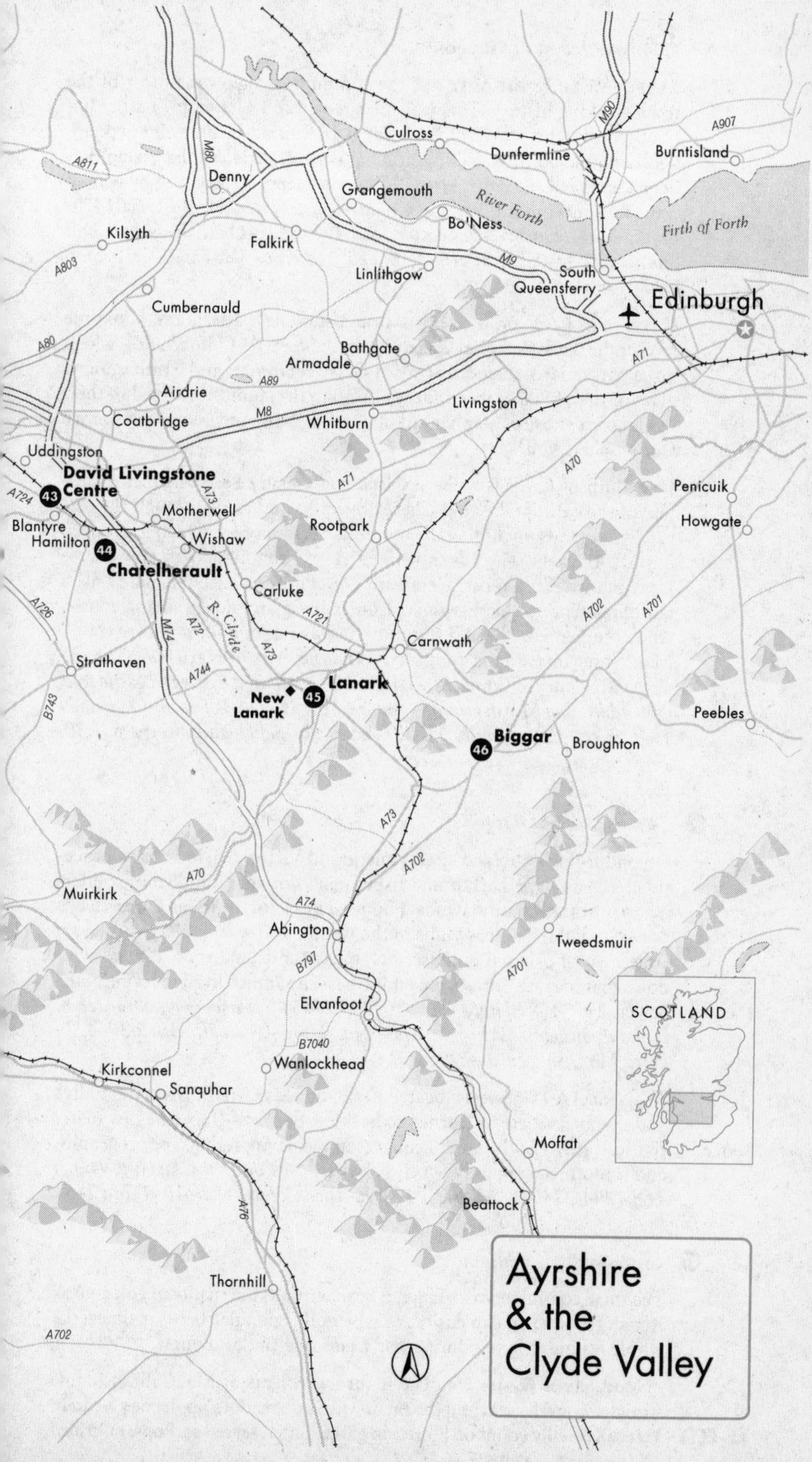

Ayrshire & the Clyde Valley

Largs

35 *42 mi southwest of Glasgow.*

At the coastal resort of Largs, the community makes the most of the town's Viking history. This was the site in 1263 of a major battle that finally broke the power of the Vikings in Scotland, and every September a commemorative Viking Festival is held. **Vikingar! the Viking Heritage Centre** tells the story of the Viking influence in Scotland by way of film, tableaux, and displays. ✉ *Barrfields, Greenock Rd.* ☎ *01475/689777* 🌐 *www.vikingar.co.uk* 🎫 *£4* ⏲ *Mar.–Oct., weekdays and Sun. 10:30–5:30, Sat. 12:30–3:30; Feb. and Nov., Sat. 12:30–3:30, Sun. 10:30–3:30.*

If you're in Largs on the seafront on a summer's afternoon, take time to visit the **Clark Memorial Church** (✉ Bath St. ☎ 01475/675186), which has a particularly splendid array of Glaswegian Arts and Crafts stained glass of the 1890s in its windows. Among the studios involved in their design were those of Stephen Adam (1848–1910) and his contemporary Christopher Wall.

Just south of Largs is **Kelburn Castle and Country Park,** the historic estate of the earl of Glasgow. There are walks and trails through the mature woodlands, including the mazelike Secret Forest, which leads deep into the thickets. The adventure center and commando-assault course wear out even the most overexcited of children. The staff here tells a tale of rescuing an elderly woman from halfway around the assault course, who commented, "Well, I did think it was rather a *hard* nature trail." Make sure you read the signposts. ✉ *Fairlie, Ayrshire* ☎ *01475/568685* 🌐 *www.kelburncountrycentre.com* 🎫 *Grounds and castle £6; castle tour is an additional £1.50; grounds only £4.50* ⏲ *Grounds Easter–Oct., daily 10–6; Nov.–Easter, daily 11–5. Castle July–Sept., daily tours at 1:30, 2:45, and 4.*

Irvine

36 *24 mi south of Glasgow.*

Beyond Irvine's cobbled streets and grand Victorians, look for a peaceful crescent-shape harbor and fishermen's cottages huddled in solidarity against the Atlantic winds. Founded in 1826, the **Irvine Burns Club** is one of the oldest Burns clubs in the world. Today its gallery displays a collection of original manuscripts, plus murals and stained-glass windows that narrate Burns's life and work. The author lived in Irvine when he was 22. ✉ *28 Eglinton St.* ☎ *01294/274511* 🌐 *www.irvineburnsclub.scotland.museum* 🎫 *Free* ⏲ *Apr.–Sept., Mon.–Wed., Fri.–Sat. 2:30–4:30; Oct.–Mar., Sat. 2:30–4:30.*

The **Vennel Art Gallery** is located in the house where Burns came to live and the shed where he learned to heckle—or dress—flax (the raw material for linen). Both buildings have on display paintings, photographs, and sculpture by mainly Scottish artists. ✉ *4 and 10 Glasgow Vennel* ☎ *01294/275059* 🎫 *Free* ⏲ *Mon.-Tues., Thurs.–Sat. 10–1 and 2–5.*

Troon

37 *28 mi south of Glasgow.*

The small coastal town of Troon is famous for its international golf course, Royal Troon. You can easily see why golf is popular here: at times, the whole 60-mi-long Ayrshire coast seems one endless course.

WHERE TO STAY & EAT
★ ££–££££

✕ **MacCallums Oyster Bar.** The main ingredients at MacCallums come straight from the sea, and the menu varies depending on the day's catch. You can usually count on lobster in garlic butter; seared scallops; or grilled langoustines. Excellent light white wines match the freshness of the food. Simple furnishings and solid wooden tables and floorboards decorate the dining room. Hidden among the boatyards and customs buildings of Troon Harbour, this top-class restaurant is easy to miss, but you can find it next to the Seacat Ferry Terminal. ✉ *The Harbour* ☎ *01292/319339* ▭ *AE, DC, MC, V* ⊙ *Closed Mon.*

£££ ✕ **Piersland House Hotel.** This hotel is set in a late-Victorian mansion, formerly the home of a whisky magnate. All the bedrooms are furnished in traditional style. Oak paneling and log fires in the restaurant provide a warm backdrop for traditional Scottish cuisine, including specialties such as beef medallions in pickled walnut sauce. ✉ *15 Craigend Rd., just north of Ayr, KA10 6HD* ☎ *01292/314747* 🖷 *01292/315613* *30 rooms* *Restaurant; no a/c* ▭ *AE, DC, MC, V* 🍽 *BP.*

GOLF **Royal Troon** was founded in 1878 and has two 18-hole courses: the Old, or Championship, Course and the Portland Course. Access for non-members is limited between May and October to Monday, Tuesday, and Thursday only; day tickets cost £150 and include two rounds and a buffet lunch. ✉ *Craigend Rd.* ☎ *01292/311555* 🌐 *www.royaltroon.co.uk* *Old Course: 18 holes, 7,107 yards, SSS 74. Portland Course: 18 holes, 6,289 yards, SSS 70.*

SHOPPING Many Glaswegians frequent **Regalia Fashion Salon** (✉ 44 Church St. ☎ 01292/312162) for its unusual collection of designer clothing for women.

Ayr

38 *34 mi south of Glasgow.*

The commercial port of Ayr is Ayrshire's chief town, a peaceful and elegant place with an air of prosperity and some good shops. Robert Burns was baptized in the Auld Kirk (Old Church) here and wrote a humorous poem about the Twa Brigs (Two Bridges), which cross the river nearby. He described Ayr as a town unsurpassed "for honest men and bonny lasses."

If you're on the Robert Burns trail, head for **Alloway,** on B7024 in Ayr's southern suburbs. In Alloway, among the middle-class residences, you'll find the one-room thatched **Burns Cottage,** where Scotland's national poet was born in 1759 and which his father built; a museum of Burnsiana is next door. Not many outside Scotland appreciate the depth of affection Scotland has for Burns. To his fellow Scots he's more than a great lyric bard; he's the champion of the underdog, the lover of noble causes, the hater of pomposity and cant, the prophet of social justice. "A man's a man for a' that"—such phrases have exalted the Scottish character, while his love songs warm the coldest hearts. January 25, Burns Night, is an anniversary of importance in Scotland. ☎ *01292/441215* *£3; £5 ticket also includes admission to Tam o' Shanter Experience and Burns Monument, plus an audio guide* ⊙ *Apr.–Oct., daily 9–6; Nov.–Mar., Mon.–Sat. 10–4, Sun. noon–4.*

Find out all about Burns at the **Tam o' Shanter Experience.** Here you can enjoy a 10-minute audiovisual journey through his life and times, then watch as one of Burns's most famous poems, "Tam o' Shanter," is brought to life on a three-screen theatrical set. It's down the road from Burns Cottage and around the corner from Alloway's ruined church. ☎ *01292/443700* *£1.50; £5 ticket also includes admission to Burns Cottage and Burns Monument, plus an audio guide* ⊙ *Apr.–Sept., daily 9–5:30; Oct.–Mar., daily 10–5.*

Auld Kirk Alloway is where Tam o' Shanter, in Burns's eponymous poem, unluckily passed a witches' revel—with Old Nick himself playing the bagpipes—on his way home from a night of drinking. Tam, in flight from the witches, managed to cross the **Brig o' Doon** (*brig* is Scots for *bridge*) just in time. His gray mare, Meg, lost her tail to the closest witch. (Any resident of Ayr will tell you that witches cannot cross running water.)

The **Burns Monument** overlooks the Brig o' Doon. ☎ *No phone* 🎫 *£1, or as part of £5 ticket for Burns Cottage and Tam o' Shanter Experience* ⏲ *Apr.–Oct., daily 9–6; Nov.–Mar., Mon.–Sat. 10–4, Sun. noon–4.*

WHERE TO EAT
★ £££–££££ ✕ **Fouter's Bistro.** Fouter's is in a long and narrow cellar, yet its white walls and decorative stenciling create a sense of airiness. The cuisine is also light and skillful—no heavy sauces here. Try the roast Ayrshire lamb with pan juices, red wine, and mint, or sample the "Taste of Scotland" appetizer—smoked salmon, trout, and other goodies. This is modern Scottish and French cooking at its best. ✉ *2A Academy St.* ☎ *01292/261391* 🌐 *www.fouters.co.uk* 💳 *AE, DC, MC, V* ⏲ *Closed Sun. and Mon.*

SHOPPING

Ayr has a good range of shops. You can watch craftspeople at work at the jewelry workshop **Diamond Factory** (✉ 26 Queen's Court ☎ 01292/280476). Particularly coveted are the handmade Celtic wedding bands. The store will export your purchases if you don't have time to wait for the work to be completed. The **Mill Shop, Begg of Ayr** (✉ Viewfield Rd. ☎ 01292/267615) sells a good selection of scarves, stoles, plaids, and travel rugs handmade on-site.

Culzean Castle & Country Park

★ 39 *50 mi south of Glasgow.*

The dramatic cliff-top Culzean (pronounced ku-*lain*) Castle and Country Park is the National Trust for Scotland's most popular property, yet it remains unspoiled. Robert Adam designed the neoclassical mansion, complete with a walled garden, in 1777. In addition to its marvelous interiors, it contains the National Guest Flat, donated by the people of Scotland in appreciation of General Eisenhower's (1890–1969) services during World War II. As president he stayed here once or twice, and his relatives still do so occasionally. Between visits it's used by the National Trust for official entertaining. The rooms on the approach to this apartment evoke the atmosphere of World War II: mementos of Glenn Miller (1904–44), Winston Churchill (1874–1965), and other personalities of the era all help create a suitably 1940s mood. On the estate grounds, shrubberies reflect the essential mildness of this coast, though some visitors, meeting the full force of a westerly gale, might think otherwise. Culzean's perpendicular sea cliff affords views across the Firth of Clyde to Arran and the Irish coast. Not a stone's throw away, it seems, the pinnacle of Ailsa Craig rears from midchannel. ☎ *01655/884400* 🌐 *www.nts.org.uk* 🎫 *Park and castle £9; park only £5* ⏲ *Park, daily 9:30–sunset; castle, Mar.–Oct., daily 10–5, last admission at 4:30. Guided tours July–Sept., daily 11:30 and 3:30; Oct.–June, daily 3:30.*

Bachelors' Club

40 *28 mi southwest of Glasgow.*

At Tarbolton, 8 mi northeast of Ayr, is the Bachelors' Club, the 17th-century house where Robert Burns learned to dance, founded a debating and literary society, and became a Freemason. ✉ *Sandgate St.* ☎ *01292/541940* 🌐 *www.nts.org.uk* 🎫 *£2.50* ⏲ *Apr.–Sep., Fri.–Tues. 1–5.*

Mauchline

41 *26 mi south of Glasgow.*

Mauchline has strong connections with Robert Burns. There's a **Burns House** here and four of his daughters are buried in the churchyard. **Poosie Nansie's Pub,** where Burns used to drink, is still serving pints today. The village is also famous for making curling stones.

Kilmarnock

20 mi south of Glasgow

This industrial town, home of Johnny Walker whisky, has more enjoyment for Burns enthusiasts: the Dick Institute, which houses the Burns
42 Museum and the Burns Federation. **Dean Castle and Country Park** is a 14th-century castle with a wonderful collection of medieval arms and armor and an attractive visitor center. Burns also inevitably gets a mention. ✉ *Off Glasgow Rd.* ☎ *01563/522702* 🎫 *Free* ⏲ *Apr.–Oct., daily noon–5; Nov.–Mar., weekends 12–4.*

Ayrshire & the Clyde Coast A to Z

BUS TRAVEL

From Glasgow, take the bus to Largs for Cumbrae; Ardrossan for Arran; Ayr and Kilmarnock for the Burns Heritage Trail; and Troon, Prestwick, and Ayr to play golf. Bus companies also operate one-day guided excursions; for details contact the tourist information center in Glasgow, Strathclyde Passenger Transport (SPT) Travel Centre.

Traveline Scotland ☎ 0870/608–2608 🌐 www.travelinescotland.com.

CAR TRAVEL

Begin your trip from Glasgow westbound on the M8, signposted for Glasgow Airport and Greenock. Join the A8 and follow it from Greenock to Gourock and around the coast past the Cloch Lighthouse. Head south on the A78 to the old Victorian village of Wemyss Bay and take the ferry over to Bute to see Mount Stuart (leave your car behind: a bus service takes you to the house from the ferry). Then continue down the A78 through Largs, Irvine, Troon, and on to Ayr and Alloway. Head to Culzean Castle, then return to Ayr and turn eastward on the B743, the Mauchline Road; but before you get here, turn left on a little road to Tarbolton and the Bachelors' Club. Return to the B743, visit Mauchline, and then head north on A76 to Kilmarnock. Glasgow is only a half hour away on the fast A77.

TRAIN TRAVEL

You can travel via train to Largs for Cumbrae; Ardrossan for Aryan; Ayr and Kilmarnock for the Burns Heritage Trail; and Troon, Prestwick, and Ayr to play golf.

National Rail ☎ 0845/748–4950 🌐 www.railtrack.co.uk.

VISITOR INFORMATION

All of the visitor centers in the area can provide you with brochures on the Burns Heritage Trail.

Ayr ✉ 22 The Sandgate ☎ 01292/678100. **Irvine** ✉ New St. ☎ 01292/678100. **Kilmarnock** ✉ 62 Bank St. ☎ 01292/678100. **Largs** ✉ Promenade ☎ 01292/678100. **Rothesay** ✉ The Winter Gardens, Rothesay, Isle of Bute ☎ 01292/678100.

Clyde Valley

The River Clyde is (or certainly was) famous for its shipbuilding and heavy industries, yet its upper reaches flow through some of Scotland's most fertile farmlands, rich with tomato crops. It's an interesting area, with ancient castles as well as museums that tell the story of manufacturing and mining prosperity.

Blantyre

8 mi southeast of Glasgow.

43 In the not-very-pretty town of Blantyre, look for signs to the **David Livingstone Centre,** a park area around the tiny (tenement) apartment where the great explorer of Africa (1813–73) was born. Displays tell of his journeys, of his meeting with Stanley ("Dr. Livingstone, I presume"), of Africa, and of the area's industrial heritage. *01698/823140 www.nts.org.uk £3.50 Apr.–Sept., Mon.–Sat. 10–5, Sun. 12:30–5; Oct.–Mar., Mon.–Sat. 10:30–4, Sun. 12:30–4; call to confirm in winter.*

Bothwell Castle, with its well-preserved walls, dates to the 13th century and stands above the River Clyde. It's close to the David Livingstone Centre. *01698/816 894 £2 Apr.–Sept., daily 9:30–6.30; Oct.–Mar., Mon.–Wed. and Sat. 9:30–4.30, Sun. 2–4.30, Thurs. 9:30–noon.*

Hamilton

9 mi southeast of Glasgow.

The **Hamilton Mausoleum,** in Strathclyde Country Park near the industrial town of Hamilton, was built in the 1840s as an extraordinary monument to the lavish eccentricities of the dukes of Hamilton, who had
44 more money than sense. Near Hamilton is **Chatelherault** (pronounced *shat*-lerro), a unique one-room-deep facade—part shooting lodge, part glorified dog kennel—designed in elegant Georgian style by William Adam (1689–1748) for the dukes of Hamilton. Within Chatelherault is an exhibition describing the glories of estate life. *Carlisle Rd., Ferniegar 01698/426213 Free Mon.–Sat. 10–5, Sun. 12–5.*

Lanark

45 *19 mi east of Glasgow.*

Set in pleasing, rolling countryside, Lanark is a typical old Scottish town. It's now most often associated with its unique neighbor New Lanark, a World Heritage Site that was home to a social experiment—a model community with well-designed workers' homes, a school, and public buildings. The River Clyde powers its way through a beautiful wooded gorge, and its waters were harnessed to drive textile mill machinery before the end of the 18th century. The owner, David Dale (1739–1806), was noted for his caring attitude toward the workers, unusual for that era. Later, his son-in-law, Robert Owen (1771–1858), took this attitude even further, founding a benevolent doctrine known as Owenism and eventually crossing the Atlantic to become involved in a similar planned-community project in Indiana, called New Harmony, which, unlike New Lanark, failed. Robert Owen's son Robert Dale Owen, 1801–77, helped found the Smithsonian Institution.

After many changes of fortune the mills eventually closed and were converted into a hotel and private residential properties. As a result, residents have moved in and New Lanark has maintained its unique environment, where those leading normal everyday lives mix easily with the tourists. One of the mills has been converted into an **interpretative center,** which tells the story of this brave social experiment. Upstream, the Clyde flows through some of the finest river scenery anywhere in Lowland Scotland, with woods and spectacular waterfalls. *01555/665876 www.newlanark.org £4.95 Daily 11–5.*

WHERE TO STAY **New Lanark Mill Hotel.** Housed in a converted cotton mill at the 18th-
£££ century model village of New Lanark, this hotel is decorated in a spare, understated style that allows the impressive architecture of barrel-vaulted ceilings and elegant Georgian windows to speak for itself. Right

next to the river in the heart of the village, the hotel has all the attractions—visitor center, shops, Falls of Clyde Wildlife Reserve—at its doorstep. ✉ *New Lanark ML11 9DB* ☎ *01555/667200* 🖷 *01555/667222* 🌐 *www.newlanark.org* *38 rooms, 8 cottages* *Restaurant; no a/c* *AE, DC, MC, V* *BP.*

SHOPPING Lanark has an interesting selection of shops within walking distance of each other. **McKellar's the Jewellers** (✉ 41 High St. ☎ 01555/661312) sells Charles Rennie Mackintosh–inspired designs in gold and silver. **Strands** (✉ 8 Bloomgate ☎ 01555/665757) carries yarns and knitwear, including Arran designs and one-of-a-kind creations by Scottish designers.

Biggar

46 *34 mi southeast of Glasgow.*

A pleasant town built of stone, Biggar is a rewarding place to spend an hour or two, out of all proportion to its size. At Biggar you are near the headwaters of the Clyde, on the moors in the center of southern Scotland. The Clyde flows west toward Glasgow and the Atlantic Ocean, and the Tweed, only a few miles away, flows east toward the North Sea. There are fine views around Biggar: to Culter Fell and to the Border Hills in the south.

Gladstone Court Museum paints a fascinating picture of life in the town in years past, with reconstructed Victorian shops, a bank, a phone exchange, and a school. ✉ *Gladstone Court* ☎ *01899/221050* *£2* *Apr.–Oct., Mon.–Sat. 10:30–5, Sun. 2–5.*

For Biggar's geology and prehistory, plus an interesting embroidery collection (including samplers and fine patchwork coverlets), visit the **Moat Park Heritage Centre,** also in the town center, in a former church. ✉ *Moat Park Church, Moat Park* ☎ *01899/221050* *£2* *Easter–mid-Oct., Mon.–Sat. 10–5, Sun. 2–5.*

The **Gasworks,** built in 1839, is a fascinating reminder of the efforts once needed to produce gas for light and heat. ✉ *Moat Park* ☎ *01899/221050* *£1* *June–Sept., daily 2–5.*

The **Greenhill Covenanters' House** is a farmhouse with Covenanting relics, 17th-century furnishings, costume dolls, and rare farm breeds. The Covenanters were breakaway supporters of Presbyterianism in the 17th century. ✉ *Moat Park* ☎ *01899/221050* *£1* *May–Sept., daily 2–5.*

Biggar Puppet Theatre regularly presents performances by Purves Puppets. Before and after performances, two half-hour hands-on tours led by the puppeteers are available. One tour goes backstage with the puppets being demonstrated on stage; the other tours the puppet museum. The theater also has games and a picnic area. ✉ *B7016, east of Biggar* ☎ *01899/220631* *Performances £5, tours £2.50* *Sept.–Easter, Mon.–Sat. 10–5; Easter–Aug., Mon.–Sat. 10–5, Sun. 2–5. Call for additional opening times and details.*

WHERE TO STAY **£££–£££££** **Shieldhill Castle.** This foursquare Norman manor has stood on this spot since 1199, though it was greatly enlarged in 1560. It's in an ideal location for touring the Borders—27 mi from Edinburgh and 31 mi from Glasgow. The rooms are named after great Scottish battles—Culloden, Glencoe, Bannockburn—and are furnished very comfortably, with miles of Laura Ashley fabrics and wallpaper. ✉ *Quothquan, near Biggar, ML12 6NA* ☎ *01899/220035* 🖷 *01899/221092* 🌐 *www.shieldhill.co.uk* *16 rooms* *2 restaurants; no a/c* *MC, V* *BP.*

Clyde Valley A to Z

BUS TRAVEL

Buses run between Glasgow and Hamilton. Inquire at the Buchanan Street bus station for details. Traveline Scotland can provide information on schedules and fares.

Buchanan Street bus station ☎ 0141/333-3708. **Traveline Scotland** ☎ 0870/608-2608 🌐 www.travelinescotland.com.

CAR TRAVEL

Take the A724 east out of Glasgow, south of the river through Rutherglen toward Hamilton; it's not a very pretty route. In Blantyre look for signs to the David Livingstone Centre. From Blantyre take the main road to Hamilton. Then travel on the A72 past Chatelherault toward Lanark. You pass the ruins of medieval Craignethan Castle, lots of greenhouses for tomatoes, plant nurseries, and gnarled old orchards running down to the Clyde. Before reaching Lanark, follow the signs down a long winding hill, to New Lanark. The A72 continues south of Lanark to join the A702 near Biggar. At the end of a full day of touring you can return to Glasgow the quick way by joining the M74 from the A744 west of Lanark (the Strathaven road). Or take a more scenic route through Strathaven (pronounced *stra*-ven) itself, A726 to East Kilbride, and enter Glasgow from south of the river.

TRAIN TRAVEL

Service runs from Glasgow Central Station to Hamilton and Lanark; for details call National Rail, or check out the timetable online. There are no trains to Biggar, but there's a connecting bus from Hamilton to Biggar.

National Rail ☎ 0845/748-4950 🌐 www.railtrack.co.uk.

VISITOR INFORMATION

Abington ✉ Welcome Break Services, M74 Junction 13 ☎ 01864/502436. **Biggar** ✉ 155 High St. ☎ 01899/221066. **Hamilton** ✉ Road Chef Services, M74 Northbound ☎ 01698/285590. **Lanark** ✉ Horsemarket, Ladyacre Rd. ☎ 01555/661661.

GLASGOW A TO Z

To research prices, get advice from other travelers, and book travel arrangements, visit www.fodors.com.

AIR TRAVEL

Airlines operating through Glasgow Airport to Europe and the rest of the United Kingdom include Aer Lingus, Air Malta, British Airways, British Midland, easyJet, Icelandair, KLM UK, and GO. Several carriers fly from North America, including Air Canada, American Airlines, Continental, and Icelandair (service via Reykjavík).

Ryanair, easyJet, and GO have sparked a major price war on the Anglo-Scottish routes (e.g., between London and Glasgow). Ryanair offers rock-bottom air fares between Prestwick and London's Stansted Airport. GO and easyJet—now owned by the same company—operate similar services from Glasgow to Stansted and Luton, respectively.

Aer Lingus ☎ 0845/084-4444 🌐 www.aerlingus.com. **Air Canada** ☎ 0870/524-7226 🌐 www.aircanada.ca. **Air Malta** ☎ 0845/607-3710 🌐 www.airmalta.com. **American Airlines** ☎ 0845/778-9789 🌐 www.aa.com. **British Airways** ☎ 0845/773-3377 🌐 www.british-airways.com. **British Midland** ☎ 0870/607-0555 🌐 www.flybmi.com. **Continental** ☎ 0800/776464 🌐 www.continental.com. **easyJet** ☎ 0870/600-0000 🌐 www.easyjet.co.uk. **GO** ☎ 0870/607-6543 🌐 www.easyjet.com. **Icelandair** ☎ 0845/

758-1111 www.icelandair.com. **KLM UK** 0870/507-4074 www.klm.com. **Ryanair** 0871/246-0000 www.ryanair.com.

AIRPORTS

Glasgow Airport is about 7 mi west of the city center on the M8 to Greenock. The airport serves international and domestic flights, and most major European carriers have frequent and convenient connections (some via airports in England) to many cities on the Continent. There's frequent shuttle service from London, as well as regular flights from Birmingham, Bristol, East Midlands, Leeds/Bradford, Manchester, Southampton, Isle of Man, and Jersey. There are also flights from Wales (Cardiff) and Ireland (Belfast, Dublin, and Londonderry). Local Scottish connections can be made to Aberdeen, Barra, Benbecula, Campbeltown, Inverness, Islay, Kirkwall, Shetland (Sumburgh), Stornoway, and Tiree.

Prestwick Airport, on the Ayrshire coast about 30 mi southwest of Glasgow and for some years eclipsed by Glasgow Airport, has grown in importance, not least because of low airfares from Ryanair.

Glasgow Airport 0141/887-1111 for information, 0141/848-4440 for tourist information desk and accommodations-booking service www.baa.co.uk. **Prestwick Airport** 01292/511006.

TRANSFERS **From Glasgow Airport:** Though there's a railway station about 2 mi from Glasgow Airport (Paisley Gilmour St.), most people travel to the city center by bus or taxi. Journey time is about 20 minutes, longer at rush hour. Metered taxis are available outside domestic arrivals. The fare should be £15–£18.

Express buses run from Glasgow Airport (terminal forecourt, outside departures lobby) to near the Central railway station, to Queen Street railway station, and to the Buchanan Street bus station. There's service every 15 minutes throughout the day. The fare is £3.50 on both Scottish Citylink and Fairline buses.

The drive from Glasgow Airport into the city center is normally quite easy, even if you're used to driving on the right. The M8 motorway runs beside the airport (Junction 29) and takes you straight into the Glasgow city center. Thereafter Glasgow's streets follow a grid pattern, at least in the city center, but a map is useful and can be supplied by the car-rental company.

Most companies that provide chauffeur-driven cars and tours will also do limousine airport transfers. Companies that are currently members of the Greater Glasgow and Clyde Valley Tourist Board are Charlton Chauffeur Drive, Corporate Travel, Little's, Peter Holmes, and Robert Neil.

From Prestwick Airport: An hourly coach service makes trips to Glasgow but takes much longer than the train. There's a rapid half-hourly train service (hourly on Sundays) direct from the terminal building to Glasgow Central. Strathclyde Passenger Transport and Scotrail offer an AirTrain discount ticket that allows you to travel for 50% of the standard rail fare. Just show a valid airline ticket, Internet booking confirmation form or original invoice (boarding cards are not accepted), for a flight to or from Prestwick Airport, at the time you purchase your rail ticket from a booking office or conductor. This discount is available only on the day you fly into or out of Prestwick Airport or the day before or after if your flight departs early or arrives late. By car the city center is reached via the fast A77 in about 40 minutes (longer in rush hour). Metered taxi cabs are available at the airport. The fare to Glasgow is about £40.

Charlton Chauffeur Drive ☎ 0141/570-2000 🌐 www.limo-drive.co.uk. **Little's Chauffeur Drive** ☎ 0141/883-2111 🌐 www.littles.co.uk. **Peter Holmes** ☎ 01389/830688. **Robert Neil** ☎ 0141/641-2125.

BUS TRAVEL

Glasgow's bus station is on Buchanan Street. The main intercity operators are National Express and Scottish Citylink, which serve numerous towns and cities in Scotland, Wales, and England, including London (8½–9 hours); there's also service to Edinburgh. Buchanan Street is close to the underground station of the same name and to the Queen Street station. Traveline Scotland can provide information on schedules and fares.

Buchanan Street bus station ☎ 0141/333-3708. **National Express** ☎ 0870/580-8080 🌐 www.nationalexpress.co.uk. **Scottish Citylink** ☎ 0870/505050 🌐 www.citylink.co.uk. **Traveline Scotland** ☎ 0870/608-2608 🌐 www.travelinescotland.com.

BUS TRAVEL WITHIN GLASGOW

Bus service is reliable within Glasgow, and connections are convenient from buses to trains and the underground. Note that buses require exact fare, which varies by the destination.

The many bus companies cooperate with the underground and ScotRail to produce the Family Day Tripper Ticket (£14 for two adults), which gets you around the whole area, from Loch Lomond to Ayrshire. The tickets are a good value and are available from Strathclyde Passenger Transport (SPT) Travel Centre and at main railway and bus stations.

Strathclyde Passenger Transport (SPT) Travel Centre ✉ St. Enoch Sq., City Center ☎ 0870/608-2608 🌐 www.spt.co.uk.

CAR RENTAL

Costs average about £30–£40 per day.

Agencies **Avis** ✉ 161 North St., City Center ☎ 0141/221-2827 🌐 www.avis.co.uk ✉ Glasgow Airport, Paisley ☎ 0141/842-7599 ✉ Prestwick Airport, Prestwick ☎ 01292/477218. **Budget Rent-a-Car** ✉ 101 Waterloo St., City Center ✉ Glasgow Airport, Paisley ☎ 0800/212636 🌐 www.budget.com. **Europcar** ✉ 38 Anderson Quay, West End ☎ 0141/248-8788 🌐 www.europcar.com ✉ Glasgow Airport, Paisley ☎ 0141/887-0414 ✉ Prestwick Airport, Prestwick ☎ 01292/678198. **Hertz** ✉ 138 Hyde Park St., City Center ☎ 0141/248-7736 🌐 www.hertz.com ✉ Glasgow Airport, Paisley ☎ 0141/887-2451.

CAR TRAVEL

If you come to Glasgow from England and the south of Scotland, you'll probably approach the city from the M6, M74, and A74. The city center is clearly marked from these roads. From Edinburgh the M8 leads to the city center and is the route that cuts straight across the city center and into which all other roads feed. From the north either the A82 from Fort William or the A/M80 from Stirling also feed into the M8 in the Glasgow city center. From then on you only have to know your exit: Exit 16 serves the the northern part of the city center, Exit 17/18 leads to the northwest and Great Western Road, and Exit 18/19 takes you to the hotels of Sauchiehall Street, and the Scottish Exhibition and Conference Centre.

You don't need a car in the city center, and you're probably better off without one; though most modern hotels have their own lots, parking here can be trying. More convenient are the park-and-ride operations at underground stations (Kelvinbridge, Bridge Street, and Shields Road), which will bring you into the city center in a few minutes. The West End museums and galleries have their own lots, as does the Burrell. Parking wardens are constantly on patrol, and fines cost upward of £26 for parking illegally. Multistory garages are open 24 hours a day at the following locations: Anderston Centre, George Street, Waterloo Place, Mitchell Street, Cambridge Street, and Concert Square. Rates run between £1 and £2 per hour.

EMERGENCIES

In case of any emergency, dial **999** to reach an ambulance or the police or fire departments (no coins are needed for emergency calls from public phones). Note that pharmacies generally operate on a rotating basis for late-night opening; hours are posted in storefront windows. Munro Pharmacy is open daily 9–9.

Dentists **Glasgow Dental Hospital** ✉ 378 Sauchiehall St., City Center ☎ 0141/211-9600 weekdays 9–3.

Hospitals **Glasgow Royal Infirmary** ✉ Castle St., near cathedral, City Center ☎ 0141/211-4000. **Glasgow Western Infirmary** ✉ Dumbarton Rd., near university, West End ☎ 0141/211-2000. **Southern General Hospital** ✉ 1345 Govan Rd., south side of Clyde Tunnel, South Side ☎ 0141/201-1100. **Stobhill Hospital** ✉ 133 Balornock Rd., near Royal Infirmary and Bishopriggs, North City ☎ 0141/201-3000.

Pharmacy **Munro Pharmacy** ✉ 693 Great Western Rd., West End ☎ 0141/339-0012.

MAIL & SHIPPING

The main post office is at St. Vincent Street, and there are many smaller post offices around the city.

Post Office **Main post office** ✉ St. Vincent St. City Center ☎ 0845/722-3344.

SIGHTSEEING TOURS

BOAT TOURS Cruises are available on Loch Lomond and to the islands in the Firth of Clyde; contact the Greater Glasgow and Clyde Valley Tourist Board for details. Contact the *Waverley* paddle steamer from June through August, and Clyde Marine Cruises from May through September.

Clyde Marine Cruises ✉ Victoria Harbour Greenock ☎ 01475/721281 🌐 www.clyde-marine.co.uk. **Greater Glasgow and Clyde Valley Tourist Board** ✉ 11 George Sq., near Queen Street station, City Center ☎ 0141/204-4400 🌐 www.seeglasgow.com. ***Waverley*** ✉ 36 Anderston Quay ☎ 0845/1304647.

BUS TOURS City Sightseeing bus tours leave daily from the west side of George Square. The Greater Glasgow and Clyde Valley Tourist Board can give further information and arrange reservations. Details of longer tours northward to the Highlands and islands can be obtained from the tourist board or Strathclyde Passenger Transport (SPT) Travel Centre.

Classic Coaches operates restored coaches from the 1950s, '60s, and '70s on tours to the north and west and to the islands. The following Glasgow companies run regular bus tours around the region: Scotguide Tours, Southern Coaches, and Weirs Tourlink.

Greater Glasgow and Clyde Valley Tourist Board ✉ 11 George Sq., near Queen Street station, City Center ☎ 0141/204-4400 🌐 www.seeglasgow.com. **Southern Coaches** ✉ Barshagra Garage, Lochlibo Rd. ☎ 0800/298-1655. **Strathclyde Passenger Transport (SPT) Travel Centre** ✉ St. Enoch Sq., City Center ☎ 0870/608-2608 🌐 www.spt.co.uk. **Weirs Tourlink** ✉ 145 Dlasetter Ave. ☎ 0141/944-6688.

PRIVATE GUIDES Little's Chauffeur Drive arranges personally tailored car-and-driver tours, both locally and throughout Scotland. The Scottish Tourist Guides Association also provides a private-guide service. Taxi firms offer city tours. If you allow the driver to follow a set route, the costs are £15 for one hour, £30 for two hours, and £45 for three hours for up to five people. If you wish the driver to follow your own route, the charge will be £15 an hour or the reading on the meter, whichever is greater. You can book tours in advance and be picked up and dropped off wherever you like. Contact the Glasgow-wide TOA Taxis.

Little's Chauffeur Drive ✉ 1282 Paisley Rd. W, South Side ☎ 0141/883-2111 🌐 www.littles.co.uk. **Scottish Tourist Guides Association** ☎☎ 01786/451-953 🌐 www.stga.co.uk. **TOA Taxis** ☎ 0141/429-7070 🌐 www.gwtoa.co.uk.

WALKING TOURS The Greater Glasgow and Clyde Valley Tourist Board can provide information on special walks on a given day.

Greater Glasgow and Clyde Valley Tourist Board ✉ 11 George Sq., near Queen Street station, City Center ☎ 0141/204-4400 🌐 www.seeglasgow.com.

SUBWAY

Glasgow is the only city in Scotland that has a subway, or underground, as it's called here. It was built at the end of the 19th century and takes the simple form of two circular routes, one going clockwise and the other counterclockwise. All trains eventually bring you back to where you started, and the complete circle takes 24 minutes. This extremely simple and efficient system operated relatively unchanged in ancient carriages (cars) until the 1970s, when it was modernized. The tunnels are small, so the trains themselves are tiny (by London standards), and this, together with the affection in which the system is held and the bright orange paint and circular routes of the trains, gave it the nickname the Clockwork Orange.

Flat fares (90 pence) and the Discovery Ticket one-day pass (£1.70, after 9:30) are available. Trains run regularly from Monday through Saturday from early morning to late evening, with a limited Sunday service, and connect the city center with the West End (for the university) and the city south of the River Clyde. Look for the orange U signs marking the 15 stations. Further information is available from Strathclyde Passenger Transport (SPT) Travel Centre.

Strathclyde Passenger Transport (SPT) Travel Centre ✉ St. Enoch Sq., City Center ☎ 0870/608-2608 🌐 www.spt.co.uk.

TAXIS

You'll find metered taxis (usually black and of the London sedan type) at stands all over the city center. Most have radio dispatch. Some have also been adapted to take wheelchairs. You can hail a cab on the street if its FOR HIRE sign is illuminated. A typical ride from the city center to the West End or the South Side costs £5.50 to £6.

TOA Taxis ☎ 0141/429-7070 🌐 www.gwtoa.co.uk.

TRAIN TRAVEL

Glasgow has two main rail stations: Central and Queen Street. Central is the arrival and departure point for trains from London's Euston station (five hours), which come via Crewe and Carlisle in England, as well as via Edinburgh from King's Cross. It also serves other cities in the northwest of England and towns and ports in the southwest of Scotland: Kilmarnock, Dumfries, Ardrossan (for the island of Arran), Gourock (for Dunoon), Wemyss Bay (for the Isle of Bute), and Stranraer (for Ireland). The Queen Street station has frequent connections to Edinburgh (50 minutes) and onward by the east-coast route to Aberdeen or south via Edinburgh to Newcastle, York, and London's King's Cross. Other services from Queen Street go to Stirling, Perth, and Dundee; northward to Inverness, Kyle of Lochalsh, Wick, and Thurso; along the Clyde to Dumbarton and Balloch (for Loch Lomond); and on the scenic West Highland line to Oban, Fort William, and Mallaig. Oban and Mallaig have island ferry connections. For details contact National Rail.

A regular bus service links the Queen Street and Central stations. Both are close to stations on the Glasgow underground. At Queen Street go to Buchanan Street, and at Central go to St. Enoch. City taxis are available at both stations.

The Glasgow area has an extensive network of suburban railway services. Locals still call them the Blue Trains, even though most are now painted maroon and cream. Look for signs to LOW LEVEL TRAINS at the Queen Street and Central stations. For more information and a free map, call Strathclyde Passenger Transport (SPT) Travel Centre or the National Rail Enquiry Line. Details are also available from the Greater Glasgow and Clyde Valley Tourist Board.

Greater Glasgow and Clyde Valley Tourist Board ✉ 11 George Sq., near Queen Street station, City Center ☎ 0141/204-4400 🌐 www.seeglasgow.com. **National Rail** ☎ 0870/748-4950 🌐 www.railtrack.co.uk. **Strathclyde Passenger Transport (SPT) Travel Centre** ✉ St. Enoch Sq., City Center ☎ 0870/608-2608 🌐 www.spt.co.uk.

TRAVEL AGENCIES

Local Agent Referrals **American Express** ✉ 115 Hope St., City Center ☎ 0141/222-1405 🌐 www.americanexpress.com. **Thomas Cook** ✉ 15-17 Gordon St., City Center ☎ 0141/201-7200 🌐 www.thomascook.com.

VISITOR INFORMATION

The Greater Glasgow and Clyde Valley Tourist Board provides information and has an accommodations-booking service, a bureau de change, a Western Union money transfer service, city bus tours, guided walks, boat trips, and coach tours around Scotland. Books, maps, and souvenirs are also available. The office is open September through June, from Monday to Saturday 9 to 6, and July through August, from Monday to Saturday 9 to 8, Sunday 10 to 6. The tourist board's branch office at the airport is open from Monday to Saturday 7:30 to 5, Sunday 8 to 3:30 (Sunday 7:30 to 5, April through September).

Greater Glasgow and Clyde Valley Tourist Board ✉ 11 George Sq., near Queen St. station, City Center ☎ 0141/204-4400 📠 0141/221-3524 🌐 www.seeglasgow.com.

THE BORDERS & THE SOUTHWEST

DUMFRIES, GALLOWAY, SIR WALTER SCOTT COUNTRY

3

FODOR'S CHOICE

Abbotsford House, *near Galashiels*

Caerlaverock Castle, *near Ruthwell*

Floors Castle, *in Kelso*

Hoebridge Inn Restaurant, *near Melrose*

Peebles Hydro Hotel, *in Peebles*

Traquair House, *near Innerleithen*

HIGHLY RECOMMENDED

RESTAURANTS
Cross Keys, *Ancrum*
Wheatsheaf Hotel and Restaurant, *near Coldstream*

HOTELS
Auchenskeoch Lodge, *near Dalbeattie*
Cringletie House, *in Peebles*
Edenwater House, *in Ednam*
Ednam House Hotel, *in Kelso*

SIGHTS
Castle Kennedy Gardens, *in Stranraer*
Dryburgh Abbey, *near Melrose*
Glen Trool, *near Newton Stewart*
Jedburgh Abbey, *in Jedburgh*
Logan Botanic Gardens, *in Portpatrick*
Melrose Abbey, *in Melrose*
Threave Gardens, *near Castle Douglas*

By Gilbert Summers
Updated by James Gracie

IF YOU ARE COMING TO SCOTLAND by road or rail from England, you'll first encounter either the Borders area or the Southwest, also known as Dumfries and Galloway, depending on the route you take. Although you'll find no checkpoints or customs posts, the Scottish tourist authorities firmly promulgate the message that it is indeed Scottish land you've entered. And you begin to notice all the idiosyncracies that distinguish Scotland—like its myriad names for things—just as soon as you pass the first Scottish signs by the main roads heading north.

The Borders region embraces the whole 90-mi course of one of Scotland's greatest rivers, the Tweed, and its tributaries. Passing mill chimneys, peel towers (small fortified towers), ruined abbeys, stately homes, and woodlands luxuriant with game birds, the rivers flow in a series of fast-rushing torrents and dark serpentine pools through the history of two nations. For at different times, parts of the region have been in English hands, just as slices of northern England (Berwick-upon-Tweed, for example) have been in Scottish hands.

All the main routes from London to Edinburgh traverse the Borders region, whose hinterland of undulating pastures, woods, and valleys is enclosed within three lonely groups of hills: the Cheviots, Moorfoots, and the Lammermuirs. Innumerable hamlets and towns dot the land, giving valley slopes a lived-in look, yet the total population is still relatively sparse. Sheep outnumber human beings by 14 to 1—which is just as Sir Walter Scott, the region's most famous resident, would have wanted it. His pseudo-baronial home at Abbotsford is the most visited of Scottish literary landmarks.

To the west is the region of Dumfries and Galloway, on the shores of the Solway Firth. It might appear to be an extension of the Borders, but the Southwest has a history and milieu all of its own. Inland, the earth rises toward high hills, forest, and bleak, yet captivating moorland, while nearer the coast are pretty farmlands, small villages, and unassuming towns. The shoreline is washed by the North Atlantic Drift (Scotland's answer to the Gulf Stream), and first-time visitors are always surprised to see palm trees and exotic plants thriving in gardens and parks along the coast.

So strong is the tartan-ribboned call of the Highlands that many people rush through the Borders and the Southwest, pause for breath at Edinburgh or Glasgow, then plunge northward, thus missing portions of Scotland that are as beautiful and historically important as elsewhere. After all, the Borders and the Southwest have more stately homes, fortified castles, and medieval monastic houses than anywhere else in Scotland. If you take the time to explore, you'll see that there's more to Scotland than brooding lochs, misty glens, and wild, kilted Highlanders.

Exploring the Borders & the Southwest

The Borders region is characterized by upland moors and hills, with fertile, farmed, and forested river valleys. Borders towns cluster around and between two great rivers—the Tweed and its tributary, the Teviot. These are mostly textile towns with plenty of personality—Borders folk are sure of their own identity and are fiercely partisan toward their own native towns.

Dumfries and Galloway, especially inland, shares the upland characteristics and, if anything, has a slightly wilder air—the highest hill in Dumfries and Galloway is the Merrick, at 2,765 ft. Easygoing and peaceful, towns in this region are usually very attractive, with wide streets and colorful frontages.

The best way to explore the region is to get off the main, and often crowded, arterial roads—the A1, A697, A68, A76, A7, M74/A74, and A75—for the little back roads. You may occasionally be delayed by a herd of cows on their way to the milking parlor, but this is often far more pleasant than, for example, tussling on the A75 with heavy-goods vehicles rushing to make the Irish ferries.

About the Restaurants & Hotels

From top-quality, full-service hotels to quaint 18th-century drovers' inns to cozy bed-and-breakfasts, the Borders has all manner of lodging options. Most good restaurants in the region tend to be within hotels rather than independent establishments. Lodging in Dumfries and Galloway tends to be a little less expensive than in the Borders. There are farmhouse B&Bs, where mornings start with hearty, extra-fresh breakfasts. Keep in mind, though, that many of these B&Bs are *working* farms, where early morning activity and the presence of animals are an inescapable part of the scene.

WHAT IT COSTS In pounds

	$$$$$	$$$$	$$$	$$	£
RESTAURANTS	over £22	£18–£22	£13–£17	£7–£12	under £7
HOTELS	over £150	£150–£110	£110–£80	£50–£80	under £50

Restaurant prices are for a main course at dinner. Hotel prices are for two people in a standard double room in high season.

Timing

Because many properties are privately owned and shut down from early autumn until early April, the area is less well suited to off-season touring than some other parts of Scotland. The region does look magnificent in autumn, however, especially along the wooded river valleys of the Borders. Late spring is the time to see the rhododendrons in the gardens of Dumfries and Galloway.

THE BORDERS

Although the Borders has many attractions, it is most famous for being the home base for Sir Walter Scott (1771–1832), the early 19th-century poet, novelist, and creator of *Ivanhoe,* who single-handedly transformed Scotland's image from that of a land of brutal savages to one of romantic and stirring deeds and magnificent landscapes. One of the best ways to approach this district is to make the theme of your tour the life and works of Scott. The novels of Scott are not read much nowadays—frankly, some of them are difficult to wade through—but the mystique that he created, the aura of historical romance, has outlasted his books and is much in evidence in the ruined abbeys, historical houses, and grand vistas of the Borders.

In addition to the Scott heritage, Borders folk take great pride in the region's fame as Scotland's main woolen-goods manufacturing area. To this day the residents possess a marked determination to defend their towns and communities. Changing times have allowed them to reposition their priorities: instead of guarding against southern raiders, they now concentrate on maintaining a fiercely competitive rugby team for the popular intertown rugby matches.

Borders communities have also reestablished their identities through the curious affairs known as the Common Ridings. Long ago it was essential that each town be able to defend its area, and over the centuries this

The driving distances between towns in the Borders and the Southwest are not lengthy, but traveling on narrow country roads can take a little longer than you might expect. Five days should be enough to see the most important sights of both regions. If you particularly enjoy sketching or taking photographs, this is not an area to be rushed; three days is the minimum time needed to sample an abbey or two and see the settings of Dumfries and Galloway towns.

Numbers in the text correspond to numbers in the margin and on the Borders and Dumfries and Galloway maps.

If you have 2 days

If you have only two days, then you will have to concentrate on either the Borders or Dumfries and Galloway. **Jedburgh** 1 ⚑ is the best place to get an idea of how important the Borders abbeys were. If you cross the border to the west, head for **Kirkcudbright** 25 for a flavor of Dumfries and Galloway.

If you have 5 days

Plan to divide your time between the Borders and Dumfries and Galloway; you'll have to be selective about which abbeys and stately homes you can fully explore. Jedburgh Abbey, in **Jedburgh** 1 ⚑, is a must-see, as is the abbey at **Melrose** 9. Melrose also has gardens to enjoy, several museums, and famous homes nearby, including **Abbotsford House** 10, home of Sir Walter Scott. Finish up at **Peebles** 15, where you should allow plenty of time to shop. In Dumfries and Galloway, two full days will give you time to visit **Sweetheart Abbey** 20, in New Abbey, and **Caerlaverock Castle** 18, near Ruthwell. Try to fit in Castle Douglas and **Threave Gardens** 24. **Kirkcudbright** 25 is also worth even a quick visit for its artistic connections.

If you have 10 days

In five days in the Borders, you can start with **Jedburgh** 1 ⚑ and **Melrose** 9, and still have time for such jewels as **Mellerstain House** 3, **Floors Castle,** and **Paxton House** 6 (though you may get stately home indigestion). Take a day to admire the views and soak up the historic atmosphere at **Smailholm Tower** 4 or **Dryburgh Abbey** 8. Next head for **Traquair House,** near **Innerleithen** 14, where, if you have kids, you should see **Robert Smail's Printing Works.** You'll also have time for a shopping visit to **Peebles** 15.

With five days in Dumfries and Galloway, you'll have time for nearly everything. At the top of your list should be **Caerlaverock Castle** 18, **Threave Gardens** 24, Threave Castle, and **Kirkcudbright** 25. Explore **Gatehouse of Fleet** 26, stopping at the Mill on the Fleet, and then travel on to **Cardoness Castle** 27 and heritage center, near the coast. Meander around the southern coastline, then penetrate the wild and wooded **Glen Trool** 30; and travel deep into the Machars to **Whithorn** 32, a site of early religious importance. Complete your Galloway experience with **Castle Kennedy Gardens** 33 and the Logan Botanic Gardens.

need became formalized in mounted gatherings to "ride the marches," or patrol the boundaries. The observance of the tradition lapsed in certain places but has now been revived. Leaders and attendants are solemnly elected each year, and Borderers who now live away from home make a point of attending their town's event. (You are welcome to watch and enjoy the excitement of clattering hooves and banners proudly displayed, but this is essentially a time for native Borderers.) The Common Ridings possess much more authenticity and historic significance than the the concocted Highland Games, so often taken to be the essence of Scotland. The little town of Selkirk claims its Common Riding is the largest mounted gathering anywhere in Europe.

A visit to at least one of the region's four great ruined abbeys makes the quintessential Borders experience. The monks in these long-abandoned religious foundations were the first to work the fleeces of their sheep flocks, thus laying the foundation for what is still the area's main manufacturing industry.

Jedburgh

❶ *50 mi south of Edinburgh, 95 mi southeast of Glasgow.*

The town of Jedburgh (*-burgh* is always pronounced *burra* in Scots) was for centuries the first major Scottish target of invading English armies. In more peaceful times it developed textile mills, most of which have since languished. The large landscaped area around the town's tourist information center was once a mill but now provides an encampment for the armies of modern tourists. The past still clings to this little town, however. The ruined abbey dominates the skyline and remains a reminder of the formerly strong, governing role of the Borders abbeys.

★ **Jedburgh Abbey,** the most impressive of the Borders abbeys, was nearly destroyed by the English earl of Hertford's forces in 1544–45, during the destructive time known as the Rough Wooing. This was English king Henry VIII's (1491–1547) armed attempt to persuade the Scots that it was a good idea to unite the kingdoms by the marriage of his young son to the infant Mary, Queen of Scots (1542–87); the Scots disagreed and sent Mary to France instead. The full story is explained in vivid detail at the **Jedburgh Abbey Visitor Centre,** which also provides information on interpreting the ruins. Ground patterns and foundations are all that remain of the once-powerful religious complex. ✉ *High St.* ☎ *01835/863925* 🌐 *www.historic-scotland.gov.uk* 🎫 *£3.50* ⏲ *Apr.–Sept., daily 9:30–6:30; Oct.–Mar., Mon.–Sat. 9:30–4:30, Sun. 2–4:30.*

The **Mary, Queen of Scots House,** a *bastel* (from the French *bastille*), was the fortified town house in which, as the story goes, Mary stayed before embarking on her famous 20-mi ride to visit her wounded lover, the earl of Bothwell (circa 1535–78), at Hermitage Castle. Interpretative displays relate the tale and illustrate other episodes in her life. Some of her possessions are also on display, as well as tapestries and furniture of the period. ✉ *Queen St.* ☎ *01835/863331* 🎫 *£3* ⏲ *Mon.–Sat. 10–4:30, Sun. 11–4:30.*

Jedburgh Castle Jail was the site of the Howard Reform Prison established in 1820. Today you can inspect prison cells, rooms arranged with period furnishings, and costumed figures. Audiovisual displays recount the history of the Royal Burgh of Jedburgh. ✉ *Castlegate* ☎ *01835/864750* 🎫 *£1.50* ⏲ *Easter–Oct., Mon.–Sat. 10–4:30, Sun. 1–4.30.*

Biking

Away from busy roads like the A68, A7, and A1, the Borders area is ideal for biking. In the Southwest, too, once you're off the beaten track, you'll discover quiet roads and country lanes that beg to be explored. Little-used roads crisscross farmlands, valleys, and upland stretches throughout the region. The Craik Forest, west of Hawick, and Galloway Forest Park, in the Galloway hills, are typical of Forestry Commission properties, with networks of forest-access roads and bike trails winding their way into the mountains. There are bike-rental shops in many towns, including Peebles, Hawick, Dumfries, and Castle Douglas. Arrange rentals in advance so you are sure to have the bicycle you need at the time you want it.

Fishing

The Solway Firth is noted for sea fishing, particularly at the Isle of Whithorn, Port William, Portpatrick, and Stranraer. The wide range of game-fishing opportunities extends from the expensive salmon beats of the River Tweed—sometimes known by its nickname, the Queen of Scottish Rivers—to undiscovered hill *lochans* (small lakes). You must have a fishing permit, available at tourist offices, tackle shops, newsstands, and post offices; and you should obtain permission from a landowner to fish on private property. Many hotels offer on-property fishing, or transportation and equipment so you can fish nearby.

Shopping

The Borders has a fairly affluent population, which is reflected in the upscale shops in several towns, including Peebles. The Borders also is well known for its knitwear industry, and mill shops are abundant. Throughout the region look for the specialty peppermint or fruit-flavor boiled sweets (hard candies)—Jethart Snails, Hawick Balls, Berwick Cockles, and Soor Plums—which, with tablet (a sugary caramel-like candy) and fudge, are available at most local confectioners. In the Southwest, shopping is concentrated mainly in medium-size and large towns such as Dumfries, Stranraer, and Newton Stewart, though many of the villages have small craft shops that sell locally made pottery, jewelry, and ornaments.

The **Harestanes Countryside Visitor Centre,** in a former farmhouse 3 mi north of Jedburgh, conveys life in the Scottish Borders with changing art exhibitions and interpretive displays on the natural history of the region. Crafts such as woodworking and tile-making are taught at the center, and finished projects are often on display. There's a gift shop and tea room, and outside are paths for countryside walks, plus the biggest children's play area in the Borders. The quiet roads are suitable for bicycle excursions. ✉ *Close to the junction of the A68 and B6400* ☎ *01835/830306* *Free* ⏲ *Apr.–Oct., daily 10–5.*

From Harestanes Countryside Visitor Centre you can see the **Waterloo Monument** on the horizon about 3 mi to the northeast. The imposing tower is an enduring reminder of the power of the landowning gentry: a marquis of Lothian built the monument in 1815, with the help of his tenants, in celebration of the victory of Wellington at Waterloo. If you have time, you can walk to the tower from the visitor center in about an hour. ✉ *Off B6400, 5 mi north of Jedburgh.*

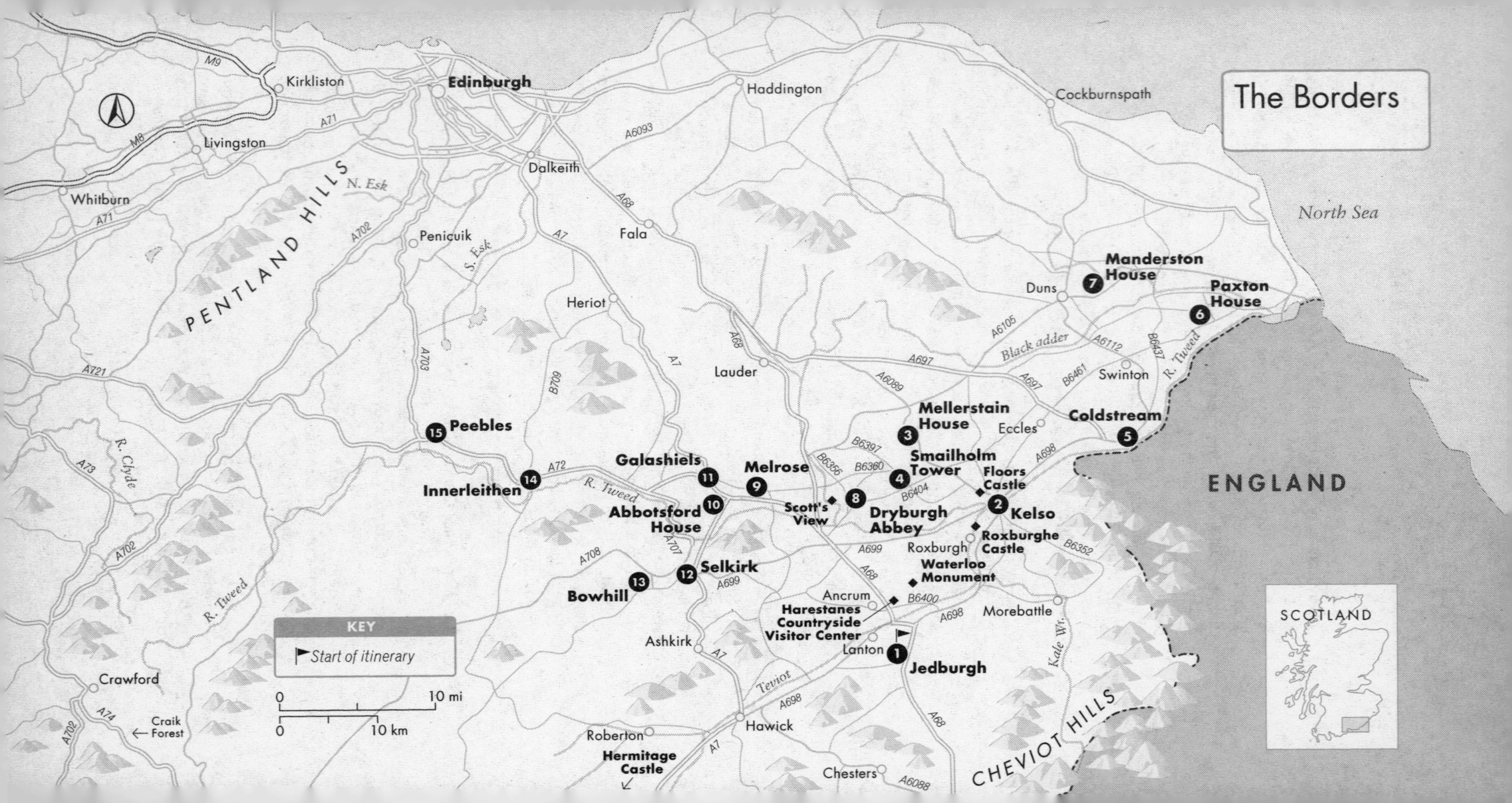
The Borders
North Sea
ENGLAND
SCOTLAND
PENTLAND HILLS
CHEVIOT HILLS
Edinburgh
Kirkliston
Livingston
Whitburn
Dalkeith
Haddington
Cockburnspath
Penicuik
Fala
Heriot
Lauder
Duns
Swinton
Eccles
Manderston House
Paxton House
Coldstream
Mellerstain House
Smailholm Tower
Floors Castle
Kelso
Roxburghe Castle
Roxburgh
Dryburgh Abbey
Scott's View
Melrose
Galashiels
Abbotsford House
Selkirk
Bowhill
Innerleithen
Peebles
Waterloo Monument
Harestanes Countryside Visitor Center
Ancrum
Lanton
Jedburgh
Morebattle
Ashkirk
Hawick
Roberton
Hermitage Castle
Chesters
Crawford
Craik Forest
R. Tweed
R. Clyde
N. Esk
S. Esk
Black adder
Teviot
Kale Wr.
M9
M8
A71
A702
A703
A721
A73
A74
A6093
A68
A7
B709
A72
A707
A708
A699
A6089
A697
A6105
A6112
B6437
B6461
A698
B6397
B6356
B6360
B6404
B6352
B6400
A6088
KEY
Start of itinerary
0 10 mi
0 10 km

off the beaten path

HERMITAGE CASTLE – To appreciate the famous 20-mi ride of Mary, Queen of Scots, to visit her wounded lover, the earl of Bothwell, travel southwest from Jedburgh to this, the most complete remaining example of the bare and grim medieval border castles, full of gloom and foreboding. Restored in the early 19th century, it was built in the 14th century (replacing an earlier structure) to guard what was at the time one of the important routes from England into Scotland. The original owner, Lord Soulis, notorious for diabolical excess, was captured by the local populace, which wrapped him in lead and boiled him in a cauldron—or so the tale goes. ✉ *On an unclassified road 2 mi west of B6399, about 15 mi south of Hawick near Liddesdale,* ☎ *01387 376222* 🌐 *www.historic-scotland.gov.uk* *£2* ⏲ *Apr.–Sept., daily 9:30–6:30.*

3

Where to Stay & Eat

★ £–£££ ✕ **Cross Keys.** This traditional pub, a national treasure, specializes in local produce, from fish to game. A splendid array of Scottish beers—real ale, as it is known here—is served. This is the quintessential village inn, right down to the green outside the front door. ✉ *The Green, Ancrum, 3 mi northeast of Jedburgh* ☎ *01835/830344* ▭ *DC, MC, V.*

£–££ **Hundalee House.** This B&B in an 18th-century manor has richly decorated Victorian-style rooms with four-poster beds, fireplaces, and modern facilities. Fifteen acres of gardens and woods surround the house, and there are splendid views across to the English border at Carter Bar and to the Cheviot hills in the southeast. ✉ *Off A68, 1 mi south of Jedburgh TD8 6PA* ☎ *01835 863011* 🌐 *www.accommodation-scotland.org* *4 rooms* *Dining room, lounge; no a/c, no room phones* ▭ *No credit cards* ⏲ *Closed Nov.–Mar.* *BP.*

£ **Spinney Guest House.** A converted farm cottage, this B&B offers simple but carefully decorated rooms. Additionally, there are two one-bedroom wood cabins (perfect for couples who like privacy), and a two-bedroom cabin where three people can sleep comfortably. Each cabin has a kitchenette and a small patio. The common room in the main house has several welcoming armchairs. ✉ *Langlee, off A68, Jedburgh TD8 6PB* ☎ *01835/863525* *01835/864883* 🌐 *www.thespinney-jedburgh.co.uk* *3 rooms, 3 cabins* *Dining room, some kitchenettes, some microwaves, some refrigerators, lounge; no a/c, no room phones* ▭ *MC, V* ⏲ *Closed Dec.–Feb.* *BP.*

Bicycling

Christopher Rainbow Tandem & Bike Hire (✉ 8 Timpendean Cottages ☎ 01835/830326 or 07799/525123 🌐 www.btinternet.com/~christopher.rainbow) rents tandems, mountain bikes, and touring bikes and is ideally placed for the four Borders abbeys, Tweed, and Borderloop cycleways. The company provides recovery service, luggage forwarding, and tour itineraries. It's on the A698, near the junction with the A68, between Jedburgh and Ancrum.

Kelso

❷ *12 mi northeast of Jedburgh.*

One of the most charming Borders burghs, Kelso is often described as having a Continental flavor—some people think it resembles a Belgian market town. The town has a broad, paved Market Square and fine examples of Georgian and Victorian Scots town architecture.

Kelso Abbey is the least intact ruin of the four great Borders abbeys—just a bleak fragment of what was once the largest of the group. It was here in 1460 that the nine-year-old James III was crowned king of Scotland. On a main invasion route, the abbey was burned three times in the 1540s alone, on the last occasion by the English earl of Hertford's forces in 1545, when the 100 men and 12 monks of the garrison were butchered and the structure all but destroyed. ✉ *Bridge St.* ☎ *0131/668–8800* 🌐 *www.historic-scotland.gov.uk* 🎟 *Free* ⏲ *24 hrs.*

Fodor's Choice ★ On the bank of the River Tweed, just on the outskirts of Kelso, stands the palatial **Floors Castle**, the largest inhabited castle in Scotland. The ancestral home of the dukes of Roxburghe, Floors is an architectural extravagance bristling with pepper-mill turrets and towers that stand on the "floors," or flat terrain, of the Tweed bank opposite the barely visible ruins of Roxburghe Castle. The enormous home was built by William Adam (1689–1748) in 1721 and modified by William Playfair (1789–1857), who added the turrets and towers in the 1840s. A holly tree in the deer park marks the place where King James II of Scotland (1430–60) was killed by a cannon that "brak in the shooting." ✉ *A6089* ☎ *01573/223333* 📠 *01573/226056* 🌐 *www.floorscastle.com* 🎟 *Joint ticket for castle and grounds, £5.75; grounds only, £3* ⏲ *Apr.–Oct., daily 10–4:30 (last admission at 4).*

Don't confuse 12th-century **Roxburghe Castle** with the comparatively youthful Floors Castle, home of the dukes of Roxburghe, nearby. Only traces of rubble and earthworks remain of this ancient structure. Although the modern-day village of **Roxburgh** is young, the original Roxburgh, one of the oldest burghs in Scotland, has virtually disappeared. Its name lives on in the duke's title and in the name of the old county of Roxburghshire. ✉ *Off A699, 4 mi southwest of Kelso.*

Where to Stay & Eat

★ £££–££££ ✕🏨 **Ednam House Hotel.** People return again and again to this large, stately hotel on the banks of the River Tweed, close to Kelso's grand abbey and old Market Square. The main hall, part of the original 1761 home, welcomes you with deep-seated armchairs, paintings, and an open fire. The restaurant's three windowed walls overlook the garden and river, and its Scottish fare includes fresh local vegetables, wild salmon, Borders beef, homemade ice cream, and traditional puddings. ✉ *Bridge St. Kelso, TD5 7HT* ☎ *01573/224168* 📠 *01573/226319* 🌐 *www.ednamhouse.com* *32 rooms* *Restaurant, golf privileges, fishing, horseback riding; no a/c* 💳 *MC, V* ⏲ *Closed late Dec.–early Jan.* *BP.*

★ ££–£££ ✕🏨 **Edenwater House.** This handsome stone house overlooks Edenwater 2 mi north of Kelso. Four well-appointed guest rooms afford superb views of the river and two of the Cheviot hills. The inn is filled with antiques and serves what connoisseurs regard as the best food in the Borders. Roast saddle of hare with foie gras, and filet of monkfish crusted with basil and coriander in beurre blanc are two of the dishes you might find on the menu. The restaurant is open Friday and Saturday for nonguests, too, and offers a £30 three-course dinner. Children under 10 are not admitted to the restaurant. ✉ *Off the B6461, Ednam, TD5 7QL* ☎ *01573/224070* 📠 *01573/226615* 🌐 *www.edenwaterhouse.co.uk* *4 rooms* *Restaurant, fishing, lounge, Internet; no a/c, no room phones* 💳 *MC, V* ⏲ *Closed Sun.–Thurs. and Jan. 1–14* *BP.*

Mellerstain House

3 *7 mi northwest of Kelso.*

One fine example of the Borders area's ornate country homes is Mellerstain House. Begun in the 1720s, it was finished in the 1770s by Robert Adam (1728–92) and is considered one of his finest creations. Sumptuous plasterwork covers almost all interior surfaces, and there are outstanding examples of 18th-century furnishings. The beautiful terraced gardens are as renowned as the house. ✉ *Off A6089* ☎ *01573/410225* 🌐 *www.mellerstain.com* 💳 *£5.50* ⏲ *May–Sept., Sun.–Fri. 12:30–5 (last admission 4:30); Oct., weekends 12:30–5 (last admission 4:30). Grounds open 1 hr before house.*

Smailholm Tower

❹ *6 mi south of Mellerstain House, 8 mi northwest of Kelso.*

This characteristic Borders structure stands uncompromisingly on top of a barren, rocky ridge in the hills south of Mellerstain. Built solely for defense, the 16th-century peel's unadorned stones contrast with the luxury of Mellerstain House. If you let your imagination wander in this windy spot, you can almost see the flapping pennants and rising dust of an advancing raiding party and hear the anxious securing of doors and bolts. Sir Walter Scott found this an inspiring spot. His grandfather lived at nearby Sandyknowe Farm (not open to the public), and the young Scott visited the tower often during his childhood. A museum here displays costumed figures and tapestries relating to Scott's Borders folk ballads. ✉ *Off B6404* ☎ *01573 460365* 🌐 *www.historic-scotland.gov.uk* 💳 *£2* ⏲ *Apr.–Sept., daily 9:30–6:30.*

Coldstream

❺ *9 mi east of Kelso.*

Three miles west of Coldstream, the England–Scotland border comes down from the hills and runs beside the Tweed for the rest of its journey to the sea. Coldstream itself, like Gretna Green, was once a Las Vegas of sorts, where runaway couples from the south could come to get married in a time when the marriage laws of Scotland were more lenient than those of England. A plaque on the former bridge tollhouse recalls this fact. The town is also celebrated in military history: in 1659 General Monck raised a regiment of foot guards here on behalf of his exiled monarch, Charles II of England (1630–85). Known as the Coldstream Guards, the successors to this regiment have become an elite corps in the British army. Today Coldstream is still a small town, with a mix of attractive 18th- and 19th-century buildings.

The **Coldstream Museum,** in the Coldstream Guards' former headquarters, examines the history of the community and the Guards. You can see 18th-century marriage contracts, pieces of masonry from the village's lost medieval convent, weapons, uniforms, and photographs. A children's play area has toys and costumes, including a child-size Coldstream Guard uniform and bearskin hat made by the Guards' regimental tailor. ✉ *Market Sq.* ☎ *01890/882630* 💳 *Free* ⏲ *Apr.–Sept., Mon.–Sat. 10–4, Sun. 2–4; Oct., Mon.–Sat. 1–4.*

Dignified houses and gardens line the stretch of the Tweed near Coldstream. The best-known house is the **Hirsel,** where a complex of farmyard buildings now serves as a crafts center and museum, with interesting walks on the extensive grounds. It's a favorite spot for bird-watchers, and superb rhododendrons bloom here in late spring. The house itself is not open to the public. ✉ *A697, immediately west of Coldstream* ☎ *01890/882834* 💳 *Free; parking £2* ⏲ *Grounds daily sunrise–sunset; museum and crafts center weekdays 10–5, weekends noon–5.*

Where to Stay & Eat

★ ££ ✕🏨 **Wheatsheaf Hotel and Restaurant.** The Wheatsheaf is a dining establishment that also provides accommodation—an important distinction according to the chef-owner. You can have an outstanding casual meal in the black-beamed bar, but it's the formal restaurant that is the real treat. Here, the sheer excellence of the Scottish cuisine, whether you order beef, salmon, or venison, has won widespread praise, yet neither the food nor the small but carefully chosen wine list is overpriced. If you don't want to leave after your meal, stay in one of the seven country-style bedrooms. The inn is on the main street of Swinton, 6 mi north of Coldstream. ✉ *Main St., Swinton TD11 3JJ* ☎ *01890/860257* 📠 *01890/860688* 🌐 *www.scottish-inns.co.uk/wheatsheaf* *7 rooms* *2 restaurants, bar; no a/c* 💳 *MC, V* *BP.*

Paxton House

❻ *15 mi northeast of Coldstream.*

Stately Paxton House is a comely Palladian mansion designed in 1758 by James and John Adam, with interiors designed by their brother Robert. There is Chippendale and Trotter furniture, and a splendid Regency picture gallery, an outstation of the National Galleries of Scotland, which houses a magnificent collection of paintings. The garden is delightful, with an ice house, squirrel hide, and a restored boathouse with a museum of salmon net fishing. A crafts shop and a tearoom are adjacent to the house. ✉ *Paxton, 15 mi northeast of Coldstream (take A6112 and B6461)* ☎ *01289/386291* 🌐 *www.paxtonhouse.com* *Joint ticket for house and garden, £5; garden only, £2.50* ⏲ *House and garden Apr.–Oct., daily 11–5, last tour at 4:15; tearoom and shops daily 10–5:30.*

Manderston House

❼ *15 mi northeast of Coldstream.*

Manderston House is a good example of the grand, no-expense-spared Edwardian country house. The family that built it made its fortune selling herring to Russia. An original 1790s Georgian house on the site was completely rebuilt from 1903 to 1905 to the specifications of John Kinross. The silver-plated staircase was modeled after the one in the Petit Trianon, at Versailles. Look for the collection of late-19th- and early 20th-century cookie tins. There's much to see downstairs in the kitchens, and outside, among a cluster of other buildings, is the octagonal, one-of-a-kind marble dairy. You can reach the house by traveling northeast from Coldstream along the A6112 to Duns, then taking the A6105 east. ✉ *Off A6105, 2 mi east of Duns* ☎ *01361/882636* 📠 *01361/882010* 🌐 *www.manderston.co.uk* *Joint ticket for house and grounds, £6.50; grounds only, £3.50* ⏲ *Mid-May–Sept., Thurs., Sun., and bank holiday Mon. 2–5, grounds open until dusk.*

Dryburgh Abbey

★ ❽ *8 mi southeast of Melrose.*

The final resting place of Sir Walter Scott and his wife, and the most peaceful and secluded of the Borders abbeys, Dryburgh Abbey sits on gentle parkland in a loop of the Tweed. The abbey suffered from English raids until, like Melrose, it was abandoned in 1544. The style is transitional, a mingling of rounded Romanesque and pointed early English. The north transept, where the Haig and Scott families lie buried, is lofty and pillared, and once formed part of the abbey church. ✉ *On the B6404, off the A68* ☎ *01835/822381* *£2.80* ⏲ *Apr.–Sept., daily 9:30–6:30; Oct.–Mar., Mon.–Sat. 9:30–4:30, Sun. 2–4:30.*

off the beaten path

SCOTT'S VIEW – There's no escaping Sir Walter in this part of the country: 3 mi north of Dryburgh on the B6356 is possibly the most photographed rural view in the south of Scotland. (Perhaps the only view used more often to summon a particular interpretation of Scotland is that of Eilean Donan Castle, far to the north.) The sinuous curve of the River Tweed and the gentle landscape unfolding to the triple peaks of the Eildons and then rolling out into shadows beyond are certainly worth seeking. You arrive at this peerless vista, where Scott often came to meditate, by taking the B6356 north from Dryburgh. A poignant tale is told about the horses of Scott's funeral cortege: on their way to Dryburgh Abbey they stopped here out of habit as they had so often in the past.

3

Melrose

9 *15 mi west of Coldstream, 5 mi southeast of Galashiels*

Though it is small, there is nevertheless a bustle about Melrose, the perfect example of a prosperous Scottish market town and one of the loveliest in the Borders. It is set round a square lined with 18th- and 19th-century buildings housing myriad small shops and cafés. Despite its proximity to the much larger Galashiels, Melrose has rejected industrialization. You'll likely hear local residents greet each other by first name in the square. Just off the square, down Abbey Street, sit the ruins ★ of **Melrose Abbey,** one of the four Borders abbeys. "If thou would'st view fair Melrose aright, go visit it in the pale moonlight," wrote Scott in *The Lay of the Last Minstrel,* and so many of his fans took the advice literally that a sleepless custodian begged him to rewrite the lines. Today the abbey is still impressive: a red-sandstone shell with slender windows, delicate tracery, and carved capitals, all carefully maintained. Among the carvings high on the roof is one of a bagpipe-playing pig. An audio tour is included in the admission price. ✉ *Abbey St.* ☎ *01896/822562* 🌐 *www.historic-scotland.gov.uk* 🎫 *£3.50* ⏲ *Apr.–Sept., daily 9:30–6:30; Oct.–Mar., Mon.–Sat. 9:30–4:30, Sun. 2–4:30.*

The National Trust for Scotland's **Priorwood Gardens,** next to Melrose Abbey, specializes in growing flowers for drying. Next to the gardens is an orchard with some old apple varieties. Dried flowers are on sale in the shop. ✉ *Abbey St.* ☎ *01896/822493* 🎫 *£2* ⏲ *Apr.–Sept., Mon.–Sat. 10–5, Sun. 1–5; Oct.–Dec., Mon.–Sat. 10–5, Sun. 1–4.*

The **Three Hills Roman Heritage Centre** exhibits such artifacts as tools, weapons, and armor, retrieved from the largest Roman settlement in Scotland, which was at Newstead, 3 mi to the east. A blacksmith's shop, several examples of pottery, and scale models of the fort are also on display. A guided four-hour walk to the site takes place each Thursday afternoon (also on Tuesday in July and August); phone for details. ✉ *The Ormiston, Melrose Square,* ☎ *01896/822651* 🌐 *www.trimontium.freeserve.co.uk* 🎫 *£1.50 (walk £2.80)* ⏲ *Apr.–Oct., weekdays 10:30–4:30, weekends 10:30–1 and 2–4:30.*

Thirlestane Castle is a large, turreted, and castellated house, part of which was built in the 13th century and part in the 16th century. It looks for all the world like a French château, and it brims with history. The former home of the Duke of Lauderdale (1616–1682), one of Charles II's advisers, Thirlestane is said to be haunted by the duke's ghost. Exquisite 17th-century plaster ceilings and rich collections of paintings, porcelain, and furniture fill the rooms. In the nursery, children are invited to play with Victorian-style toys and to dress up in masks and costumes. ✉ *Off A68, Lauder, 9 mi north of Melrose* ☎ *01578/722430* 🌐 *www.*

thirlestanecastle.co.uk *Joint ticket for castle and grounds, £5.30; grounds only, £1.50* *Apr.–Oct., Sun.–Fri. 10:30–5, last admission 4:15; grounds open until 6. Tours are available 11–2.*

Where to Stay & Eat

££–£££ Fodor's Choice ★ **Hoebridge Inn.** Whitewashed walls, oak-beamed ceilings, and an open fire welcome you into this converted and modernized 19th-century bobbin mill. The cuisine is a blend of British and Mediterranean styles with occasional Asian influences. You might have pan-fried tiger prawns with chili and lime syrup, accompanied by bean-sprout and *mangetout* (peas in their edible pods) salad; or try the duck with roast figs, Parma ham, and a port-and-balsamic reduction. The inn lies in Gattonside, just next to Melrose but a 2-mi drive along the B6360, thanks to the intervention of the Tweed; you can also reach the inn by a footbridge from the town. *Off B360, Gattonside* *01896/823082* *MC, V.*

£££ **Burts Hotel.** This hotel is in a 1722 building in the center of Melrose. Floral pastels fill the rooms and public areas. The bar is particularly welcoming, with a cheerful open fire and a wide selection of fine malt whiskies; it is ideal for a quiet dram before or after a meal. The restaurant has high-back upholstered chairs, and white-linen tablecloths. Cannon of venison and roast duck terrine are typical entrées on the prix-fixe, multi-course menu. Fishing can be arranged. *Melrose Sq., TD6 9PL* *01896/822285* *01896/822870* *www.burtshotel.co.uk* *20 rooms* *Restaurant, fishing; no a/c* *AE, MC, V* *BP.*

£££ **Dryburgh Abbey Hotel.** Mature woodlands and verdant lawns surround this imposing, 19th-century mansion, which is right next to the abbey ruins on a sweeping bend of the River Tweed. The rooms are large and sumptuous, with canopied beds and lace-trimmed curtains, and throughout the hotel you'll feel a sense of quiet and peace in keeping with the location. The restaurant specializes in traditional Scottish fare. *Off B6404, St. Boswells, TD6 0RQ* *01835/822261* *01835/823945* *www.dryburgh.co.uk* *36 rooms, 2 suites* *Restaurant, golf privileges, pool, fishing* *AE, MC, V* *BP.*

The Arts

The Wynd Theatre (3 Buccleuch St. 01896/823854) has a monthly program of four nights of drama from national touring companies, two concerts of folk, blues, jazz, or oratorio from touring national and international companies, plus classic film on two Fridays. There's also an art gallery highlighting top contemporary Scottish artists, plus a bar and nearby parking. Tickets cost £8 for performances, £6 for films.

Abbotsford House

10 *2 mi west of Melrose.*

Fodor's Choice ★

In 1811 Sir Walter Scott, already an established writer, bought a farm on this site named Cartleyhole, which was a euphemism for the real name, Clartyhole (*clarty* is Scots for "muddy" or "dirty"). The name was surely not romantic enough for Scott, who renamed the property Abbotsford House after a ford in the nearby Tweed used by the abbot of Melrose. Scott eventually had the house entirely rebuilt in the Scots Baronial style. The result was called "the most incongruous pile that gentlemanly modernism ever devised" by art critic John Ruskin. That was Mr. Ruskin's idiosyncratic take; most people have found this to be one of the most fetching of all Scottish abodes. A gently seedy mansion chockfull of Scottish curios, paintings, and mounted deer heads, this is an appropriate domicile for a man of such an extraordinarily romantic imagination. It's worth visiting just to feel the atmosphere that the most successful writer of his day created and to see the condition in which

THE VERSE OF SIR WALTER SCOTT

SIR WALTER SCOTT *(1771–1832) was probably Scottish tourism's best propagandist. Thanks to his fervid "Romantik" imagination, his long narrative poems—such as* The Lady of the Lake*—and a truly long string of historical novels, including* Ivanhoe, Waverley, Rob Roy, Redgauntlet, *and* The Heart of Midlothian, *the world fell in love with the image of heroic Scotland. Seriously told and thoroughly documented, his works lifted fiction high above the Gothic romances of his contemporaries. As part of the Romantic movement in Britain (the English poets William Wordsworth and Samuel Taylor Coleridge were his near-contemporaries), Scott wrote of Scotland as a place of Highland wilderness and clan romance, shaping outsiders' perceptions of Scotland in a way that to an extent survives even today.*

Scott was born in College Wynd, Edinburgh. A lawyer by training, he was an assiduous collector of old ballads and tales. As a young boy recovering from illness, Scott was sent to his grandfather's farm, near Smailholm in the Borders, where he first heard the stirring tales of Borders history. After qualifying as an advocate in 1792 and after his marriage in 1797 to Margaret Charlotte Charpentier, daughter of a French refugee, Scott seriously began to devote his spare time to writing. The Lay of the Last Minstrel, *a romantic poem published in 1805, brought him fame and was soon followed by further romantic verse narratives.*

In 1811 Scott bought the house that was to become Abbotsford, his Borders mansion near Melrose, which he rebuilt and which gradually became a storehouse of Scottish history: Bonnie Prince Charlie's quaich (drinking bowl), library ceiling plaster casts from Rosslyn Chapel, Rob Roy's broadsword, and an entrance porch copied from Linlithgow Palace are examples of the wealth of artifacts he amassed, all of which can still be seen today.

Scott started on his series of Waverley novels in 1814, at first anonymously, and by 1820 had produced Waverley, Guy Mannering, The Antiquary, Tales of My Landlord *(three series), and* Rob Roy. *Between 1820 and 1825 there followed an additional 11 titles, including* Ivanhoe *and* The Pirate, *which was partly written during a voyage around Scotland with lighthouse builder Robert Stevenson, grandfather of novelist Robert Louis Stevenson. Many of his verse narratives and novels focused on real-life settings, in particular the Trossachs, northwest of Stirling, an area which rapidly became, and still remains, extremely popular with visitors.*

In 1826 Ballantyne's publishing house, in which Scott was a partner, went bankrupt, and Scott took it as a matter of honor to personally clear the debts. Until his death six years later, he produced a copious amount of work, including additional novels, a biographical Life of Napoleon, *and translations of German works. Scott's health started to fail under the pressure of work (and those mounting bills), and he died on September 21, 1832. His remaining debts were paid off when the copyright to his works were sold soon after his death.*

Abbotsford can be visited in spring and summer, and other houses associated with Scott can be seen (from the outside only) in Edinburgh: 25 George Square, which was his father's house, and 39 Castle Street. The site of his birthplace, in College Wynd, is marked with a plaque. The most obvious structure associated with Scott is the Scott Monument on Princes Street, which looks for all the world like a Gothic rocket ship with a statue of Scott and his pet dog as passengers.

he wrote, driving himself to pay off his endless debts. To Abbotsford came most of the famous poets and thinkers of Scott's day, including Wordsworth and Washington Irving. With some 9,000 volumes in the library, Abbotsford is the repository for the writer's collection of Scottish memorabilia and historic artifacts. Scott died here in 1832, and the house is today owned by his descendants. ✉ *B6360, Galashiels* ☎ *01896/752043* 🎫 *£4.20* ⏲ *3rd Monday in March–May and Oct., Sun. 2–5; June–Sept., daily 9:30–5.*

Galashiels

⓫ *5 mi northwest of Melrose.*

A busy gray-stone Borders town, Galashiels is still active with textile mills and knitwear shops. The **Lochcarron of Scotland Cashmere and Wool Centre** houses a museum, where you can go on a mill tour and learn about the manufacture of tartans and tweeds. ✉ *Waverley Mill, Huddersfield St.* ☎ *01896/752091* 🎫 *Free; tour £2.50* ⏲ *June–Sept., Mon.–Sat. 9–5, Sun. noon–5; Oct.–Dec. and Jan.–May, Mon.–Sat. 9–5. Guided tours Mon.–Thurs. at 10:30, 11:30, 1:30, and 2:30; Fri. at 10:30 and 11:30.*

Dating from 1583, **Old Gala House,** a short walk from the town center, is the former home of the lairds (landed proprietors) of Galashiels. It now serves as a museum with displays on the building's history and the town of Galashiels, as well as a contemporary art gallery and exhibition space. You can trace your family history at a comprehensive genealogy facility. ✉ *Scott Cres.* ☎ *01750/20096* 🎫 *Free* ⏲ *Apr.–May and Sept., Tues.–Sat. 10–4; June–Aug., Mon.–Sat. 10–4, Sun. 1–4; Oct., Tues.–Sat. 1–4.*

Shopping

Lochcarron of Scotland Cashmere and Wool Centre (✉ Waverley Mill ☎ 01896/752091) sells a wide selection of woolens and tweeds.

Selkirk

⓬ *7 mi south of Galashiels.*

Selkirk is a hilly outpost with a smattering of antiques shops and an assortment of bakers selling the Selkirk Bannock (fruited sweet bread-cake) and other cakes. Sir Walter Scott was sheriff (judge) of Selkirkshire from 1800 until his death in 1832, and his statue stands in Market Place. **Sir Walter Scott's Courtroom,** where he presided, contains a display examining Scott's life, his writings, and his time as sheriff, and it includes an audiovisual presentation. ✉ *Market Pl.* ☎ *01750/20096* 🎫 *Free* ⏲ *Apr.–May, Mon.–Sat. 10–4; June–Sept., Mon.–Sat. 10–4, Sun. 2–4; Oct., Mon.–Sat. 1–4.*

Halliwell's House Museum, tucked off the main square in Selkirk, was once an ironmonger's shop, which is now re-created downstairs. Upstairs, an exhibit tells the town's tale, with useful background information on the Common Ridings. ✉ *Market Pl.* ☎ *01750/20096* 🎫 *Free* ⏲ *Apr.–May and Sept.–Oct., Mon.–Sat. 10–5, Sun. 2–4; July–Aug., Mon.–Sat. 10–6, Sun. 2–5.*

Bowhill

⓭ *3 mi west of Selkirk.*

Bowhill, one of the stately homes in the Borders, and home of the duke of Buccleuch, dates from the 19th century and houses an outstanding collection of works by Gainsborough, Van Dyck, Canaletto, Reynolds, and Raeburn, as well as porcelain and period furniture. The house itself is open in July only (parties, however, can book at other times); the grounds and playground have more friendly hours. ✉ *Off A708* ☎ *01750/22204* *Joint ticket for house and grounds and playground, £4.50; grounds and playground only, £1* ⏲ *House July, daily 1–5. Grounds and playground Easter–June and Aug., Sat.–Thurs. noon–5; July, daily noon–5.*

Innerleithen

⓮ *15 mi northwest of Selkirk.*

The main reason to come to the linear community of Innerleithen is to see **Robert Smail's Printing Works.** The fully operational, restored print shop with a reconstructed waterwheel fascinates adults and older children, who can try their hand at old-fashioned typesetting. ✉ *7–9 High St.* ☎ *01896/830206* *£3.50* ⏲ *Mar.–June and Sept.–Oct., Mon.–Thur. 12–5, Sun. 1–5; July–Aug., Thurs.–Mon. 10–6, Sun. 1–5; last admission 45 mins before closing.*

Fodor'sChoice ★ Near the town of Innerleithen stands **Traquair House,** said to be the oldest continually occupied house in Scotland. Inside you are free to discover secret stairs, a maze, intricate embroidery, more than 3,000 books, and a bed used by Mary, Queen of Scots, in 1566. Ale is still brewed in the 18th-century brew house here, and it's recommended. You may even spend the night. ✉ *B709, Traquair, 1 mi from Innerleithen* ☎ *01896/830323* 📠 *01896/830639* 🌐 *www.traquair.co.uk* *£5.60* ⏲ *Easter–May, 12:30–5; June–Aug., 10:30–5:30; Oct., 11–4; last admission half hour before closing.*

Where to Stay

££££ **Traquair House.** To stay in one of the three guest rooms in the 12th-century part of Traquair House is to experience a slice of Scottish history. Each spacious room is individually decorated with antiques and canopied beds. During your stay you may explore those parts of the house that are open to the public, or walk in the parkland and gardens. In the 18th-century lower drawing room you can savor a glass of the house ale before an open fire. Dinner can be arranged. ✉ *B709, Traquair, EH44 6PW* ☎ *01896/830323* 📠 *01896/830639* 🌐 *www.traquair.co.uk* *3 rooms* *Dining room; no a/c* *MC, V* *BP.*

Peebles

⓯ *6 mi west of Innerleithen.*

Thanks to its excellent though pricey shopping, Peebles gives the impression of catering primarily to leisured country gentlefolk. Architecturally the town is nothing out of the ordinary, a very pleasant Borders burgh. Don't miss the splendid dolphins ornamenting the bridge crossing the River Tweed.

Neidpath Castle, a 15-minute walk upstream along the banks of the Tweed from Peebles, perches artistically above a bend in the river, and comes into view through the tall trees. The castle is a medieval structure remodeled in the 17th century, with dungeons hewn from solid rock. You can return on the opposite riverbank after crossing an old, finely skewed railroad viaduct. ✉ *Off A72* ☎ *01721/720333* *£3* ⏲ *Easter week, two bank holiday weekends in May, and Mid-June–early Sept., Mon.–Sat. 10:30–4.30, Sun. 12:30–4.30.*

Where to Stay & Eat

£££££ Fodor's Choice ★ **Peebles Hydro.** Not only does the Hydro have something for everyone, but it has it in abundance: pony trekking, a putting green, and a giant chess and checkers game are just a few of the diversions you'll find here. The elegant Edwardian building stands on 30 acres of land, and you are welcome to explore all of it. The public areas and most rooms have lofty ceilings and elegant, antique-reproduction furnishings. The restaurant has a Scottish menu that includes local salmon, lamb, and beef. *Innerleithen Rd., EH45 8LX 01721/720602 01721/722999 www.peebleshydro.com 132 rooms Restaurant, putting green, tennis court, pool, gym, hot tub, sauna, bicycles, croquet, recreation room, baby-sitting, children's programs (ages infant–16), playground, laundry service; no a/c AE, DC, MC, V BP.*

★ **£££–£££££** **Cringletie House.** With turrets and crow-step gables, Cringletie manages to be fancy *and* homey. A British-country-house style predominates, and bedrooms are individually decorated. From the drawing room there are views over the valley. A walled garden grows produce used in the restaurant. Locals come here for Scottish fare such as boned quail stuffed with trompette mushrooms, and loin of deer from the neighboring estate. The afternoon tea, served in the conservatory, is especially recommended. *Edinburgh Rd., Off A703, EH45 8PL 01721/730233 01721/730244 www.cringletie.com 14 rooms Restaurant, putting green, tennis court, croquet, fishing; no a/c AE, MC, V BP.*

£££–££££ **Park Hotel.** An intimate retreat on the banks of the River Tweed at the northern tip of the Ettrick Forest, the Park Hotel offers tranquil, green surroundings and airy, modern rooms in florals and pastels. The restaurant serves superior Scottish cuisine; many of the dishes use local salmon and trout. You are welcome to use the facilities at the Peebles Hydro Hotel, ½ mi away. *Innerleithen Rd., EH45 8BA 01721/720451 01721/723510 www.parkpeebles.co.uk 24 rooms Restaurant, fishing; no a/c AE, DC, MC, V BP.*

£ **Drummore.** An acre of wild gardens full of bird life surrounds this hillside B&B. The house, built in the 1960s, has rooms with contemporary, functional furniture, plus a lounge with a vast picture window overlooking the town. *Venlaw High Rd., EH45 8RL 01721/720336 01721/723004 arthur@trails.scottishborders.co.uk 2 rooms Lounge; no a/c, no room phones, no room TVs MC, V Closed Nov.–Mar. BP.*

Shopping

Be prepared for temptations at every turn as you browse the shops on High Street and in the courts and side streets leading off it.

GIFTS **Head to Toe** (43 High St. 01721/722752) stocks natural beauty products, handsome linens—from patchwork quilts to silk flowers—handmade pine furniture, candles, and cards. If you need a rest after a heavy day of shopping, repair to the **Country Shop** (56 High St. 01721/720630), a gift store with souvenirs aplenty and a coffee shop upstairs, with views over the town and bustling High Street. There are also cooking and garden departments.

JEWELRY & ANTIQUES The German-born and Swiss-trained watchmaker Jurgen Tubbecke sells antiques alongside his handcrafted chronometers at the **Clockmaker** (3 High St. 01721/723599). Among the many craftspeople and jewelers on High Street is **Keith Walter** (28 High St. 01721/720650), a gold- and silversmith who makes items on the premises and stocks jewelry made by other local designers.

DUMFRIES & GALLOWAY

Galloway covers the southwestern portion of Scotland, west of the main town of Dumfries. Here a gentle coastline gives way to farmland and then breezy uplands that gradually merge with coniferous forests. Use caution when negotiating the A75—you are liable to find aggressive trucks bearing down on you as these commercial vehicles race for the Irish ferries at Stranraer and Cairnryan (anything as environmentally sensible as a direct east–west railway link was closed in the early 1960s in an attempt to save money by slimming down Britain's rail network). Trucks notwithstanding, once you are off the main roads, Dumfries and Galloway offer some of the most pleasant drives in Scotland—though the occasional herd of cows on the way to be milked is a potential hazard.

Gretna Green

16 *10 mi north of Carlisle, 87 mi south of Glasgow, 92 mi southwest of Edinburgh.*

Gretna Green is, quite simply, an embarrassment to native Scots. What else can you say about a place that advertises "amusing joke weddings," as does one of the visitor centers here? These strange goings-on are tied to the reputation this community developed as a refuge for runaway couples from England, who once came north to take advantage of Scotland's more lenient marriage laws. This was the first place they reached on crossing the border. At one time anyone could perform a legal marriage in Scotland, and the village blacksmith (known as the "anvil priest") did the honors in Gretna Green. The blacksmith's shop is still standing, and today it contains a collection of blacksmithing tools, including the anvil over which many weddings were conducted.

Ruthwell

21 mi west of Gretna, 83 mi south of Glasgow, 88 mi southwest of Edinburgh.

North of the upper Solway Firth the countryside is flat, fertile farmland. Progressing west, however, a pleasant landscape of low, round hills begins to take over. But there are two historical features among the flat-
17 lands which mustn't be ignored. Inside **Ruthwell Parish Church** is the 8th-century **Ruthwell Cross**, a Christian sculpture admired for the detailed biblical scenes carved onto its north and south faces. The east and west faces have carvings of vines, birds, and animals, plus verses from an Anglo-Saxon poem called *The Dream of the Rood.* Considered an idolatrous monument, it was removed and demolished by Church of Scotland zealots in 1642 but was later reassembled.

The **Savings Banks Museum,** near the church in Ruthwell, tells the story of the savings-bank movement, founded by the Reverend Dr. Henry Duncan in 1810. It is said that Duncan's bank was the first in Western history to encourage ordinary people to invest their money in savings accounts in return for interest. ✉ *6½ mi west of Annan* ☎ *01387/870640* 🌐 *www.savingsbanksmuseum.co.uk* *Free* ⏲ *Easter–Oct., daily 10–1 and 2–5; Nov.–Easter, Tues.–Sat. 10–1 and 2–5.*

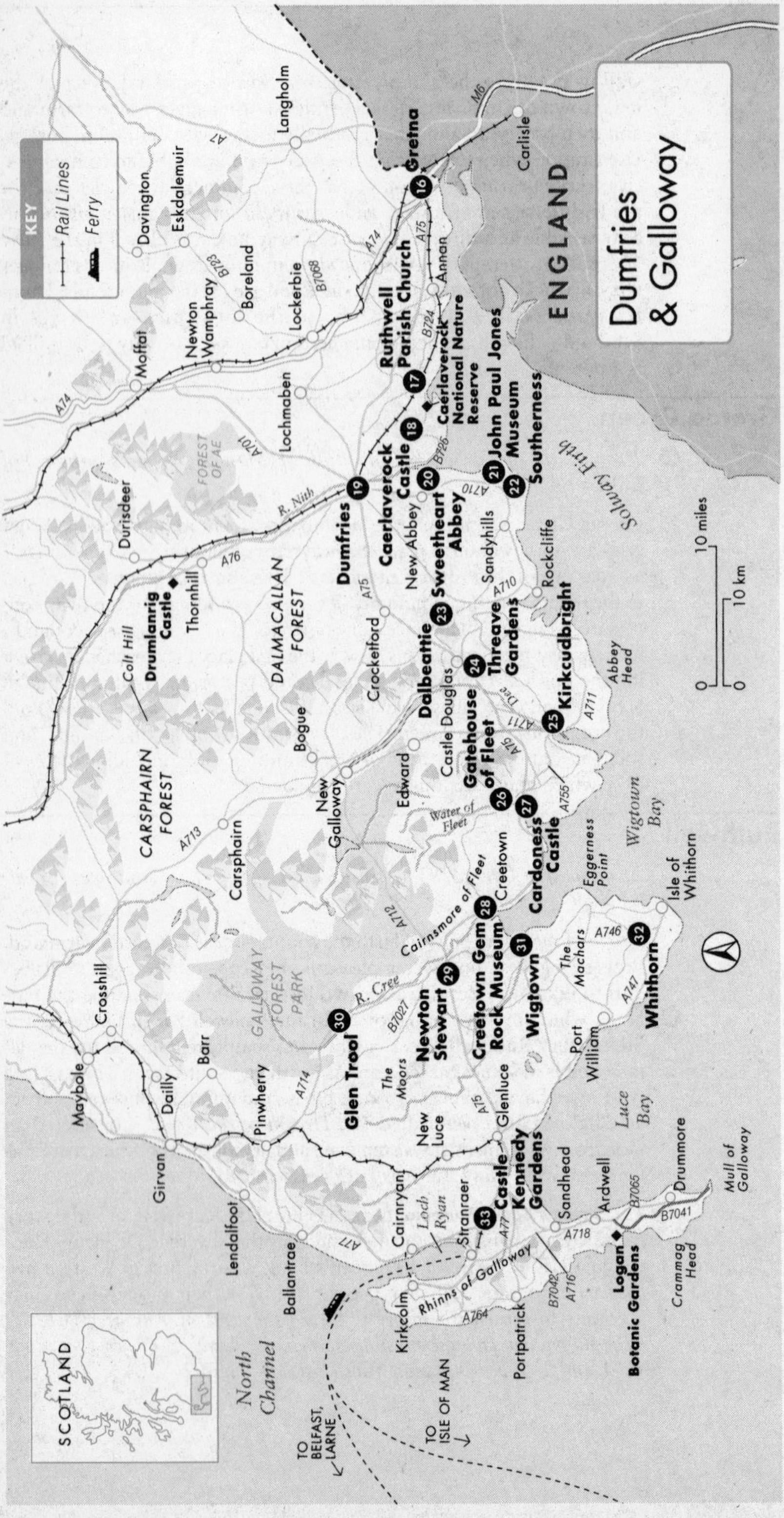
Dumfries & Galloway
KEY
Rail Lines
Ferry
SCOTLAND
ENGLAND
North Channel
TO BELFAST, LARNE
TO ISLE OF MAN
Solway Firth
Luce Bay
Wigtown Bay
Loch Ryan
CARSPHAIRN FOREST
DALMACALLAN FOREST
GALLOWAY FOREST PARK
FOREST OF AE
The Moors
The Machars
Rhinns of Galloway
Mull of Galloway
Crammag Head
Eggerness Point
Abbey Head
R. Nith
R. Cree
Water of Fleet
Dee
Cairnsmore of Fleet
Colt Hill
16 Gretna
17 Ruthwell Parish Church
18 Caerlaverock National Nature Reserve
19 Dumfries
20 Caerlaverock Castle
21 John Paul Jones Museum
22 Southerness
23 Sweetheart Abbey
24 Threave Gardens
25 Kirkcudbright
26 Gatehouse of Fleet
27 Cardoness Castle
28 Creetown Gem Rock Museum
29 Newton Stewart
30 Glen Trool
31 Wigtown
32 Whithorn
33 Castle Kennedy Gardens
Drumlanrig Castle
Dalbeattie
Logan Botanic Gardens
Carlisle
Langholm
Davington
Eskdalemuir
Boreland
Lockerbie
Moffat
Newton Wamphray
Lochmaben
Annan
Durisdeer
Thornhill
New Abbey
Sandyhills
Rockcliffe
Crocketford
Castle Douglas
Bogue
New Galloway
Edward
Carsphairn
Creetown
Isle of Whithorn
Port William
Glenluce
New Luce
Crosshill
Maybole
Barr
Dailly
Girvan
Pinwherry
Lendalfoot
Ballantrae
Cairnryan
Stranraer
Kirkcolm
Portpatrick
Sandhead
Ardwell
Drummore
M6
A74
A7
A75
A701
B723
B7068
B724
B725
A710
A76
A713
A711
A755
A712
B7027
A714
A746
A747
A77
A718
A716
B7042
B7065
B7041
A764
0 10 miles
0 10 km

Caerlaverock Castle

18 *5 mi west of Ruthwell.*

Fodor's Choice ★

The moated Caerlaverock Castle overlooks a nature reserve on a coastal loop of the B725. Built in a triangular design unique in Britain, this 13th-century moated fortress has solid-sandstone masonry and an imposing double-tower gatehouse. King Edward I of England (1239–1307) besieged the castle in 1300, when his forces occupied much of Scotland as the Wars of Independence commenced. The castle suffered many times in Anglo-Scottish skirmishes, as the video presentation attests. ✉ *Off B725, 5 mi west of Ruthwell* ☎ *01387/770244* 💷 *£3* ⏱ *Apr.–Sept., daily 9:30–6:30; Oct.–Mar., Mon.–Sat. 9:30–4:30, Sun. 2–4:30.*

The **Caerlaverock National Nature Reserve** lets you observe wintering wildfowl, including various species of geese, ducks, swans, and raptors, from blinds and a visitor center. ✉ *Off B725, east of Caerlaverock Castle* ☎ *01387/770275* 💷 *Free* ⏱ *Daily.*

Dumfries

19 *15 mi northwest of Ruthwell, 76 mi south of Glasgow, 81 mi southwest of Edinburgh.*

The town of Dumfries, where Scotland's national poet Robert Burns (1759–96) spent the last years of his short life, is a no-nonsense, red-sandstone community. The playwright J. M. Barrie (1860–1937) spent his childhood in Victoria Terrace here in the 1870s, and the garden of Moat Brae House is said to be the playground that inspired his boyish dreams in *Peter Pan*. The **River Nith** meanders through Dumfries, and the pedestrians-only town center makes wandering and shopping a pleasure. The town also contains Robert Burns's favorite *howff* (pub), the Globe Inn; one of the houses he lived in; and his mausoleum.

Not surprisingly, in view of its close association to the poet, Dumfries has a **Robert Burns Centre,** housed in a sturdy former mill overlooking the river. The center has an audiovisual program and an extensive exhibit on the life of the poet. ✉ *Mill Rd.* ☎ *01387/264808 or 01387/263666* 💷 *Free; small charge for audiovisual show* ⏱ *Apr.–Sept., Mon.–Sat. 10–8, Sun. 2–5 (café, daily 11–4); Oct.–Mar., Tues.–Sat. 10–1 and 2–5.*

off the beaten path

DRUMLANRIG CASTLE – This spectacular estate is as close as Scotland gets to the treasure houses of England—which is not surprising, since it's owned by the dukes of Buccleuch, one of the wealthiest British peerages. Ornate, square built, and resplendent with romantic turrets, this pink-sandstone palace was constructed between 1679 and 1691 by the first duke of Queensbury, who, after nearly bankrupting himself building the place, found it disappointing on his first overnight stay and never returned. The Buccleuchs inherited the palace and soon filled the richly decorated rooms with French furniture from the period of Louis XIV, family portraits, and a valuable collection of paintings by Holbein, Rembrandt, da Vinci, and Murillo. There are also crafts workshops, a working forge, a playground, a gift shop, and a tearoom. ✉ *Near Thornhill, about 18 mi northwest of Dumfries off A76* ☎ *01848/330248* 💷 *Joint ticket for castle and park, £6; park only, £3* ⏱ *Castle: May–Aug., Mon.–Sat. 11–4, Sun. noon–4, last entry at 4; country park, gardens, and adventure playground: May–Sept., daily 11–5.*

MUSEUM OF LEAD MINING – There are underground trips for the stouthearted at this museum devoted to one of Scotland's lesser-known industries. The Miners' Library not only shows how the miners educated themselves but also has a genealogical computer database. To reach the museum follow Mennock Pass through rounded moorland hills to remote Wanlockhead, Scotland's highest village. ✉ *Goldscaur Rd., Wanlockhead, on B797 east of Sanquhar, 27 mi northwest of Dumfries* ☎ *01659/74387* 🌐 *www.leadminingmuseum.co.uk* 🎫 *£4.95* ⏲ *Apr.–Oct., daily 10–4:30, last tour at 4.*

The Arts

Gracefield Arts Centre (✉ 28 Edinburgh Rd. ☎ 01387/262084) has public art galleries and studios with a constantly changing exhibition program. The **Dumfries and Galloway Arts Festival** is usually held at the end of May at several venues throughout the region. Contact the Gracefield Arts Centre for more information. The **Robert Burns Centre Film Theatre** (✉ Mill Rd. ☎ 01387/264808) screens mainstream, special-interest, foreign, and other films.

Bicycling

Cycles can be rented from **Greirson and Graham** (✉ 10 Academy St. ☎ 01387/259483), and the staff can provide advice on where to ride.

Shopping

Dumfries is the main shopping center for the region, with all the big-name chain stores as well as specialty shops. **Greyfriars Crafts** (✉ 56 Buccleuch St. ☎ 01387/264050) sells mainly Scottish goods, including glass, ceramics, and jewelry. If you are visiting Drumlanrig Castle, don't miss the **crafts center** (☎ 01848/331555) in the stable block, chock-full of all types of crafts, including leather goods, landscape and portrait works, stainless-steel jewelry, and cutlery. The center is open May through August, daily 9 to 5; September through April, by appointment. For a souvenir that's easy to pack, try **David Hastings** (✉ Maryng, Shieldhill, near Amisfield ☎ 01387/710451), with more than 100,000 old postcards and postal history items. The store is open weekdays 10 to 5 or by appointment. The shop is in a house called Maryng in a group of houses called Shieldhill.

New Abbey

7 mi south of Dumfries, 83 mi south of Glasgow, 88 mi southwest of Edinburgh.

At the center of the village of New Abbey is the red-tinted and roofless
⑳ **Sweetheart Abbey.** "Sweetheart" is a translation of the abbey's previous name, St. Mary of the Dolce Coeur. The abbey was founded in 1273 by the Lady of Galloway, Devorgilla (1210–1290), in memory of her husband, John Balliol (?–1269), who was buried in Bardard Castle in England. It is said Devorgilla had his heart embalmed and placed in a casket, which she carried everywhere. After she died, Devorgilla was laid to rest before the High Altar of Sweetheart Abbey with the casket resting on her breast. The couple's son, also named John (1250–1315), was the puppet king installed in Scotland by Edward of England when the latter claimed sovereignty over Scotland. After John's appointment the Scots gave him a scathing nickname that would stay with him for the rest of his life: Toom Tabard (Empty Shirt). ✉ *A710 at New Abbey* ☎ *01387/850397* 🎫 *£1.80.* ⏲ *Apr.–Sept., daily 9:30–6:30; Oct.–Mar., Mon.–Wed. and Sat. 9:30–4:30, Thurs. 9:30–noon, Sun. 2–4:30.*

John Paul Jones Museum

21 *5 mi south of New Abbey, 88 mi south of Glasgow, 94 mi southwest of Edinburgh.*

The little community of Kirkbean (blink and you've missed it) set in a bright green landscape is the backdrop for Arbigland estate. It was in a cottage on the property that John Paul (1747–1792), the son of an estate gardener, was born. He eventually left Scotland, added "Jones," to his name, and became the founder of the U.S. navy. The cottage where he was born is furnished as it would have been when John was a boy, and audio headsets describe what life was like in the mid-18th century. John Paul Jones returned to raid the coastline of his native country in 1778. The story of this exploit is told in an adjoining visitor center, where there is a replica of Jones's ship cabin. A gift shop sells souvenirs. Follow signs to Arbigland from Kirkbean. ✉ *Off A710 by Kirkbean* ☎ *01387/880613* £2 ⏲ *Apr.–June and Sept., daily 10–5; July–Aug., daily 10–5.*

Southerness

22 *3 mi south of Kirkbean, 91 mi south of Glasgow, 97 mi southwest of Edinburgh.*

The minor road to Southerness (off the A710) ends in a welter of recreational vehicles and trailer homes in the shadow of one of Scotland's earliest lighthouses, built in 1749 by the port authorities of Dumfries who were anxious to make the treacherous River Nith approaches safer.

en route

After the turn-off to Southerness, the A710 turns west and becomes faintly Riviera-like. At Colvend, you can detour down a minor road to Rockcliffe, a sleepy coastal community overlooking the creeping tides and endless shallows of the Solway coast.

Dalbeattie

23 *12 mi northwest of Southerness, 89 mi south of Glasgow, 95 mi southwest of Edinburgh.*

Like the much larger Aberdeen, far to the northeast, Dalbeattie contains buildings constructed with local gray granite from the town's quarry. The well-scrubbed gray glitter makes Dalbeattie atypical of Galloway towns, where housefronts are usually painted in pastels.

Where to Stay

★ ££ **Auchenskeoch Lodge.** This quaint and informal Victorian country house, a former hunting lodge, has three bedrooms and serves delicious breakfasts and multi-course dinners (for guests only). The antique furnishings have a comfortable, faded elegance that will make you feel at home. You'll find full bookshelves in the sitting room, a billiards table in the game room, and a private loch and croquet lawn outdoors. Many of the vegetables and herbs used in the kitchen are grown in the hotel's gardens. ✉ *B793, 5 mi southeast of Dalbeattie, DG5 4PG* ☎ *01387/780277* *www.auchenskeochlodge.com* *3 rooms* *Dining room, fishing, billiards, croquet; no a/c* *MC, V* ⏲ *Closed Nov.–Easter* *BP.*

Horseback Riding

Barend Riding School and Trekking Centre (✉ Sandyhills ☎ 01387/780632 or 01387/780533) helps you to a "horse-high" view of the beautiful coast and countryside of this region. The school is 6 mi southeast of Dalbeattie on the A710.

Castle Douglas

6 mi west of Dalbeattie, 94 mi south of Glasgow, 99 mi southwest of Edinburgh.

This is a pleasant town, with a long main street where the bakeries vie for business. The main reason to come to Castle Douglas is to visit

★ 24 **Threave Gardens.** As Scotland's best-known charitable conservation agency, the National Trust for Scotland cares for several garden properties, including the sloping parkland around the mansion house of Threave. This horticultural undertaking demands the employment of many gardeners—and it is at Threave that the gardeners train, thus ensuring there is always some fresh development or experimental planting here. There's a good visitor center as well. ✉ *South of A75, 1 mi west of Castle Douglas* ☎ *01556/502575* 🌐 *www.nts.org.uk* 💷 *House and gardens £8.50; gardens only £5* ⏲ *Gardens and estate daily 9:30–sunset; walled garden and greenhouses daily 9:30–5; visitor center, plant center, exhibition, shop, and restaurant Mar.–Oct., daily 9:30–5:30 and Nov.–Dec., daily 10–4; house tours Mar.–Oct., Thur.–Sun. 11–4.*

Threave Castle, not to be confused with the mansion house in Threave Gardens, was an early home of the Black Douglases, who were the earls of Nithsdale and lords of Galloway. The castle was dismantled in the religious wars of the mid-17th century, though enough of it remains to have housed prisoners from the Napoleonic Wars of the 19th century. It's a few minutes from Castle Douglas by car and is signposted from the main road. To get there, you must leave your car in a farmyard and walk the rest of the way. Make your way down to the reeds by the river on an occasionally muddy path. At the edge of the river you can then ring a bell, and, rather romantically, a boatman will come to ferry you across to the great stone tower looming from a marshy island in the river. ✉ *North of A75, 3 mi west of Castle Douglas* ☎ *07711/223101* 💷 *£2.20, includes ferry* ⏲ *Apr.–Sept., daily 9:30–6:30.*

Sports & the Outdoors

BIKING You can rent bicycles from **Castle Douglas Cycle Centre** (✉ Church St. ☎ 01556/504542).

WATER SPORTS The **Galloway Sailing Centre** (✉ Loch Ken ☎ 01644/420626 🌐 www.lochken.co.uk) rents dinghies, windsurfing equipment, and canoes. It also runs sailing, windsurfing, canoeing, mountain biking, archery, and climbing courses.

Shopping

BOOKS It's well worth the short drive north from Castle Douglas (A75 then B794) to visit **Benny Gillies Books, Maps and Prints** (✉ 31–33 Victoria St., Kirkpatrick Durham 🌐 www.bennygillies.co.uk ☎ 01556/650412). The shop has an outstanding selection of secondhand and antiquarian Scottish books, hand-colored antique maps, and prints depicting areas throughout Scotland.

GIFTS The **Posthorn** (✉ 26–30 St. Andrew St. ☎ 01556/502531) is renowned for its display of figurines by Border Fine Art as well as Scotland's biggest display of Moorcroft glazed and enamel pottery.

JEWELRY **Galloway Gems** (✉ 130–132 King St. ☎ 01556/503254) sells mineral specimens, polished stone slices, and art materials.

Kirkcudbright

25 *11 mi southwest of Castle Douglas, 103 mi south of Glasgow, 109 mi southwest of Edinburgh.*

Kirkcudbright (pronounced "Kirk-*coo*-bray") is an 18th-century town of Georgian and Victorian houses, some of them color-washed in pastel shades and roofed with the blue slates of the district. For much of this century it has been known as an artists' town, and its L-shape main street is full of crafts and antiques shops. Conspicuous in the town center is **MacLellan's Castle,** the shell of a once-elaborate castellated mansion dating from the 16th century. You can walk around the interior, though the stone walls and rooms are bare. There are lovely views over the town from the windows. ✉ *Off High St.* ☎ *01557/331856* *£2* *Apr.–Sept., daily 9:30–6:30.*

The 18th-century **Broughton House** was once the home of the artist E. A. Hornel, one of the "Glasgow Boys" of the late 19th century. Many of his paintings hang in the house, which is furnished in period style and contains an extensive library specializing in local history. There's also a Japanese garden. ✉ *12 High St.* ☎ *01557/330437* *£3.50* *Apr.–June and Sept.–Oct., daily 1–5:30; July–Aug., daily 11–5:30; last admission at 4:45.*

Stuffed with all manner of local paraphernalia, the delightfully old-fashioned **Stewartry Museum** allows you to putter and absorb as much or as little as takes your interest in the display cases. ✉ *St. Mary St.* ☎ *01557/331643* *Free* *Oct.–Apr., Mon.–Sat. 11–4; May, Mon.–Sat. 11–5; June–Sept., Mon.–Sat. 10–6, Sun. 2–5.*

The **Tolbooth Arts Centre,** in the old tolbooth, gives a history of the town's artists' colony and its leaders E. A. Hornel, Jessie King, and Charles Oppenheimer, and displays some of their paintings as well as works by modern artists and craftspeople. ✉ *High St.* ☎ *01557/331556* *£1.50* *Oct.–Apr., Mon.–Sat. 11–4; May, Mon.–Sat. 11–5; June and Sept., Mon.–Sat. 11–5, Sun. 2–5; July–Aug., Mon.–Sat. 10–6, Sun. 2–5.*

Gatehouse of Fleet

26 *9 mi west of Kirkcudbright, 108 mi southwest of Glasgow, 114 mi southwest of Edinburgh.*

A peaceful, pleasant backwoods sort of place, Gatehouse of Fleet has a
27 castle guarding its southern approach from the A75. **Cardoness Castle** is a typical Scottish tower house, severe and uncompromising. The 15th-century structure once was the home of the McCullochs of Galloway, then the Gordons—two of the area's important and occasionally infamous families. ✉ *A75, 1 mi southwest of Gatehouse of Fleet* ☎ *01557/814427* *£2.20* *Apr.–Sept., daily 9:30–6:30; Oct.–Mar., Sat. 9:30–4:30, Sun. 2–4:30.*

The **Mill on the Fleet** heritage center is a converted cotton mill in which you can learn the history behind this small town's involvement in the cotton industry. Arts and crafts are exhibited, and the tearoom serves light lunches and delicious home-baked goods. ✉ *High St.* ☎ *01557/814099* *£2.75* *Easter–Oct., daily 10:30–5:30.*

Where to Stay

££££ **Cally Palace.** Many of the public rooms in this Georgian hotel, built in 1763 as a private mansion, retain their original grandeur, with elaborate plaster ceilings and marble fireplaces. The bedrooms are individually decorated and well equipped. Surrounding the house are 150 acres of parkland, with gardens, a loch, and a golf course. Fresh produce stars in the restaurant in such dishes as seared medallions of Kirroughtree venison. The staff is exceptionally friendly and prepared to spoil you. ✉ *Off the A75, DG7 2DL* ☎ *01557/814341* 📠 *01557/814522* 🌐 *www.mcmillanhotels.co.uk* *56 rooms* *Restaurant, cable TV, 18-hole golf course, putting green, tennis court, pool, hot tub, sauna, bar; no a/c in some rooms* 💳 *AE, MC, V* ⏲ *Closed Jan.–Feb.* *BP.*

£–££ **High Auchenlarie Farmhouse.** You are sure to get a hearty breakfast at this 300-year-old working beef farm, which has been a B&B since 1972. Set high on a hillside overlooking Wigtown Bay, the house provides tremendous views—on a clear day you can see all the way to the Isle of Man. The rooms have solid, wood farmhouse furniture, and the breakfasts are traditional (sausage, bacon, eggs, and grilled tomatoes), though lighter options are also available. ✉ *DG7 2HB* ☎ *01557/840231* *3 rooms* *Dining room; no a/c, no room phones* 💳 *No credit cards* *BP.*

Shopping

The merchandise shop at **Galloway Lodge Preserves** (✉ 24– 28 High St. ☎ 01557/814357) sells its own marmalades, mustards, chutneys, jams, and jellies (all made in the village) plus Scottish pottery. There's a well-stocked gift and crafts shop at the **Mill on the Fleet** heritage center (✉ High St. ☎ 01557/814099).

en route

If you want to avoid the A75, take a right by the Anwoth Hotel in Gatehouse of Fleet, where the signpost points to Gatehouse Station. This route eventually leads to Creetown and will provide you with a taste of the Dumfries and Galloway hinterland. Beyond the wooded valley where the Water of Fleet runs (local rivers are often referred to as "Water of" something), dark hills and conifer plantings lend a brooding, empty air to this lonely stretch.

Creetown Gem Rock Museum

28 *12 mi west of Gatehouse of Fleet, 95 mi southwest of Glasgow, 112 mi southwest of Edinburgh.*

The village of Creetown is noted for its Gem Rock Museum. The museum has an eclectic mineral collection, a dinosaur egg, an erupting volcano, and a crystal cave. Also here are an audiovisual display, Internet café, tearoom, and a shop selling stones and crystals—both loose and in settings. ✉ *Chain Rd., off A75, Creetown* ☎ *01671/820357* *£3.25* ⏲ *Easter–Sept., daily 9:30–5:30; Oct.–Nov., daily 10–4; Dec.–Feb., weekends 10–4; Mar.–Easter, daily 10–4; last admission 30 mins before closing.*

Newton Stewart

29 *8 mi northwest of Creetown, 89 mi southwest of Glasgow, 108 mi southwest of Edinburgh.*

The solid and bustling little town of Newton Stewart makes a good touring base for the western region of Galloway. The A712 heading northeast from town takes you to the **Galloway Forest Park,** where you can take nature walks or go cycling. At the Clatteringshaws Visitor Centre, there are exhibits about the wildlife of Galloway, plus a reconstruction of an Iron Age dwelling. ✉ *A712, 7 mi northeast of Newton Stewart* ☎ *01671/402420* 🌐 *www.cast.org.uk/clatteringshaws.htm* *Free* ⏲ *Apr.–Sept., daily 10:30–5; Oct., daily 10:30–4:30.*

Birders may prefer the **Wood of Cree Nature Reserve,** owned and managed by the Royal Society for the Protection of Birds. To get there, take the minor road that travels north from Newton Stewart alongside the River Cree east of the A714. The entrance is next to a small parking area at the side of the road. In the reserve, you can see such species as the redstart, pied flycatcher, and garden warbler. ✉ *4 mi north of Newton Stewart* ☎ *01671/402861* 💷 *Donations accepted* ⏲ *Daily.*

Glen Trool

★ 30 *12 mi north of Newton Stewart, 77 mi southwest of Glasgow, 96 mi southwest of Edinburgh.*

Glen Trool is one of Scotland's best-kept secrets. With high purple-and-green hilltops shorn rock-bare by glaciers, and with a dark, winding loch and thickets of birch trees sounding with birdcalls, the setting almost looks more highland than the real Highlands. Note **Bruce's Stone,** just above the parking lot, marking the site where in 1307 Scotland's champion Robert the Bruce (King Robert I, 1274–1329) won his first victory in the Scottish Wars of Independence. To get here, follow the A714 north and turn right at the signpost for Glen Trool. This road leads you toward the hills that have thus far been the backdrop for the woodlands. Watch for another sign for Glen Trool. Follow this little road through increasingly wild woodland scenery to its terminus at a parking lot. Only after you have left the car and climbed for a few minutes onto a heathery knoll does the full, rugged panorama become apparent.

Wigtown

31 *8 mi south of Newton Stewart, 96 mi southwest of Glasgow, 114 mi southwest of Edinburgh.*

More than twenty bookshops have sprung up on the brightly painted main street of sleepy Wigtown, which has been voted Scotland's national book town. In an area of grassy marshland near the muddy shores of Wigtown Bay there's a monument to the Wigtown Martyrs, two women who were tied to a stake and left to drown in the incoming tide in 1685, during Covenanting times. Dumfries and Galloway's history is inextricably linked with the ferocity of the so-called Killing Times (roughly 1650–1699), when the Covenanters were persecuted for their belief that there should be no bishops in the Church of Scotland, and that the king should not be head of the church. Wigtown's **Bladnoch Distillery** is Scotland's southernmost malt whisky producer. It has a visitor center and a gift shop, and tours are available. ☎ *01988/402605 or 01988/402235* 🌐 *www.bladnoch.co.uk* 💷 *Free; tours £1* ⏲ *Weekdays 9–5, tours weekdays 10–4:15.*

Whithorn

32 *11 mi south of Wigtown, 107 mi southwest of Glasgow, 125 mi southwest of Edinburgh.*

The Machars, the triangle promontory south of Newton Stewart, are well known for their early Christian sites. The road that is now the A746 used to be a pilgrims' way that led to the royal burgh of Whithorn, where sat **Whithorn Priory,** one of Scotland's great medieval cathedrals, and now an empty shell. It was built in the 12th century and is said to occupy the site of a former stone church, the Candida Casa, built by St. Ninian in the 5th century. As the story goes, the church housed a shrine to Ninian, the earliest of Scotland's saints, and kings and barons sought to visit the shrine at least once in their lives. As you approach the priory, observe the royal arms of pre-1707 Scotland—that is, Scotland before the Union with England—carved and painted above the arch of the *pend* (covered way) that leads to the site. The **Whithorn Story and Visitor Centre** explains the significance of what is claimed to be the site of the earliest Christian community in Scotland. A museum has a collection of early Christian crosses. ✉ *45–47 George St.* ☎ *01988/500508* 🌐 *www.whithorn.com* 💳 *£2.70* ⏲ *Apr.–Oct., daily 10:30–5; last tour at 4.*

Three miles away, in the Isle of Whithorn (which is a small seaport, not an island) are the ruins of **St. Ninian's Chapel,** where pilgrims who came by sea prayed before traveling inland to Whithorn Priory. Some people claim that this, and not Whithorn Priory, is the site of Candida Casa.

Stranraer

34 mi northwest of Whithorn, 89 mi southwest of Glasgow via A77, 133 mi southwest of Edinburgh.

The town of Stranraer is not a very scenic place itself, but nearby are Castle Kennedy Gardens, the highlight of this region. Stranraer is also the main ferry port to Northern Ireland—if you happen to make a purchase in one of its shops, you may wind up with some Irish coins in your change.

★ 33 The **Castle Kennedy Gardens** surround the shell of the original Castle Kennedy, which was burned in 1716. The current 14th earl of Stair, lives on the grounds, at Lochinch Castle, built in 1864 (not open to the public). Pleasure grounds dispersed throughout the property were built by the second earl of Stair in 1733. The earl was a field marshal and used his soldiers to help with the heavy work of constructing banks, ponds, and other major landscape features. When the rhododendrons are in bloom, the effect is kaleidoscopic. There's also a pleasant tearoom. ✉ *North of A75, 3 mi east of Stranraer* ☎ *01776/702024* 💳 *£3* ⏲ *Apr. (or Easter, if earlier)–Sept., daily 10–5.*

Portpatrick

8 mi southwest of Stranraer, 97 mi southwest of Glasgow, 143 mi southwest of Edinburgh.

The holiday town of Portpatrick lies across the Rhinns of Galloway from Stranraer. Once an Irish ferry port, Portpatrick's harbor eventually proved too small for larger vessels. Today the village is the starting point for Scotland's longest official long-distance footpath, the **Southern Upland Way,** which runs a switchback course for 212 mi to Cockburnspath, on the east side of the Borders. The path begins on the cliffs just north of the town and follows the coastline for 1½ mi before turning inland. Just south of Portpatrick are the lichen-yellow ruins of 16th-century **Dunskey Castle,** accessible from a cliff-top path off the B7042.

★ The spectacular **Logan Botanic Gardens,** one of the National Botanic Gardens of Scotland, are a must-see for garden lovers. Displayed here are plants that enjoy the prevailing mild climate, especially tree ferns, cabbage palms, and other southern-hemisphere exotica. ✉ *Off B7065 at Port Logan* ☎ *01776/860231* 💳 *£3.50* ⏲ *Mar. and Oct., daily 10–5; May–Sept., 10–6.*

If you wish to visit the southern tip of the Rhinns of Galloway, called the **Mull of Galloway,** follow the B7065/B7041 until you run out of land. The cliffs and seascapes here are rugged, and there is a lighthouse and a bird reserve.

THE BORDERS & THE SOUTHWEST A TO Z

To research prices, get advice from other travelers, and book travel arrangements, visit www.fodors.com.

AIR TRAVEL

The nearest Scottish airports are at Edinburgh, Glasgow, and Prestwick (outside of Glasgow).

BOAT & FERRY TRAVEL

P&O European Ferries runs a service from Larne, in Northern Ireland, to Cairnryan several times daily, with a crossing time of one hour on their "Superstar Express" service, and one hour forty five minutes on other services. Stena Line operates a ferry service between Stranraer and Belfast.

P&O European Ferries ✉ Cairnryan Port, Cairnryan, near Stranraer ☎ 0870/242-4666. **Stena Line** ☎ 08705/707070.

BUS TRAVEL

From the south the main bus services use the M6 or A1, with appropriate feeder services into the hinterland; contact Scottish Citylink or National Express. For bus links from Edinburgh and Glasgow contact First or Stagecoach Western. First offers the flexible tickets Reiver Rover (£28 weekly, £8 daily) and Waverley Wanderer (£33.50 weekly, £11.50 daily), which provide considerable savings for travel in the Borders. Stagecoach Western serves towns and villages in Dumfries and Galloway.

First ☎ 0870/608-2608. **National Express** ☎ 08705/808080 🌐 www.nationalexpress.co.uk. **Scottish Citylink** ☎ 08705/505050 🌐 www.citylink.co.uk. **Stagecoach Western** ☎ 01563/525192, 01387/253496, or 01776/704484.

CAR TRAVEL

The main route into both the Borders and Galloway from the south is the M6, which becomes the M74 at the border. Or you can take the scenic and leisurely A7 northeastward through Hawick toward Edinburgh or the A75 and other parallel routes westward into Dumfries and Galloway and to the ferry ports of Stranraer and Cairnryan.

There are, however, several other routes: starting from the east, the A1 brings you from the English city of Newcastle to the border in about an hour. The A1 has the added attraction of Berwick-Upon-Tweed, on the English side of the border, but traffic on the route is heavy. Moving west, the A697, which leaves the A1 north of Morpeth (in England) and crosses the border at Coldstream, is a leisurely back-road option. The A68 is probably the most scenic route to Scotland: after climbing to Carter Bar, it reveals a view of the Borders hills and windy skies before dropping into the ancient town of Jedburgh.

EMERGENCIES

Dial 999 for an ambulance, the police, or the fire department (no coins are needed for emergency calls from public telephone booths). All towns in the region have at least one pharmacy. Pharmacies are not found in rural areas, where general practitioners often dispense medicine. The police will provide assistance in locating a pharmacist in an emergency.

SPORTS & THE OUTDOORS

FISHING *Scottish Borders Angling Guide* is the best way to find your way around the many Borders waterways. *Fishing in Dumfries and Galloway* covers the Southwest. The tourist boards for Dumfries and Galloway and the Borders carry these and other publications, including a comprehensive information pack.

GOLF There are more than 30 courses in Dumfries and Galloway and 21 in the Borders. The Freedom of the Fairways Pass (five-day pass, £90; three-day pass, £65, no play on weekends) allows play on all 21 Borders courses and is available from the Scottish Borders Tourist Board. The Gateway to Golf Pass (10-round pass, £95; six-round pass, £75; plus a supplement for championship courses) is accepted by all clubs in Dumfries and Galloway and is available from the tourist board.

TOURS

The bus companies mentioned under ⇨ Bus Travel also run orientation tours in the area. Tours are primarily conducted by Edinburgh- and Glasgow-based companies (⇨ Chapters 2 and 3). James French runs coach tours in the summer. Margot McMurdo arranges custom-tailored, chauffeur-driven tours, and golf and fishing packages. Her "Splendour of Scott Country" tour covers the Borders area.

James French ✉ French's Garage, Coldingham ☎ 01890/771283. **Margot McMurdo** ✉ Tweedview Farmhouse, Oliver Farm, Tweedsmuir. ☎📠 01721/720845 🌐 www.aboutscotland.co.uk/tour/guide/margot.

TRAIN TRAVEL

The Borders and the Southwest suffered badly in the shortsighted contraction of Britain's rail network in the 1960s, but there are now moves to reintroduce a Borders line between Carlisle and Edinburgh. For now, however, there is no train service in the Borders, apart from the Edinburgh–London King's Cross line. Trains stop at Berwick-Upon-Tweed, just south of the border. The Scottish Borders Rail Link is actually a bus service linking Hawick, Selkirk, and Galashiels with rail services at Carlisle, Edinburgh, and Berwick.

There is only limited service in the Southwest. Trains from London's Euston to Glasgow stop at Carlisle, just south of the border, and some also stop at Lockerbie. There are direct trains from Carlisle to Dumfries and the Nith Valley, stopping at Gretna Green and Annan. From Glasgow, there are services to Stranraer, the Nith Valley, and Dumfries.

National Rail ☎ 08457/484950. **Scottish Borders Rail Link** ☎ 01896/752237.

VISITOR INFORMATION

Seasonal information centers are at Castle Douglas, Coldstream, Eyemouth, Galashiels, Gatehouse of Fleet, Gretna Green, Hawick, Kelso, Kirkcudbright, Langholm, Melrose, Moffat, Newton Stewart, Sanquhar, and Selkirk.

Scottish Borders Tourist Board ✉ Murray's Green, Jedburgh TD8 6BE ☎ 01835/863435 📠 01835/864099 🌐 www.scot-borders.co.uk ✉ High St. Peebles, EH45 8AG ☎ 01721/720138 📠 01721/724401.

Dumfries and Galloway Tourist Board ✉ Whitesands, Dumfries DG1 2RS ☎ 01387/253862 🌐 www.dumfriesandgalloway.co.uk ✉ 26 Harbour Street, Stranraer DG9 7RA ☎ 01387/253862 📠 01387/245555.

FIFE & ANGUS

ST. ANDREWS, DUNDEE, AND GLAMIS CASTLE

4

FODOR'S CHOICE

Crail, *in Fife*

Falkland, *in Fife*

Glamis Castle, *in Glamis*

Het Theatercafe, *in Dundee*

Ostlers Close Restaurant, *in Cupar*

The Peat Inn Restaurant, *in Cupar*

HIGHLY RECOMMENDED

RESTAURANTS But 'n' Ben, *in Auchmithie*

Drovers Inn, *in Memus*

HOTELS Redroofs, *in Forfar*

SIGHTS Falkland Palace, *in Falkland*

House of Dun, *in Montrose*

Scottish Fisheries Museum, *in Anstruther*

GOLF The New Course, *in St. Andrews*

By Gilbert Summers
Updated by Nick Bruno

THE REGIONS OF FIFE AND ANGUS sandwich Scotland's fourth-largest—and often overlooked—city, Dundee. This is typical eastern-seaboard country: open beaches, fishing villages, and breezy cliff-top walkways. Scotland's east coast has only light rainfall throughout the year; northeastern Fife, in particular, may claim the record for the most sunshine and the least rainfall in Scotland, which all adds to the enjoyment when you're touring the East Neuk (*neuk*, pronounced nyook, is Scots for corner) or exploring St. Andrews's nooks and crannies.

"Farewell Scotland, I'm awa' to Fife," cried the fishwife of Newhaven, setting sail for the opposite shore of the Firth of Forth. It was all of 6 mi away, but she expressed what many Lothian people used to feel: that Fife was a foreign place. It proudly styles itself as a "kingdom," and its long history—which really began when the Romans went home in the 4th century and the Picts moved in—lends some substance to the boast. From medieval times its earls were first among Scottish nobility and crowned her kings. For many, however, the most historic event in the region was the birth of golf, in the 15th century, which, legend has it, occurred in St. Andrews, an ancient university town with stone houses and seaside ruins. The Royal & Ancient Golf Club, the ruling body of the game worldwide, still has its headquarters here.

Not surprisingly, fishing and seafaring have also played a role in the history of the East Neuk coastal region. From the 16th through 19th centuries, a large population lived and worked in the small ports and harbors that form a continuous chain around Fife's coast, which James V once called "a beggar's mantle fringed with gold." Although some fancy it a Scottish equivalent of the Italian Riviera, James V's golden fringe—today a series of waterfront villages darkened by the shrubbery of masts and rigging—is not all that golden in terms of sand or sunshine. The outlook of black rocks and seaweed may seem rather dreary to some, but the villages, with no two windows or chimney pots alike, have character, with brownstone or color-washed fronts, rusty charm, fishy weather vanes, outdoor stone stairways to upper floors, and crude carvings of anchors and lobsters on their lintels—all crowded on steep, narrow *wynds* (narrow streets) and hugging pint-size harbors that in the golden era supported village fleets of 100 ships apiece.

North, across the Firth of Tay, lies the region of Angus, whose particular charm is its variety: in addition to its seacoast and pleasant Lowland market centers, there's also a hinterland of lonely rounded hills with long glens running into the typical Grampian Highland scenery beyond. One of Angus's interesting features, which it shares with the eastern Lowland edge of Perthshire, is its fruit-growing industry. Seen from roadside or railway, what at first sight appear to be sturdy grapevines on field-length wires turn out to be soft-fruit plants, mainly raspberries. The chief fruit-growing area is Strathmore, the broad vale between the northwesterly Grampian Mountains and the small coastal hills of the Sidlaws behind Dundee. Striking out from this valley, you can make a number of day trips to uplands or seacoast.

About the Restaurants

With an affluent population, St. Andrews supports several stylish hotel restaurants. Because it is a university town and popular tourist destination, there are also many good cafés and bistro-style restaurants. In some of the West Fife towns, such as Kirkcaldy and Dunfermline, and in Dundee, restaurants serve not only traditional Scottish fare, but also Italian, Indian, and Chinese specialties. Bar lunches are the rule in large and small hotels throughout the region, and in seaside places the "carry *oot*" (to go) meal is an old tradition.

Fife and Angus cover a compact area, so getting around is straightforward. You can visit everything in a series of excursions off the main north–south artery, the A90/M90, which leads from Edinburgh to Aberdeen.

Numbers in the text correspond to numbers in the margin and on the Fife Area, St. Andrews, and Angus Area maps.

If you have **2 days**

Two days allow you to sample the extremes of the area in every sense. Make your way to **St. Andrews** 1–7 to take in this most attractive of Scottish east-coast Lowland towns. The next day travel north of **Dundee** 16–24 to visit **Kirriemuir** 29, a typical Angus town, where J. M. Barrie (the author of *Peter Pan*) was born, and to see the castle at **Glamis** 31—and perhaps to explore the hills via the glens of Angus west of Kirriemuir.

If you have **5 days**

With five days, you can spend two or three days sampling not just **St. Andrews** 1–7 but also the rest of the East Neuk, with its characteristic pantile-roof fishing villages—**Crail** 8, Anstruther and its **Scottish Fisheries Museum** 9, **Pittenweem** 10, and, just inland, Kellie Castle—all strung along the south-facing coast. Also worth exploring are the inland communities of **Falkland,** with its gorgeous palace; **Cupar** 14, close to Hill of Tarvit House; and **Ceres,** home to the **Fife Folk Museum** 15. For a real treat have a meal and stay overnight at The Peat Inn. If you golf, you could allocate a day on a golf course as well. In Angus you can first travel along the breezy coast toward **Arbroath** 25 and **Montrose** 26, near to which you'll find the **House of Dun** 27. Staying overnight near **Forfar** 30 will bring the inland communities of **Kirriemuir** 29, **Glamis** 31, and **Meigle** 32, with its outstanding collection of early medieval sculpture, within easy reach the next day.

About the Hotels

If you're staying in Fife, the obvious base is St. Andrews, with ample accommodations of all kinds. Other towns also have a reasonable selection, and you'll find good hotels and guest houses at Dunfermline and Kirkcaldy. Along the coastal strip and in the Howe of Fife between Strathmiglo and Cupar are some superior country-house hotels, many with their own restaurants.

WHAT IT COSTS In Pounds

	$$$$$	$$$$	$$$	$$	$
RESTAURANTS	over £22	£18–£22	£13–£17	£7–£12	under £7
HOTELS	over £150	£110–£150	£80–£110	£50–£80	under £50

Restaurant prices are for a main course at dinner. Hotel prices are for two people in a standard double room in high season. All prices include the 17.5% VAT.

Exploring Fife & Angus

Fife lies north of the Firth of Forth, stretching far up the Forth Valley (which is west and a little north of Edinburgh), with St. Andrews on its eastern coast. Northwest of Fife and across the Firth of Tay, the city of

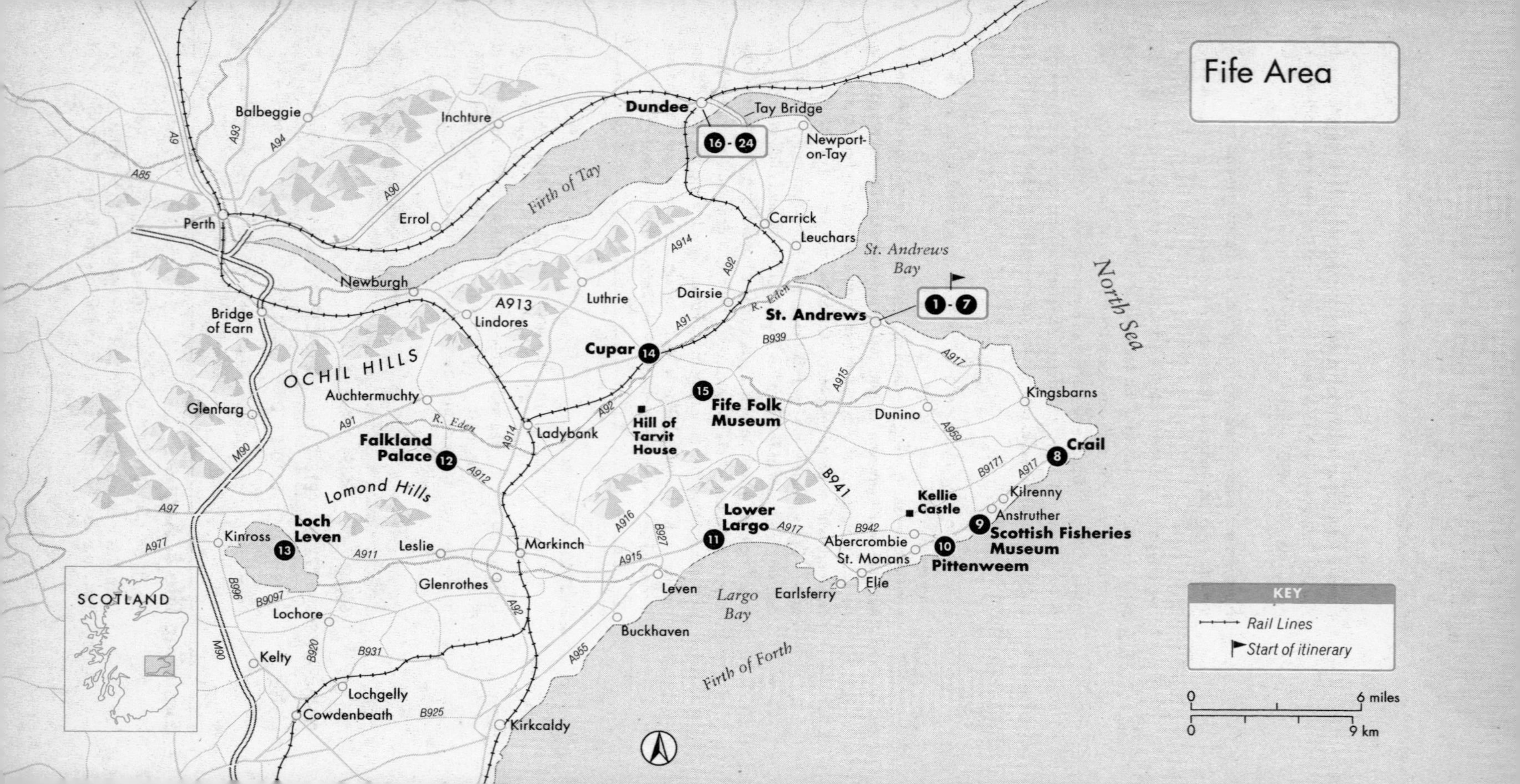
Fife Area
Dundee
Tay Bridge
16 - 24
Newport-on-Tay
Balbeggie
Inchture
A9
A93
A94
A85
A90
Firth of Tay
Perth
Errol
Carrick
Leuchars
St. Andrews Bay
North Sea
A914
A92
Newburgh
Luthrie
Dairsie
R. Eden
Bridge of Earn
A913
Lindores
A91
St. Andrews
1 - 7
B939
Cupar
14
OCHIL HILLS
A917
A915
Auchtermuchty
Glenfarg
15
Fife Folk Museum
Kingsbarns
Dunino
A959
A91
R. Eden
A914
Ladybank
A92
Hill of Tarvit House
Falkland Palace
12
M90
A912
B941
Crail
8
B9171
A917
Kilrenny
Lomond Hills
Kellie Castle
Anstruther
9
Scottish Fisheries Museum
A97
Loch Leven
13
Lower Largo
11
A916
B927
A917
B942
Abercrombie
St. Monans
10
Pittenweem
Kinross
A977
A911
Leslie
Markinch
A915
Glenrothes
Leven
Largo Bay
Earlsferry
Elie
SCOTLAND
B996
B9097
Lochore
A92
Buckhaven
M90
B920
Kelty
B931
A955
Firth of Forth
Lochgelly
Cowdenbeath
B925
Kirkcaldy
KEY
Rail Lines
Start of itinerary
0
6 miles
0
9 km

Beaches

Scotland's east coast enjoys many hours of sunshine, compared with its west coast, and is blessed with lots of sandy beaches under the ever-changing backdrop of the sky. In Fife, Tentsmuir's beach near St. Andrews is popular with kite flyers and horseback riders, while the small cove beach at Elie, just south of Crail, hosts local cricket matches in summer. In Angus, Broughty Ferry's beach fills with families and children on weekends and during school holidays—even on the most blustery of days you'll find well-wrapped *bairns* (small children) making pictures in the sand. North of Arbroath lies Auchmithie beach, more shingly than the others and offering a bracing breath of North Sea air. And finally, near the Montrose basin, you can discover the enchanting crescent of Lunan Bay, home to many species of seabird.

Golf

What serious golfer doesn't dream of playing at world-famous St. Andrews? Once you're in Fife, that dream can be easily realized. Six St. Andrews courses, all part of the St. Andrews Trust, are open to visitors, and more than 40 other courses in the region offer golf by the round or by the day. Many area hotels have golfing packages or will arrange a day of golf. A round on a municipal course costs very little, and most clubs, apart from some pretentious spots, charge only comparatively modest greens fees.

Dundee and its rural hinterland, Angus, stretch still farther north and west toward the foothills of the Grampian Mountains.

Timing

Spring in the Angus glens can be quite captivating, with the highest mountains still snow-covered. Similarly, the moorland colors of autumn are appealing. In fall and winter, some hotels in rural Angus fill with foreign sportspeople intent on hunting the local wildfowl. However, Fife and Angus are really spring and summer destinations, when most of the sights are open to visitors.

ST. ANDREWS & THE EAST NEUK VILLAGES

In its western parts, Fife still bears the scars of heavy industry, especially coal mining, but these signs are less evident as you move east. Northeastern Fife, around the town of St. Andrews, seems to have played no part in the industrial revolution; instead, its residents earned a living from the grain fields or from the sea. Fishing has been a major industry, and in the past a string of Fife ports traded across the North Sea. Today the legacy of Dutch-influenced architecture—crow-step gables (the stepped effect on the ends of the roofs) and distinctive town houses—is still plain to see and gives these East Neuk villages a distinctive character.

St. Andrews is unlike any other Scottish town. Once Scotland's most powerful ecclesiastical center as well as the seat of the country's oldest university and then, much later, the very symbol and spiritual home of golf, the town has a comfortable, well-groomed air, sitting almost smugly apart from the rest of Scotland. This air of superiority has received a huge boost from Prince William's presence as a student here, which has also led to a record number of foreign students enrolling at the university.

St. Andrews

52 mi northeast of Edinburgh, 83 mi northeast of Glasgow.

It may have a ruined cathedral and a grand university—the oldest in Scotland—but the modern claim to fame for St. Andrews is mainly its status as the home of golf. Forget that Scottish kings were crowned here, or that John Knox preached here, or that Reformation reformers were burned at the stake here. Thousands flock to St. Andrews to play at the Old Course, home of the Royal & Ancient Club, and to follow in the footsteps of Hagen, Sarazen, Jones, and Hogan. Of course, nongolfers can tread the city streets to take in historic sights. In fact, St. Andrews's layout is still pure Middle Ages: its three main streets—North, Market, and South—converge on the city's earliest religious site, near the cathedral. Like most of the town's ancient monuments, the cathedral ruins are impressive in their desolation—but this is no dusty museum-city. The streets are busy, the shops are stylish, the gray houses sparkle in the sun, and the scene is particularly brightened during the academic year by bicycling students in scarlet gowns. You may want to take a cue from their mode of transport: car parking in St. Andrews is notoriously difficult. If possible, visit without a car, as the town is small enough to explore on foot or by bicycle.

Local legend has it that St. Andrews was founded by one St. Regulus, or Rule, who, acting under divine guidance, carried relics of St. Andrew by sea from Patras in Greece. He was shipwrecked on this Fife headland and founded a church. The holy man's name survives in the square-shape **St. Rule's Tower,** consecrated in 1126 and the oldest surviving building in St. Andrews. You can enjoy dizzying views of town from the top of the tower, reached via a steep set of stairs. ✉ *Off Pends Rd.* ☎ *01334/472563* 🌐 *www.historic-scotland.gov.uk* 🎫 *£2.50, includes admission to cathedral* ⏲ *Apr.–Sept., daily 9:30–6; Oct.–Mar., daily 9:30–4.*

❷ **St. Andrew's Cathedral,** near St. Rule's Tower, is today only a ruined, poignant fragment of what was formerly the largest and most magnificent church in Scotland. Work on it began in 1160, and consecration was finally celebrated in 1318 after several setbacks. The cathedral was subsequently damaged by fire and repaired, but fell into decay in the 16th century, during the Reformation. Only ruined gables, parts of the nave south wall, and other fragments survive. The on-site museum helps you interpret the remains and gives a sense of what the cathedral must once have been like. ✉ *Off Pends Rd.* ☎ *01334/472563* 🌐 *www.historic-scotland.gov.uk* 🎫 *£2.20, includes admission to St. Rule's Tower; combined admission to cathedral, tower, and St. Andrews Castle, £4* ⏲ *Apr.–Sept., daily 9:30–6; Oct.–Mar., daily 9:30–4.*

❸ On the shore north of the cathedral stands **St. Andrews Castle,** which was started at the end of the 13th century. Although now a ruin, the remains include a rare example of a cold and gruesome bottle-shape dungeon, in which many prisoners spent their last hours. Even more atmospheric is the castle's mine and countermine. The former was a tunnel dug by besieging forces in the 16th century; the latter, a tunnel dug by castle defenders in order to meet and wage battle below ground. You can stoop and crawl into this narrow passageway—an eerie experience, despite the addition of electric light. The visitor center has a good audiovisual presentation on the castle's history. ✉ *End of North Castle St.* ☎ *01334/*

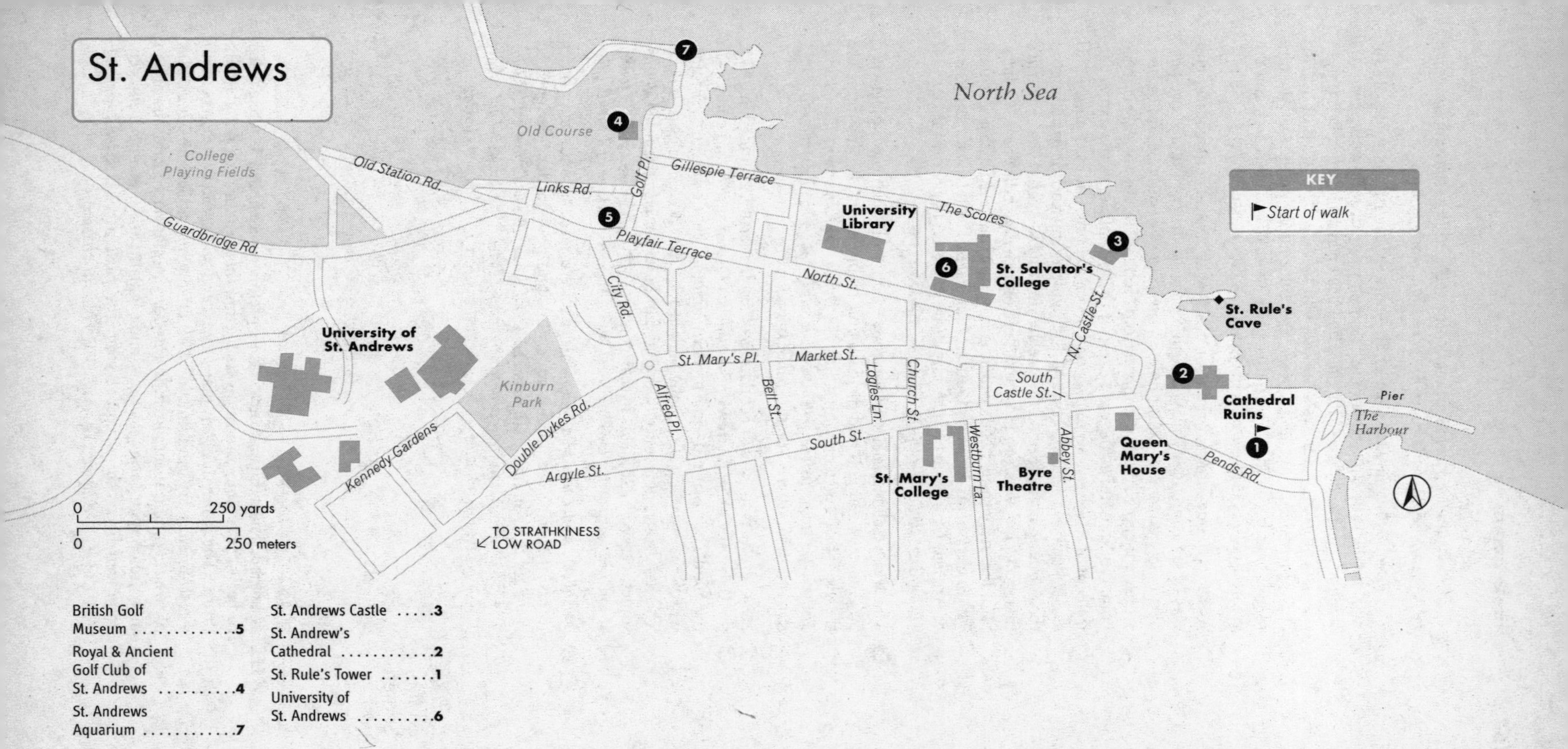
St. Andrews
North Sea
KEY
Start of walk
Old Course
College Playing Fields
Old Station Rd.
Links Rd.
Golf Pl.
Gillespie Terrace
The Scores
University Library
Guardbridge Rd.
Playfair Terrace
North St.
St. Salvator's College
St. Rule's Cave
City Rd.
N. Castle St.
University of St. Andrews
St. Mary's Pl.
Market St.
Logies Ln.
Church St.
South Castle St.
Cathedral Ruins
Pier
The Harbour
Kinburn Park
Alfred Pl.
Bell St.
Double Dykes Rd.
South St.
Westburn La.
Abbey St.
Queen Mary's House
Pends Rd.
Kennedy Gardens
Argyle St.
St. Mary's College
Byre Theatre
0
250 yards
0
250 meters
TO STRATHKINESS LOW ROAD
British Golf Museum 5
Royal & Ancient Golf Club of St. Andrews 4
St. Andrews Aquarium 7
St. Andrews Castle 3
St. Andrew's Cathedral 2
St. Rule's Tower 1
University of St. Andrews 6

477196 🌐 www.historic-scotland.gov.uk 🎫 £2.80; castle and cathedral, £4 ⏲ Apr.–Sept., daily 9:30–6; Oct.–Mar., daily 9:30–4.

4 The **Royal & Ancient Golf Club of St. Andrews,** the ruling house of golf worldwide, is the spiritual home of all who play or follow the game. Its clubhouse on the dunes—a dignified building open to club members only—is adjacent to St. Andrews's famous Old Course. The town of St. Andrews prospers on golf, golf schools, and golf equipment (the manufacture of golf balls has been a local industry for more than 100 years), and the greatest golfers in the world play on the Old Course.

As to the game and its origins on the Royal & Ancient's course, golf was perhaps originally played with a piece of driftwood, a shore pebble, and a convenient rabbit hole on the sandy, coastal turf. It has been argued that golf came to Scotland from Holland, but historical evidence points to Scotland as the cradle, if not the birthplace, of the game. Citizens of St. Andrews were playing golf on the town links (public land) as far back as the 15th century. Rich golfers, instead of gathering on the common links, formed themselves into clubs. Arguably, the world's first golf club was the Honourable Company of Edinburgh Golfers, founded in Leith in 1744, which is now at Muirfield in East Lothian. The Society of St. Andrews Golfers, founded in 1754, became the Royal & Ancient Golf Club of St. Andrews in 1834. ✉ *The Scores* ☎ *01334/460000* 📠 *01334/460001* 🌐 *www.randa.org.*

5 The **British Golf Museum** explores the centuries-old relationship between St. Andrews and golf and displays golf memorabilia. It's just opposite the Royal & Ancient Golf Club. ✉ *Bruce Embankment* ☎ *01334/460046* 🌐 *www.britishgolfmuseum.co.uk* 🎫 *£4* ⏲ *Easter–mid-Oct., daily 9:30–5:30; mid-Oct.–Easter, hrs vary.*

St. Andrews is the site of Scotland's oldest university. Founded in 1411,
6 the **University of St. Andrews** now consists of two stately old colleges in the middle of town and some modern buildings on the outskirts. A third, weatherworn college, originally built in 1512, has become a girls' school. The handsome university buildings can be explored on guided walks, sometimes led by students in scarlet gowns. ☎ *01334/462245* 🌐 *www.st-andrews.ac.uk* 🎫 *£4* ⏲ *Tours: June–Aug., weekdays at 11 and 2:30.*

7 At the **St. Andrews Aquarium,** seals, fish, crustaceans, and many other forms of marine life inhabit aquariums and pool gardens designed to simulate their natural habitats. ✉ *The Scores, West Sands* ☎ *01334/474786* 🌐 *www.standrewsaquarium.co.uk* 🎫 *£4.85* ⏲ *Easter–Oct., daily 10–6; Nov.–Easter, daily 10–5; last admission 1 hr before closing.*

off the beaten path

LEUCHARS – This small town has a 12th-century church with some of the finest Norman architectural features to be seen anywhere in Scotland. Note in particular the blind arcading (arch shapes on the wall) and the beautifully decorated chancel and apse. ✉ *A919, 5 mi northwest of St. Andrews.*

Where to Stay & Eat

£££ ✕ **Balaka.** The handsome gray-stone premises here hide a 1-acre garden of herbs, vegetables, and flowers used in this restaurant's Bangladeshi dishes. The Rouf family displays its exceptional cookery prowess amid a restrained dusty pink interior with crisp white tablecloths and vases of roses. Popular dishes include *mas bangla* (marinated salmon fried in mustard oil with garlic, scallions, and eggplant) and green-herb chicken, enhanced by fresh coriander from the garden. ✉ *3 Alexandra Pl.* ☎ *01334/474825* 💳 *AE, MC, V* ⏲ *No lunch Sun.*

££££ **Rufflets Country House Hotel.** Ten acres of formal and informal gardens surround this creeper-covered country house just outside St. Andrews. All the rooms are beautifully decorated and comfortable, with the amenities you would expect of a top-class hotel. Dinner is served in the roomy Garden Restaurant, famous for its use of local produce in memorable Scottish dishes. Try the Tay salmon or the pan-seared Rannoch venison in a raspberry-tea glaze served with fresh asparagus. Lighter and less expensive meals are available at the bar. ✉ *Strathkinness Low Rd., KY16 9TX* ☎ *01334/472594* 📠 *01334/478703* 🌐 *www.rufflets.co.uk* *20 rooms, 4 suites* *Restaurant, some in-room hot tubs, some minibars, cable TV, bar, no-smoking rooms; no a/c* 💳 *AE, DC, MC, V* *BP.*

££ **Aslar Guest House.** Inside this 1865 terraced town house you'll find large rooms decorated with antique and reproduction furniture, and striped or pattern wallpaper. One room has a four-poster bed, another a fireplace. St. Andrews's historic center is within walking distance. ✉ *120 North St., KY16 9AF* ☎ *01334/473460* 📠 *01334/477540* 🌐 *www.aslar.com* *5 rooms* *Cable TV, lounge, Internet; no a/c, no room phones* 💳 *MC, V* *BP.*

££ **University of St. Andrews.** For accommodation within walking distance of all attractions, it's hard to beat the university for value and convenience. Room sizes—mainly singles—vary from adequate in the New Hall building to happily spacious in the older buildings. The newer rooms have private bathrooms. Self-catering accommodation is also available, at Albany Park. ✉ *79 North St., KY16 9AD* ☎ *01334/462000* 📠 *01334/462500* 🌐 *www.st-andrews.ac.uk* *120 rooms (72 with shower)* *Restaurant, bar, lounge, laundry facilities; no a/c, no room phones, no room TVs* 💳 *MC, V* *Closed early Sept.–early June.*

Nightlife & the Arts

PUBS **Chariots** (✉ The Scores ☎ 01334/472451), inside the Scores Hotel, is popular with locals in their thirties and forties.

THEATER **Byre Theatre** (✉ Abbey St. ☎ 01334/475000 🌐 www.byretheatre.com) puts on its own productions, working with various theater groups, and also hosts visiting productions. Experimental and youth theater, small-scale operatic performances, contemporary dance, and Sunday night jazz (in the foyer) also take place regularly. There's also an excellent café-bar.

Golf

One 9-hole and five 18-hole courses, all part of the St. Andrews Links Trust, are open to visitors. For information about availability—there's usually a waiting list, which varies according to the time of year—contact the **Reservations Department** (✉ St. Andrews Links Trust, Pilmour House, St. Andrews KY16 9SF ☎ 01334/466666 📠 01334/477036 🌐 www.standrews.org.uk 🌐 www.golfagent.com). Greens fees range from £72 to £105 for a round on the Old Course and from £7 to £50 for a round on the five other courses.

Balgove Course. Redesigned and -opened in 1993, Balgove is a beginner-friendly course at which you can turn up and tee off without prior reservation. *9 holes, 1,520 yards, par 30.*

Eden Course. The inland and aptly-named Eden, designed in 1914 by Harry S. Colt, has an easy charm compared to the other St. Andrews Links courses. *18 holes, 6,162 yards, par 70.*

Jubilee Course. This windswept course, opened in 1897, offers quite a challenge even for very experienced golfers. *18 holes, 6,805 yards, par 72.*

★ **New Course.** Not exactly new—it opened in 1895—the New Course is rather overshadowed by the Old Course, but it has a firm following of golfers who appreciate the loop design. *18 holes, 6,604 yards, par 71.*

Old Course. Believed to be the oldest golf course in the world, the Old Course was first played in the 15th century. Each year, more than 44,000 rounds are teed off, and no doubt most get stuck in one of its 112 bunkers. A handicap certificate is required. *18 holes, 6,566 yards, par 72.*

Strathtyrum Course. Those with a high handicap will enjoy a toddle around this course, opened in 1993, without the worry or embarrassment of holding up more experienced golfers. *18 holes, 5,094 yards, par 69.*

Shopping

Bonkers (✉ 80 Market St. ☎ 01334/473919) carries a huge selection of books, cards, pottery, soft toys, and gift items. **Renton Oriental Rugs** (✉ 72 South St. ☎ 01334/476334) is the best place in the region, if not in all Scotland, to buy Oriental rugs and carpets of all colors, patterns, and sizes—many of them antiques. **St. Andrews Fine Art** (✉ 84A Market St. ☎ 01334/474080) is the place to go for Scottish paintings—oils, watercolors, drawings, and prints—from 1800 to the present. The **St. Andrews Pottery Shop** (✉ Church Sq. between South St. and Market St. ☎ 01334/477744) sells decorative domestic stoneware, porcelain, ceramics, enamel jewelry, and terra-cotta pots.

Crail

8 *10 mi south of St. Andrews via A917.*

Fodor'sChoice ★

One of numerous fishing communities along the Fife coast, Crail is the oldest, most palatial by local standards, and most aristocratic of East Neuk burghs, where fish merchants retired and built cottages. The town landmark is a picturesque Dutch-influenced town house, or *tolbooth*, which contains the oldest bell in Fife, cast in Holland in 1520. As you head into East Neuk from this tiny port, look about for tolbooths, market crosses, and merchant houses and their little *doocots* (dovecotes, where pigeons were kept for winter meat)—typical picturesque touches of this region. Full details on the heritage and former trading links of Crail can be found in the **Crail Museum and Heritage Center.** ✉ *62–64 Marketgate* ☎ *01333/450869* *Free* *Easter and June–Sept., Mon.–Sat. 10–1 and 2–5, Sun. 2–5; after Easter–end of May, weekends and holidays 2–5.*

Anstruther

4 mi southwest of Crail via A917.

Anstruther, locally called Ainster, has a picturesque waterfront with a few shops brightly festooned with children's pails and shovels, a gesture to seaside vacationers. Facing Anstruther harbor is the ★ 9 **Scottish Fisheries Museum,** housed in a colorful cluster of buildings, the earliest of which dates from the 16th century. The museum illustrates the life of Scottish fisherfolk, past and present, through documents, artifacts, ship models, paintings, and tableaux. These displays, complete with the reek of tarred rope and net, have been known to induce nostalgic tears in not a few old deckhands. There are also floating exhibits at the quayside. ✉ *Anstruther harbor* ☎ *01333/310628* *www.scottish-fisheries-museum.org* *£3.50* *Apr.–Oct., Mon.–Sat. 10–5:30, Sun. 11–5; Nov.–Mar., Mon.–Sat. 10–4:15, Sun. noon–4:15; last admission 45 mins before closing.*

Where to Eat

£££££ ✕ **The Cellar.** Specializing in fish but with a selection of Scottish beef and lamb as well, the Cellar serves prix-fixe, three-course meals made from top-quality ingredients cooked simply in modern Scottish style. The crayfish-and-mussel bisque is famous, and the wine list reflects high standards. You enter this unpretentious, old-fashioned restaurant through a small courtyard. It's popular with the locals, but its fame is widespread. ✉ *24 E. Green* ☎ *01333/310378* 💳 *AE, DC, MC, V* ⏲ *Closed Sun. and Mon. Nov.–Easter.*

Nightlife

The **Dreel Tavern** (✉ 16 High St. W ☎ 01333/310727) is a 16th-century coaching inn famous for its hand-drawn ales.

Bicycling

The back roads of Fife make pleasant biking terrain. You can rent bicycles from **East Neuk Outdoors** (✉ Cellardyke Park ☎ 01333/311929), which also has archery, rappeling, climbing, orienteering, and canoeing equipment, and provides instruction.

Pittenweem

⑩ *1½ mi southwest of Anstruther via A917.*

Many examples of East Neuk architecture serve as the backdrop for the working harbor at Pittenweem. Look for the crow-step gables, white *harling* (Scots for roughcasting, the rough mortar finish on walls), and red pantiles (S-shape in profile). The *weem* part of the town's name comes from the Gaelic *uaime,* or cave. This town's particular cave is **St. Fillan's Cave,** which contains the shrine of St. Fillan, a 6th-century hermit who lived inside it. It's up a close (alleyway) behind the waterfront. ✉ *Cove Wynd, near harbor* ☎ *01333/311495 (Gingerbread Horse Craft Shop has key)* 🎫 *£1* ⏲ *Mon.–Sat. 10–5, Sun. noon–5.*

Kellie Castle, dating from the 16th and 17th centuries and restored in Victorian times, stands among the grain fields and woodlands of northeastern Fife. Four acres of pretty gardens surround the castle, which is in care of the National Trust for Scotland. ✉ *B9171, 3 mi northwest of Pittenweem* ☎ *01333/720271* 🎫 *Garden and grounds £2; combined ticket to castle and gardens £5* ⏲ *Castle Apr.–Sept., Thurs.–Mon. noon–5; garden and grounds year-round, daily 9:30–sunset.*

Lower Largo

⑪ *10 mi west of Pittenweem via A917 and A915.*

Lower Largo's main claim to fame is that it was the birthplace of Alexander Selkirk (1676–1721), the Scottish sailor who was the inspiration for Daniel Defoe's (1660–1731) *Robinson Crusoe.* Once a juvenile delinquent, he grew up to terrorize the region and then departed to sail the seas. In 1704, having quarreled with his captain, Selkirk was put ashore on the isle of Juan Fernandez off the coast of Chile. Four years later a British privateer picked him up; his rescuers found him dressed in goatskins and surrounded by tame goats. Piratical adventures on the way home earned him a fortune, and he returned to Largo so richly dressed his mother didn't recognize him. His statue can be seen above the doorway of the house on Main Street, where he was born.

Shopping

At nearby Upper Largo, in a converted barn, **Scotland's Larder** (✉ Upper Largo ☎ 01333/360414) is a shop-restaurant that sells a huge assortment of Scottish preserves, baked goods, and seasonal produce—anything from Dundee cakes (a light fruit cake with a distinctive, circular pattern of split almonds on the top) and shortbread to smoked salmon and oysters. It also has tastings, talks, and cooking demonstrations, all of which show off the savory foods of Scotland.

Falkland

Fodor's Choice ★ *14 mi northwest of Lower Largo.*

One of the loveliest communities in Scotland, Falkland is a royal burgh ★ 12 of twisting streets and crooked stone houses. **Falkland Palace,** a former hunting lodge of the Stuart monarchs, dominates the town. The palace is one of the earliest examples in Britain of the French Renaissance style. Overlooking the main street is the palace's most impressive feature—the walls and chambers on its south side, all rich with Renaissance buttresses and stone medallions, built for King James V (1512–42) in the 1530s by French masons. He died here, and the palace was a favorite resort of his daughter, Mary, Queen of Scots (1542–87). The gardens behind the palace contain a most unusual survivor: a royal tennis court—not at all like its modern counterpart—built in 1539. In the beautiful gardens, overlooked by the palace turret windows, you may easily imagine yourself back at the solemn hour when James on his deathbed pronounced the doom of the house of Stuart: "It cam' wi' a lass and it'll gang wi a lass." ✉ *Main St.* ☎ *01337/857397* 🎫 *Palace and gardens £7; gardens only, £3* ⏲ *Mar.–Oct., Mon.–Sat. 10–6, Sun. 1–5.*

Loch Leven

13 *10 mi southwest of Falkland via A911.*

Scotland's largest Lowland loch, Loch Leven is famed for its fighting trout. The area is also noted for abundant bird life, particularly its wintering wildfowl. Mary, Queen of Scots, was forced to sign the deed of abdication in her island prison in the loch. On the southern shore overlooking the lock, **Vane Farm Nature Reserve,** a visitor center run by the Royal Society for the Protection of Birds, provides information about Loch Leven's ecology. ✉ *Vane Farm, Rte. B9097, just off M90 and B996* ☎ *01577/862355* 🎫 *£3* ⏲ *Daily 10–5.*

Cupar

14 *21 mi northwest of Loch Leven via M90 and A91, 10 mi west of St. Andrews via A91.*

Cupar is a busy market town, with a station on the Edinburgh–Aberdeen line. On rising ground near the town stands the National Trust for Scotland's **Hill of Tarvit House.** Originally a 17th-century mansion, the house was altered in the high-Edwardian style in the late 1890s and early 1900s by the Scottish architect Sir Robert Lorimer (1864–1929). Inside the house are fine collections of antique furniture, Chinese porcelain, bronzes, tapestries, and Dutch paintings. Lorimer also designed the formal Edwardian gardens. A tearoom is also on the premises. ✉ *2 mi south of Cupar off A916* ☎ *01334/653127* 🎫 *£5 house and gardens; gardens only, £2* ⏲ *House Apr.–Oct., daily noon–5. Tearoom Apr.–Sept., daily noon–5; Oct., weekends noon–5. Garden and grounds daily 9:30–sunset.*

At the **Scottish Deer Centre,** red deer can be seen at close quarters on ranger-guided tours. There are also nature trails, a winery, falconry displays, an adventure playground (a wood and tire fortress suitable for older children), five shops, and a coffee bar. ✉ *A91, near Rankelour Farm, just outside Cupar* ☎ *01337/810391* *£4.50* ⊙ *Easter–Oct., daily 10–6; Nov.–Easter, daily 10–5.*

off the beaten path

DAIRSIE BRIDGE – A few minutes east of Cupar at Dairsie, an unclassified road goes off to the right from the A91 and soon runs by the River Eden. The Dairsie Bridge, which goes over the river, is 450 years old and has three arches, one above the other. Above the trees rises the spire of Dairsie Church, dating from the 17th century. The stark ruin of Dairsie Castle, often overlooked, stands gloomily over the river nearby. With wild-rose hedges, grazing cattle, and pheasants calling from the woody thickets, this is the very essence of rural Lowland Fife, yet it's only about 15 minutes from the Old Course.

4

Where to Eat

£££ Fodor's Choice ★ ✕ **Ostlers Close Restaurant.** This long-established, unpretentious, cottage-style restaurant, with plain painted walls and stick-back chairs, has earned a well-deserved reputation for top-quality cuisine that is imaginative without being trendy. Wild mushrooms in season are a particular favorite with the chef, and the fish and shellfish dishes are especially good. Ostlers Close is tucked away in an alley off of Cupar's main street. It's a good idea to reserve ahead, particularly for lunch. ✉ *Bonnygate* ☎ *01334/655574* *www.ostlersclose.co.uk* *AE, MC, V* ⊙ *Closed Sun. and Mon. No lunch Tues.–Thurs.*

Shopping

With its wide selection of British and international designer-clothing labels, **Margaret Urquhart** (✉ 13–17 Lady Wynd ☎ 01334/652205) attracts customers from as far away as Edinburgh and Glasgow.

Ceres

3 mi southeast of Cupar via A916 and B939, 9 mi southwest of St. Andrews.

15 To learn more about the history and culture of rural Fife, visit the **Fife Folk Museum,** in Ceres. The life of local rural communities is reflected in artifacts and documents housed in a former weigh house and adjoining weavers' cottages. ✉ *High St.* ☎ *01334/828180* *£2.50* ⊙ *Easter and mid-May–Sept., daily 2–5.*

Where to Stay & Eat

££££ Fodor's Choice ★ ✕ **The Peat Inn.** This popular inn is best known for its outstanding modern Scottish-style restaurant, generally considered one of the finest in Scotland. Mouthwatering entrées might include roast scallops with potatoes and leeks and a pea puree, or medallions of monkfish and lobster with artichoke hearts in a lobster sauce. Book well in advance. A detached building houses eight bright and contemporary two-room suites. ✉ *Jct. B940 and B941, 6 mi southwest of St. Andrews* *Peat Inn, Cupar, Fife, KY15 5LH* ☎ *01334/840206* *01334/840530* *www.thepeatinn.co.uk* *8 suites* *Restaurant, bar, free parking; no a/c* *AE, MC, V* ⊙ *Closed Sun.–Mon.* *CP.*

DUNDEE & ANGUS

The small city of Dundee sits near the mouth of the river Tay surrounded by the farms and glens of rural Angus, and the coastal grassy banks and golf courses of northeastern Fife. A vibrant, industrial city, Dundee's onetime reliance on oft-quoted "jam, jute, and journalism" has been replaced by its significant role in the biotech and computer-games industries. People in and around Dundee are often described as the friendliest in Britain and the self-deprecating Dundonian patter is rather more endearing than, say, the sharper humor of the Glaswegians. Dundee has a large student population, a lively music and nightlife scene, many smart restaurants, and several historical and nautical sights.

Angus combines coastal agriculture on rich, red soils with dramatic inland glens that pierce their way into the foothills of the Grampian mountain ranges to the northwest. Although the peaceful back roads in this area are uncluttered, the main road from Perth/Dundee to Aberdeen—the A90—requires drivers to take special care, with its mix of fast cars, lorries, and unexpectedly slow farm traffic.

Dundee

14 mi northwest of St. Andrews, 58 mi north of Edinburgh, 79 mi northeast of Glasgow.

The city of Dundee makes an excellent base at any time of year for exploring Fife and Angus. The West End, especially its main thoroughfare Perth Road, has beguiling shops, intimate cafés, and excellent bars. As you walk along the cobbled streets, you may catch a glimpse of the 1888 Tay Rail Bridge, and if you head southwest you'll reach Roseangle and Magdalen Green, where the famous landscape artist James McIntosh Patrick (1907–1998) found inspiration from the wonderful views and ever changing skyscapes. The popular comics *The Beano* and *The Dandy* were first published here in the 1930s, and, in tribute to the comics, statues depicting Desperate Dan, Gnasher, and a catapult-wielding Minnie the Minx, were erected in the City Square.

16 For sweeping views of the city and the Tayside region, head to the **The Law**—*law* means hill in Scottish—an extinct volcano whose summit reaches 1,640 feet above sea level in the center of Dundee. A World War II memorial and outdoor viewing area cap the hill. ✉ *Law Rd.*

17 In a former jute mill, the **Verdant Works** houses a multifaceted exhibit on the story of jute and Dundee's historical involvement in the jute trade. Restored machinery, audiovisuals, and tableaux all vividly re-create the hard, noisy life of the jute worker. ✉ *W. Hendersons Wynd* ☎ *01382/225282* 💰 *£5.95* ⏲ *Apr.–Oct., Mon.–Sat. 10–5, Sun. 11–5; Nov.–Mar., Wed.–Sat. 10:30–4:30, Sun. 11–4:30.*

An innovative building designed by architect Richard Murphy houses
18 one of Britain's most exciting artistic venues, **Dundee Contemporary Arts.** Its galleries specialize in the best works of both Scottish and international artists. Creative facilities include a print studio and a visual research center linked to the University of Dundee. The presence of working artists encourages many meet-the-artist events year-round. There are also two movie theaters, a craft and design shop, and a café. ✉ *152 Nethergate* ☎ *01382/909900* 💰 *Free* ⏲ *Tues.–Sat. 10:30–midnight, Sun. 10:30 AM–11 PM; galleries close at 5:30 Tues.–Wed. and weekends, at 8 Thurs.–Fri.; print-studio hrs vary.*

You'll see the world upside down when you're strapped into the gyro-
19 scope at **Sensation**, a hands-on science center focusing on the five senses. Although the general noise level testifies to the child-friendly nature of the place, enthusiastic staff members persuade visitors of all ages to participate. Among the many experiments and activities, you can "age" yourself (or make yourself look younger) on computer screens or practice

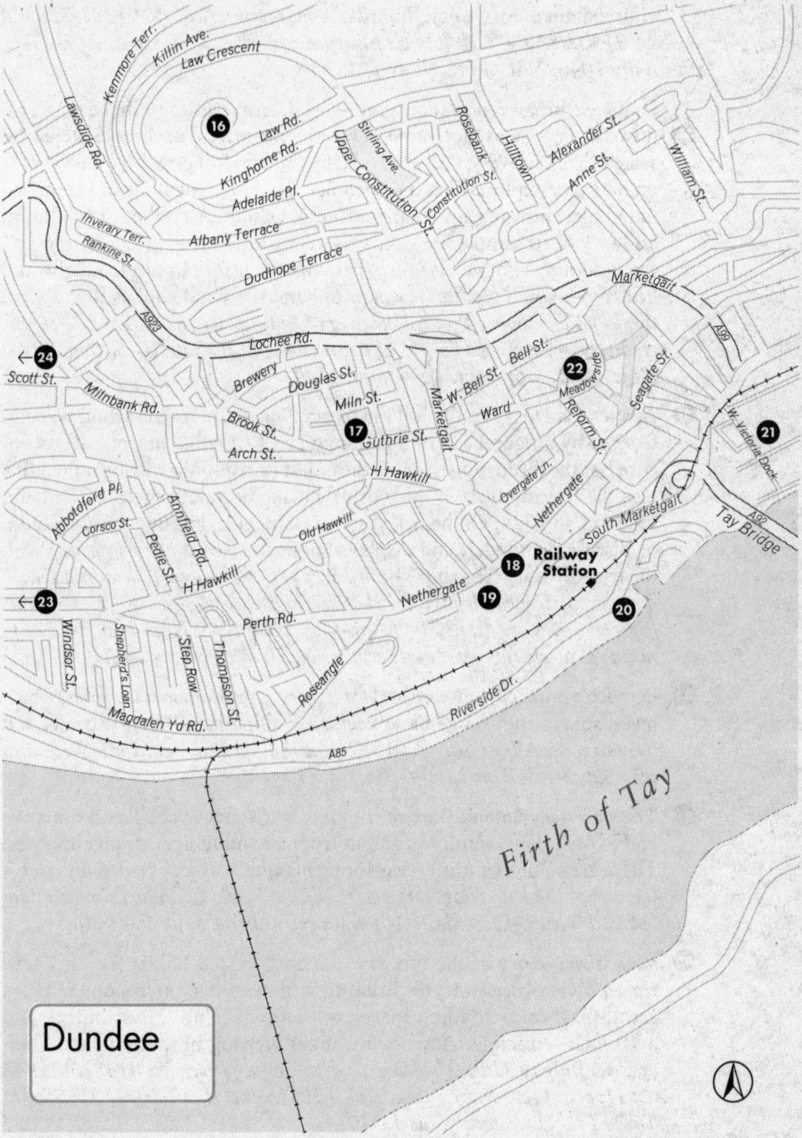

Dundee
Contemporary Arts 18

The Law 16

McManus Galleries 22

Mills Observatory 24

RRS Discovery 20

Sensation 19

Unicorn 21

University
Botanic Garden 23

Verdant Works 17

your balance on wobble boards. ✉ *Greenmarket* ☎ *01382/228800* 🖷 *01382/868602* 🌐 *www.sensation.org.uk* 🎟 *£5.50* ⏲ *Apr.–Oct., daily 10–6; Nov.–Mar., daily 10–5.*

20 Dundee's urban renewal program—its determination to shake off its industrial past—was motivated in part by the arrival of the **RRS (Royal Research Ship) *Discovery***, the vessel used by Captain Robert Scott (1868–1912) on his polar explorations. The steamer was originally built and launched in Dundee; now it's a permanent tourist exhibit. An onboard exhibition allows you to sample life as it was aboard the intrepid *Discovery,* and the *Polarama* exhibit lets you experience life in Antarctica hands-on and heads-in—you'll feel the temperature and the wind chill as if you were there. ✉ *Discovery Point, Discovery Quay* ☎ *01382/201245* 🌐 *www.rrsdiscovery.com* 🎟 *£5.95* ⏲ *Apr.–Oct., Mon.–Sat. 10–5, Sun. 11–5; Nov.–Mar., Mon.–Sat. 10–4, Sun. 11–4.*

21 At Victoria Dock, you'll find the frigate ***Unicorn***, a 46-gun wood warship fronted by a figurehead of a galloping, crested white unicorn. The *Unicorn* has the distinction of being the oldest British-built warship afloat (it's also the fourth-oldest in the world), having been launched at Chatham, England, in 1824. On board, you can clamber right down into the hold, or discuss the models and displays about the Royal navy's history with the friendly staff. The ship's hours may vary in winter. ✉ *Victoria Dock, just east of Tay Rd. bridge* ☎ *01382/200900 or 01382/200893* 🌐 *www.frigateunicorn.org* 🎟 *£3.50* ⏲ *Apr.–Oct., daily 10–5; Nov.–Mar., Wed.–Fri. noon–4, weekends 10–4, last admission 20 mins before closing.*

22 Dundee's principal museum and art gallery is the **McManus Galleries**, which has displays on a range of subjects, including local history, trade, and industry. ✉ *Albert Sq.* ☎ *01382/432084* 🎟 *Free* ⏲ *Mon.–Wed. and Fri.–Sat. 10–5, Thurs. 10–7, Sun. 12:30–4.*

23 The **University Botanic Garden** contains an extensive collection of native and exotic plants outdoors and in tropical and temperate greenhouses. There are some beautiful areas for picnicking, a visitor center, and a coffee shop. ✉ *Riverside Dr.* ☎ *01382/647190* 🌐 *www.dundee.ac.uk* 🎟 *£2* ⏲ *Mar.–Oct., daily 10–4:30; Nov.–Feb., daily 10–3:30.*

24 **Mills Observatory** at the top of a thickly forested hill, is the only full-time public observatory in Britain, with a resident astronomer. There are displays on astronomy, space exploration, scientific instruments, and a 10-inch refracting telescope for night viewing of the stars and planets. ✉ *Balgay Hill, 2 mi west of the city center* ☎ *01382/435846* 🎟 *Free* ⏲ *Oct.–Mar., weekdays 4–10, weekends 12:30–4; Apr.–Sept., Tues.–Fri. 11–5, weekends 12:30–4.*

off the beaten path

CLAYPOTTS CASTLE – In the eastern suburbs of Dundee, away from the surviving Victorian architecture of the city center, lies this well-preserved 16th-century tower house laid out in a Z plan. You can view the castle from the outside only. ✉ *South of A92, 3 mi east of the city center.*

BROUGHTY CASTLE – Originally built to guard the Tay estuary, Broughty Castle is now a museum focusing on fishing, ferries, and the history of the town of Broughty Ferry's whaling industry. There's also a display of arms and armor. ✉ *Broughty Ferry, 4 mi east of the city center* ☎ *01382/436916* 🎟 *Free* ⏲ *Apr.–Sept., Mon.–Sat. 10–4, Sun. 12:30–4; Oct.–Mar., Tues.–Sat. 10–4, Sun. 12:30–4.*

Where to Stay & Eat

££ ✕ **Dandilly's.** Heavy wooden tables, large windows, and a quirky-casual staff distinguish this West End eatery, as does the innovative Italian cuisine. Try the signature chicken with apricot and ginger, and save room for dessert. ✉ *183 Perth Rd.* ☎ *01382/669218* ▭ *MC, V.*

££ ✕ **The Tapas Bar.** An attractive wood-filled eatery with a helpful staff and a superb menu, including such goodies as calamari in tomato sauce, and pork cooked in cider, the Tapas Bar is great for either a quiet lunch or an up-tempo, sangria-fueled evening. ✉ *16 Commercial St.* ☎ *01382/200527* ▭ *MC, V.*

£–££ ✕ **Het Theatercafe.** At the lively Rep Theatre, you have a choice of the café-bar upstairs, which serves drinks, snacks, and good coffee, or the restaurant downstairs. The international dishes at the restaurant include chicken *satay* (grilled on skewers) and Cajun chicken or fish cakes. Theater posters of past productions and stills of actors hang on the walls. ✉ *Dundee Repertory Theatre, Tay Sq.* ☎ *01382/206699* 🌐 *www.het-theatercafe.co.uk* ▭ *MC, V* ⊗ *Closed Sun.*

Fodor's Choice ★

£££££ ✕🏨 **Kinnaird.** A luxurious country house set in extensive grounds above the Tay Valley northwest of Dundee, Kinnaird has elegant, individually decorated bedrooms with king-size beds and antique furniture. Reception rooms welcome you with open fires and fresh flowers, and imaginative Scottish cuisine rounds out a memorable experience. ✉ *Kinnaird Estate, PH8 0LB* ☎ *01796/482440* 📠 *01796/482289* 🌐 *www.kinnairdestate.com* *9 rooms* *2 restaurants, tennis court, massage, fishing, croquet, free parking, no-smoking rooms; no a/c, no kids under 12* ▭ *MC, V* 🍽 *BP.*

£££–£££££ ✕🏨 **Queen's Hotel.** This handsome Victorian former railway hotel in the lively west end of Dundee is thoroughly up-to-date inside. Modern oak furniture, green carpets, and simple burgundy, gold, or yellow curtains and bedspreads decorate the spacious rooms. Nosey Parkers Bistro (££–£££), decorated with bright, primary colors and white tablecloths, is popular with locals for its international dishes or a quick drink after work. ✉ *160 Nethergate, DD1 4DU* ☎ *01382/322515* 📠 *01382/202668* 🌐 *www.queenshotel-dundee.com* *52 rooms, 1 suite* *Restaurant, cable TV, bar, free parking; no a/c* ▭ *AE, DC, MC, V* 🍽 *BP.*

£££–££££ ✕🏨 **Hilton Dundee.** This hotel has a central, riverside location as well as the usual high standards of the Hilton chain. Wood furniture, and green and blue bedspreads and curtains, decorate the bedrooms. Add the fine international Unicorn Restaurant and the river views, and this modern hotel is hard to resist. ✉ *Earl Grey Place, DD1 4DE* ☎ *01382/229271* 📠 *01382/200072* 🌐 *www.hilton.com* *129 rooms* *Restaurant, room service, in-room data ports, cable TV, indoor pool, gym, bar, casino, business services, meeting rooms, free parking, no-smoking rooms; no a/c* ▭ *AE, DC, MC, V* 🍽 *BP.*

££–££££ ✕🏨 **Swallow Hotel.** This Victorian mansion sits among 5 acres of landscaped gardens, which is unusual for the city of Dundee. The fairly spacious bedrooms are done in pink or yellow, with geometric- or floral-patterned curtains and modern wooden furniture. The Conservatory Restaurant (££–£££) serves Scottish-influenced international fare and gives the impression that you are actually sitting in the garden. ✉ *Kingsway West, Invergowrie, DD2 5JT* ☎ *01382/631200* 📠 *01382/631201* *104 rooms, 3 suites* *Restaurant, pool, gym, sauna, steam room; no a/c* ▭ *AE, DC, MC, V* 🍽 *BP.*

£££ ✕🏨 **Apex City Quay.** This stylish, contemporary quayside hotel has sleek, Scandinavian-style rooms with easy chairs, satiny pillows, and CD/DVD players to help you unwind. To relax further, or to exercize, head for the Japanese spa and fitness center. Both the restaurant and brasserie have globally influenced menus and views of the Tayside landscape. ✉ *1*

West Victoria Dock Rd., DD1 3JP ☎ 01382/202404 📠 01382/201401 🌐 www.apexhotels.com 145 rooms, 8 suites 2 restaurants, in-room data ports, cable TV, indoor pool, health club, spa, lounge, business services, meeting rooms, free parking ▭ MC, V 🍽 CP.

Nightlife & the Arts

BARS & PUBS Dundee's pub scene, centered in the West End-Perth Road area, is one of the liveliest in Scotland. The **Speedwell Bar** (✉ 165–168 Perth Rd. ☎ 01382/667783), or Mennie's, as it is known locally, is in a mahogany-filled Edwardian building brimming with Dundonian character. It's renowned for its superb cask beers and its turn-of-the-20th-century, whale-bone-like, Shanks urinals. The old-fashioned **Tay Bridge Bar** (✉ 129 Perth Rd. ☎ 01382/643973) and its more sophisticated Walnut Lounge are both packed on weekends. **The Art Bar** (✉ 140 Perth Rd. ☎ 01382/227888) has won a loyal following with its program of live jazz, cajun, and folk music, plus its resident DJ, Howard. There's also a good chance you may catch a performance by Michael Marra, widely regarded as Scotland's finest poet and songwriter. **Mickey Coyle's** (✉ 21–23 Old Hawkhill ☎ 01382/225871) has live acoustic sets by local bands as well as DJ nights. The crowd is friendly and, like most pubs in the city, it is frequented by all age groups. The intimate, second-floor **West Port Bar** (✉ Henderson's Wynd ☎ 01382/200993) showcases up-and-coming indie-rock bands.

DANCE CLUBS Dundee is well supplied with dance clubs. **Fat Sam's Disco** (✉ 31 S. Ward Rd. ☎ 01382/228181) attracts clubbers of all ages to its Thursday rock-and-indie night, Friday funk, and Saturday house sounds. **The Reading Rooms** (✉ Blackscroft ☎ 01382/450432) is one of Scotland's top clubs, with dance and hip-hop sounds every weekend and live bands during the week. **Oasis Night Club** (✉ St. Andrews La. ☎ 01382/221061) is strictly for those over 25, with a musical medley covering the 1960s to the 1990s.

MUSIC **Bonar Hall** (✉ Park Pl. ☎ 01382/345466) hosts classical, jazz, and rock concerts. **Caird Hall** (✉ City Sq. ☎ 01382/434451) is one of Scotland's finest concert halls, staging a wide range of music.

THEATER The **Dundee Repertory Theatre** (✉ Tay Sq. ☎ 01382/223530) includes an exhibition gallery and is home to the nationally respected Dundee Rep Ensemble as well as Scotland's preeminent contemporary-dance group, Scottish Dance Theatre. **Whitehall Theatre** (✉ 12 Bellfield St. ☎ 01382/322684) has mostly musical-theater productions, including light opera.

Sports

Dundee Olympia Leisure Centre (✉ Earl Grey Pl. ☎ 01382/434173) has four swimming pools, a diving pool, sauna, water slides, exercise equipment, a climbing wall, and a restaurant.

Shopping

COFFEE & TEA **J. Allan Braithwaite** (✉ 6 Castle St. ☎ 01382/322693) carries 13 freshly roasted coffees and more than 30 blended teas, including mango and apricot.

HOME FURNISHINGS & TEXTILES Rich fabrics, Moroccan light fixtures, Asian furnishings, and sumptuous soaps are just some of the largely Eastern-oriented goodies on display at **Indigo House** (✉ 69 Perth Rd. ☎ 01382/206726).The **Westport Gallery** (✉ 44 West Port ☎ 01382/229707) stocks contemporary designer homeware, including ceramics and glass, plus highly stylized clothing and jewelry.

SCOTTISH SPECIALTIES Dundee is lucky to have a particularly impressive branch of **Hector Russell** (✉ 6a Castle St. ☎ 01382/206805 🌐 www.hector-russell.com), kiltmakers extraordinaire, where every item necessary for correct Highland dress can be purchased, made-to-measure or off the rack.

SHOPPING MALLS **Overgate** (✉ Overgate ☎ 01382/314201) is a modern shopping mall housing upscale chain stores. Many of the major retail chains can be found at **Wellgate Shopping Centre** (✉ Off Panmure St. ☎ 01382/225454). For bargain hunting, try **City Quay** (✉ Victoria Docks, Camperdown St. ☎ 01382/220583), where factory and designer outlet shops cluster conveniently together.

Arbroath

25 *15 mi north of Dundee via A92.*

You'll find traditional boatbuilding in the holiday resort and fishing town of Arbroath. It also has several small curers and processors, and shops sell the town's most famous delicacy, "Arbroath smokies"—whole haddock gutted and lightly smoked. A few miles north along the coast is the old fishing village of Auchmithie, with a beautiful little beach that you can walk to via a short path. The jagged, reddish cliffs and caves are home to a flourishing seabird population.

Arbroath Abbey, founded in 1178, is an unmistakable presence in the town center; it seems to straddle whole streets, as if the town were simply ignoring the red-stone ruin in its midst. Surviving today are remains of the church, as well as one of the most complete examples in existence of an abbot's residence. From here in 1320 a passionate plea was sent by King Robert the Bruce (1274–1329) and the Scottish Church to Pope John XXII (circa 1245–1334) in far-off Rome. The pope had until then sided with the English kings, who adamantly refused to acknowledge Scottish independence. The Declaration of Arbroath stated firmly, "For as long as but a hundred of us remain alive, never will we on any conditions be brought under English rule. It is in truth not for glory, nor riches, nor honours that we are fighting, but for freedom—for that alone, which no honest man gives up but with life itself." Some historians describe this plea, originally drafted in Latin, as the single most important document in Scottish history. The pope advised English king Edward II (1284–1327) to make peace, but warfare was to break out along the border from time to time for the next 200 years. The excellent visitor center recounts this history in well-planned displays. ✉ *Arbroath town center* ☎ *01241/878756* 🌐 *www.historic-scotland.gov.uk* *£3* *Apr.–Sept., daily 9:30–6; Oct.–Mar., Mon.–Wed. and Sat. 9:30–4, Thurs. 9:30–12:30, Sun. 2–4.*

Arbroath was the shore base for the construction of the Bell Rock lighthouse on a treacherous, barely exposed offshore rock in the early 19th century. A signal tower was built to facilitate communication between the mainland and the builders working offshore. In the tower now is the **Signal Tower Museum,** which tells the story of the lighthouse, built by Robert Stevenson (1772–1850) in 1811. (The name Stevenson is strongly associated with the building of lighthouses throughout Scotland, though the most famous son of that family is remembered for another talent: Robert Louis Stevenson [1850–94] gravely disappointed his family by choosing to be a writer instead of an engineer.) The museum also houses a collection of items related to the history of the town, its folk life, and the local fishing industry. ✉ *Ladyloan, west of harbor* ☎ *01241/875598* 🌐 *www.angus.gov.uk* *Free* *Sept.–June, Mon.–Sat. 10–5; July–Aug., Mon.–Sat. 10–5, Sun. 2–5.*

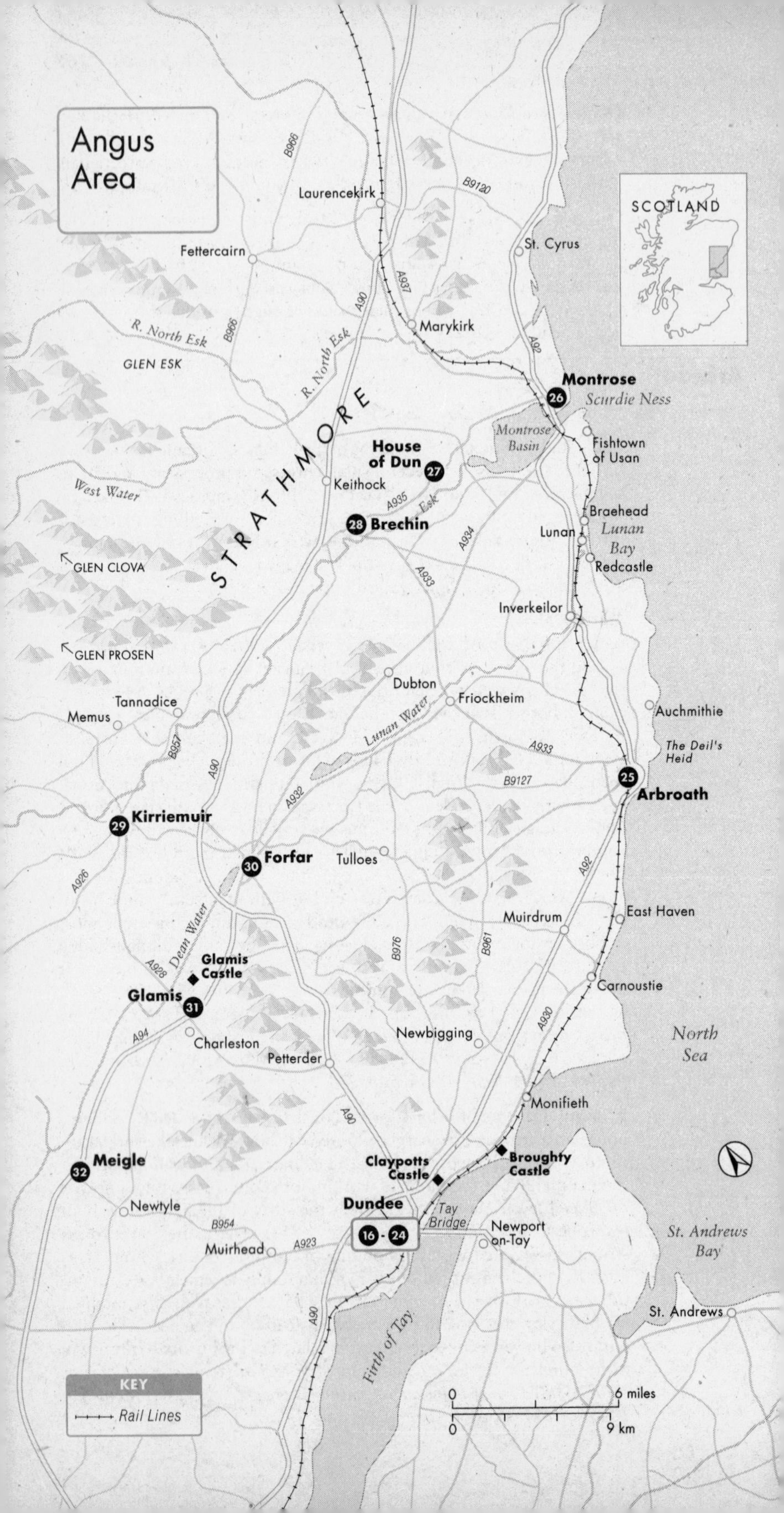
Angus Area
SCOTLAND
Laurencekirk
B966
B9120
St. Cyrus
Fettercairn
A937
A90
Marykirk
R. North Esk
B966
R. North Esk
GLEN ESK
A92
Montrose
26
Scurdie Ness
STRATHMORE
Montrose Basin
Fishtown of Usan
House of Dun
27
Keithock
West Water
A935
Esk
28 Brechin
Braehead
Lunan
Lunan Bay
A934
Redcastle
GLEN CLOVA
A933
Inverkeilor
GLEN PROSEN
Dubton
Friockheim
Auchmithie
Tannadice
Memus
Lunan Water
B957
A933
The Deil's Heid
A90
B9127
25
Arbroath
A932
29 Kirriemuir
30 Forfar
Tulloes
A926
A92
East Haven
Muirdrum
Dean Water
B976
B961
Glamis Castle
A928
Glamis
31
Carnoustie
A930
North Sea
A94
Charleston
Newbigging
Petterder
Monifieth
A90
Broughty Castle
32 Meigle
Claypotts Castle
Dundee
Tay Bridge
Newtyle
16 - 24
Newport on-Tay
St. Andrews Bay
B954
Muirhead
A923
St. Andrews
A90
Firth of Tay
KEY
Rail Lines
0
6 miles
0
9 km

Where to Eat

★ £–££ ✕**But 'n' Ben.** This restaurant offers a taste of quality Scottish home cooking, including smoked fish and mince dishes, at reasonable prices. After lunch, stroll down to the Auchmithie's lovely, shingle beach. ✉ *Auchmithie, near Arbroath, 3 mi off A92* ☎ *01241/877223* ⏲ *Closed Tues.* 💳 *MC, V.*

Nightlife

For a good pint, seek out the **Foundry Bar** (✉ E. Mary St. ☎ 01241/872524), a spartan bar frequented by locals and enlivened by impromptu music sessions on Wednesday and Friday—customers often bring along their fiddles and accordions, and all join in.

Montrose

㉖ *14 mi north of Arbroath via A92.*

An unpretentious and attractive town with a museum and a selection of shops, Montrose is also noted for its beach. Behind Montrose the River Esk forms a wide estuary known as the Montrose Basin. The **Montrose Basin Wildlife Centre,** run by the Scottish Wildlife Trust, is a nature reserve with a good number of geese, ducks, and swans. Several nature trails can take you up close to the reserve's residents if you are quiet. ✉ *Rossie Braes* ☎ *01674/676336* 🌐 *www.montrosebasin.org.uk* 🎫 *£2.50* ⏲ *Reserve daily, 24 hrs. Visitor center Apr.–Oct., daily 10:30–5; Nov.–Mar., daily 10:30–4.*

House of Dun

★ ㉗ *4 mi west of Montrose via A935.*

The National Trust for Scotland's leading attraction in this area is the House of Dun, which overlooks the Montrose Basin. The mansion was built in the 1730s for David Erskine, otherwise known as Lord Dun (1670–1755), a lawyer and a Jacobite. Designed by architect William Adam (1689–1748), the house is particularly noted for its ornate plasterwork and curious Masonic masonry. Some of Lord Dun's heirlooms, including samples from the family's collection of embroidery, tell the story of the Seat of Dun and the eminent family's history. The sprawling grounds have a number of restored workshops, plus an enchanting Victorian walled garden. ✉ *A935* ☎ *01674/810264* 🌐 *www.nts.org.uk* 🎫 *House and garden, £7; garden only, £1* ⏲ *House Apr.–June and Sept.–Oct., Fri.–Tues. noon–5; July–Aug., Fri.–Tues. 11–6. Garden and grounds daily 9:30–sunset. Restaurant daily 11–6.*

Brechin

㉘ *10 mi southwest of Montrose.*

The small market town of Brechin, in Strathmore, has a cathedral that was founded circa 1200 and contains an interesting selection of antiquities, including the Mary Stone, a Pictish relic. The town's 10th-century **Round Tower,** next to the cathedral, is one of only two on mainland Scotland (they are more frequently found in Ireland). It was originally built for the local Culdee monks. 🎫 *Free* ⏲ *Daily 9–5.*

The first arrivals in this part of Scotland were the Picts, who came sometime in the first millennium AD. **Pictavia** explores what is known about this race of Celts using actual artifacts, replicas, and interactive exhibits. ✉ *Brechin Castle Centre, off the A90* ☎ *01307/473785* 🌐 *www.pictavia.org.uk* 🎫 *£3.25* ⏲ *Apr.–Oct., Mon.–Sat. 9–6, Sun. 10–6; Nov.–Mar., Mon.–Sat. 9–5, Sun. 10–5.*

Nightlife

Arena (✉ 79–81 High St. ☎ 01356/624313) has a mix of live bands and DJs and attracts young people from a wide area.

en route

You can rejoin the hurly-burly of the A90 for the return journey south; the more pleasant route, however, leads southwesterly on minor roads (there are several options) that go along the face of the Grampians, following the fault line that separates Highland and Lowland. The **glens of Angus** extend north from various points on Route A90. Known individually as the glens of Isla, Prosen, Clova, and Esk, these long valleys run into the high hills of the Grampians and offer a choice of clearly marked walking routes. Those in Glen Clova are especially appealing.

Kirriemuir

29 *15 mi southeast of Brechin.*

Kirriemuir stands at the heart of Angus's red-sandstone countryside and was the birthplace of the writer and dramatist Sir James Barrie (1860–1937), best known abroad as the author of *Peter Pan.* **Barrie's birthplace** now has upper floors furnished as they might have been in Barrie's time, with manuscripts and personal mementos displayed. The outside washhouse is said to have been Barrie's first theater. Next door, at 11 Brechin Road, is an exhibition called *The Genius of J. M. Barrie,* which provides literary and theatrical information on the author. ✉ *9 Brechin Rd.* ☎ *01575/572646* 🌐 *www.nts.org.uk* *£3.50; combined ticket with Camera Obscura £5* ⏲ *Apr.–Oct., Sat.–Wed. noon–5.*

J. M. Barrie donated the **Camera Obscura,** housed in a cricket pavilion on Kirriemuir Hill, just northeast of Kirriemuir, to the town—one of only three in the country. It affords magnificent views of the surrounding area on a clear day. ✉ *Kirriemuir Hill* ☎ *no phone* *£3.50; combined ticket with Barrie's birthplace £5* ⏲ *Apr.–Sept., daily noon–5.*

Where to Eat

★ ££ ✕ **Drovers Inn.** The Drovers, set in the heart of the Angus farmlands, is a rare find in Scotland, with more the feeling of an English country pub than a Scottish inn. Plain but friendly surroundings, decorated with old farm implements and historic photographs, form the backdrop for simple, top-quality bar food: savory pies, nourishing soups, venison, and Aberdeen Angus steak. Everything is homemade, from bread to sorbets, and only local produce is used. The inn is popular with locals; weekends it's best to make reservations, even for bar meals. ✉ *Off A90, Memus, near Kirriemuir* ☎ *01307/860322* *MC, V.*

Forfar

30 *7 mi east of Kirriemuir.*

Forfar goes about its business of being the center of a farming hinterland without being preoccupied with tourism. This means it's an everyday, friendly, and pleasant-enough Scottish town, bypassed by the A90 on its way north. A high point of the town is the **Meffan Museum and Art Gallery,** which displays an impressive collection of Pictish carved stones and frequently changing art exhibitions. ✉ *20 W. High St.* ☎ *01307/464123* *Free* ⏲ *Mon.–Sat. 10–5.*

off the beaten path

ABERLEMNO – You can see excellent examples of Pictish stone carvings about 5 mi northeast of Forfar alongside the B9134. Carvings of crosses, angels, serpents, and other animals adorn the stones, which date to the 7th–early 9th centuries. Note the stone in the nearby churchyard—one side is carved with a cross and the other side depicts the only known battle scene in Pictish art, with horsemen and foot soldiers.

Where to Stay & Eat

££ **Royal Hotel.** Now fully modernized, this former coaching inn in the center of Forfar serves as a welcoming base for exploring or golfing. The bedrooms are well equipped, though those in the more modern part of the hotel are on the small side. All have a green-and-peach color scheme, with stained-wood finishes and floral fabrics. The public rooms have retained their 19th-century charm. The leisure complex has a pool, gym, and roof garden. The restaurant turns out well-cooked bar meals—such as fish-and-chips and lasagna—served by a friendly staff. *Castle St., DD8 3AE 01307/462691 www.royalhotelforfar.co.uk 19 rooms Restaurant, pool, gym, sauna; no a/c AE, DC, MC, V BP.*

★ £ **Redroofs.** This former cottage hospital is now a hospitable private home and B&B set among trees. Rooms are spacious and very comfortable, and the hosts go out of their way to help you plan your sightseeing. Curios collected by the owners on their travels decorate the sitting room. Evening meals can be arranged. *Balgavies, Guthrie, by Forfar, DD8 2TH 01307/830268 3 rooms Refrigerators, no-smoking rooms; no a/c, no room phones No credit cards BP.*

Glamis

31 *5 mi southwest of Forfar, 6 mi south of Kirriemuir via A928.*

Set in pleasantly rolling countryside is the village of Glamis (pronounced Glahms), with a village green, a line of cottages, a folk museum, and Glamis Castle. The latter is the second-most visited residence in Scotland, after Balmoral Castle in Deeside. A row of 19th-century cottages with unusual stone-slab roofs makes up the **Angus Folk Museum,** whose exhibits focus on the crafts and tools of domestic and agricultural life in the region during the past 200 years. *Off A94 01307/840288 £5 Apr.–Oct., Sat.–Wed. noon–5.*

Fodor's Choice ★ **Glamis Castle,** one of Scotland's best-known and most beautiful castles, connects Britain's royalty through 10 centuries, from Macbeth ("Thane of Glamis") to the late Princess Margaret—born here in 1930 in the ancestral home of her mother—the first royal princess born in Scotland in 300 years. The property of the earls of Strathmore and Kinghorne since 1372, the castle was largely reconstructed in the late 17th century; the original keep, which is much older, is still intact. One of the most famous rooms in the castle is Duncan's Hall, the legendary setting for Shakespeare's *Macbeth*. Guided tours allow you to see fine collections of china, tapestries, and furniture. Other facilities include shops, a produce stall, and a restaurant. *A94, 1 mi north of Glamis 01307/840393 www.strathmore-estates.co.uk Castle and grounds, £6.70; grounds only, £3.50 Apr.–June and Sept.–Oct., daily 10:30–5:30; July–Aug., daily 10–5:30; last tour at 4:45.*

Meigle

32 *7 mi southwest of Glamis, 15 mi west of Dundee.*

The town of Meigle, in the wide swath of Strathmore, has one of the most notable medieval collections in Western Europe, housed at the **Meigle Museum.** This magnificent collection consists of some 25 sculptured monuments from the Celtic Christian period (8th to 10th centuries), nearly all of which were found in or around the local churchyard. ✉ *A94* ☎ *0131/640612* 🌐 *www.historic-scotland.gov.uk* £2 ⏲ *Apr.–Nov., daily 9:30–6.*

FIFE & ANGUS A TO Z

To research prices, get advice from other travelers, and book travel arrangements, visit www.fodors.com.

AIRPORTS

Dundee Airport is off the A85 2 mi west of the city center. ScotAirways operates a popular direct flight from London City Airport, and Easter Airways flies in from Manchester.

Eastern Airways ☎ 01652/680600 🌐 www.easternairways.com.**ScotAirways** ☎ 0870/6060707 🌐 www.scotairways.com.

BUS TRAVEL

Buses connect Edinburgh's St. Andrew Square bus station and Glasgow's Buchanan Street bus station to Fife and Angus. Scottish Citylink operates hourly service to Dundee from both Glasgow and Edinburgh. Stagecoach Fife Buses serves Fife and St. Andrews.

Local service connects St. Andrews and Dundee to many of the smaller towns throughout Fife and Angus. A Day Rover ticket (£5 with Strathtay Scottish; £10 with Stagecoach Fife) is a good value. The Strathtay pass covers Dundee and Angus, and Stagecoach covers all of Fife.

Bus Information**Scottish Citylink** ☎ 08705/505050 🌐 www.citylink.co.uk. **Stagecoach Fife Buses** ☎ 01592/261461. **Strathtay Scottish** ☎ 01382/228345 🌐 www.strathtaybuses.com.

CAR RENTAL

Agencies**Arnold Clark** ✉ E. Dock St., Dundee ☎ 01382/225382 🌐 www.arnoldclark.co.uk. **Avis c/o DIS** ✉ Old Glamis Rd., Dundee ☎ 01382/832264 🌐 www.avis.co.uk. **Hertz** ✉ 18 W. Marketgate, Dundee ☎ 01382/223711 🌐 www.hertz.com.

CAR TRAVEL

The M90 motorway from Edinburgh takes you to within a half hour of St. Andrews and Dundee. If you're coming from Fife, you can use the A91 and the A914 and then cross the Tay Bridge to reach Dundee, though the quickest way is to use the fast-paced, less-scenic M90/A90. Travel time from Edinburgh to Dundee is about one hour, from Edinburgh to St. Andrews, 1½ hours.

Fife is an easy area in which to get around—although it can be difficult to find a place to park in St. Andrews. Most roads are quiet and uncongested. The most interesting sights are in the east, which is served by a network of cross-country roads. Angus is likewise an easy region to explore because it's serviced by a fast main road, the A90, plus the A92, a gentler road, and rural roads that run between the Grampians and the A90.

EMERGENCIES

Dial ☎ 999 in case of an emergency to reach an ambulance, or the fire or police departments (no coins are needed for emergency calls made from public phone booths). Consult your hotel, a tourist information center, or the yellow pages of the telephone directory for listings of local doctors and dentists. Late-night pharmacies are not found outside the larger cities. In St. Andrews, Dundee, and other larger centers, pharmacies use a rotating system for off-hours and Sunday prescription service.

TOURS

Travel Greyhound runs several general orientation bus tours of the main cities and the region from late July to early August. Fishers Tours has bus tours year-round both within and outside the region. Lochs and Glens operates bus tours of Scotland year-round. Heritage Golf Tours Scotland specializes in golf vacations that include hotel and car rental and course reservations. Links Golf St. Andrews tailors tours to individual requirements.

Bus Tours **Fishers Tours** ✉ 16 West Port, Dundee ☎ 01382/227290 🌐 www.fisherstours.co.uk. **Lochs and Glens** ✉ Gartocharn, West Dunbartonshire ☎ 01389/713713 🌐 www.lochsandglens.com. **Travel Greyhound** ✉ Unit 56, The Forum Centre, Commercial St., Dundee ☎ 01382/340006 or 01382/340007.

Golf Tours **Heritage Golf Tours Scotland** ✉ Swilken House, 21 Loch Dr., Helensburgh, G84 8PY ☎ 01436/674630 🌐 www.golftours-scotland.co.uk. **Links Golf St. Andrews** ✉ 7 Pilmour Links, St. Andrews, KY16 9JG ☎ 01334/478639 🌐 www.linksgolfstandrews.com.

TRAIN TRAVEL

ScotRail stops at Kirkcaldy, Markinch (for Glenrothes), Cupar, Leuchars (for St. Andrews), Dundee, Arbroath, and Montrose. For details of the various services, call National Rail.

National Rail ☎ 08457/484950 🌐 www.railtrack.co.uk.

VISITOR INFORMATION

The Arbroath, Dundee, Forth Bridges, Kirkcaldy, and St. Andrews tourist offices are open year-round. Smaller tourist information centers operate seasonally in the following towns: Anstruther, Brechin, Carnoustie, Crail, Forfar, Kirriemuir, and Montrose.

Arbroath ✉ Market Pl., Arbroath, DD11 1HR ☎ 01241/872609. **Dundee** ✉ 7–21 Castle St., Dundee, DD1 3AA ☎ 01382/527527 🌐 www.angusanddundee.co.uk. **Forth Bridges** ✉ c/o Queensferry Lodge Hotel, St. Margaret's Head, North Queensferry, KY11 1HP ☎ 01383/417759. **Kirkcaldy** ✉ 19 Whytescauseway, Kirkcaldy, KY1 1XF ☎ 01592/267775. **St. Andrews** ✉ 70 Market St., St. Andrews, KY16 9NU ☎ 01334/472021 🌐 www.standrews.com.

5

THE CENTRAL HIGHLANDS

STIRLING, THE TROSSACHS AND LOCH LOMOND, PERTHSHIRE

FODOR'S CHOICE

Blair Castle, *near Pitlochry*
Cameron House, *in Alexandria*
Doune, *near Stirling*
Gleneagles Hotel, *in Auchterarder*
Roman Camp, *in Callander*
Scone Palace, *in Perth*
Stirling Castle, *in Stirling*

HIGHLY RECOMMENDED

HOTELS
Auchterarder House Hotel, *in Auchterarder*
Sunbank House Hotel, *in Perth*
West Plean, *in Stirling*

SIGHTS
Bannockburn Heritage Centre, *in Stirling*
Dunblane, *near Stirling*
Loch Katrine, *in the Trossachs*
Pass of Killiecrankie, *in Pitlochry*

By Gilbert Summers
Updated by Beth Ingpen

STAND ON STIRLING CASTLE ROCK TO SURVEY the whole Central Highland region, and you will see Scotland coast to coast. This is where Scotland draws in her waist, from the Clyde in the west to the Forth in the east. You can judge just how near the area is to the well-populated Midland Valley by looking out from the ramparts of Edinburgh Castle: the Highland hills, which meander around the Trossachs region and above Callander, are clearly visible. Similarly, the high-tower blocks of some of Glasgow's peripheral housing developments are noticeable from many of the countryside's higher peaks, particularly Ben Lomond.

5

Today the old county seats of Perth and Stirling still play important roles as the primary administrative centers of the counties of Perthshire and Stirlingshire, which make up the Central Highlands. Geographically, it's no surprise that this region has been a favorite vacation getaway for Edinburghers and Glaswegians for centuries. So beloved is the area, in fact, that 720 square mi of it were designated part of Scotland's first national park, Loch Lomond and the Trossachs National Park, in 2002.

As early as 1794 the local minister in Callander, on the very edge of the Highlands, wrote: "The Trossachs are often visited by persons of taste, who are desirous of seeing nature in her rudest and unpolished state." What these early visitors came to see was a series of lochs and hills, whose crags and slopes were hung harmoniously with shaggy birch, oak, and pinewoods. The tops of the hills are high but not too savage—real wilderness would have been too much for these fledgling nature lovers. The Romantic poets, especially William Wordsworth (1770–1850), sang the praises of such locales. Though Wordsworth is more closely associated with the Lake District in England, his travels through Scotland and the Trossachs inspired several of his poems. But it was Sir Walter Scott (1771–1832) who definitively put this area on the tourist map by setting his 1810 dramatic verse narrative, *The Lady of the Lake,* in the landscape of the Trossachs. Scott's verse was an immediate and huge success, and visitors flooded in to trace the events of the poem across the region. The poem mentions every little bridge and farmhouse and is still the most comprehensive guide to the area. Various engineering schemes of the Glasgow Water Department, however, have rendered some of the topography out of date.

Just as the Trossachs have long attracted those with discriminating tastes, so has Loch Lomond, Scotland's largest loch in terms of surface area. The hard rocks to the north confine it to a long thin ribbon, and the more yielding Lowlands allow it to spread out and assume a softer, wider form. Here the Lowlands' fields and lush hedgerows quickly give way to dark woods and crags—just a half hour's drive north from Glasgow. The song, "The Banks of Loch Lomond," said to have been written by a Jacobite prisoner incarcerated in Carlisle, England, captures beautifully a particular style of Scottish sentimentality, resulting in the popularity of the "bonnie, bonnie banks" around the world, especially wherever Scots are to be found.

Scots, in particular, prize the sights of this region, for they are some of the most hallowed in their history. "Scots Wha He Wi' Wallace Bled," a rousing pipe-band tune generally regarded as the Scottish national anthem, is played much here. It deals with William Wallace who, like Robert the Bruce, waged war against England in the 13th and 14th centuries. The most notable battles of Wallace and Bruce were fought at Stirling Bridge and Bannockburn, respectively. In nearby Callander, Rob Roy MacGregor, the Scottish Robin Hood, lived (and looted and terrorized) his way into the storybooks.

Within the region the physical contrast between Lowland and Highland is quite pronounced because of the Highland boundary fault. This geological divide also marked the boundary between Scotland's two languages and cultures, Gaelic and Scots, with the Gaels ensconced northwest behind the mountain barrier. In the Central Highlands the fault runs through Loch Lomond, close to Callander, to the northeast above Perth, and into the old county of Angus. Remember that even though the Central Highlands are easily accessible, there is still much high, rough country in the region. Ben Lawers, near Killin, is the ninth-highest peak in Scotland, and the moor of Rannoch is as bleak and empty a stretch as can be seen anywhere in the northlands. But if the glens and lochs prove to be too lonely or intimidating, it's only a short journey to the softer and less harsh Lowlands.

Exploring the Central Highlands

The main towns of Stirling and Perth serve as roadway hubs for the area, making both places natural starting points for tours. Stirling itself is worth covering in some detail on foot. The successive waves of development of this important town can easily be traced—from castle and Old Town architecture to Victorian developments and urban and industrial sprawl.

The Trossachs are a short distance from Stirling, all easily covered in a loop. You can get to Loch Lomond from either Glasgow or Stirling. The main road up the west bank (A82) is not recommended for leisurely touring, as the traffic is heavy and it's not a relaxing drive. Do use this road, however, if you are on your way to Oban, Kintyre, or Argyll.

Loch Lomond is best seen from one of two cul-de-sac roads: by way of Drymen at the south end, up to Rowardennan, or if you are pressed for time, west from Aberfoyle to reach Loch Lomond near its northern end, at Inversnaid. Note that in the Trossachs, the road that some maps show going all the way around Loch Katrine is a private road belonging to the Strathclyde Water Board and is open only to walkers and cyclists.

Getting around Perthshire is made interesting by the series of looped tours accessible from the A9, a fast main artery. Exercise caution while driving the A9 itself, however; there have been many auto accidents in this area. The entire route can be completed in a single day, but if you have time on your hands and are seeking a little spontaneity, you may want to overnight in a village or two along the way.

About the Restaurants

Regional country delicacies—loch trout, river salmon, lamb, and venison—appear regularly on even modest menus in Central Highlands restaurants. The urban areas south and southwest of Stirling, in contrast, lack refined dining spots. Here you will find simple pubs, often crowded and noisy, but serving substantial food at lunchtime (eaten balanced on your knee, perhaps, or at a shared table).

About the Hotels

In Stirling and Callander, as well as in the small towns and villages throughout the region, you'll find a selection of accommodations out of all proportion to the size of the communities (industrial towns are the exceptions). The grand hotels, though few, were brought into existence by the carriage trade of the 19th century, when travel in Scotland was the fashion. The level of service at these places has, by and large, not slipped. Alternatively, many country-house inns are a match for the grand hotels in comfort, while adding a personal touch to the service.

Scotland's beautiful interior is excellent touring country. The glens, in some places, run parallel to the lochs, including those along Lochs Earn, Tay, and Rannoch, making for satisfying loops and round-trips.

Numbers in the text correspond to numbers in the margin and on the Central Highlands and Stirling maps.

If you have 2 days

There's enough to see in **Stirling** 1–18 to fill up at least a day. The second day, cover the Trossachs loop, which includes **Loch Venachar** 23, Loch Achray, and **Loch Katrine** 24, and the historic towns of **Dunblane** 19, **Doune** 20, **Callander** 21, and **Aberfoyle** 25.

If you have 6 days

Spend a day in **Stirling** 1–18. If you are shopping for Scottish woolens, wander into Mill Trail country east of Stirling. Then visit **Dunblane** 19 and **Doune** 20, staying overnight at **Callander** 21 to explore the fine country northward toward **Balquhidder Glen** 22. Spend a day in the **Trossachs** around **Loch Venachar** 23 and **Loch Katrine** 24, and take a boat ride to see the landscape at its best. The next day travel to **Drymen** 26 for a morning around **Loch Lomond** 27 before driving into Perthshire. Spend a night at **Auchterarder** 36, with its antiques shops, or travel straight to **Perth** 28, where you should base yourself for two days while exploring Perthshire. Go west for **Crieff** 35 and Drummond Castle Garden or north for Highland resort towns such as **Dunkeld** 29, with its cathedral; **Pitlochry** 30, close to the historic Pass of Killiecrankie; impressive **Blair Castle** 31; and **Aberfeldy.** Between Pitlochry and Aberfeldy, make time for the bleak landscapes of **Loch Rannoch**—a great contrast to the generally pastoral Perthshire countryside.

WHAT IT COSTS In Pounds

	$$$$	$$$	$$	$	¢
RESTAURANTS	over £22	£18–£22	£12–£18	£7–£12	under £7
HOTELS	over £150	£110–£150	£80–£110	£50–£80	under £50

Restaurant prices are for a main course at dinner. Hotel prices are for two people in a standard double room in high season. Prices generally include the 17.5% VAT.

Timing

The Trossachs and Loch Lomond can get quite busy and crowded in high summer, so the area makes a good choice for off-season touring. Fall colors are spectacular, and winter brings dramatic Highland light.

STIRLING

26 mi northeast of Glasgow, 36 mi northwest of Edinburgh.

In some ways, Stirling is a little Edinburgh with similar "crag-and-tail" foundations and a royal half mile. Its castle, built on a steep-sided plug of rock, dominates the landscape, and its esplanade affords views of the surrounding valley plain of the River Forth. Stirling's strategic position, commanding the lowest bridge on the Forth, was appreciated by the Stewart kings, and they spent a lot of time at its castle—a fact that, together with the relics of freedom fighters in the neighborhood, has led some

Scottish nationalists to declare that Stirling, not Edinburgh, should really be the capital city.

Exploring Stirling

The historic part of town is tightly nestled around the castle—everything is within easy walking distance. You can either take a taxi or walk—if you're feeling energetic—out to Bannockburn Heritage Centre or the National Wallace Monument, on the town's outskirts.

a good tour

Stirling is one of Britain's great historic towns. An impressive proportion of the Old Town walls remain and can be seen from Dumbarton Road, as soon as you step outside the tourist information center. If you're an art lover, make a foray west along Dumbarton Road to visit the **Smith Art Gallery and Museum** 1 ►. Back near the information center, on Corn Exchange Road, is a modern statue of Robert MacGregor (1671–1734), better known as Rob Roy, notorious cattle dealer and drover, part-time thief and outlaw, Jacobite (most of the time), and hero of Sir Walter Scott's namesake novel (1818). Rob is practically inescapable if you visit Callander and the Trossachs, where he had his home.

About 25 yards up the hill on Corn Exchange from Rob Roy's statue is another statue, of Campbell Bannerman, where you should make a sharp left on to the upper **Back Walk** 2. This gentle but relentless uphill path follows the Old Town walls, eventually leading to the castle. After about 110 yards north, at a junction, follow the sign to the right for the Old Town Jail along Academy Road, which passes behind the Stirling Highland Hotel, formerly the Old High School, built in 1854 on the site of the former Greyfriars Monastery. At the junction of Academy Road and Spittal Street/St. John's Street, look across to **Darrow House** 3, a fine example of Scottish domestic architecture, now a private home.

Turn left on to St. John's Street and walk uphill, passing another typical town house, **Bothwell Ha** 4, on the left-hand side. Behind Bothwell Ha is the **Old Town Jail** 5, the former military detention barracks. It now contains exhibits on life in a 19th-century Scottish prison. Adjacent to the Old Town Jail is the Youth Hostel, housed in Erskine Marykirk, a neoclassical church built in 1824. Walk a little farther north on St. John's Street; at the junction with Castle Wynd is a path to your left. Walk up this path to find **Cowane's Hospital** 6, which was built as almshouses in 1639. The medieval **Church of the Holy Rude** 7 is on your right, and straight ahead is the **cemetery** 8, with some unusual monuments.

Walk back down the path to St. John's Street. Directly across the road from the end of the path is **Mar Place House** 9, a restored Georgian town house. Turn left onto Castle Wynd, and immediately on your left is the long and ornate facade of the distinctively Renaissance **Mar's Wark** 10. Continue up the hill, following signs to **Stirling Castle** 11 and the **Royal Burgh of Stirling Visitor Centre** 12. At this point you can appreciate the strategic position of the castle and the wonderful views toward the Highlands. You can also see the Wallace Monument and Old Stirling Bridge from here. After exploring the castle, walk back down Castle Wynd. On your left-hand side is **Argyll's Lodging** 13.

Turn left onto Broad Street; 100 yards down on the right-hand side is the **Tolbooth** 14. The Mercat Cross, where proclamations were made, stands opposite. Continue down Broad Street, and turn right onto Bow Street, following it around to the left downhill toward the more modern part of Stirling, with its many shops. Alternatively, walk a few minutes down

Biking

The big attraction for cyclists is the Lowland/Highland Trail, passing through Drymen, Aberfoyle, the Trossachs, Callander, Lochearnhead, and Killin. This route runs along former railroad-track beds, as well as private and minor roads, to reach well into the Central Highlands. Another almost completely traffic-free option is the roadway around Loch Katrine. Paths flanking the canals make for equally easygoing riding. Mountain bikes can tackle many of the forest roads and trails enjoyed by walkers. Avoid main roads, which can be busy with holiday traffic.

Fishing

Coarse and game fishing, loch and river fishing, and sea angling are among the fishing options in the area. Statutory fishing season for salmon and sea trout on the Tay River system is from January 15 to October 15. Coarse fishing for grayling, pike, perch, and roach on the Earn River system is reserved February through October. In some cases, Sunday fishing is illegal. Visitor information centers have publications that show the best locations.

Golf

There are many excellent courses in this inland region, from classic parkland courses with mature trees and velvet greens to tricky, hilly, and heathery courses where the challenge is to keep the ball moving forward. Few courses are crowded and most welcome visitors, though possibly with restricted tee times. The Golf Discount Pass, valid for 10 consecutive days, is good for play on more than 30 golf courses throughout the Central Highlands. You can buy the pass at local visitor information centers. Two favorite places to play in the region are the Callander and Killin golf courses.

Hiking

Hill walking and "Munro-bagging" (climbing all the mountains more than 3,000 feet high; so-called in honor of the mountaineer who first listed them) are very popular in the Highlands. Even in the wilder parts, you will find locals and visitor centers able to give advice on routes. Some trails, such as the West Highland Way and the Forest Enterprise routes are well-marked, but most are simply well-trod paths. The most popular trails are on Ben Lawers, Ben Ledi, and Ben Lomond. You should have the proper boots and safety equipment for high-elevation routes. The publications *Walk Loch Lomond and the Trossachs* and *Walk Perthshire,* available at bookstores or visitor information centers, are invaluable for hikers and trekkers.

---

from the castle (via Barn Road, Castlehill, and Lower Bridge Street) to see the medieval **Old Stirling Bridge** 15. Drive north–northeast down Causewayhead Road from the castle to get to the Gothic pencil that is the **National Wallace Monument** 16, commemorating Scotland's great freedom fighter. Due east of the castle and most easily reached from the monument are the ruins of **Cambuskenneth Abbey** 17, in an idyllic riverside setting. The historic battle site of **Bannockburn Heritage Centre** 18—rather incongruously set in the middle of a housing development—is south of town, off Glasgow Road (A80).

TIMING Stirling is a compact town, and this tour, though it has many sights to admire, can be done at high speed in a day or in a more leisurely fashion over two days.

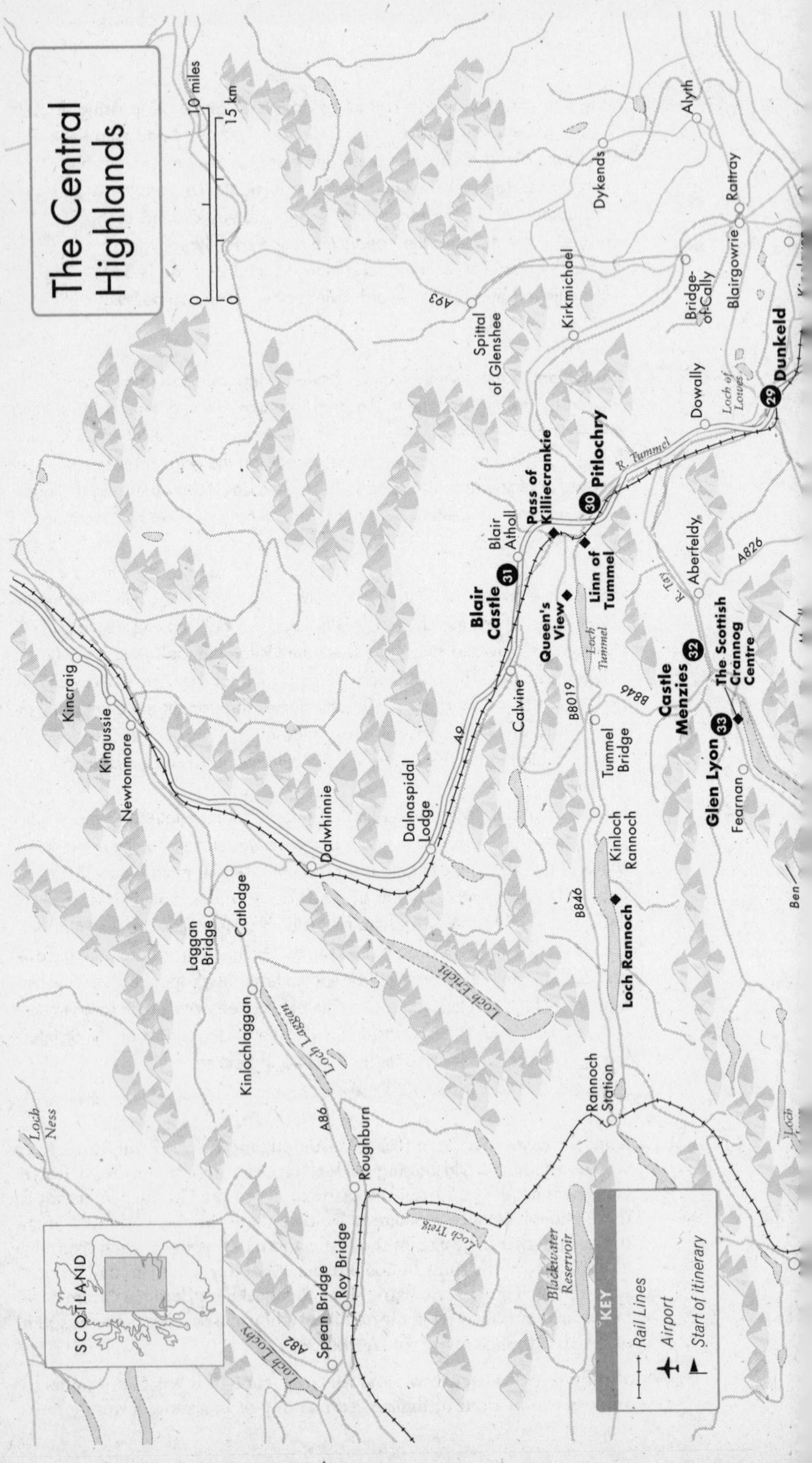
The Central Highlands
0 10 miles
0 15 km
SCOTLAND
KEY
Rail Lines
Airport
Start of itinerary
Loch Ness
Loch Lochy
A82
Spean Bridge
Roy Bridge
Roughburn
A86
Loch Treig
Blackwater Reservoir
Rannoch Station
Kinlochlaggan
Loch Laggan
Laggan Bridge
Catlodge
Loch Ericht
Newtonmore
Kingussie
Kincraig
Dalwhinnie
Dalnaspidal Lodge
A9
Calvine
Blair Castle 31
Blair Atholl
Pass of Killiecrankie
Pitlochry 30
Linn of Tummel
Queen's View
Loch Tummel
B8019
Tummel Bridge
Kinloch Rannoch
B846
Loch Rannoch
Castle Menzies 32
The Scottish Crannog Centre
Glen Lyon 33
Fearnan
Aberfeldy
R. Tay
A826
R. Tummel
Dowally
Loch of Lowes
Dunkeld 29
Spittal of Glenshee
A93
Kirkmichael
Bridge-of-Cally
Blairgowrie
Rattray
Dykends
Alyth
Ben

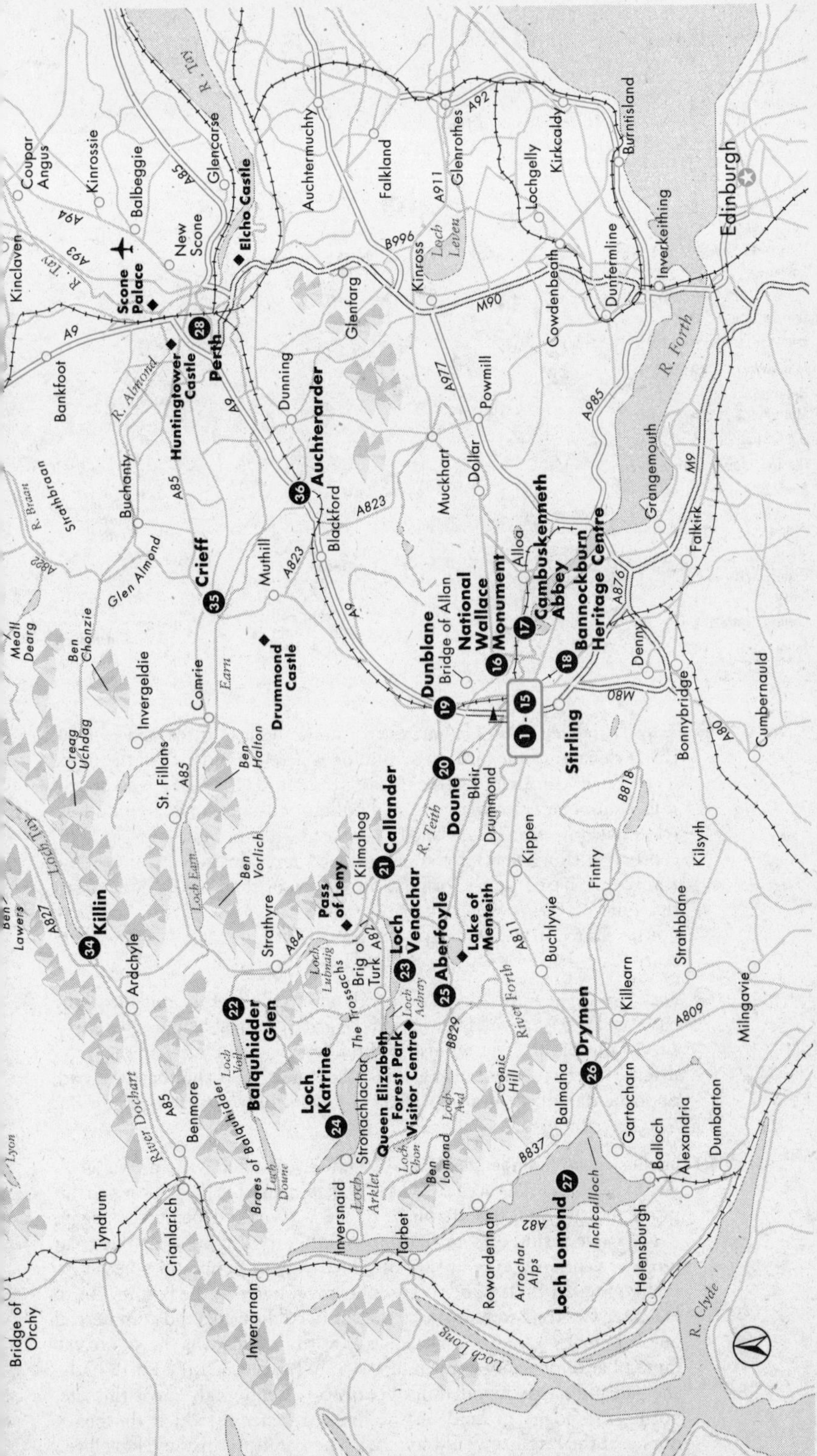
Perth
Scone Palace
Elcho Castle
Huntingtower Castle
Auchterarder
Crieff
Drummond Castle
Dunblane
Bridge of Allan
National Wallace Monument
Cambuskenneth Abbey
Bannockburn Heritage Centre
Stirling
Doune
Callander
Pass of Leny
Loch Venachar
Aberfoyle
Lake of Menteith
Balquhidder Glen
Loch Katrine
Queen Elizabeth Forest Park Visitor Centre
Drymen
Loch Lomond
Killin
Edinburgh
Kinclaven
Coupar Angus
Kinrossie
Balbeggie
New Scone
Glencarse
Bankfoot
Auchtermuchty
Falkland
Glenrothes
Kirkcaldy
Burntisland
Lochgelly
Kinross
Loch Leven
Glenfarg
Dunning
Cowdenbeath
Dunfermline
Inverkeithing
R. Forth
Powmill
Muckhart
Dollar
Alloa
Grangemouth
Falkirk
Denny
Bonnybridge
Cumbernauld
Kilsyth
Blackford
Muthill
Buchanty
Strathbraan
Glen Almond
Meall Dearg
Ben Chonzie
Invergeldie
Comrie
Creag Uchdag
St. Fillans
Ben Halton
Ben Vorlich
Loch Earn
Loch Tay
Ben Lawers
Strathyre
Kilmahog
Brig o' Turk
The Trossachs
Loch Lubnaig
Loch Achray
Blair Drummond
Kippen
Fintry
Buchlyvie
Killearn
Strathblane
Milngavie
Conic Hill
Balmaha
Gartocharn
Balloch
Alexandria
Dumbarton
Helensburgh
Inchcailloch
Rowardennan
Arrochar Alps
Loch Long
R. Clyde
Ben Lomond
Loch Ard
Loch Chon
Stronachlachar
Inversnaid
Loch Arklet
Tarbet
Inverarnan
Crianlarich
Tyndrum
Bridge of Orchy
Benmore
River Dochart
Braes of Balquhidder
Loch Doune
Loch Voil
Ardchyle
R. Tay
R. Almond
R. Teith
River Forth
A9
A85
A93
A94
A911
A92
B996
M90
A977
A985
M9
A823
A822
A876
M80
A80
B818
A811
A809
A81
A84
A827
B829
B837
A82
A821

Argyll's Lodging 13
Back Walk 2
Bannockburn Heritage Ctr. . . 18
Bothwell Ha . . . 4
Cambuskenneth Abbey 17
Cemetery 8
Church of the Holy Rude 7
Cowane's Hospital 6
Darrow House . . 3
Mar Place House 9
Mar's Wark . . . 10
National Wallace Monument . . . 16
Old Stirling Br. 15
Old Town Jail . . 5
Royal Burgh of Stirling Visitor Centre 12
Smith Art Gallery and Museum 1
Stirling Castle . 11
Tolbooth 14

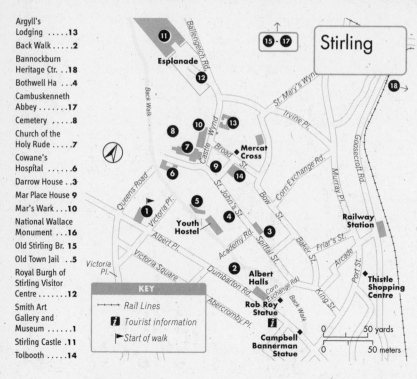

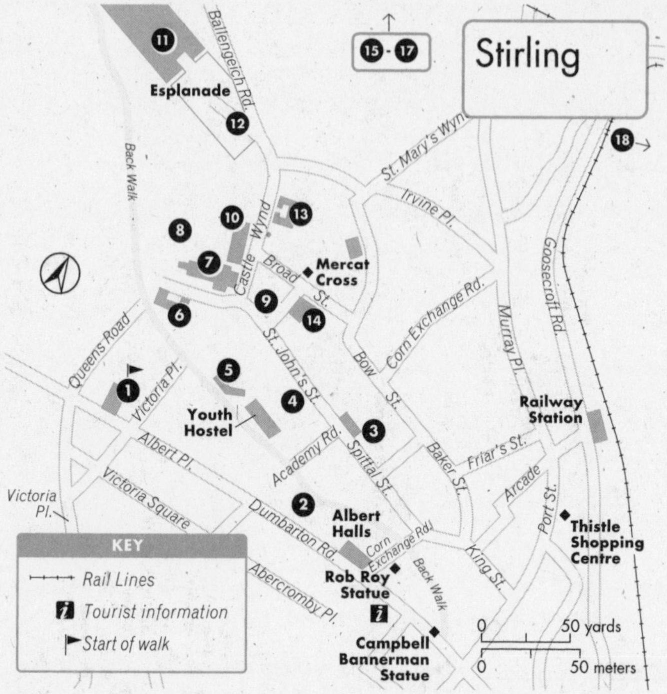

What to See

13 **Argyll's Lodging.** A nobleman's town house built in three phases from the 16th century onward, this building is actually older than the name it bears—that of Archibald, the ninth earl of Argyll (1629–85), who bought it in 1666. It was for many years a military hospital, then a youth hostel. It has now been refurbished to show how the nobility lived in 17th-century Stirling. Specially commissioned reproduction furniture and fittings are based on the original inventory of the house's contents at that time. ✉ *Castle Wynd* ☎ *0131/668–8800* 🌐 *www.historic-scotland.gov.uk* 🎫 *£3.30; £7.50 with admission to Stirling Castle* ⏲ *Apr.–Sept., daily 9:30–5:15; Oct.–Mar., daily 9:30–4:15.*

2 **Back Walk.** The upper Back Walk will take you along the outside of the city's walls, past a watchtower and the grimly named Hangman's entry, carved out of the great whinstone boulders that once marked the outer defenses of the town. One of several access areas is off Dumbarton Road, opposite the tourist information center. ✉ *Runs from Dumbarton Rd. to Castle Rock.*

★ 18 **Bannockburn Heritage Centre.** In 1298, the year after William Wallace's victory, Robert the Bruce (1274–1329) materialized as the nation's champion, and the final bloody phase of the Wars of Independence began. Bruce's rise resulted from the uncertainties and timidity of the great lords of Scotland (ever unsure of which way to jump and whether to bow to England's demands). This tale is recounted at the Bannockburn Heritage Centre, hidden among the sprawl of housing and commercial development on the southern edge of Stirling. This was the site of the famed Battle of Bannockburn in 1314. In Bruce's day the Forth had a shelved and partly wooded floodplain. So he cunningly chose this site, noting the boggy ground on the lower reaches in which the heavy horses of the English would founder. The events of this time have been re-created within the center by means of an audiovisual presentation, models and costumed figures, and an arresting mural depicting the battle in detail. ✉ *Off A80* ☎ *01786/812664* 🌐 *www.nts.org.uk* 🎫 *£3.50* 🕑 *Site daily. Heritage Centre Apr.–Oct., daily 10–5:30; Feb.–Mar. and Nov.–mid-Dec., daily 10:30–4.*

4 **Bothwell Ha.** This 16th-century hall (*ha* is Scots for hall) is said to have been owned by the earl of Bothwell (circa 1535–78), the third husband of Mary, Queen of Scots (1542–87). It is closed to the public. ✉ *St. John's St.*

17 **Cambuskenneth Abbey.** On the south side of the Abbey Craig, the scanty remains of this 13th-century abbey lie in a sweeping bend of the River Forth, with the dramatic outline of Stirling Castle as a backdrop. Important meetings of the Scottish Parliament were once held here, and King Edward I (1239–1307) of England visited in 1304. The abbey was looted and damaged during the Scots Wars of Independence in the late 13th and early 14th centuries. The reconstructed tomb of King James III (1452–88) can be seen near the outline of the high altar. ✉ *Ladysneuk Rd.* ☎ *0131/668–8800* 🌐 *www.historic-scotland.gov.uk* 🎫 *Free* 🕑 *Daily.*

8 **Cemetery.** Among the most notable of the many unusual monuments in the cemetery near the Church of the Holy Rude is the **Star Pyramid** of 1858. Also look for the macabre, glass-walled **Martyrs Monument,** erected in memory of two Wigtownshire girls who were drowned in 1685 for their Covenanting faith. The castle dominates the foreground, and from **Ladies' Rock,** a high perch within the cemetery, there are excellent views of the looming fortress. ✉ *Top of St. John's St.*

7 **Church of the Holy Rude.** The nave of this handsome church survives from the 15th century, and a portion of the original medieval timber roof can also be seen. This is the only Scottish church still in use to have witnessed the coronation of a Scottish monarch—James VI (1566–1625) in 1567. ✉ *Top of St. John's St.*

6 **Cowane's Hospital.** Built in 1639 for *decayed breithers* (unsuccessful merchants), this building has above its entrance a small, cheery statue of the founder himself, John Cowane, which is said to come alive on Hogmanay Night (December 31) to walk the streets with the locals and join in their New Year's revelry. ✉ *St. John's St.*

3 **Darrow House.** Dating from the 17th century, this house displays the characteristic crow-step gables, dormer windows, and projecting turn-pike stair of the period. It is closed to the public. ✉ *Spittal St.*

9 **Mar Place House.** This handsome Georgian building was saved from dereliction and painstakingly restored through the town council's ongoing Old Town renovation program. It is closed to the public. ✉ *Mar Pl.*

10 **Mar's Wark.** These distinctive windowless and roofless ruins are the stark remains of a Renaissance palace built in 1570 by Lord Erskine (died 1572), earl of Mar and Stirling Castle governor. The name means "Mar's work," or building. Look for the armorial carved panels, the gargoyles, and the turrets flanking a railed-off *pend* (archway). During the 1745 Jacobite rebellion, Mar's Wark was laid siege to and severely damaged, but its admirably worn shell survives. The ruins are enclosed by a fence; you may view them from outside only. ✉ *Castle Wynd* ☎ *0131/668–8800* 🌐 *www.historic-scotland.gov.uk.*

16 **National Wallace Monument.** It was near Old Stirling Bridge that the Scottish freedom fighter William Wallace (circa 1270–1305) and a ragged army of Scots won a major victory in 1297. The movie *Braveheart,* di-

rected by and starring Mel Gibson, was based on Wallace's life. A more accurate version of events is told in an exhibition and audiovisual presentation at this pencil-thin museum on the Abbey Craig. Up close, this Victorian shrine to William Wallace, built between 1856 and 1869, becomes less slim and soaring, revealing itself to be a substantial square tower with a creepy spiral stairway. To reach the monument, follow the Bridge of Allan signs (A9) northward, crossing the River Forth by Robert Stephenson's (1772–1850) New Bridge of 1832, next to the historic old one. The National Wallace Monument is signposted at the next traffic circle. ✉ *Abbey Craig* ☎ *01786/472140* 🎫 *£5* ⏲ *Mar.–May and Oct., daily 10–5; June, daily 10–6; July–Aug., daily 9:30–6:30; Sept., daily 9:30–6; Nov.–Feb. daily 10:30–4.*

15 **Old Stirling Bridge.** North of Stirling Castle, on the edge of town, is a narrow, humped 15th-century bridge, now open only to pedestrians. ✉ *Off Drip Rd., A84.*

5 **Old Town Jail.** The original town jail, now restored, has living exhibitions about life in a 19th-century Scottish prison. Furnished cells, models, and staff—dressed as prisoners, wardens, and prison reformers—bring the past vividly to life. From October through March, these living-history performances take place only on weekends. ✉ *Access from St. John's St.* ☎ *01786/450050* 🌐 *www.visitscotland.com* 🎫 *£3.95* ⏲ *Apr.–Sept., daily 9:30–6; Oct. and Mar., daily 9:30–5; Nov.–Feb., daily 9:30–4; last admission 1 hr before closing.*

12 **Royal Burgh of Stirling Visitor Centre.** This visitor center at the foot of the Castle Esplanade houses a shop and exhibition hall with an audiovisual presentation on the town and surrounding area. Groups perform Highland dancing on the Esplanade Tuesday evenings from mid-June through August. The dancers wear tartan and step to fiddle or bagpipe music. ☎ *01786/462517* 🎫 *Free* ⏲ *Apr.–mid-June and Sept.–Oct., daily 9:30–6; mid-June–Aug., Tues. 9:30-8, Wed.–Mon. 9:30–6; Nov.–Mar., daily 9:30–5.*

1 **Smith Art Gallery and Museum.** This community art gallery, founded in 1874 with the bequest of a local collector, showcases a varied exhibition program of paintings and sculpture. ✉ *Albert Pl./Dumbarton Rd.* ☎ *01786/471917* 🎫 *Free* ⏲ *Tues.–Sat. 10:30–5, Sun. 2–5.*

Fodor's Choice ★

11 **Stirling Castle.** Its magnificent strategic position made Stirling Castle the grandest prize in the Scots Wars of Independence in the late 13th and early 14th centuries. The Battle of Bannockburn in 1314 was fought within sight of its walls, and the victory by Robert the Bruce yielded both the castle and freedom from English subjugation for almost four centuries.

The daughter of King Robert I (Robert the Bruce), Marjory, married Walter Fitzallan, the high steward of Scotland. Their descendants included the Stewart dynasty of Scottish monarchs (Mary, Queen of Scots, was a Stewart, though she preferred the French spelling, *Stuart*). The Stewarts were responsible for many of the works that survive within the castle walls today. They made Stirling Castle their court and power base, creating fine Renaissance-style buildings that were not completely obliterated, despite subsequent reconstruction for military purposes.

You'll enter the castle through its outer defenses, which consist of a great curtain wall and batteries that date from 1708, built to bulwark earlier defenses by the main gatehouse. From this lower square the most conspicuous feature is the **palace,** built by King James V (1512–42) between 1538 and 1542. The decorative figures festooning the ornately worked outer walls of this edifice show the influence of French masons. Overlooking the upper courtyard is the **Great Hall,** built by King James IV (1473–1513) in 1503. Before the Union of Parliaments in 1707, when the Scottish aristocracy sold out to England, this building had been used as one of the seats of the Scottish Parliament. After 1707 it sank into decline, becoming a riding school, then a barracks. It has since been restored to its original splendor.

Among the later works built for regiments stationed here, the **King's Old Building** stands out; it is a 19th-century baronial revival on the site of an earlier building. The oldest building on the site is the **Mint,** or **Coonzie Hoose,** perhaps dating as far back as the 14th century. Below is an arched passageway leading to the westernmost section of the ramparts, the **Nether Bailey.** You'll have the distinct feeling here of being in the bow of a warship sailing up the *carselands* (valley plain) of the Forth Valley, which fans out before the great superstructure of the castle. Among the gun platforms and the crenellations of the ramparts, you may find yourself pondering the strategic significance of Stirling. To the south lies the hump of the Touch and the Gargunnock hills (part of the Campsie Fells), which diverted potential direct routes from Glasgow and the south. For centuries all roads into the Highlands across the narrow waist of Scotland led to Stirling. If you look carefully northward, you can still see the Old Stirling Bridge, once the lowest and most convenient place to cross the river. For all these geographic reasons, the castle was perhaps the single most important fortress in Scotland. ✉ *Castlehill* ☎ *0131/668–8800* 🌐 *www.historic-scotland.gov.uk* 🎫 *£7.50, including admission to Argyll's Lodging* ⏲ *Apr.–Sept., daily 9:30–5:15; Oct.–Mar., daily 9:30–4:15.*

⓮ **Tolbooth.** The Tolbooth, built in 1705, has a traditional Scottish steeple and gilded weathercock. For centuries the Burgh Court handed down sentences here, and the Tolbooth also served as a jail. ✉ *Broad St.*

Where to Stay & Eat

££–£££ ✕ **Hermann's Brasserie.** You can dine in the main dining room, with its Black-Watch–tartan carpet, Austrian-landscape wall murals, and green-shaded lighting, or in the bright conservatory, with its pine tables and thistle arrangements. Run by Austrian-born Hermann and his Glaswegian wife, the brasserie has a loyal clientele of locals and returning visitors. The *Cullen skink* (an archetypal Scottish soup made with smoked fish and potato) and seared salmon fillet with pink-peppercorn sauce are delicious. ✉ *58 Broad St.* ☎ *01786/450632* 💳 *AE, MC, V.*

£ ✕ **Berties Restaurant.** Berties serves coffees and light lunches in the impressive Victorian-style Albert Halls, by the Rob Roy statue. Try the Brie melted over a bacon baguette, or salmon fish cakes with red-pepper coulis. In summer you can sit outside on the cobblestones; on Sunday local musicians play Scottish music. ✉ *Albert Halls, Dumbarton Rd.* ☎ *01786/473544* 💳 *MC, V* ⏲ *No dinner.*

££££–£££££ ✕🏨 **Stirling Highland Hotel.** The attractive 1854 building this hotel occupies was once the Old High School, and many original architectural features remain. Furnishings are old-fashioned, with solid wood, tartan, florals, and low-key, neutral color schemes. The modern-Scottish Scholars Restaurant offers outstanding seafood, game, and Aberdeen Angus beef. ✉ *Spittal St., FK8 1DU* ☎ *01786/272727* 📠 *01786/272829* 🌐 *www.paramount-hotels.co.uk* 🛏 *96 rooms* 👍 *Restaurant, pool, health club, sauna, bar, Internet, some pets allowed (fee); no a/c* 💳 *AE, DC, MC, V* 🍽 *BP.*

£££ ✕🏨 **Park Lodge Hotel.** A French family runs this elegant 18th-century establishment. The interior is all fanlights, antique furniture, and candles. The Heritage Restaurant (£££) serves prix-fixe dinners that typically include French classics such as *filet au poivre* (pepper beef steak) and *magret de canard* (duck breast). ✉ *32 Park Terr., FK8 2JS* ☎ *01786/474862* 📠 *01786/449748* 🌐 *www.parklodge.net* *10 rooms* *Restaurant, lounge, Internet, some pets allowed; no a/c* ▭ *MC, V* 🍽 *BP.*

£££ **Terraces Hotel.** This central hotel is in a compact Georgian town house. Each room is individually decorated with modern furniture, pastel walls, and striped upholstery. The restaurant (£££) serves a traditional Scottish prix-fixe meal; steak is a specialty. ✉ *4 Melville Terr., FK8 2ND* ☎ *01786/472268* 📠 *01786/450314* 🌐 *www.hotelnet.co.uk/terraceshotel* *17 rooms* *Restaurant, lounge, Internet; no a/c* ▭ *AE, DC, MC, V* 🍽 *BP.*

£–££ **Castlecroft.** Tucked beneath Stirling Castle, this warm and comfortable modern house is well situated for sightseeing in the Old Town, and it overlooks fine views of the plain of the River Forth toward the Highland hills. ✉ *Ballengeich Rd., FK8 1TN* ☎ *01786/474933* 📠 *01786/466716* *6 rooms* *Lounge, Internet, no-smoking rooms; no a/c, no room phones* ▭ *MC, V* 🍽 *BP.*

£ **Lochend Farm.** Extensive country views, wholesome farm cooking, and a pleasantly relaxing pace are the hallmarks of this peaceful working farm. Only 5 mi from the M9/M80, southwest of Stirling, it also makes a good touring base. The traditionally furnished—and very comfortable—bedrooms have sinks and share a bathroom. ✉ *Carronbridge, Denny, Stirlingshire FK6 5JJ* ☎ *01324/822778* 🌐 *www.lochendfarm.com* *2 rooms without bath* *Lounge, Internet; no a/c, no room phones, no smoking* ▭ *No credit cards* ⏲ *Closed Nov.–Mar.* 🍽 *BP.*

£ **Stirling Youth Hostel.** A former neoclassical church houses this hostel, with high-grade four- and six-bed rooms (and a few doubles) with in-room bath facilities. Use of the television room, the dining room, and the self-service, fully equipped kitchen is included in the bargain price of £11.50 (£12.75 in July and August) per person, including breakfast. ✉ *Erskine Marykirk, St. John's St., FK8 1EA* ☎ *01786/473442* 🌐 *www.syha.org.uk* *126 beds* *Dining room, lounge, shop, laundry facilities, Internet; no a/c, no room phones* ▭ *MC, V* 🍽 *BP.*

★ £ **West Plean.** This handsome rambling, early Georgian house is part of a working farm, with a walled garden and woodland walks. Well-prepared food and spacious rooms make this bed-and-breakfast an excellent bargain. ✉ *Denny Rd., FK7 8HA* ☎ *01786/812208* 📠 *01786/480550* ✉ *west.plean@virgin.net* *3 rooms* *Lounge, no-smoking rooms; no a/c* ▭ *No credit cards* ⏲ *Closed Dec.–Jan.* 🍽 *BP.*

The Arts

The **Macrobert Arts Centre** (✉ Stirling University ☎ 01786/466666 🌐 www.macrobert.stir.ac.uk) has a theater, art gallery, and studio with programs that range from films to pantomime.

Shopping

Though in a nondescript 1970s building, the downtown **Thistle Shopping Centre** nevertheless has a good selection of stores. Many locals travel to the nearby town of **Bridge of Allan,** which has interesting specialty shops, including **Glass Works** (✉ The Avenue ☎ no phone), for original glassware made on the premises, and **Fotheringham Gallery** (✉ The Avenue ☎ 01786/832861), for special gifts and paintings.

Ceramics

South of Stirling, at Larbert (and signposted off the A9), is **Barbara Davidson's pottery studio** (✉ Muirhall Farm ☎ 01324/554430), run by one of the best-known potters in Scotland, in an 18th-century farm setting. It's open from Monday to Saturday, 10 to 5. You can make an appointment to paint a pot, which will be glazed, fired, and mailed to you; and in July and August you can even try throwing your own pot.

Knitwear

East of Stirling is **Mill Trail** country, along the foot of the Ochil Hills. A leaflet from any local tourist information center will lead you to the delights of a real mill shop and low mill prices—even on cashmere—at Tillicoultry, Alva, and Alloa.

Scottish Specialties

House of Henderson (✉ 6– 8 Friars St. ☎ 01786/473681), a Highland outfitters, sells tartans, woolens, and accessories and offers a made-to-measure kilt service.

THE TROSSACHS & LOCH LOMOND

Immortalized by Wordsworth and Sir Walter Scott, the Trossachs (the name means "bristly country") may contain some of Scotland's loveliest forest, hills, and glens, well justifying the area's designation as country's first national park. The Trossachs has a very peculiar charm, for it combines the wildness of the Highlands with the prolific vegetation of an old Lowland forest. Its open ground is a dense mat of bracken and heather, and its woodland is of silver birch, dwarf oak, and hazel—trees that fasten their roots into the crevices of rocks and stop short on the very brink of lochs. The most colorful season is fall, particularly October, a lovely time when most visitors have departed and the hares, deer, and game birds have taken over. Even in rainy weather the Trossachs of "darksome glens and gleaming lochs" are memorable: the water filtering through the rocks comes out so pure and clear that the lochs are like sheets of crystal glass.

Dunblane

★ ⓳ *7 mi north of Stirling.*

The oldest part of Dunblane—with its twisting streets and lovely town houses—huddles around the square where the partly restored ruins of **Dunblane Cathedral** stand. Bishop Clement oversaw construction of the cathedral in the early 13th century on the site of St. Blane's tiny 8th-century cell. It is contemporary with the Borders abbeys but more mixed in its architecture—part early English and part Norman. Dunblane ceased to be a cathedral, as did most others in Scotland, at the time of the Reformation, in the mid-16th century. ☎ *0131/668–8800* 🌐 *www.historic-scotland.gov.uk* 🎫 *Free* 🕐 *Apr.–Sept., daily 9:30–6; Oct.–Mar., Mon.–Sat. 9:30–4, Sun. 2–4.*

Where to Stay & Eat

£££££ ✕🏨 **Cromlix House Hotel.** Cherished furniture and paintings, the original conservatory, and a library enhance the period atmosphere of this Victorian former hunting lodge. Food is served in two elegant, country-house-style dining rooms. Specialties include game and lamb from the hotel estate. Try the delicious confit of guinea fowl as a starter, followed by beef with pickled walnuts. ✉ *Kinbuck, on B8033, 3 mi northeast of Dunblane, FK15 9JT* ☎ *01786/822125* 📠 *01786/825450* 🌐 *www.cromlixhouse.com* 🛏 *6 rooms, 8 suites* 🛎 *Restaurant, tennis court, fishing, library, lounge, Internet, no-smoking rooms; no a/c* 💳 *AE, DC, MC, V* 🍽 *BP.*

Doune

20 *5 mi west of Dunblane.*

Fodor's Choice ★

The Highland-edge community of Doune was once a center for pistol making. No self-respecting Highland chief's attire was complete without a prestigious and ornate pair of pistols. Today Doune is more widely known for one of the best-preserved medieval castles in Scotland. **Doune Castle** looks like an early castle is supposed to look: grim and high-walled, with echoing, drafty stone vaults. Construction of the fortress began in the early 15th century on a now-peaceful riverside tract. The best place to photograph this squat, walled fort is from the bridge, a little way upstream, west on A84. The castle is signposted to the left as you enter the town from the Dunblane road. ✉ *Off A84* ☎ *0131/668–8800* 🌐 *www.historic-scotland.gov.uk* 🎫 *£2.80* ⏲ *Apr.–Sept., daily 9:30–6; Oct.–Mar., Mon.–Wed. and Sat. 9:30–4, Sun. 2–4.*

Callander

21 *8 mi northwest of Doune.*

A traditional Highland-edge resort, Callander bustles throughout the year, even during off-peak times, simply because it is a gateway to Highland scenery, and Loch Lomond and the Trossachs National Park. As a result, there's plenty of window-shopping here, plus nightlife in pubs and a good selection of accommodations.

Callander's **Rob Roy and Trossachs Visitor Centre** provides another encounter with the overly romanticized "tartan Robin Hood," Rob Roy MacGregor. A man of great physical strength and courageous energy, MacGregor is known as a defender of the downtrodden and scourge of authorities. He was, in fact, a medieval throwback, a cattle thief, an embezzler of lairds' rents, and the operator of a vicious protection racket among poor farmers. You can learn more about his high jinks from the high-tech account—replete with displays and tableaux—in the modern visitor center. Hollywood paid homage to this local folk legend with the 1995 film *Rob Roy,* starring actors Liam Neeson and Jessica Lange. The visitor center also provides information about the national park. ✉ *Ancaster Sq.* ☎ *01877/330342* 🌐 *www.visitscotland.com* 🎫 *£3.25* ⏲ *July–Aug., daily 9–6; Mar.–June and Sept.–Dec., daily 10–5; Jan.–Feb., weekdays 11–3, weekends 11–4.*

A walk is signposted from the east end of the main street to the **Bracklinn Falls,** over whose lip Sir Walter Scott once rode a pony to win a bet. It's a 1½-mi walk through the woods up to the **Callander Crags,** with views of the Lowlands as far as the Pentland Hills behind Edinburgh. The walk begins at the west end of the main street.

Where to Stay & Eat

£ ✕ **Pip's Coffee House.** Come to this cheerful little place just off the main street for light meals, soups, and salads, as well as exquisite Scottish home baking, including fresh scones daily. ✉ *Ancaster Sq.* ☎ *01877/330470* ⏲ *Closed Wed. Oct.–Feb.* 💳 *No credit cards.*

££££–£££££ ✕🏨 **Roman Camp.** This former hunting lodge, dating to 1625, has 20 acres of gardens with river frontage, yet it is within easy walking distance of Callander's town center. The antiques-filled sitting rooms and library are more reminiscent of a stately family home than a hotel. The restaurant has a good reputation for its salmon, trout, and other seafood, all cooked in an imaginative, modern Scottish style. Also delicious is the fillet of Scotch beef with an herb-potato scone and wild-mushroom mousseline. ✉ *Main St., Callander, Perthshire FK17 8BG* ☎ *01877/330003* 📠 *01877/331533*

Fodor's Choice ★

www.roman-camp-hotel.co.uk *11 rooms, 3 suites* *Restaurant, fishing, bar, lounge, library; no a/c* *AE, DC, MC, V* *BP.*

Sports & the Outdoors

HIKING **Wheels/Trossachs Backpackers** (Invertrossachs Rd. 01877/331100 www.scottish-cycling.co.uk) is a friendly firm that can help with route planning and also arranges organized walks, bike and canoe trips, and hostel accommodations.

GOLF **Callander golf course,** designed by Tom Morris in 1890, has fine views and a tricky moorland layout. Keep between the trees on the 15th hole and you may end up with a hole-in-one. *Aveland Rd., 01877/330090* *18 holes, 5,151 yards, par 66.*

Shopping

The **Edinburgh Woollen Mill Group** operates three mill shops in and near Callander. All the stores have a vast selection of woolens on display and will provide overseas mailing and tax-free shopping. *Callander Woollen Mill: 12–18 Main St. 01877/330273* *Kilmahog Woollen Mill: North of town at Trossachs Turning 01877/330268* *Trossachs Woollen Mill: North of town at Trossachs Turning 01877/330178.*

en route

Callander is the gateway to the Trossachs, but because it is on the main road, the A84, it also attracts overnight visitors on their way to Oban, Fort William, and beyond. All this traffic enters the proper Highlands just north of Callander, where the slopes squeeze both the road and rocky river into the narrow **Pass of Leny.** An abandoned railway—now a pleasant walking or bicycling path—also goes through the pass, past Ben Ledi and Loch Lubnaig.

Balquhidder Glen

22 *12 mi north of Callander.*

A 20-minute drive from Callander, through the Pass of Leny and beyond Strathyre, is Balquhidder Glen (pronounced *bal*-whidd-*er*), a typical Highland glen that runs westward. The glen has characteristics seen throughout the north: a flat-bottom U-shape profile, formed by prehistoric glaciers; extensive Forestry-Commission plantings replacing much of the natural woodlands above; a sprinkling of farms; and farther up the glen, hill roads bulldozed into the slopes to provide access for foresters. You may notice a boarded-up look of some of the area's houses, many of which are second homes for affluent residents of the south. The glen is also where Loch Voil and Loch Doune spread out, adding to the stunning vistas. This area is often known as the Braes (Slopes) of Balquhidder and was once the home of the MacLarens and the MacGregors. **Rob Roy MacGregor's** grave is signposted beside Balquhidder village. The site of his house, now a private farm, is beyond the parking lot at the end of the road up the glen. The glen has no through road, though there is a right-of-way (on foot) from the churchyard where Rob Roy is buried, through the plantings in Kirkton Glen and then on to open windy grasslands and a blue *lochan* (little lake). This path eventually drops into the next valley, Glen Dochart, and rejoins the A84.

The Trossachs

10 mi west of Callander.

With its harmonious scenery of hill, loch, and wooded slopes, the Trossachs has been a popular touring region since the late 18th century, at the dawn of the age of the Romantic poets. Influenced by the writings of Sir Walter Scott, early visitors who strayed into the Highlands from the central belt of Scotland admired this as the first "wild" part of Scotland they encountered. Perhaps because the Trossachs represent the very essence of what the Highlands are supposed to be, the whole of this area, including Loch Lomond, is now protected as a national park, Scotland's first. Here you'll find birch and pine forests, vistas down lochs where the woods creep right to the water's edge, and, in the background, peaks that rise high enough to be called mountains, though they're not as high as those to the north and west. The Trossachs are almost a Scottish visual cliché. They're popular right through the year, drawing not only first-time visitors from all around the world, but also Scots out for a Sunday drive.

23 The A821 runs west together with the first and gentlest of the Trossachs lochs, **Loch Venachar.** A sturdy gray-stone building, with a small dam at the Callander end, controls the water that feeds into the River Teith (and, hence, into the Forth). A few minutes after it passes Loch Venachar the A821 becomes muffled in woodlands and twists gradually down to the village of **Brig o' Turk.** (*Turk* is Gaelic for the Scots *tuirc,* meaning wild boar, a species that has been extinct in this region since about the 16th century.) ✉ *On A821.*

Loch Achray, stretching west of Brig o' Turk, dutifully fulfills expectations of what a verdant Trossachs loch should be: small, green, reedy meadows backed by dark plantations, rhododendron thickets, and lumpy, thickly covered hills. The parking lot by Loch Achray is the place to begin the ascent of steep, heathery **Ben An,** which affords some of the best Trossachs' views. The climb requires a couple of hours and good lungs. ✉ *On A821.*

★ 24 At the end of Loch Achray, a side road turns right into a narrow pass, leading to **Loch Katrine,** the heart of the Trossachs. During the time of Sir Walter Scott, the road here was narrow and almost hidden by the overhanging crags and mossy oaks and birches. Today it ends at a slightly anticlimactic parking lot with a shop, café, and visitor center. To see the finest of the Trossachs lochs properly, you must—even for just a few minutes—walk a bit farther along the level, paved road beyond the parking lot (open only to Strathclyde Water Board vehicles). Loch Katrine's water is taken by aqueduct and tunnel to Glasgow—a Victorian feat of engineering that has ensured the purity of the supply to Scotland's largest city for more than 100 years. The steamer **SS *Sir Walter Scott*** (☎ 01877/376316 💷 £6.80 morning, £5.80 afternoon) embarks on cruises of Loch Katrine during summer, leaving from Trossachs Pier. Take the cruise if time permits, as the shores of Katrine remain undeveloped and scenic. This loch is the setting of Scott's narrative poem, *The Lady of the Lake,* and Ellen's Isle is named after his heroine. ✉ *Off the A821* ☎ *01877/376316* 🌐 *www.lochkatrine.org.uk* ⏲ *Visitor center, Apr.–late-Oct., daily 9–5; Cruises, Apr.–late-Oct., Thurs.–Tues. at 11, 1:45, and 3:15, Wed. at 1:45 and 3:15.*

en route

For more exquisite nature viewing after your visit to Loch Katrine, drive back through the pass to the main A821 and turn right, heading south to higher moorland blanketed with conifer plantations—some of which have near-mature timber planted in the 1940s by the Forestry Commission. The conifers hem in the views of Ben Ledi and Ben Venue, which can be seen over the spiky green waves of trees as the road snakes around heathery knolls and hummocks. There's another viewing area, and a small parking lot, at the highest point of the road. Soon the road swoops off the Highland edge and leads downhill. Near the start of the descent, the **Queen Elizabeth Forest Park Visitor**

Centre can be seen on the left. The center has displays on the life of the forest, a summer-only café, some fine views over the Lowlands to the south, and a network of footpaths. The Trossachs end here.

Aberfoyle

㉕ *11 mi south of Loch Katrine, in the Trossachs.*

Aberfoyle has numerous souvenir shops and an attraction that appeals mainly to children. The **Scottish Wool Centre** tells the story of Scottish wool "from the sheep's back to your back." You can see live specimens of the main breeds in the sheep amphitheater and try your hand at spinning in the textile display area. In the Border collie training area, dogs in training to assist shepherds practice herding ducks. The shop stocks a huge selection of woolen garments and knitwear. ⊠ *Off Main St.* ☎ *01877/382850* ⊠ *£3* ☉ *Apr.–Sept., daily 9:30–6; Oct.–Dec. and Feb.–Mar., daily 10–5; Jan., daily 10–4:30.*

The tiny island of **Inchmahome**, on the Lake of Menteith, was a place of refuge in 1547 for the young Mary, Queen of Scots. ⊠ *Off the A81, 4 mi east of Aberfoyle.*

off the beaten path

ALONG THE B829 – From Aberfoyle you can take a trip to see the more enclosed northern portion of **Loch Lomond.** During the off-season the route has an untamed and windswept air when it extends beyond the shelter of trees. Take the B829 (signposted INVERSNAID and STRONACHLACHAR), which runs west from Aberfoyle and offers outstanding views of Ben Lomond, especially in the vicinity of Loch Ard. The next loch, where the road narrows and bends, is **Loch Chon**, which appears dark and forbidding. Its ominous reputation is further enhanced by the local legend: the presence of a dog-headed monster prone to swallowing passersby. Beyond Loch Chon, the road climbs gently from the plantings to open moor with a breathtaking vista over **Loch Arklet** to the Arrochar Alps, the name given to the high hills west of Loch Lomond. Hidden from sight in a deep trench, Loch Arklet is dammed to feed Loch Katrine. Go left at the road junction (a right will take you to the town of Stronachlachar) and take the open road along Loch Arklet. These deserted green hills were once the rallying grounds of the Clan Gregor. Near the dam on Loch Arklet, on your right, **Garrison Cottage** recalls the days when the government had to billet troops here to keep the MacGregors in order. From Loch Arklet the road zigzags down to **Inversnaid**, where you will see a hotel, house, and parking lot, with **Loch Lomond** stretching out of sight above and below. The only return to Aberfoyle is by retracing the same route.

Where to Stay & Eat

£££££ ✕🏨 **Macdonald Forest Hills Hotel.** A traditional-Scottish-country-house theme pervades this hotel, from the rambling white building itself to the wood-paneled lounges, log fires, and numerous sporting activities. More than 20 acres of gardens and grounds surround the building, which sits on a grassy hillside overlooking Loch Ard. Chintz drapes and reproduction antiques fill the bedrooms. The restaurant's tartan decor makes an appropriate backdrop for excellent Scottish cuisine—sometimes prepared with a Mediterranean touch. The menu emphasizes game, salmon, shellfish, and the best Scottish beef and lamb. ⊠ *Kinlochard, FK8 3TL* ☎ *01877/387277* 🖨 *01877/387307* ⊕ *www.foresthills-hotel.co.uk* ⇨ *56 rooms* ᣔ *Restaurant, tennis court, indoor pool, gym, sauna, bicycles, boating, fishing, horseback riding, children's programs (ages 5–12); no a/c, no children under 5* 🖃 *AE, DC, MC, V* ⊧◯⊧ *BP.*

Sports & the Outdoors

BIKING **Trossachs Cycle Hire** (✉ Trossachs Holiday Park ☎ 01877/382614 🌐 www.trossachsholidays.co.uk) rents out bicycles from March through October and will provide advice on what routes to take.

WALKING The long-distance walkers' route, the **West Highland Way,** which runs 95 mi from Glasgow to Fort William, follows the bank of Loch Lomond at Inversnaid, which you can reach from the B829. A brief stroll up the path is very pleasant, particularly if you're visiting during the spring, when birdsong fills the oak-tree canopy. You may get an inkling of why Scots wax so romantic about their bonnie, bonnie banks.

Drymen

26 *11 mi southwest of Aberfoyle.*

Drymen is a respectable and cozy town in the Lowland fields, with stores, tea shops, and pubs catering to the well-to-do Scots who have moved here from Glasgow. For the most outstanding Loch Lomond view from the south end, drive west from Drymen and take just a few minutes to clamber up bracken-covered **Duncryne Hill.** At dusk you may be rewarded by a spectacular sunset. You can't miss this distinctive dumpling-shape hill, south of Gartocharn on the Drymen–Balloch road, the A811.

Shopping

The Rowan Gallery (✉ 36 Main St. ☎ 01360/660996) displays original paintings and prints, and specializes in contemporary work by Scottish artists. Also here is a fine selection of ceramics, woodwork, cards, and jewelry.

Loch Lomond

27 *3 mi west of Drymen via B837, signposted* ROWARDENNAN *and* BALMAHA; *14 mi west of Aberfoyle.*

The upper portion of Loch Lomond, Scotland's largest loch in terms of surface area, is a sparkling ribbon of water snaking into the hills. Toward the south, the more yielding Lowlands allow the loch to spread out. Wooded islands, some of which can be visited, dot this portion of the loch. As you drive along the B837, you may notice Conic Hill, a wavy ridge of bald, heathery domes behind Balmaha. If you have a regional map, note how Inchcailloch and the other islands line up with Conic Hill. This geographic line is indicative of the Highland boundary fault, which runs through Loch Lomond and the hill.

Before starting your exploration of the loch, take time to visit **Loch Lomond Shores** at Balloch on the southern tip of the loch. Opened in 2002, this castle-like structure contains the **Loch Lomond and Trossachs National Park Gateway Centre,** your introduction to Scotland's first national park. A film about the area is shown, and there are shops, restaurants, slipways, and beaches. ✉ *Off A82, near Balloch* ☎ *01389/721500* 🌐 *www.lochlomondshores.com* 🕓 *Weekdays 11–5, weekends 11–6.*

At the little settlement of **Balmaha,** the versatile recreational role filled by Loch Lomond is clear: cruising craft are at the ready, hikers appear out of woodlands on the West Highland Way, and day-trippers stroll at the loch's edge. The heavily wooded offshore islands look alluringly close. One of the best ways to explore them is by taking a cruise or renting a boat. ✉ *On B837.*

The island of **Inchcailloch** (*inch* comes from *innis,* Gaelic for island), just offshore, can be explored in an hour or two. Pleasant pathways thread through oak woods planted in the 18th century, when the bark was used by the tanning industry. ✉ *On B837.*

Loch Lomond is seldom more than a narrow field's length away from the B837 as the road runs northwest to the town of **Rowardennan.** Where the drivable road ends, in a parking lot crunchy with pinecones, you can ramble along one of the marked loch-side footpaths or make your way toward Ben Lomond, 3½ mi away. ✉ *End of B837.*

Where to Stay & Eat

££££ Fodor'sChoice ★ **Cameron House.** This luxury hotel combines top-quality service with country-club facilities, all on the shores of Loch Lomond. Pastel shades and antique reproductions decorate the bedrooms. The outstanding restaurants serve excellent Scottish-French cuisine, such as poached salmon with hollandaise sauce. There's also a nautical-style diner called Breakers. ✉ *Loch Lomond, Alexandria, Dumbartonshire G83 8QZ ☎ 01389/755565 🖷 01389/759522 🌐 www.devereonline.co.uk/cameronhouse 96 rooms, 7 suites 3 restaurants, cable TV, 9-hole golf course, 2 tennis courts, 2 pools, hair salon, health club, hot tub, sauna, steam room, fishing, croquet, squash, bar, children's programs (ages 5–12); no a/c AE, DC, MC, V BP.*

Boat Tours

MacFarlane and Son (✉ Boatyard, Balmaha, Loch Lomond ☎ 01360/870214) runs cruises on Loch Lomond and rents rowboats and small powerboats to those who prefer to do their own exploring. From Tarbet, on the western shore, **Cruise Loch Lomond** (✉ Boatyard, Tarbet ☎ 01301/702356 🌐 www.cruiselochlomondltd.com) runs tours all year.

Shopping

At **Thistle Bagpipe Works** (✉ Luss, Dunbartonshire ☎ 01436/860250), on the western shore of Loch Lomond, you can commission your own made-to-order set of bagpipes. You can also order a complete Highland outfit, including kilt and jacket.

PERTHSHIRE

Although Perth has an ancient history dating to the Dark Ages, it has been rebuilt and recast innumerable times, and sadly, no trace remains of the pre-Reformation monasteries that once dominated the skyline. In fact, modern Perth has swept much of its colorful history under a grid of busy streets. The town serves a wide rural hinterland and has a well-off air, making it one of Scotland's most interesting shopping towns outside of Edinburgh and Glasgow.

Perth's rural hinterland is grand in several senses. On the Highland edge, prosperous-looking farms are scattered across heavily wooded countryside, and even larger properties are screened by trees and parkland. All this changes as the mountain barrier is penetrated, giving rise to grouse moors and deer forest (in this case, *forest* has the Scots meaning of, paradoxically, *open hill*). Parts of Perthshire are quite remote without ever losing their cozy feel.

Perth

28 *36 mi northeast of Stirling, 43 mi north of Edinburgh, 61 mi northeast of Glasgow.*

Perth has long been a focal point in Scottish history, and several critical events took place here, including the assassination of King James I of Scotland (1394–1437) and John Knox's (1514–72) preaching in St. John's Kirk in 1559. Later, the 17th-century religious wars in Scotland saw the town occupied, first by the marquis of Montrose (1612–50), then later by Oliver Cromwell's (1599–1658) forces. The Jacobites also occupied the town in the 1715 and 1745 rebellions.

Perth's attractions—with the exception of the shops—are scattered and take time to reach on foot. Some, in fact, are far enough away to necessitate the use of a car, bus, or taxi. A modest selection of castles is within easy reach of Perth.

The cruciform-plan **St. John's Kirk**, dating from the 12th century, was internally divided into three parts at the Reformation, but was restored to something closer to its medieval state by Sir Robert Lorimer in the 1920s. ✉ *St. John St.* ☎ *01738/626159* 🎫 *£1 donation* ⏲ *Weekdays 10–2 and 2–4, and for Sun. services.*

The **Perth Art Gallery and Museum** has a wide-ranging collection of natural history, local history, and archaeology exhibits. ✉ *78 George St.* ☎ *01738/632488* 🎫 *Free* ⏲ *Mon.–Sat. 10–5.*

On the North Inch of Perth, look for **Balhousie Castle** and the **Regimental Museum of the Black Watch.** Some will tell you the Black Watch was a Scottish regiment whose name is a reference to the color of its tartan. An equally plausible explanation, however, is that the regiment was established to keep an undercover watch on rebellious Jacobites. *Black* is the Gaelic word *dubh,* meaning, in this case, "hidden" or "covert," used in the same sense as the word *blackmail.* The castle is closed on the last Saturday in June. ✉ *Facing North Inch Park (entrance from Hay St.)* ☎ *0131/310–8530* 🎫 *Free* ⏲ *May–Sept., Mon.–Sat. 10–4:30; Oct.–Apr., weekdays 10–4.*

The Round House contains the **Fergusson Gallery,** displaying a selection of 6,000 works—paintings, drawings, and prints—by the Scottish artist J. D. Fergusson (1874–1961). ✉ *Marshall Pl.* ☎ *01738/441944* 🎫 *Free* ⏲ *Mon.–Sat. 10–5.*

Off the A9 west of town is **Caithness Glass,** where you can watch glass-workers creating silky-smooth bowls, vases, and other glassware. Also here are a small museum, restaurant, and shop. ✉ *Inveralmond* ☎ *01738/492320* 🎫 *Free* ⏲ *Factory weekdays 9–4:30. Shop Easter–Nov., Mon.–Sat. 9–5, Sun. 10–5; Dec.–Easter, Mon.–Sat. 9–5, Sun. noon–5.*

Huntingtower Castle, a curious double tower that dates from the 15th century, is associated with an attempt to wrest power from the young James VI in 1582. Some early painted ceilings survive, offering the vaguest hint of the sumptuous interiors, once found in many such ancient castles, that are now reduced to bare and drafty rooms. ✉ *Off A85* ☎ *0131/668–8800* 🌐 *www.historic-scotland.gov.uk* 🎫 *£2.20* ⏲ *Apr.–Sept., daily 9:30–6; Oct.–Mar., Mon.–Wed. and Sat. 9:30–4, Thurs. 9:30–noon, Sun. 2–4.*

Elcho Castle, a fortified mansion on the east side of Perth, is the abandoned 15th-century seat of the earls of Wemyss. All that remains is a shell. ✉ *On River Tay* ☎ *0131/668–8800* 🌐 *www.historic-scotland.gov.uk* 🎫 *£2.20* ⏲ *Apr.–Sept., daily 9:30–6; Oct.–Nov., daily 9:30–4.*

Fodor'sChoice ★

Scone Palace is much more cheerful and vibrant than Perth's other castles. The palace is the current residence of the earl of Mansfield but is open to visitors. Although it incorporates various earlier works, the palace today has mainly a 19th-century theme, with mock castellations that were fashionable at the time. There's plenty to see if you're interested in the acquisitions of an aristocratic Scottish family: magnificent porcelain, furniture, ivory, clocks, and 16th-century needlework. A coffee shop, restaurant, gift shop, and play area are on-site, and the extensive grounds have a pine plantation. The palace has its own mausoleum nearby, on the site of a long-gone abbey on **Moot Hill**, the ancient coronation place of the Scottish kings. To be crowned, they sat on the Stone of Scone, which was seized in 1296 by Edward I of England, Scotland's greatest enemy, and placed in the coronation chair at Westminster Abbey, in London. It was returned to Scotland in November 1996 and is now on view in Edinburgh Castle. Some Scots hint darkly that Edward was fooled by a substitution and that the real stone is hidden, waiting for Scotland to regain its independence. ✉ *Braemar Rd.* ☎ *01738/552300* 🌐 *www.scone-palace.co.uk* *£6.35* ⏲ *Apr.–Oct., daily 9:30–5:30; last admission at 4:45.*

Where to Stay & Eat

££–£££ ✕ **Parklands.** This top-quality hotel, a stylish Georgian town house overlooking lush woodland, is perhaps best known for its restaurant, Acanthus Restaurant and Colourist Bistro (££–£££), serving Scottish fish, game, and beef. A sense of elegance permeates the low-key, contemporary interior. ✉ *2 St. Leonard's Bank, PH2 8EB* ☎ *01738/622451* *01738/622046* *14 rooms* *2 restaurants; no a/c* *AE, DC, MC, V* *BP.*

★ **££** ✕ **Sunbank House Hotel.** A lesson in traditional style, this early Victorian gray-stone mansion in a fine residential area near Perth's Branklyn Gardens provides solid, unpretentious comforts along with great views over the River Tay and the city. The restaurant (££££) serves imaginatively prepared, Continental-style (with Italian overtones), prix-fixe dinners and specializes in locally raised meats and game. ✉ *50 Dundee Rd., PH2 7BA* ☎ *01738/624882* *01738/442515* 🌐 *www.sunbankhouse.com* *9 rooms* *Restaurant, lounge, no-smoking rooms; no a/c* *MC, V* *BP.*

Nightlife & the Arts

The Victorian **Perth Repertory Theatre** (✉ 185 High St. ☎ 01738/621031) stages plays and musicals. In the summer it's the main venue for the Perth Festival of the Arts. The **Perth City Hall** (✉ King Edward St. ☎ 01738/624055) hosts musical performances of all types.

Shopping

CLOTHING **C & C Proudfoot** (✉ 104 South St. ☎ 01738/632483) sells a comprehensive selection of sheepskins, leather jackets, rugs, slippers, and handbags.

GLASS & CHINA Perth is an especially popular hunting ground for china and glass. **Caithness Glass** (✉ Inveralmond, off A9 at northern town boundary ☎ 01738/492320) sells all types of glassware in its factory shop. **Watson of Perth** (✉ 163–167 High St. ☎ 01738/639861) has sold exquisite bone china and cut crystal since 1900 and can pack your purchase for shipment overseas.

JEWELRY & ANTIQUES Perth proffers an unusual buy: Scottish freshwater pearls from the River Tay, in delicate settings, some of which take their theme from Scottish flowers. The Romans coveted these pearls. If you do, too, then you can make your choice at **Cairncross Ltd., Goldsmiths** (✉ 18 St. John's St. ☎ 01738/624367), where you can also admire a display of some of the more unusual shapes and colors of pearls. Antique jewelry and silver, including a few Scottish items, can be found at **Timothy Hardie** (✉ 25 St. John's St. ☎ 01738/633127). **Whispers of the Past** (✉ 15 George St. ☎ 01738/635472) has a collection of jewelry, linens, and other items.

Dunkeld

29 *14 mi north of Perth.*

Thomas Telford's sturdy river bridge of 1809 carries the road into the town of Dunkeld. Here, the National Trust for Scotland not only cares for grand mansions and wildlands but also actively restores smaller properties. The effects of its Little Houses project can be seen in the square off the main street, opposite the fish-and-chips shop. All the houses on the square were rebuilt after the 1689 defeat of the Jacobite army here, which occurred after its early victory in the Battle of Killiecrankie.

At **Loch of Lowes,** a Scottish Wildlife Trust reserve near Dunkeld, the domestic routines of the osprey, one of Scotland's conservation success stories, can be observed in relative comfort. ✉ *Off A923, about 2 mi northeast of Dunkeld* ☎ *01350/727337* ⌚ *Apr.–Sept., daily 10–5.*

Shopping

Dunkeld Antiques (✉ Tay Terr. ☎ 01350/728832), facing the river as you cross the bridge, stocks mainly 18th- and 19th-century items, from large furniture to ornaments, books, and prints. At the **Jeremy Law of Scotland's Highland Horn and Deerskin Centre** (✉ City Hall, Atholl St. ☎ 01350/727569), you can purchase stag antlers and cow horns shaped into walking sticks, cutlery, and tableware. Deerskin shoes and moccasins, small leather goods made from deerskin, and a specialty malt-whisky collection of more than 200 different malts are also sold. The center has a worldwide postal service and a tax-free shop.

Pitlochry

30 *15 mi north of Dunkeld.*

A typical central Highland resort, always full of hustle and bustle, Pitlochry has wall-to-wall souvenir and gift shops, large hotels, and a mountainous golf course. Most Scottish dams have salmon passes or ladders of some kind, enabling the fish to swim upstream to their spawning grounds. In Pitlochry, the **Pitlochry Dam and Fish Ladder,** just behind the main street, leads into a glass-paneled pipe that allows the fish to observe the visitors.

If you have a whisky-tasting bent visit **Edradour Distillery,** which claims to be the smallest single-malt distillery in Scotland (but then, so do others). ✉ *2½ mi east of Pitlochry* ☎ *01796/472095* 💳 *Free* ⌚ *Tours Mar.–Oct., Mon.–Sat. 9:30–5, Sun. noon–5; Nov.–Dec., Mon.–Sat. 10–4.*

The **Linn of Tummel** (🌐 www.nts.org.uk), a series of marked walks along the river and through tall, mature woodlands, is a little north of Pitlochry. Above the Linn, the A9 rises on stilts and gives an exciting view of the ★ valley. The **Pass of Killiecrankie,** set among the oak woods and rocky river just north of the Linn of Tummel, was the site of a famous battle won by the Jacobites in 1689. The National Trust for Scotland's **visitor center** at Killiecrankie explains the significance of this battle, which was the first attempt to restore the Stewart monarchy. The battle was noted for the death of the central Jacobite leader, John Graham of Claverhouse (1649–89), also known as Bonnie Dundee, who was hit by a stray bullet. The rebellion fizzled after Claverhouse's death. ✉ *Off A9, 4 mi north of Pitlochry* ☎📠 *01796/473233* 🌐 *www.nts.org.uk* 💳 *£2* ⌚ *Site year-round, daily; visitor center Apr.–June and Sept.–Oct., daily 10–5:30; July–Aug., daily 9:30–6.*

off the beaten path

LOCH RANNOCH – With its shoreline of birch trees framed by dark pines, this is the quintessential Highland loch. Fans of Robert Louis Stevenson (1850–94), especially of *Kidnapped* (1886), will not want to miss the last, lonely section of road. Stevenson describes the setting: "The mist rose and died away, and showed us that country lying as waste as the sea; only the moorfowl and the peewees crying upon it, and far over to the east a herd of deer, moving like dots.

Much of it was red with heather, much of the rest broken up with bogs and hags and peaty pools." Apart from the blocks of alien conifer plantings in certain places, little here has changed. To reach the lake, take the B8019 at the Linn of Tummel north of Pitlochry. Travel west past the Queen's View scenic lookout at the east end of Loch Tummel. At the Tummel Bridge, pick up the B846, which travels along the shores of Loch Rannoch. ✉ *Off B846, 20 mi west of Pitlochry.*

Nightlife & the Arts

Pitlochry Festival Theatre (☎ 01796/484626 for box office, 01796/484600 for general inquiries 🌐 www.pitlochry.org.uk), open May through October, presents six plays each season and hosts eight Sunday concerts.

Blair Castle

31 *10 mi north of Pitlochry.*

Fodor's Choice ★

Thanks to its historic contents and its war-torn past, Blair Castle is one of Scotland's most highly rated sights. The turreted white castle was home to successive dukes of Atholl and their families, the Murrays, until the death of the 10th duke. One of the castle's many fascinating details is a preserved piece of floor still bearing marks of the red-hot shot fired through the roof during the 1745 Jacobite rebellion—the last occasion in Scottish history that a castle was besieged. The castle holds not only military artifacts—historically, the duke was allowed to keep a private army, the Atholl Highlanders—but also a fine collection of furniture and paintings. Outside is a Victorian walled garden. ✉ *From Pitlochry take the A9 to Blair Atholl and follow signs* ☎ *01796/481207* 🌐 *www.blair-castle.co.uk* 🎫 *£6.50* ⏲ *Apr.–Oct., daily 9:30–5 (last admission at 4).*

Shopping

The **House of Bruar** (✉ on the A9 just north of Blair Atholl ☎ 01796/483236) is an Aladdin's cave for shopaholics who love top-quality Scottish clothing, crystal and glassware, and decorative items. There's also a good restaurant.

Aberfeldy

15 mi southwest of Pitlochry; 25 mi southwest of Blair Castle.

The sleepy town of Aberfeldy is a popular tourist base. Aberfeldy Bridge (1733), with five arches and a humpback, was designed by William Adam

32 (1689–1748). **Castle Menzies,** a 16th-century fortified tower house, contains the **Clan Menzies Museum,** which displays many relics of the clan's history. The castle stands west of Aberfeldy, on the opposite bank of the River Tay. ✉ *Off B846* ☎ *01887/820982* 🎫 *£3.50* ⏲ *Apr.–mid-Oct., Mon.–Sat. 10:30–5, Sun. 2–5; last admission at 4:30.*

33 **Glen Lyon,** just a few miles away from Aberfeldy, is one of central Scotland's most attractive glens; it has a rushing river, forests, high hills on both sides, prehistoric sites (complete with legendary tales), and the typical *big hoose* (big house) hidden on private grounds. There's even a dam at the head of the loch, a reminder that little of Scotland's scenic beauty is unadulterated. You can reach the glen by a high road from Loch Tay: take the A827 to Fearnan, then turn north to Fortingall. The **Fortingall yew,** in the churchyard near the Fortingall Hotel, wearily rests its great limbs on the ground. This tree is thought to be more than 3,000 years old. Legend has it that Pontius Pilate was born beside it, during the time

his father was serving as a Roman legionnaire in Scotland. After viewing the yew, turn west into Glen Lyon. ✉ *Off A827, 15 mi from Aberfeldy via Fortingall and Fearnan.*

off the beaten path

THE SCOTTISH CRANNOG CENTRE – Here's your chance to travel back 5,000 years to a time when the local inhabitants of this area, in common with others across Scotland and Ireland, started building defensive homesteads, known as *crannogs,* on wooden piles standing in lochs. They were approachable only by narrow bridges that could be easily defended. This practice continued until as late as the 17th century. Archaeologists have found many remains of crannogs in lochs throughout Scotland. One of the best-preserved was found several feet under the surface of Loch Tay, off the north shore at Fearnan, and it's now possible to visit an accurate replica built on the south shore. An exhibition gives details about crannog construction and the way of life in and around crannogs. The Crannog Centre is just west of Aberfeldy, on the southern shore of Loch Tay. ✉ *Kenmore, South Loch Tay* ☎ *01887/830583* 🌐 *www.crannog.co.uk* 🎫 *£4.25* ⏲ *Mid-Mar.–Oct., daily 10–5:30; Nov., daily 10–4; last entry one hr before closing.*

Boating

Loch Tay Boating Centre (✉ Pier Rd., Kenmore ☎ 01887/830291) rents cabin cruisers, speedboats, fishing boats, and canoes. It's open from April through mid-October daily from 9 to 7 PM.

en route

Between Aberfeldy and Killin, take the north-bank road by Loch Tay, the A827, which affords fine views west along the loch toward the mountains Ben More and Stobinian and north to Ben Lawers.

Killin

34 *24 mi southwest of Aberfeldy, 39 mi north of Stirling, 45 mi west of Perth.*

A village with an almost alpine flavor, known for its modest but surprisingly diverse selection of crafts and woolen wares, Killin is also noted for its scenery. The **Falls of Dochart,** white-water rapids overlooked by a pine-clad islet, are at the west end of the village. ✉ *Off A827.*

The **Breadalbane Folklore Centre,** by the Falls of Dochart, focuses on the area's heritage and folk tales. The most curious of these are the "Healing Stones of St. Fillan"—water-worn stones that have been looked after lovingly for centuries for their supposed curative powers. ✉ *Off A827* ☎ *01567/820254* 🎫 *£2* ⏲ *Mar.–May and Oct., daily 10–5; June and Sept., daily 10–6; July–Aug., daily 9:30–6:30.*

Across the River Dochart and near the golf course sit the ruins of **Finlarig Castle,** built by Black Duncan of the Cowl, a notorious Campbell laird. The castle can be visited at any time. ✉ *Off A827.*

Where to Stay & Eat

£–££ ✕🏨 **Lodge House.** Few other guest houses in Scotland can match the mountain views from this 100-year-old property; it's certainly worth the short drive 15 mi west from Killin to Crianlarich. Informal and cozy, the guest house is successful thanks to what the Scots call good "crack"—conviviality, in this case between host and guests. The food is good Scots fare: haggis, salmon, and oatcakes; and it's a good value at £15 for a prix-fixe four-course dinner. The bedrooms are plain and unfussy, but more than adequate. You may wish to walk along the riverbank after dinner, or have a wee dram in the tiny bar instead. ✉ *Crianlarich, Perthshire FK20 8RU* ☎ *01838/300276* 🌐 *www.lodgehouse.co.uk* 🛏 *6 rooms* ♨ *No a/c, no room phones, no smoking* 💳 *MC, V* 🍽 *BP.*

Biking

If you want to explore the north end of the Glasgow–Killin cycleway, rent a mountain bike from **Killin Outdoor Centre and Mountain Shop** (✉ Main St. ☎ 01567/820652 🌐 www.killinoutdoor.co.uk). Also available are canoes, crampons, skis, and ice axes.

5

en route

Southwest of Killin the A827 joins the main A85. By turning south over the watershed, you will see fine views of the hill ridges behind Killin. The road leads into **Glen Ogle,** "amid the wildest and finest scenery we had yet seen . . . putting one in mind of prints of the Khyber Pass," as Queen Victoria (1819–1901) recorded in her diary when she traveled this way in 1842.

Crieff

35 *25 mi southwest of Killin.*

The hilly town of Crieff offers walks with Highland views from **Knock Hill** above the town. Signs point the way there from Crieff's center. If you wish to discover the delights of whisky distilling, sign up for the **Famous Grouse Experience** at the Glenturret Distillery. A guide takes you through the distillery and to the Pavilion Bar where you can have a glass of Famous Grouse Finest and try your skill at "nosing." The finale comprises two films, one about what makes Famous Grouse such distinctive whisky, the other an interactive "Flight of the Famous Grouse over Scotland." You might cap your tour with lunch or dinner at either of the two Scottish restaurants. Signs lead to the distillery on the west side of the town. ✉ *The Hosh, off A822* ☎ *01764/656565* 🌐 *www.famousgrouse.co.uk/experience* 🎫 *£6* ⏲ *July–Aug., daily 9–6:30 (last tour 5); Sept.–June, daily 9–6 (last tour 4:30).*

Just south of Crieff is a glass paperweight manufacturer, part of a complex called the **Crieff Visitors Centre.** Adjacent to the complex are a small pottery factory, a restaurant, and a shop, where you can purchase Thistle hand-painted pottery and intricate millefiori, among other things. ✉ *A822, ½ mi south of Crieff* ☎ *01764/654014* 🎫 *Free* ⏲ *Apr.–Oct., daily 9–5:30; Nov.–Mar., daily 9–5.*

Drummond Castle Garden is a very large, formal Victorian parterre celebrating family and Scottish heraldry. The flower beds are planted and trimmed in the shapes of various heraldic symbols, such as a lion rampant and a checkerboard, associated with the coat of arms of the family who own the castle and the Scottish Royal Coat of Arms. It's regarded as one of the finest of its kind in Europe, and it even made an appearance in the film *Rob Roy.* ✉ *Off A822, 6 mi southwest of Crieff* ☎ *01764/681257* 🎫 *£3.50* ⏲ *Easter weekend and May–Oct., daily 2–6; last admission at 5.*

Shopping

Crieff is a center for china and glassware, which you can purchase along with pottery at the **Crieff Visitors Centre** (✉ A822 ☎ 01764/654014), ½ mi south of town. **Stuart Crystal** (✉ Muthill Rd. ☎ 01764/654004), a factory shop, sells not only its own Stuart crystal but also Waterford, Dartington, and Wedgwood wares.

Auchterarder

36 *11 mi southeast of Crieff.*

Famous for the Gleneagles Hotel and nearby golf courses, Auchterarder also has a flock of tony antiques shops to amuse Gleneagles's golf widows and widowers.

Where to Stay & Eat

★ £££££ **Auchterarder House Hotel.** This secluded and richly furnished Victorian country mansion has a plush dining room filled with glittering glassware; it's an appropriate setting for the unusual and creative presentation of local foods. *On B8062 at Auchterarder, 15 mi southwest of Perth, PH3 1DZ 01764/663646 01764/662939 www.auchterarderhouse.com 15 rooms Dining room, golf privileges, croquet, lounge; no a/c AE, DC, MC, V BP.*

£££££ Fodor'sChoice ★ **Gleneagles Hotel.** One of Britain's most famous hotels, Gleneagles is the very essence of modern grandeur. Like a vast, secret palace, it stands hidden in breathtaking countryside amid world-famous golf courses. Recreation facilities are nearly endless: four restaurants, a shopping arcade, a spa, the Gleneagles Equestrian Centre, the Falconry Centre, and more, all of which make a stay here a luxurious and unforgettable experience. *Auchterarder, near Perth, PH3 1NF 01764/662231 01764/662134 www.gleneagles.com 216 rooms, 13 suites 4 restaurants, room service, in-room data ports, minibars, cable TV, 3 18-hole golf courses, 9-hole golf course, 5 tennis courts, pro shop, 2 indoor pools, gym, hot tub, outdoor hot tub, sauna, spa, steam room, fishing, bicycles, horseback riding, squash, children's programs (ages 4–10), concierge, Internet; no a/c AE, DC, MC, V BP.*

THE CENTRAL HIGHLANDS A TO Z

To research prices, get advice from other travelers, and book travel arrangements, visit www.fodors.com.

AIR TRAVEL

Perth and Stirling can be reached easily from the Edinburgh, Dundee, and Glasgow airports by train, car, or bus.

BUS TRAVEL

A good network of buses connects with the central belt via Edinburgh and Glasgow. For more information contact Scottish Citylink or National Express. The Perth and Kinross Council supplies a map showing all public transport routes in Perthshire, marked with nearby attractions. This map can be obtained from any tourist information center in Perthshire.

The following companies organize reliable service on routes throughout the Central Highlands: First Ltd., Scottish Citylink, and Stagecoach.

First Ltd Goosecroft Rd. bus station, Stirling 01324/613777. **National Express** 08705/808080 www.gobycoach.com. **Scottish Citylink** Leonard St. bus station, Perth 08705/505050 www.citylink.co.uk. **Stagecoach** Ruthvenfield Rd., Inveralmond Industrial Estate, Perth 01738/629339.

CAR RENTAL

Agencies **Arnold Clark** St. Leonard's Bank, Perth 01738/638511. **Avis** Texaco Service Station, Bannockburn Rd., Stirling 01786/816828 www.avis.co.uk. **Europcar** 26 Glasgow Rd., Perth 01738/636888 www.europcar.com.

CAR TRAVEL

You'll find easy access to the area from the central belt of Scotland via the motorway network. The M9 runs within sight of the walls of Stirling Castle, and Perth can be reached via the M90 over the Forth Bridge. Two signed touring routes are useful: the Perthshire Tourist Route, and the Deeside Tourist Route, with a spectacular journey via Blairgowrie and Glenshee to Deeside and Aberdeen. Local tourist information centers can supply maps of these routes.

visitscotland ✉ Box 121, Livingston EH54 8AF ☎ 0845/225-5121 or 01506/832121 from outside the United Kingdom 🌐 www.visitscotland.com.

EMERGENCIES

In case of an emergency, dial **999** to reach an ambulance or the police or fire departments (no coins are needed for emergency calls from phone booths). If you need to see a doctor or dentist, ask for recommendations from the nearest tourist information center, your hotel receptionist, or B&B host. Late-night pharmacies are found only in the larger towns and cities. In an emergency the police will help you find a pharmacist.

Hospitals **Perth Royal Infirmary** ✉ Taymount Terr., Perth ☎ 01738/623311. **Stirling Royal Infirmary** ✉ Livilands Gate, Stirling ☎ 01786/434000. **Vale of Leven Hospital** ✉ Main St., Alexandria ☎ 01389/754121.

TOURS

The bus companies listed under ⇨ Bus Travel run a number of general orientation tours. The nearest visitor center is your best source for contacts and reservations. Don't miss the opportunity to take a boat trip on a loch, especially in the Trossachs (Loch Katrine) and Loch Lomond; consult a visitor center for details.

TRAIN TRAVEL

The Central Highlands are linked to Edinburgh and Glasgow by rail, with through routes to England (some direct-service routes from London take fewer than five hours). Several Savers ticket options are available, although in some cases on the ScotRail system, the discount fares must be purchased before your arrival in the United Kingdom. Contact National Rail or ScotRail for details.

The West Highland Line runs through the western portion of the area. Services also run to Stirling, Dunblane, Perth, and Gleneagles; stops on the Inverness–Perth line include Dunkeld, Pitlochry, and Blair Atholl.

National Rail ☎ 08457/484950 🌐 www.railtrack.co.uk. **ScotRail** ☎ 08457/550033 🌐 www.scotrail.co.uk.

VISITOR INFORMATION

The tourist offices listed below are open year-round. Seasonal tourist information centers are also open (generally from April to October) in the following towns: Aberfoyle, Balloch, Callander, Drymen, Dunblane, Helensburgh, Killin, Pirnhall, Tarbet, and Tyndrum.

Aberfeldy ✉ The Square ☎ 01887/820276 🌐 www.perthshire.co.uk. **Alva** ✉ Mill Trail Visitor Centre, W. Stirling St. ☎ 08707/200605. **Auchterarder** ✉ 90 High St. ☎ 01764/663450 🌐 www.perthshire.co.uk. **Blairgowrie** ✉ 26 Wellmeadow ☎ 01250/872960 🌐 www.perthshire.co.uk. **Crieff** ✉ Town Hall, High St. ☎ 01764/652578 🌐 www.perthshire.co.uk. **Dumbarton** ✉ A82 north-bound ☎ 08707/200612. **Dunkeld** ✉ The Cross ☎ 01350/727688 🌐 www.perthshire.co.uk. **Falkirk** ✉ 2/4 Glebe St. ☎ 08707/200614. **Kinross** ✉ Heart of Scotland Visitor Centre, Service Area Junction 6 M90 ☎ 01577/863680 🌐 www.perthshire.co.uk. **Loch Lomond & the Trossachs National Park Gateway Centre** ✉ Loch Lomond Shores, near Balloch ☎ 08707/200631 **Perth** ✉ Lower City Mills, W. Mill St. ☎ 01738/450600 🌐 www.perthshire.co.uk. **Pitlochry** ✉ 22 Atholl Rd. ☎ 01796/472215 🌐 www.perthshire.co.uk. **Stirling** ✉ 41 Dumbarton Rd. ☎ 08707/200620 ✉ Royal Burgh of Stirling Visitor Centre, Castle Esplanade ☎ 08707/200622 🌐 www.visitscottishheartlands.org.

ABERDEEN & THE NORTHEAST

6

FODOR'S CHOICE

King's College, *in Aberdeen*
Marcliffe at Pitfodels, *near Aberdeen*
Silver Darling, *in Aberdeen*

HIGHLY RECOMMENDED

RESTAURANTS
Old Monastery, *near Buckie*

HOTELS
Academy House, *in Fordyce*
Kildrummy Castle Hotel, *near Alford*
Minmore House, *in Glenlivet*

SIGHTS
Craigievar Castle, *near Alford*
Cullen, *near Findochty*
Dufftown, *in Speyside*
Elgin Cathedral, *in Elgin*
Glenlivet, *near Aberlour*
Glen Muick, *near Ballater*
Haddo House, *near Ellon*
Kildrummy Castle, *near Alford*
Marischal College, *in Aberdeen*
Provost Ross's House, *in Aberdeen*

By Gilbert Summers
Updated by Beth Ingpen

HERE, IN THIS GRANITE SHOULDER of Grampian, are Royal Deeside, the countryside that Queen Victoria made her own; the Castle Country route, where fortresses stand hard against the hills; and the Malt Whisky Trail, where peaty streams embrace the country's greatest concentration of distilleries. The region's gateway is the city of Aberdeen, constructed of granite and now aglitter with new wealth and new blood drawn together by North Sea oil.

Because of its isolation, Aberdeen has historically been a fairly autonomous place. Even now it's perceived by many U.K. inhabitants as lying almost out of reach in the northeast. In reality, it's only 90 minutes' flying time from London or a little more than two hours by car from Edinburgh. Its magnificent, confident 18th- and early 19th-century city center amply rewards exploration, and there are also many surviving buildings from earlier centuries for you to seek out. Yet even if Aberdeen vanished from the map, an extensive portion of the northeast would still remain at the top of many travelers' wish lists, studded as it is with some of Scotland's most enduring travel icons.

Some credit Sir Walter Scott with having opened up Scotland for tourism through his poems and novels. Others say General Wade did it when he built the Highland roads. But it was probably Queen Victoria who gave Scottish tourism its real momentum when, in 1842, she first came to Scotland and when, in 1847—on orders of a doctor, who thought the relatively dry climate of upper Deeside would suit her—she bought Balmoral. At first sight she described it as "a pretty little castle in the old Scottish style." The pretty little castle was knocked down to make room for a much grander house in full-flown Scottish baronial style, designed, in fact, by her husband, Prince Albert. Before long the entire Deeside and the region north were dotted with handsome country houses and mock-baronial châteaux, as the ambitious rich thought it wise to stake a claim in the neighborhood. The locals, bless 'em, took it all in stride. To this day, the hundreds who line the road when the queen and her family arrive for services at the family's parish church at Crathie are invariably visitors to Deeside—one of Balmoral's great attractions for the monarch has always been the villagers' respect for royal privacy.

Balmoral is merely the most famous castle in the area. There are so many others that in one part of the region a Castle Trail has been established, leading you to such fortresses as the ruined medieval Kildrummy Castle, which once controlled the strategic routes through the valley of the River Don. Later structures, such as Craigievar, a narrow-turreted castle resembling an illustration from a fairy-tale book, reflect the changing times of the 17th century, when defense became less of a priority. Later still, grand mansions such as Haddo House, with its symmetrical facade and elegant interior, surrender any defensive role entirely and instead make statements about their owner's status.

A trail leading to a more ephemeral kind of pleasure can be found south of Elgin and Banff, where the glens embrace Scotland's greatest concentration of malt-whisky distilleries. With so many in Morayshire, where the distilling is centered in the valley of the River Spey and its tributaries, there's now a Whisky Trail. Follow it to experience a surprising wealth of flavors, considering that whisky is made of three basic ingredients.

The Northeast's chief attraction lies in the gradual transition from high mountain plateau—by a series of gentle steps through hill, forest, and farmland—to the Moray Firth and North Sea coast, where the word "unadulterated" is redefined. Here you'll find some of the United Kingdom's most perfect wild shorelines, both sandy and sheer cliff. The Grampian Mountains, to the west, contain some of the highest ground in the nation, in the area of the Cairngorms. In recognition of this area's very special nature, Cairngorms National Park (Scotland's second, after Loch Lomand and the Trossachs National Park) was created in early 2003. The Grampian hills also have shaped the character of the folk who live in the northeast. In earlier times the massif made communication with the south somewhat difficult. As a result, native northeasterners still speak the richest Lowland Scottish.

Exploring Aberdeen & the Northeast

Once you have spent time in Aberdeen, you may be inclined to venture west into Deeside, with its royal connections and looming mountain backdrop, and then pass over the hills into the Castle Country to the north. You might head farther west to touch on Speyside and the Whisky Trail, before meandering back east and south along the pristine coastline at Scotland's northeasternmost tip.

About the Restaurants & Hotels

The northeast has some splendid country hotels with log fires and old Victorian furnishings, where you can also be sure of eating well. Many hotels in Aberdeen offer competitive rates on weekends. Partly in response to the demands of spendthrift oilmen, restaurants have cropped up all over Aberdeen, and the quality of the food improves yearly.

WHAT IT COSTS In Pounds

	£££££	££££	£££	££	£
RESTAURANTS	over £22	£18–£22	£13–£17	£7–£12	under £7
HOTELS	over £150	£110–£150	£80–£110	£50–£80	under £50

Restaurant prices are for a main course at dinner. Hotel prices are for two people in a standard double room in high season. All prices include the 17.5% VAT.

Timing

Because the National Trust for Scotland tends to close its properties in winter, many of the northeast's castles are not suitable for off-season travel, though you can always see them from the outside. Duff House, Macduff Marine Aquarium, and some of the distilleries are open much of the year, but May and June are probably the best times to visit.

ABERDEEN, THE SILVER CITY

In the 18th century local granite quarrying produced a durable silver stone that would be used boldly in the glittering blocks, spires, columns, and parapets of Victorian-era Aberdonian structures. The city remains one of the United Kingdom's most distinctive, although some would say it depends on the weather and the brightness of the day. The mica chips embedded in the rock look like a million mirrors in the sunshine. In rain and heavy clouds, however, their sparkle is snuffed out.

The North Sea has always been important to Aberdeen. In the 1850s the city was famed for its sleek, fast clippers that sailed to India for cargoes of tea. In the late 1960s the course of Aberdeen's history was unequivocally altered when oil and gas were discovered offshore, sparking rapid growth and further industrialization.

Exploring Aberdeen

Aberdeen centers on Union Street, with its many fine survivors of the Victorian and Edwardian streetscape. Old Aberdeen is very much a separate area of the city, north of the modern center and clustered around

Although the Grampian area isn't huge, it has many different terrains. To get a real flavor of this most authentic of Scottish regions, sample both the coastline and the mountains.

Numbers in the text correspond to numbers in the margin and on the Royal Deeside, Aberdeen, and the Northeast maps.

If you have 3 days

Setting out from **Aberdeen** 1–20, follow in the footsteps of Queen Victoria and tour the castles and glens of Royal Deeside. Head for **Crathes Castle** 22 and **Banchory** 23, with its largely unchanged Victorian High Street. After lunch follow the river upstream to Aboyne, turning north on B9094, then left onto B9119 for 6 mi for a panorama (signposted on B9119) known as the Queen's View, a bit north of Dinnet. Then continue on B9119, dropping gently downhill through the birch woods to A93 and **Ballater** 26, to the west. The next morning visit Her Majesty's **Balmoral Castle** 27 (note that it's open only for three months in the summer)—explore the ballroom and grounds, take a pony ride, and then treat yourself to a walk in nearby Glen Muick. Here you'll find the famous climb of Lochnagar, so beloved by Victoria. Overnight in **Braemar.** The next morning set off for Castle Country and some serious castle hopping—**Corgarff Castle** 29, **Kildrummy Castle** 30, **Craigievar Castle** 32, and **Castle Fraser** 33—before returning to Aberdeen.

If you have 5 days

Downtown **Aberdeen's** 1–20 silver granite certainly deserves two days. Then travel into Speyside to visit distilleries in **Dufftown** 34, **Craigellachie** 35, **Aberlour** 36, and **Elgin** 40. Spend a morning exploring Elgin before moving east along the coast to stay overnight in **Fordyce** 45. Visit the magnificent Duff House gallery in **Banff** 46 before returning to Aberdeen. On the last day see a castle or two: **Drum** 21 or **Crathes** 22, in Deeside; **Haddo House** 48 or **Fyvie Castle** 47, northwest of **Ellon** 49; or loop northwestward for **Corgarff** 29, the ruined castle at **Kildrummy** 30, fairy-tale **Craigievar** 32, or **Castle Fraser** 33.

St. Machar's Cathedral and the many fine buildings of the University of Aberdeen.

a good tour

Start your walk at the east end of **Union Street** 1. Here within the original old town is the Castlegate. The actual castle once stood somewhere behind the Salvation Army Citadel (1896), an imposing baronial granite tower whose design was inspired by Balmoral Castle. On the north side of Castle Street stands the 17th-century **Tolbooth** 2, a reminder of Aberdeen's earliest days. The impressive **Mercat Cross** 3 is just beyond King Street. Turn north down Broad Street to reach **Marischal College** 4, whose sparkling granite frontage dominates the top end of the street.

A survivor from an earlier Aberdeen can be found opposite Marischal College, beyond the concrete supports of St. Nicholas House (which houses the tourist information center): **Provost Skene's House** 5 was once part of a closely packed area of town houses and is now a museum portraying civic life. Just around the corner on Upperkirkgate, at the lowest point, are two modern shopping malls—the St. Nicholas Centre on the left, the Bon-Accord Centre on the right.

Upperkirkgate becomes Schoolhill, where there's a complex of silver-tone buildings in front of which stands a statue of General Charles Gordon (1833–85), the military hero of Khartoum (1885). Interestingly, he is not the Gordon for whom **Robert Gordon University** 6, behind the statue, was named. The university's next-door neighbor is **Aberdeen Art Gallery** 7, which plays an active role in the city's cultural life and is a popular rendezvous for locals.

Three buildings, the Central Library, St. Mark's Church, and the restored Edwardian His Majesty's Theatre, on **Rosemount Viaduct** 8 are collectively known to all Aberdonians as Education, Salvation, and Damnation. **The Village** 9, great for kids, is off Rosemount Viaduct on Rosemount Place.

Union Terrace 10, a 19th-century development, runs back toward Union Street. Smug cats decorate **Union Bridge** 11, where Union Terrace meets Union Street. Here you can turn left across the bridge and follow Union Street to **St. Nicholas Kirk** 12. It's set in a peaceful green churchyard that's screened by a colonnaded facade (1829) and is popular with office workers at lunchtime in summer.

You're now almost back at your starting point. Turn right, opposite Broad Street, and head down Ship Row to enjoy the Aberdeen Maritime Museum, housed partly in **Provost Ross's House** 13 and partly in a magnificent modern glass extension. Below Ship Row is the harbor, which contains some fine 18th- and 19th-century architecture. Explore it if time permits and you don't mind the traffic. An essential place to visit if you have children with you is **Satrosphere** 14, a hands-on exhibition of science and technology. On Constitution Street, off Justice Street/Park Road beyond the eastern end of Union Street, it's worth the 10-minute walk.

For the second part of your city tour, hop on a bus traveling north from a stop near Marischal College, or up King Street, off the Castlegate, to reach Old Aberdeen. Many of the University of Aberdeen's departments are housed in the 18th- and 19th-century buildings of Old Aberdeen, such as those in **College Bounds** 15. **King's College** 16 was founded in 1494 and is now part of the University of Aberdeen. This area has some fine Georgian houses, including the **Town House** 17. Behind it the modern intrusion of St. Machar's Drive destroys some of the old-town ambience, but you can recapture it on a stroll along the Chanonry, past the elegant structures that once housed officials connected with the cathedral nearby.

North on the Chanonry is **St. Machar's Cathedral** 18. The structure was first built in AD 580, but nothing remains of the original foundation; much of what you see is from the 15th and 16th centuries. Beyond St. Machar's lies **Seaton Park** 19, full of daffodils in spring. Until the early 19th century the only way north out of Aberdeen was over the River Don on the **Brig o'Balgownie** 20 (constructed in 1314), at the far end of Seaton Park—a 15-minute walk.

TIMING You can devote a day to each half of this walk, or you can spend a long morning in the center of Aberdeen, then take a bus out to Old Aberdeen after a late lunch, and do the tour in a (long) day.

What to See

7 **Aberdeen Art Gallery.** Locals take great pride and pleasure in this collection—from 18th-century art to contemporary works—of paintings, prints and drawings, sculpture, porcelain, costumes, and much else. It also hosts frequent temporary exhibitions and has a good café. ✉ *Schoolhill* ☎ *01224/523700* 🌐 *www.aagm.co.uk* 🎟 *Free* ⏲ *Mon.–Sat. 10–5, Sun. 2–5.*

Biking

Northeast Scotland is superb biking country, with networks of minor roads crisscrossing rolling fields and carrying little other than farm traffic. A few converted railway track beds serve as bicycle and pedestrian pathways. The Formartine and Buchan Way, formerly the Buchan railway line from Aberdeen to Fraserburgh and Peterhead, is a good route, as is the River Dee Walkway, in Aberdeen, which runs from Duthie Park west to the suburb of Peterculter. Mountain biking on forestry and ski trails is another popular option. Local tourist information centers have lists of bike rental shops; reserve your bike at least a day in advance.

Fishing

With major rivers, including the Dee, Don, Deveron, Spey, and Ythan, as well as popular smaller rivers, like the Ugie, plus loch and estuary fishing, the Northeast is one of Scotland's leading game-fishing areas. Ballater is a good base for exploring the River Dee's famous pools, while Craigellachie, Aberlour, Fochabers are on the edge of the River Spey. Most fishing areas are privately owned, and a fishing permit is required even for a day. Some beats on the Dee and Spey cannot be fished at all, unless you are the guest of the owner; some hotels offers private fishing areas for guests. You can obtain details about beats, boats, and permits from local tourist information centers.

Golf

The northeast has more than 50 golf clubs, some of which have championship courses, including Inchmarlo Golf Centre at Banchory, Moray Golf Club at Lossiemouth, near Elgin, and Spey Bay Golf Club, near Fochabers. But it's not just the championship courses that offer a rewarding game. There are some real surprises among the far less famous: try Lumphanan Golf Club, near Banchory, or the coastal Royal Tarlair at Macduff, just over the River Deveron from Banff. All towns and many villages have their 9- and 18-hole municipal links, where greens fees are a modest £15–£20 per round.

The Malt Whisky Trail

South of Elgin and Banff, where streams jostle for elbow room on their race down from the Grampians to the sea, the glens embrace Scotland's greatest concentration of malt-whisky distilleries. Just as the Gironde in France has famous vineyards clustered around it, the valley of the River Spey has famous single-malt distilleries, all connected by the signposted Malt Whisky Trail. Instead of Lafite-Rothschild, Pétrus, and Haut-Brion, there's Glenfiddich, Glen Grant, Tamdhu, or Tamnavulin. Speyside malts are known for being sweeter and less peaty than Scotland's island malts.

Skiing

With some of the highest ground in the country, the Northeast offers a slew of skiing options. January, February, and March are typically the best months for the deepest snow. The largest and most popular ski area is Glenshee Ski Centre, just south of Braemar. The season here can be brief and the runs are short, but Glenshee's four mountains provide enough variety to satiate even the most die-hard skiers. About 18 mi north of Ballater, in Strathdon, is the Lecht, a lower-altitude ski area that's good for beginners. Cairngorm, near Aviemore, is the most reliably snowy mountain, but high winds often cause certain runs to be closed. Finally, Alford Ski Centre, just west of Aberdeen, has an artificial "dry" slope, made of plastic-bristle matting. Ski passes in Scotland cost approximately £20–£30.

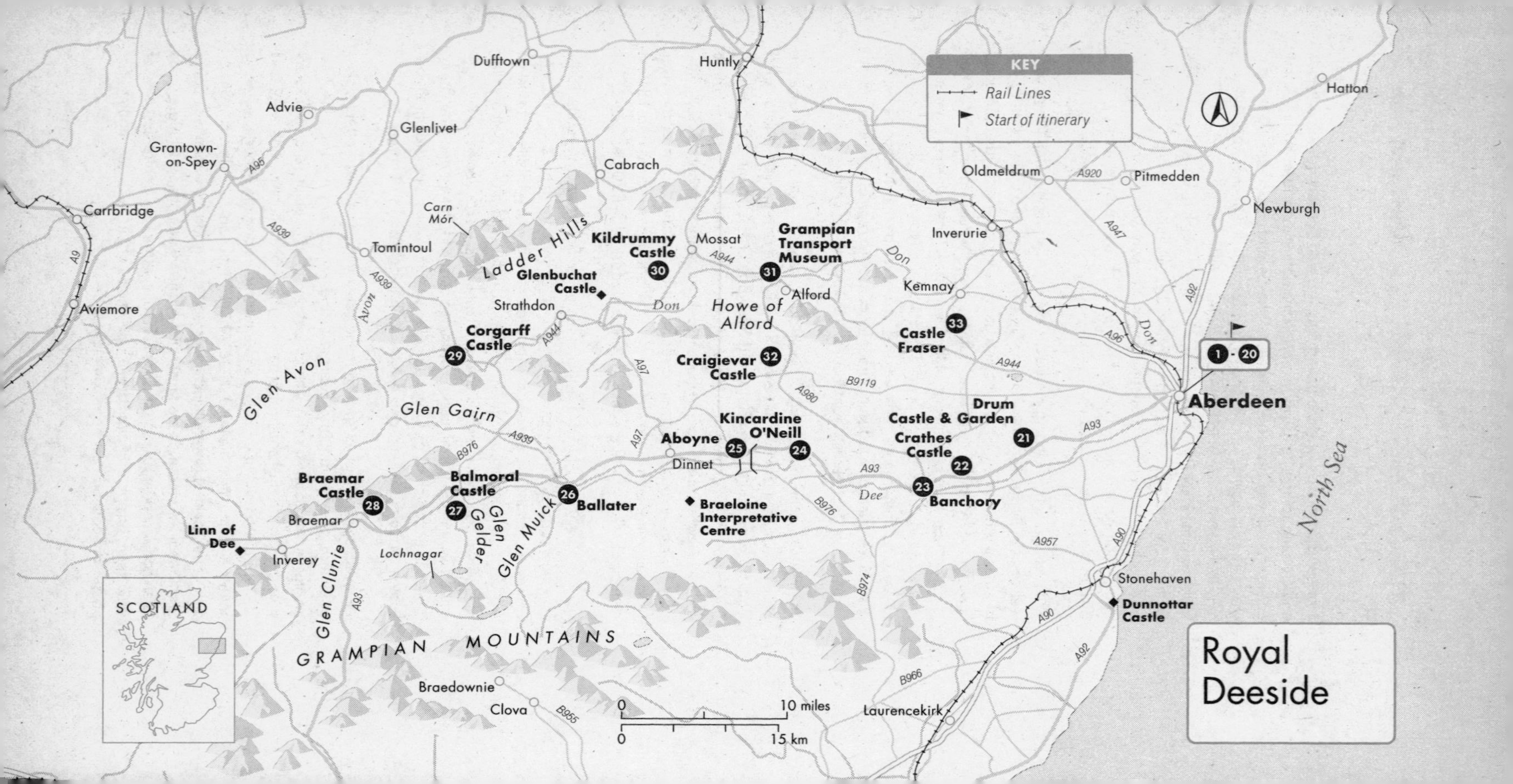
Royal Deeside
KEY
Rail Lines
Start of itinerary
SCOTLAND
Aberdeen
1 - 20
North Sea
Hatton
Newburgh
Pitmedden
Oldmeldrum
Inverurie
Kemnay
Castle Fraser 33
Drum Castle & Garden 21
Crathes Castle 22
Banchory 23
Stonehaven
Dunnottar Castle
Laurencekirk
Grampian Transport Museum 31
Alford
Howe of Alford
Craigievar Castle 32
Kincardine O'Neill 24
Aboyne 25
Dinnet
Braeloine Interpretative Centre
Ballater 26
Balmoral Castle 27
Braemar Castle 28
Braemar
Inverey
Linn of Dee
Corgarff Castle 29
Strathdon
Glenbuchat Castle
Kildrummy Castle 30
Mossat
Ladder Hills
Carn Mór
Cabrach
Huntly
Dufftown
Glenlivet
Advie
Tomintoul
Grantown-on-Spey
Carrbridge
Aviemore
Glen Avon
Glen Gairn
Glen Gelder
Glen Muick
Glen Clunie
Lochnagar
GRAMPIAN MOUNTAINS
Braedownie
Clova
Don
Dee
Avon
A9
A95
A939
A944
A97
A980
B9119
A96
A92
A947
A920
A93
B976
B974
A957
A90
B966
B955
0
10 miles
0
15 km

Aberdeen Art Gallery 7
Brig o'Balgownie . .20
College Bounds 15
King's College 16
Marischal College 4
Mercat Cross 3
Provost Ross's House 13
Provost Skene's House 5
Robert Gordon University 6
Rosemount Viaduct 8
St. Machar's Cathedral 18
St. Nicholas Kirk 12
Satrosphere . .14
Seaton Park . .19
Tolbooth 2
Town House 17
Union Bridge 11
Union Street 1
Union Terrace 10
The Village 9

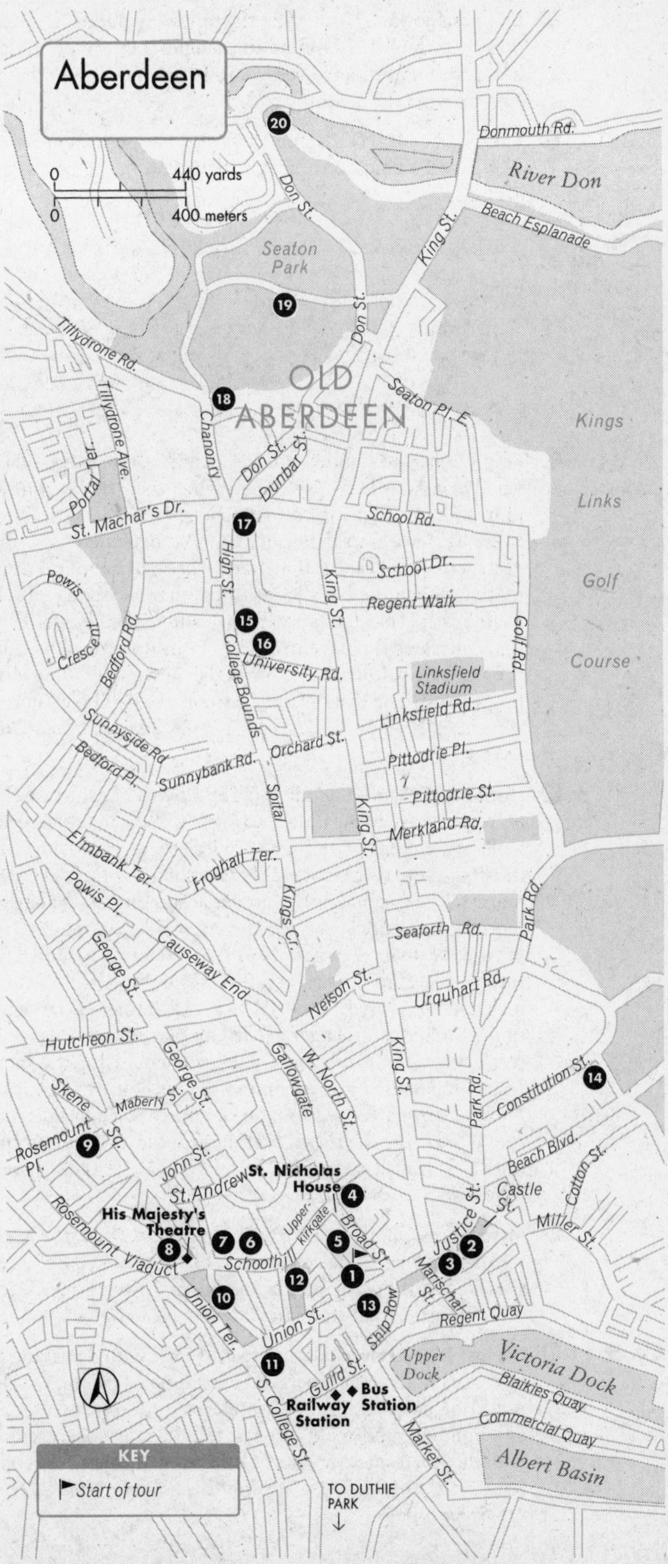

20 **Brig o'Balgownie.** Until 1827 the only way out of Aberdeen going north was over the River Don on this single-arch bridge. It dates from 1314 and is thought to have been built by Richard Cementarius, Aberdeen's first provost. ✉ *Seaton Park.*

15 **College Bounds.** Handsome 18th- and 19th-century houses line this cobbled street (which has paved sidewalks) in the oldest part of the city. ✉ *Old Aberdeen.*

off the beaten path

DUTHIE PARK AND WINTER GARDENS – A great place to feed the ducks, Duthie Park also has a boating pond and trampolines, carved wooden animals, and playgrounds. In the very attractive (and warm!) Winter Gardens are fish in ponds, free-flying birds, and turtles and terrapins among the luxuriant foliage and flowers. The park lies close beside Aberdeen's other river, the Dee. ✉ *Polmuir Rd., Riverside Dr., about 1 mi south of city center* 🎫 *Free* ⏲ *Gardens daily 10–dusk.*

16 **King's College.** Founded in 1494, King's College is now part of the University of Aberdeen. Its **chapel**, which was built around 1500, has an unmistakable flying (or crown) spire. That it has survived at all was because of the zeal of the principal, who defended his church against the destructive fanaticism that swept through Scotland during the Reformation, when the building was less than a century old. Today the renovated chapel plays an important role in university life. The tall oak screen that separates the nave from the choir, the ribbed wooden ceiling, and the stalls constitute the finest medieval wood carvings found anywhere in Scotland. The **King's College Centre** will tell you more about the university. ✉ *High St.* ☎ *01224/273702* 🌐 *www.abdn.ac.uk/kcc* ⏲ *Weekdays 9:30–5, Sat. 11–4.*

Fodor's Choice ★

★ 4 **Marischal College.** Founded in 1593 by the Earl Marischal as a Protestant alternative to the Catholic King's College in Old Aberdeen, Marischal College combined with King's College to form the University of Aberdeen in 1860 (the earls Marischal held hereditary office as keepers of the king's mares). The original university buildings on this site have undergone extensive renovations, and the current facade was built in 1891. The spectacularly ornate work is set off by the gilded flags, and this turn-of-the-20th-century creation is still the world's second-largest granite building. Only El Escorial, outside Madrid, is larger. The main part of the building, no longer needed by the university, is at present the subject of various plans, one of which would turn it into a hotel. The **Marischal Museum**'s two main galleries house the *Encyclopaedia of the North East,* an A-to-Z look at the northeast's heritage, and *Collecting the World,* the worldwide ethnographic collections of 19th-century northeast travelers. ✉ *Broad St.* ☎ *01224/274301* 🌐 *www.abdn.ac.uk* 🎫 *Free* ⏲ *Museum weekdays 10–5, Sun. 2–5.*

3 **Mercat Cross.** Built in 1686 and restored in 1820, the Mercat Cross (the term stems from "marketplace"), always the symbolic center of a Scottish medieval burgh, stands just beyond King Street. Along its parapet are 12 portrait panels of the Stewart monarchs.

★ 13 **Provost Ross's House.** Dating from 1593, with a striking modern extension, this houses the **Aberdeen Maritime Museum.** Displays here, composed of paintings, model ships, and equipment used in the fishing, shipbuilding, and oil industries, tell the story of the city's involvement with the sea, from early inshore fisheries to the North Sea oil boom. ✉ *Ship Row* ☎ *01224/337701* 🌐 *www.aberdeencity.gov.uk* 🎫 *Free* ⏲ *Mon.–Sat. 10–5, Sun. noon–3.*

5 **Provost Skene's House.** *Provost* is Scottish for mayor, and this former mayor's domestic dwelling was once part of a closely packed area of town houses. Steeply gabled and built of rubble, it survives in part from 1545. It is now a museum portraying civic life, with a painted chapel and rooms restored and furnished in period style. ✉ *Guestrow off Broad St.* ☎ *01224/641086* 🌐 *www.aagm.co.uk* 🎫 *Free* 🕒 *Mon.–Sat. 10–5, Sun. 1–4.*

6 **Robert Gordon University.** When it was built in 1731, this institution was called Robert Gordon's Hospital and was used to educate poor boys. Adjacent is the independent Robert Gordon School. It is closed to the public. ✉ *Schoolhill.*

8 **Rosemount Viaduct.** Three silvery, handsome buildings on this bridge are collectively known by all Aberdonians as Education, Salvation, and Damnation. The **Central Library** and **St. Mark's Church** date from the last decade of the 19th century, and **His Majesty's Theatre** (1904–08) has been restored inside to its full Edwardian splendor. If you're taking photographs, you can choose an angle that includes the statue of Scotland's first freedom fighter, Sir William Wallace (1270–1305), in the foreground pointing majestically to Damnation.

18 **St. Machar's Cathedral.** It is said that St. Machar was sent by St. Columba to build a church on a grassy platform near the sea, where a river flowed in the shape of a shepherd's crook. This spot fit the bill. Founded in AD 580, this cathedral has nothing of its original structure. Much of the existing building dates from the 15th and 16th centuries. The central tower collapsed in 1688, reducing the building to half its original length. The twin octagonal spires on the western towers date from the first half of the 16th century. The nave is thought to have been rebuilt in red sandstone in 1370, but the final renovation was completed in granite by the middle of the 15th century. Along with the nave ceiling, the twin spires were finished in time to take a battering in the Reformation, when the barons of the Mearns stripped the lead off the roof of St. Machar's and stole the bells. The cathedral suffered further mistreatment—including the removal of stone by Oliver Cromwell's (1599–1658) English garrison in the 1650s—until it was fully restored in the 19th century. ✉ *Chanonry* ☎ *01224/485988* 🕒 *Mon.–Sat. 9–5, Sun. 9–7.*

12 **St. Nicholas Kirk.** The original burgh church, the Mither Kirk, as this edifice is known, is curiously not within the bounds of the early town settlement; that was located to the east, near the end of present-day Union Street. During the 12th century the port of Aberdeen flourished, and there wasn't room for the church within the settlement. Its earliest features are its pillars—supporting a tower built much later—and its clerestory windows: both date from the 12th century. St. Nicholas was divided into east and west kirks at the Reformation, followed by a substantial amount of renovation from 1741 on. Some early memorials and other works have survived. ✉ *Union St.* 🕒 *Weekdays 10–1, Sun. for services.*

14 **Satrosphere.** The hands-on exhibits at Satrosphere bring science and technology to life. Children (and adults) of even the most unscientific bent love displays such as the see-through sheep that eats grass, digests it, then produces pellets from its bottom. ✉ *179 Constitution St.* ☎ *01224/640340* 🌐 *www.satrosphere.net* 🎫 *£5* 🕒 *Mon.–Sat. 10–5, Sun. 11:30–5.*

19 **Seaton Park.** With its spring daffodils, tall trees, and boldly colored herbaceous borders, this park is typical of Aberdeen's exceptionally high standards of civic horticulture. The city is a frequent prizewinner in the annual Britain in Bloom contest. ✉ *Don St., Old Aberdeen.*

2 **Tolbooth.** The city was governed from this 17th-century building for 200 years. It was also the burgh court and jail. You can see it from the outside only. ✉ *Castle St.*

17 **Town House.** This Georgian work, plain and handsome, incorporates parts of an earlier building from 1720. It is not open to the public. ✉ *High St., Old Aberdeen.*

11 **Union Bridge.** Built in the early 19th century, as was much of Union Street, this bridge has a gentle rise—or descent, if you're traveling east—and the street is carried on a series of blind arches. The north side of Union Bridge is the most obvious reminder of the artificial raising of the grand thoroughfare's levels (despite appearances, you'll discover you're not at ground level). Much of the original work remains. ✉ *Union St.*

1 **Union Street.** This great thoroughfare is to Aberdeen what Princes Street is to Edinburgh: the central pivot of the city plan and the product of a wave of enthusiasm to rebuild the city in a contemporary style in the early 19th century.

10 **Union Terrace.** In the 19th-century development of Union Terrace stands a statue of Robert Burns (1759–96) addressing a daisy. Behind Burns are the **Union Terrace Gardens,** faintly echoing Edinburgh's Princes Street Gardens in that both separate the older part of the city, to the east, from the 19th-century development to the west. Most buildings around the grand-looking Caledonian Hotel are late Victorian.

9 **The Village.** This museum and educational center has interactive displays that show you what life was like in a village 2,000 years ago. You can dress up in costumes, play jigsaw puzzles, watch puppet shows, and try your hand at spinning, weaving, and mosaic making. ✉ *Rosemount Pl.* ☎ *01224/648041* £3 ⏲ *Mon., Wed., and Fri.–Sat. 10–noon; Sun. 2:30–4:30.*

off the beaten path

DUNNOTTAR CASTLE – For an afternoon trip out from Aberdeen, it's hard to beat this magnificent cliff-top castle, which straddles a headland overlooking Stonehaven, 15 mi south of Aberdeen. Building began in the 14th century, when Sir William Keith, Marischal of Scotland (i.e., keeper of the king's mares and one of the king's right-hand men), decided to build a tower house as a status symbol to demonstrate his power. Subsequent generations continued to add on to the structure over the centuries, and important visitors included Mary, Queen of Scots. The castle is most famous for holding out for eight months against Oliver Cromwell's army in 1651–2, and thereby saving the Scottish crown jewels, which had been stored here for safekeeping. Reach the castle via the A90; take the Stonehaven turnoff and follow the signs. Wear sensible shoes to investigate the ruins. ✉ *Stonehaven* ☎ *01569/762173* £3.50 ⏲ *Easter–Oct., Mon.–Sat. 9–6, Sun. 2–5.*

Where to Stay & Eat

££££ Fodor's Choice ★ ✕ **Silver Darling.** Huge windows afford panoramic views of the harbor at the quayside Silver Darling, one of Aberdeen's most acclaimed restaurants. It specializes, as its name suggests, in fish (a silver darling is a herring). Try the ravioli with langoustine, mushrooms, samphire, and vanilla or the macadamia nut–crusted North Sea halibut with a spicy lemongrass-and-coconut emulsion. ✉ *Pocra Quay, Footdee* ☎ *01224/576229* *Reservations essential* *AE, DC, MC, V* ⏲ *Closed Sun. No lunch Sat.*

££–£££ ✕ **Lascala Ristorante.** Glowing blues and reds, sparkling chandeliers, and plants everywhere set the scene for a classic Italian restaurant. Veal and fish are prominent on the menu, and the daily specials make the most of fresh produce. Reserve ahead, as the restaurant can get busy. ✉ *51 Huntly St.* ☎ *01224/626566* ▭ *AE, DC, MC, V.*

££££–£££££ ✕ **Marcliffe at Pitfodels.** This spacious country-house hotel in the West End combines old and new in the individually decorated rooms to impressive effect—some have reproduction antique furnishings, others are more modern. The restaurant (££££) serves the freshest local seafood and top-quality Aberdeen Angus beef, and you can choose from more than 500 wines to go with your meal. ✉ *N. Deeside Rd., Pitfodels, AB15 9YA* ☎ *01224/861000* 🖷 *01224/868860* 🌐 *www.marcliffe.com* *40 rooms, 2 suites* *Restaurant, room service, cable TV, bar, laundry service, no-smoking rooms; no a/c* ▭ *AE, DC, MC, V* *BP.*

Fodor'sChoice ★

£££££ **Thistle Aberdeen Caledonian Hotel.** This large downtown hotel, generally considered the city's best, offers pleasant views over the city gardens. Rooms are decorated with dark-wood furniture and chintz drapes and bedcovers, and the restaurant serves tasty dishes from a menu best described as eclectic Scottish. Ask about special weekend deals that include dinner and breakfast. ✉ *10–14 Union Terr., AB10 1WE* ☎ *01224/640233* 🖷 *01224/641627* 🌐 *www.thistlehotels.com* *72 rooms, 4 suites* *Restaurant, in-room data ports, bar, no-smoking rooms; no a/c* ▭ *AE, DC, MC, V* *BP.*

£££–££££ **Craighaar Hotel.** Perhaps because it's convenient to the airport, the Craighaar is popular with businesspeople. A rustic cinnamon and terra-cotta color scheme and modern teak furnishings decorate the hotel. The gallery suites—split-level rooms—are outstanding. The restaurant's menu has a Scottish slant, with dishes such as lamb with an herb crust, whisky-and-mint sauce, and *skirlie* (oatmeal-stuffed) tomato. ✉ *Waterton Rd., Bankhead, AB21 9HS* ☎ *01224/712275* 🖷 *01224/716362* 🌐 *www.craighaar.co.uk* *49 rooms, 6 suites* *Restaurant, in-room data ports, bar, laundry service, no-smoking rooms; no a/c* ▭ *AE, DC, MC, V* *BP.*

£££ **Palm Court.** Slightly removed from the city center, the Palm Court is relatively quiet, with high standards of accommodation and service. Rooms, though not large, are attractively furnished with warm, floral fabrics. Traditional Scottish meals are served in the conservatory, where your attention may well be distracted from a plate of fresh salmon or roasted chicken by the wealth of decorative artifacts surrounding you. Ask about the special weekend rates. ✉ *81 Seafield Rd., AB15 7YX* ☎ *01224/310351* 🖷 *01224/312707* *info@palmcourt.co.uk* *23 rooms* *Restaurant, bar, laundry service, no-smoking rooms; no a/c* ▭ *AE, MC, V* *BP.*

££–£££ **Atholl Hotel.** The granite Atholl, with its many turrets and gables, is set in a leafy residential area to the west of the city. Rooms are done in rich, dark colors; if space is more important than a view, opt for a room on the first floor. The restaurant prepares such traditional Scottish dishes as lamb cutlets and roasted rib of beef. ✉ *54 Kings Gate, AB15 4YN* ☎ *01224/323505* 🖷 *01224/321555* 🌐 *www.atholl-aberdeen.com* *35 rooms* *Restaurant, in-room data ports, bar, laundry service, no-smoking rooms; no a/c* ▭ *AE, DC, MC, V* *BP.*

Nightlife & the Arts

In part because of the oil-industry boom, Aberdeen has a fairly lively nightlife scene, though much of it revolves around pubs and hotels; theaters, concert halls, arts centers, and cinemas are also well represented. The principal newspapers—the *Press and Journal* and the *Evening Ex-*

press—and *Aberdeen Leopard* magazine can fill you in on what's going on anywhere in the northeast. Aberdeen's tourist information center has a monthly publication with an events calendar.

The Arts

ARTS CENTERS **Aberdeen Arts Centre** (✉ 33 King St. ☎ 01224/635208 🌐 www.aberdeenartscentre.org.uk) hosts experimental plays, poetry readings, and exhibitions by local and Scottish artists, among other arts presentations. At **Haddo House** (✉ Off B9005 near Methlick ☎ 01651/851770), 20 mi north of Aberdeen, the Haddo House Arts Trust runs a mixed-bag of events, from opera and ballet to Shakespeare, Scots-language plays, and puppetry. The **Lemon Tree** (✉ 5 W. North St. ☎ 01224/642230) has an innovative and international program of dance, stand-up comedy, folk, jazz, rock and roll, and art exhibitions.

CONCERT HALL The **Music Hall** (✉ Union St. ☎ 01224/641122) presents seasonal programs of concerts by the Scottish National Orchestra, the Scottish Chamber Orchestra, and other major groups. Events also include folk concerts, crafts fairs, and exhibitions.

DANCE Many avant-garde dance companies perform at the popular **Aberdeen Arts Centre** (✉ 33 King St. ☎ 01224/635208). **His Majesty's Theatre** (✉ Rosemount Viaduct ☎ 01224/637788) is a regular venue for classical and modern ballet, as well as musicals.

FESTIVALS August sees the world-renowned **Aberdeen International Youth Festival** (box office ✉ Music Hall, Union St. ☎ 01224/641122), which attracts youth orchestras, choirs, dance troupes, and theater companies from many countries. During the festival some companies take their productions to other venues in the northeast.

FILM **The Belmont** (✉ 49 Belmont St. ☎ 01224/343536) screens independent and classic films. **UGC Cinemas** (✉ Queen's Link Leisure Park, Links Rd. ☎ 0870/155–0502) shows general-release films.

THEATER & OPERA **Haddo House Arts Trust** (✉ Off B9005 near Methlick ☎ 01651/851770) presents an enterprising mix of semiprofessional and professional productions. At **His Majesty's Theatre** (✉ Rosemount Viaduct ☎ 01224/637788), shows are presented throughout the year, many of them in advance of their official opening in London's West End.

Nightlife

CASINO If you're interested in trying your luck at the gaming tables, you can place bets at the **Gala Casino** (✉ 59–61 Summer St. ☎ 01224/645273). Membership is granted within 24 hours.

DANCE CLUBS Most clubs don't allow jeans or sneakers, and it's best to check beforehand that a particular dance club is not closed for a private function. **Cotton Club** (✉ 491 Union St. ☎ 01224/581858), though a bit dingy, is always busy with a young clientele in the 18 to 30 age range. The popular front bar is cheerfully noisy with karaoke performers. **Franklyn's** (✉ 44 Justice Mill La. ☎ 01224/212817), popular with a varied age group, has live and occasionally DJ-ed music. The somewhat upscale **G's Nightclub** (✉ 70–78 Chapel St. ☎ 01224/642112) is where local professionals come to let down their hair. You can dance the night away to mainstream music from the 60s on up at **Hotel Metro** (✉ 17 Market St. ☎ 01224/583275).

MUSIC CLUBS The **Lemon Tree** (✉ 5 W. North St. ☎ 01224/642230), with a wide-ranging music program, is the main rock venue and stages frequent jazz events. There's live music on Saturday night at the **Masada Bar** (✉ Rosemount Viaduct ☎ 01224/641587).

Sports & the Outdoors

Biking

The tourist information center can provide a leaflet with suggestions for cycle tours. The average rate for a mountain bike is £15 a day. **Alpine Bikes** (✉ 70 Holburn St. ☎ 01224/211455) rents mountain bikes and will give you advice on where to bike.

Golf

Greens fees range from £30 to £80 per round at courses in and around Aberdeen. Make reservations at least 24 hours in advance. Some private courses restrict tee times for visiting golfers to certain days or hours during the week, so be sure to check that the course you wish to play is open when you want to play it.

Royal Aberdeen Golf Club, Balgownie. Founded in 1780, this club is the sixth oldest in the world, and there are fine views of Aberdeen from its fairways. ✉ *Bridge of Don* ☎ *01224/702571* *18 holes, 6,415 yards, SSS 70.*

Murcar. Sea views and variety of terrain are the highlights of this course, founded in 1909, but it is most famous for its 7th hole, which course designer Archibald Simpson considered to be one of his finest. ✉ *Bridge of Don* ☎ *01224/704354* *18 holes, 6,241 yards, SSS 71.*

Westhill. This parkland course, founded in 1977, overlooks Royal Deeside. ✉ *Westhill Heights* ☎ *01224/742567* *18 holes, 5,849 yards, SSS 69.*

Shopping

Department Stores

You'll find most of the large national department stores in the Bon Accord, St. Nicholas, and Trinity shopping malls or along Union Street.

The spacious **John Lewis** (✉ George St., reached via Bon Accord Centre ☎ 01224/625000) resembles a double-decker sandwich with its filling illuminated. You'll find clothing, household items, giftware, and much more. It's closed on Monday. **Esslemont & Macintosh** (✉ 26 Union St. ☎ 01224/647331) is a long-established Aberdeen store. The favorite haunt of well-off ladies who lunch, it has an excellent stock of upscale clothing and accessories, cosmetics, and furniture.

Specialty Shops

There are clusters of small specialty shops in the **Chapel Street–Thistle Street** area at the west end of **Union Street** and on the latter's north side. **Colin Wood** (✉ 25 Rose St. ☎ 01224/643019) is the place to go for small antiques, Scottish maps, and prints. At the **Aberdeen Family History Society Shop** (✉ 158–164 King St. ☎ 01224/646323) you can browse through publications related to local history and genealogical research. For a small fee the Aberdeen & North East Family History Society will undertake some research on your behalf. **Nova** (✉ 20 Chapel St. ☎ 01224/641270), where the locals go for gifts, stocks major U.K. brand names, such as Neal's Yard, Dartington Glass, and Crabtree and Evelyn, as well as Scottish silver jewelry. The **Early Learning Centre** (✉ Bon-Accord Centre, George St. ☎ 01224/624188) specializes in toys with educational value. The **Toy Bazaar** (✉ 45 Schoolhill ☎ 01224/640021) stocks toys for children preschool age and up.

ROYAL DEESIDE & CASTLE COUNTRY

Deeside, the valley running west from Aberdeen down which the River Dee flows, earned its "royal" appellation when discovered by Queen Victoria. To this day, where royalty goes, lesser aristocracy and freshly minted millionaires follow. It's still the aspiration of many to own a grand shooting estate in Deeside. In a sense this yearning is understandable because piney hill slope, purple moor, and blue river intermingle tastefully here. Royal Deeside's gradual scenic change adds a growing sense of excitement as you travel deeper into the Grampians.

There are castles along the Dee as well as to the north in Castle Country, a region that also illustrates the gradual geological change in the northeast: uplands lapped by a tide of farms. All the Donside and Deeside castles are picturesquely sited, with most fitted out with tall slender turrets, winding stairs, and crooked chambers that epitomize Scottish baronial. All have tales of ghosts and bloodshed, siege and torture. Many were tidied up and "domesticated" during the 19th century. Although best toured by car, much of this area is accessible either by public transportation or on tours from Aberdeen.

Drum Castle & Garden

❷❶ *11 mi west of Aberdeen.*

Drum Castle is a foursquare tower that dates from the 13th century, with later additions. Note the tower's rounded corners, said to make battering-ram attacks more difficult. Nearby, fragments of the ancient Forest of Drum still stand, dating from the days when Scotland was covered by great woodlands of oak and pine. The Garden of Historic Roses lays claim to some old-fashioned roses not commonly seen today. ✉ *Off A93* ☎ *01330/811204* 🌐 *www.nts.org.uk* 🎫 *Castle and garden £7; garden only, £2.50* ⏲ *Castle and garden Apr.–May and Sept., daily 12:30–5:30; June–Aug., daily 10–5:30; grounds daily 9:30–dusk.*

Crathes Castle

❷❷ *5 mi west of Drum Castle, 16 mi west of Aberdeen.*

Crathes Castle was once the home of the Burnett family. Keepers of the Forest of Drum for generations, the family acquired lands here by marriage and later built a new castle, completed in 1596. The National Trust for Scotland cares for the castle and the grand gardens, with their calculated symmetry and clipped yew hedges. Sample the tasty home baking in the tearoom. ✉ *Off A93, 3½ mi east of Banchory* ☎ *01330/844525* 🌐 *www.nts.org.uk* 🎫 *Castle £7; garden £7; castle and garden £9* ⏲ *Castle Apr.–Sept., daily 10–5:30; Oct., daily 10–4:30 (last admission 45 min. before closing). Tearoom and shop Apr.–Sept., daily 10–5:30; Oct., daily 10–4:30; Nov.–March., Wed.–Sun. 10–4; garden daily 9–dusk.*

Banchory

❷❸ *3 mi west of Crathes Castle, 19 mi west of Aberdeen via A93.*

Banchory is an immaculate town, with pinkish granite buildings. It's usually bustling with ice-cream-eating strollers, out on a day trip from Aberdeen. If you visit in autumn and have time to spare, drive for a mile along the B974 south of Banchory to the **Brig o'Feuch** (pronounced fy-ooch, the *ch* as in loch). The area around this bridge is very pleasant: salmon leap in season, and the fall colors and foaming waters make for an attractive scene.

Where to Stay & Eat

££££ ✕🅿 **Banchory Lodge.** With the River Dee flowing a few yards beyond the garden, tranquil Banchory Lodge is an ideal spot for anglers. The house was built in the 17th century and it retains its period charm. Rooms are individually decorated, though all have bold color schemes and tartan or floral fabrics. The restaurant (££££) serves Scottish cuisine with French overtones; try the salmon, roast duckling, or guinea fowl. ✉ *Banchory, Kincardineshire AB31 5HS* ☎ *01330/822625* 🖷 *01330/825019* 🌐 *www.banchorylodge.co.uk* *22 rooms* *Restaurant, fishing, bicycles, bar, lounge; no a/c* ▭ *AE, DC, MC, V* 🍽 *BP.*

Kincardine O'Neill

24 *9 mi west of Banchory.*

The ruined kirk in the little village of Kincardine O'Neill was built in 1233 and once sheltered travelers: it was the last hospice before the Mounth, the name given to the massif that shuts off the south side of the Dee Valley. Beyond Banchory (and the B974), no motor roads run south until you reach Braemar (A93), though the Mounth is crossed by a network of tracks once used by Scottish soldiers, invading armies (including the Romans), and cattle drovers. Photography buffs won't want to miss the bridge at Potarch, just to the east.

Aboyne

25 *5 mi west of Kincardine O'Neill.*

Aboyne is a pleasant, well-laid-out town, with a village green (unusual for Scotland) that hosts an annual Highland Games. However, there's not a lot to detain you here, except a good coffee shop. The **Braeloine Interpretative Centre,** in Glen Tanar beyond Aboyne, has a natural history display, a picnic area, and walks. ✉ *Glen Tanar; cross River Dee, take right on B976, and left into glen* ☎ *013398/86072* ⏲ *Apr.–Sept., Wed.–Mon. 10–5; Oct.–Mar., Thurs.–Mon. 10–5.*

off the beaten path

QUEEN'S VIEW – To reach one of the most spectacular vistas in northeast Scotland—stretching across the Howe of Cromar to Lochnagar—take the B9094 due north from Aboyne, then turn left onto the B9119 for 6 mi.

Where to Eat

£ ✕ **At the Sign of the Blackfaced Sheep.** Filled rolls, soups, salads, steak sandwiches, and delicious home-baked goods are served here, but another good reason to visit is the upscale gifts and paintings that you can buy in this coffee and crafts shop. ✉ *Ballater Rd.* ☎ *013398/87311* ▭ *MC, V.*

en route

Look for a large granite boulder next to the A93 on which is carved YOU ARE NOW ENTERING THE HIGHLANDS. You may find this piece of information superfluous, given the quality of the scenery.

Ballater

26 *12 mi west of Aboyne, 43 mi west of Aberdeen.*

The handsome holiday resort of Ballater, once noted for the curative properties of its local well, has profited from the proximity of the royals, nearby at Balmoral. You might be amused by the array of BY ROYAL APPOINTMENT signs proudly hanging from many of its various shops (even

CloseUp

DO YE KEN WHOT EHM SAYIN', LADDIE?

*M***UCH," SAID DOCTOR JOHNSON,** *"may be made of a Scotchman if he be caught young." This quote sums up, even today, the attitude of some English people—confident in their English, the language of parliament and much of the media—to the Scots language. The Scots have long been made to feel uncomfortable about their mother tongue and have partly themselves to blame, for until the 1970s (and in some private schools, even today) they were actively encouraged to ape the dialect of the Thames Valley ("standard English") in order to "get on" in life.*

The Scots language (that is, Lowland Scots, not Gaelic) was a northern form of Middle English and in its day was the language used in the court and in literature. It borrowed from Scandinavian, Dutch, French, and Gaelic. After a series of historical body blows—such as the decamping of the Scottish court to England after 1603 and the printing of the King James Bible in English but not in Scots—it declined as a literary or official language. It survives in various forms but is virtually an underground language, spoken at home, in shops, and on the playground, the farm, and the quayside among ordinary folk, especially in its heartland, in the Northeast. There they describe Scots who use the brayed diphthongs of the English Thames Valley as speaking with a bool in the mou*—marble in the mouth. You may even find yourself exporting a few useful words, such as* dreich *(gloomy),* glaikit *(acting and looking foolish), or* dinna fash *(don't worry), all of which are much more expressive than their English equivalents.*

Scottish Gaelic, an entirely different language, is still spoken across the Highlands and Hebrides. There's also a large Gaelic-speaking population in Glasgow—a result of the Celtic diaspora, islanders migrating to Glasgow in search of jobs in the 19th century. Speakers of Gaelic in Scotland were once persecuted, after the failure of the 18th-century Jacobite rebellions. Official persecution has now turned to guilt-tinged support, as the promoters of Gaelic now lobby for substantial public funds to underwrite television programming and language classes for new learners. One of the joys of Scottish television is watching Gaelic news programs to see how the ancient language copes with such topics as nuclear reprocessing, the Internet, and the latest band to go number one.

monarchs need bakers and butchers). Take time to stroll around this well-laid-out community. The railway station houses the tourist information center and a display on the glories of the Great North of Scotland branch railway line, closed in the 1960s along with so many others in this country.

★ As long as you have your own car, you can capture the feel of the eastern Highlands yet still be close to town. Start your expedition into **Glen Muick** (Gaelic for pig, pronounced mick) by crossing the River Dee and turning upriver on the south side, shortly after the road forks. The native red deer are quite common throughout the Scottish Highlands, but the flat valley floor here is one of the very best places to see them. Beyond the lower glen, the prospect opens to reveal not only grazing herds but also fine views of the battlement of cliffs edging the mountain called Lochnagar.

Where to Stay & Eat

££££–£££££ ✕🏨 **Darroch Learg Hotel.** Amid tall trees on a hillside, the Darroch Learg is everything a Victorian Scottish country house should be. Most guest rooms are decorated with mahogany furniture and rich fabrics. The Scottish food in the conservatory restaurant (£££££) is sophisticated but also substantial, with the rich flavors of local beef, venison, and fish. Note that the less expensive rooms are in the neighboring Oak Hall, another handsome Victorian house. ✉ *Braemar Rd., Ballater, AB35 5UX* ☎ *013397/55443* 🖶 *013397/55252* ✉ *nigel@darroch-learg.demon. co.uk* ➫ *18 rooms* ♻ *Restaurant, laundry service, no-smoking rooms; no a/c* ⊟ *AE, DC, MC, V* ⊘ *Closed Jan.* ❙◯❙ *BP.*

££££ ✕🏨 **Balgonie Country House.** A tranquil Edwardian country house on 3 acres of gardens overlooking Ballater's golf course, Balgonie delivers top-quality food and accommodations. Bedrooms are individually decorated in soft greens, blues, or pinks, with either antiques or, in the attic rooms, modern Swedish-style furniture. The dining room (£££££) is a peaceful setting for a four-course meal of classic French cuisine. ✉ *Braemar Pl., Ballater AB35 5NQ* ☎🖶 *013397/55482* ⊕ *www.royaldeesidehotels. com* ➫ *9 rooms* ♻ *Restaurant, bar, laundry service, no-smoking rooms; no a/c* ⊟ *AE, DC, MC, V* ⊘ *Closed Jan.–mid-Feb.* ❙◯❙ *BP.*

££££ ✕🏨 **Hilton Craigendarroch Hotel.** This magnificent country-house hotel, just outside Ballater on a hillside overlooking the River Dee, manages to keep everyone happy. Choose between a luxurious room in the main house and a private, less-expensive pine lodge set among the trees. Fitted with every kind of labor-saving appliance, the lodges are perfect for families. The hotel's restaurants (££–£££££) include the Oaks, for modern Scottish food à la carte, and the Club House poolside brasserie. ✉ *Braemar Rd., Ballater AB35 5XA* ☎ *013397/55858* 🖶 *013397/ 55447* ⊕ *www.hilton.com* ➫ *39 rooms, 6 suites* ♻ *2 restaurants, room service, some in-room hot tubs, some kitchens, some microwaves, some refrigerators, cable TV, tennis court, 2 pools, wading pool, gym, hair salon, hot tub, sauna, squash, 2 bars, laundry facilities, laundry service, business services, no-smoking rooms; no a/c* ⊟ *AE, DC, MC, V.*

Shopping

At either location of **Countrywear** (✉ 15 and 35 Bridge St. ☎ 013397/ 55453), you'll find everything you need for Highland country living, including fishing tackle, tweeds, children's clothes, and that flexible garment popular in Scotland between seasons: the body warmer. Head to the **Clothes Shop** (✉ 1 Braemar Rd. ☎ 013397/55947) for fleeces and waterproofs to keep you dry on the hills. For a low-cost gift you could always see what's being boiled up at **Dee Valley Confectioners** (✉ Station Sq. ☎ 013397/55499). The **McEwan Gallery** (✉ On A939, 1 mi west of Ballater ☎ 013397/55429) displays fine paintings, watercolors, prints, and books (many with a Scottish or golf theme) in an unusual house built by the Swiss artist Rudolphe Christen in 1902.

Balmoral Castle

㉗ *7 mi west of Ballater.*

The enormous parking lot is indicative of the popularity of Balmoral Castle, one of Queen Elizabeth II's favorite family retreats. Balmoral is a Victorian fantasy, designed, in fact, for Queen Victoria (1819–1901) by her consort, Prince Albert (1819–61) in 1855. "It seems like a dream to be here in our dear Highland Home again," Queen Victoria wrote. "Every year my heart becomes more fixed in this dear Paradise." Balmoral's visiting hours depend on whether the royals are in residence. In truth, there are more interesting and historic buildings to explore, as the only part of the castle on view is the ballroom, with an exhibition of royal artifacts. The Carriage Hall has displays of commemorative china, carriages, and native wildlife. Perhaps it's just as well that most of the house is closed to the public, for Balmoral suffers from a bad rash of tartanitis. Thanks to Victoria and Albert, stags' heads abounded, the bagpipes wailed incessantly, and the garish Stuart tartan was used for every item of furnishings, from carpets to chair covers. A more somber Duff tartan, black and green to blend with the environment, was later adopted, and from the brief glimpse you may get of Balmoral's interior, it's clear that royal taste is now more restrained. Queen Elizabeth II, however, follows her predecessors' routine in spending a holiday of about six weeks in Deeside, usually from mid-August to the end of September. During this time Balmoral is closed to visitors.

Victoria loved Balmoral more for its setting than its house, so be sure to take in its pleasant gardens. Year by year Victoria and Albert added to the estate, taking over neighboring houses, securing the forest and moorland around it, and developing deer stalking and grouse shooting here. In consequence, Balmoral is now a large property, as the grounds run 12 mi along the Deeside road. Its privacy is protected by belts of pinewood, and the only view of the castle from the A93 is a partial one, from a point near Inver, 2 mi west of the gates. But there's an excellent bird's-eye view of it from an old military road, now the A939, which climbs out of Crathie, northbound for Cockbridge and the Don Valley. This view embraces the summit of Lochnagar, in whose *corries* (hollows) the snow lies year-round. Around and about Balmoral are some notable spots—Cairn O'Mount, Cambus O'May, and the Cairngorms from the Linn of Dee—and some of them may be seen on pony-trekking expeditions, which use Balmoral stalking ponies and go around the grounds and estate. When the royals are in residence, even the grounds are closed to the public. ✉ *A93* ☎ *013397/42334* 🌐 *www.balmoralcastle.com* 🎫 *£4.50* ⏲ *Apr.–July, daily 10–5; last admission at 4.*

en route

As you continue west into Highland scenery, further pine-framed glimpses appear of the "steep frowning glories of dark Lochnagar," as it was described by the poet Lord Byron (1788–1824). Lochnagar (3,786 feet) was made known to an audience wider than hill walkers by the Prince of Wales, who published a children's story, *The Old Man of Lochnagar.*

Braemar

17 mi west of Ballater, 60 mi west of Aberdeen, 51 mi north of Perth via A93.

The village of Braemar is associated with the Braemar Highland Gathering, held every September. Although there are many such gatherings celebrated throughout Scotland, this one is distinguished by the presence of the royal family. Competitions and events include hammer throwing, caber tossing, running races, Highland dancing, and bagpipe playing. You can find out more at the **Braemar Highland Heritage Centre,** in a converted stable block in the middle of town. It tells the history of the village with displays and a film, and it also has a gift shop. ✉ *The Mews, Mar Rd.* ☎ *013397/41944* 🎫 *Free* ⏲ *Apr.–Sept., daily 9–6; Oct., daily 9–5; Nov.–Mar., daily 10–noon and 1–5.*

28 Braemar is dominated by **Braemar Castle** on its outskirts. The castle dates from the 17th century, although its defensive walls, designed in the shape of a pointed star, came later. At Braemar (the *braes,* or slopes, of the

district of Mar) the standard, or rebel flag, was first raised at the start of the spectacularly unsuccessful Jacobite Rebellion of 1715. Thirty years later, during the last rebellion, Braemar Castle was strengthened and garrisoned by Hanoverian (government) troops. ✉ *A93* ☎ *013397/41219* 🌐 *www.braemarcastle.co.uk* 🎫 *£3* ⏲ *Apr.–Oct., Mon.–Thurs., Sat. and Sun. 10–6.*

off the beaten path

LINN OF DEE – Although the main A93 slinks off to the south from Braemar, a little unmarked road will take you farther west into the hilly heartland. In fact, even if you do not have your own car, you can still explore this area by catching the post bus that leaves from the Braemar post office once a day. The road offers views over the winding River Dee and the blue hills before passing through the tiny hamlet of Inverey and crossing a bridge at the Linn of Dee. *Linn* is a Scots word meaning "rocky narrows," and the river's gash here is deep and roaring. Park beyond the bridge and walk back to admire the sylvan setting.

Where to Stay & Eat

££ **Invercauld Arms.** This handsome stone Victorian hotel in the center of Braemar makes a good base for exploring Royal Deeside. The entrance lounge, with plush sofas and elegant velvet chairs, leads to beautifully restored public rooms and to comfortable guest rooms with floral drapes and reproduction antique furniture. The restaurant (£££) serves a three-course dinner; dishes might include Aberdeen Angus steak with tomato and wild-mushroom sauce or chicken with bean sprouts and water chestnuts in oyster sauce. ✉ *Braemar AB35 5YR* ☎ *013397/41605* 📠 *013397/41428* *68 rooms* *Restaurant, in-room safes, cable TV, bar, laundry service, business services, meeting rooms, no-smoking rooms; no a/c* 💳 *AE, DC, MC, V* *BP.*

Golf

The tricky 18-hole **Braemar golf course,** founded in 1902, is laden with foaming waters. Erratic duffers take note: the compassionate course managers have installed, near the water, poles with little nets on the end for those occasional shots that may go awry. ✉ *Cluny Bank Rd.* ☎ *013397/41618* *18 holes, 4,916 yds, SSS 65.*

en route

From Braemar retrace the A93 as far as Balmoral. From Balmoral look for a narrow road going north, signposted B976. Be careful on the first twisting mile through the trees. You'll soon emerge from scattered pines into the open moor in upland Aberdeenshire. Behind is the massif of Lochnagar again, and to the west are snow-tipped domes of the big Cairngorms. Roll down to a bridge and go left on the A939, which comes in from Ballater. Another high moor section follows: as the road leaves the scattered buildings by the bridge, see if you can spot the roadside inscription to the company of soldiers who built the A939 in the 18th century.

Corgarff Castle

29 *23 mi northeast of Braemar, 14 mi northwest of Ballater.*

Eighteenth-century soldiers paved a military highway, now the A939, north from Ballater to Corgarff Castle, a lonely tower house with a star-shape defensive wall—a curious replica of Braemar Castle. Corgarff was built as a hunting seat for the earls of Mar in the 16th century. After an eventful history that included the wife of a later laird being burned alive in a family dispute, the castle ended its career as a garrison for Hanoverian troops. The troops were responsible for preventing illegal whisky distilling. ⊠ *Signposted off A939* ☎ *0131/668–8800* ⊕ *www.historic-scotland.gov. uk* ⊠ *£3* ⊘ *Apr.–Sept., daily 9:30–6; Oct.–Mar., Sat. 9:30–4, Sun. 2–4.*

en route | If you return east from Corgarff Castle to the A939/A944 junction and make a left onto the A944, the thorough castle signposting indicates you are on the **Castle Trail.** The A944 meanders along the River Don to the village of Strathdon, where a great mound by the roadside—on the left—turns out to be a *motte,* or the base of a wooden castle, built in the late 12th century. Although it takes considerable imagination to become enthusiastic about a great grass-covered heap, surviving mottes have contributed greatly to the understanding of the history of Scottish castles. The A944 then joins the A97 (go left), and just a few minutes later a sign points to Glenbuchat Castle, a plain Z-plan tower house.

Kildrummy Castle

★ ③⓪ *18 mi northeast of Corgarff, 23 mi north of Ballater, 22 mi north of Aboyne.*

Kildrummy Castle is significant because of its age—it dates to the 13th century—and because it has ties to the mainstream medieval traditions of European castle building. It shares features with Harlech and Caernarfon, in Wales, as well as with Château de Coucy, near Laon, France. Kildrummy underwent several expansions at the hands of England's King Edward I (1239–1307); the castle was back in Scottish hands in 1306, when it was besieged by King Edward I's son. The defenders were betrayed by a certain Osbarn the Smith, who was promised a large amount of gold by the English forces. They gave it to him after the castle fell, pouring it molten down his throat, or so the ghoulish story goes. Kildrummy's prominence ended after the collapse of the 1715 Jacobite uprising. It had been the rebel headquarters and was consequently dismantled. ⊠ *A97* ☎ *0131/668–8800* ⊕ *www.historic-scotland.gov. uk* ⊠ *£2.20* ⊘ *Apr.–Sept., daily 9:30–6.*

Kildrummy Castle Gardens, behind the castle and with a separate entrance from the main road, are built in what was the original quarry for the castle. This sheltered bowl within the woodlands has a broad range of shrubs and alpine plants and a notable water garden. ⊠ *A97* ☎ *019755/71203 or 019755/71277* ⊕ *www.kildrummy-castle-gardens. co.uk* ⊠ *£2.50* ⊘ *Apr.–Oct., daily 10–5; call to confirm opening times late in season.*

Where to Stay & Eat

★ ×▥ **Kildrummy Castle Hotel.** A grand late-Victorian country house, this
££££–£££££ hotel offers a peaceful stay and attentive service. Oak paneling, beautiful plasterwork, and gentle color schemes create a serene environment, enhanced by the views of Kildrummy Castle Gardens next door. The Scottish cuisine (£££–££££) uses local game as well as seafood. ⊠ *A97, Kildrummy, by Alford, Aberdeenshire AB33 8RA* ☎ *019755/71288* ⊟ *019755/71345* ⊕ *www.kildrummycastlehotel.co.uk* ⊠ *16 rooms* △ *Restaurant, fishing, bar, laundry service, no-smoking rooms; no a/c* ⊟ *MC, V* ⊘ *Closed Jan.* ⫝̸ *BP.*

Alford

9 mi east of Kildrummy, 28 mi west of Aberdeen.

A plain and sturdy settlement in the Howe (Hollow) of Alford, this town gives those who have grown somewhat weary of castle hopping a break:
③① it has a museum instead. The **Grampian Transport Museum** specializes in

road-based means of locomotion, backed up by a library and archives. One of its more unusual exhibits is the *Craigievar Express*, a steam-driven creation invented by the local postman to deliver mail more efficiently. ✉ *Alford* ☎ *019755/62292* 🌐 *www.gtm.org.uk* 🎫 *£4.50* ⏲ *Apr.–Sept., daily 10–5; Oct., daily 10–4.*

Craigievar Castle

★ 32 *5 mi south of Alford.*

Craigievar Castle is much as the stonemasons left it in 1626, with its pepper-pot turrets and towers. It was built in relatively peaceful times by William Forbes, a successful merchant in trade with the Baltic Sea ports (hence he was also known as Danzig Willie). Centuries of care and wise stewardship have ensured that the experience is as authentic as possible. Guided tours take you past family portraits and beautiful 17th- and 18th-century furniture. ✉ *5 mi south of Alford on A980* ☎ *013398/83635* 🌐 *www.nts.org.uk* 🎫 *Castle and grounds £9; grounds only, £1* ⏲ *Castle Apr.–Sept., Fri.–Tues. noon–5:30; grounds daily 9:30–sunset.*

Castle Fraser

33 *8 mi southeast of Alford.*

The massive Castle Fraser, southeast of Alford, is the largest of the castles of Mar. Although it shows a variety of styles reflecting the taste of its owners from the 15th through the 19th centuries, its design is typical of the cavalcade of castles that exist here in the northeast, and for good reason, as this—along with many other of the region's castles, including Midmar, Craigievar, Crathes, and Glenbuchat—was designed by a family of master masons called Bell. The walled garden includes a recreation of a 19th-century knot garden, with colorful flowerbeds, box hedging, gravel paths, and splendid herbaceous borders. Have lunch in the tearoom or the picnic area. ✉ *8 mi southeast of Alford off A944* ☎ *01330/833463* 🌐 *www.nts.org.uk* 🎫 *£7* ⏲ *Castle Apr.–June and Sept., Fri.–Tues. noon–5:30; July–Aug., daily 11–5:30; gardens daily 9:30–6; grounds daily 9:30–sunset.*

THE NORTHEAST

This route starts inland, traveling toward Speyside—the valley, or strath, of the River Spey—famed for its whisky distilleries, which it promotes in yet another signposted trail. Distilling scotch is not an intrinsically spectacular process. It involves pure water, malted barley, and sometimes peat smoke, then a lot of bubbling and fermentation, all of which cause a number of odd smells. The result is a prestigious product with a fascinating range of flavors that you either enjoy immensely or not at all.

Instead of assiduously following the Malt Whisky Trail, just dip into it and blend it with some other aspects of the lower end of Speyside—the county of Moray. Whisky notwithstanding, Moray's scenic qualities, low rainfall, and other reassuring weather statistics are also worth remembering. The suggested route then allows you to sample the northeastern seaboard, including some of the best but least-known coastal scenery in Scotland.

Dufftown

★ 34 *54 mi from Aberdeen via A96 and A920 (turn west at Huntly).*

On one of the Spey tributaries, Dufftown was planned in 1817 by the earl of Fife. In the center of town, the conspicuous battlemented **clock**

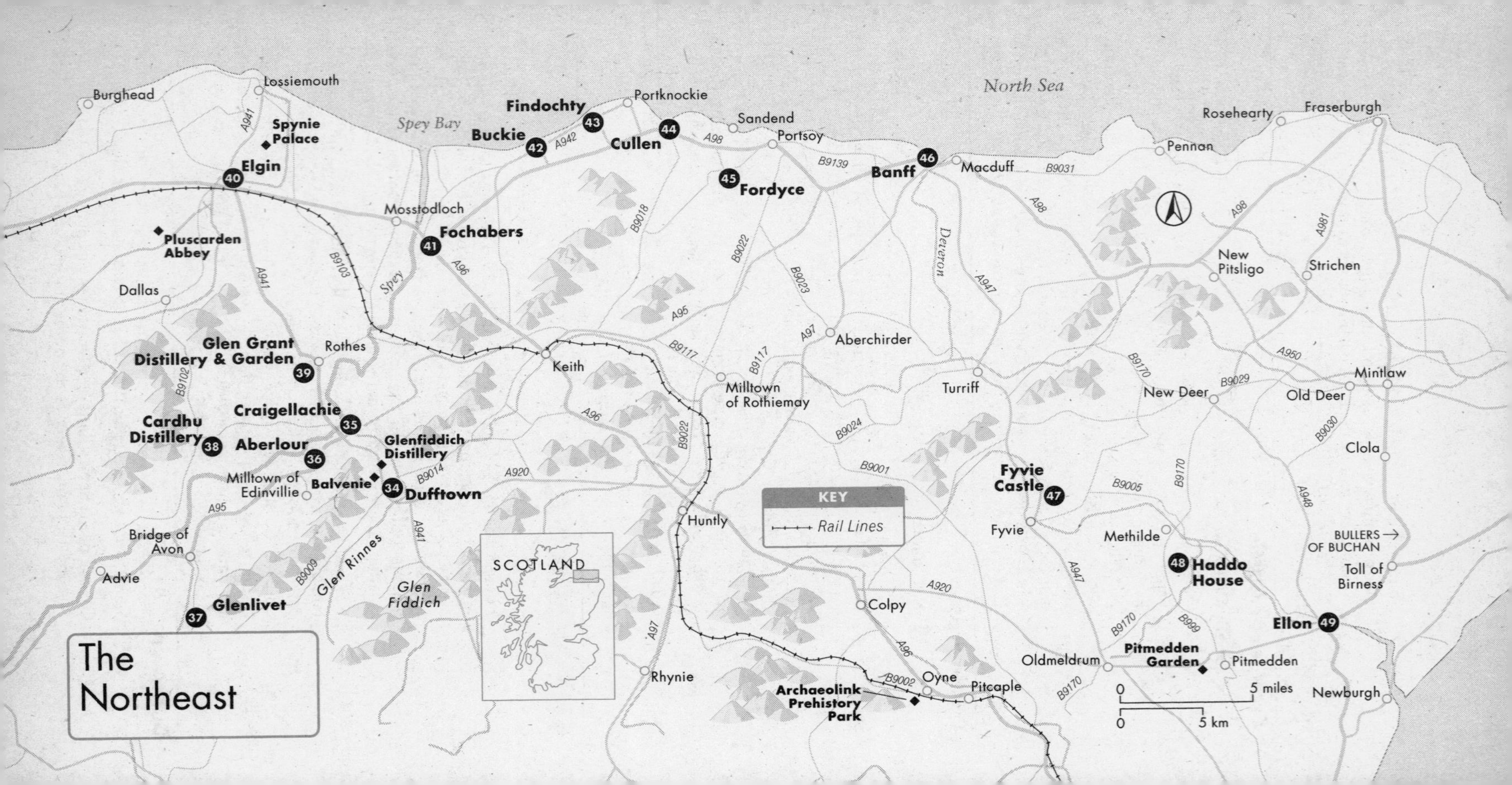

The Northeast
North Sea
Spey Bay
KEY
Rail Lines
SCOTLAND
0 5 miles
0 5 km
Burghead
Lossiemouth
Spynie Palace
40 Elgin
Pluscarden Abbey
Dallas
Mosstodloch
41 Fochabers
42 Buckie
43 Findochty
Portknockie
44 Cullen
Sandend
Portsoy
45 Fordyce
46 Banff
Macduff
Pennan
Rosehearty
Fraserburgh
New Pitsligo
Strichen
Mintlaw
Old Deer
New Deer
Clola
BULLERS OF BUCHAN
Toll of Birness
49 Ellon
Newburgh
Pitmedden
Pitmedden Garden
48 Haddo House
Methilde
Oldmeldrum
47 Fyvie Castle
Fyvie
Turriff
Aberchirder
Milltown of Rothiemay
Keith
Huntly
Rhynie
Colpy
Oyne
Pitcaple
Archaeolink Prehistory Park
Glen Grant Distillery & Garden 39
Rothes
Craigellachie 35
Cardhu Distillery 38
Aberlour 36
Glenfiddich Distillery
Balvenie
34 Dufftown
Milltown of Edinvillie
Bridge of Avon
Advie
37 Glenlivet
Glen Rinnes
Glen Fiddich
Spey
Deveron
A941
A942
A98
A96
A95
A97
A920
A947
A950
A948
A981
B9103
B9102
B9018
B9022
B9139
B9031
B9023
B9117
B9024
B9001
B9014
B9009
B9170
B9029
B9030
B9005
B999
B9002

tower—the centerpiece of the planned town and a former jail—houses the local tourist information center. ✉ *The Square* ☎ *01340/820501* ⏲ *Apr.–Oct., daily 9–5.*

Many make **Glenfiddich Distillery,** a half mile north of Dufftown, their first stop on the Malt Whisky Trail. The independent company of William Grant and Sons Limited was the first to realize the tourist potential of the distilling process. The company began offering tours and subsequently built an entertaining visitor center. The audiovisual show and displays are as worthwhile as the tour, and the traditional stone-walled premises with the typical pagoda-roof malting buildings are pleasant. You don't have to like whisky to come away feeling you've learned something about a leading Scottish export. ✉ *North of Dufftown on A941* ☎ *01340/820373* 🌐 *www.glenfiddich.com* 🎫 *Free* ⏲ *Easter–mid-Oct., Mon.–Sat. 9:30–4:30, Sun. noon–4:30; mid-Oct.–Easter, weekdays 9:30–4:30.*

On a mound just above the Glenfiddich Distillery is a grim, gray, and squat curtain-walled castle, **Balvenie.** This fortress, which dates from the 13th century, once commanded the glens and passes toward Speyside and Elgin. ✉ *Dufftown* ☎ *0131/668–8800* 🎫 *£1.80* ⏲ *Apr.–Sept., daily 9:30–6.*

Mortlach Church, set in a hollow by the Dullan Water, is thought to be one of Scotland's oldest Christian sites, perhaps founded by St. Moluag, a contemporary of St. Columba, as early as AD 566. Note the weathered Pictish cross in the churchyard and the even older stone under cover in the vestibule, with a strange Pictish elephantlike beast carved on it. Though much of the church was rebuilt after 1876, some early work survives, including three lancet windows from the 13th century and a leper's squint (a hole extended to the outside of the church so that lepers could hear the service but be kept away from the rest of the congregation).

Craigellachie

35 *4 mi northwest of Dufftown via A941.*

Renowned as an angling resort, Craigellachie, like so many Speyside settlements, is sometimes enveloped in the malty reek of the local industry. Just before the village you'll notice the huge **Speyside Cooperage and Visitor Centre,** a major stop on the Malt Whisky Trail. Inside, you can watch craftspeople make and repair oak barrels used in the local whisky industry. ✉ *Dufftown Rd.* ☎ *01340/871108* 🎫 *£3.10* ⏲ *Jan.–mid-Dec., weekdays 9:30–4:30.*

The Spey itself is crossed by a handsome **suspension bridge,** designed by Thomas Telford (1757–1834) in 1814 and now bypassed by the modern road.

Aberlour

36 *2 mi southwest of Craigellachie via A95.*

Aberlour, often listed as Charlestown of Aberlour on maps, is a handsome little burgh, essentially Victorian in style, though actually founded in 1812 by the local landowner. The names of the noted local whisky stills are Cragganmore, Aberlour, and **Glenfarclas,** which is just west of town. Tour guides tell the story of Glenfarclas and the Grant family, and tours end with tastings in the Ship Room, the intact lounge of the former ocean liner, *Empress of Australia.* ☎ *01807/500245* 🌐 *www.*

CloseUp

WHISKY, THE WATER OF LIFE

C **ONJURED FROM AN INNOCUOUS MIX** *of malted barley, water, and yeast, malt whisky is for many synonymous with Scotland. Clans produced whisky for hundreds of years before it emerged as Scotland's national drink and major export. Today those centuries of expertise result in a sublimely subtle drink with many different layers of flavor. Each distillery produces a malt with—to the expert—instantly identifiable, predominant notes peculiarly its own.*

There are two types of whisky: malt and grain. Malt whisky, generally acknowledged to have a more sophisticated bouquet and flavor, is made with malted barley—barley that is soaked in water until the grains germinate and then dried to halt the germination, all of which adds extra flavor and a touch of sweetness to the brew. Grain whisky also contains malted barley, but with the addition of unmalted barley and maize. Blended whiskies, which make up many of the leading brands, usually balance malt and grain whisky distillations; deluxe blends contain a higher percentage of malts. Blends that contain several malt whiskies are called "vatted malts." Whisky connoisseurs often prefer to taste the single malts: the unblended whisky from a single distillery. In simple terms, malt whiskies may be classified into "eastern" and "western" in style, with the whisky made in the east of Scotland, for example in Speyside, being lighter and sweeter than the products of the western isles, which often have a taste of peat smoke or even iodine.

The production process is, by comparison, relatively straightforward: just malt your barley, mash it, ferment it and distill it, then mature to perfection. To find out the details, join a distillery tour, and be rewarded with a dram.

---

glenfarclas.co.uk 🎫 *£3.50* ⏲ *Apr.–Sept., weekdays 10–5, also Jun.–Sept., Sat. 10-5; Oct.–Mar., weekdays 10–4.*

Where to Eat

£ ✕ **Old Pantry.** This corner restaurant, overlooking Aberlour's pleasant, tree-shaded central square, serves everything from a cup of coffee with a sticky cake to a three-course spread of soup, roast meat, and traditional pudding. ✉ *The Square* ☎ *01340/871617* 💳 *MC, V.*

Shopping

Country Cousins (✉ 110 High St., Aberlour ☎ 01340/871142) sells designer women's clothing. Beneath Country Cousins is **The Basement** (✉ 110 High St. ☎ 01340/871142), with an eclectic mix of antique furniture, books, pictures and ceramics. A couple of miles west of Aberlour, at Marypark, look for **Speyside Pottery** (✉ Ballindalloch ☎ 01807/500338), where Thomas and Anne Gough produce domestic stoneware in satisfying, traditional shapes.

Glenlivet

★ ㊲ *10 mi southwest of Aberlour via A95 and B9008.*

Glenlivet is a very small village with a very famous distillery by the same name. Founded in 1824 by George Smith, today Glenlivet Distillery produces one of the best-known 12-year-old single malts in the world. Take the distillery tour for a chance to see inside the huge bonded warehouse where the whisky steeps in oak casks. The River Livet runs through the glen and by the distillery in an area renowned for its birdlife. ✉ *Glenlivet, Ballindalloch* ☎ *01542/783220* 🌐 *www.theglenlivet.com* 🎫 *£3* ⏲ *Apr.–Oct., Mon.–Sat. 10–4, Sun. 12:30–4.*

Where to Stay & Eat

★ £££–££££ **Minmore House.** Minmore has the distinctive feel of a private home, with faded chintz in the drawing room (where afternoon tea is served) and a paneled library. An eclectic mix of antique furnishings decorate the guest rooms. The restaurant (££££) serves a prix-fixe dinner of exceptional contemporary Scottish cuisine that may include Aberdeen Angus beef. After dinner, enjoy one of more than 100 malt whiskies in the library bar. The Speyside Way long-distance footpath passes below the house, and the area is famous for bird-watching. ✉ *Glenlivet, Ballindalloch, Banffshire AB37 9DB* ☎ *01807/590378* 📠 *01807/590472* 🌐 *www.minmorehousehotel.com* *10 rooms* *Restaurant, bar; no a/c, no room TVs, no kids under 10* *AE, MC, V* ⏲ *Closed mid-Feb.–Mar.* *BP.*

en route

From Glenlivet, make your way back to Bridge of Avon, and turn right (north) onto the A95 toward Aberlour. When you reach Marypark, turn west onto a minor road, signed Knockando, that takes you over the river Spey. Once across the river, turn north onto the B9102 and within a few minutes you will arrive at Cardhu, another Malt Whisky Trail stop.

Cardhu Distillery

38 *10 mi north of Glenlivet via B9008, A95, and B9102.*

Cardhu Distillery was established by John and Helen Cumming in 1811, though officially they founded it in 1824, after distilling was made legal by the Excise Act of 1823. Today its product lies at the heart of Johnnie Walker Blends. Guided tours take you to the mashing, fermenting, and distilling halls. You may even taste the remarkably smooth single malt before it gets near any blending vats. ✉ *Knockando* ☎ *01340/872555* *£4* ⏲ *Jan.–Easter, weekdays 11–3; Easter–June, weekdays 10–5; July–Sept., Mon.–Sat. 10–5, Sun. noon–4; Oct., weekdays 11–4; Nov.–Dec., weekdays 11–3. Last tour one hour before closing.*

Glen Grant Distillery & Garden

39 *12 mi northeast of Cardhu via B9102 and A941.*

Glen Grant will come as a welcome relief to less-than-enthusiastic companions of dedicated Malt Whisky Trail followers. In addition to a distillery tour, there are large and beautiful garden. James Grant founded the distillery in 1840 when he was only 25, and it was the first distillery to be electrically powered. Now owned by Chivas Regal, Glen Grant produces a distinctive pale-gold, clear whisky, with an almost floral or fruity finish, using peculiarly tall stills and special purifiers. The gardens are planted and tended as Major Grant planned them, with orchards and woodland walks, log bridges over waterfalls, a magnificent lily pond, and azaleas and rhododendrons in profusion. ✉ *A941, Rothes* ☎ *01542/783318* 🌐 *www.chivas.com* *£3* ⏲ *Apr.–Oct., Mon.–Sat. 10–4; Sun. 12:30–4.*

Elgin

40 *10 mi north of Rothes via A941, 69 mi northwest of Aberdeen, 41 mi east of Inverness via A96.*

As the center of the fertile Laigh (low-lying lands) of Moray, Elgin has been of local importance for centuries. Like Aberdeen, it's self-supporting and previously remote, sheltered by great hills to the south and lying between two major rivers, the Spey and the Findhorn. Beginning in the 13th century, Elgin became an important religious center, a cathedral city with a walled town growing up around the cathedral and adjacent to the original settlement. Left in peace for at least some of its history, Elgin prospered, and by the early 18th century it became a mini-Edinburgh of the north and a place where country gentlemen spent their winters. It even echoed Edinburgh in carrying out wide-scale reconstruction in the early part of the 18th century: much of the old town was swept away in a wave of rebuilding, giving Elgin the fine neoclassical buildings that survive today.

The town's old street plan survived almost intact until the late 20th century, when it succumbed to the modern madness of demolishing great swaths of buildings for the sake of better traffic flow: Elgin suffered from its position on the Aberdeen–Inverness main road. However, the central main-street plan and some of the older little streets and *wynds* (alleyways) remain. You'll also see Elgin's past in the arcaded shop fronts—some of which date from the late-17th century—on the main shopping street.

At the center of Elgin, the most conspicuous structure is **St. Giles Church,** which divides High Street. The grand foursquare building constructed in 1828 exhibits the Greek revival style: note the columns, the pilasters, and the top of the spire, surmounted by a representation of the Lysicrates Monument. Past the arcaded shops at the east end of High Street, you can see the **Little Cross** (17th century), which marked the boundary between the town and the cathedral grounds. The **Elgin Museum,** near the Little Cross, has an especially interesting collection of dinosaur relics. ✉ *High St.* ☎ *01343/543675* ⏲ *Apr.–Oct., weekdays 10–5, Sat. 11–4, Sun. 2–5; Nov.–Mar. by appointment only.*

★ Cooper Park contains a magnificent ruin, the **Elgin Cathedral,** consecrated in 1224. Its eventful story included devastation by fire: a 1390 act of retaliation by Alexander Stewart (circa 1343–1405), the Wolf of Badenoch. The illegitimate-son-turned-bandit of King David II (1324–71) had sought revenge for his excommunication by the bishop of Moray. The cathedral was rebuilt but finally fell into disuse after the Reformation in 1560. By 1567 the highest authority in the land, the regent earl of Moray, had stripped the lead from the roof to pay for his army. Thus ended the career of the religious seat known as the Lamp of the North. Some traces of the cathedral settlement survive—the gateway Pann's Port and the Bishop's Palace—although they've been drastically altered. Cooper Park is a five-minute walk northeast of Elgin Museum, across the bypass road. ☎ *0131/668–8800* 🌐 *www.historic-scotland.gov.uk* 🎫 *£3; combined admission with Spynie Palace £3.50* ⏲ *Apr.–Sept., daily 9:30–6; Oct.–Mar., Mon.–Wed. and Sat. 9:30–4, Thurs. 9:30–noon, Sun. 2–4.*

Just north of Elgin is **Spynie Palace,** the impressive 15th-century former headquarters of the bishops of Moray. It has now fallen into ruin, though the top of the tower has good views over the Laigh of Moray. Find it by turning right off the main A941 Elgin–Lossiemouth road. ☎ *0131/668–8800* 🌐 *www.historic-scotland.gov.uk* 🎫 *£2.20; combined admission with Elgin Cathedral £3.50* ⏲ *Apr.–Sept., daily 9:30–6; Oct.–Mar., Sat. 9:30–4, Sun. 2–4.*

off the beaten path

PLUSCARDEN ABBEY – Given the general destruction caused by the 16th-century upheaval of the Reformation, abbeys in Scotland tend to be ruinous and deserted, but at Pluscarden Abbey the monks' way of life continues. Originally a 13th-century structure, the abbey was abandoned by the religious community after the Reformation. The third marquis of Bute bought the remains in 1897 and initiated a restoration program that continues today. Monks from Prinknash Abbey near Gloucester, England, returned here in 1948, and the abbey is now an active community. ✉ *6 mi southwest of Elgin, off B9010* 💷 *Free* ⏲ *Daily 5 AM–8:30 PM.*

Where to Stay & Eat

££££–£££££ ✕🏨 **Mansion House Hotel.** The crenelated tower is the first thing you are likely to see as you drive up to this 19th-century baronial mansion set amid woodland on a flawless green lawn overlooking the River Lossie. The rooms are individually decorated; all are pleasant and comfortable. The restaurant (£££££) serves fine Scottish cuisine, such as loin of venison roasted with juniper berries. ✉ *The Haugh, IV30 1AW* ☎ *01343/548811* 📠 *01343/547916* 🌐 *www.mansionhousehotel.co.uk* *23 rooms* *Restaurant, room service, cable TV, pool, gym, hair salon, massage, sauna, bar; no a/c* 💳 *AE, DC, MC, V* 🍽 *BP.*

Shopping

Gordon and MacPhail (✉ 58 South St. ☎ 01343/545110), an outstanding delicatessen and wine merchant, also stocks rare malt whiskies. This is a good place to shop for gifts for those foodies among your friends. **Johnstons of Elgin** (✉ Newmill ☎ 01343/554099) is a woolen mill with a worldwide reputation for its luxury fabrics, especially cashmere. The bold color range is particularly appealing. The large visitor-center shop stocks not only the firm's own products but also top-quality Scottish crafts and giftware. There's also a restaurant. **Sonya Designer Clothing** (✉ 137 High St. ☎ 01343/549111) may occupy small premises, but the shop is big on ideas and choices for casual wear, clubbing glitter-wear, and swimwear. A half mile outside of Elgin on the A96 toward Inverness, you'll find **The Oakwood** (✉ Forest Rd., Burghead ☎ 01343/543200), a 1920s Swiss-chalet-style former roadhouse with an excellent antiques center stocking everything from large furniture to lead soldiers. At the restaurant here you can have a delicious bowl of homemade soup and French bread for £2.50. Don't miss the upstairs display area, with its art nouveau stained-glass windows.

Fochabers

41 *9 mi east of Elgin.*

Just before reaching the Fochabers village center, you'll see the works of a major local employer, Baxters of Fochabers. From Tokyo to New York, upmarket stores stock their soups, jams, chutneys, and other gourmet products—all of which are made here, close to the River Spey. The **Baxters Visitors Centre** presents a video, *Baxters Experience,* about the history of the business, plus interactive exhibits and cooking demonstrations. You can have a look in a re-creation of the Baxters' first grocery shop, a real shop that stocks Baxters' goods, and a shop called the Best of Scotland, specializing in a range of Scottish products. A restaurant serves up an assortment of delectables. ✉ *1 mi west of Fochabers on the A96* ☎ *01343/820666* 🌐 *www.baxters.com* 💷 *Free; small charge for cooking demonstrations and other special features* ⏲ *Apr.–Oct., daily 9–6; Nov.–Dec., daily 9–5; Jan.–Mar., daily 10–5; check ahead to see if all areas are operating in winter months.*

Once over the Spey Bridge and past the cricket ground (a very unusual sight in Scotland), you'll find the symmetrical, 18th-century Fochabers village square lined with antiques dealers. Through one of these shops, Pringle Antiques, you can enter the **Fochabers Folk Museum,** a converted church that has a fine collection of items relating to past life in the village and surrounding area. Exhibits include carts and carriages, farm implements, and Victorian toys. ✉ *Behind Pringle Antiques* ☎ *01343/821204* 🎫 *Free* ⏲ *Easter–Oct., daily 9:30–1 and 2–5.*

One of the village's lesser-known treasures is the **Gordon Chapel** (✉ Duke St., just off the Square), which has an exceptional set of stained-glass windows by Pre-Raphaelite artist Sir Edward Burne-Jones.

Consider diverting onto the road that runs south directly opposite the Fochabers Folk Museum. Leaving the houses behind for well-hedged country lanes, you will discover a Forestry Commission sign to the **Earth Pillars.** These curious eroded sandstone pillars are framed by tall-trunk pines and overlook a wide prospect of the lower Spey Valley.

off the beaten path

STRATHISLA DISTILLERY – Whisky lovers should take the A96 a few minutes southwest from Fochabers to see this distillery in the small town of Keith. Strathisla Distillery was built in 1786 and now produces the main component of the Chivas Regal blend. Guided tours take you through the mash house, tun room, and still house, ending with a tasting session. ✉ *Seafield Ave., Keith* ☎ *01542/783044* 🌐 *www.chivas.com* 🎫 *£4* ⏲ *Apr.–Oct., Mon.–Sat. 10–4, Sun. 12:30–4.*

Shopping

Antiques (Fochabers) (✉ Hadlow House, The Square ☎ 01343/820838) carries quirky old kitchenware, stripped pine, china, pictures, jewelry, and antique furniture. **Pringle Antiques** (✉ High St. ☎ 01343/820362) is a good place to shop for small furniture, pottery, glassware, silver, and jewelry. **Watts Antiques** (✉ 45 High St. ☎ 01343/820077) has small collectibles, jewelry, ornaments, and china. **Art and Antiques** (✉ 33 High St. ☎ 01343/829104) combines an unusual mix of original art by the owners with ceramic, glassware, and small pieces of furniture.Take a break from all the white elephants by stopping into **Balance Natural Health** (✉ 59 High St. ☎ 01343/821443), which stocks homeopathic remedies, potpourris, and the like. If you're interested in contemporary art, some by local artists, head to **Just Art** (✉ 64 High St. ☎ 01343/820500), a fine gallery with high-quality ceramics and paintings. The **Boogie Woogie** (✉ 2 Regent Sq., Fife Keith ☎ 01542/888077 🌐 www.boogiewoogieshop.com) is an emporium of unusual gifts, home furnishings, jewelry, clothes, and shoes; plus a coffee shop that serves simple warm meals, coffee, and baked goods. The shop is open daily. At **the Quaich** (✉ 85 High St. ☎ 01343/820981) you can stock up on cards and small gifts, then sit with a cup of tea and a home-baked snack.

Buckie

42 *8 mi east of Fochabers via A98 and A942.*

The fishing port of Buckie and its satellite villages are gray and workaday, with plenty of Victorian architecture added to the original fishermen's cottages, which sit almost on the sea. The **Buckie Drifter Maritime Heritage Centre,** housed in premises reminiscent of an old fishing drifter (a fishing vessel with sails), is a hands-on visitor center that tells the story of the herring industry and of Buckie's development as a port. Upstairs, you enter a 1920s quayside scene, with a replica steam drifter that you can board and barrels you can pack with herring. ✉ *Freuchny Rd. off Commercial Rd.* ☎ *01542/834646* 🌐 *www.moray.org/bdrifter* 🎫 *£2.75* ⏲ *Apr.–Oct., Mon.–Sat. 10–5, Sun. noon–5.*

The **Peter Anson Gallery** displays a selection of watercolor works related to the development of the fishing industry. The gallery is housed in a room reached through a library. ✉ *Cluny Pl.* ☎ *01542/832121* 🎫 *Free* ⏲ *Weekdays 10–8, Sat. 10–noon.*

Where to Eat

★ ££££ **Old Monastery.** On a broad, wooded slope set back from the coast near Buckie, with westward views as far as the hills of Wester Ross, sits the Old Monastery, once a Victorian religious establishment. The monastic theme carries through to the restrained interior of the Cloisters Bar and the Chapel Restaurant, where the cream-painted walls are hand stencilled in shades of terra-cotta and green. Local specialties—fresh fish, venison, and Aberdeen Angus beef—make up the Scottish prix-fixe menu. The restaurant is on an unclassified road off the A98. Follow signs to Drybridge, but instead of turning into the village, continue up the hill for 1½ mi. ✉ *Drybridge, Buckie* ☎ *01542/832660* ▭ *AE, MC, V* ⏲ *Closed Mon.–Tues. No dinner Sun.*

en route

Driving east you'll pass a string of salty little fishing villages. They paint a colorful scene with their gabled houses and fishing nets set out to dry amid the rocky shoreline.

Findochty

43 *2 mi east of Buckie on A942.*

The residents of Findochty are known for their fastidiousness and creativity in painting their houses, taking the art of house painting to a new level. Some residents even paint the mortar between the stonework a different color from the exterior. The harbor, with many colorful small sailing boats tied up to the quay, has a faint echo of the Mediterranean about it. A 15-minute stroll about the older part of the village will take you past several blocks of painted homes.

Cullen

★ 44 *3 mi east of Findochty.*

Look for some wonderfully painted homes at Cullen, in the old fishermen's town below the railway viaduct. But the real attractions of this little resort are its white-sand beach and the fine view west toward the aptly named Bowfiddle Rock. A stroll along the beach reveals the shape of the fishing settlement below and the 18th-century town above. Most unusual for a town of its size, Cullen has numerous specialty shops—antiques and gift stores, butchers, an ironmonger, a baker, a pharmacy, and a locally famous ice cream shop among them—as well as several hotels and cafés.

Where to Stay & Eat

££ **The Seafield Hotel.** A former coaching inn built in 1822, this hotel has high standards in every department. Deep, rich colors prevail, and comfort and friendliness are key. The restaurant (£££), with its golden walls and tartan carpet, has an extensive à la carte Scottish menu that includes seafood, game, beef, and lamb. ✉ *Seafield St., Cullen AB56 4SG* ☎ *01542/840791* 🖷 *01542/840736* 🌐 *www.theseafieldhotel.com* *20 rooms* *Restaurant, room service, bar, laundry service, Internet, no-smoking rooms; no a/c* ▭ *AE, MC, V* *BP.*

Fordyce

45 *5 mi east of Cullen.*

The conservation village of Fordyce lies among the barley fields of Banffshire like a small slice of rural England gone far adrift. You can stroll by the churchyard, picnic on the old bleaching green (a notice board explains everything), or visit a restored 19th-century carpenter's workshop, where musical instruments are made.

Where to Stay

★ ££ Academy House. This B&B offers accommodations in what was once the headmaster's house for the local secondary school. Well-chosen antiques decorate the spacious rooms. Evening meals are served on request at £13 per person. *School Rd., AB45 2SJ 01261/842743 www.fordyceaccommodation.com 2 rooms Dining room, exercise equipment, Internet; no a/c, no room phones No credit cards BP.*

Banff

46 *36 mi east of Elgin, 47 mi north of Aberdeen.*

Midway along the northeast coast, overlooking Moray Firth and the estuary of the River Deveron, Banff is a fishing town of considerable elegance that feels as though it's a million miles from tartan-clad Scotland. Part Georgian, like Edinburgh's New Town, and part 16th-century small burgh, like Culross, Banff is an exemplary east-coast salty town, with a tiny harbor and fine architecture. It's also within easy reach of plenty of unspoiled coastline—cliff and rock to the east, at Gardenstown (known as Gamrie) and Pennan, or beautiful little sandy beaches westward toward Sandend and Cullen.

The jewel in Banff's crown is the grand mansion of **Duff House,** a splendid William Adam–designed (1689–1748) baroque mansion that has been restored as an outstation of the National Galleries of Scotland. Many fine paintings are displayed in rooms furnished to reflect the days when the house was occupied by the dukes of Fife. A good tearoom and a shop are in the basement. *Off the A98 01261/818181 www.duffhouse.com £4.50 Apr.–Oct., daily 11–5; Nov.–Mar., Thurs.–Sun. 11–4.*

Across the river in Banff's twin town, Macduff, on the shore east of the harbor, stands **Macduff Marine Aquarium.** A 250,000-gallon central tank and many smaller display areas and touch pools show the sea life of the Moray Firth and North Atlantic. *High Shore 01261/833369 www.marine-aquarium.com £4 Daily 10–5.*

Fyvie Castle

47 *18 mi south of Banff, 18 mi northwest of Ellon.*

In an area rife with castles, Fyvie Castle stands out as the most complex. Five great towers built by five successive powerful families turned a 13th-century foursquare castle into an opulent Edwardian statement of wealth. There are some superb paintings on view, including 12 Raeburns, as well as myriad sumptuous interiors and many walks on the castle grounds. Fyvie is impressive for its sheer impact—if you like your castles oppressive and gloomy. *Off A947 between Oldmeldrum and Turriff 01651/891266 www.nts.org.uk £7 Castle Apr.–June and Sept., Fri.–Tues. noon–5; July–Aug., daily 11–5; grounds daily 9:30–dusk.*

Haddo House

★ 48 *12 mi southeast of Fyvie Castle.*

Created as the home of the Gordon family, earls and marquesses of Aberdeen, Haddo House—designed by William Adam—is now cared for by the National Trust for Scotland. Built in 1732, the elegant mansion has a light and graceful Georgian design, with curving wings on either side of a harmonious, symmetrical facade. The interior is late-Victorian ornate, with magnificent paintings (including works by Pompeo Batoni and Sir Thomas Lawrence) and objets d'art. Pre-Raphaelite stained-glass windows by Sir Edward Burne-Jones grace the chapel. Outside is a terrace garden with a fountain, and few yards farther is Haddo Country Park, which has walking trails leading to memorials about the Gordon family. ✉ *Off B999, 8 mi northwest of Ellon* ☎ *01651/851440* 🌐 *www.nts.org.uk* 🎫 *£7* ⏲ *House June, Fri.–Mon. 11–4:30; July–Aug., daily 11–4:30. Shop and tearoom Good Fri.–Easter Mon., daily 11–5; May–Jun. and Sept.–Oct., Fri.–Mon. 11–5; Jul.–Aug., daily 11–5. Park and garden daily 9:30–6.*

Ellon

49 *8 mi southeast of Haddo House, 32 mi southwest of Banff.*

Formerly a market center on what was then the lowest bridging point of the River Ythan, Ellon, a bedroom suburb of Aberdeen, is a small town at the center of a rural hinterland. It's also well placed for visiting several of Castle Country's splendid properties.

Five miles west of Ellon, at Pitmedden, is a unique re-creation by the National Trust for Scotland of a 17th-century garden. **Pitmedden Garden** is best visited in high summer, from July onwards, when annual bedding plants form intricate formal patterns. The 100-acre estate also has woodland and farmland walks, as well as the Museum of Farming Life. ☎ *01651/842352* 🌐 *www.nts.org.uk* 🎫 *£5* ⏲ *Garden, shop, museum, and tearoom May–Sept., daily 10–5:30; grounds daily 10–5:30.*

off the beaten path

ARCHAEOLINK PREHISTORY PARK – A strange grass-covered dome rises from the hillside halfway between Huntly and Aberdeen. This example of modern architecture houses an exhibition about far older structures: the many stone circles, symbol stones, and other prehistoric monuments scattered all over this part of the northeast. Dedicated to the "exploration of life before history," Archaeolink also includes open-air exhibits, such as a replica of an Iron Age farm. ✉ *Off A96 at Oyne, 20 mi west of Ellon* ☎ *01464/851500* 🎫 *£4.25* ⏲ *Apr.–Oct., daily 10–5; Nov.–Mar., Sun.–Tues. 11–3.*

ABERDEEN & THE NORTHEAST A TO Z

To research prices, get advice from other travelers, and book travel arrangements, visit www.fodors.com.

AIR TRAVEL

CARRIERS Airlines linking Aberdeen with Europe include KLM U.K., with flights to Amsterdam (the Netherlands), to Bergen and Stavanger (Norway), and within the United Kingdom; SAS (Scandinavian Airlines), serving Stavanger; British Airways, serving Paris via Manchester and offering domestic flights as well; and British Midland, with flights to Esbjerg (Denmark) and within the United Kingdom. In addition to British Airways, British Midland, and KLM U.K., domestic service between Aberdeen and most major U.K. airports is offered by Brymon, a British Airways subsidiary, and easyJet.

British Airways ☎ 08457/733377 🌐 www.ba.com. **British Midland** ☎ 0870/607-0555 🌐 www.flybmi.com. **Brymon** ☎ 01224/770596. **easyJet** ☎ 0870/600-0000 🌐 www.easyjet.com. **KLM U.K.** ☎ 0870/507-4074 🌐 www.klmuk.com. **SAS** (Scandinavian Airlines) ☎ 087060/727727 🌐 www.scandinavian.net.

AIRPORTS

Aberdeen Airport—serving both international and domestic flights—is in Dyce, 7 mi west of the city center on the A96 (Inverness).

Aberdeen Airport ☎ 01224/722331 🌐 www.baa.co.uk.

AIRPORT TRANSFERS

First Aberdeen Bus 27 operates between the airport terminal and Union Street in the center of Aberdeen. Buses (£1.45) run frequently at peak times, less often at midday and in the evening; the journey time is approximately 40 minutes.

The drive to the center of Aberdeen is easy via the A96 (which can be busy during rush hour).

Dyce is on ScotRail's Inverness–Aberdeen route. The rail station is a short taxi ride from the terminal building. The ride takes 12 minutes, and trains run approximately every two hours. If you intend to visit the western region first, you can travel northwest, from Aberdeen, by rail, direct to Elgin via Inverurie, Insch, Huntly, and Keith.

First Aberdeen ☎ 01224/650000 www.firstaberdeen.co.uk. **National Rail** ☎ 08457/484950 www.railtrack.co.uk.

BOAT & FERRY TRAVEL

There's ferry service between Aberdeen, Lerwick (Shetland), and Kirkwall (Orkney) operated by Northlink Ferries. From Lerwick, you can catch the Smyril Line ferry to Bergen (Norway); this ferry runs between May and September.

Northlink Ferries ✉ The New Harbour Building, Ferry Rd., Stromness, Orkney, KW16 3BH ☎ 01856/851144 fax 01856/851155 www.northlinkferries.co.uk. **Smyril Line** ✉ Holmsgarth Terminal, Lerwick, ZE1 0PR ☎ 01595/690845 www.smyril-line.com.

BUS TRAVEL

Long-distance buses run to and from most parts of Scotland, England, and Wales. Contact National Express for bus connections with English towns. Contact Scottish Citylink for bus connections with Scottish towns.

First Aberdeen operates services within the city of Aberdeen. Timetables are available from the tourist information center at St. Nicholas House.

First Aberdeen ☎ 01224/650000 www.firstaberdeen.co.uk. **National Express** ☎ 08705/808080 www.gobycoach.com. **Scottish Citylink** ☎ 08705/505050 www.citylink.co.uk.

CAR RENTAL

Agencies **Alamo National Car Rental** ✉ Aberdeen Airport ☎ 01224/770955. **Avis** ✉ Aberdeen Airport ☎ 0870/6060100 www.avis.co.uk. **Arnold Clark** ✉ Citroen Garage, Girdleness Rd. ☎ 01224/249159 www.arnoldclark.co.uk. **Budget Rent-a-Car** ✉ Wellheads Dr. and Aberdeen Airport ☎ 0800/181181 www.budget.co.uk. **Enterprise Rentacar** ✉ 80 Skene Sq. ☎ 01224/642642 www.erac.com. **Europcar** ✉ Aberdeen Airport ☎ 01224/770770 www.europcar.com ✉ 121 Causeway End ☎ 01224/631199. **Hertz** ✉ Aberdeen Airport ☎ 01224/722373 www.hertz.com.

CAR TRAVEL

You can travel from Glasgow and Edinburgh to Aberdeen on a continuous stretch of the A90/M90, a fairly scenic route that runs up Strathmore, with a fine hill view to the west. The coastal route, the A92, is a more leisurely alternative, with its interesting resorts and fishing villages. The most scenic route, however, is the A93 from Perth, north to Blairgowrie and into Glen Shee. The A93 then goes over the Cairnwell Pass, the highest main road in the United Kingdom. (This route isn't recommended in winter, when snow can make driving difficult.)

Aberdeen is a compact city with good signage. Its center is Union Street, the main thoroughfare running east–west, which tends to get crowded with traffic. Anderson Drive is an efficient ring road on the city's west side; be extra careful on its many traffic circles. It's best to leave your car in one of the parking garages (arrive early to get a space) and walk around, or use the convenient park-and-ride stop at the Bridge of Don, north of the city. Street maps are available from the tourist information center, newsdealers, and booksellers.

Around the northeast roads are generally not busy, but speeding and erratic driving can be a problem on the main A roads. The rural side roads are a pleasure to drive.

EMERGENCIES

Dial ☎ 999 in case of an emergency to reach an ambulance, or the fire, coast guard, or police departments (no coins are needed for emergency calls made from public phone booths). For a doctor or dentist, consult your hotel receptionist, B&B proprietor, or the yellow pages.

There's a lost-property office at the Grampian Police headquarters.

Notices on pharmacy doors will guide you to the nearest open pharmacy at any given time. Anderson Pharmacy (open Monday–Saturday, 9–6) and Boots the Chemists Ltd. (open weekdays 8:30–5, Saturday 8:30–6, Sunday noon–5), both in Aberdeen, keep longer hours than most. There's an in-store pharmacist at Safeway Food Store (open weekdays 8–10, Saturday 8–8, Sunday 9–9), also in Aberdeen.

Emergency Contact **Grampian Police** ✉ Force Headquarters, Queen St., Aberdeen ☎ 01224/386000.

Hospitals **Aberdeen Royal Infirmary** ✉ Accident and Emergency Department, Foresterhill, Aberdeen ☎ 01224/681818. **Dr. Gray's Hospital, Elgin** ✉ Accident and Emergency Department, at end of High St. on A96 ☎ 01343/543131.

Late-Night Pharmacies **Anderson Pharmacy** ✉ 34 Holburn St. ☎ 01224/587148. **Boots the Chemists Ltd.** ✉ Bon Accord Centre, George St. ☎ 01224/626080. **Safeway Food Store** ✉ 215 King St. ☎ 01224/624398.

SKIING

The main ski area is at Glenshee, just south of Braemar, though the season can be brief here. Those accustomed to long alpine runs and extensive choices will find the runs here short, unlike the lift lines. The Lecht lies at a lower altitude than Glenshee and is mainly suitable for beginners. The area at Cairngorm, by Aviemore, is another ski option. There's an artificial "dry" slope at Alford.

Contacts **Alford** ✉ Greystone Rd., Alford, Aberdeenshire ☎ 019755/63024. **Cairngorm** ✉ Aviemore, Inverness-shire ☎ 01479/861261 🌐 www.cairngormmountain.com. **Glenshee** ✉ A93, Cairnwell, by Braemar, Aberdeenshire ☎ 013397/41320 🌐 www.ski-glenshee.co.uk. **Lecht** ✉ A939, between Cock Bridge and Tomintoul, Strathdon, Aberdeenshire ☎ 01975/651440 🌐 www.lecht.co.uk.

TAXIS

You'll find taxi stands throughout the center of Aberdeen: along Union Street, at the railway station at Guild Street, at Back Wynd, and at Regent Quay. The taxis have meters and are mostly black, though some are beige, maroon, or white.

TOURS

BUS TOURS First Bus (operated by First Aberdeen) conducts city tours, available on most days between July and mid-September. Grampian Coaches (operated by First Aberdeen) run tours encompassing the northeast coastline and countryside. Some tours are based on one of the area's various trails: Malt Whisky, Coastal, Castle, or Royal. Whyte's Coaches offers tours throughout the northeast and beyond.

First Bus ☎ 01224/650000 🌐 www.firstgroup.com. **Grampian Coaches** ☎ 01224/650024 🌐 www.grampian-coaches.co.uk. **Whyte's Coaches** ☎ 01651/862211 🌐 www.whytescoachtours.co.uk.

PRIVATE GUIDES The Scottish Tourist Guides Association can supply experienced personal guides, including foreign-language-speaking guides if necessary.

Scottish Tourist Guides Association ✉ The Old Town Jail, St. John's St., Stirling FK8 1EA ☎ 01786/447784 🌐 www.stga.co.uk.

TRAIN TRAVEL

You can reach Aberdeen directly from Edinburgh (2½ hours), Glasgow (3 hours), and Inverness (2½ hours). Get a ScotRail timetable for full details, or call National Rail. There are also London–Aberdeen routes that go through Edinburgh and the east-coast main line.

Train Information **National Rail** ☎ 08457/484950 🌐 www.railtrack.co.uk. **ScotRail** ☎ 08457/550033 🌐 www.scotrail.co.uk.

VISITOR INFORMATION

The tourist information center in Aberdeen has a currency exchange and supplies information on all of Scotland's northeast. There are also year-round tourist information offices in Braemar and Elgin. In summer, also look for tourist information centers in Alford, Banchory, Banff, Crathie, Dufftown, Forres, Fraserburgh, Huntly, Stonehaven, and Tomintoul.

Tourist Information **Aberdeen** ✉ 23 Union St. ☎ 01224/288828 🌐 www.castlesandwhisky.com. **Ballater** ✉ The Old Royal Station, Station Sq. ☎ 013397/55306. **Braemar** ✉ The Mews, Mar Rd. ☎ 013397/41600. **Elgin** ✉ 17 High St. ☎ 01343/542666. **Inverurie** ✉ 18 High St., Inverurie ☎ 01467/625800.

ARGYLL & THE ISLES

7

FODOR'S CHOICE

The George Hotel, *in Inveraray*
Iona, *near Mull*

HIGHLY RECOMMENDED

HOTELS	Allt-Na-Craig, *near Crinan*
	Dungrianach, *on Oban*
	The Lagg Inn, *near Lamlash*
RESTAURANT	Harbour Inn, *in Bowmore*
SIGHTS	Auchindrain Museum, *near Inveraray*
	Brodick Castle and Country Park, *in Brodick*
	Crarae Gardens, *near Inveraray*
	Inveraray, *on Loch Fyne*
	Islay Woollen Mill, *near Port Askaig*
	Kilchurn Castle, *near Lochawe*
	Kildalton Cross, *near Port Ellen*
	Kilmartin House Museum, *near Crinan*
	Machrie Moor Stone Circles, *in Machrie*
	Torosay Castle, *near Craignure*

By Gilbert Summers

Updated by Willie Wallace

DIVIDED IN TWO by the long peninsula of Kintyre, western Scotland is characterized by a complicated, splintered seaboard. The west is an aesthetic delight, though it does catch those moist (yes, that's a euphemism) Atlantic weather systems. But the occasional wet foray is a small price to pay for the glittering freshness of oak woods and bracken-covered hillsides and for the bright interplay of sea, loch, and rugged green peninsula. Only a few decades ago the Clyde estuary was a coastal playground for people living in Glasgow and along Clydeside: their annual holiday was a steamer trip to any one of a number of Clyde resorts, known as going *doon the watter.* From the faded Clyde resort of Dunoon, Scotland's first national park stretches to the north. A quarter of Loch Lomond and the Trossachs National Park is in Argyll, mostly consisting of the Argyll Forest. Signs and visitor centers lead you into an exploration of the park's natural attractions.

Some impressive castles gaze out over this luxuriant landscape. Ruined Dunstaffnage and Kilchurn castles once guarded the western seaboard; turreted Inveraray Castle and magnificent Brodick, on the Isle of Arran, now guard their own historic interiors, with hundreds of antiques and portraits. The Kilmartin area has stone circles, carved stones, and burial mounds from the Bronze Age and earlier, taking imaginative travelers thousands of years back in time. Gardens are another Argyll specialty thanks to the temperate west-coast climate—Crarae Gardens, south of Inveraray, invites you down winding paths through plantings of magnolias and azaleas that reach their colorful peaks in late spring. The Brodick Castle grounds have fine azalea plantings, and Ardkinglas Woodland Garden adds an outstanding conifer collection.

Western Scotland's tiny islands are essentially microcosms of Scotland: each has its jagged cliffs or tongues of rock, its smiling sands and fertile pastures, its grim and ghostly fortress, and its tale of clan outrage or mythical beast. The pace of life is gentle out here, and the roads narrow and tortuous—not designed for heavy vehicles (beware pilgrim buses to Iona in summer, as they can cause major delays on the southside routes). Arran is the place for hill walking on Goat Fell, the mountain that gives the island its distinctive profile. On Islay you can hunt down peaty, iodine-scented malt whisky. The process of choosing your favorite makes for a pleasant evening in the island's friendly pubs and hotels. Mull has yet more castles, a short stretch of narrow-gauge railway, and the pretty port of Tobermory, with its brightly painted houses. Iona (just off Mull's western tip) is famous as an early seat of Christianity in Scotland and the burial place of Scottish kings in the Dark Ages. You could spend all your time touring these larger islands, but plenty of small islands are just as lovely, and they're blissfully uncrowded.

Exploring Argyll & the Isles

With long sea lochs carved into its hilly, wooded interior, Argyll is a beguiling interweaving of water and land. The Kintyre Peninsula stretches between the islands of the Firth of Clyde (including Arran) and the islands of the Inner Hebrides. Loch Fyne tends to get in the way of a breezy mainland tour: it's a long haul around the end of this fjord-like sea loch to Inveraray. Ferry services allow all kinds of interisland tours and can shorten mainland trips as well.

About the Restaurants

This part of Scotland has a few restaurants of distinction, and local ingredients are high in quality: the seafood, fresh from the sparkling lochs and sea, could hardly be better. Beef, lamb, and game are also common.

You could easily spend a week exploring the islands alone, so consider spending at least a few nights in this region.

Numbers in the text correspond to numbers in the margin and on the Argyll and the Isles map.

If you have
2 days

From Glasgow make your way to **Inveraray** 3 via Loch Lomond (A82) and the Rest and Be Thankful Pass (A83). Continue south via the **Crarae Gardens** 5, then south to Lochgilphead, where you take A816 north to the **Crinan Canal** 7. Continue north on A816 and stay overnight in **Oban** 1. The next day follow A85 east to see **Dunstaffnage Castle** and **Kilchurn Castle** 2 before returning to the Loch Lomond/Glasgow area.

If you have
4 days

Starting from Ardrossan, in Ayrshire, take the ferry to **Brodick** and stay overnight on the island of Arran, visiting **Brodick Castle and Country Park** 12. Cross to Kintyre Peninsula by taking the ferry from **Lochranza** 15 for Claonaig; then cross the peninsula itself to Kennacraig. For a lovely day trip head south to the Isle of Gigha and its **Achamore House Gardens** 10; then return north to the **Crinan** area. The next day go up to **Oban** 1 and make an excursion to Mull for **Iona** 25, **Tobermory** 27, and **Torosay Castle** 23. Finally, return to Oban *or* leave Mull via Fishnish Pier, where you can take a ferry to Lochaline and travel north on the mainland from there.

If you have
7 days

This noncircular route provides a good flavor of the islands. Starting from Ardrossan, take the ferry to **Brodick** and stay overnight on Arran, visiting **Brodick Castle and Country Park** 12. Take the ferry from **Lochranza** 15 to Claonaig, cross the Kintyre Peninsula to Kennacraig, and continue west to the island of **Islay** 16–20, staying two nights to sample its wildlife preserves, coastal scenery, and malt whisky and perhaps to take the short ferry trip to **Jura** 22 to enjoy its wilder terrain. Return to the mainland to explore the area around Knapdale, staying in the **Crinan** area for at least one night. Go north to **Oban** 1 and take the ferry to Mull to see **Iona** 25, **Tobermory** 27, and **Torosay Castle** 23, staying two nights. Finally, return to Oban and head east on A85 to see **Dunstaffnage Castle** and **Kilchurn Castle** 2. If you are more interested in wandering about deserted beaches than visiting castles and distilleries, consider taking three days to visit **Colonsay** 30. You can take the ferry out on Wednesday and return on Friday.

In rural districts it's prudent to choose a hotel or guest house that serves a decent evening meal as well as breakfast.

About the Hotels

Accommodations in Argyll and on the isles range from château-like hotels to modest inns. Many traditional provincial hotels and small coastal resorts have been equipped with modern conveniences yet retain their personalized service and historic charm. Apart from these, however, your choices are limited; the best overnight option is usually a simple guest house offering bed, breakfast, and an evening meal.

WHAT IT COSTS In Pounds					
	£££££	££££	£££	££	£
RESTAURANTS	over £22	£18–£22	£13–£17	£7–£12	under £7
HOTELS	over £150	£110–£150	£80–£110	£50–£80	under £50

Restaurant prices are for a main course at dinner. Hotel prices are for two people in a standard double room in high season. All prices include the 17.5% VAT.

Timing

This part of the mainland is close enough to Glasgow that it's convenient to reach year-round. You can take advantage of quiet roads and plentiful accommodations in early spring and late autumn. In winter, short daylight hours and strong wind can make island stays rather bleak.

AROUND ARGYLL

Topographical grandeur and rocky shores are what make Argyll special. Try to take to the water at least once, even if your time is limited. The sea and the sea lochs have played a vital role in the history of western Scotland since the time of the war galleys of the clans. Oban is the major ferry gateway and transport hub, with a main road leading south into Kintyre.

Oban

❶ *96 mi northwest of Glasgow, 125 mi northwest of Edinburgh, 50 mi south of Fort William, 118 mi southwest of Inverness.*

It's almost impossible to avoid Oban when touring the west. Luckily it has a waterfront with some character and serves as a launch point for several ferry excursions. A traditional Scottish resort town, Oban has *ceilidhs* (song, music, and dance festivals) and tartan kitsch as well as late-night revelry in pubs and hotel bars. There's an inescapable sense, however, that just over the horizon, on the islands or down Kintyre, lie more peaceful and traditional environs.

Four miles north of Oban stands **Dunstaffnage Castle,** once an important stronghold of the MacDougall clan in the 13th century. From the ramparts you have outstanding views across the **Sound of Mull** and the **Firth of Lorne,** a nautical crossroads of sorts, once watched over by Dunstaffnage Castle and commanded by the galleys (*birlinn* in Gaelic) of the Lords of the Isles. ✉ *Off A85* ☎ *01631/562465* 🌐 *www.historic-scotland.gov.uk* 🎫 *£2.20* ⏲ *Apr.–Sept., daily 9:30–6; Oct.–Mar., Sat.–Wed. 9:30–4.*

At the **Scottish Sealife Sanctuary** kids, as well as adults, love the outstanding display of marine life, including shoals of herring, sharks, rays, catfish, otters, and seals. There's even a children's adventure playground and, of course, a gift shop. The restaurant serves morning coffee with homemade scones, plus a full lunch menu, and afternoon tea. To get here drive north from Oban for 10 mi on A828. ✉ *Barcaldine, Connel* ☎ *01631/720386* 🌐 *www.sealsanctuary.co.uk* 🎫 *£6.95* ⏲ *Jan.–mid-Feb., weekends 10–4; mid-Feb.–June and Sept.–Dec., daily 10–4; July–Aug., daily 10–5.*

Where to Stay & Eat

£££££ **Isle of Eriska.** A severe, baronial-style granite facade belies the luxurious welcome within this hotel, set on its own island 10 mi north of Oban and accessible by a bridge from the mainland. Every detail in the spacious rooms has been carefully chosen for your comfort. The restau-

Biking

As both a vacation destination and a ferry gateway, Oban gets a lot of bike traffic. Arran, too, is popular for cycling, with a large number of bike-rental shops. Biking on the forest-service roads in Loch Lomond and the Trossachs National Park is another option. Many roads have one lane only, so wear high-visibility clothing, especially in the busy summer months—and, above all, bring rain gear.

Fishing

The largest skate in Britain are found in the waters off the island of Mull. Local charter-boat companies offer sea-angling trips for pollock, saith, dogfish, conger, and mackerel, as well as skate. A catch-and-release policy is sometimes required, and always encouraged. Lochs and rivers yield salmon, brown and rainbow trout, pike, perch, Arctic char, and eels. Local fishing literature, available in tourist offices, identifies at least 50 loch and river sites for game fishing and at least 20 coastal settlements suited to sea angling.

Golf

Western Scotland has about two dozen golf courses, notably some fine coastal links. Machrihanish, near Campbeltown, and Machrie, on Islay, are the best known. Both were founded in the late-19th century and both have lots of holes where you can't see the flag from the tee. Fees at both start at £35. Arran has seven golf courses, none of which are particularly difficult. All have breathtaking views of the sea and the mountains. Try the 12-hole course at Shiskine. Fees on Arran start at £10.

---

rant serves innovative Scottish cuisine made with local ingredients: try the scallop and zucchini timbale with lobster, artichoke, and champagne butter sauce. You can take a stroll to watch seals and otters offshore or herons and badgers on the grounds. ✉ *Ledaig, by Oban, Argyll PA37 1SD* ☎ *01631/720371* 🖷 *01631/720531* 🌐 *www.eriska-hotel.co.uk* *17 rooms* *Restaurant, 6-hole golf course, tennis court, pool, health club; no a/c* ▭ *AE, MC, V* ⊙ *Closed Jan.* 🍽 *MAP.*

££££ **Manor House Hotel.** On the shore just outside Oban, this 1780 stone house, once the home of the duke of Argyll, has wonderful sea views. The public areas are furnished with antiques, the bedrooms with reproductions. The restaurant serves a five-course prix-fixe meal of Scottish and French dishes, including lots of local seafood and game in season, complemented by a carefully selected wine list. The house is within walking distance of downtown Oban and the bus, train, and ferry terminals. ✉ *Gallanach Rd., Oban, Argyll PA34 4LS* ☎ *01631/562087* 🖷 *01631/563053* 🌐 *www.manorhouseoban.com* *11 rooms* *Restaurant, bar, lounge; no a/c, no kids under 12* ▭ *AE, MC, V* 🍽 *MAP.*

££ **Kilchrenan House.** A fully refurbished Victorian stone house just a few minutes' walk from the town center, this is a high-grade bed-and-breakfast. Rooms overlook the sea and the islands. ✉ *Corran Esplanade, Oban, Argyll PA34 5AQ* ☎🖷 *01631/562663* 🌐 *www.kilchrenanhouse.co.uk* *10 rooms* *Dining room, lounge; no a/c* ▭ *MC, V* ⊙ *Closed Dec.–Jan.* 🍽 *BP.*

££ **Ronebhal Guest House.** You can see Loch Etive and the mountains beyond from this stone house east of Oban, set back within its own grounds. Rooms are light and modern with large windows. The front bedrooms have the best views of the loch. ✉ *Connel, Argyll PA37 1PJ*

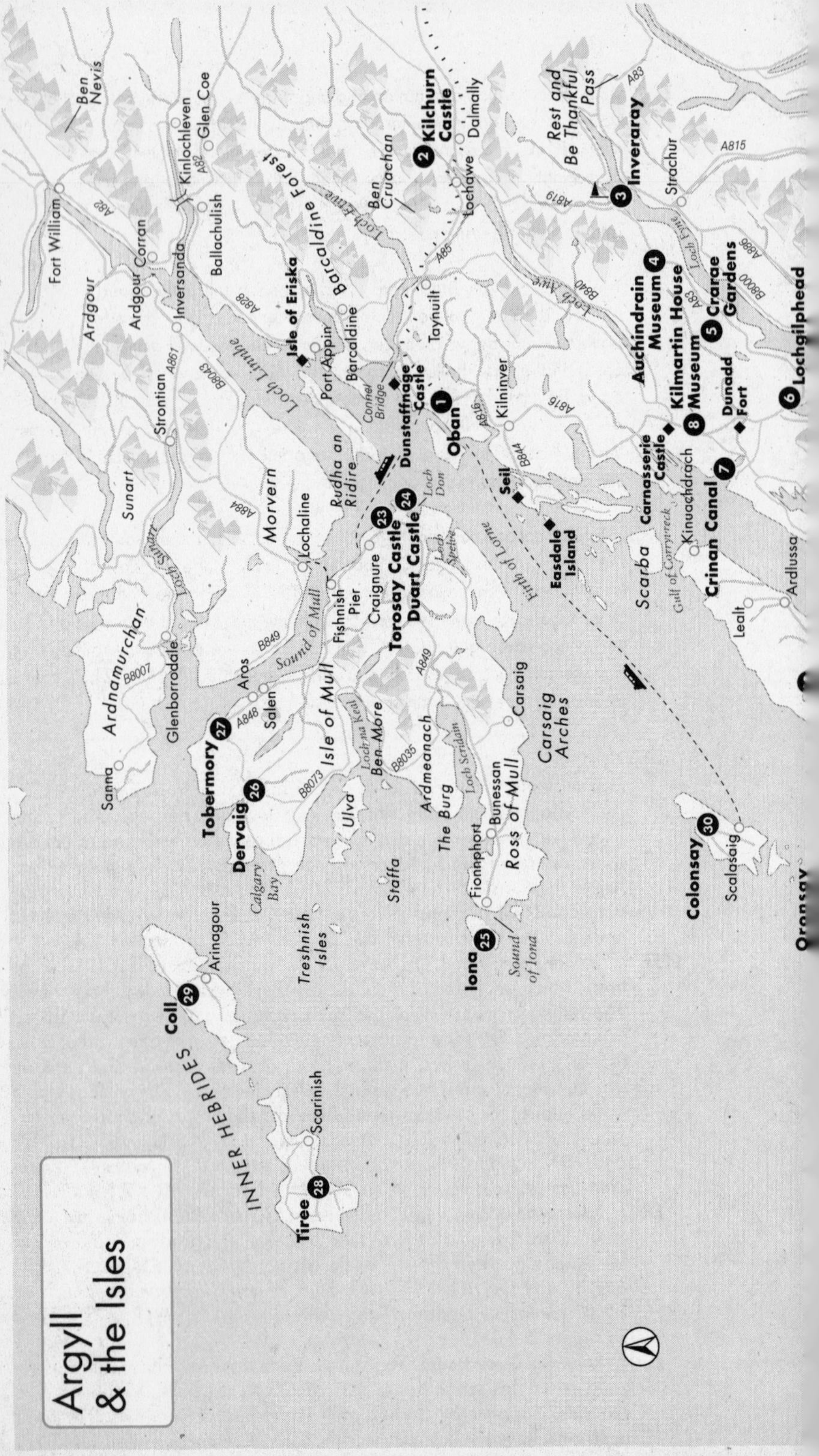
Argyll & the Isles
Ben Nevis
Fort William
A82
Kinlochleven
Glen Coe
Ballachulish
Corran
Ardgour
Ardgour
Inversanda
A861
Strontian
B8043
Sunart
Loch Sunart
Morvern
A884
Lochaline
Ardnamurchan
B8007
Glenborrodale
Sanna
Loch Linnhe
A828
Isle of Eriska
Port Appin
Barcaldine
Barcaldine Forest
Ben Cruachan
Loch Etive
2 Kilchurn Castle
Dalmally
Lochawe
A85
Taynuilt
Connel Bridge
Dunstaffnage Castle
1 Oban
A816
Kilninver
B844
Rudha an Ridire
Loch Don
23 Torosay Castle
24 Duart Castle
Craignure
Fishnish Pier
Sound of Mull
B849
Aros
Salen
A848
27 Tobermory
26 Dervaig
Calgary Bay
Isle of Mull
B8073
Loch na Keal
Ben More
B8035
A849
Ulva
Staffa
Ardmeanach
The Burg
Loch Scridain
Bunessan
Ross of Mull
Fionnphort
25 Iona
Sound of Iona
Carsaig
Carsaig Arches
Treshnish Isles
29 Coll
Arinagour
28 Tiree
Scarinish
INNER HEBRIDES
Seil
Easdale Island
Loch Spelve
Firth of Lorne
Scarba
Gulf of Corryvreck
Kinuachdrach
Lealt
Ardlussa
30 Colonsay
Scalasaig
Oronsay
7 Crinan Canal
Carnasserie Castle
8 Kilmartin House Museum
Dunadd Fort
6 Lochgilphead
5 Crarae Gardens
4 Auchindrain Museum
3 Inveraray
Loch Awe
B840
Loch Fyne
A83
A819
Strachur
A815
A886
B8000
Rest and Be Thankful Pass

KEY
Rail Lines
Ferry
Start of itinerary
SCOTLAND
10 miles
15 km
0
0
ATLANTIC OCEAN
NORTHERN IRELAND
Oronsay
Nave Island
Kilnave
Loch Gruinart
B8017
B8018
Loch Gorm
Port Charlotte
17
Machir Bay
A847
Rhinns of Islay
Portnahaven
Port Wemyss
Loch Indaal
Laggan Bay
Kintra
The Oa
18
Mull of Oa
16
Bowmore
Bridgend
A846
Islay
20
Islay Woollen Mill
Port Askaig
Loch Finlaggan
21
Feolin Ferry
Sound of Islay
Loch Tarbert
Paps of Jura
22
Jura
Lagg
A846
Craighouse
Small Isles Bay
Sound of Jura
19
Port Ellen
Ardbeg
Kildalton Cross
Achamore House Gardens
10
Gigha
Sound of Gigha
Castle Sween
Loch Caolisport
Kilberry
Knapdale
B8024
Loch Gilp
Lochgilphead
9
Tarbert
Kennacraig
Claonaig
B8000
Portavadie
Tayinloan
A83
Kintyre
Kilchenzie
Machrihanish
Campbeltown
Southend
Mull of Kintyre
Catacol
15
Lochranza
Sound of Bute
Arran
Goat Fell
Sannox
Corrie
12
Brodick Castle and Country Park
11
Isle Of Arran Heritage Museum
B842
Drumadoon Point
14
Machrie Moor Stone Circles
Blackwaterfoot
Lagg
A841
Kilmory
13
Lamlash
Brodick
Holy Island
Whiting Bay
Bute
Rothesay
Millport
Colintraive
Dunoon
Wemyss Bay
Wemyss Bay
Largs
A78
Ardrossan
Firth of Clyde
Maidens

☎ 01631/710310 🌐 www.ronebhal.co.uk ⇨ 6 rooms (4 with bath) ♁ Dining room, lounge; no a/c, no room phones, no kids under 7, no smoking ▭ MC, V ⊗ Closed Dec.–Jan. 🍴 BP.

★ £ **Dungrianach.** Aptly named with a word meaning "the sunny house on the hill," this late-Victorian house is set high in woodland with superb views of the ocean and islands. Yet it's only a few minutes' walk from Oban's ferry piers and town center. Antique and reproduction furniture fill the guest rooms. ✉ *Pulpit Hill, Oban, Argyll PA34 4LU ☎ 01631/562840 🌐 www.dungrianach.com ⇨ 2 rooms ♁ Dining room, lounge; no a/c, no room phones ▭ No credit cards ⊗ Closed Oct.–Mar. 🍴 BP.*

Sports & the Outdoors

BIKING You can rent bicycles from **Oban Cycles** (✉ 29 Lochside St. ☎ 01631/566996), whose shopkeepers will give you advice on waterside routes to take as far out as Ganavan Bay and Dunstaffnage Castle.

FISHING **The Gannet** (✉ 3 Kiel Croft, Benderloch ☎ 01631/720262 🌐 www.fishntrip.co.uk), a charter-fishing company run by Adrian Lauder, offers sea-angling trips for £400 a day. Fishing parties are limited to 10 people (eight for skate-fishing).

Shopping

The factory store **Caithness Glass Oban** (✉ Railway Pier ☎ 01631/563386 🌐 www.caithnessglass.co.uk) is a good place to buy a memento of Scotland. The paperweights with swirling colored patterns are particularly lovely.

Lochawe

18 mi east of Oban.

Lochawe is a loch-side community squeezed between the broad shoulder of Ben Cruachan and Loch Awe itself. The road gets busy in peak season, filled with people trying to park near Lochawe Station.

★ ❷ **Kilchurn Castle,** a ruined fortress at the east end of Loch Awe, was built in the 15th century by Sir Colin Campbell (d. 1493) of Glenorchy, and rebuilt in the 17th century. Airy vantage points amid the towers have fine panoramas of the surrounding highlands and loch. ✉ *1 mi northeast of Lochawe on A85 ☎ 0131/668–8800 🌐 www.historic-scotland.gov.uk 🎫 Free ⊗ Daily 24 hrs.*

The **Duncan Ban Macintyre Monument** was erected in honor of this Gaelic poet (1724–1812), sometimes referred to as the Robert Burns of the Highlands. The view from here is one of the finest in Argyll, taking in Ben Cruachan and the other peaks nearby, as well as Loch Awe and its scattering of islands. To find the monument from Dalmally, just east of Loch Awe, follow an old road running southwest toward the banks of Loch Awe—you'll see the round, granite structure from the road's highest point, often called Monument Hill.

en route

The A819 south to Inveraray initially runs alongside Loch Awe, the longest loch in Scotland, but soon leaves these pleasant banks to turn east and join the A83, which carries traffic from Glasgow and Loch Lomond by way of the high Rest and Be Thankful pass. The Rest and Be Thankful, a quasi-alpine pass among high green slopes and gray rocks, is one of the most scenic points along the road.

Inveraray

★ ⚑ ❸ *21 mi south of Lochawe, 61 mi north of Glasgow, 29 mi west of Loch Lomond.*

On the approaches to Inveraray, note the ornate 18th-century bridgework that carries the road along the loch side. This is your first sign that Inveraray is not just a jumbled assembly of houses; in fact, much of it was designed as a planned town for the third duke of Argyll in the mid-18th century. The current seat of the Campbell duke is **Inveraray Castle,** a smart, grayish-green turreted stone house with a self-satisfied air, visible through trees from the town itself. Like the town, the castle was built around 1743. Tours of the interior convey the history of the powerful Campbell family. ☎ *01499/302203* 🌐 *www.inveraray-castle.com* 🎫 *£5.50* ⏲ *Apr.–May and Oct., Mon.–Thurs. and Sat. 10–1 and 2–5:45, Sun. 1–5:45; Jun–Sept., Mon.–Sat. 10–5:45, Sun. 1–5:45.*

The **Inveraray Jail** is one of the latest generation of visitor centers. The old town jail and courtroom now house realistic courtroom scenes, period cells, and other paraphernalia that give you a glimpse of life behind bars in Victorian times—and today. The site includes a Scottish crafts shop. ✉ *Inveraray* ☎ *01499/302381* 🌐 *www.inverarayjail.co.uk* 🎫 *£5.75* ⏲ *Apr.–Oct., daily 9:30–6; Nov.–Mar., daily 10–5; last admission 1 hr before closing.*

The 1911 lightship ***Arctic Penguin*** is a rare example of a riveted iron vessel. It now houses exhibits and displays on the maritime heritage of the River Clyde and Scotland's west coast. Beside it rests the "puffer" *Eilean Eisdeal*, a tiny inter-island freight boat. ☎ *01499/302213* 🌐 *www.skwebpages.com/arctic* 🎫 *£3.60* ⏲ *Apr.–Sept., daily 10–6; Oct.–Mar., daily 10–5.*

Ardkinglas Woodland Garden has one of Britain's finest collections of conifers, set off by rhododendron blossoms in early summer. You'll find it around the head of Loch Fyne, about 4 mi east of Inveraray. ✉ *A83, Cairndow* ☎ *01499/600261* 🌐 *www.ardkinglas.com* 🎫 *£3* ⏲ *Daily dawn–dusk.*

At **Loch Fyne Oysters,** about 11 mi northeast of Inveraray, you can purchase these delicious shellfish to go, order them to be shipped, or sit down and consume a dozen with a glass of wine. ✉ *A83, Clachan Farm, Cairndow* ☎ *01499/600264* 🌐 *www.loch-fyne.com* ⏲ *Daily 9–8.*

Where to Stay & Eat

££ Fodor's Choice ★ ✕🏨 **The George Hotel.** This 18th-century former coaching inn has been in the Clark family for six generations, and the warmth of the welcome reflects the benefit of continuity. Roaring log fires invite repose in the common rooms, while antiques and oil paintings in the rooms make you feel as though you were in another, slower-paced era. Locals fill the restaurant (££) to sample the excellent food, such as king scallop and bacon kebabs with lemon basil and shallots. ✉ *Main St. E, Inveraray, Argyll PA32 8TT* ☎ *01499/302111* 📠 *01499/302098* 🌐 *www.thegeorgehotel.co.uk* 🛏 *15 rooms* 🛎 *Restaurant, some in-room hot tubs, 2 bars; no a/c* 💳 *MC, V* 🍽 *BP.*

Auchindrain Museum

★ ❹ *5 mi south of Inveraray.*

Step a few centuries back in time at the Auchindrain Museum, once an 18th-century communal tenancy farm. The old bracken-thatch and iron-roof buildings give you a feel for early farming life in the Highlands, and the interpretation center explains it all. ✉ *A83* ☎ *01499/500235* 🎫 *£4* ⏲ *Apr.–Sept., daily 10–5.*

Crarae Gardens

★ 5 *10 mi southwest of Inveraray.*

Well worth a visit for plant lovers are the Crarae Gardens, where magnolias, azaleas, and rhododendrons flourish in the moist, lush environment. The flowers and trees attract several different species of birds and butterflies. ✉ *Off A83, about 10 mi southwest of Inveraray* ☎ *01546/886614* 🌐 *www.nts.org.uk/crarae.html* 🎫 *£3.50* ⏲ *Gardens daily 9–6 or dusk; visitor center April–Sept., 10–5.*

Lochgilphead

6 *26 mi south of Inveraray.*

Lochgilphead, the largest town in this region, looks best when the tide is in, as Loch Gilp (really a bite out of Loch Fyne) reveals a muddy shoreline at low tide. With a series of well-kept, colorful buildings along its main street, this neat little town is worth a look.

off the beaten path

CARNASSERIE CASTLE – This tower house has the distinction of having belonged to the writer of the first book printed in Gaelic. The writer, John Carswell, bishop of the isles, translated a text by the Scottish reformer John Knox into Gaelic and published it in 1567. ✉ *Off A816, 9 mi north of Lochgilphead* ☎ *0131/668–8800* 🌐 *www.historic-scotland.gov.uk* 🎫 *Free* ⏲ *Daily 24 hrs.*

Horseback Riding

Castle Riding Centre and Argyll Trail Riding (✉ Brenfield, Ardrishaig, Argyll ☎ 01546/603274 🌐 www.brenfield.co.uk), south of Lochgilphead, offers guided rides along routes throughout Argyll and farther afield into the West Highlands.

Shopping

The factory shop at the **Highbank Collection** (✉ Highbank Industrial Estate ☎ 01546/602044) sells glassware made on-site, model wooden boats, hand-painted pottery, and ceramic giftware.

Crinan

1 mi north of Lochgilphead.

Crinan is synonymous with its canal, the reason for this tiny community's existence and its mainstay. The narrow road beside the Crinan Hotel bustles with yachting types waiting to pass through the locks, bringing a surprisingly cosmopolitan feel to such an out-of-the-way corner of Scotland. To reach Crinan, take the A816 Oban road north from Lochgilphead for about a mile, then turn left.

7 The **Crinan Canal** was opened in 1801 to enable fishing vessels to reach Hebridean fishing grounds without making the long haul south around the Kintyre Peninsula. At its west end the canal drops to the sea in a series of locks. This area gets busy at times, with yachting enthusiasts strolling around and drinking coffee at the shop beside the Crinan Hotel.

★ 8 For an exceptional encounter with early Scottish history, visit the **Kilmartin House Museum,** about 8 mi north of Crinan on the A816. The museum explores the stone circles and avenues, burial mounds, and carved stones dating from the Bronze Age and earlier that are scattered thickly around this neighborhood. Nearby **Dunadd Fort,** a rocky hump rising out of the level ground between Crinan and Kilmartin, was once the capital of the early kingdom of Dalriada, founded by the first wave of Scots who migrated from Ireland around AD 500. Clamber up the rock to see a basin, a footprint, and an outline of a boar carved on the smooth upper face of the knoll. ✉ *At Kilmartin, on A816* ☎ *01546/510278* 🌐 *www.kilmartin.org* 🎫 *£4.50* ⏲ *Daily 10–5:30.*

off the beaten path

CASTLE SWEEN – The oldest stone castle on the Scottish mainland, dating from the 12th century, sits on a rocky bit of coast about 12 mi south of Crinan. You can reach it by an unclassified road from Crinan that grants outstanding views of the Paps of Jura (the mountains on Jura), across the sound. There are some temptingly deserted white-sand beaches here.

7

Where to Stay & Eat

★ ££ ✕🏨 **Allt-Na-Craig.** This large stone Victorian house was once the home of *Wind in the Willows* author Kenneth Graham. The house is set in lovely gardens overlooking Loch Fyne on the edge of the village. Nearby is the yacht-filled eastern basin of the Crinan Canal. Charlotte Nicol's food is well worth a stay. ✉ *4 mi south of Lochgilphead Ardrishaig, PA30 8EP* ☎ *01546/603245* *5 rooms, 1 cottage* *Restaurant; no a/c* 💳 *MC, V* 🍽 *BP.*

Kintyre Peninsula

52 mi (to Campbeltown) south of Lochgilphead.

Rivers and streams crisscross this long, narrow strip of green pasture-
9 lands and hills stretching south from Lochgilphead. **Tarbert,** a name that appears throughout the Highlands, is the Gaelic word for "place of portage," and a glance at the map tells you why it was given to this little town with a workaday waterfront: Tarbert sits on the narrow neck of land between East and West Loch Tarbert, where long ago boats were actually carried across the land to avoid looping all the way around the peninsula. The **Tairbeart Heritage Centre,**just south of the village, will tell you more about the area's history. ✉ *Tarbert* ☎ *01880/821116* 🎫 *Free* ⏲ *Mid-Mar.–Dec., daily 10–sunset.*

The **Isle of Gigha,** barely 5 mi long, is sheltered in a frost-free, sea-warmed climate between Kintyre and Islay. The island was long favored by British aristocrats as a summer destination. One relic of the Isle of
10 Gigha's aristocratic legacy is the **Achamore House Gardens,** which produce lush shrubberies with spectacular azalea displays in late spring. For a nimble day trip, take the 20-minute ferry to Gigha from Tayinloan and walk right over to the gardens. You may not want to take your car, as the walk is fairly easy. ☎ *01583/505267* 🌐 *www.isle-of-gigha.co.uk* 🎫 *Gardens £2; ferry £4.50 per person plus £15.80 per car* ⏲ *Gardens daily dawn–dusk. Ferry Mon.–Sat. 9–5, Sun. 11, 2, and 3.*

Golf

You can play **Machrihanish Golf Club's** perfectly manicured 18 holes warmed by Gulf Stream breezes. U.S. Navy Seal teams-in-training have been known to drop from the air into a chilly nearby loch. ✉ *Campbeltown* ☎ *01586/810213* 🌐 *www.machgolf.com* *18 holes, 6,228 yards, par 70.*

ARRAN

Many Scots, especially those from Glasgow and the west, are well disposed toward Arran, as it reminds them of unhurried childhood holidays. Called "Scotland in Miniature" by the tourist board, Arran really does have it all: mountains, glens, beaches, waterfalls, standing stone circles, Viking forts, castles, and a malt whisky distillery, one of more than 40 illegal stills that hid in the remote glens of 18th-century Arran.

To get to Arran, take the ferry from Ardrossan, on the mainland. (It's also possible to take the ferry from Claonaig on the Kintyre Peninsula in summer.) You'll see a number of fellow travelers wearing hiking boots: they're ready for the delights of Goat Fell, the impressive peak (2,868 feet) that gives Arran one of the most distinctive profiles of any island in Scotland. As the ferry approaches Brodick, you'll see Goat Fell's cone. Arran's southern half is less mountainous; the Highland Boundary Fault crosses just to the north of Brodick Bay. Exploring the island is easy, as the A841 road neatly circles it.

Brodick

▶ *1 hr by ferry from Ardrossan.*

The largest township on Arran, Brodick is really a village, its frontage lined by a number of Victorian hotels, set spaciously back from a promenade and beach. The **Isle of Arran Heritage Museum** documents life on the island from ancient times to the present. Several buildings, including a cottage and *smiddy* (smithy), have period furnishings as well as displays on prehistoric life, farming, fishing, and other aspects of the island's social history. ✉ *Rosaburn, Brodick* ☎ *01770/302636* ⊕ *www. arranmuseum.co.uk* ☞ *£2.25* ⊙ *Apr.–Oct., daily 10:30–4:30.*

★ ⑫ Arran's biggest cultural draw is **Brodick Castle and Country Park,** on the north side of Brodick Bay. The red sandstone structure, parts of which date back to the 13th century, is cosseted by trees and parkland and several rooms are open to the public. The castle's furniture, paintings, and silver are opulent in their own right—try counting the number of deer heads on the hall walls—but the real attraction is the garden, where brilliantly colored rhododendrons bloom, particularly in late spring and early summer. There are many unusual varieties of azalea, though the ordinary yellow kind is unmatched for its scent: your first encounter with these is like hitting a wall of perfume. Save time to visit the Servants' Hall, where an excellent restaurant serves morning coffee (with hot scones—try the date-and-walnut variety), a full lunch menu that changes daily, and afternoon teas with home-baked goods. ✉ *1 mi north of Brodick Pier* ☎ *01770/302202* ⊕ *www.nts.org.uk* ☞ *Castle and gardens £7; gardens only, £3.50* ⊙ *Castle and gardens Apr.–Oct., daily 10–5. Reception center and restaurant Apr.–Oct., daily 10–5; Nov.–Dec., Fri.–Sun. 10–5. Country park daily 9:30–dusk.*

Where to Stay & Eat

££–£££ ✕ **The Brodick Bar.** Local beef, lamb, and game, plus the most succulent scallops you'll ever taste, are what keeps the locals (and visitors) coming back to this casual, friendly, small-town pub and restaurant. ✉ *Alma Rd, Brodick* ☎ *01770/302169* ☐ *MC, V.*

£–££ ✕▦ **Glencloy Farmhouse.** This 19th-century sandstone house is surrounded by colorful gardens and nestled in a peaceful valley. Brodick and views of the hills and sea are a few minutes' walk away. The owner conducts courses in embroidery in March, April, and October, and you can see evidence of her skills throughout the house. Breakfast is a treat, with organic eggs, homemade jam, and fresh-baked bread and muffins. ✉ *Brodick, Isle of Arran, KA26 8DA* ☎ *01770/302251* ✐ *mvpglencloy@compuserve.com* ⇆ *5 rooms (2 with bath)* ⚲ *Dining room; no a/c, no room phones* ☐ *MC, V* ⦿ *BP.*

Shopping

Arran's shops are well stocked with island-produced goods. The Home Farm is a popular shopping area with a small restaurant. The **Duchess Court Shops** (✉ The Home Farm ☎ 01770/302831) include Bear Necessities, with everything bearly; the Nature Shop, with nature-oriented books and gifts; and Arran Aromatics, one of Scotland's top makers of toiletries and supplying many top hotels. **The Island Cheese Company,** (✉ The Home Farm ☎ 01770/302788) stocks Arran blue cheese among other handmade Scottish cheeses.

Lamlash

13 *4 mi south of Brodick.*

With views offshore to Holy Island, now a Buddhist retreat, which is flanked by steep cliffs, Lamlash has a breezy seaside-holiday atmosphere. To reach the highest point accessible by car, go through the village and turn right beside the bridge onto Ross Road, which climbs steeply from a thickly planted valley, **Glen Scorrodale,** and yields fine views of Lamlash Bay. From Lamlash you can explore the southern part of Arran: 10 mi southwest is the little community of **Lagg,** sitting peacefully by the banks of the Kilmory Water, and **Whiting Bay** has a waterfront string of hotels and well-kept properties.

Where to Stay & Eat

★ ££ **The Lagg Inn.** Arran's oldest inn is an 18th-century lodge with fireplaces in the common rooms and gardens that reach down to the river. Each room is quiet and bright, if a little flowery, and many overlook the riverside garden or woodland. Simple home cooking in the restaurant (££) and friendly locals in the bar add up to a fine evening. The inn is 8 mi west of Whiting Bay. ✉ *Kilmory, Isle of Arran, KA278PQ* ☎ *01770/870255* 📠 *01770/870250* 🌐 *www.arran.uk.com/lagg/inn* *9 rooms* *Restaurant, golf privileges, bar, lounge; no a/c* *MC, V* *BP.*

Biking

You can rent bicycles at **Whiting Bay Cycle Hire** (✉ Elim, Silverhill, Whiting Bay ☎ 01770/700382), open May through September.

Shopping

Patterson Arran Ltd. (✉ The Old Mill, Lamlash ☎ 01770/600606) is famous for its mustards, preserves, and marmalades.

Machrie

11 mi north of Lagg.

The area surrounding Machrie, which has scattered homesteads and a popular beach, is littered with prehistoric sites: chambered cairns, hut circles, and standing stones dating from the Bronze Age. From Machrie, a well-surfaced track takes you to a grassy moor by a ruined farm, where you
★ 14 can see the **Machrie Moor Stone Circles:** small, rounded granite-boulder circles and much taller, eerie red-sandstone monoliths. Out on the bare moor, the lost and lonely stones are very evocative, well worth a walk to see if you like the feeling of solitude. The stones are about a mile outside of Machrie; just follow the HISTORIC SCOTLAND sign pointing the way.

Sports & the Outdoors

HORSEBACK RIDING Even novices can enjoy a guided ride on a mount from **Cairnhouse Riding Centre** (✉ Blackwaterfoot, 2 mi south of Machrie on A84 ☎ 01770/860466).

GOLF **Machrie Golf Links** would be a lot more crowded if it were a little more accessible. The course was designed in 1891, and except for minor changes in the 1970s, has changed little. Watch out for the sand dunes! ✉ *1 mi from the airport, 4 mi from Port Ellen* ☎ *01496/302310* 🌐 *www.machrie.com* *18 holes, 5,894 yards, par 71.*

Shopping

The **Old Byre Showroom** (✉ Auchencar Farm, 2 mi north of Machrie on A841 ☎ 01770/840227 🌐 www.oldbyre.co.uk) sells sheepskin goods, hand-knit sweaters, designer knitwear, leather goods, and rugs.

en route

Continuing to Blackwaterfoot, you can return to Brodick via the String Road: from the Kinloch Hotel, head up the hill. As you drive, there are more fine views of the granite complexities of Arran's hills: gray notched ridges beyond brown moors and, past the watershed, a vista of Brodick Bay.

Lochranza

15 *14 mi north of Brodick.*

North of Brodick is Lochranza, a crafts community sheltered by the Bay of Loch Ranza, which spills into the flat-bottom glacial glen. The village is set off by a picturesque ruin, **Lochranza Castle,** set on a low sand spit. This is said to have been the landing place of Robert the Bruce when he returned from Rathlin Island in 1307 to start the campaign that won Scotland's independence. A sign indicates where you can pick up the key to get in. ☎ *0131/668–8800* 🌐 *www.historic-scotland.gov.uk* *Free* *Apr.–Sept., daily 9:30–6; Oct.–Mar, Mon.–Sat. 9:30–4, Sun. 2–4.*

ISLAY & JURA

Islay has a character distinct from that of the rest of the Hebrides. In contrast to areas where most residents live on crofts (generally worked by someone who has another job, i.e., fisherman, teacher, postman), Islay's western half in particular has large self-sustaining farms. Many of the island's best beaches, wildlife preserves, and historical sites are also on its western half, whereas the southeast is mainly an extension of Jura's inhospitable quartzite hills. Islay is particularly known for its birds, including the rare chough (a crow with red legs and beak) and, in winter, its barnacle geese. Several distilleries produce delectable malt whiskies and provide jobs for the locals. Islay's sheer number of distilleries will spoil you for choice. A peaty taste characterizes the island's malt whiskies, which are available in local pubs, off-license shops, and distillery shops. Though not all have shops, most distilleries welcome visitors by appointment; some charge a small fee for a tour, which you can redeem against a purchase of whisky.

Although it's possible to meet an Islay native in a local pub, such an event is statistically less likely on Jura, with its one road, one distillery, one hotel, and six sporting estates. In fact, you have a better chance of bumping into one of the island's red deer, which outnumber the human population by at least 20 to 1. The island has a much more rugged look than Islay, with its profiles of the Paps of Jura, a hill range at its most impressive when basking in the rays of a west-coast sunset.

Bowmore

16 *11 mi north of Port Ellen.*

Compact Bowmore is about the same size (population 1,000) as Port Ellen, but it works slightly better as a base for touring because it's central to the island's main routes. Sharing its name with the whisky made in the distillery by the shore (founded 1779), Bowmore is a tidy town, its grid pattern having been laid out in 1768 by the local landowner Daniel Campbell, of Shawfield. Main Street stretches from the pier head to the commanding parish church, built in 1767 in an unusual circular design—so the devil could not hide in a corner.

Where to Stay & Eat

££££ ✕🏨 **Harbour Inn.** The cheerfully noisy bar is frequented by locals and off-duty distillery workers, who are happy to rub elbows with travelers and exchange island gossip. The superb restaurant (££) serves morning coffee, lunch, and dinner. Menus highlight local lobster, crab, prawns, and island lamb and beef. The rooms are bright and contemporary, with simple wood or velvet-upholstered furniture. ✉ *The Square, Bowmore, Islay PA43 7JR* ☎ *01496/810330* 📠 *01496/810990* 🌐 *www.harbour-inn.com* *7 rooms* *Restaurant, lounge; no a/c* 💳 *AE, MC, V* *BP.*

Shopping

You can purchase whisky and take a tour at **Bowmore distillery** (✉ School St. ☎ 01496/810671).

en route

Traveling north out of Bowmore (past a sign for Bridgend), the road skirts the sand flats at the head of Loch Indaal, where a daily mail plane used to land until an airport was built in the 1930s. To reach Port Charlotte, follow the loch shores all the way past Bruichladdich, which, like Bowmore, produces a malt whisky with the same name.

Port Charlotte

17 *11 mi west of Bowmore via A846/A847.*

Above the road on the north side in a converted kirk (church) is the **Museum of Islay Life,** a haphazard but authentic and informative display of times past. ✉ *A847* ☎ *01496/850358* *£2* ⏲ *Apr.–Oct., Mon.–Sat. 10–5, Sun. 2–5; Nov.–Mar., Mon. and Sat. 10–4.*

South of Port Charlotte, a loop road lets you explore the wild landscapes of the **Rhinns of Islay.** At the south end of the Rhinns are the scattered cottages of **Portnahaven** and its twin, **Port Wemyss.** Take the A847 to the villages, then return by the bleak, unclassified road that loops north and east, passing by the recumbent stone circle at Coultoon and the chapel at Kilchiaran. The strange whooping sound you may hear as you turn away from Portnahaven comes from Scotland's first wave-powered generator, sucking and blowing as it supplies electricity for both villages. It's well worth the climb down to the shore to see it in action.

en route

When you reach the B8018 north of Bruichladdich, you can turn left to reach **Machir Bay,** with its lovely (and usually deserted) sandy beach. The derelict kirk of **Kilchoman,** a short walk up from the shore, has some interesting grave slabs and a late-medieval Celtic stone cross. Heading back on the B8017 towards Bridgend, you reach an important reserve, managed by the Royal Society for the Protection of Birds, at **Loch Gruinart.** The loch is the winter nesting ground for many thousands of white-fronted and barnacle geese, which fill the air in clouds when they take off and settle, in the midst of a cacophony of honking. As you continue on the B8017, you'll pass the ruined chapel at **Cill Naoimh** (Kilnave), which carries a dark tale of a group of Maclean clansmen defeated in a nearby battle with the Macdonalds in 1598: the Macleans sought sanctuary in the chapel, but their pursuers set its roof aflame, and the clansmen perished within. There's a weathered 8th-century carved cross in the graveyard. You'll reach the main island road shortly before Bridgend.

The Oa

⓲ *13 mi south of Bowmore.*

The southern Oa peninsula is a region of caves that's rich in smuggling lore. At its tip, the Mull of Oa, is a monument recalling the 650 men who lost their lives in 1918 when the troopships *Tuscania* and *Otranto* went down nearby. To get here, drive south on the A846: before you reach Port Ellen, go straight ahead; when the A846 turns to a minor road to Imeraval, make a right at the junction, then a left. Bring good strong shoes for walking.

Port Ellen

⓳ *11 mi south of Bowmore.*

The sturdy community of Port Ellen was founded in the 1820s, and much of its architecture dates from the 19th century. It has a harbour, a few shops, and some inns. The road traveling east from Port Ellen for 3 mi passes three top distilleries and makes a very pleasant afternoon's "whisky walk." **Ardbeg Distillery** (☎ 01496/302244) is the farthest from Port Ellen. **Laphroaig Distillery** (☎ 01496/302418) is a little less than a mile from Port Ellen toward Ardberg. The whisky it produces is one of the most distinctive in the Western Isles, with a tangy, peaty seaweed-and-iodine flavor. **Lagavulin Distillery** (☎ 01496/302400) has the whisky with the strongest iodine scent of all the island malts. Tours are free at all three distilleries by appointment only.

About 8 mi northeast of Port Ellen is one of the highlights of Scotland's Celtic heritage. After passing through a pleasantly rolling, partly wooded landscape, take a narrow road (it's signposted KILDALTON CROSS) from Ardbeg. This leads to a ruined chapel with surrounding kirkyard, in which stands the finest carved cross anywhere in Scotland: ★ the 8th-century **Kildalton Cross.** Carved from a single slab of epidiorite rock, the ringed cross is encrusted on both sides with elaborate designs in the style of the Iona school. The surrounding grave slabs date as far back as the 12th and 13th centuries. 🌐 *www.historic-scotland.gov.uk.*

Islay Woollen Mill

★ ⓴ *3 mi north of Bowmore via A846; follow signs for Port Askaig.*

The mill, set in a wooded hollow by the river, has a fascinating array of working machinery; the proud owner will take you around. The shop here sells high-quality products that were woven on-site. Beyond the usual tweed, there's a distinctive selection of hats, caps, and clothing made from the mill's own cloth. All the tartans and tweeds worn in the film *Braveheart* originated here. Look for the sign for the mill on the main road about a mile east beyond the tiny community of Bridgend. ✉ *Off A846* ☎ *01496/810563* 🌐 *www.islaywoollenmill.co.uk* 🎫 *Free* ⏲ *Mon.–Sat. 10–5.*

Port Askaig

㉑ *3 mi northeast of Loch Finlaggan via A846.*

Serving as the ferry port for Jura, Port Askaig is nothing more than a cluster of cottages by the pier. Uphill, just outside the village, a side road travels along the coast, giving impressive views of Jura on the way. At road's end, the **Bunnahabhain Distillery** (☎ 01496/840646) sits on the shore. You can also purchase whisky at the **Caol Ila Distillery** (☎ 01496/840207). Call ahead for tour times.

Where to Stay & Eat

££ ✕▦ **Port Askaig Hotel.** The hotel grounds extend all the way to the shore at this modernized roadside drovers' inn overlooking the Sound of Islay and the island of Jura, beside the ferry terminal. Accommodations are comfortable without being luxurious, and the traditional Scottish food (£) is well prepared, using homegrown produce. ⊠ *Port Askaig, Isle of Islay, Argyll PA46 7RD* ☎ *01496/840245* ▤ *01496/840295* ⊕ *www.portaskaig.co.uk* ⊅ *8 rooms, 6 with bath* ⚘ *Restaurant, 2 bars; no a/c, no room phones* ▤ *MC, V* ⊺◯⊺ *BP.*

Jura

㉒ *5 mins by ferry from Port Askaig.*

The rugged, mountainous landscape of Jura, home to only 200 people, looms immediately east of Port Askaig. Having crossed the Sound of Islay from Port Askaig, you will find it easy to choose which road to take—Jura has only one, starting at Feolin, the ferry pier. Apart from the initial stretch it's all single-lane. The A846 starts off below one of the many raised beaches, then climbs across moorland, providing scenic views across the Sound of Jura. The ruined Claig Castle, on an island just offshore, was built by the Lords of the Isles to control the sound.

Beyond the farm buildings of Ardfin, and Jura House (with gardens occasionally open to the public), the road turns northward across open moorland with scattered forestry blocks and the faint evidence, in the shape of parallel ridges, of the original inhabitants' lazy beds or strip cultivation. The original settlements were cleared with the other parts of the Highlands when the island became more of a sheep pasture and deer forest. The community of Craighouse has the island's only distillery, the **Isle of Jura Distillery** (⊠ A846 ☎ 01496/820240), producing malt whisky. Phone ahead to reserve your place on a tour.

The settlement of **Kinuachdrach** once served as a crossing point to Scarba and the mainland. To get to Kinuachdrach after crossing the river at Lealt, follow the track beyond the surface road for 5 mi. The coastal footpath to Corryvreckan lies beyond, over the bare moors. This area has two enticements: the first, for fans of George Orwell (1903–50), is the house of **Barnhill** (not open to the public), where the author wrote *1984*; the second, for wilderness enthusiasts, is the whirlpool of the **Gulf of Corryvreckan** and the unspoiled coastal scenery.

Where to Stay & Eat

££–£££ ✕▦ **Jura Hotel.** In spite of its monopoly, this hotel set in pleasant gardens can be relied on for high-quality accommodations and good, simple food prepared with local ingredients. ⊠ *Craighouse, Isle of Jura, PA60 7XU* ☎ *01496/820243* ▤ *01496/820249* ⊅ *17 rooms (11 with bath)* ⚘ *Restaurant; no a/c, no room phones* ▤ *AE, DC, MC, V* ⊺◯⊺ *BP.*

IONA & THE ISLE OF MULL

Though Mull certainly has an indigenous population, the island is often called the Officers' Mess because of its popularity with retired military personnel. Across from the Ross of Mull is the island of Iona, cradle of Scottish Christianity and ancient burial site of the kings of Scotland.

Craignure

40-min ferry crossing from Oban, 15-min ferry crossing to Fishnish (5 mi northwest of Craignure) from Lochaline.

Craignure, little more than a pier and some houses, is close to Mull's two best-known castles, Torosay and Duart. Reservations for the year-round ferry trip from Oban to Craignure are advisable in summer. The ferry from Lochaline to Fishnish, just northwest of here, accepts no reservations and does not run on Sundays.

★ 23 A trip to **Torosay Castle** can include the novelty of steam-and-diesel service on a narrow-gauge railway, which takes 20 minutes to run from the pier at Craignure to the grounds of Torosay (about ½ mi). Scottish baronial in style, the turreted mid-19th-century castle has a friendly air. Between Easter and October you have the run of much of the house, which is full of intrigue and humor by way of idiosyncratic information boards and informal family albums. The castle's garden has an Italian statue walk. ✉ *Off the A849, about 1 mi southeast of Craignure* ☎ *01680/812421* 🖷 *812470* 🌐 *www.torosay.com* 🎫 *Castle and gardens £5; gardens £4; train £2.50* ⏲ *Castle: Easter–Oct., daily 10:30–5:30; last admission at 5. Gardens: Easter–Oct., daily 9–7; Nov.–Easter, daily dawn–dusk. Train departs between 4 and 8 times a day when castle is open.*

24 The 13th-century **Duart Castle,** the ancient Maclean seat, was ruined by the Campbells in 1691, but was purchased and restored by Sir Fitzroy Maclean in 1911. Inside, one display depicts the wreck of the *Swan,* a Cromwellian vessel sunk offshore in 1653 and excavated in the 1990s by marine archaeologists. Outside, you can visit nearby **Millennium Wood,** planted with groups of Mull's indigenous trees. If you're an enthusiastic hiker you can walk 4 mi along the shore from Torosay to Duart Castle.; if you have less energy, you can drive (or walk) the 3 mi from Craignure. To reach Duart by car, take the A849 and turn left around the shore of Duart Bay. ✉ *3 mi southeast of Craignure* ☎ *01680/812309* 🌐 *www.duartcastle.com* 🎫 *£4* ⏲ *Apr., Sun.–Fri. 11–4; May–mid-Oct., daily 10:30–6.*

Where to Stay & Eat

££ ✕🏨 **Craignure Inn.** This 18th-century whitewashed drover's inn, a short walk from the ferry pier, has a lively bar and often hosts local musicians. Hearty, home-cooked bar meals (£–££) include shepherd's pie, fish and chips, and hamburgers. The rooms are warm and snug, with polished-wood furniture, exposed beams, and views of the Sound of Mull. ✉ *Craignure, Isle of Mull, Argyll PA65 6AY* ☎ *01680/812305* 🌐 *www.craignure-inn.co.uk* *3 rooms* *Restaurant, bar; no a/c* 💳 *MC, V* 🍽 *BP.*

en route

Between Craignure and Fionnphort at the end of the Ross of Mull the double-lane road narrows as it heads southwest, touched by sea inlets at Lochs Don and Spelve. Inland, vivid grass and high rock faces in Glen More make gray and green the prevalent hues. These stepped-rock faces, the by-product of ancient lava flows, reach their highest point in Ben More, the only island *munro* outside Skye (a munro is a Scottish mountain more than 3,000 feet high). Stay on the A849 for a pleasant drive the length of the Ross of Mull, a wide promontory with scattered settlements. The National Trust for Scotland cares for the rugged stretch of coast, known as The Burg and home to a 40-million-year-old fossil tree (at the end of a long walk from the B8035, signposted west off the A849). The A849 continues through the village of Bunessan and eventually ends in a long parking lot opposite the houses of Fionnphort. The vast parking space is a testament to the popularity of the nearby island of Iona, which does not allow cars. Ferry service is frequent in summer.

Iona

25 *5 mins by ferry from Fionnphort, which is 36 mi west of Craignure.*

Fodor'sChoice ★

No less a travel writer than Dr. Samuel Johnson (1709–84) wrote, "We were now treading that illustrious Island which was once the luminary of the Caledonian regions." The fiery and argumentative Irish monk Columba (circa 521–97) chose Iona for the site of a monastery in 563 because it was the first landing place from which he could *not* see Ireland. Christianity had been brought to Scotland (Galloway) by St. Ninian (circa 360–432) in 397, but until St. Columba's church was founded, the word had not spread widely among the ancient northerners, the Picts. As the most important Christian site in the land, Iona was the burial place of the kings of Scotland until the 11th century, so many Dark Age kings, 48 of them Scottish (others were Pictish and Celtic), are interred here, not to mention princes and bishops. The tombstones that are still visible are near the abbey. Many carved slabs also commemorate clan chiefs.

Columba's monastery survived repeated Norse sackings but finally fell into disuse around the time of the Reformation. Restoration work began at the turn of the 20th century, and in 1938 the **Iona Community** was founded. Today the restored buildings, including the abbey, serve as a spiritual center under the jurisdiction of the Church of Scotland. Beyond the ancient cloisters, the island's most delightful aspect is its almost mystical tranquillity—enhanced by the fact that most visitors make only the short walk from the ferry pier to the abbey (by way of the nunnery), rather than press on to the island's farther reaches. Guided tours are every half hour in summer and on demand in winter. ☎ *01681/700793* 🌐 *www.historic-scotland.gov.uk* *£2.80* ⊙ *Apr.–Sept., daily 9:30–6; Oct.–Mar., daily 9:30–4.*

Where to Stay & Eat

£££–££££ ✕ **St. Columba Hotel.** An 1846 former manse, St. Columba stands next to the cathedral about ¼ mi from the ferry pier. All front rooms have glorious views across the Sound of Iona to Mull. Chefs in the restaurant (£££) cook exceptional three-course meals using organic ingredients. ✉ *Isle of Iona, Argyll PA76 6SL* ☎ *01680/700304* *01680/700688* 🌐 *www.stcolumba-hotel.co.uk* *18 rooms* *Restaurant, lounge; no a/c* ⊙ *Closed mid-Oct–mid-Apr.* *MC, V* *BP.*

Shopping

Iona has a few pleasant surprises for shoppers, the biggest of which is the **Old Printing Press Bookshop** (✉ Beside St. Columba Hotel), an excellent antiquarian and secondhand bookstore. The **Iona Community Shop** (☎ 01681/700404), across the road from the abbey itself, carries a nice selection of Celtic-inspired gift items, plus locally made crafts, sheet music and songbooks, and CDs and tapes.

en route

Back on Mull, turn west onto the B8035 at Loch Scridain: the road rises away from the loch to the conifer plantations and green slopes of Gleann Seilisdeir. The main road through the glen breaches the stepped cliffs and drops to the shore, revealing inspiring views of the island of Ulva guarding Loch na Keal. High ledges eventually give way to vistas of the screes of Ben More. Continue to skirt the coast on the B8073, and you'll take in a succession of fine coastal views with Ulva in the foreground. Beyond Calgary Bay the landscape is gentler as you approach the village of Dervaig.

Dervaig

26 *60 mi north of Fionnphort, 27 mi northwest of Craignure.*

Dervaig is a pretty riverside village 8 mi west of Tobermory. Its circular, pointed church tower is reminiscent of the Irish-Celtic style of the 8th and 9th centuries. The Bellart is a good trout- and salmon-fishing river, and Calgary Bay, 5 mi away, offers one of the best beaches on Mull. At the **Old Byre Heritage Centre,** an audiovisual presentation on the history of Mull plays hourly on the half hour; there's also a crafts shop. The restaurant's wholesome fare, particularly the thick, hearty homemade soup, is a boon to weary travelers. Driving on the B8073 you'll see signs for the center just before the village of Dervaig. ✉ *Dervaig* ☎ *01688/400229* *£3* *Easter–Oct., daily 10:30–6:30; last admission at 5:30.*

Where to Stay & Eat

££ **Calgary Hotel.** In a small wooded valley above the beautiful sandy bay, this former farmhouse is quite secluded, but warm and welcoming. Rooms have colorful quilts and drapes, and some have views over the woods to Calgary Bay. The restaurant, in a converted dovecote, attracts locals from all over the island as well as visitors. ✉ *Calgary, by Dervaig, PA75 6QW* ☎ *01688/400256* *www.calgary.co.uk* *9 rooms* *Restaurant, lounge; no a/c* *MC, V* *Closed Dec.–Feb.* *BP.*

The Arts

With just 43 seats the aptly named **Mull Little Theatre** (☎ 01688/302828) has the not-insignificant distinction of being the smallest professional theater in the United Kingdom. The theater stages a varied program of plays throughout the summer.

Tobermory

27 *5 mi northeast of Dervaig.*

Founded as a fishing station, Tobermory gradually declined, hastened by the arrival of railroad service in Oban. Still, the brightly painted crescent of 18th-century buildings around the harbor—now a popular mooring for yachtsmen—gives Tobermory a Mediterranean look.

Where to Stay & Eat

££–£££ **The Tobermory Hotel.** This hotel is made up of a row of former fishermen's cottages right on on Tobermory's waterfront. Most rooms have views of the bay, and superior rooms have king-size beds; one has a four-poster. The restaurant (££–£££) menu highlights local produce, but the dishes are prepared with a twist: for example, the spiced-salmon fillet is served over a haddock-and-prawn roll and topped with lemon-and-coriander cream, and the Angus-beef casserole is accompanied by a cheese trencher and crusty bread. ✉ *Tobermory, Isle of Mull, Argyll PA75 6PR* ☎ *01688/302091* *01688/302254* *www.thetobermoryhotel.com* *15 rooms* *Restaurant, bar, lounge; no a/c* *MC, V* *BP.*

££ **Fairways Lodge.** Between the third and fourth fairways of the local golf course, this modern bungalow has a breathtaking view out over Tobermory Bay. Rooms are prettily furnished with antique and reproduction items. You can walk into town in a few minutes, though it's a bit of a steep climb back. ✉ *Tobermory, Isle of Mull, Argyll PA75 6PS*

☎ 01688/302238 🌐 *www.fairwaysmull.com* 5 *rooms* *Dining room, golf privileges, lounge; no a/c* MC, V BP.

en route

To reach the ferry at Fishnish, drive south from Tobermory on the A848, which yields pleasant, if unspectacular, views across to the mountainous region of Morvern, on the mainland. On the coast just beyond Aros, across the river flats, stands the ruined 13th-century **Aros Castle.** The road runs through Salen to Fishnish (for the ferry to Lochaline) and then continues onto Craignure (for the ferry to Oban).

THE SMALLER ISLANDS

Caledonian MacBrayne ferries travel from Oban to three other fairly sizeable islands, Tiree, Coll, and Colonsay, with populations of only about 800, 150, and 100, respectively. The islands have pristine beaches and prehistoric artifacts much as other Scottish islands do, but their remoteness means you'll likely be exploring all by yourself.

Tiree

28 *4 hours sail from Oban, via Coll.*

A fertile, low-lying island with its own microclimate, Tiree is windswept, but it has more hours of sunshine per year than any other part of the British Isles. Long, rolling Atlantic swells attract surfers, and summer visitors can raise the population to the nearly 4,500 it supported in the 1830s. Among Tiree's several archaeological sites are a large boulder near Vaul covered with more than 50 Bronze-Age cup marks, and an excavated *broch* (stone tower) at Dun Mor Vaul.

Coll

29 *3 hours sail from Oban.*

Neighboring Tiree, Coll is even lower lying but also rockier and less fertile. The island is rich in archaeology, with standing stones at Totronald, a cairn at Annagour, and the remains of several Iron Age forts around the island. The keep of Breachacha Castle, on the south end of the island, dates to 1450. A former stronghold of the Maclean clan, the castle is very similar to Kisimul Castle on the Isle of Barra. Today Breachacha is privately owned, but you may view it from the road near Uig.

Colonsay & Oronsay

2½ hours sail from Oban.

30 **Colonsay** is one of Scotland's quietest, most unspoiled, and least populous islands. The beautiful beach at Kiloran Bay is an utterly peaceful place even at the height of summer.

The standing stones at Kilchattan Farm are known as Fingal's Limpet Hammers. Fingal, or Finn, MacCoul is a warrior of massive size and strength in Celtic mythology. Standing before the stones, you can imagine Fingal wielding them like hammers to cull equally large limpets from Scotland's rocky coast. The island's social life revolves round the bar at the 19th-century Colonsay Hotel, 100 yards from the ferry pier.

The adjacent island of **Oronsay** can be reached at low tide, at the expense of wet legs, in a wade across a sandy sound separating the two islands (after which an intake of reviving malt whisky never tastes better). Mesolithic shell mounds show the island was populated from before 4,000 BC, though only a handful of people live here now. The cloister ruins of a formerly rich and influential 14th-century Augustinian priory, including a stone cross, are well worth the paddle.

ARGYLL & THE ISLES A TO Z

To research prices, get advice from other travelers, and book travel arrangements, visit www.fodors.com.

AIR TRAVEL

British Airways Express flies from Glasgow to Campbeltown (on the Kintyre Peninsula) and the island of Islay.

British Airways Express ☎ 08457/733377 🌐 www.britishairways.com.

BOAT & FERRY TRAVEL

Caledonian MacBrayne (CalMac) operates car-ferry service to and from the main islands. An Island Hopscotch ticket reduces the cost of island-hopping. Serco Denholm Ltd. operates the Islay–Jura ferry.

Caledonian MacBrayne main office ✉ Ferry Terminal, Gourock ☎ 01475/650100 for schedules, 08705/650000 for reservations 🌐 www.calmac.co.uk. **Serco Denholm Ltd.** ☎ 01475/731540.

BUS TRAVEL

Scottish Citylink runs daily bus service from Glasgow's Buchanan Street station to the mid-Argyll region and Kintyre. The other companies listed below provide local service within the region.

Alex Dunuachie ✉ Jura ☎ 01496/820314 or 01496/820221. **B. Mundell Ltd.** ✉ Islay ☎ 01496/840273. **Bowmans Coaches** ✉ Mull ☎ 01680/812313 🌐 www.bowmanscoaches.sagenet.co.uk. **Oban & District Buses** ✉ Oban and Lorne ☎ 01631/562856. **Scottish Citylink** ☎ 08705/505050 🌐 www.citylink.co.uk. **Stagecoach Western Buses** ✉ Arran ☎ 01770/302000. **West Coast Motor Service** ✉ Mid-Argyll and Kintyre ☎ 01586/552319 🌐 www.westcoastmotors.co.uk.

CAR TRAVEL

Negotiating this area is easy except in July and August, when the roads around Oban may be congested. There are some single-lane roads, especially on the east side of the Kintyre Peninsula and on the islands.

You'll probably have to board a ferry at some point; all ferries take cars as well as pedestrians. The A85 takes you to Oban, the main ferry terminal for Mull. The A83 rounds Loch Fyne and heads down Kintyre to Kennacraig, the ferry terminal for Islay. Farther down the A83 is Tayinloan, the ferry port for Gigha. You can reach Brodick on Arran by ferry from Ardrossan, on the Clyde coast (A8/A78 from Glasgow), or, in summer, you can travel to Lochranza from Claonaig on the Kintyre Peninsula. *See* Boat and Ferry Travel for more information.

EMERGENCIES

Dial **999** in case of an emergency to reach an ambulance, coast guard, or the fire or police departments (no coins are needed for emergency calls made from public phone booths). Lorne and Islands District General Hospital has an emergency room. If you need medical or dental care, inquire at your hotel, the local tourist office, the police station, or look under "Doctors" or "Dentists" in the local yellow pages.

Hospital **Lorne and Islands District General Hospital** ✉ Glengallen Rd., Oban ☎ 01631/567500.

TOURS

BOAT TOURS Gordon Grant Tours leads a Three Isles ferry excursion to Mull, Iona, and Staffa and leaves Mull on other trips to Treshnish Isles and Staffa. From Taynuilt, near Oban, boat trips are available from Loch Etive Cruises. Sea Life Surveys offers four- and six-hour whale-watching and wildlife day trips from Tobermory, on the Isle of Mull. Turas Mara runs daily excursions in summer from Oban and Mull to Staffa, Iona, and the Treshnish Isles and specializes in wildlife tours.

Gordon Grant Tours ✉ Waterfront, Railway Pier, Oban ☎ 01631/562842. **Loch Etive Cruises** ✉ Taynuilt ☎ 01866/822430 or call Oban tourist office. **Sea Life Surveys** ✉ Torrbreac, Dervaig, Mull 🌐 www.sealifesurveys.co.uk/trips.cfm ☎ 01688/400223. **Turas Mara** ✉ Penmore Mill, Dervaig, Mull ☎ 01688/400242.

BUS TOURS Many of the bus companies listed in Bus Travel arrange general sightseeing tours. Bowmans Tours runs trips from Oban to Mull, Staffa, and Iona between March and October.

Bowmans Tours ✉ Scallastle Farm, Craignure, Mull ☎ 01680/812313 📠 01631/563221.

TRAIN TRAVEL

Oban and Ardrossan are the main rail stations. For information call National Rail. All trains connect with ferries. A narrow-gauge railway takes ferry passengers from the pier head at Craignure (Mull) to Torosay Castle, a distance of about half a mile.

National Rail ☎ 08457/484950.

VISITOR INFORMATION

The tourist offices in Lochgilphead, Tarbert, and Tobermory (Mull) are open April through October only; the rest are open year-round.

Bowmore, Islay ✉ The Square ☎ 08707/200617 🌐 www.scottish.heartlands.org. **Brodick, Arran** ✉ The Pier ☎ 01770/302140 📠 01770/302395 🌐 www.ayrshire-arran.com. **Campbeltown** ✉ Mackinnon House, The Pier ☎ 08707/200609. **Craignure, Mull** ✉ The Pierhead ☎ 08707/200610. **Dunoon** ✉ 7 Alexandra Parade ☎ 08707/20062. **Inveraray** ✉ Front St. ☎ 08707/200616. **Lochgilphead** ✉ Lochnell St. ☎ 08707/200618. **Oban** ✉ Argyll Square ☎ 08707/200630 **Tarbert, Loch Fyne** ✉ Harbour St. ☎ 08707/200624. **Tobermory, Mull** ✉ Main St. ☎ 08707/200625.

AROUND THE GREAT GLEN

INVERNESS, LOCH NESS, CAWDOR CASTLE, FORT WILLIAM

8

FODOR'S CHOICE

Brodie Castle, *near Nairn*
Cawdor Castle, *near Nairn*
Fort George, *near Nairn*
The Lodge at Daviot Mains, *near Inverness*
Osprey Hotel, *in Kingussie*

HIGHLY RECOMMENDED

RESTAURANTS
Crannog Seafood Restaurant, *in Fort William*

HOTELS
Boath House, *near Nairn*
Clach Mhuilinn, *in Inverness*
Crolinnhe, *in Fort William*
Isles of Glencoe Hotel, *in Ballachulish*
Polmaily House, *in Drumnadrochit*
The Cross, *in Kingussie*

SIGHTS
Cairngorm National Park, *near Aviemore*
Loch an Eilean, *near Aviemore*

By Gilbert Summers
Updated by Beth Ingpen

THE ANCIENT RIFT VALLEY of the Great Glen is a dramatic feature on the map of Scotland, giving the impression that the top half of the country has slid southwest. Geologists confirm that this actually occurred, after matching granite from Strontian, in Morvern, west of Fort William, with the same type of rock found at Foyers, on the east side of Loch Ness, some 65 mi away. The Great Glen, with its sense of openness, lacks the grandeur of Glencoe or the mountains of the Torridons, but the highest mountain in the United Kingdom, Ben Nevis (4,406 feet), looms over its southern portals, and spectacular scenery lies within a short distance of the main glen.

A map of Scotland gives a hint of the grandeur and beauty to be found here: fingers of inland lochs, craggy and steep-sided mountains, rugged promontories, and deep inlets. But no map can convey the area's brilliant purple and emerald moorland, its forests and astonishingly varied wildlife (mountain hares, red deer, golden eagles, ospreys), or the courtesy of its soft-spoken inhabitants and the depth of their ancestral memory and clan mythology.

Though it's the capital of the Highlands, Inverness has the flavor of a Lowland town, its winds blowing in a sea-salt air from the Moray Firth. Inverness is also home to one of the world's most famous monster myths: in 1933, during a quiet news week, the editor of a local paper decided to run a story about a strange sighting of something splashing about in Loch Ness. Seventy years later the story lives on, and the dubious Loch Ness phenomenon continues to keep cameras trained on the deep waters.

Fort William, without a monster on its doorstep, makes do with Ben Nevis and the Road to the Isles, a title sometimes applied to the breathtaking scenic route to Mallaig. This is best seen by rail, since the road to Mallaig is still narrow, winding, and single track in places, and meeting an oncoming bus can be alarming—especially if you are distracted by the view. On the way, road and rail routes pass Loch Morar, the country's deepest body of water, which lays claim to its own monster, Morag. Away from the Great Glen to the north lie the heartlands of Scotland, a bare backbone of remote mountains.

The great hills that loom to the southeast form the border of Strathspey, the broad valley of the River Spey. This area, commonly called Speyside, is known as one of Scotland's main whisky-distilling areas and is traversed by the Malt Whisky Trail.

Impressive and historic castles are also on the agenda in the Great Glen, perhaps one of the best known of which is Urquhart Castle, a favorite haunt of Nessie-watchers because of its location halfway down Loch Ness. It was once a great royal base and dates to the 13th and 14th centuries, though it's largely in ruins now. To the east are two top-of-the-list castles that are still inhabited: Cawdor Castle, with its happy marriage of different furnishings—modern and ancient, mellow and brightly colored—and Brodie Castle, with its magnificent library and a collection of paintings that extend well into the 20th century.

Exploring the Great Glen

The first possible route originates in Fort William and heads to Mallaig, taking in the unique qualities of the birch-knoll and blue-island West Highland views. The second route centers on Inverness, moving east into Speyside, then west down the Great Glen. There are many romantic and historic associations with this area. It was here that the rash adventurer Prince Charles Edward Stuart (1720–88) arrived for the final Jacobite

Rebellion, of 1745–46, and it was from here that he departed after the last battle.

About the Restaurants & Hotels

Inverness, Fort William, and Aviemore have plenty of hotels, B&Bs, cafés, and restaurants in all price ranges. Fort William has a particularly good seafood restaurant. Outside of the towns, there is a wealth of country-house hotels serving superb meals. Because this is an established vacation area, you should have no trouble finding a room for a night; however, the area is quite busy in peak season.

WHAT IT COSTS In Pounds	£££££	££££	£££	££	£
RESTAURANTS	over £22	£18–£22	£13–£17	£7–£12	under £7
HOTELS	over £150	£110–£150	£80–£110	£50–£80	under £50

Restaurant prices are for a main course at dinner. Hotel prices are for two people in a standard double room in high season. All prices include the 17.5% VAT.

Timing

This is a spring and autumn kind of area—summer contends with pesky midges, and winter brings raw chill. However, in summer, if the weather is settled, it can be very pleasant in the far west, perhaps on the Road to the Isles, toward Mallaig. Early spring is a good time to sample Scottish skiing at Nevis Range or Glencoe.

SPEYSIDE & LOCH NESS

Because Jacobite tales are interwoven with landmarks throughout this entire area, you should first learn something about this thorny but colorful period of Scottish history in which the Jacobites tried to restore the exiled Stuarts to the British monarchy. One of the best places to do this is at Culloden, just east of Inverness, where a major battle ended in final, catastrophic defeat for the Jacobites. Inverness itself is not really a town in which to linger, unless you need to do some shopping. Other areas to concentrate on are the inner Moray Firth moving down into Speyside, before moving west into the Great Glen. Loch Ness is just one of the attractions hereabouts. In the Great Glen and Speyside, the best sights are often hidden from the main road, an excellent reason to favor peaceful rural byways and to avoid as far as possible the busy A82 (down Loch Ness's western shore), as well as the A96 and A9, which carry much of the eastern traffic in the area.

Inverness

❶ *176 mi north of Glasgow, 109 mi northwest of Aberdeen, 161 mi northwest of Edinburgh.*

Inverness seems designed for the tourist, with its banks, souvenirs, high-quality woolens, and well-equipped visitor center. Compared with other Scottish towns, however, Inverness has less to offer visitors who have a keen interest in Scottish history. Throughout its past, Inverness was burned and ravaged by one or another of the restive Highland clans competing for dominance in the region. Thus, a decorative wall panel here and a fragment of tower there are all that remain amid the modern shopping facilities and 19th-century downtown developments. This does make a good base, however, for exploring the northern end of the Great Glen.

One of Inverness's few historic landmarks is the **castle** (the local Sheriff Court), nestled above the river. The current structure is Victorian,

The road from Fort William northwest to Mallaig, though narrow and winding, is one of the classic routes of Scottish touring and is popularly known as the Road to the Isles. Similarly, the Great Glen road (A82), from Fort William northeast to Inverness, is a vital coast-to-coast link.

Numbers in the text correspond to numbers in the margin and on the Around the Great Glen map.

If you have 2 days — Base yourself at **Fort William** 21 so that you can take in the spectacular scenery of **Glencoe** 19 and Glen Nevis and also get a glimpse of the western seaboard toward **Mallaig** 24.

If you have 4 days — Spend two days at one of two bases at each end of the Great Glen, say, **Inverness** 1 or **Nairn** 3, at the north end, and **Fort William** 21 or **Ballachulish** 20, at the south end. On the first day travel to Nairn from Inverness, and from Nairn go eastward to take a quick glance at Findhorn and/or Forres before travelling southward via **Cawdor Castle** 5 and/or **Brodie Castle** 6 to **Grantown-on-Spey** 9. Then follow the Spey as far as you like via **Boat of Garten,** with its ospreys in spring and early summer; **Aviemore** and its mountain scenery; and **Kingussie** 14, where the Highland Folk Museum does a good job of explaining what life was really like before modern domestic and agricultural equipment made things easy. The next day explore **Loch Ness** 17, traveling down the eastern bank as far as **Fort Augustus** 16 and returning up the western bank via **Drumnadrochit** 18; if you have time on a long summer evening, divert northward at Drumnadrochit to discover the beautiful glens Affric and Cannich, before returning to Inverness. On the third day travel to Fort William, taking in the **Caledonian Canal** 15. Spend a day doing the suggested loop to **Mallaig** 24 and go back through **Glenfinnan** 25 to Fort William, or go straight to **Arisaig** 23 and take an unforgettable day cruise among the Small Isles.

If you have 7 days — Seven days will give you plenty of time to visit all the highlights of the Great Glen area. Base yourself at **Inverness** 1 (or **Nairn** 3) for two nights, taking time to investigate the ecological community at Findhorn, then spend a night at **Kingussie** 14 and a night at **Drumnadrochit** 18. Moving west to the Fort William area, either stay in **Fort William** 21 itself, or go farther west and spend two nights in the excellent accommodations of **Arisaig** 23 for two nights. Either base will allow for exploration of the suggested circular route, a day at sea among the Small Isles, and a half day or day amid the grandeur of **Glencoe** 19 or Glen Nevis, behind Fort William. You may also want to make excursions farther north and west.

---

built after a former fort was blown up by the Jacobites in the 1745 campaign. The excellent, although small, **Inverness Museum and Art Gallery** (✉ Castle Wynd ☎ 01463/237114) covers archaeology, art, local history, and the natural environment in its lively displays.

Where to Stay & Eat

£££££ ✕ **Dunain Park Hotel.** You'll receive individual attention in this 18th-century mansion set amid 6 acres of wooded gardens. An open fire awaits you in the living room, a good place to sip a drink and browse through books and magazines. Antiques and traditional touches make the bedrooms equally cozy and attractive. The restaurant serves French-influenced Scottish dishes such as Shetland salmon baked in sea salt and medallions of venison rolled in oatmeal with a claret–and–crème-de-cassis sauces. ✉ *Dunain, 2½ mi southwest of Inverness on A82, IV3 8JN* ☎ *01463/230512* 🖷 *01463/224532* 🌐 *www.dunainparkhotel.co.uk* *5 rooms, 6 suites, 2 cottages* *Restaurant, pool, sauna, laundry service, Internet, no-smoking rooms; no a/c* ▭ *AE, MC, V* 🍽 *BP.*

££££–£££££ **Inverness Marriott Hotel.** Families appreciate this central rambling mansion set among 4 acres of gardens on the edge of a golf course: kids under 14 stay free, and the heated indoor pool and extensive leisure facilities—including privileges at the golf course next door—offer plenty to do. The bedrooms are spacious, comfortable, and well equipped, if a bit characterless. Six two-bedroom, two-bathroom apartments (each with kitchen) are a good value. The restaurant serves well-prepared and reliable steaks, seafood tagliatelle, and game pâté. ✉ *Culcabock Rd., IV2 3LP* ☎ *01463/237166* 🖷 *01463/712984* 🌐 *www.marriotthotels.com/invkm* *76 rooms, 6 apartments* *Restaurant, room service, in-room data ports, minibars, cable TV, golf privileges, pool, health club, hair salon, hot tub, sauna, lounge, laundry service, Internet; no a/c* ▭ *AE, DC, MC, V* 🍽 *BP.*

£££ **Culduthel Lodge.** Overlooking the River Ness sits an elegant 1840s stone villa, its white-pillar portico inviting you into a relaxing country-house environment: crackling log fires, flowers, sherry, luxury toiletries, and even a complimentary newspaper are all part of the deal. You can enjoy good Scottish cuisine in the dining room, with a menu that changes daily. ✉ *14 Culduthel Rd., IV2 4AG* ☎🖷 *01463/240089* 🌐 *www.culduthel.com* *12 rooms* *Restaurant, lounge, laundry service, no-smoking rooms; no a/c, no kids under 11* ▭ *MC, V* 🍽 *BP.*

££ **Ballifeary House.** The particularly helpful proprietors at this well-maintained bed-and-breakfast, in a pretty 19th-century villa, offer high standards of comfort and service. Rooms and common areas are decorated with Victorian-style furnishings. You can walk from the house to downtown Inverness and several good restaurants. ✉ *10 Ballifeary Rd., IV3 5PJ* ☎ *01463/235572* 🖷 *01463/717583* 🌐 *www.ballifearyhousehotel.co.uk* *5 rooms* *Lounge; no a/c, no room phones, no kids under 15, no smoking* ▭ *MC, V* 🍽 *BP.*

★ **££** **Clach Mhuilinn.** This pretty, modern cottage home sits amid a lush garden in a residential area. Floral fabrics and a mahogany bed are in one bedroom; the other has pinewood and tartan, and its own sitting room. Breakfast, including homemade Scottish oatcakes, is served before a view of the flower-filled garden. ✉ *7 Harris Rd., IV2 3LS* ☎ *01463/237059* 🖷 *01463/242092* 🌐 *www.ness.co.uk* *1 room, 1 suite* *Lounge, Internet; no a/c, no room phones, no kids under 16, no smoking* ▭ *MC, V* ⏲ *Closed Nov.–Mar.* 🍽 *BP.*

££ Fodor'sChoice ★ **The Lodge at Daviot Mains.** Built in Highland-lodge style and 5 mi south of Inverness on the A9, the Lodge at Daviot Mains provides the perfect setting for home comforts and traditional Scottish cooking (for guests only); you might find wild salmon on the menu. Rooms are very tastefully decorated, with carpets and plush, Victorian-style furnishings. The master bedroom has a four-poster canopy bed and bay windows. ✉ *Daviot Mains, Inverness IV2 5ER* ☎ *01463/772215* 🌐 *www.thelodgeatdaviotmains.co.uk* *6 rooms* *Dining room, in-room data ports; no a/c, no smoking* ▭ *MC, V* 🍽 *BP.*

££ **Moyness House.** Scottish author Neil M. Gunn (1891–1973), known for short stories and novels that evoke images of the Highlands, such as *Morning Tide, Highland River,* and *Butcher's Broom,* once lived in

Biking

A dedicated bicycle path, created by Scotland's National Cycle Networks, runs from Glasgow to Inverness, passing through Fort William and Kingussie. Additionally, a good network of back roads snakes around Inverness and toward Nairn. The B862/B852, which runs by the southeast side of Loch Ness, has little traffic and is a good bet for cyclists. Stay off the A9, however, as it's busy with vehicular traffic on both sides of Aviemore. The very busy A82 main road, along the northwest bank of Loch Ness via Drumnadrochit, is for the same reason not recommended for cyclists.

Fishing

The Great Glen is laced with rivers and lochs where you can fly-fish for salmon and trout. The fishing seasons are as follows: salmon, from early February through September or early October (depending on the area); brown trout, from March 15 to September 30; sea trout, from May through September or early October; rainbow trout, no statutory-close season. Sea angling from shore or boat is also possible. Tourist centers can provide information on locations, permits, and fishing rights.

Hiking

The Great Glen area is renowned for its hill walking. Some of the best routes are around Glen Nevis, Glencoe, and on Ben Nevis, the highest mountain in Great Britain. If you head for the hills, you should be fit and properly outfitted. Ben Nevis is a large and often dangerous mountain, because weather conditions can change very rapidly and unpredictably. Remember that it can snow on the summit plateau at any time of the year.

The Malt Whisky Trail

The two westernmost distilleries on the Malt Whisky Trail are in Forres. Benromach is the smallest distillery in Moray, while Dallas Dhu, where whisky is no longer in production, is preserved as a museum. Here you can scramble all around the rooms and machinery that, in working distilleries, are not usually open to visitors.

---

this lovely Victorian villa. Just past the well-trimmed hedges is a quiet residential street a few minutes' walk from downtown Inverness. Careful decorative touches grace each colorful room. The friendly owners provide excellent service and sound sightseeing advice. ⊠ *6 Bruce Gardens, Inverness, IV3 5EN* ☎🖷 *01463 233636* 🌐 *www.moyness.co.uk* *7 rooms* *Lounge, Internet; no a/c, no smoking* ▭ *AE, MC, V* *BP.*

£–££ **Atholdene House.** This family-run 1879 stone villa extends a warm welcome with a fire, games, and drinks in the common room. Rooms are simply decorated, with a mix of contemporary and antique furnishings. Downtown Inverness is a short walk away. ⊠ *20 Southside Rd., IV2 3BG* ☎ *01463/233565* 🖷 *01463/729101* 🌐 *www.atholdenehouse.com* *11 rooms (2 with shared bath)* *Lounge, Internet; no a/c, no room phones, no smoking* ▭ *MC, V* *CP, BP.*

Nightlife & the Arts

BARS & LOUNGES **Blackfriars Pub** (⊠ Academy St. ☎ 01463/233881) prides itself on its cask-conditioned ales, which you can enjoy to the accompaniment of regular live entertainment, including *ceilidhs* (a mix of country dancing, music, and song; pronounced *kay*-lees) and poetry readings. **The Gellion's Bar** (⊠ 14 Bridge St. ☎ 01463/233648) claims to be Inverness's oldest pub,

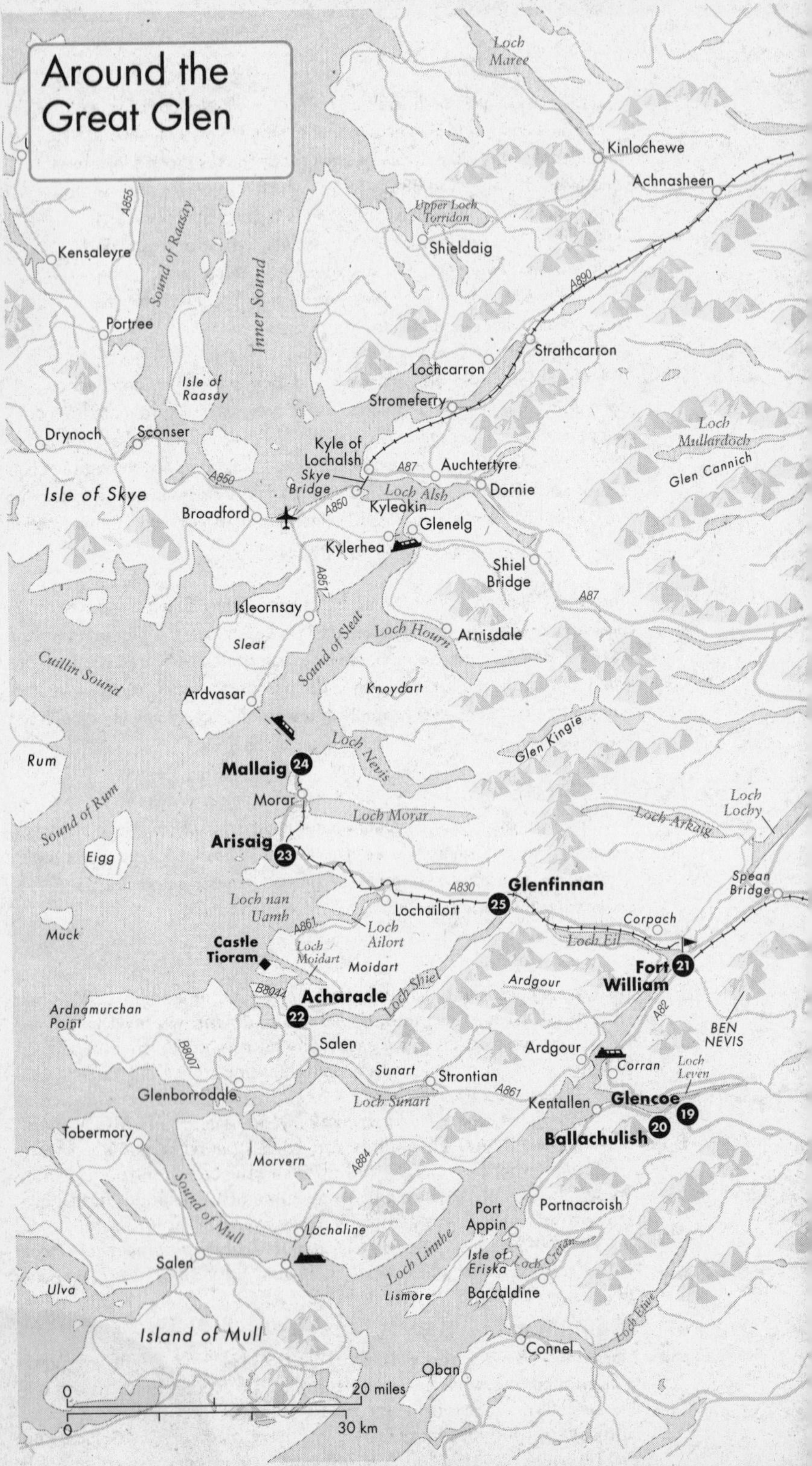
Around the Great Glen
Loch Maree
Kinlochewe
Achnasheen
Upper Loch Torridon
Shieldaig
A890
Kensaleyre
A855
Sound of Raasay
Inner Sound
Portree
Strathcarron
Lochcarron
Isle of Raasay
Stromeferry
Loch Mullardoch
Drynoch
Sconser
Kyle of Lochalsh
Skye Bridge
A87
Auchtertyre
Glen Cannich
A850
Loch Alsh
Dornie
Isle of Skye
Broadford
A850
Kyleakin
Glenelg
Kylerhea
Shiel Bridge
A851
A87
Isleornsay
Loch Hourn
Arnisdale
Sleat
Sound of Sleat
Cuillin Sound
Ardvasar
Knoydart
Loch Nevis
Glen Kingie
Rum
Mallaig
24
Morar
Loch Morar
Loch Arkaig
Loch Lochy
Sound of Rum
Eigg
Arisaig
23
A830
Glenfinnan
Spean Bridge
Loch nan Uamh
Lochailort
25
A861
Loch Ailort
Corpach
Muck
Castle Tioram
Loch Moidart
Moidart
Loch Eil
Fort William
21
Loch Shiel
Ardgour
B8044
Acharacle
22
Ardnamurchan Point
A82
BEN NEVIS
B8007
Salen
Ardgour
Sunart
Strontian
Corran
Loch Leven
A861
Glenborrodale
Loch Sunart
Kentallen
Glencoe
19
Tobermory
Ballachulish
20
Morvern
A884
Sound of Mull
Portnacroish
Port Appin
Lochaline
Salen
Isle of Eriska
Loch Creran
Loch Linnhe
Ulva
Lismore
Barcaldine
Island of Mull
Loch Etive
Connel
Oban
0
20 miles
0
30 km

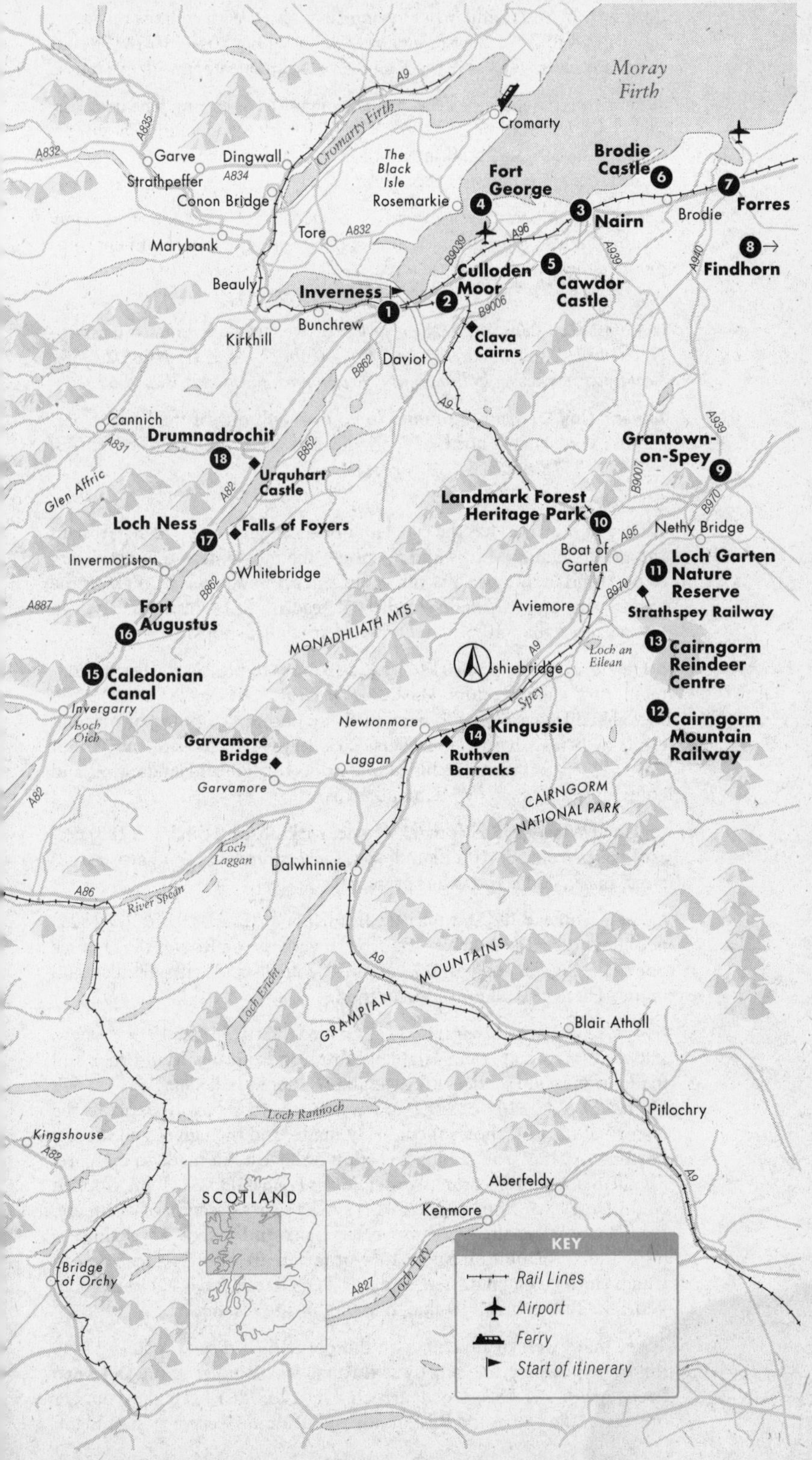

Moray Firth
Cromarty
Cromarty Firth
A9
A835
A832
Garve
Dingwall
Strathpeffer
A834
Conon Bridge
The Black Isle
Rosemarkie
Brodie Castle 6
Fort George 4
3 Nairn
7 Forres
Brodie
Marybank
Tore
A832
B9039
A96
A939
A940
8 Findhorn
Culloden Moor
5 Cawdor Castle
Beauly
Inverness 1
2
B9006
Bunchrew
Kirkhill
Clava Cairns
Daviot
B862
A9
Cannich
Drumnadrochit
18
A831
Urquhart Castle
B852
Glen Affric
A82
A939
Grantown-on-Spey 9
B9007
B970
Landmark Forest Heritage Park 10
Loch Ness 17
Falls of Foyers
A95
Nethy Bridge
Boat of Garten
Invermoriston
Whitebridge
B862
11 Loch Garten Nature Reserve
B970
Strathspey Railway
A887
Fort Augustus 16
Aviemore
MONADHLIATH MTS.
A9
Loch an Eilean
13 Cairngorm Reindeer Centre
15 Caledonian Canal
Invergarry
Loch Oich
Spey
Newtonmore
14 Kingussie
12 Cairngorm Mountain Railway
Garvamore Bridge
Ruthven Barracks
Laggan
Garvamore
CAIRNGORM NATIONAL PARK
A82
Loch Laggan
Dalwhinnie
A86
River Spean
Loch Ericht
A9
GRAMPIAN MOUNTAINS
Blair Atholl
Loch Rannoch
Pitlochry
Kingshouse
A82
A9
SCOTLAND
Aberfeldy
Kenmore
Bridge of Orchy
A827
Loch Tay
KEY
Rail Lines
Airport
Ferry
Start of itinerary

dating from 1841, and hosts live music nightly, with ceilidhs on Saturday from 4 to 7 PM. **The Harlequin** (✉ 1 View Pl. ☎ 01463/718178) has castle and river views and a welcoming beer garden, along with live music.

CABARET June through September, **Scottish Showtime** (✉ Spectrum Theatre, Faraline Park Bus Station ☎ 0800/015–8001 or 🌐 www.scottishshowtime.com for details and bookings) presents Scottish cabaret of the tartan-clad-dancer and bagpipe/accordion variety.

THEATER **Eden Court Theatre** (✉ Bishops Rd. ☎ 01463/234234) offers not only drama but also a program of music, film, and light entertainment, plus an art gallery and an excellent café.

Golf

Inverness Golf Club, established in 1883, welcomes visitors to its parkland course 1 mi from downtown. ✉ *Culcabock Rd.* ☎ *01463/239882* 🌐 *www.invernessgolfclub.co.uk* *18 holes, 6,256 yards, par 69.*

Torvean Golf Course is a municipal course with one of the longest par-5s (565 yards) in the north of Scotland. ✉ *Glenurquhart Rd.* ☎ *01463/711434* *18 holes, 5,784 yards, par 69.*

Shopping

Although Inverness has the usual indoor shopping malls and department stores—including Marks and Spencer—the most interesting goods are to be found in the specialty outlets in and around town. Don't miss the atmospheric indoor **Victorian Market** (✉ Academy St.), built in 1870, which houses more than 40 privately owned specialist shops.

FINE ART & ARTS & CRAFTS **art.tm** (✉ 20 Bank St. ☎ 01463/712240) aims to present the best of contemporary arts and crafts. The **Castle Gallery** (✉ 43 Castle St. ☎ 01463/729512) displays contemporary British painting, sculpture, prints, and crafts by British artists. The **Riverside Gallery** (✉ 11 Bank St. ☎ 01463/224781) sells paintings, etchings, and prints of Highland landscapes, and contemporary work by Highland artists.

SCOTTISH SPECIALTIES **Highland Wineries** (✉ Moniack Castle, Kirkhill ☎ 01463/831283) creates wines from Scottish ingredients, such as birch sap, and also makes jams, marmalade, and other preserves.

Made in Scotland (✉ Station Rd., Beauly, IV4 7EH ☎ 01463/782821) is well worth a 14-mi drive west from Inverness (on Route A862) to see one of the biggest and best selections of Scottish-made gifts, textiles, and crafts. There's a restaurant here, too.

Duncan Chisholm and Sons (✉ 47–51 Castle St. ☎ 01463/234599 🌐 www.kilts.co.uk) specializes in Highland dress and tartans. Mail-order and made-to-measure services are available. **Hector Russell Kiltmakers** (✉ 4–9 Huntly St. ☎ 01463/222781 🌐 www.hector-russell.com) explains the history of the kilt, shows them being made, and then gives you the opportunity to buy from a huge selection or have a kilt made to measure. The firm offers overseas mail order. **James Pringle Ltd.** (✉ Holm Woollen Mills, Dores Rd. ☎ 01463/223311) stocks a vast selection of cashmere, lamb's-wool, and Shetland knitwear, tartans, and tweeds; a weaving exhibit and an exhibit on the history of tartan are also on-site. You can watch cloth being made here and, for a £3 charge, have a go on a loom yourself. Take a break for lunch in the on-site restaurant.

Three miles west of Inverness on the Fort William road, you can stop for a bowl of soup and a browse through the antiques at the **Oakwood Dochgarroch** (✉ A82, Dochgarroch ☎ 01463/861481), the younger brother of the Oakwood Restaurant and Antiques Centre west of Elgin.

Midway between Inverness and Nairn on the A96 is the **Taste of Moray** (✉ Gollanfield ☎ 01667/462340 🌐 www.tasteofmoray.co.uk), well worth a stop for its restaurant, but especially for the Food Hall, which stocks a huge selection of Scottish, and especially Morayshire, produce. There's an excellent selection of gift items and household wares.

Culloden Moor

❷ *5 mi east of Inverness via B9006.*

Culloden Moor was the scene of the last major battle fought on British soil—to this day considered one of the most infamous and tragic in all of warfare. Here, on a cold April day in 1746, the outnumbered Jacobite forces of Bonnie Prince Charlie were destroyed by the superior firepower of George II's army. The victorious commander, the duke of Cumberland (George II's son), earned the name of "Butcher" Cumberland for the bloody reprisals carried out by his men on Highland families, Jacobite or not, caught in the vicinity. In the battle itself, the duke's army—greatly outnumbering the Scots—killed more than 1,000 soldiers. The National Trust for Scotland has re-created a slightly eerie version of the battlefield as it looked in 1746. The uneasy silence of the open moor overshadows the merry clatter from the visitor center's coffee shop and the tinkle of cash registers. ✉ *B9006* ☎ *01463/790607* 🌐 *www.nts.org.uk* 🎫 *£5* ⏲ *Site daily, 24 hrs; visitor center, Feb. and Nov.–Dec., daily 11–4; Mar., daily 10–4; Apr.–June and Sept.–Oct., daily 9–6; July–Aug., daily 9–7; last entry 30 mins before closing.*

Not far from Culloden, on a narrow road southeast of the battlefield, are the **Clava Cairns,** dating from the Bronze Age. In a cluster among the trees, these stones and monuments form a large ring with passage graves, which consist of a central chamber below a cairn, reached via a tunnel. Placards explain the graves' significance. ✉ *B851.*

Nairn

❸ *12 mi east of Culloden Moor, 17 mi east of Inverness via B9006/B9091; 92 mi west of Aberdeen.*

Although Nairn has the air of a Lowland town, it's actually part of the Highlands. A once-prosperous fishing village, Nairn has something of a split personality. King James VI (1566–1625) once boasted of a town so large the residents in either end spoke different languages. This was a reference to Nairn, whose fisherfolk, living by the sea, spoke Lowland Scots, whereas its uptown farmers and crofters spoke Gaelic.

The fishing boats have moved to larger ports, but Nairn's historic flavor has been preserved at the **Nairn Museum** in Viewfield House, a handsome Georgian building in the center of town. Exhibits emphasize artifacts, photographs, and model boats relating to Nairn's fishing past. A genealogy service is also offered. A library in the same building has a strong local-history section. ✉ *Viewfield House, Viewfield Drive* ☎ *01667/456791* 🎫 *£1.50* ⏲ *May–Sept., Mon.–Sat. 10–4:30.*

Where to Stay & Eat

★ **£££££** ✕🏨 **Boath House.** After a night in this stunning 1820s mansion, you may never want to leave. The château-like manor is surrounded by 20 manicured acres, and, inside, the spacious rooms have handsome 19th-century furniture and contemporary Scottish art. An Aveda health-and-beauty spa awaits you in the basement. The restaurant chefs use local produce, game in season, and fresh fish and seafood delivered daily by the fisherfolk themselves. ✉ *Auldearn, near Nairn, IV12 5TE* ☎ *01667/454896* 📠 *01667/455469* 🌐 *www.boath-house.com* *5 rooms, 1 cottage* *Restaurant, spa, Internet; no a/c* ▭ *AE, MC, V* *BP.*

Golf

Nairn's courses are highly regarded by golfers and are very popular, so be sure to book far in advance. **Nairn Golf Club,** founded in 1887, hosted the 1999 Walker Cup on its Championship Course, a traditional Scottish coastal golf links with what are claimed to be the finest greens in Scotland. ✉ *Seabank Rd.* ☎ *01667/453208* 🌐 *www.nairngolfclub.co.uk* *18 holes, 6,721 yards, par 79.*

Nairn Dunbar Golf Club, founded in 1899, is a difficult course with gorse-lined fairways and lovely sea views. ✉ *Lochloy Rd.* ☎ *01667/452741* 🌐 *www.nairndunbar.com* *18 holes, 6,765 yards, par 72.*

Shopping

At **Auldearn Antiques** (✉ Dalmore Manse, Auldearn, near Nairn ☎ 01667/453087) it's easy to spend an hour or more wandering around the old church—filled with furniture, fireplaces, architectural antiques, and linens—and the converted farmsteads, with their tempting antique (or just old) chinaware and textiles. Visit **Brodie Country Fare** (✉ Brodie, east of Nairn ☎ 01309/641555) only if you are feeling flush: you may covet the unusual knitwear, quality designer clothing and shoes, gifts, and toys, but they are *not* cheap. You'll also find a food store and delicatessen and an excellent and inexpensive restaurant. Not surprisingly, this establishment is extremely popular with the locals. **Nairn Antiques** (✉ St. Ninian Pl., near the traffic circle ☎ 01667/453303) carries a wide selection of antique jewelry, silver, glassware, furniture, pottery, prints, and some unusual giftware.

Fort George

4 *10 mi west of Nairn.*

Fodor's Choice ★

As a direct result of the battle at Culloden, the nervous government in London ordered the construction of a large fort on a promontory reaching into the Moray Firth: Fort George was started in 1748 and completed some 20 years later. It survives today as perhaps the best-preserved 18th-century military fortification in Europe. A visitor center and tableaux at the fort portray the 18th-century Scottish soldier's way of life, as does the **Regimental Museum of the Queen's Own Highlanders.** To get here take the B9092 north from A96 west of Nairn. ✉ *Ardersier* ☎ *0131/668–8800* 🌐 *www.historic-scotland.gov.uk* *Fort £5.50, museum free* ⏲ *Apr.–Sept., daily 9:30–6; Oct.–Mar., Mon.–Sat. 9:30–4, Sun. 2–4; last admission 45 mins before closing.*

Cawdor Castle

5 *5 mi southwest of Nairn.*

Fodor's Choice ★

Shakespeare's (1564–1616) Macbeth was Thane of Cawdor, but the sense of history that exists within the turreted walls of Cawdor Castle is more than fictional. Cawdor is a lived-in castle, not an abandoned, decaying structure. The earliest part of the castle is the 14th-century central tower; the rooms contain family portraits, tapestries, fine furniture, and paraphernalia reflecting 600 years of history. Outside the castle walls are sheltered gardens and woodland walks. ✉ *Cawdor, off B9090, 5 mi southwest of Nairn* ☎ *01667/404615* 🌐 *www.cawdorcastle.com* *Castle £6.30, garden and grounds £3.50* ⏲ *June–mid-Oct., daily 10–5.*

Brodie Castle

6 *8 mi east of Nairn.*

Fodor's Choice ★

The original medieval castle here was rebuilt and extended in the 17th and 19th centuries. Fine examples of late-17th-century plasterwork are preserved in the Dining Room and Blue Sitting Room; an impressive library and a superb collection of pictures extend into the 20th century. Brodie Castle is in the care of the National Trust for Scotland. ✉ *Off A96, Brodie, by Nairn* ☎ *01309/641371* 🌐 *www.nts.org.uk* 🎫 *Castle £5; grounds only, £1 (honesty box)* ⏲ *Castle, Apr. and July–Aug., daily noon–4; May–June and Sept., Sun.–Thurs. noon–4. Grounds, year-round, daily 9:30–sunset.*

Forres

7 *10 mi east of Nairn via A96.*

The burgh of Forres is everything a Scottish medieval town should be, with a handsome tolbooth (the former courthouse and prison) as its centerpiece. It is remarkable how well the old buildings have adapted to their modern retail uses. With two distilleries, one still operating, the other preserved as a museum, Forres is a key point on the Malt Whisky Trail. At the eastern end of town, don't miss **Sueno's Stone,** a soaring pillar of stone carved with ranks of cavalry, foot soldiers, and dying victims. The stone is said to commemorate a 10th-century victory.

Benromach Distillery is the smallest distillery in Moray and was founded in 1898. It is now owned by whisky specialists Gordon and MacPhail, whose shop in Elgin stocks a vast range of malts. The firm's history is outlined in a video, which also explains the production process at Benromach. Tutored nosing and tasting is one of the special features of a tour here. The distillery is part of the Malt Whisky Trail. ✉ *Invererne Rd.* ☎ *01309/675968* 🌐 *www.benromach.com* 🎫 *£2.50* ⏲ *Oct.–Mar., weekdays 10–4; Apr.–Sept., Mon.–Sat. 9:30–5.*

Dallas Dhu Historic Distillery, the last port of call on the Malt Whisky Trail, was the last distillery built in the 19th century. No longer a working distillery, the entire structure is open to visitors and you can explore it from top to bottom. An audiovisual presentation tells the story of Scotch whisky. ✉ *Mannachie Rd.* ☎ *01309/676548* 🎫 *£3.30* ⏲ *Apr.–Sept., daily 9:30–6; Oct.–Mar., Mon.–Wed. 9:30–4, Thurs. 9:30–noon, Sat. 9:30–4, Sun. 2–4.*

Findhorn

8 *6 mi north of Forres via A96 and B9011.*

Findhorn stretches along the edge of the semi-enclosed Findhorn Bay, which provides excellent birdwatching territory. At the southern end of the tiny town is the **Findhorn Foundation ecovillage,** a community dedicated to developing "new ways of living infused with spiritual values." Village inhabitants farm and garden to sustain themselves through direct connection with the earth. A visit affords a glimpse into the lives of the ultra-independent villagers, homes made out of whisky barrels, and the Universal Hall, made of wood and beautiful engraved glass. The **Phoenix Shop** sells organic foodstuff and handmade crafts. ✉ *The Park, Findhorn, IV36 3TZ* ☎ *01309/690311* 🌐 *www.findhorn.org.*

Grantown-on-Spey

9 *24 mi south of Forres via A940 and A939.*

The sturdy settlement of Grantown-on-Spey, set amid tall pines that flank the River Spey, is a classic Scottish planned town. This means it's a community that was planned and laid out by the local landowner, in this case Sir James Grant in 1776. It has handsome buildings in silver granite and some good shopping for Scottish gifts.

Shopping

Ewe and Me (✉ 82 High St. ☎ 01479/872911) is a well-stocked, high-quality gift shop with Scottish silver jewelry, glassware, Highland Stoneware platters and jugs, stuffed toys, and a large selection of greetings cards. **Speyside Heather Centre** (✉ Skye of Curr ☎ 01479/851359) has 200–300 varieties of heather for sale. A crafts shop, floral-art sundries, an antiques shop, a heather exhibition, and the Clootie Dumpling tearoom are also here.

Boat of Garten

11 mi southwest of Grantown via B970.

In the peaceful village of Boat of Garten, the scent of pine trees mingles with an equally evocative smell—that of steam trains. Boat of Garten is the terminus of the **Strathspey Steam Railway** (☎ 01479/810725 🌐 www.strathspeyrailway.co.uk), and the oily scent of smoke and steam hangs faintly in the air near the authentically preserved train station. From here you can take a 5-mi train trip to Aviemore, offering a chance to wallow in nostalgia and enjoy superb views of the high and often white domes of the Cairngorm Mountains.

10 **Landmark Forest Heritage Park** has a working steam-powered sawmill and a Clydesdale horse to haul the logs; a forestry workshop, where you can try out skills such as crosscut sawing; a bookstore; and a restaurant. Outdoors you'll find nature trails, a treetop trail, and a giant, climbable fire tower. Diversions for children include the Wild Forest Maze, terrifyingly steep water slides, a climbing wall, miniature cars and trucks, and an adventure playground. Reach Carrbridge on the quiet B9153—keep off the A9. ✉ *On B9153, Carrbridge, 3 mi north of Boat of Garten* ☎ *01479/841613* 🌐 *www.landmark-centre.co.uk* *£2.60–£7.95* ⏲ *Apr.–mid-July, daily 10–6; mid-July–Aug., daily 10–7; Sept.–Mar., daily 10–5; last admission 1 hr before closing.*

11 The **Loch Garten Nature Reserve** achieved fame when the osprey, a bird that was facing extinction in the early part of the 20th century, returned to breed here. Instead of cordoning off the nest site, conservation officials encouraged visitors by constructing a blind for bird-watching. Now thousands of bird lovers visit annually to get a glimpse of the domestic arrangements of this fish-eating bird, which has since bred in many other parts of the Highlands. The sanctuary, which is about 1 mi east of Boat of Garten via the B970, is administered by the Royal Society for the Protection of Birds (RSPB). ☎ *01479/821409 or 01463/715000* 🌐 *www.rspb.org.uk* *£2.50* ⏲ *Osprey observation post Apr.–Aug., daily 10–6; other areas of reserve year-round, daily.*

Aviemore

6 mi southwest of Boat of Garten via B970.

Once a quiet junction on the Highland Railway, Aviemore now has all the brashness and concrete boxiness of a year-round holiday resort. The

Aviemore area is a versatile walking base, but you must be dressed properly and carry emergency safety gear for high-level excursions onto the near-arctic plateau.

★ For skiing and rugged hiking follow the B970 from Aviemore to **Cairngorm National Park.** Past Loch Morlich at the high parking lots on the exposed shoulders of the Cairngorm Mountains are dozens of trails for hiking and cycling. Cairngorm became Scotland's second national park in March 2003.

12 The **CairnGorm Mountain Railway,** a funicular railway to the top of Cairn Gorm (the mountain that gives its name to the Cairngorms), operates both during and after the ski season and affords extensive views of the broad valley of the Spey. At the top is an interpretation center and restaurant. Be forewarned: it can get very cold above 3,000 feet, and weather conditions can change rapidly, even in the middle of summer. ✉ *Off B9152* ☎ *01479/861261* 🌐 *www.cairngormmountain.com* 🎫 *£7.50* ⏲ *Daily 9–4:30.*

On the high slopes of the Cairngorms, you may see the reindeer herd
13 that was introduced here in the 1950s. You can inquire at the **Cairngorm Reindeer Centre,** by Loch Morlich, about accompanying the herders on their daily rounds. The reindeer are docile creatures and seem to enjoy human company. Be sure to wear waterproof gear, as conditions can be wet and muddy. ✉ *Loch Morlich, Glen More Forest Park* ☎📠 *01479/861228* 🌐 *www.reindeer-company.demon.co.uk* 🎫 *Reindeer Centre £6; paddocks £2* ⏲ *Reindeer Centre, Feb.–Dec., daily 10–5 or dusk; paddocks, Easter–Dec. 10–5 or dusk; herder rounds, May–Sept., daily at 11 and 2:30; Oct.–Apr., daily at 11 (weather permitting).*

★ The place that best sums up Speyside's piney ambience is probably **Loch an Eilean** (signs guide you to it from Aviemore). On the Rothiemurchus Estate (☎ 01479/810858 🌐 www.rothiemurchus.net), a converted cottage beside Loch an Eilean is a visitor center (the area is a National Nature Reserve). The estate also offers several diversions, including stalking, fly-fishing for salmon and trout, guided walks, safari tours, off-road driving, clay-pigeon shooting, and farm-shop tastings of estate-produced beef, venison, and trout.

Kingussie

14 *13 mi southwest of Aviemore, via A9 and A86.*

The village of Kingussie (pronounced Kin-*yoo*-see) is of interest primarily for its **Highland Folk Museum.** The interior exhibits are in what was an 18th-century shooting lodge, its paneled and varnished ambience still apparent. Displays include 18th-century furniture, clothing, and implements. Outside, various types of Highland buildings have been reconstructed. The museum also maintains a Victorian schoolhouse in nearby Newtownmore. ✉ *Kingussie* ☎ *01540/661307* 🌐 *www.highlandfolk.com* 🎫 *Kingussie £2, Newtonmore £5* ⏲ *Kingussie, Apr.–Sept., Mon.–Sat. 9:30–5:30; Oct., weekdays 9:30–4:30; Nov.–Mar., weekdays, guided tours only, at 11 and 1. Newtonmore, Apr.–Aug., daily 10:30–5:30; Sept., daily 11–4:30; Oct., weekdays 11–4:30.*

Ruthven Barracks, which from a distance looks like a ruined castle on a mound, is redolent with tales of the '45 (as the last Jacobite Rebellion is often called). The defeated Jacobite forces rallied here after the battle at Culloden, but then abandoned and blew up the government outpost they had earlier captured. You'll see it as you approach Kingussie. ✉ *B970, ½ mi south of Kingussie* ☎ *0131/668–8800* 🌐 *www.historic-scotland.gov.uk* 🎫 *Free* ⏲ *Daily, 24 hrs.*

Where to Stay & Eat

★ **£££££** **The Cross.** Meals are superb and the wine list extensive at this "restaurant with rooms." Dinner, which could be fillet of local venison with port and red currants or pike mousse with a prawn sauce, is included in the price of your room, though you can dine here even if you are not an overnight guest. Bedrooms—all with king-size beds—are individually decorated and may have a balcony, canopy bed, or antique dressing table. *Tweed Mill Brae, Inverness-shire PH21 1TC 01540/661166 01540/661080 www.thecross.co.uk 9 rooms Restaurant; no a/c, no room TVs MC, V Closed Dec.–Feb. No dinner Tues. MAP.*

£ Fodor's Choice ★ **Osprey Hotel.** In a great stone house surrounded by woodlands and near to a nature reserve, you'll find worn yet elegant rooms filled with with delicate antiques. An impressive wine list complements the much praised cuisine, which might include breast of duck with grape and red wine sauce or monkfish with Bloody Mary sauce. This is an ideal base for skiing and hiking. *Ruthven Rd., Inverness-shire PH21 1EN 01540/661510 www.ospreyhotel.co.uk 8 rooms Restaurant, 2 lounges, Internet; no a/c, no room phones AE, MC, V.*

en route

Eleven miles southwest of Kingussie on the A86 at Laggan Bridge, where the main road crosses the River Spey, an unnamed road runs west up the glen to Garvamore. If you're not pressed for time, it's worth taking this road to view the **Garvamore Bridge** (about 6 mi north of the junction, at the south side of Corrieyairack Pass). This dual-arched bridge was built in 1735 by General Wade (1673–1748), who had been ordered to improve Scotland's roads by a British government concerned that its troops would not be able to travel the Highlands quickly enough to quell an uprising.

A stretch of the **A86**, quite narrow in some places, hugs the western shore of Loch Laggan. It has superb views of the mountainous heartlands to the north, and, over the silvery spine of hills known as the Grey Corries, culminating with views of Ben Nevis to the south.

Caledonian Canal

15 *40 mi west of Kingussie.*

Traveling north up the Great Glen takes you parallel to Loch Lochy (on the eastern shore) and over the Caledonian Canal at Laggan Locks. From this beautiful spot, which offers stunning vistas of lochs, mountains, and glens in all directions, you can look back on the impressive profile of Ben Nevis. The canal, which links the lochs of the Great Glen—Loch Lochy, Loch Oich, and Loch Ness—owes its origins to a combination of military as well as political pressures that emerged at the time of the Napoleonic Wars with France: for the most part, the British needed a better and faster way to get naval vessels from one side of Scotland to the other. The great Scottish engineer Thomas Telford (1757–1834) surveyed the route in 1803. The canal, which took 19 years to complete, has 29 locks and 42 gates. Telford ingeniously took advantage of the three lochs that lie in the Great Glen, which have a combined length of 45 mi, so that only 22 mi of canal had to be constructed to connect the lochs and complete the waterway from coast to coast.

Where to Stay & Eat

£££–££££ **Glengarry Castle Hotel.** This rambling, pleasantly old-fashioned mansion makes a good touring base; Invergarry is just south of Loch Ness and within easy reach of the Great Glen's best sights. Rooms have traditional Victorian decor; some have superb views over Loch Oich. The food is classic Scottish fare. Try the poached salmon with hollandaise or the loin of lamb with rosemary. The grounds include the ruins of Glengarry Castle, a seat of the MacDonnell clan. The hotel entrance is south of the A82–A87 road junction. ✉ *Invergarry, Inverness-shire PH35 4HW* ☎ *01809/501254* 🖷 *01809/501207* 🌐 *www.glengarry.net* *26 rooms* *Restaurant, tennis court, fishing, library, Internet, no-smoking rooms; no a/c* 💳 *MC, V* ⊗ *Closed Nov.–Mar.* 🍴 *BP.*

8

Fort Augustus & Loch Ness

53 mi north of Laggan.

The best place to see the locks of the Caledonian Canal in action is at **16** **Fort Augustus,** at the southern tip of Loch Ness. In the village center considerable canal activity takes place at a series of locks that rise from Loch Ness. Fort Augustus itself was captured by the Jacobite clans during the 1745 Rebellion. Later the fort was rebuilt as a Benedictine abbey, but monks no longer live here. The **Caledonian Canal Heritage Centre** (✉ Ardchattan House, Canalside, Fort Augustus ☎ 01320/366493), in a converted lockkeeper's cottage, gives the history of the canal and its uses over the years.

From the B862, just east of Fort Augustus, you'll get your first good **17** long view of the formidable and famous **Loch Ness,** which has a greater volume of water than any other Scottish loch, a maximum depth of more than 800 feet, and its own monster—at least according to popular myth. Early travelers who passed this way included English lexicographer Dr. Samuel Johnson (1709–84) and his guide and biographer, James Boswell (1740–95), who were on their way to the Hebrides in 1783. They remarked at the time about the condition of the population and the squalor of their homes. Another early travel writer and naturalist, Thomas Pennant (1726–98), noted that the loch kept the locality frost-free in winter. Even General Wade came here, his troops blasting and digging a road up much of the eastern shore. None of these observant early travelers ever made mention of a monster. Clearly, they had not read the local guidebooks.

en route

A more leisurely alternative to the fast-moving traffic on the busy A82 to Inverness, and one that combines monster-watching with peaceful road touring, is to take the B862 from Fort Augustus and follow the east bank of Loch Ness; join the B852 just beyond Whitebridge and take the opportunity to view the waterfalls at Foyers. The B862 runs around the end of Loch Ness, then climbs into moorland and forestry plantation. The half-hidden track beside the road is a remnant of the military road built by General Wade. Loch Ness quickly drops out of sight but is soon replaced by the peaceful, reedy Loch Tarff.

Drumnadrochit

18 *21 mi north of Fort Augustus via A82.*

If you're in search of the infamous beast Nessie, head to Drumnadrochit: here you'll find **Loch Ness 2000,** a visitor center that explores the facts and the fakes, the photographs, the unexplained sonar contacts, and the sincere testimony of eyewitnesses. You'll have to make up your own mind on Nessie. All that's really known is that Loch Ness's huge volume of water has a warming effect on the local weather, making the lake conducive to mirages in still, warm conditions. These are often the circumstances in which the "monster" appears. Whether or not the *bestia aquatilis* lurks in the depths—more than ever in doubt since 1994, when the man who took one of the most convincing photos of Nessie confessed on his deathbed that it was a fake—plenty of camera-toting, sonar-wielding, and submarine-traveling scientists and curiosity seekers haunt the lake. ✉ *Off the A82* ☎ *01456/450573 or 01456/450218* 🌐 *www.loch-ness-scotland.com* *£5.95* ⏲ *Easter–May, daily 9:30–5; June and Sept., daily 9–6; July and Aug., daily 9–8; Oct., daily 9:30–5:30; Nov.–Easter, daily 10–3:30; last admission 30 mins before closing.*

Urquhart Castle, near Drumnadrochit, is a favorite Loch Ness monster–watching spot. This weary fortress stands on a promontory overlooking the loch, as it has since the Middle Ages. Because of its central and strategic position in the Great Glen line of communication, the castle has a complex history involving military offense and defense, as well as its own destruction and renovation. The castle was begun in the 13th century and was destroyed before the end of the 17th century to prevent its use by the Jacobites. The ruins of what was one of the largest castles in Scotland were then plundered for building material. A visitor center relates these events and gives an idea of what life was like here in medieval times. Today swarms of bus tours pass through after investigating the Loch Ness phenomenon. ✉ *2 mi southeast of Drumnadrochit on A82* ☎ *0131/668–8800* 🌐 *www.historic-scotland.gov.uk* *£5.50* ⏲ *Apr.–Sept., daily 9:30–6; Oct.–Mar., daily 9:30–4; last admission 45 mins before closing.*

Where to Stay & Eat

★ **££££** **Polmaily House.** This country house amid lovely parkland is on the northern edge of Loch Ness; sailing on the loch is even possible. Books, log fires, and a helpful staff contribute to an atmosphere that is warmer and more personal than that found at grander, more expensive hotels, and families are sincerely welcomed. The restaurant is noted for its traditional British cuisine using fresh Highland produce. Tay salmon in pastry with dill sauce, roast rack of lamb with rosemary, and cold smoked venison with melon are examples of some flavorful dishes. ✉ *A831, 1½ mi northwest of Urquhart Castle, IV63 6XT* ☎ *01456/450343* 📠 *01456/450813* 🌐 *www.polmaily.co.uk* *9 rooms, 5 suites* *Restaurant, tennis court, pool, boating, fishing, croquet, horseback riding, recreation room, Internet; no a/c* *MC, V* *BP, MAP.*

TOWARD THE SMALL ISLES

Fort William has enough points of interest—a museum, exhibits, and shopping—to compensate for its less-than-picturesque setting. The town's primary purpose is to serve the west Highland hinterland; its role as a tourist stop is secondary. Because this is a relatively wet part of Scotland and because Fort William itself can always be explored if it rains, strike west toward the coast if the weather looks clear: on a sunny day the Small Isles—Rum, Eigg, Canna, and Muck—look as blue as the sea and sky together. From here you can also visit Skye via the ferry at Mallaig, or take a day cruise from Arisaig to the Small Isles for a glimpse of traffic-free island life. South of Fort William, Ballachulish and Glencoe are within easy striking distance.

Glencoe

19 *92 mi north of Glasgow, 44 mi northwest of Edinburgh.*

Glencoe, where great craggy buttresses loom darkly over the road, has a special place in the folk memory of Scotland: it was the site of an infamous massacre in 1692, still remembered in the Highlands for the treachery with which soldiers of the Campbell clan, acting as a government militia, treated their hosts, the MacDonalds. According to Highland code, in his own home a clansman should give shelter even to his sworn enemy. In the face of bitter weather, the Campbells were accepted as guests by the MacDonalds. Apparently acting on orders from the British government, the Campbells turned on their hosts, committing murder "under trust." **The National Trust for Scotland's Visitor Center** at Glencoe (at the west end of the glen) tells the story of the MacDonald massacre and also has an excellent display on mountaineering. ☎ *01855/811307* *£3.50* ⊙ *Site daily. Visitor center Mar., daily 10–4; Apr.–Aug., daily 9:30–5:30; Sept.–Oct., daily 10–5; Nov.–Feb., weekdays 10–4.*

Skiing

The **Glencoe Ski Centre** (✉ Kingshouse, Glencoe ☎ 01855/851226 🌐 www.ski-glencoe.co.uk), at the east end of the glen, has challenging black runs, well-maintained beginner and intermediate runs on the lower plateau, and snowboarding facilities.

Ballachulish

20 *1 mi west of Glencoe, 15 mi south of Fort William, 39 mi north of Oban.*

Ballachulish, once a slate-quarrying community, acts as gateway to the western approaches to Glencoe (though there is a Glencoe village as well).

Where to Stay & Eat

£££££ ✕ **Airds Hotel.** This former ferry inn, dating to the 17th century, has some of the finest views in all of Scotland. Set in a peaceful village midway between Ballachulish and Oban, the long white building, backed by trees, has a congenial air to it. Quilted bedspreads and family mementos make you feel at home. Fishing trips can be arranged. The restaurant serves Scottish cuisine, including venison and grouse. ✉ *Port Appin, Argyll PA38 4DF* ☎ *01631/730236* *01631/730535* 🌐 *www.airds-hotel.com* *12 rooms* *Restaurant, fishing, bicycles, lounge, Internet; no a/c* *MC, V* *MAP.*

★ **£££££** ✕ **Isles of Glencoe Hotel.** An excellent base for families, this hotel has its own leisure facilities including a toy corner. The interior is modern, with streamlined, fitted furniture in the bedrooms and original landscape paintings. Though neither original nor inventive, the cuisine—a choice of well-cooked beef, chicken, fish, and game dishes—is satisfying after a hard day's sightseeing. In keeping with its youth-friendly environment, there is also a separate children's menu. ✉ *Ballachulish PA39 4HL* ☎ *01855/821582* *01855/821463* 🌐 *www.freedomglen.co.uk* *59 rooms* *Restaurant, golf privileges, pool, sauna, steam room, recreation room, playground, Internet; no a/c* *MC, V* *MAP.*

Fort William

21 *15 mi north of Ballachulish, 69 mi southwest of Inverness, 108 mi northwest of Glasgow, 138 mi northwest of Edinburgh.*

As its name suggests, Fort William originated as a military outpost, first established by Oliver Cromwell's General Monk in 1655 and refortified by George I (1660–1727) in 1715 to help combat an uprising by the turbulent Jacobite clans. It remains the southern gateway to the Great Glen and the far west, and it's a bustling, tourist-oriented place. The **West Highland Museum,** in the town center, explores the history of Prince Charles Edward Stuart and the 1745 Rebellion. Included in the museum's folk exhibits are a costume and tartan display and a famous collection of Jacobite relics. ✉ *Cameron Sq.* ☎ *01397/702169* *£2* ⊙ *June* *and Sept., Mon.–Sat. 10–5; July–Aug., Mon.–Sat. 10–5 and Sun. 2–5; Oct.–May, Mon.–Sat. 10–4.*

Britain's highest mountain, the 4,406-foot **Ben Nevis,** looms over Fort William less than 4 mi from Loch Linnhe, an inlet of the sea. A trek to its summit is a rewarding experience, but you should be fit and well prepared—food and water, map and compass, first-aid kit, whistle, hat, gloves, and warm clothing (yes, even in summer) for starters—as the unpredictable weather can make it a hazardous hike. Ask for advice at the local tourist office before you begin.

A huge collection of gemstones, crystals, and fossils, including a 26-pound uncut emerald, are displayed at **Treasures of the Earth,** in a converted church near Fort William. ✉ *A830, Corpach* ☎ *01397/772283* 🎫 *£3.50* ⏲ *July–Sept., daily 9:30–7; Oct.–Dec. and Feb.–June, daily 10–5.*

Where to Stay & Eat

★ £££–£££ ✕ **Crannog Seafood Restaurant.** Set conspicuously on a small pier jutting out over the waters of Loch Linnhe, the Crannog has transformed Fort William dining. The sight of a fishing boat drawing up to the pier to take its catch straight to the kitchen says it all about the freshness of the seafood. The chef's capable touch ensures the fresh flavors are not overwhelmed. From the window seats you can watch the sun setting behind the steep hills on the far side of the loch. ✉ *Town Pier* ☎ *01397/705589* 💳 *MC, V.*

£££££ ✕🏨 **Inverlochy Castle.** A red-granite Victorian castle, Inverlochy stands on 50 acres of woodlands in the shadow of Ben Nevis, with striking Highland landscape on every side. Dating from 1863, the hotel retains all the splendor of its period, with a fine fresco ceiling, crystal chandeliers, a handsome staircase in the Great Hall, and plush, comfortable bedrooms. The restaurant is exceptional, serving such local specialties as roast saddle of roe deer or wood-pigeon consommé, with orange soufflé as the final touch. ✉ *Torlundy, 3 mi northeast of Fort William on A82, PH33 6SN* ☎ *01397/702177* 📠 *01397/702953* 🌐 *www.inverlochycastlehotel.com* ↩ *14 rooms, 3 suites* ♨ *Restaurant, tennis court, fishing, billiards, croquet, library, Internet; no a/c* 💳 *AE, MC, V* ⏲ *Closed Jan.–Feb.* 🍽 *BP.*

£££ 🏨 **The Grange.** A delightful, white-frosted confection of a Victorian villa stands in pretty gardens a 10-minute walk from downtown. Antiques, flowers, log fires, and views of Loch Linnhe await you here. The owners delight in giving sightseeing advice. ✉ *Grange Road, Fort William PH33 6JF* ☎ *01397/705516* 📠 *01397/701595* 🌐 *www.thegrange-scotland.co.uk* ↩ *4 rooms* ♨ *Lounge; no a/c, no room phones, no children under 12* 💳 *No credit cards* ⏲ *Closed Dec.–Feb.* 🍽 *BP.*

££–£££ 🏨 **Ashburn House.** This large white Victorian surrounded by an expansive lawn is a short walk from downtown. Chintz-draped bedrooms in shades of pink and blue are furnished with king-size beds. The conservatory lounge overlooks the loch, and the breakfast includes home-baked scones served in a delightful Victorian-corniced dining room. ✉ *Achintore Rd., PH33 6RQ* ☎ *01397/706000* 📠 *01397/702024* 🌐 *www.highland5star.co.uk* ↩ *7 rooms* ♨ *Dining room, lounge, Internet; no a/c, no room phones, no smoking* 💳 *AE, MC, V* ⏲ *Closed Dec.* 🍽 *BP.*

★ ££–£££ 🏨 **Crolinnhe.** An elegant Victorian house with colorful gardens, overlooking Loch Linnhe yet only a 10-minute walk from town, Crolinnhe is an exceptionally comfortable B&B. Antique and high-quality reproduction furniture is set off by pastel walls and bold-tone drapes. The breakfasts are among the best served in any establishment in Scotland. ✉ *Grange Rd., PH33 6JF* ☎ *01397/702709* 📠 *01397/700506* 🌐 *www.crolinnhe.co.uk* ↩ *3 rooms* ♨ *Dining room, lounge; no a/c, no room phones, no smoking* 💳 *No credit cards* ⏲ *Closed Nov.–Mar.* 🍽 *BP.*

Sports & the Outdoors

BIKING For a thrilling ride down Ben Nevis, take the gondola up to the beginning of the **Nevis Range mountain bike track** (open from May to September, weather permitting) and then shoot off on a 2,000-foot descent. Rent mountain and road bikes from **Off Beat Bikes** (✉ 117 High St. ☎ 01397/704008 🌐 www.offbeatbikes.co.uk).

GOLF The **Fort William golf course** has spectacular views of Ben Nevis and welcomes visitors. ✉ *Torlundy, Fort William* ☎ *01397/704464* *18 holes, 5900 yards, par 68.*

HIKING This area—especially around Glen Nevis, Glencoe, and Ben Nevis—is very popular with hikers, however, routes are not well-marked, so contact the Fort William tourist information center before you go. The center will provide you with route advice based on your interests, level of fitness, and hiking experience. **Ben Nevis** is a large and dangerous mountain, where snow can fall on the summit plateau any time of the year. Several excellent guides are available locally; they should be consulted for high-altitude routes.

For a walk in **Glen Nevis,** drive north from Fort William on the A82 toward Fort Augustus. On the outskirts of town, just before the bridge over the River Nevis, turn right up the unclassified road signposted Glen Nevis. Drive about 6 mi, past a youth hostel, a campground, and a few houses, and cross the River Nevis over the bridge at Achraibhach. Notice the southern flanks of Ben Nevis rising steeply to the east and the Mamores mountains to the west. Park at a parking lot about 2½ mi from the Achraibhach bridge. Starting here, a footpath leads to waterfalls and a steel-cabled bridge (1 mi), and then to Steall, a ruined croft beside a boulder-strewn stream (a good picnic place). You can continue up the glen for some distance without danger of becoming lost, so long as you stay on the path and keep the river to your right. Watch your step going through the tree-lined gorge. The return route is back the way you came.

SKIING **Nevis Range** (☎ 01397/705825 🌐 www.nevis-range.co.uk), is a modern development on the flanks of Aonach Mor, 7 mi north of Fort William, has good and varied skiing, as well as views of Ben Nevis. There are runs for all ability levels and a gondola system.

Shopping

The majority of shops here are along High Street, which in summer attracts ever-present, bustling crowds intent on stocking up for excursions to the west. The **Ben Nevis Woollen Mill** (✉ Belford Rd. ☎ 01397/704244), at the north end of town, is a major supplier of tartans, woolens, and tweeds. The **Granite House** (✉ 74 High St. ☎ 01397/703651) stocks Scottish contemporary jewelry, china and crystal giftware, wildlife sculptures, folk music CDs, ethnic clothing, musical instruments, toys and collectibles, and cards. The **Scottish Crafts and Whisky Centre** (✉ 135–139 High St. ☎ 01397/704406) has the usual souvenirs, but it also sells homemade chocolates and a vast range of malt whiskies, including miniatures and limited-edition bottlings. **Treasures of the Earth** (✉ Corpach ☎ 01397/772283) stocks an Aladdin's cave assortment of gemstone jewelry, crystal ornaments, mineral specimens, polished stones, fossils, and books on related subjects. The shop is closed in January.

en route For a lovely ferry ride, travel down the east side of Loch Linnhe to Corran, where a frequent ferry shuttles cars and foot passengers across the loch to Ardgour. (You can avoid the ferry by driving around the head of Loch Eil, but it's not a particularly scenic route.) From Ardgour the two-lane A861 runs south along Loch Linnhe before heading into Glen Sanda, crossing the watershed, and running down to the long shores of **Loch Sunart.** This is a typical western Highlands sea loch: orange kelp marks the tide lines, and herons stand muffled and miserable, wondering if it's worth risking a free meal at the local fish farm. As for the fish farms themselves, you'll grow accustomed to their floats and cages turning up in the foreground of every sea-loch view. The farms created jobs and were originally hailed as the savior of the Highland economy, but questions are now being raised about their environmental impact, at the same time that the market for their product is threatened by Scandinavian imports.

At the little village of Salen, either turn north immediately or divert to the westernmost point of mainland Scotland, at **Ardnamurchan Point,** reached along a narrow road with blind curves, in part through thickets of rhododendrons. The Ardnamurchan Peninsula is a must-see if you love unspoiled coastal scenery. Here you'll find small farming communities and vacation homes.

Acharacle

22 *3 mi north of Salen.*

On the way north to Acharacle (pronounced ach-*ar*-ra-kle with a Scots *ch*), you'll pass through deep-green plantations and moorland lily ponds. This spread-out settlement, backed by the hills of Moidart, lies at the shallow and reedy west end of **Loch Shiel**; the north end is more dramatic and sits deep within the rugged hills.

en route

Traveling between Acharacle and Arisaig, you'll reach the upper sandy shores of Loch Moidart by climbing on the A861 over a high moorland pass. On the next ascent, from Loch Moidart, you'll be greeted by stunning sea views. You can reach the sea coast by the mouth of Loch Ailort (pronounced *eye*-ort), and there are plenty of places to pull off among the boulders and birch scrub and sort out the view of the islands. In the distance you'll be able to spot Eigg, a low island marked by the dramatic black peak of An Sgurr. Beyond Eigg is the larger Rum, with its range of hills and the Norse-named, cloud-capped Rum Coullin looming over the island. You'll meet the main road again at the junction with the A830, the main route from Fort William to Mallaig. Turn left here. The breathtaking seaward views should continue to distract you from the road beside Loch nan Uamh (from Gaelic, meaning "cave" and pronounced *oo*-am). This loch is associated with Prince Charles Edward Stuart's nine-month stay on the mainland, during which he gathered a small army, marched as far south as Derby in England, alarmed the king, retreated to unavoidable defeat at Culloden in the spring, and then spent a few months as a fugitive in the Highlands. A cairn by the shore marks the spot where the prince was picked up by a French ship; he never returned to Scotland.

Arisaig

23 *27 mi north of Acharacle.*

Considering its small size, Arisaig, gateway to the Small Isles, offers a surprising choice of high-quality options for dining and lodging. To the north of Arisaig, the road cuts across a headland to reach a stretch of coastline where silver sands glitter with the mica in the local rock; clear water, blue sky, and white sand lend a tropical flavor to the beaches—when the sun is shining.

From Arisaig try to visit a couple of the **Small Isles: Rum, Eigg, Muck,** and **Canna,** each very small with few or no inhabitants. Rum is a wildlife reserve. **Arisaig Marine Ltd.** (Arisaig Harbour, Arisaig, Inverness-shire PH39 4NH 01687/450224) runs a boat service from the harbor at Arisaig to the islands at Easter and from May to September, daily at 11. The MV *Sheerwater,* delivers supplies and sometime visitors to the tiny island communities.

Where to Stay & Eat

£££ **Arisaig Hotel.** A 1720 former coaching inn close to the water, this hotel has magnificent views of the Small Isles. The inn has retained its provinciality with simple furnishings and home cooking (££). High-quality local ingredients are used to good advantage; lobster, langoustines, and crayfish are specialties, as are "proper" puddings, such as fruit crumbles. *Arisaig PH39 4NH 01687/450210 01687/450310 www.arisaighotel.co.uk 13 rooms Restaurant, 2 bars, lounge, recreation room, shop; no a/c MC, V.*

££–£££ **Old Library Lodge and Restaurant.** This converted 1722 barn on the waterfront houses good-size rooms decorated with contemporary furnishings, framed prints, and comforters, plus a fine restaurant with reasonable prices. Local produce is prepared in a French-bistro style and served in a whitewashed, airy dining room. *Arisaig PH39 4NH 01687/450651 01687/450219 www.oldlibrary.co.uk 6 rooms Restaurant, Internet; no a/c, no kids under 18 AE, MC, V Closed Dec.–Feb. BP.*

Mallaig

24 *8 mi north of Arisaig, 44 mi northwest of Fort William.*

After the approach along the coast, the workaday fishing port of Mallaig itself is anticlimactic. It has a few shops, and there is some bustle by the quayside when fishing boats unload or the Skye ferry departs: this is the departure point for the southern ferry connection to the Isle of Skye, the largest island of the Inner Hebrides. Mallaig is also the starting point for day cruises up the Sound of Sleat, which separates Skye from the mainland. The sound offers views into the rugged Knoydart region and its long, fjord-like sea lochs, Lochs Nevis and Hourn. The area to the immediate north and west beyond Loch Nevis, one of the most remote in Scotland, is often referred to as the Rough Bounds of Knoydart. For cruises to Loch Nevis, which operate all year, contact **Bruce Watt Sea Cruises** (Western Isles Guest House, East Bay, Mallaig, PH41 4QG 01687/462320).

The **Heritage Centre** of Mallaig has exhibits, films, photographs, and models on all aspects of the local history. *Station Rd. 01687/462085 www.mallaigheritage.org.uk £2 Apr.–Oct., Mon.–Sat. 9:30–4:30, Sun. 12:30–4:30.*

Beside the harbor, **Mallaig Marine World** shows you what goes on beneath the surface of the Sound of Sleat: live fish and shellfish and a display on the local fishing traditions are among the attractions here. *The Harbour 01687/462292 £3 Daily 9:30–5:30; call to confirm hrs.*

A small, unnamed side road just south of Mallaig leads east to an even smaller road that will bring you to **Loch Morar,** the deepest of all the Scottish lochs (more than 1,000 feet); the next deepest point is miles out into the Atlantic, beyond the continental shelf. The loch is said to have its own resident monster, Morag, who undoubtedly gets less recognition than its famous cousin Nessie. Apart from this short public road, the area around the loch is all but roadless.

Glenfinnan

25 *26 mi southeast of Mallaig.*

Glenfinnan, perhaps the most visitor-oriented stop on the route between Mallaig and Fort William, has much to offer if you're interested in Scottish history. Here the National Trust for Scotland has capitalized on the romance surrounding the story of the Jacobites and their intention of returning a Stuart monarch and the Roman Catholic religion to a country that had become staunchly Protestant. In Glenfinnan in 1745, the sometimes-reluctant clans joined forces and rallied to Prince Charles Edward Stuart's cause.

The raising of the prince's standard is commemorated by the **Glenfinnan Monument,** an unusual tower on the banks of Loch Shiel; the story of his campaign is told in the nearby visitor center. Note that the figure at the top of the monument is of a Highlander, not the prince. The view down Loch Shiel from the Glenfinnan Monument is one of the most photographed views in Scotland. ✉ *A830* ☎ *01397/722250* 🌐 *www.nts.org.uk* 🎫 *£2* ⏲ *Site, year-round, daily. Visitor center Apr.–June and Sept.–Oct., daily 10–5; July–Aug., daily 9:30–5:30.*

As impressive as the Glenfinnan Monument (especially if you've tired of the Jacobite "Will He No Come Back Again" sentiment) is the curving railway viaduct that stretches across the green slopes behind the monument. The **Glenfinnan Viaduct,** 21 spans and 1,248 feet long, was in its time the wonder of the Highlands. The railway's contractor, Robert MacAlpine, known as Concrete Bob by the locals, pioneered the use of mass concrete for viaducts and bridges when his company built the Mallaig extension, which opened in 1901. Now the viaduct is famous again, this time for its appearance in the "Harry Potter" films.

The train is the most relaxing way to take in the landscape of birch- and bracken-covered wild slopes; diesel **rail services** (☎ 08457/484950) run all year on the stretch of line between Fort William and Mallaig. The best ride is on the **Jacobite Steam Train** (☎ 01463/239026), which runs between July and September.

AROUND THE GREAT GLEN A TO Z

To research prices, get advice from other travelers, and book travel arrangements, visit www.fodors.com.

AIR TRAVEL

Inverness Airport has flights from London, Edinburgh, and Glasgow. Domestic flights covering the Highlands and islands are operated by British Airways, Servisair, easyJet, Eastern Airways, and Highland Airways. Fort William has bus and train connections with Glasgow, so Glasgow Airport can be an appropriate access point.

British Airways ☎ 08457/733377 🌐 www.britishairways.com. **easyJet** ☎ 0870/600-0000 🌐 www.easyjet.com. **Servisair** ☎ 01667/464040.

Glasgow Airport ☎ 0141/887-1111. **Inverness Airport** ✉ Dalcross ☎ 01667/464000.

BUS TRAVEL

A long-distance Scottish Citylink service connects Glasgow and Fort William. Inverness is also well served from the central belt of Scotland; for information call the Inverness coach station.

There is limited service available within the Great Glen area and some local service running from Fort William. Highland Country Buses operates buses down the Great Glen and around Fort William. A number of postbus services will help get you to the more remote corners of the area. A timetable is available from the Royal Mail.

Highland Country Buses ✉ Fort William Bus Station, Ardgour Rd, Fort William ☎ 01397/702373. **Inverness coach station** ✉ off Academy St., Inverness ☎ 01463/233371. **Royal Mail Post Buses** ✉ 7 Strothers La., Inverness IV1 1AA ☎ 01463/256273. **Scottish Citylink** ☎ 08705/505050 🌐 www.citylink.co.uk.

8

CAR RENTAL

Agencies **Avis** ✉ Dalcross Airport, Inverness ☎ 01667/464070 🌐 www.avis.co.uk. **Budget** ✉ Burns Cottage, Railway Terr., Inverness ☎ 0800/181181 🌐 www.budget.com. **Europcar Ltd.** ✉ Friar's Bridge Service Station, Telford St., Inverness ☎ 01463/235337. **Hertz** ✉ Dalcross Airport, Inverness ☎ 01667/462652 🌐 www.hertz.com.

CAR TRAVEL

The fast A9 brings you to Inverness in roughly three hours from Glasgow or Edinburgh, even if you take your time.

As in all areas of rural Scotland, a car is a great asset for exploring the Great Glen and Speyside, especially since the best of the area is away from the main roads. You can use the main A82 from Inverness to Fort William, or use the smaller B862/B852 roads (former military roads) to explore the much quieter east side of Loch Ness. The same applies to Speyside, where several options open up away from the A9, especially through the pinewoods by Coylumbridge and Feshiebridge, east of the main road. Mallaig, west of Fort William, has improving road connections, but the road is still narrow and winding in many places, and rail remains the most enjoyable way to experience the rugged hills and loch scenery between these two places. In Morvern, the area across Loch Linnhe southwest of Fort William, you may encounter single-lane roads, which require slower speeds and concentration.

EMERGENCIES

In case of any emergency, dial **999** for an ambulance, the police, the coast guard, or the fire department (no coins are needed for emergency calls from phone booths). Pharmacies are not common away from the larger towns, and doctors often dispense medicines in very rural areas. In an emergency, the police will assist you in locating a pharmacist. In Fort William, Boots the Chemist is open weekdays from 8:45 to 6, Saturday from 8:45 to 5:30. In Inverness, Kinmylies Pharmacy is open weekdays until 6 and Saturdays until 5:30. The pharmacy at the Scottish Co-Op superstore is open Monday though Wednesday, from 9 to 8, Thursday and Friday from 9 to 9, Saturday from 9 to 6, and Sunday from 10 to 6.

Hospitals **Belford Hospital** ✉ Belford Rd., Fort William ☎ 01397/702481. **Raigmore Hospital** ✉ Old Perth Rd., Inverness ☎ 01463/704000. **Town and County Hospital** ✉ Cawdor Rd., Nairn ☎ 01667/452101.

Late-Night Pharmacies **Boots the Chemist** ✉ High St., Fort William ☎ 01397/705143. **Kinmylies Pharmacy** ✉ 1 Charleston Ct., Kinmylies Inverness ☎ 01463/221094. **Scottish Co-Op** ✉ Milton of Inshes, Perth Rd., outside Inverness ☎ 01463/712188.

TOURS

BOAT TOURS

Arisaig Marine operates Hebridean day cruises for whale-, seal-, and bird-watching. Your vessel is the MV *Sheerwater,* which travels to the Small Isles at Easter and daily from May through September, when charter trips also go to Skye. Also available for charter from Arisaig Marine is a fast twin-engine motor yacht, which can take up to 12 passengers around the

Small Isles and farther afield. Caledonian MacBrayne runs scheduled service and cruises from Mallaig to Skye, the Small Isles, and Mull.

Jacobite Cruises Ltd. runs morning and afternoon cruises on Loch Ness to Urquhart Castle and boat and coach excursions to the Monster Exhibition in Drumnadrochit.

An unusual option from Inverness is a day trip to Orkney: John o'Groats Ferries runs day tours from Inverness to Orkney, daily from June through August. Moray Firth Cruises provides trips by boat from Inverness harbor into the Moray Firth, offering you the chance to see dolphins in their breeding area.

Arisaig Marine ☎ 01687/450224 🌐 www.arisaig.co.uk. **Caledonian MacBrayne** ☎ 01475/650100 🌐 www.calmac.co.uk. **Jacobite Cruises Ltd.** ☎ 01463/233999 🌐 www.jacobite.co.uk. **John o'Groats Ferries** ☎ 01955/611353 🌐 www.jogferry.co.uk. **Moray Firth Cruises** ☎ 01463/717900.

PERSONAL GUIDES

James Johnstone is based in Inverness but will drive you anywhere; he has a particularly good knowledge of the Highlands and islands, including the Outer Isles.

James Johnstone ☎ 01463/798372 📠 01463/790179 🌐 www.jajcd.com.

TRAIN TOURS

From Fort William, ScotRail runs services on the outstandingly beautiful West Highland Line to Mallaig. The Jacobite Steam Train is an exciting summer (July to September) option on the same route.

Jacobite Steam Train ☎ 01463/239026. **ScotRail** ☎ 08457/550033 🌐 www.scotrail.co.uk.

TRAIN TRAVEL

There are connections from London to Inverness and Fort William (including overnight sleeper service), as well as reliable links from Glasgow and Edinburgh. For information call National Rail Enquiries.

Though there is no rail connection among towns within the Great Glen, this area has the West Highland line, which links Fort William to Mallaig; a trip on this scenic line is recommended (steam trains are a bonus in the summer months). There's train service between Glasgow (Queen Street) and Inverness, via Aviemore, which gives access to the heart of Speyside. For information call National Rail.

National Rail ☎ 08457/484950. **Jacobite Steam Train** ☎ 01463/239026 for bookings. **ScotRail** ☎ 08457/550033 🌐 www.scotrail.co.uk.

VISITOR INFORMATION

Aviemore, Fort William, and Inverness have year-round tourist offices. Other tourist centers, open seasonally, include those at Ballachulish, Fort Augustus, Grantown-on-Spey, Kingussie, Mallaig, Nairn, and Strontian. The Web site for the whole area is www.host.co.uk.

Aviemore ✉ Grampian Rd. ☎ 01479/810363. **Fort William** ✉ Cameron Centre, Cameron Sq. ☎ 01397/703781. **Inverness** ✉ Castle Wynd ☎ 01463/234353 🌐 www.host.co.uk.

THE NORTHERN HIGHLANDS

SUTHERLAND, ISLE OF SKYE, OUTER HEBRIDES

9

FODOR'S CHOICE

Ceilidh Place, *in Ullapool*
Eilean Donan Castle, *in Dornie*
Loch Maree, *in Gairloch*
The Mountain Restaurant and Lodge, *in Gairloch*
Three Chimneys Restaurant with Rooms, *in Dunvegan*

HIGHLY RECOMMENDED

RESTAURANT

Loch Bay Seafood Restaurant, *in Stein*

HOTELS

Ardvourlie Castle, *on the Isle of Harris*
Craigvar, *in Strathpeffer*
Dornoch Castle Hotel, *in Dornoch*
Hotel Eilean Iarmain, *Armadale*
Ptarmigan, *in Broadford*

SIGHTS

Calanais Standing Stones, *in Calanais*
Corrieshalloch Gorge, *in Wester Ross*
Glen Brittle, *on the Isle of Skye*
Glen Torridon, *in Shieldaig*
Inverewe Gardens, *in Poolewe*

By Gilbert Summers
Updated by Chris Townsend

MUCH OF THE ROMANCE of "Caledonia stern and wild"—the splendid and tranquil landscape, the Highland clans, red deer and golden eagles, Celtic mists and legends—is concentrated in this region. This is where you'll find Eilean Donan, the most romantic of Scottish castles; the land's end at John o'Groats; and Skye, the mysterious island immortalized by the exploits of Bonnie Prince Charlie. The old counties of Ross and Cromarty (sometimes called Easter and Wester Ross), Sutherland, and Caithness constitute the most northern portion of mainland Scotland. The population is sparse, mountains and moorland limit the choice of touring routes, and distances are less important than whether the winding, hilly roads you sometimes encounter are two lanes or one.

Much of Sutherland and Wester Ross is made up of a rocky platform of Lewisian gneiss, certainly the oldest rocks in Britain, scoured and hollowed by glacial action into numerous lochs. On top of this rolling, wet moorland landscape sit strangely shaped quartzite-capped sandstone mountains, eroded and pinnacled. Take a walk here, and the Ice Age doesn't seem so far away. One of the region's leitmotivs is the sea lochs that thrust salty fingers into the loneliest landscapes in Scotland, carrying the Atlantic's salty tang among the moors and deep forests. Strange, solitary peaks rear up out of the heather, and if you're lucky, you may sight a golden eagle soaring overhead in search of rabbits.

Many place-names in this region reflect its early links with Scandinavia. Sutherland, the most northern portion of mainland Scotland, was once the southernmost land belonging to the Vikings. Cape Wrath, got its name from the Viking word *hvarth* (turning point), and Laxford, Suilven, and dozens of other names in the area have Norse rather than Gaelic derivations.

The island of Skye and the Outer Hebrides, which are now often referred to as the Western Isles, are the stronghold of the Gaelic language. Skye, famous for its misty mountains, called the Cuillins, has a surprisingly wide variety of landscape, considering its relatively small size. The south of the island is generally flatter; its coastline is the place to hunt out hidden beaches, perhaps overlooked by a ruined castle, and its interior moorlands are dotted with lochans (small lakes). As you travel northward, however, the landscape becomes increasingly mountainous, with green pastures surrounding the scattered crofting (farming) communities and sea inlets strewn with jewel-like islets, miniature versions of Skye itself.

Exploring the Northern Highlands

From Inverness, the gateway to the Northern Highlands, roads fan out like the spokes of a wheel to join the coastal route around the rim of mainland Scotland. Many roads here are single lane, requiring you to pause at passing places to allow ongoing traffic to pass: do not underestimate driving times, especially when driving on minor roads or on the islands. There are simply no roads into the wilder areas, and few roads at all—so you're bound to be sharing the roads with heavy trucks and buses. Ferry services are generally very reliable, weather permitting.

On a map, this area may seem far from major urban centers, but it's easy to reach. Inverness has an airport with direct links to London, Edinburgh, Glasgow, and even Amsterdam, and you can reach destinations such as the fishing town of Ullapool in an hour by car from Inverness.

About the Restaurants & Hotels

Charming, earthy, inexpensive inns and a few good modern hotels will welcome you with warmth and vivacity as you come in after a day of touring in the cool, moist Highlands air. Although the scope of dining

The quality of the northern light and the sheer beauty of the landscapes add to the adventure. Above all, don't rush things. Multiple-journey ferry tickets—the Island Hopscotch, for example—can help you stay flexible.

Numbers in the text correspond to numbers in the margin and on the Northern Highlands & Skye map and the Outer Hebrides map.

9

If you have 2 days

If you only have two days, head to the fabled isle of Skye, whose mists shroud so many legends. Stay in towns with remarkable hotels, such as ☒ **Broadford** ⑲ ⚑ or ☒ **Armadale** ⑳, then tour the spectacular countryside, including the celebrated Cuillin Ridge near **Glen Brittle** ㉖. Be sure to detour to see **Eilean Donan Castle** ⑱, once you're back on the mainland.

If you have 5 days

If the weather looks settled, head for Skye, and base yourself at ☒ **Portree** ㉑ ⚑. The next day, visit **Glen Brittle** ㉖ and the Cuillin Ridge. On your third day, take the ferry from Uig, in the north of Skye, to ☒ **Tarbert** ㉛, in the Western Isles, and visit the **Calanais Standing Stones** ㉚, the **Arnol Black House** ㉙, and some deserted beaches. The next day, travel to ☒ **Stornoway** ㉗ and catch the ferry to ☒ **Ullapool** ③ on the mainland. On your fifth day, return to Inverness by way of the **Corrieshalloch Gorge** ② and **Strathpeffer** ①.

If you have 8 days

Tackle the coastal loop of the north of Scotland counterclockwise. Start at ☒ **Ullapool** ③ ⚑, then take the ferry for ☒ **Stornoway** ㉗ and the Western Isles. Spend your second day visiting Stornoway's harbor and museum, and on your third day, drive north to visit **Port of Ness**, the **Butt of Lewis Lighthouse** ㉘, the **Arnol Black House** ㉙, and the **Calanais Standing Stones** ㉚. The fourth day, drive to ☒ **Tarbert** ㉛ and then **Northton** for a visit to the **Seallam! Visitor Centre and Co Leis Thu? Genealogical Research Centre**. The next day, take the ferry to North Uist, returning to Tarbert in the evening. On your sixth day, take the ferry to Uig on Skye and travel to ☒ **Portree** ㉑. Spend your seventh day visiting **Glen Brittle** ㉖, then move on to ☒ **Broadford** ⑲. On your last day, cross the Skye Bridge and return to Inverness.

options is more limited than in populous areas of Scotland, several restaurants of very high standard dot the region, especially on Skye. Most country-house inns serve reliable, hearty, seafood and meat-and-potatoes meals.

WHAT IT COSTS In Pounds				
£££££	**££££**	**£££**	**££**	**£**
RESTAURANTS over £22	£18–£22	£13–£17	£7–£12	under £7
HOTELS over £150	£110–£150	£80–£110	£50–£80	under £50

Restaurant prices are for a main course at dinner. Hotel prices are for two people in a standard double room in high season.

Timing

The Northern Highlands and islands are best seen in late spring, summer, and early autumn. The earlier in the spring or later in the autumn you go, the greater the chances of your encountering the elements in their extreme form, and the fewer attractions and accommodations you will find open; even tourist-friendly Skye closes down almost completely by the end of October. As a final deciding factor, you may not want to take a western sea passage in a gale, a frequent occurrence in the winter months.

THE NORTHERN LANDSCAPES

Weater Ross and Sutherland have some of the most distinctive mountain profiles in all of Scotland, although the coastal rim roads are more interesting than the cross-country routes. The essence of Caithness, the area at the top of Scotland, is space, big skies, and distant blue hills beyond endless rolling moors (although "tax-break" conifer planting has encroached on the views in some areas). There's a surprising amount to see and do on the east coast beyond Inverness—try to allow enough time to take in the visitor centers and croft houses open to view.

Strathpeffer

❶ *19 mi northwest of Inverness via A9, A835, and A834.*

At the former Victorian spa town of Strathpeffer you can take a walk to admire Victorian "holiday houses" and the Eagle Stone, a boulder carved with Pictish signs in the 7th century, now perched on a hill just outside the town. The Highland Museum of Childhood displays early Highlands toys in the former railway station. Not far from Strathpeffer are the tumbling **Falls of Rogie** (signposted off the A835), where an interestingly bouncy suspension bridge presents you with a fine view of the splashing waters below.

Where to Stay

★ **££** 🖾 **Craigvar.** Host Margaret Scott is a delight and stocks plenty of tourist leaflets to keep you busy at this pretty Georgian bed-and-breakfast. The Beige Room has white walls and cream furnishings, with a swag of dried hydrangea above the bed. Idiosyncratic pictures—from 18th-century portraits to Japanese-style still lifes—hang on the walls. The Blue Room has a four-poster bed and Victorian bath. ☒ *The Square, Strathpeffer, Ross-shire IV14 9DL* ☎ *01997/421622* 🖷 *01997/421796* 🌐 *www. craigvar.com* ↪*3 rooms* ↺ *Lounge; no a/c, no smoking* ⊟*MC, V* 🍴*BP.*

Corrieshalloch Gorge

★ **❷** *39 mi northwest of Strathpeffer.*

For a thrilling touch of vertigo, don't miss Corrieshalloch Gorge. A river draining the high moors plunges 150 feet into a 200-foot-deep, thickly wooded gorge. There's a suspension-bridge viewpoint and a heady atmosphere of romantic grandeur, like an old Scottish print come to life. A short walk leads from a parking area to the viewpoint.

Ullapool

❸ *12 mi northwest of Corrieshalloch Gorge, 238 mi north of Glasgow.*

By the shores of salty **Loch Broom**, Ullapool was founded in 1788 as a fishing station to exploit the local herring stocks. The town has a cosmopolitan air and comes to life when the Lewis ferry docks and departs. Ullapool is an ideal base for hiking and taking wildlife and nature cruises. In the **Ullapool Museum**, a film, photographs, and audiovisual displays tell the story of the area from the ice age to modern times. ☒ *7–8 W. Argyle St.* ☎🖧 *01854/612987* 🖾 *£2* ☉ *Apr.–Oct., Mon.–Sat. 9:30–5:30; Nov.–Mar., Thurs.–Sat. 11–3.*

Biking

For the strong and prepared biker, there is perhaps no better way to see the Northern Highlands landscapes than by pedaling over them. There are a number of lovely, unclassified lanes that wind through the hills and along coastal cliffs. Although some of these narrow, sometimes unpaved, roads are seldom used by motor vehicles, the occasional car may come along and force you onto the shoulder. You'll likely find yourself on main roads, contending with traffic, at least some of the time, so avoid taking a bike trip in high season (July and August). High-visibility clothing is advised.

Fishing

The possibilities for fishing are endless here, as a glance at the loch-covered map of Sutherland suggests. Brown trout and salmon are abundant. You can fish from the banks of Loch Assynt, 5 mi east of Lochinver, from April through October 15. Loch Garve, 4 mi west of Strathpeffer, is another favorite fishing spot; the season there is from March 15 through October 6. Boat fishing is also popular on Loch Maree, southeast of Gairloch and north of Poolewe, from May through October. Fishing permits are available at local post offices, shops, and hotels.

Where to Stay & Eat

£££–££££ Fodor'sChoice ★ **Ceilidh Place.** You can borrow one of the many books scattered throughout this comfortable house and while away the hours on deep, luxurious sofas in the sitting room, which overlooks the bay. Rooms have cream bedspreads and rich, warm colors. The inn's restaurant (££) specializes in seafood and vegetarian food; try the rocket pancakes with wild mushrooms. *Ceilidhs* (country dancing, music, and song; pronounced *kay*-lees) and concerts of chamber music, folk music, and opera are held frequently during summer. The bunkhouse across the road is an inexpensive alternative, with access to the hotel's facilities. ✉ *W. Argyle St., IV26 2TY* ☎ *01854/612103* 🖷 *01854/612886* 🌐 *www.theceilidhplace.com* *26 rooms, 10 with bath* *Restaurant; no a/c, no phones in some rooms, no room TVs* 💳 *AE, DC, MC, V* *BP.*

en route Drive north of Ullapool into **Coigach and Assynt,** and you'll enter a different kind of landscape. Here you won't find the broad flanks of great hills that hem you in, as you would in the Great Glen or Glen Coe. Instead, in Wester Ross the mountains rear out of the hummocky terrain and seem to shift their position, hiding behind one another in bewitching ways. Even their names seem different from those of the *bens* (mountain peaks or high hills) elsewhere: Cul Mor, Cul Beag, Stac Polly, Canisp, Suilven. Some owe their origins to Norse words rather than to undiluted Gaelic—a reminder that Vikings used to sail this northern seaboard. Much of this area lies within the Inverpolly National Nature Reserve.

Achiltibuie

4 *25 mi northwest of Ullapool.*

Achiltibuie is a crofting community set in magnificent mountain and coastal scenery. Offshore are the attractive **Summer Isles,** whose history dates back to Viking raids. Cruises from Ullapool visit the largest and only inhab-

The Northern Highlands & Skye
Eddrachillis Bay
Eye Peninsula
Stornoway
TO STORNOWAY
The Minch
Stoer
Lochinver
Laxay
Enard Bay
Isle of Lewis
Achiltibuie 4
Summer Isles
SCOTLAND
Shiant Islands
Gruinard Bay
Little Loch Broom
Loch Ewe
B8057
Isle of Ewe
Melvaig
Dundonnel
An Teallach
Inverewe Gardens
Fionn Loch
Gairloch 17
A832
Badachro
Loch Maree
Skye Museum of Island Life
Flodigarry
Staffin Bay
Quiraing
Kilmuir
Brogaig
Kilt Rock
Waternish Peninsula 23
Uig
Uig Bay
Trotternish Peninsula 22
Trotternish
Loch Snizort
Loch Torridon
Lower Diabaig
Kinlochewe
Beinn Eighe
Liathach
Inveralligin
A896
Glen Torridon
Island of Rona
Stein
Greshornish
Old Man of Storr
Loch Shieldaig
Upper Loch Torridon
Visitor Center
Loch Dunvegan
Kensaleyre
Sound of Raasay
Shieldaig 16
Edinbane
A855
A856
A890
24 Dunvegan Castle
Applecross
Inner Sound
21 Portree
Lochcarron 15
Strathcarron
25 Glendale
A863
B885
Isle of Skye
Isle of Raasay
Loch Kishorn
Loch Carron
Talisker
Drynoch
Carbost
Sconser
Scalpay
Kyle of Lochalsh
Eilean Donan Castle 18
Sligachan
Luib
Auchtertyre
Kyleakin
Skye Bridge
Dornie
Glen Brittle 26
Broadford 19
A850
Blaven
Kylerhea
Glenelg
Glenbrittle House
Cuillin Hills
Torrin
A851
Shiel Bridge
Strathaird
Sound of Sleat
Soay
Elgol
Isleornsay
A87
Sleat
Arnisdale
Cuillin Sound
Armadale 20
Armadale Castle Gardens and Museum of the Isles
Ardvasar
Mallaig

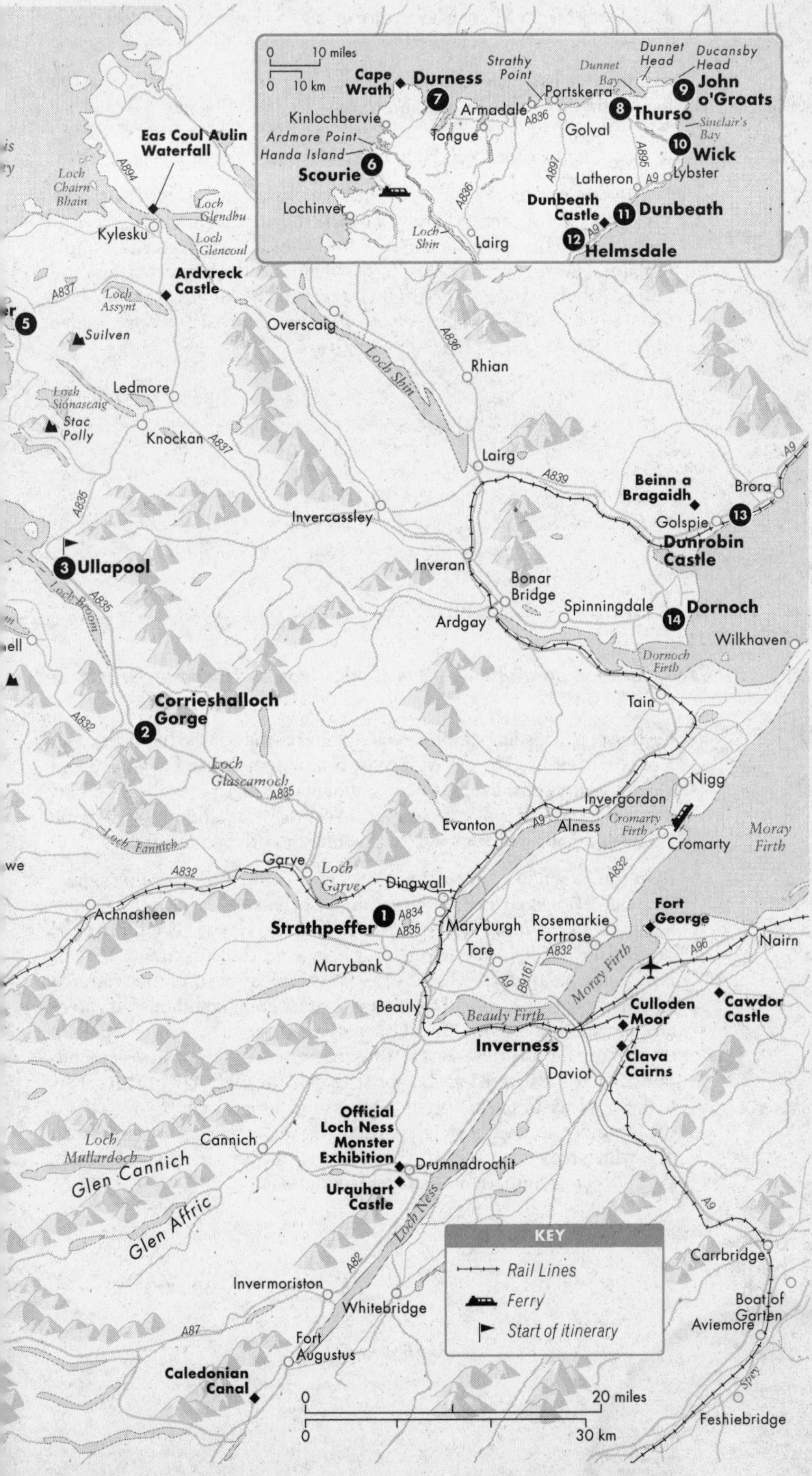

0 10 miles
0 10 km
Cape Wrath
Durness
Strathy Point
Dunnet Head
Dunnet Bay
Ducansby Head
John o'Groats
Portskerra
Armadale
Thurso
Kinlochbervie
Tongue
Golval
Sinclair's Bay
Ardmore Point
Handa Island
Wick
Scourie
Latheron
Lybster
Dunbeath Castle
Dunbeath
Lochinver
Loch Shin
Lairg
Helmsdale
Eas Coul Aulin Waterfall
Loch Chairn Bhain
Loch Glendhu
Kylesku
Loch Glencoul
Ardvreck Castle
Loch Assynt
Suilven
Overscaig
Rhian
Ledmore
Loch Sionascaig
Stac Polly
Knockan
Lairg
Beinn a Bragaidh
Brora
Invercassley
Golspie
Dunrobin Castle
Ullapool
Inveran
Bonar Bridge
Ardgay
Spinningdale
Dornoch
Wilkhaven
Dornoch Firth
Loch Broom
Tain
Corrieshalloch Gorge
Loch Glascarnoch
Nigg
Invergordon
Evanton
Alness
Cromarty Firth
Cromarty
Moray Firth
Loch Fannich
Garve
Loch Garve
Dingwall
Achnasheen
Strathpeffer
Maryburgh
Rosemarkie
Fortrose
Fort George
Nairn
Tore
Marybank
Beauly
Beauly Firth
Moray Firth
Culloden Moor
Cawdor Castle
Inverness
Clava Cairns
Daviot
Official Loch Ness Monster Exhibition
Loch Mullardoch
Cannich
Glen Cannich
Drumnadrochit
Urquhart Castle
Glen Affric
Loch Ness
KEY
Rail Lines
Ferry
Start of itinerary
Carrbridge
Invermoriston
Whitebridge
Boat of Garten
Aviemore
Fort Augustus
Caledonian Canal
Spey
0 20 miles
0 30 km
Feshiebridge

ited island, Tanera Mhor, where you can buy special Summer Isle stamps—Tanera Mhor is the only Scottish island to have a private postal service.

At the **Achiltibuie Smokehouse,** Summer Isles Foods smokes all sorts of fish—salmon, haddock, eel, and trout—which can be purchased in the small shop; mail order is also available. ✉ *Altandhu* ☎ *01854/622353* 🌐 *www.summerislesfoods.com.* ⏲ *Easter–mid-Oct., Mon.–Sat. 9:30–5.*

The **Hydroponicum** produces luscious fruit and vegetables year-round. The plants are suspended above nutrient-filled pools from which their roots draw required sustenance by means of a wick. You can sample tomatoes, beans, lettuce, pears, figs, and more in the Lilypond Cafe, and buy perishable and nonperishable items in the shop. ✉ *Achiltibuie* ☎ *01854/622202* 🌐 *www.thehydroponicum.com* 🎫 *£4.75 for guided tour* ⏲ *Apr.–Sept., daily 10–6; Oct., weekdays 11:30–3.*

en route

A single-lane unclassified road winds north from Achiltibuie through a wild though harmonious landscape of bracken and birch trees, heather and humped-hill horizons, with outstanding sea views on the second half of the route. Don't fall victim to the breathtaking landscape views, however; the road has several blind curves that demand extreme care. Just before Inverkirkaig is a parking lot next to the River Kirkaig, and a short stroll away is Achins Book and Craft Shop—perhaps Scotland's most remote bookstore.

Lochinver

❺ *18 mi north of Achiltibuie via unclassified road, 38 mi north of Ullapool via A835/A837.*

Lochinver is a bustling shoreside community of whitewashed cottages, with a busy harbor used by the west coast fishing fleet, and a few dining and lodging options. Behind the town the mountain Suilven rises abruptly. This unusual monolith is best seen from across the water, however. Take the cul-de-sac, **Baddidarroch Road,** for the finest photo opportunity.

Bold souls spending time at Lochinver may enjoy the interesting single-lane B869 **Drumbeg loop** to the north of Lochinver—it has several challenging hairpin turns along with breathtaking views. (The junction is on the north side of the River Inver bridge on the outskirts of the village, signposted as STOER and CLASHNESSIE.) Just beyond the scattered community of Stoer, a road leads west to **Stoer Point Lighthouse.** If you're an energetic walker, you can hike across the short turf and heather along the cliff top for fine views east toward the profiles of the northwest mountains. There's also a red-sandstone sea stack: the **Old Man of Stoer.** This makes a pleasant excursion on a long summer evening. If you stay on the Drumbeg section, there's a particularly tricky hairpin turn in a steep dip, which may force you to take your eyes off the fine view of Quinag, yet another of Sutherland's shapely mountains.

off the beaten path

ARDVRECK CASTLE – Beside Loch Assynt on the A837 stand the ruins of Ardvreck Castle, a clan MacLeod stronghold, built in the 15th century and now in the care of Historic Assynt. ✉ *A837, 11 mi east of Lochniver* 🎫 *Free.*

EAS COUL AULIN WATERFALL – This is the longest waterfall in the United Kingdom, with a drop of 685 feet. A rugged hike leads to the falls, which are at the head of Loch Glencoul; in summer, cruises offer a less taxing alternative. The falls are 3 mi southeast of the Kylesku Bridge off the A894. *Assynt Visitor Center* ☎ *0157/844330.*

Where to Stay & Eat

££–£££ **Inver Lodge Hotel.** On a hillside above Lochinver, this modern hotel has stunning views of the sea from all its bedrooms. Floral fabrics and traditional mahogany furniture decorate the smart guest rooms. The restaurant (£££££) makes the most of fresh, local seafood on its Scottish menu; try the lobster, straight from the sea the day you dine. Anglers feel especially at home here, with three salmon rivers and many trout lochs within easy reach. *Iolaire Rd., Sutherland, IV27 4LU 01571/844496 01571/844395 www.inverlodge.com 20 rooms Restaurant, room service, sauna, fishing, recreation room; no kids under 7 AE, DC, MC, V Closed Nov.–Easter BP.*

£ **Davar.** Rooms are light-filled, airy, and simple at this modern, comfortable B&B with views over Lochinver Bay. Green carpets set off pastel walls, and the bedrooms are spacious. *Lochinver, Sutherland, IV27 4LS 01571/844501 am-gordon@talk21.com 3 rooms No a/c, no room phones, no smoking No credit cards Closed Dec.–Mar. BP.*

£ **Polcraig Guest House.** This quiet detached house with views toward Lochinver Bay has high-quality B&B accommodations. Rooms are pretty and uncluttered with pine furniture, floral prints, and a green, blue, or pink color scheme. *Cruamer, Sutherland, IV27 4LD 01571/844429 cathelmac@aol.com 5 rooms In-room hot tub, no-smoking rooms; no a/c, no room phones No credit cards BP.*

£ **Tigh-Na-Sith.** The name means "house of peace" in Gaelic, and the owners do their best to make you feel at home. You can relax before panoramic harbor views in the lounge, or walk to the harbor and nearby shops and restaurants. Ground-floor bedrooms are modern with bright colors. *Sutherland, IV27 4LD 01571/844740 julie@tigh-na-sith.freeuk.com 2 rooms Lounge; no a/c; no room phones, no room TVs, no smoking No credit cards Closed Nov.–Mar. BP.*

Shopping

Highland Stoneware (Baddidarroch 01571/844376) manufactures tableware and decorative items with hand-painted designs of Highland wildflowers, animals, and landscapes. In the showroom you can browse and purchase wares.

At Inverkirkaig, just south of Lochinver, don't miss **Achins Book and Craft Shop** (Inverkirkaig 01571/844262), which also has a pleasant café. The shop is a great place for Scottish books on natural history, hill walking, fishing, and crafts. It also sells well-chosen craft items—knitwear, tweeds, and pottery—along with artwork and traditional music. The shop is open daily from 9:30 to 6 between Easter and October (phone ahead in winter to check opening times), and its pleasant coffee shop is open from Easter through October, daily 10 to 5.

Scourie

6 *28 mi north of Lochinver.*

Scourie is a small settlement catering to visitors—fisherfolk especially—with a choice of local accommodations. It also makes a good base for a trip to the bird sanctuary on the island of Handa.

off the beaten path

HANDA ISLAND – Just off the coast of Scourie is a bird sanctuary that shelters huge seabird colonies, especially impressive at nesting time in spring and early summer. It's administered by the Scottish Wildlife Trust. In spring and summer only, Handa can be reached by a small open boat from Tarbet; contact the tourist information center in Lochinver or Durness for details.

Where to Stay & Eat

£££ ✕ **Eddrachilles Hotel.** This long-established, traditional inn has one of the best views of any hotel in Scotland—across the islands of Eddrachillis Bay (which can be explored by boat from the hotel). The hotel sits on 320 acres of private moorland and is just south of the Handa Island bird sanctuary. The bedrooms are modern and comfortable, with chandeliers and photographs on the walls. The chef uses local produce to prepare meals in straightforward Scottish style, with the emphasis on fish and game; try the poached salmon or the saddle of venison. ✉ *Badcall Bay, IV27 4TH* ☎ *01971/502080* 📠 *01971/502477* 🌐 *www.eddrachilles.com* *11 rooms* *Restaurant, bar; no a/c* 💳 *MC, V* *Closed Nov.–Feb.* *BP.*

en route

From Scourie northward, the A894/A838 traverses the most northerly landscapes, with the empty quarter below Cape Wrath on its west side. You can sample this wild landscape by hiking 4 mi to Sandwood Bay, at the end of the B801, beyond the fishing port of Kinlochbervie. Sandwood has rock stacks, a white beach, and its own ghost, said to frequent ruined Sandwood Cottage; so this is a truly haunting area in all senses of the word.

Durness

7 *27 mi north of Scourie, 55 mi north of Lochinver.*

The sudden patches of green at Durness, on the north coast, are caused by the richer limestone outcrops among the acid moorlands. The limestone's most spectacular feature is **Smoo Cave,** a cave system hollowed out of the limestone by water action. Access is via a steep cliff path. Boat tours run daily from April through September; reservations are advised because there's a limit of six per 20-minute tour. The seasonal **tourist information center** (✉ Durine, Durness IV27 4PN ☎ 01971/511259) has complete information.

Craftspeople and artists sell pottery, leatherwork, weaving, paintings, and more from their studios at **Balnakeil Craft Village** (☎ 01971/511777). The village, on an unnamed road but clearly signed from Durness, is open April through October. Hours at the studios vary, but most places stay open daily from 10 to 5, and even later on summer evenings.

If you've made it this far north, you'll probably want to go all the way to **Cape Wrath,** at the northwest tip of Scotland. You can't drive your own vehicle. May through September, a small boat (☎ 01971/511376) ferries people across the Kyle of Durness, a sea inlet, from Keoldale; a minibus (☎ 01971/511287) will then take you to the lighthouse. The highest mainland cliffs in Scotland, including **Clo Mor,** at 920 feet, lie between the Kyle and Cape Wrath.

en route

The north-coast road along the top of Scotland is both attractive and severe. It runs, for example, around the head of Loch Eriboll, which was a World War II convoy assembly point and was usually referred to as "Loch 'orrible" by the crews. Yet it has its own desolate charm. There are little beaches and settlements to explore along this road, and the landscape gradually softens as you journey east.

Thurso

8 *74 mi east of Durness.*

The town of Thurso, which is quite substantial for a community so far north, is hard to categorize. Since the 1950s its development has been related to the atomic reactor (Britain's first) along the coast at Doun-reay—presumably situated there to be as far as possible from the seat of government, in London. In town are the Thurso Heritage Museum and Old St. Peter's Kirk, which dates back to the 12th century. There are also fine beaches, particularly to the east, at Dunnet Bay. And with several restaurants and hotels, Thurso is one of the few towns that make a good starting point for exploring the far north. Many people make the trip to the northernmost point of mainland Britain, which is at **Dunnet Head,** with its fine views to Orkney.

Where to Stay & Eat

£££ ✕⛉ **Forss Country House Hotel.** Despite its stark, gray exterior, this 1810 house surrounded by woodland makes a good base for fishing (guide service and instruction provided) or touring. Plain, soft-tone walls and spare, dark-wood antique and reproduction furniture, along with log fires and sturdy Scottish cuisine make for a charming place to stay. Prix-fixe meals might include haggis-stuffed sirloin with Glenmorangie whisky sauce. ✉ *Forss, about 4 mi west of Thurso, KW14 7XY* ☎ *01847/861201* 🖷 *01847/861301* ⊕ *www.forsscountryhouse. co.uk* ⇨ *14 rooms* ⛾ *Restaurant, golf privileges, fishing; no a/c* ☐ *AE, MC, V.*

£–££ ⛉ **Murray House.** This Victorian town house in the center of Thurso is convenient to the Orkney ferry. Floral wallpaper and bedding decorate the rooms. You may sit in the garden or watch a film in the lounge. ✉ *1 Campbell St., Thurso KW14 7HD* ☎ *01847/895759* ⊕ *www. murrayhousebb.com* ⇨ *4 rooms* ⛾ *Lounge; no a/c, no smoking* ☐ *No credit cards* ⦿❙ *BP.*

Biking

Bikes can be rented from **Wheels Cycle Shop** (✉ 35 High St. ☎🖷 01847/896124); the staff here is also happy to advise on routes.

John o'Groats

❾ *21 mi east of Thurso via A836.*

The windswept little outpost of John o'Groats is usually taken to be the most northern community in the Scottish mainland, though that is not strictly accurate, as an exploration of the little network of roads between Dunnet Head and John o'Groats will confirm. A crafts center has a few high-quality shops selling knitwear, candles, and gifts. Go east to **Duncansby Head** for spectacular views of cliffs and sea stacks by the light-house—and puffins, too.

The Arts

The **Lyth Arts Centre** (✉ Lyth, 4 mi off A9 ☎ 01955/641270), between Wick and John o'Groats, is in an old country school. From April through November each year, it hosts performances by professional touring music and theater companies, as well as exhibitions of contemporary fine art. Check local papers or tourist information centers for opening times, schedules, and fees.

Cruising

John o'Groats Ferries (☎ 01955/611353 ⊕ www.jogferry.co.uk) operates wildlife cruises from John o'Groats Harbor. The 1½-hour trip takes you past spectacular cliff scenery and bird life into the Pentland Firth, to Duncansby Stacks, and to the island of Stroma. Cruises cost £14 and are available daily from mid-June through August, at 2:30.

Wick

10 *17 mi south of John o'Groats, 22 mi southeast of Thurso via A882.*

Wick is a substantial town that was built on its fishing industry. The gaunt, bleak ruins of **Castle Sinclair** and **Castle Girnigoe** teeter on a cliff top 3 mi north of the town.

To learn how this town grew, visit the **Wick Heritage Centre**—it's run by local people in part for the local community, and they're real enthusiasts. The center is the largest museum in the Northern Highlands and has on display a restored fisherman's house, a fish kiln, and a blacksmith's shop, as well as collections of fossils and 19th-century toys and clothing. An art gallery and terraced gardens overlooking the town round out the offerings. ✉ *19 Bank Row* ☎ *01955/605393 or 01955/603385* 🎫 *£ 2* ⏲ *May–Sept., Mon.–Sat. 10–5; last admission at 3:45.*

The **Northlands Viking Centre,** which highlights the role of Scandinavian settlers in this area, has models of the Viking settlement at Freswick and of a Viking long ship, as well as coins and other artifacts. ✉ *The Old School, Auckengill, near Keiss, 10 mi north of Wick via A9* ☎ *01955/607771* 🎫 *£1.40* ⏲ *June–Sept., daily 10–4.*

Where to Stay

£ **Greenvoe.** This B&B is a well-appointed modern house, fresh and beautifully maintained, with unfussy, functional, and comfortable bedrooms. A delicious, generous breakfast is included in the room rate, and late-night snacks are a hospitable touch. ✉ *George St., Caithness KW1 4DE* ☎ *01955/603942* *3 rooms share bath* *No a/c, no room phones, no smoking* *No credit cards* ⏲ *Closed last 2 wks in Dec.* *BP.*

Shopping

Perhaps the best-known purveyor of crafts in the area is **Caithness Glass** (✉ Airport Industrial Estate, Wick Airport ☎ 01955/602286). Producing a distinctive style of glassware and paperweights—most of the better gift shops stock Caithness Glass—the factory has tours of the glass-blowing workshops and a shop with the full product range. It's open year-round daily from 9 or 11 until 5.

en route

Signposted west off the A9 about 10 mi south of Wick are the extraordinary **Grey Cairns of Camster,** two Neolithic chambered cairns, dating from 4000 to 3000 BC, that are among the best preserved in Britain. **Camster Round Cairn** is 20 yards in diameter and 13 yards high, and **Camster Long Cairn** reaches nearly 77 yards in length. Nineteenth-century excavations revealed skeletons, pottery, and flint tools in the round cairn's internal chamber. If you don't mind dirty knees, you can crawl into the chambers in both cairns.

Dunbeath

11 *21 mi south of Wick.*

The moors of Caithness roll down to the sea at Dunbeath, where you find the **Dunbeath Heritage Centre** in a former school. Inside are photographs and domestic and crofting artifacts that relay the area's history from the Bronze Age to the oil age. It's particularly helpful to those researching family histories. ✉ *Off A9* ☎ *01593/731233* 🌐 *www.dunbeath-heritage.org.uk* 🎫 *£2* ⏲ *Apr.–Oct., daily 10–5; phone for winter hrs.*

The **Laidhay Croft Museum,** just north of Dunbeath, feels more like a private home than a museum. It was built in the 18th century, comprises a longhouse and barn—animals and people lived under the same long roof—and is furnished as it would have been during its working life. ✉ *Off A9* ☎ *01593/731244* 🎫 *£1* 🕐 *Easter–Oct., daily 10–6.*

Helmsdale

12 *15 mi south of Dunbeath.*

The **Timespan Heritage Centre,** a thought-provoking mix of displays, artifacts, and audiovisual materials, portrays the history of the area, from the Stone Age to the 1869 gold rush in the Strath of Kildonan. The complex also includes a café and an art gallery, with changing exhibitions that cover the whole breadth of the arts. ✉ *Helmsdale* ☎ *01431/821327* 🌐 *www.timespan.org.uk* 🎫 *£3.50* 🕐 *Apr.–Oct., Mon.–Sat. 9:30–5, Sun. 2–5; last admission 1 hr before closing.*

Golspie

18 mi south of Helmsdale.

Golspie is a little coastal town with a number of shops and accommodations, though it has the air of a place that visitors merely pass through.
13 The Scottish home of the dukes of Sutherland is **Dunrobin Castle,** an ancient seat developed by the first duke into a 19th-century flamboyant white-turreted behemoth. Trains so fascinated the duke that he built his own railroad in the park and staffed it with his servants. This duke, who also owned one of the largest palaces in London, was in good part responsible for the Sutherland Clearances of 1810–20, which devastated this region in the 19th century. Thousands of native Gaels were shamefully evicted from settlements in the interior and forced to emigrate or settle at sites on the coast. Traveling south on the A9, you'll see the controversial statue of the duke, in which he looks like some Eastern Bloc despot, on Beinn a Bragaidh (Ben Braggie), the hilltop to the west. Many people strongly feel that it should be removed, as the "improvement" policies of the duke were ultimately responsible for the brutality associated with the Clearances. ✉ *A9* ☎ *01408/633177* 🎫 *£6.25* 🕐 *Apr.–May and early Oct., daily 10:30–4:30; June–Sept., daily 10:30–5:30; last entry 30 mins before closing.*

Shopping

The **Orcadian Stone Company** (✉ Main St. ☎ 01408/633483) makes stone products, including giftware crafted from local Caithness slate, jewelry, incised plaques, and prepared mineral specimens. There's also a geological exhibit. The shop is open from Easter to October, Monday to Saturday, 9 to 5:30.

Dornoch

14 *10 mi south of Golspie, 40 mi north of Inverness.*

A town of sandstone, tiny rose-filled gardens, and a 13th-century cathedral with stunning traditional and modern stained-glass windows, Dornoch is also noted for its golf. You may hear it referred to as the St. Andrews of the North, but because of the town's location so far north, the courses here are delightfully uncrowded. Royal Dornoch is the jewel in its crown, praised by the world's top golfers.

Where to Stay & Eat

★ **£££** ✕🏨 **Dornoch Castle Hotel.** A genuine late-15th-century castle, once the palace of the bishops of Caithness, this hotel blends the very old and the more modern. Some rooms are a wing built in 1974. The lounge is a relaxing Adamesque room of soft green and cream, and bedrooms wear pastel stripes and floral fabrics. This is not a luxury hotel, but it's clean and comfortable, with friendly staff and satisfying, well-cooked Scottish food in the restaurant (££££): try the roast haunch of venison with juniper-and-cranberry sauce. ✉ *Dornoch, Sutherland, IV25 3SD* ☎ *01862/810216* 📠 *01862/810981* 🌐 *www.dornochcastlehotel.com* *18 rooms* *Restaurant, room service; no a/c* 💳 *AE, MC, V* 🍽 *BP.*

££ **Highfield House.** On its own grounds on the edge of town, the Highfield delivers B&B accommodations in a modern family home. Rooms are light and airy, with pastel colors and natural-wood furnishings. ✉ *Evelix Rd., IV25 3HR* ☎ *01862/810909* 📠 *01862/811605* 🌐 *www.highfieldhouse.co.uk* *3 rooms* *Dining room; no a/c, no room phones, no kids under 12, no smoking* 💳 *No credit cards* 🍽 *BP.*

Golf

Were it not for its remote northern location, **Royal Dornoch** would undoubtedly be a candidate for the British Open Championship. It's a superb, breezy, and challenging links course. ✉ *Golf Rd., Dornoch* ☎ *01862/810219* *18 holes, 6,200 yards, par 70.*

en route

If you're driving south toward Inverness on the A9, consider detouring first to Tain (look for signs to the town) for a visit to its excellent heritage center **Tain through Time.** The complex consists of a museum, the Collegiate Church, and the Pilgrimage Centre, all inviting you to explore Tain's history as an important pilgrimage site, thanks to the shrine of St. Duthus, in the late 15th-century. King James IV (1473–1513) was a frequent pilgrim here. ✉ *Tower St.* ☎ *01862/894089* 🌐 *www.tainmuseum.demon.co.uk* *£3.50* *3rd Mon. in Mar.–Mar. 31, daily 12–4; Apr.–Oct., daily 10–6; Nov.–3rd Mon. in Mar., Sat. noon–4.*

TORRIDON

Torridon has a grand, rugged, and wild air that feels especially remote, yet it doesn't take much more than an hour from Inverness before you reach Kinlochewe, near the east end of Glen Torridon. The western side is equally spectacular. Walking trails and mountain panoramas abound.

The A890, which runs from the A832 into the heart of Torridon, is a single-lane road in some stretches, with plenty of open vistas across the deserted heart of northern Scotland.

Lochcarron

15 *66 mi west of Inverness via A9/A835/A832/A890.*

Lochcarron, a village strung along the shore, functions as a local shopping hub. **The Smithy Heritage Centre,** in a restored blacksmith's forge, provides visitor information about the area, and also arranges woodland walks. ✉ *Ribhuachan, by Lochcarron* ☎ *01520/722246* *Apr.–Oct., Mon.–Sat. 10–5:30.*

Shopping

At **Lochcarron Weavers** (✉ Mid Strome ☎ 01520/722212) you can observe a weaver at work, producing pure-wool worsted tartans that can be bought on-site or at the firm's other outlets in the area.

en route

Driving north by the A896, you pass **Rassal Ash Wood,** on your right. The lushness of the fenced-in area within this small nature reserve is a reminder of what Scotland might have been like had sheep and deer not been kept here in such high numbers. The combined nibbling of these animals ensures that Scotland's natural tree cover does not regenerate without human intervention.

Shieldaig

16 *16 mi northwest of Lochcarron.*

Just west of the southern coast of Upper Loch Torridon is Shieldaig, a village that sits in an attractive crescent overlooking a loch of its own, **Loch Shieldaig.** For an atmospheric evening foray, walk north toward Loch Torridon, at the northern end of the village by the church. The path is fairly well made, though hiking shoes are recommended, passing exquisite views and tiny rocky beaches.

★ The scenic spectacle of **Glen Torridon** lies east of Shieldaig. Some say that Glen Torridon has the finest mountain scenery in Scotland. It consists mainly of the long gray quartzite flanks of **Beinn Eighe** (rhymes with *say*) and **Liathach** (*leea*-gach), with its distinct ridge profile that looks like the keel of an upturned boat. At the end of the glen the National Trust for Scotland operates a **visitor center** that explains the ecology and geology of the area. ☎ *01445/791221* *Audiovisual display and deer museum £2* ⏲ *Countryside center May–Sept., daily 10–6; estate, deer park, and deer museum year-round, daily 9–5.*

off the beaten path

APPLECROSS – The tame way to reach this small community facing Skye is by a coastal road from near Shieldaig; the exciting route turns west off the A896 a few miles farther south. A series of hairpin turns corkscrews up the steep wall at the head of a corrie (a glacier-cut mountain valley), over the **Bealach na Ba** (Pass of the Cattle). There are spectacular views of Skye from the bare plateau on top, and you can brag afterward that you've been on what is probably Scotland's highest drivable road.

Where to Stay & Eat

£££–££££ ✕ **Loch Torridon Hotel.** Forest and mountains make up the impressive backdrop for this former shooting lodge, now a hotel on the shore of Loch Torridon. Log fires, handsome plasterwork ceilings, mounted stag heads, and traditional furnishings set the mood downstairs, and bedrooms are decorated in restrained pastel shades with antique mahogany furniture. The four-course dinner may include seafood, beef, lamb, and game, and the cellar has many fine wines. ✉ *Torridon, by Achnasheen, Wester Ross, IV22 2EY* ☎ *01445/791242* *01445/791296* *www.lochtorridonhotel.com* *20 rooms* *Restaurant, fishing, library; no a/c* *AE, DC, MC, V* *BP.*

Gairloch

17 *38 mi north of Shieldaig.*

This region's main center, with some shops and accommodations, Gairloch has one further advantage: lying just a short way from the mountains of the interior, this small oasis often escapes the rain clouds that sometimes cling to the high summits. You can enjoy a game of golf here and perhaps stay dry, even when the nearby Torridon hills are deluged. In the village is the **Gairloch Heritage Museum,** with exhibitions covering prehistoric times to the present. ✉ *Junction of A832 and B8031* ☎ *01445/712287* *www.gairlochheritagemuseum.org.uk* *£2.50* ⏲ *Apr.–Sept., Mon.–Sat. 10–5; Oct., weekdays 10–1:30; Nov.–Mar. by appointment.*

Fodor'sChoice ★ Southeast of Gairloch stretches one of Scotland's most scenic lochs, **Loch Maree.** Its harmonious environs, with tall Scots pines and the mountain Slioch looming as a backdrop, witnessed the destruction of much of the tree cover in the 18th century. Iron ore was shipped in and smelted using local oak to feed the furnaces. Oak now grows here only on the northern limits of the range. Scottish Natural Heritage has an **information center** and nature trails by the loch and in the Beinn Eighe Nature Reserve. Red deer sightings are virtually guaranteed; locals say the best place to spot another local denizen, the pine marten, is around the trash containers in the parking turnoffs.

★ The highlight of this area is **Inverewe Gardens,** 6 mi northeast of Gairloch. The main attraction lies in the contrast between the bleak coastal headlands and thin-soiled moors and the lush plantings of the garden behind its dense shelterbelts. These are proof of the efficacy of the warm North Atlantic Drift, part of the Gulf Stream, which takes the edge off winter frosts. Inverewe is sometimes described as subtropical, but this is an inaccuracy that irritates the head gardener; do not expect coconuts and palm trees here. ☒ *A832, Poolewe* ☎ *01445/781200* 🌐 *www.nts.org.uk* 🎫 *£7* 🕒 *Gardens Apr.–Oct., daily 9–9; Nov.–Mar., daily 9:30–5. Visitor center, shop, and restaurant Apr.–Oct., daily 10–5. Guided walks Apr.–Sept., weekdays at 1:30.*

Where to Stay & Eat

££££ **Dundonnell Hotel.** This excellent family-run hotel, set on the roadside by Little Loch Broom, east of Gairloch, has cultivated a solid reputation for its hospitality and cuisine. Light floral curtains and bedspreads and contemporary furnishings fill the fresh, modern bedrooms. Many of the guest rooms and public rooms have stunning views of pristine hills and lochs. The restaurant serves homemade soups and fresh seafood, as well as desserts well worth leaving room for. ☒ *Dundonnell, near Garve, Ross-shire, IV23 2QR* ☎ *01854/633204* 📠 *01854/633366* 🌐 *www.dundonnellhotel.com* *30 rooms* *Restaurant, bar, lounge; no a/c* 💳 *AE, MC, V* *BP.*

££ Fodor'sChoice ★ **The Mountain Restaurant and Lodge.** A restaurant, lodge, and book shop all rolled into one, this property is a center of activity in Gairloch. The restaurant has a conservatory with a widespread view over the sea. Huge, fresh-baked scones, both savory and sweet, are excellent for breakfast and lunch. Books of all subjects are everywhere, spilling over from the shop into the restaurant. Mountaineering memorabilia decorate the walls. ☒ *Strath Sq., IV21 2BX* ☎ *01445/712316* *4 rooms* *Restaurant, no-smoking rooms; no a/c* 💳 *MC, V* 🕒 *Closed Jan.–Feb.* *BP.*

Golf

Gairloch Golf Club is one of the few on this stretch of coast. ☎ *01445/712407* *9 holes, 1,942 yards, SSS 62.*

en route

The road between Gairloch and the Corrieshalloch Gorge initially passes coastal scenery with views of Gruinard Bay and its white beaches, then woodlands around Dundonnell and Loch Broom. Soon the route traverses wild country: the toothed ramparts of the mountain An Teallach (pronounced *tyel*-lack) are visible on the horizon. The moorland route you travel is known chillingly as Destitution Road. It was built in the 1840s to give the local folk (long vanished from the area) some way of earning a living after the failure of the potato crop; it's said the workers were paid only in food. At Corrieshalloch the A832 joins the A835 for Inverness.

SKYE, THE MISTY ISLAND

Skye ranks near the top of most visitors' priority lists: the romance of Prince Charles Edward Stuart (1720–88), known as Bonnie Prince Charlie, combined with the misty Cuillin Hills and their proximity to the mainland all contribute to its popularity. Today Skye remains fey, mysterious, and mountainous, an island of sunsets that linger brilliantly until late at night and of beautiful, soft mists. Much photographed are the really old crofts, one or two of which are still inhabited, with their thick stone walls and thatch roofs. Much written about is the story known as the Adventure—the sad history of the "prince in the heather" and pretender to the British throne, Bonnie Prince Charlie. At the disastrous Battle of Culloden, George II's army outnumbered and destroyed the Jacobite forces of Prince Charles Edward Stuart. After the battle Bonnie Prince Charlie wandered over the Highlands, a passive object, handed like a bale of contraband from one smuggler to another, numbed with constant applications of whisky—the beginnings of the alcoholism that finally killed him. He then escaped to the isles of Harris and South Uist, where he met Flora Macdonald (1722–90), the woman who took him, disguised as her maid, "over the sea to Skye" and then back to the mainland. His Scottish exploits were the stuff of legend. *Will ye no' come back again . . . Speed, bonnie boat . . . Charlie is my darling . . .* the tunes and lyrics of Lady Nairn, jaunty or mournful, composed long after the events, are as good an epitaph as any adventurer could wish for.

To reach Skye these days, you can cross over the bridge spanning the narrow channel of Kyle Akin, between Kyle of Lochalsh and Kyleakin, or take the (more romantic) ferry options between Mallaig and Armadale or between Glenelg and Kylerea. You can tour comfortably around the island in two or three days. Orientation is easy: follow the only roads around the loops on the northern part of the island and enjoy the road running the length of the Sleat Peninsula in southern Skye, taking the loop roads that exit to the north and south as you please. There are some stretches of single-lane road, but none poses a problem.

Kyle of Lochalsh

55 mi west of Inverness, 120 mi northwest of Glasgow.

This little town is the mainland gateway to Skye. Time used to mean nothing in this part of Scotland—so many other things were of greater importance. But the area has seen great changes as the Skye Bridge has transformed not only travel to Skye but the very seascape itself. The most noticeable attraction, though (in fact, almost a cliché), is not in Kyle at all, but 8 mi farther east at Dornie—Eilean Donan Castle.

Guarding the confluence of lochs Long, Alsh, and Duich stands that most
18 picturesque of all Scottish castles, **Eilean Donan Castle,** perched on a lit-
Fodor's Choice ★ tle islet connected to the mainland by a stone-arched bridge. Dating from the 14th century, this romantic icon has all the massive stone walls, timber ceilings, and winding stairs that you could ask for. Empty and neglected for years after being bombarded by frigates of the Royal Navy during an abortive Spanish-Jacobite landing in 1719, it was almost entirely rebuilt from a ruin in the early 20th century. Now the hero of travel brochures, Eilean Donan has appeared in many Hollywood movies and TV shows. ✉ *Off A97, Dornie* ☎ *01599/555202* 🌐 *www.eileandonancastle.com* 💰 *£3.75* ⏲ *Apr.–Oct., daily 10–5:30.*

Broadford

19 *8 mi west of Kyle of Lochalsh via Skye Bridge.*

One of the larger of Skye's settlements, Broadford lies along the shore of Broadford Bay, which has on occasion welcomed whales to its sheltered waters. You can observe and handle snakes, frogs, lizards, and tortoises at the **Serpentarium,** in the town center. *The Old Mill, Harrapool 01471/822209 £2.50 Easter–Oct., Mon.–Sat. 10–5.*

An unlikely but worthwhile stop is **Sutherlands** (A850 01471/822225), where the Esso gas station offers a lot more than gasoline: 24-hour car rental (with pickup service at Armadale Pier or Kyle of Lochalsh), a bureau de change, Internet access, a launderette, a well-stocked gift and book shop, and fresh foods and ready-made snacks.

off the beaten path

THE ROAD TO ELGOL – The B8083 leads from Broadford to one of the finest views in Scotland. This road passes through **Strath Suardal** and little **Loch Cill Chriosd** (Kilchrist) by a ruined church. If there are cattle wading in the loch and the light is soft—typical of Skye—then this place takes on the air of a romantic oil painting. Skye marble, with its attractive green veining, was produced from the marble quarry at **Torrin.**

You can appreciate breathtaking views of the mountain called **Blaven** as the A881 continues to Elgol, a gathering of crofts along this road that descends to a pier. Admire the heart-stopping profile of the Cuillin peaks from the shore, or at a point about halfway down the hill, you can find the path that goes toward them across the rough grasslands. For even better views, take a boat trip on the **Bella Jane** (Elgol Jetty 0800/731–3089 www.bellajane.co.uk) from Elgol jetty toward Loch Coruisk; you'll be able to land and walk up to the loch itself, as well as see seals during your boat trip. The boat excursion is available from April through October, daily, and advance booking is essential (ticket price is £18.50).

Where to Stay

★ ££ **Ptarmigan.** This top-notch B&B is run by a couple that knows Skye inside out and can help with planning your route (whether driving or hiking). The three bedrooms, all with sea views, have modern dark-wood furnishings, neutral wall coverings, and sophisticated green-and-purple tartan drapes. Large-scale maps of the island line the walls of the cozy sitting room, which has a window looking right onto the water's edge, ideal for spotting birds, otters, and the occasional whale. There's also a separate cottage with cooking facilities. *Broadford, Isle of Skye, IV49 9AQ 01471/822744 01471/822745 www.ptarmigan-cottage.com 3 rooms, 1 cottage No a/c, no room phones, no smoking AE, MC, V BP.*

Biking

Fairwinds Bicycle Hire (Fairwinds, Elgol Rd. 01471/822270) rents bicycles year-round.

Shopping

Craft Encounters (A850 01471/822754) stocks Skye crafts, including pottery and jewelry.

Armadale

20 *17 mi south of Broadford, 43 mi south of Portree, 5 mi (ferry crossing) west of Mallaig.*

Rolling interior moorlands, scattered with rivers and lochans, give way to enchanting hidden coves and scattered waterside communities here in **Sleat,** the southernmost part of Skye. Sleat well rewards a day or two spent exploring its side roads and its many craft outlets. For most visitors, Armadale is the first town to visit.

The popular **Armadale Castle Gardens and the Museum of the Isles,** including the Clan Donald Centre, tell the story of the Macdonalds and their proud title—the Lords of the Isles—with the help of an excellent audiovisual presentation. In the 15th century the clan was powerful enough to threaten the authority of the Stuart monarchs of Scotland. There are extensive gardens and nature trails, plus a gift shop, restaurant, library, and archive facility. Also on the grounds are high-quality accommodations in seven cottages with kitchen facilities. ✉ *½ mi north of Armadale Pier* ☎ *01471/844305 or 01471/844275* 🌐 *www.cland.demon.co.uk* *£4* ⏲ *Clan Donald Centre Apr.–Oct., daily 9:30–5:30, last entry at 5; gardens daily 24 hrs.*

Where to Stay & Eat

££££££ ✕ **Kinloch Lodge.** This country-house hotel, run by Lord and Lady Macdonald with flair and professionalism, provides dinner, bed, and breakfast for one price. Antiques, chintz fabrics, bookcases, and family photographs fill the warm, restful lounges, and the elegant bedrooms are individually decorated with more antiques and quilted bedspreads. The dinner menu might include Skye langoustines, Highland lamb with a peppercorn and pinhead-oatmeal crust, and "dark-chocolate nemesis" for dessert. ✉ *Off A851, Sleat, Isle of Skye, IV43 8QY* ☎ *01471/833214* *01471/833277* 🌐 *www.kinloch-lodge.co.uk* *14 rooms* *Restaurant, fishing, 2 lounges, helipad; no a/c* *AE, MC, V* *MAP.*

★ ££££–£££££ ✕ **Hotel Eilean Iarmain.** The Isle Ornsay Hotel (as it is also more pronounceably known) sits beside the shore and is an enchanting collection of wood paneling, chintz, antiques, and soft country-house-style color schemes. Each room is an atmospheric individual: try the Tower Room, with its nooks and crannies, or the room with the canopy bed from Armadale Castle. The menu in the dining room changes daily but might include such dishes as seared venison with juniper and rowan, or steamed mussels with cream and whisky. ✉ *Isleornsay, Sleat, Isle of Skye, IV43 8QR* ☎ *01471/833332* *01471/833275* 🌐 *www.eileaniarmain.co.uk* *12 rooms, 4 suites* *Restaurant, fishing, lounge, helipad; no a/c, no room TVs* *AE, MC, V* *BP.*

Biking

The Skye Ferry Filling Station (✉ Ardvasar ☎ 01471/844249) rents bicycles in summer and can provide information on scenic routes.

Shopping

Local designer Chryssy Gibbs creates colorful wool sweaters and sells them at **Harlequin Knitwear** (✉ Off A851, Duisdale, Sleat ☎ 01471/833321). She works from her home, which is up a rather bumpy, steep track. It's worth the trek because once you arrive (and after being greeted by her cats), you will find distinctive sweaters—with descriptive names such as Stained Glass, Mosaic, and Tudor—of Shetland wool, mohair, or chenille in colors that reflect the tones of the Skye landscape.

CLANS & TARTANS

WHATEVER THE ORIGINS *of the clans—some with Norman roots, intermarried into Celtic society; some of Norse origin, the product of Viking raids on Scotland; others traceable to the monastic system; yet others possibly descended from Pictish tribes—by the 13th century the clan system was at the heart of Gaelic tribal culture. By the 15th century the clan chiefs of the Scottish Highlands were a threat even to the authority of the Stewart monarchs.*

The word clann means "family" or "children" in Gaelic, and it was the custom for clan chiefs to board out their sons among nearby families, a practice that helped to bond the clan unit and create strong allegiances: the chief became "father" of the tribe and was owed loyalty by lesser chiefs and ordinary clansmen.

The clan chiefs' need for strong men-at-arms, fast-running messengers, and bards for entertainment and the preservation of clan genealogy was the probable origin of the Highland Games, still celebrated in many Highland communities each year, and which are an otherwise rather inexplicable mix of sports, music, and dance.

Gradually, by the 18th century, increasing knowledge of Lowland agricultural improvements, and better roads into the Highlands that improved communication of ideas and "southern" ways, began to weaken the clan system: fine clothes, French wines, and even a Lowland education became more common in chiefly households. Even before Culloden, where Bonnie Prince Charles, supported by some of the clans, was defeated by George II's army, the clan system had lost its tight grip on the Highlands. After Culloden, as more modern economic influences took hold, those on the "wrong" side lost all; many chiefs lost their lands, tartan was banned, and clan culture withered.

Tartan's own origins as a part of the clan system are disputed; the Gaelic word for striped cloth is breacan*—piebald or spotted—so even the word itself is not Highland. However, it is indisputable that in the days before mass manufacture, when cloth was locally spun, woven, and dyed using plant derivatives, each neighborhood would have different dyestuffs—bilberry, iris, bramble, water lily—and therefore different colors available. In this way, particular combinations of colors and favorite patterns of the local weavers could become associated with a particular area and therefore clan, but were not in any sense a clan's "own by exclusive right."*

Between 1746 and 1782 the wearing of tartan was generally prohibited. By the time the ban was lifted, many recipes for dyes and weaving patterns had been forgotten. In addition, some neighborhoods stopped making and coloring their own cloth because of the mechanization and use of chemical dyes in cloth production.

It took the influence of Sir Walter Scott, with his romantic, and fashionable, view of Highland history, to create the "modern myth" of clans and tartan. Sir Walter engineered George IV's visit to Scotland in 1822, which turned into a tartan extravaganza. The idea of one tartan or group of tartans "belonging" to one particular clan was created at this time—literally created, with new patterns and color ways dreamed up and "assigned" to particular clans. Queen Victoria and Prince Albert, with their passion for all things Scottish and for tartan in particular at Balmoral, reinforced the tartan culture later in the century, and it persists on and off to this day.

It is considered "proper" in some circles to wear the "right" tartan, that is, that of your clan. You may be able to find a clan connection with the help of expertise such as that available at **Scotland's Clan Tartan Centre** (✉ 70– 74 Bangor Rd., Leith, Edinburgh ☎ 0131/553–5161).

Ragamuffin (✉ Armadale Pier ☎ 01471/844217) specializes in designer knitwear and clothing. The friendly staff can make you a cup of coffee while you browse, then mail your purchases back home for you.

Portree

21 *43 mi north of Armadale.*

Portree, the population center of the island, is not overburdened by historical features, but it's a pleasant center clustered around a small and sheltered bay, and it makes a good touring base. On the outskirts of town is **Tigh na Coille: The Aros Experience** (*Tigh na Coille* is Gaelic for "house of the forest," and *Aros* means "home" or "homestead"), where the story of Skye, told via tableaux and a taped guide, continues where the Armadale Castle audiovisual tour left off; together the two provide an excellent account of Skye's often turbulent history over the centuries. You'll find a gift shop, restaurant, and theater, which hosts musical events. Forest walks can be enjoyed in the surrounding woodlands: discover the link between the Gaelic alphabet and tree names. ✉ *Viewfield Rd.* ☎ *01478/613649* *www.scotlandcreates.com/aros* *£3 for taped guide* *Daily 10–5.*

Where to Stay & Eat

£££££ **Cuillin Hills Hotel.** Just outside Portree, this gabled hotel has many rooms with views over Portree Bay toward the Cuillin Hills. Bold floral patterns decorate the bedrooms. The seafood dishes in the restaurant (££££) are especially good: try the local prawns, lobster, or scallops, or the glazed ham carved from the bone. ✉ *Isle of Skye, IV51 9QU* ☎ *01478/612003* *01478/613092* *www.cuillinhills.demon.co.uk* *30 rooms* *Restaurant, cable TV, bar; no a/c* *AE, MC, V* *BP.*

£££–££££ **Bosville Hotel.** Wood furniture and tartan and floral fabrics fill the traditional guest rooms, most of which have harbor views, at this comfortable, family-run hotel. You have an excellent choice of eating options (£–££): fine cuisine in the Chandlery Seafood Restaurant, or a more homey supper of Scottish fare in the lounge bar. ✉ *Bosville Terrace, IV51 9DG* ☎ *01478/612846* *01478/613434* *www.macleodhotels.co.uk/bosville* *15 rooms* *Restaurant, bar, lounge; no a/c* *AE, DC, MC, V* *BP.*

££–£££ **Rosedale Hotel.** Converted 19th-century buildings right on the harbor house modern accommodations—rooms are done in pastels and florals—and a restaurant serving delicious Scottish cooking. The menu (££££) might include breast of duck with cranberries and parsnip puree, or pasta rolls with smoked haddock and lemon butter. Ask for a room at the front for harbor views. ✉ *Beaumont Crescent, Isle of Skye, IV51 9DB* ☎ *01478/613131* *01478/612531* *www.rosedalehotelskye.co.uk* *23 rooms* *Restaurant, bar, lounge; no a/c* *MC, V* *Closed Dec.–Mar.* *BP.*

Shopping

An Tuireann Arts Centre (✉ Struan Rd. ☎ 01478/613306) is a showcase for locally made crafts and is a good place to look for unusual gifts or greetings cards. **Croft Comforts** (✉ 2 Wentworth St. ☎ 01478/613762) has a wonderful selection of silver, porcelain, antique and modern jewelry, and pottery, as well as larger items. In addition, it provides a mine of information about Skye: just ask David or Fiona Middleton for advice on places to eat, attractions to visit, or hidden coves to enjoy, and you won't be disappointed. **Skye Batiks** (✉ The Green ☎ 01478/613331) stocks unique Celtic-influenced batik clothing, cushion covers, and wall hangings; chunky handwoven cotton smocks, jackets, and skirts; silver jewelry; wood carvings; and much more. **Skye Original Prints** (✉ 1 Wentworth St. ☎ 01478/612544) sells prints by local artist Tom Mackenzie.

Trotternish Peninsula

22 *16 mi north of Portree via A855.*

As the road (A855) goes north from Portree, cliffs rise to the left. They're actually the edge of an ancient lava flow, set back from the road and running for miles as your rugged companion. In some places the hardened lava has created spectacular features, including a curious pinnacle called the **Old Man of Storr.** The A855 travels past neat white croft houses and forestry plantings to **Kilt Rock.** Everyone on the Skye tour circuit stops here to peep over the cliffs (there is a safe viewing platform) for a look at the geology of the cliff edge: columns of two types (and colors) of rock create a folded, pleated effect, just like a kilt.

The spectacular **Quiraing** dominates the horizon 5 mi past Kilt Rock. For a closer view of the strange pinnacles and rock forms, make a left onto a small road at Brogaig by Staffin Bay. There's a parking lot near the point where this road breaches the ever-present cliff line, though you have to walk back toward the Quiraing itself, where the rock formations and cliffs are most dramatic. The trail is on uneven, stony ground, and it's a steep scramble up to the rock formations. In ages past, stolen cattle were hidden deep within the Quiraing's rocky jaws.

The main A855 reaches around the top end of Trotternish, to the **Skye Museum of Island Life** at Kilmuir, where you can see the old crofting ways brought to life. Included in the displays and exhibits are documents and photographs, reconstructed interiors, and implements. Flora Macdonald, helpmate of Bonnie Prince Charlie, is buried nearby. ✉ *Kilmuir* ☎ *01470/552206* 🌐 *www.skyemuseum.co.uk* *£1.75* ⏲ *Easter–Oct., daily 9–5:30.*

Where to Stay & Eat

£££–££££ **Flodigarry Country House Hotel.** Close links with Flora Macdonald, Prince Charles Edward Stuart's helpmate, are not the least of the attractions at this country-house hotel, which is well placed for exploring the north and west of Skye. Yes, you can actually have a room in Flora's own cottage, adjacent to the hotel, where six of her children were born. The main hotel is a bit grander, and excellent seafood is served in the restaurant. ✉ *Staffin, Isle of Skye, IV51 9HZ* ☎ *01470/552203* *01470/552301* 🌐 *www.flodigarry.co.uk* *19 rooms* *Restaurant, bar; no a/c, no room TVs* *MC, V* *BP.*

Waternish Peninsula

23 *20 mi northwest of Portree via A850.*

The northwest corner of Skye has scattered crofting communities, magnificent coastal views, and two good restaurants, well worth the trip in themselves. In the Hallin area look westward for an islet-scattered sea loch with small cliffs rising from the water—and looking like miniature models of full-size islands. Just above the village of Stein, on the left side of the road, is a restored and inhabited "black house"—a thatched cottage blackened over time because a hole in its roof stood in for a chimney—today a rare sight on Skye and, in any event, now painted white.

Stoneware pottery is fired in a wood-fired kiln at the **Edinbane Pottery Workshop and Gallery,** in southern Waternish. You can watch the potters work, then buy from the showroom. ✉ *Edinbane* ☎ *01470/582234*

⊕ *www.edinbane-pottery.co.uk* ⊗ *Easter–Oct., daily 9–6; Nov.–Easter, weekdays 9–6.*

Where to Stay & Eat

★ ✕ **Loch Bay Seafood Restaurant.** Down on the waterfront at Stein stands
£££–£££££ a distinctive black-and-white-painted restaurant known as the place where
the island's top chefs eat and relax on their nights off. The fish and seafood
is freshly caught and simply prepared, the goal being to enhance the natural flavors of the ingredients rather than overwhelm the senses with
extraneous sauces. ⊠ *Near fishing jetty, Stein* ☏☏ *01470/592235*
▤ *MC, V* ⊗ *Closed Nov.–Easter and weekends except Sat. July–Oct.*

£££–£££££ ✕▣ **Greshornish House.** Your room rate includes dinner and breakfast,
so you can't miss out on this hotel's best feature: its restaurant, where
mahogany tables are laid with damask, crystal, and candelabra. The menu
might include scallops poached in white wine with flakes of smoked haddock and cream, freshly caught local lobster or king prawns with salad
and mayonnaise, or Skye lamb cutlets with heather honey and ginger,
served with wild Skye berries. Greshornish is a quirky hotel with spacious, if rather eclectically furnished, public rooms and bedrooms of all
shapes and sizes. ⊠ *Greshornish, Isle of Skye, IV51 9PN* ☏ *01470/
582266* ☐ *01470/582345* ⊕ *www.greshornishhotel.co.uk* 📨 *8 rooms*
♨ *Restaurant, tennis court, fishing, croquet; no a/c, no room phones,
no room TVs* ▤ *MC, V* ⊗ *MAP.*

Dunvegan Castle

㉔ *22 mi west of Portree.*

In a commanding position above a sea loch, Dunvegan Castle has been
the seat of the chiefs of Clan MacLeod for more than 700 years. Though
the structure has been greatly changed over the centuries, a gloomy ambience prevails, and there's plenty of family history on display, notably
the Fairy Flag—a silk banner, thought to be originally from Rhodes or
Syria and believed to have magically saved the clan from danger. The banner's powers are said to suffice for only one more use. Make time to visit
the gardens, with their water garden and falls, fern house, a walled garden, and viewing points. Dunvegan Sea Cruises runs a boat trip from the
castle to the nearby seal colony. ⊠ *At junction of A850 and A863, Dunvegan* ☏ *01470/521206* ⊕ *www.dunvegancastle.com* 🎫 *Garden only £4;
castle and garden £6; boat trips to see the seals £4* ⊗ *Mid-Mar.–Oct., daily
10–5:30, last admission at 5; Nov.–mid-Mar., daily 11–4, last entry at 3:30.*

Where to Stay & Eat

££ ▣ **Roskhill House.** A white 19th-century croft house, which once housed
the local post office in the dining room, Roskhill is more of a home away
from home than a country-house hotel. Bold colors decorate the bedrooms, and the lounge has books and games. Stone walls, dark stick-
back chairs, and a scarlet carpet lend the dining room a publike air. In
the morning, a full Scottish breakfast, including vegetarian options, is
served. ⊠ *Roskhill, by Dunvegan, Isle of Skye, IV55 8ZD* ☏ *01470/
521317* ☐ *01470/521827* ⊕ *www.roskhillhouse.co.uk* 📨 *4 rooms*
♨ *Dining room; no a/c, no room phones, no room TVs* ▤ *MC, V*
⊗ *BP.*

Glendale

㉕ *2 mi south of Dunvegan.*

The Glendale Visitor Route, a signed driving trail off the A863 through
the westernmost area of northwest Skye, leads past crafts outlets, museums, and other attractions. The **Toy Museum,** though badly damaged

by fire in 2002, salvaged and restored many items from its collection of dolls, trains, games, puzzles, and books. Its new facilities are slated to open in late 2003. ✉ *Glendale* ☎ *01470/511240* 🌐 *www.toy-museum.co.uk* 🎫 *£2.50* ⏲ *Mon.–Sat. 10–6.*

Borreraig Park has a fascinating museum of island life—rightly described by the owner as "a unique gallimaufry for your delight and edification"—that includes a detailed series of panels on the making of bagpipes and on the history of the MacCrimmons, hereditary pipers to the Clan MacLeod. A superb gift shop stocks unique island-made sweaters (the exact sheep can be named), wool, bagpipes, Celtic silver and gold jewelry, and CDs of traditional music. ✉ *Borreraig Park, by Dunvegan* ☎ *01470/51131* 🌐 *www.craftsonskye.org.uk/borreriag-museum.html* 🎫 *£2* ⏲ *Daily 10–6.*

Where to Stay & Eat

£££££ Fodor'sChoice ★ ✕🏨 **Three Chimneys Restaurant with Rooms.** One of Skye's top-notch restaurants, Shirley Spear's shoreside cottage might be small on space, but it's big on flavor: fresh local seafood, beef, lamb, and game are transformed into dishes such as prawn and lobster bisque, or grilled loin of Skye lamb with honey-roasted root vegetables and sherried button-mushroom sauce. Skye soft fruits—raspberries, strawberries, black currants—may follow. Adjacent to the restaurant are luxury accommodations in a courtyard wing, with magnificent sea views from all the rooms. ✉ *B884, Colbost, by Dunvegan, Isle of Skye, IV55 8ZT* ☎ *01470/511258* 📠 *01470/511358* 🌐 *www.threechimneys.co.uk* 🛏 *6 rooms* 👍 *In-room VCRs; no a/c* 💳 *AE, MC, V* ⏲ *No lunch Sun.* 🍽 *BP.*

Shopping

Skye Silver (✉ The Old School, Colbost, Glendale ☎ 01470/511263), west of Dunvegan, designs gold and silver jewelry with a Celtic theme and also has more unusual pieces that reflect the natural forms of the seashore and countryside: silver-coral earrings, silver-leaf pendants, and starfish and cockleshell earrings.

Glen Brittle

★ 26 *28 mi southeast of Glendale.*

You can safely enjoy spectacular mountain scenery in Glen Brittle, with some fine views of the Cuillin Ridge (which is not for the casual walker, as there are many steep and dangerous cliff faces). Glen Brittle extends off the A863/B8009 on the west side of the island.

THE OUTER HEBRIDES

The Outer Hebrides—the Western Isles in common parlance—stretch about 130 mi from end to end and lie about 50 mi from the Scottish mainland. This splintered archipelago extends from the Butt of Lewis in the north to the 600-foot Barra Head on Berneray in the south, whose lighthouse has the greatest arc of visibility in the world. The Isle of Lewis and Harris is the northernmost and largest of the group. The island's only major town, Stornoway, is on a nearly landlocked harbor on the east coast of Lewis; it's probably the most convenient starting point for a driving tour of the islands if you're approaching the Western Isles from the Northern Highlands.

Just south of the Sound of Harris is North Uist, rich in monoliths, chambered cairns, and other reminders of a prehistoric past. Though it is one of the smaller islands in the chain, Benbecula, sandwiched between

North and South Uist and sometimes referred to as the Hill of the Fords, is in fact less bare and neglected looking than its bigger neighbors to the north. South Uist, once a refuge of the old Catholic faith, is dotted with ruined forts and chapels; in summer its wild gardens burst with alpine and rock plants. Eriskay and a scattering of islets almost block the 6-mi strait between South Uist and Barra, an isle you can walk across in an hour.

Harris tweed is available at many outlets on the islands, including some of the weavers' homes; keep an eye out for signs directing you to weavers' workshops. Sunday on the islands is strictly observed as a day of rest, and nearly all shops and visitor attractions are closed.

Stornoway

27 *2½-hr ferry trip from Ullapool.*

The port capital for the Outer Hebrides is Stornoway, the only major town on Lewis. In the Town Hall, the **An Lanntair Gallery** has exhibitions of contemporary and traditional art that change monthly, as well as a coffee and gift shop and frequent traditional Gaelic musical and theatrical events. ✉ *Town Hall, S. Beach St.* ☎ *01851/703307* 🌐 *www.lanntair.com* *Free* *Mon.–Sat. 10–5:30.*

Where to Stay

£ **27 Springfield Road.** A quiet residential area backing onto open fields is the setting for this modern detached house with very comfortable accommodations. Modern furniture fills the rooms: one is done in blue and pink florals; another has navy and beige geometric prints. Immaculate gardens surround the house, which is just a short walk from downtown. ✉ *27 Springfield Rd., Stornoway, Isle of Lewis, HS1 2PS* ☎ *01851/703254* 🌐 *www.davinamacdonald.co.uk* *3 rooms* *Lounge; no a/c, no room phones, no smoking* *No credit cards.*

Biking

Alex Dan Cycle Centre (✉ 67 Kenneth St. ☎ 01851/704025) rents bicycles and can give you advice on where to ride.

Port of Ness

30 mi north of Stornoway via the A857.

The stark, windswept community of Port of Ness cradles a small harbor squeezed in among the rocks and overlooked by **Harbour View,** a small gallery and café. ☎ *07833/697065.*

28 At the northernmost point of Lewis stands the **Butt of Lewis Lighthouse,** designed by David and Thomas Stevenson (of the prominent engineering family whose best-known member was not an engineer at all: the novelist Robert Louis Stevenson [1850–94]). The lighthouse was first lit in 1862. The adjacent cliffs provide a good vantage point for viewing seabirds, whales, and porpoises. The lighthouse is a few minutes northwest of Port of Ness along the B8014.

Shopping

At **Borgh Pottery** (✉ Fivepenny House, Borve, on the road to Ness ☎ 01851/850345 🌐 www.borghpottery.com), open from Monday to Saturday 9:30 to 6, you can buy attractive hand-thrown studio pottery made on the premises, including lamps, vases, mugs, and dishes.

The Outer Hebrides
ATLANTIC OCEAN
Butt of Lewis Lighthouse
28
Butt of Lewis
Port of Ness
A857
Isle of Lewis and Harris
Arnol Black House
29
Barvas
Shawbost
Arnol
Tolsta
Gearrannan
B895
East Loch Roag
Shawbost School Museum
Loch Roag
Dun Carloway
Tiumpan Head
Valtos
Stornoway
Eye Peninsula
Callanish
27
Stornoway
30
Calanais Standing Stones
Brenish
SCOTLAND
MORSGAIL FOREST
LEWIS
A859
TO ULLAPOOL
Amhuinnsuidhe
FOREST OF HARRIS
Seaforth Island
Amhuinnsuidhe Castle
B887
Rhenigidale
Tarbert
Luskentyre
31
Loch Seaforth
A859
HARRIS
The Minch
Northton
St. Clement's Church
Leverburgh
32
Rodel
Sound of Harris
Newtonferry (Port nan Long)
33
A865
Balranald Nature Reserve
North Uist
Trinity Temple
A867
Bayhead
A865
Lochmaddy
A855
Uig
Barpa Longass Chambered Cairn
Clachan-a-Luib
Trotternish
A865
Grimsay
Benbecula
Rueval Hill
Our Lady of the Isles
Isle of Skye
South Uist
Sandwick
A865
Loch Druidibeg National Nature Reserve
Ormaclete Castle
Howmore
A863
Sea of Hebrides
Flora Macdonald's birthplace
Kildonan
34
Lochboisdale
Eriskay
Barra
Eoligarry
Cille Bharra
Traigh Moor
Castlebay
KEY
Kissimul Castle
Ferry
Berneray
Barra Head
TO OBAN
0
10 miles
0
15 km

Arnol Black House

29 *21 mi southwest of Port of Ness, 16 mi northwest of Stornoway.*

In the small community of Arnol, look for signs off the A858 for the Arnol Black House, a well-preserved example of an increasingly rare type of traditional Hebridean home. Once common throughout the islands—even into the 1950s—these dwellings were built without mortar and thatched on a timber framework without eaves. Other characteristic features include an open central peat hearth and the absence of a chimney—hence the soot and the designation *black*. On display inside are many of the house's original furnishings. To reach Arnol from Port of Ness, go back south on the A857 and pick up the A858 at Barvas. ✉ *Off the A858, Arnol* ☎ *01851/710395* 🌐 *www.historic-scotland.gov.uk* 🎫 *£2.80* ⏲ *Apr.–Sept., Mon.–Sat. 9:30–6; Oct.–Mar., Mon.–Sat. 9:30–4.*

en route

The journey along the A857 to the Calanais Standing Stones takes you past several interesting sights. The rather dusty but illuminating **Shawbost School Museum** (✉ Off A857, Shawbost ☎ 01851/710212) survives from the Highland Village Competition in 1970, during which students gathered artifacts and contributed to displays aimed at illustrating a past way of life in Lewis. The museum is open all year, Monday through Saturday 10 to 5. **Dun Carloway** (✉ Off A857), one of the best-preserved Iron Age *brochs* (circular stone towers) in Scotland, dominates the scattered community of Carloway. The mysterious tower was probably built around 2,000 years ago as protection against seaborne raiders. The interpretative center explains more about the broch and its setting. Up a side road north from Carloway at **Gearrannan** (☎ 01851/643416 🌐 www.gearrannan.com) an old black-house village has been brought back to life with a museum and guided tours explaining the old island way of life.

Calanais Standing Stones

★ 30 *22 mi southeast of Arnol.*

At Calanais (Callanish) are the Calanais Standing Stones, lines of megaliths reminiscent of those in Stonehenge, in England. Probably positioned in several stages between 3000 and 1500 BC, this grouping consists of an avenue of 19 monoliths extending northward from a circle of 13 stones, with other rows leading south, east, and west. It's believed they may have been used for astronomical observations. The site is accessible at any time. The **visitor center** has an exhibit on the stones, a shop, and a tearoom. ✉ *Off A858, Calanais* ☎ *01851/621422* 🎫 *Exhibit £1.75* ⏲ *Visitor center Apr.–Sept., Mon.–Sat. 10–7, tearoom closes at 5:30; Oct.–Mar., Wed.–Sat. 10–4, tearoom closes at 3:30.*

The restored black house next to the gate leading to the Calanais Standing Stones is the site of the **Callanish Stones Tearoom** (☎ 01851/621373), an interesting spot in which to take refreshment or browse among the crafts on display.

Tarbert

31 *47 mi south of Calanais.*

Tarbert is the main port of Harris, with one or two shops and accommodations. **Traigh Luskentyre,** roughly 5 mi southwest of Tarbert, is a spectacular example of Harris's tidy selection of beaches—2 mi of yellow sands adjacent to **Traigh Seilebost** beach, with superb views northward to the hills of the Forest of Harris. Turreted **Amhuinnsuidhe Castle** (pronounced avun-*shooee*) was built in the 1860s by the earls of Dunmore as a base for fishing and hunting in the North Harris deer forest. The castle stands about 10 mi northwest of Tarbert on the B887, and you can view it from the outside only.

Where to Stay

★ ££££ **Ardvourlie Castle.** Ardvourlie, a former Victorian hunting lodge, sits in splendid isolation amid the dramatic mountain scenery of Harris, an ideal habitat for hill walking. The decor is bold, idiosyncratic, and entirely in keeping with the High Victorian atmosphere of the castle. A well-stocked library and roaring fires complement the country-house hospitality. The cooking (for guests only) is along traditional lines and of a high standard, favoring fresh local produce and, often, wild game. ✉ *Isle of Harris, 15 mi north of Tarbert, signed off the A859, HS3 3AB* ☎ *01859/502307* 📠 *01859/502348* *4 rooms* *Dining room, library; no a/c, no room phones* *MC, V* ⏲ *Closed Nov.–Mar.*

Northton

16 mi south of Tarbert.

The little community of Northton has two attractions. The **McGillivray Centre** focuses on the life and work of William McGillivray (1796–1852), a noted naturalist with strong links to Harris. McGillivray authored the five-volume *History of British Birds* as well as biographies of other naturalists and zoologists. Some of his original drawings are on display in the center (others can be seen in the British Museum of Natural History in London). ✉ *Off A859* ☎ *01859/502011* *Donations accepted* ⏲ *Mon.–Sat. 9–9.*

The **Seallam! Visitor Centre and Co Leis Thu? Genealogical Research Centre** is where you can trace your Western Isles ancestry. Photographs and interpretive signs describe the history of Harris and its people. The owners organize guided walks and cultural evenings weekly between May and September. ✉ *Off A859* ☎ *01859/520258* 🌐 *www.seallam.com* *£2.50 for exhibitions* ⏲ *Mon.–Sat. 9–5.*

St. Clement's Church

32 *20 mi south of Tarbert.*

At the southernmost point of Harris is the community of Rodel, where you'll find St. Clement's Church, a cruciform church standing on a hillock. This is the most impressive pre-Reformation church in the Outer Hebrides; it was built around 1500 and contains the magnificently sculptured tomb (1528) of the church's builder, Alasdair Crotach, MacLeod chief of Dunvegan Castle. An arched recess has sculpted panels showing, among other scenes, St. Michael and Satan weighing souls. There are also other effigies and carvings within the building.

North Uist

8 mi south of Rodel via ferry from Leverburgh, Harris.

The island of North Uist is particularly known for its prehistoric remains.
33 At **Newtonferry (Port nan Long)**, by Otternish and the ferry pier for the Leverburgh (Harris) ferry service, stand the remains of what was reputed to be the last inhabited broch in North Uist, **Dun an Sticar.** This defensive tower, reached by a causeway over the loch, was home to Hugh Macdonald, a descendant of MacDonald of Sleat, until 1602.

You can explore the ruins of **Trinity Temple (Teampull na Trionaid),** a medieval college and monastery said to have been founded in the 13th century by Beathag, daughter of Somerled, the progenitor of the Clan Donald. The ruins stand 8 mi southwest of Lochmaddy, off the A865.

The **Barpa Langass Chambered Cairn,** dating from the 3rd millennium BC, is the only chambered cairn in the Western Isles known to have retained its inner chamber fully intact. You can peek inside, but don't venture too far without a light. It sits very close to the A867 between Lochmaddy and Clachen.

The **Balranald Nature Reserve,** administered by the Royal Society for the Protection of Birds (RSPB), shelters large numbers of waders and seabirds, including red-necked phalaropes, living in a varied habitat of loch, marsh, *machair* (grasslands just behind the beach), and sandy and rocky shore. The reserve can be viewed anytime (guided walks by an RSPB warden May–August), but you are asked to keep to the paths during breeding season (April–June) so as not to disturb the birds. It's on the west side of North Uist. Ask for information at the Goular visitor center. ✉ *Off the A865, 3 mi northwest of Bayhead* ☎ *01876/560287 or 01463/715000.*

Horseback Riding

Uist Community Riding School (✉ The Stables, Balivanich, Isle of Benbecula ☎ 01870/604283 🌐 www.ucrs.freeserve.co.uk) offers rides out into the countryside.

South Uist

34 mi south of Newtonferry via Grimsay, Benbecula, and 3 causeways.

Carpets of wildflowers in spring and early summer, superb deserted beaches, and historical connections to Flora Macdonald and Bonnie Prince Charlie head the list of reasons to visit South Uist. You can travel the length of South Uist along Route A865, making short treks off this main road on your way to Lochboisdale, on the southeast coast of the island. At Lochboisdale you can catch ferries to Barra, the southernmost principal island of the Outer Hebrides, or to Oban, on the mainland.

About 5 mi south of the causeway from Grimsay to Benbecula, atop Rueval Hill, stands the 30-foot-high statue of the Madonna and Child known as ***Our Lady of the Isles.*** The local Catholic community erected the statue, the work of sculptor Hew Lorimer, in 1957.

One of only two remaining British native—that is, nonmigrating—populations of greylag geese make their home at **Loch Druidibeg National Nature Reserve** in a fresh and brackish loch environment. Stop at the warden's office for information about access and nature trails. ✉ *Off A865* ☎ *01870/620–0238.*

A few miles south of Howmore, just west of A865, stand the ruins of **Ormaclete Castle,** built in 1708 for the chief of the Clan Ranald but accidentally destroyed by fire in 1715 on the eve of the Battle of Sheriffmuir, during which the chief was killed.

The **Kildonan Museum and Heritage Centre** houses South Uist artifacts collected in the 1950s and 1960s by Father John Morrison, a local priest. There are also archaeological displays that explain what South Uist was like from the bronze age until the Viking raids. You can shop for gifts in the crafts shop and have a bite in the tearoom. ✉ *A865, Kildonan* ☎ *01878/710343* 🎟 *£1.50* ⏲ *Easter–Oct., Mon.–Sat. 10–5, Sun. 2–5.*

34 At Gearraidh Bhailteas, you can see the site of **Flora Macdonald's birthplace.** South Uist's most famous daughter, Flora helped the Young Pretender, Prince Charles Edward Stuart, avoid capture and was feted as a heroine afterward. Legend has it that Flora helped the fugitive prince escape from South Uist in a rowboat with the prince disguised as Flora's maid. ✉ *¼ mi west of A865, ½ mi north of Milton* 🎫 *Free* ⏲ *Daily, 24 hrs.*

Shopping

Hebridean Jewelry (✉ Garrieganichy, Lochdar ☎ 01870/610288) sells decorative jewelry and framed pictures; the owners also run a crafts shop on the premises.

THE NORTHERN HIGHLANDS A TO Z

To research prices, get advice from other travelers, and book travel arrangements, visit www.fodors.com.

AIR TRAVEL

The main airports for the Northern Highlands are Inverness and Wick (both on the mainland). Loganair has direct air service from Edinburgh and Glasgow to Inverness and from Edinburgh to Wick. You can fly from London's Luton Airport to Inverness on one of the daily easyJet flights and from Gatwick to Inverness on British Airways. Loganair also operates flights among the islands of Barra, Benbecula, and Lewis, in the Outer Hebrides (weekdays only). Highland Airways operates flights from Inverness to Stornoway and Benbecula.

British Airways ☎ 08457/733377 🌐 www.britishairways.com. **Loganair** ☎ 08457/733377 🌐 www.loganair.co.uk. **easyJet** ☎ 0870/600-0000 🌐 www.easyjet.com. **Highland Airways** ☎ 01851/701282 🌐 www.highlandairways.co.uk

Inverness Airport ☎ 01667/464000 🌐 www.hial.co.uk/inverness-airport.html.

BOAT & FERRY TRAVEL

Ferries run from Ullapool to Stornoway, from Oban to Castlebay and Lochboisdale, and from Uig, on the Isle of Skye, to Tarbert and Lochmaddy. Causeways link North Uist, Benbecula, and South Uist. The Island Hopscotch planned-route ticket and the Island Rover pass, both offered by Caledonian MacBrayne, called CalMac, give considerable reductions on interisland ferry fares.

Caledonian MacBrayne ✉ Ferry Terminal, Gourock PA19 1QP ☎ 01475/650100 🌐 www.calmac.co.uk. **Oban to Castlebay and Lochboisdale ferry** ☎ 01631/566688. **Ullapool to Stornoway ferry** ☎ 01854/612358. **Uig to Tarbert and Lochmaddy ferry** ☎ 01470/542219.

BUS TRAVEL

Scottish Citylink and National Express run buses from England to Inverness, Ullapool, Thurso, Scrabster, and Wick. There are also coach connections between the ferry ports of Tarbert and Stornoway; consult the local tourist information center for details.

Highland Country Buses provides bus service in the Highlands area. On the Outer Hebrides several small operators run regular routes to most towns and villages. The post-bus service—which also delivers mail—becomes increasingly important in remote areas; it supplements the regular bus service, which runs only a few times per week. A full timetable of services for the Northern Highlands (and the rest of Scotland) is available from the Royal Mail.

Highland Country Buses in the mainland and Skye ☎ 01463/222244. **National Express** ☎ 08705/808080 🌐 www.nationalexpress.co.uk. **Royal Mail Post Buses** ✉ 7 Strothers La., Inverness, IV1 1AA ☎ 01463/256273. **Scottish Citylink** ☎ 08705/505050 🌐 www.citylink.co.uk.

CAR RENTAL

Agencies **Avis** ✉ Inverness Airport ☎ 01667/464070. **Budget Rent-a-Car** ✉ Burns Cottage, Railway Terrace, Inverness ☎ 01463/713333. **Europcar Ltd.** ✉ Friar's Bridge Service Station, Telford St., Inverness ☎ 01463/235337. **Hertz** ✉ Inverness Airport, Inverness ☎ 01667/462652.

CAR TRAVEL

Because of the infrequent bus services and sparse railway stations, a car is definitely the best way to explore this region. The twisting, winding single-lane roads demand a degree of driving dexterity. Local rules of the road require that when two cars meet, whichever driver reaches a passing place first must stop in it or opposite it and allow the oncoming car to continue. Small cars tend to yield to large commercial vehicles. Never park in passing places, and remember that these sections of the road can also allow traffic behind you to pass. Note that in this sparsely populated area, distances between gas stations can be considerable.

DISCOUNTS & DEALS

It is in the Highlands and islands that the Freedom of Scotland Travelpass really becomes useful, saving you money on ferries, trains, and some buses (⇨ Train Travel *in* Smart Travel Tips).

EMERGENCIES

Dial 999 in an emergency for an ambulance, the police, the fire department, or the coast guard (no coins are needed for emergency calls from public phone booths). Pharmacies are not found in rural areas. Pharmacies in the main towns—Thurso, Wick, Stornoway—keep normal shop hours. In an emergency the police will provide assistance in locating a pharmacist. General practitioners may also dispense medicine in rural areas.

TOURS

BOAT TOURS

Several small firms run cruises along the spectacular west-coast seaboard. On Skye there's also a broad selection of mountain guides. Contact the local tourist information center for details about local operators.

Dunvegan Sea Cruises, at Dunvegan Castle, Skye, runs a boat trip to the nearby seal colony for £4. John o'Groats Ferries operates wildlife cruises from John o'Groats harbor daily from mid-June through August. The trip takes passengers into the Pentland Firth, to Duncansby Stacks, and the island of Stroma, passing by spectacular cliff scenery and bird life. John o'Groats Ferries also runs guided day tours to Orkney from Inverness, daily June through early September.

Dunvegan Sea Cruises ☎ 01470/531500. **John o'Groats Ferries** ☎ 01955/611353 🌐 www.jogferry.co.uk.

SPECIAL-INTEREST TOURS

Highland Heritage Tours will take you on a minibus day trip to the Isle of Skye from Inverness. James Johnstone will drive you anywhere and knows a lot about the Highlands and islands, including the Outer Hebrides. Puffin Express runs unusual "Wildlife and Stone Age" day tours from Inverness between Easter and October, with limited tours in the winter (when the owner goes wolf-watching in Poland). Raasay Outdoor Centre organizes courses in kayaking, sailing, windsurfing, climbing, rappeling, archery, walking, and navigation skills.

Highland Heritage Tours ☎ 01463/798618. **James Johnstone** ☎ 01463/798372. **Puffin Express** ☎ 01463/717181 📠 01463/717188 🌐 www.puffinexpress.co.uk. **Raasay Outdoor Centre** ☎ 01478/660266 📠 01478/660200 🌐 www.raasayoutdoorcentre.co.uk.

TRAIN TRAVEL

Main railway stations in the area include Oban (for Barra and the Uists) and Kyle of Lochalsh (for Skye), on the west coast, or Inverness (for points north to Thurso and Wick). There's direct service from London to Inverness and connecting service from Edinburgh and Glasgow. For information contact National Rail.

Stops on the northern lines (Inverness to Thurso–Wick and Inverness to Kyle of Lochalsh) include Beauly, Muir of Ord, and Dingwall; on the Thurso–Wick line, Alness, Invergordon, Fearn, Tain, Ardgay, Culrain, Invershin, Lairg, Rogart, Golspie, Brora, Helmsdale, Kildonan, Kinbrace, Forsinard, Altnabreac, Scotscalder, and Georgemas Junction; and on the Kyle line, Garve, Lochluichart, Achanalt, Achnasheen, Achnashellach, Strathcarron, Attadale, Stromeferry, Duncraig, Plockton, and Duirinish.

National Rail ☎ 08457/484950 🌐 www.nationalrail.co.uk. **ScotRail** ☎ 08457/550033 🌐 www.scotrail.co.uk.

VISITOR INFORMATION

The tourist information centers at Dornoch, Dunvegan, Durness, Portree, Stornoway, Tarbert, Ullapool, and Wick are open year-round, with limited winter hours at Dunvegan, Durness, Ullapool, and Wick.

Seasonal tourist information centers are at Bettyhill, Broadford (Skye), Castlebay (Barra, Outer Hebrides), Gairloch, Helmsdale, John o'Groats, Kyle of Lochalsh, Lairg, Lochboisdale (South Uist, Outer Hebrides), Lochcarron, Lochinver, Lochmaddy (North Uist, Outer Hebrides), North Kessock, Shiel Bridge, Strathpeffer, Thurso, and Uig.

Dornoch ✉ The Square, Dornoch IV25 3SD ☎ 01862/810400. **Dunvegan** ✉ 2 Lochside, Dunvegan, Isle of Skye IV55 8WB ☎ 01470/521581. **Durness** ✉ Sango, IV27 4PZ ☎ 01971/511259. **Portree** ✉ Bayfield House, Bayfield Rd., Portree, Isle of Skye, IV51 9EL ☎ 01478/612137. **Stornoway** ✉ 26 Cromwell St., Isle of Lewis and Harris, HS1 2DD ☎ 01851/703088 🌐 www.witb.co.uk. **Tarbert** ✉ Pier Rd., Tarbert, Isle of Lewis and Harris ☎ 01859/502011. **Ullapool** ✉ Argyll St., Ullapool IV26 2UR ☎ 01854/612135. **Wick** ✉ Whitechapel Rd. off High St., Wick KW1 4EA ☎ 01955/602596.

THE NORTHERN ISLES

ORKNEY, SHETLAND

10

FODOR'S CHOICE

Creel Inn, *in St. Margaret's Hope*
Jarlshof, *near Virkie*
Maes Howe, *near Finstown*
Old Scatness, *in Virkie*
Ring of Brogar, *near Stromness*
Skara Brae, *near Stromness*

HIGHLY RECOMMENDED

SIGHTS

Busta House, *in Brae*
Earl Patrick's Palace, *in Kirkwall*
Hermaness National Nature Reserve, *near Haroldswick*
St. Magnus Cathedral, *in Kirkwall*
Shetland Croft House Museum, *in South Voe*

By Gilbert Summers

Updated by Beth Ingpen

BOTH ORKNEY AND SHETLAND possess a Scandinavian heritage that gives their collective 200 islets an ambience different from any other region of Scotland. For mainland Scots, visiting this archipelago is a little like traveling abroad without having to worry about a different language or currency. Both Orkney and Shetland are essentially bleak and austere, but have awe-inspiring seascapes and genuinely warm, friendly people. Neither has yet been overrun by tourism.

An Orcadian has been defined as a farmer with a boat, whereas a Shetlander has been called a fisherman with a croft (small farm). Orkney is the greener archipelago and is rich with artifacts that testify to the many centuries of continuous settlement here: stone circles, burial chambers, ancient settlements, and fortifications. Shetland, with its ocean views and sparse landscapes—trees are a rarity because of ever-present wind—is endowed with a more remote air than neighboring Orkney. However, don't let Shetland's desolate countryside fool you: it has a wealth of historic interest and is far from being a backwater island. Oil money from its mineral resources and its position as a crossroads in the northern seas for centuries have helped make Shetland a cosmopolitan place.

Exploring the Northern Isles

Both Orkney and Shetland require at least a couple of days if you are to do more than just scratch the surface. Since getting to Shetland isn't easy, you may want to spend three or four days here. In any case, the Northern Isles generate their own laid-back approach to life, and once here, you may want to take it slowly.

About the Restaurants

The seafood is first class and so is Orkney's malt whisky. Meals are usually of the stick-to-your-ribs variety, as vegetable gardeners do face some extra challenges from the northerly latitude. For local tastes, try the cheeses, *bere bannocks* (barley-and-oat cakes), and Orkney ales (with names full of foreboding, like Skullsplitter).

About the Hotels

Accommodations in the Northern Isles are on par with mainland Scotland. However, to experience a simpler lifestyle, check out the unique "camping bods" in Shetland—old cottages providing inexpensive, basic lodging (log fires, cold water, and sometimes no electricity). For details, contact the Shetland visitor center.

WHAT IT COSTS In Pounds

	£££££	££££	£££	££	£
RESTAURANTS	over £22	£18–£22	£13–£17	£7–£12	under £7
HOTELS	over £150	£110–£150	£80–£110	£50–£80	under £50

Restaurant prices are for a main course at dinner. Hotel prices are for two people in a standard double room in high season.

Timing

The bird colonies are at their most lively in early summer, which is also when the long northern daylight hours allow you plenty of sightseeing time.

AROUND ORKNEY

Most of Orkney's many prehistoric sites are open to view, providing an insight into the life of bygone eras. At Maes Howe, for example, it be-

Getting around is quite straightforward—the roads are good on both Shetland and Orkney. A fast and frequent interisland passenger and car ferry service makes island-hopping perfectly practical.

Numbers in the text correspond to numbers in the margin and on the Shetland Islands and the Orkney Islands maps.

If you have 1 day — From Inverness take a day trip to Orkney—though it will be a long one—via the bus and ferry. Start by visiting the historic sites in **Kirkwall** 8, then visit **Skara Brae** 4, **Maes Howe** 3, and the **Ring of Brogar** 2.

If you have 5 days — Get a good taste of Orkney by taking in the main sights—St. Magnus Cathedral, Earl Patrick's Palace, and the Bishop's Palace in **Kirkwall** 8—then go out to **Skara Brae** 4, **Maes Howe** 3, and the **Ring of Brogar** 2. You could also see a bit of Shetland in this length of time. Don't miss the **Shetland Croft House Museum** 12, **Old Scatness** 13, **Jarlshof** 14, Sumburgh Head, and **St. Ninian's Isle** 15. Stay overnight in **Lerwick** 10 and make a quick exploration of Lerwick itself and **Scalloway** 16; then make a trip up to Esha Ness to get the flavor of the north of Mainland. If you have enough time on your fifth day, you might visit the **Hermaness National Nature Reserve.**

comes evident that graffiti is not solely an expression of today's youths: the Vikings left their marks here way back in the 12th century. You can purchase the Historic Scotland joint-entry ticket at the first site you visit; the ticket costs less than paying separately for entry into each site.

Stromness

1 *1¾ hrs north of Thurso via ferry from Scrabster.*

Stromness makes a good base for visiting the northern and western parts of Orkney, and the town holds two points of interest. The **Pier Arts Centre,** a former Stromness merchant's house (circa 1800), has adjoining buildings that now serve as a gallery with a permanent collection of 20th-century paintings and sculptures. ✉ *28–30 Victoria St.* ☎ *01856/850209* 📠 *01856/851462* *Free* ⏲ *Sept.–May, Tues.–Sat. 10:30–12:30 and 1:30–5; June–Aug., Tues.–Sat. 10:30–5.*

The **Stromness Museum** displays a varied collection of local natural-history material. Also here are ship models, a feature on the German fleet that was scuttled on Scapa Flow in 1919, and exhibits on fishing, shipping, whaling, and the Hudson Bay Company, which recruited workers in Stromness between the late 18th and 19th centuries. ✉ *52 Alfred St.* ☎ *01856/850025* *£2.50* ⏲ *Apr.–Sept., daily 10–5; Oct.–Mar., Mon.–Sat. 11–3:30.*

Where to Stay

££ **Mill of Eyrland.** White-painted stone walls, country antiques, and the rippling sound of the mill stream running beneath the windows make for a pleasant stay at this 1861 former water mill. The mill's old machinery can still be seen, and attractive gardens surround the house. Evening meals are available on request. This makes a good base for visiting the main archaeological sites. ✉ *Stenness, KW16 3HA*

☎ 01856/850136 🖷 01856/851633 ⇐ 4 rooms, 2 with bath ♨ Dining room, lounge, Internet; no a/c, no room phones, no smoking ▭ No credit cards 🍽 BP.

Ring of Brogar

❷ *5 mi northeast of Stromness.*

Fodor'sChoice ★

The Ring of Brogar is a magnificent circle of 36 neolithic stones (originally 60) surrounded by a deep ditch. When the fog descends over the stones—a frequent occurrence—their looming shapes seem to come alive. Though their original use is uncertain, it's not hard to imagine strange rituals taking place here in the misty past. The stones stand between Loch of Harray and Loch of Stenness, 5 mi northeast of Stromness. ✉ *Off A965* ☎ *0131/668–8800* 🌐 *www.historic-scotland.gov.uk* 🎫 *Free* ⏲ *Year-round.*

Maes Howe

❸ *1 mi northeast of Ring of Brogar on the A965.*

Fodor'sChoice ★

The huge burial mound of Maes Howe (circa 2500 BC) measures 115 feet in diameter and contains an enormous burial chamber. It was raided by Vikings in the 12th century, and Norse crusaders found shelter here, leaving a rich collection of runic inscriptions. Maes Howe is 1 mi northeast of the Ring of Brogar. ✉ *On A965* ☎ *0131/668–8800* 🌐 *www.historic-scotland.gov.uk* 🎫 *£3* ⏲ *Apr.–Sept., daily 9:30–6; Oct.–Mar., Mon.–Sat. 9:30–4, Sun. 2–4.*

Skara Brae

❹ *8 mi north of Stromness.*

Fodor'sChoice ★

At the Neolithic village of Skara Brae you'll find houses, joined by covered passages, with stone beds, fireplaces, and cupboards that have survived since the village was first occupied around 3000 BC. The site was preserved in sand until it was uncovered in 1850. It can be found 8 mi north of Stromness. ✉ *Off A967/B9056* ☎ *0131/668–8800* 🌐 *www.historic-scotland.gov.uk* 🎫 *£5, £4 Oct.–Mar.* ⏲ *Apr.–Sept., daily 9:30–6; Oct.–Mar., Mon.–Sat. 9:30–4, Sun. 2–4.*

Marwick Head Nature Reserve

❺ *5 mi north of Skara Brae.*

The Royal Society for the Protection of Birds tends the Marwick Head Nature Reserve, whose cliffs are home to thousands of seabirds. The Kitchener Memorial, which recalls the 1916 sinking of the cruiser HMS *Hampshire* with Lord Kitchener aboard, can also be seen in the reserve, on a cliff-top site. Access to the reserve, which is unstaffed, is along a path north from Marwick Bay. Take care near cliff edges. ✉ *Off B9056* ☎ *01856/850176* 🎫 *Free* ⏲ *Daily.*

Birsay

12 mi north of Stromness, 25 mi northwest of Kirkwall.

❻ Just before you reach Birsay (via the A966), you'll see the **Earl's Palace,** the impressive remains of a 16th-century palace built by the earls of Orkney. Some of its walls stand 20–30 feet high. The structure is unstaffed, but you may wander inside the ruins.

Birdwatching

Shetland is renowned for its seabirds. Every summer, more than a million birds alight on the islands' dramatic cliff faces to nest and breed, feeding on the abundance of North Atlantic fish. Birders can spot more than 20 different species, from tiny storm petrels to gannets with 6-foot wing spans. Perhaps most popular with visitors are the puffins, with their short necks, striped beaks, and comical orange feet. The visitor center in Lerwick has leaflets that indicate the main nesting sites. Orkney, too, has a share of seabird nesting sites, and the visitor centers in Kirkwall and Stromness provide details on how to find them.

Diving

Orkney, especially the former wartime anchorage of Scapa Flow on Hoy, claims to have the best dive sites in Britain. Part of the attraction lies in the remains of German navy ships that were scuttled here in 1919. Many boat-rental companies arrange diving charters; contact the tourist information centers. Shetland also has exceptional underwater visibility, perfect for viewing the wrecks and abundant marine life.

Festivals

Shetland has quite a strong cultural identity, thanks to its Scandinavian heritage. There are, for instance, books of local dialect verse, a whole folklore contained in knitting patterns, and a strong tradition of fiddle playing. In the middle of the long winter, at the end of January, the Shetlanders celebrate their Viking culture with the Up Helly Aa Festival, which involves much merrymaking, dressing up, and the burning of a replica of a Viking long ship. The Shetland Folk Festival, held in April, and October's Shetland Accordion and Fiddle Festival both attract large numbers of visitors. Orkney's St. Magnus Festival, a musical celebration, is based in Kirkwall and usually held the third week in June. Orkney also hosts a jazz festival in April, an annual folk festival at the end of May, the unique Boys' Ploughing Match in mid-August, and The Ba' (ball; street rugby-football played by the Uppies and Doonies residents of Kirkwall) on Christmas and New Year's Day.

Fishing

Sea fishing is such a popular sport in Orkney that the local tourist board advises anglers to book early. Several companies rent sea-angling boats, with fishing rods available in most cases. Loch angling in Orkney is also popular; Loch of Harray and Loch of Stenness are the best-known spots. Shetland, also renowned for sea angling, holds several competitions throughout the year. Contact the tourist information centers for directions to fishing spots, lists of equipment-rental shops, and tour-operator recommendations.

The **Brough of Birsay** is the remains of an early Pictish and then Norse settlement, including a Romanesque church. (*Brough* is another word for burgh.) The collection of roofless stone structures are on a tiny island, close to Birsay, accessible only at low tide. To ensure you won't be swept away, check the tide tables before setting out.

❼ **Gurness Broch** is an Iron Age tower standing more than 10 feet high, surrounded by stone huts. It's about 8 mi from Birsay along Orkney's northern coast. ✉ *On A966, Aikerness* ☎ *0131/668–8800* 🌐 *www.historic-scotland.gov.uk* 🎫 *£3* ⏲ *Apr.–Sept., daily 9:30–6.*

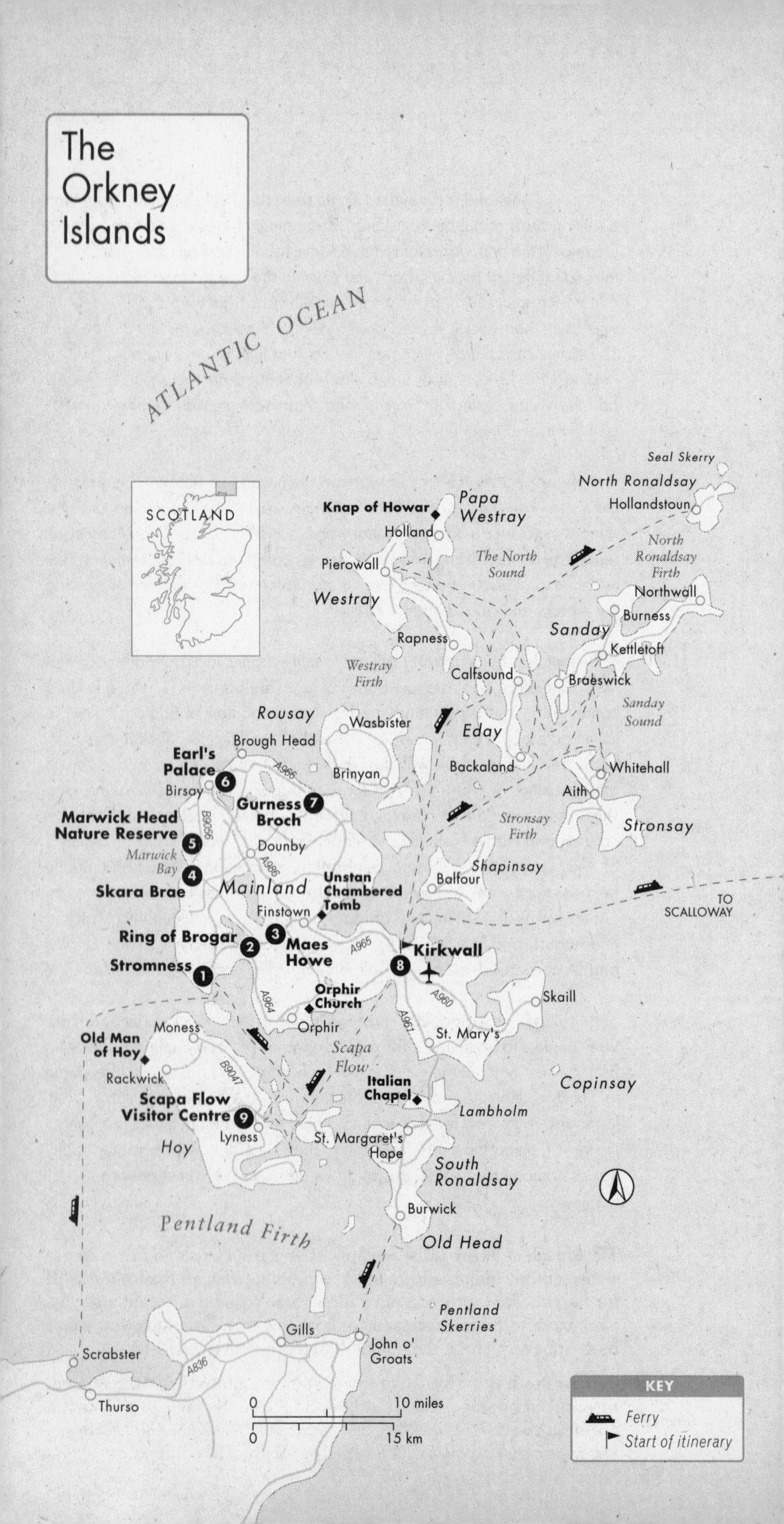

The Orkney Islands
ATLANTIC OCEAN
SCOTLAND
Seal Skerry
North Ronaldsay
Hollandstoun
Papa Westray
Knap of Howar
Holland
Pierowall
Westray
The North Sound
North Ronaldsay Firth
Northwall
Burness
Sanday
Kettletoft
Rapness
Westray Firth
Calfsound
Braeswick
Sanday Sound
Rousay
Wasbister
Eday
Brough Head
Earl's Palace
Birsay
A966
Brinyan
Backaland
Whitehall
Aith
Stronsay
Gurness Broch
Marwick Head Nature Reserve
B9056
Marwick Bay
Dounby
A986
Stronsay Firth
Shapinsay
Balfour
Skara Brae
Mainland
Unstan Chambered Tomb
Finstown
TO SCALLOWAY
Ring of Brogar
Maes Howe
A965
Kirkwall
Stromness
A960
Orphir Church
A964
Orphir
A961
Skaill
Moness
Old Man of Hoy
Rackwick
B9047
Scapa Flow
St. Mary's
Italian Chapel
Copinsay
Lambholm
Scapa Flow Visitor Centre
Lyness
Hoy
St. Margaret's Hope
South Ronaldsay
Burwick
Pentland Firth
Old Head
Pentland Skerries
Gills
John o' Groats
Scrabster
A836
Thurso
0
10 miles
0
15 km
KEY
Ferry
Start of itinerary

Kirkwall

8 *16 mi east of Stromness.*

In bustling Kirkwall, the main town on Orkney, there's plenty to see in the narrow, winding streets extending from the harbor, which retain a ★ strong medieval feel. **Earl Patrick's Palace,** built in 1607, is perhaps the best surviving example of Renaissance architecture in Scotland. There are no tours, so you can explore the palace ruins at your own pace. *Palace Rd., Kirkwall 0131/668–8800 £2.20, includes Bishop's Palace Apr.–Sept., daily 9:30–6.*

The **Bishop's Palace,** near Earl Patrick's Palace, dates to the 12th century. It was rebuilt in the late 15th century, and its round tower was added in the 16th century. *Palace Rd., Kirkwall 0131/668–8800 £2.20, includes Earl Patrick's Palace Apr.–Sept., daily 9:30–6.*

★ Founded by Jarl Rognvald in 1137 and named for his uncle, **St. Magnus Cathedral** was built mainly between 1137 and 1200, though more work was carried out during the following 300 years. The cathedral is still in use and contains some of the best examples of Norman architecture in Scotland. The ornamentation on some of the tombstones is particularly striking. *Mon.–Sat. 9–1 and 2–6; Sun. for services and 2–6.*

The **Orkney Wireless Museum** tells the story of wartime communications at Scapa Flow. Thousands of servicemen and -women were stationed here and used the equipment displayed in the museum to protect the Home Fleet. The museum also contains many handsome 1930s wireless radios and examples of the handicrafts produced by Italian prisoners of war. Check with the tourist center for the museum's hours. *Kiln Corner, Junction Rd. 01856/871400 £2 Apr.–Sept., hrs vary.*

The **Unstan Chambered Tomb** lies within a 5,000-year-old cairn. You enter the tomb via a short passageway through the side of the cairn. Pottery found within is known as Unstan ware. *On A964, 7½ mi west of Kirkwall 0131/668–8800 Free Daily.*

off the beaten path

ITALIAN CHAPEL – Created from a corrugated-iron hut by Italian prisoners of war during World War II, this beautiful and inspiring chapel has interior frescoes that were painted with whatever came to hand—bits of metal, colorful stones, leftover paints. It can be found in Lambholm, on the A961, 7 mi south of Kirkwall and just across from the first of the Churchill Barriers. *Free Daily.*

ORKNEYINGA SAGA CENTRE – This makes a good starting point for an exploration of Orkney's Norse heritage. Exhibits include the remains of the 12th-century Orphir Church, Scotland's only circular medieval church, and also the outline of a Viking drinking hall. The center is off the A964, 8 mi southwest of Kirkwall. *01856/811319 Free Daily 9–5.*

Where to Stay & Eat

££££ **Foveran Hotel.** Thirty-four acres of grounds surround this modern-built, ranch-style hotel just outside Kirkwall and overlooking Scapa Flow. The Foveran has an attractive light-wood, Scandinavian-style dining room, and a sitting room with a fireplace. The restaurant (££–£££) serves home-made soups, pâtés, and fresh seafood. *St. Ola, KW15 1SF 01856/872389 01856/876430 www.foveranhotel.co.uk 8 rooms Restaurant, lounge, Internet; no a/c MC, V BP.*

££ Fodor'sChoice ★ **Creel Inn.** Right on the waterfront, this outstanding small "restaurant with rooms" affords magnificent sea views from all three of its guest rooms, which are decorated in a simple, country style. The kitchen (£££) prepares imaginative modern Scottish cuisine using the freshest Orcadian seafood, meat, and locally grown vegetables. The Creel is well worth the 13-mi drive south from Kirkwall. ✉ *Front Rd., St. Margaret's Hope, South Ronaldsay, KW17 2SL* ☎ *01856/831311* 🌐 *www.thecreel.co.uk* *3 rooms* *Restaurant; no a/c, no room phones, no children under 5* ▭ *MC, V* ⊙ *Closed Oct.–Nov. and Jan.–Mar.* *BP.*

£££ **Merkister Hotel.** On the edge of Loch Harray, this hotel is an angler's dream, with rental equipment and boats, instruction for novices, and experienced gillies (guides). The comfortable, traditional-style bedrooms encourage a good night's sleep after a hard day on the water. The restaurant serves Scottish cuisine. Even if you're not interested in fishing, the Merkister makes a good base for touring the region. ✉ *Harray Loch, Harray, KW17 2LF* ☎ *01856/771366* 🖷 *01856/771515* *14 rooms* *Restaurant, fishing, Internet; no a/c* ▭ *AE, MC, V* *BP.*

£ **Polrudden Guest House.** This modern guest house sits in a quiet area, yet it's within walking distance of the town center and public parks. Multicolor matching curtains and quilt covers complement the simple pine furnishings. ✉ *Peerie Sea Loan, KW15 1UH* ☎ *01856/874761* 🖷 *01856/870950* 🌐 *www.polrudden.com* *7 rooms* *Dining room; no a/c, no room phones* ▭ *MC, V* *BP.*

The Arts

Orkney's cultural highlight is the **St. Magnus Festival** (☎ 01856/871445 🌐 www.stmagnusfestival.com), a music festival based in Kirkwall and usually held the third week in June. Orkney also hosts an annual folk festival at the end of May.

Sports & the Outdoors

BIKING Bicycles can be rented from **Bobby's Cycle Centre** (✉ Tankerness La. ☎🖷 01856/875777), open year-round.

FISHING The **Merkister Hotel** (✉ Harray ☎ 01856/771366) arranges fishing packages, with all equipment, including boats, available to rent.

Shopping

Kirkwall is Orkney's main shopping hub. At **Judith Glue** (✉ 25 Broad St. ☎ 01856/874225) you can purchase designer knitwear with traditional patterns, as well as Orkney-made crafts and hampers of Orkney produce. Don't miss **Ola Gorrie at the Longship** (✉ 7–15 Broad St. ☎ 01856/888790), which sells a huge array of giftwares and gold and silver jewelry with Celtic and Norse themes, including a delightful representation of a dragon originally drawn on the wall of the burial chamber at Maes Howe. **Ortak Jewelry** (✉ Hatston ☎ 01856/872224), a visitor center and shop, stocks Celtic-theme jewelry and has exhibits and jewelry-making demonstrations.

After all your shopping, you will have earned a dram of the local single malt at the **Highland Park Distillery** (✉ Holm Rd. ☎ 01856/874619 🌐 www.highlandpark.co.uk). Highland Park is a mellow whisky, less sweet than the Speyside malts, yet without the peat or iodine tinge of the western malts. It can be purchased all over Orkney (and farther afield), as well as from the distillery itself, which has a visitor center and shop.

Scapa Flow Visitor Centre

9 *On Hoy, 14 mi southwest of Kirkwall, 6 mi south of Stromness via ferry.*

The Scapa Flow Visitor Centre, on Hoy, portrays the strategic role of the sheltered anchorage of Scapa Flow—said to be Britain's best diving site—in two world wars. Note that if you want to take your car over to Hoy, you will need to book well in advance with Orkney Ferries, as this is a very popular route and space is limited. The center is a short walk from the ferry terminal. ✉ *Off B9047, Lyness* ☎ *01856/791300 center, 01856/872044 ferry* 🎫 *Free* ⏲ *June–Sept., Mon.–Sat. 9–4, Sun. 10–4; Oct.–May, weekdays 9–4.*

AROUND SHETLAND

10

The Shetland coastline is an incredible 900 mi because of all the indentations, and there isn't a point on the island farther than 3 mi from the sea. Settlements away from Lerwick, the primary town, are small and scattered.

Lerwick

10 *14 hrs by ferry from Aberdeen.*

Lerwick was founded by Dutch fishermen in the 17th century. Handsome stone buildings front the town's twisting flagstone lanes and harbor, which is still a very active port. **Fort Charlotte,** a 17th-century Cromwellian stronghold, was built to protect the Sound of Bressay. ✉ *Market St.* ☎ *0131/668–8800* 🎫 *Free* ⏲ *Daily.*

The **Shetland Museum** gives an interesting account of the development of the town, with displays on archaeology, art and textiles, shipping, and folk life. ✉ *Lower Hillhead* ☎ *01595/695057* 🌐 *www.shetland-museum.org.uk* 🎫 *Free* ⏲ *Mon., Wed., and Fri. 10–7; Tues., Thurs., and Sat. 10–5.*

Clickhimin Broch, on the site of what was originally an Iron Age fortification, makes a good introduction to these mysterious Pictish buildings, possibly intended as a place of retreat and protection in the event of attack. South of the broch are vivid views of the cliffs at the south end of the island of Bressay, which shelters Lerwick Harbor. ✉ *1 mi south of Lerwick off A970* ☎ *0131/668–8800* 🎫 *Free* ⏲ *Daily.*

off the beaten path

NOSS NATIONAL NATURE RESERVE – The island of Noss (*noss* means "nose" in old Norse) rises to a point called the Noup, where high cliffs seem to heave with birdlife. The seabirds nest in orderly fashion: black and white guillemots (45,000 pairs) and razorbills at the bottom; gulls, gannets, cormorants, and kittiwake in the middle; and fulmars and puffins at the top. The smell and noise of the birds, and the vertiginous cliff faces, make for a violent assault on the senses, not soon forgotten. Noss is reached via ferry to Bressay, then inflatable boat to Noss itself; call the reserve office, managed by Scottish Natural Heritage, for boat trip schedules. ✉ *Bressay* ☎ *01595/693345* 🎫 *£3* ⏲ *Mid-May–Aug., Tues.–Wed. and Fri.–Sun. 10–5, weather permitting.*

Where to Stay & Eat

£££ ✕🏨 **Shetland Hotel.** Modern and well-appointed—a result of the oil boom in the area and the needs of high-flying oil executives—the Shetland is done up in an attractive blend of burgundy and blue color schemes. The food is rich and filling, with sometimes wildly clashing flavors. One entrée consists of saddle of Shetland lamb filled with haggis forcemeat stuffing, sliced and served with a rich Orkney malt-whisky-and-rosemary jus—enough of a meal to sink the Shetland ferry! The hotel sits directly opposite the ferry terminal. ✉ *Holmsgarth Rd., ZE1 0PW* ☎ *01595/695515* 📠 *01595/695828* 🌐 *www.shetlandhotels.com* ↪ *64* *rooms, 1 suite* ♁ *2 restaurants, room service, cable TV, 2 bars, business service, meeting rooms; no a/c* ▭ *AE, DC, MC, V* 🍽 *BP.*

£ **Lerwick Youth Hostel.** Now a converted hostel, the stone Islesburgh House in the center of Lerwick offers very affordable double, family, and group-size rooms with white-painted walls, pine furniture, and colorful curtains and bedding. The turn-of-the-20th-century house has pretty architectural features, like big windows, pine shutters, and handsome fireplaces. The café serves healthy meals using whole foods and fresh vegetables. ✉ *King Harald St., Lerwick, Shetland, ZE1 0EQ* ☎ *01595/692114* 📠 *01595/696470* 🌐 *www.islesburgh.org.uk* *60 beds* ♁ *Café, laundry facilities, Internet; no a/c, no kids under 5* ▭ *MC, V* ⊙ *Closed Oct.–Mar.*

Biking

Bicycles can be rented from **Eric Brown Cycles** (✉ Grantfield Garage, North Rd. ☎ 01595/692709), open year-round.

Shopping

Anderson & Co. (✉ Shetland Warehouse, 60–62 Commercial St. ☎ 01595/693714) carries handmade knitwear and souvenirs. **The Spider's Web** (✉ 51 Commercial St. ☎ 01595/695246) sells hand-spun and -knitted woolen clothing.

Hjaltasteyn (✉ 161 Commercial St. ☎ 01595/696224) sells handcrafted gold and silver jewelry set with gemstones. **J. G. Rae Limited** (✉ 92 Commercial St. ☎ 01595/693686) stocks gold and silver jewelry with Norse and Celtic motifs. **Shetland Jewelry** (✉ Sound Side, Weisdale ☎ 01595/830275) sells gold and silver Celtic-inspired jewelry.

Broch of Mousa

⓫ *14 mi south of Lerwick via A970.*

The community of Sandwick is the departure point for the passenger ferry to the tiny isle of Mousa, where you can see the Broch of Mousa, which is in excellent condition. The broch's towering walls give a real sense of enclosure and security, which must have been reassuring for islanders subject to attacks from ship-borne raiders. ✉ *Mousa* ☎ *0131/668–8800, 01950/431367 ferry* 🌐 *www.historic-scotland.gov.uk* *Broch free, ferry £8 round-trip* ⊙ *Broch, year-round; ferry departs mid-Apr.–mid-Sept., Mon.–Thurs. and Sat. at 2, Fri. and Sun. at 12:30 and 2, weather permitting.*

Shopping

Lawrence J. Smith Ltd. (✉ Hoswick, 2 mi west of Sandwick ☎ 01950/431215) sells Shetland knitwear—both handmade and machine-made—for all ages in a wide selection of colors.

Shetland Croft House Museum

★ ⓬ *7 mi south of Sandwick.*

The scattered village of Voe (one of several with this name on Shetland; *voe* means "coastal inlet" in old Norse) is the home of the Shetland Croft House Museum. This 19th-century thatched house contains artifacts that depict the former way of life of the rural Shetlander, which the museum attendant will be delighted to discuss with you. You'll find domestic and crofting implements, including a handmill for preparing meal and willow baskets for carrying fish; and clothing, such as shawls, some thick for warmth, some so fine and lacy that they could be pulled through a wedding ring. ✉ *South Voe, Dunrossness, unclassified road east of A970*

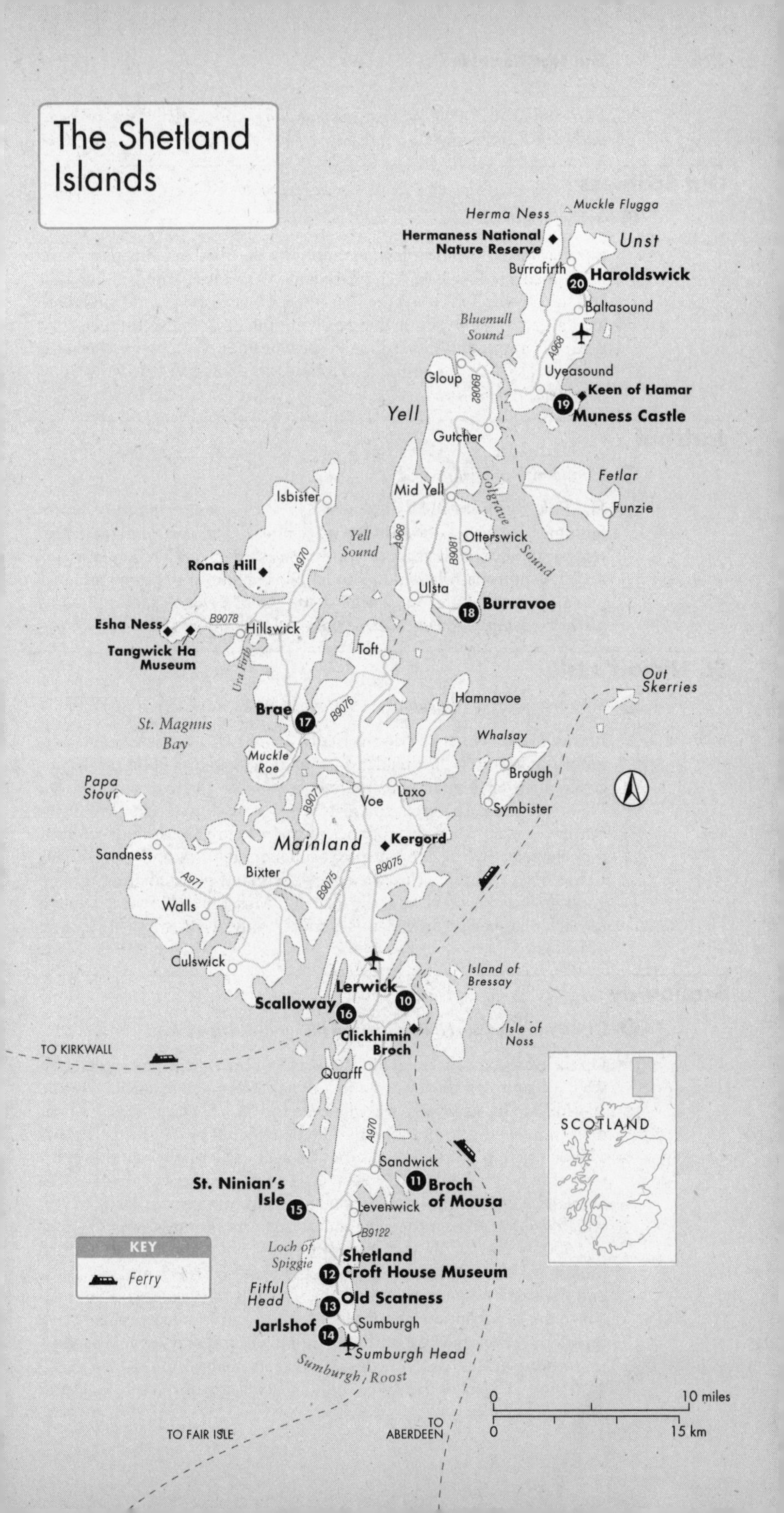

The Shetland Islands
Herma Ness
Muckle Flugga
Hermaness National Nature Reserve
Unst
Burrafirth
20 Haroldswick
Baltasound
Bluemull Sound
A968
Uyeasound
Gloup
B9082
Keen of Hamar
19 Muness Castle
Yell
Gutcher
Fetlar
Funzie
Mid Yell
Colgrave Sound
Isbister
Yell Sound
A968
Otterswick
B9081
Ronas Hill
A970
Ulsta
18 Burravoe
Esha Ness
B9078
Hillswick
Tangwick Ha Museum
Ura Firth
Toft
Out Skerries
Hamnavoe
Brae
17
B9076
St. Magnus Bay
Whalsay
Muckle Roe
Brough
Papa Stour
Voe
Laxo
B9071
Symbister
Mainland
Kergord
Sandness
Bixter
B9075
A971
B9075
Walls
Culswick
Island of Bressay
Lerwick
10
Scalloway
16
Clickhimin Broch
Isle of Noss
TO KIRKWALL
Quarff
SCOTLAND
A970
Sandwick
11 Broch of Mousa
St. Ninian's Isle
15
Levenwick
B9122
KEY
Ferry
Loch of Spiggie
12 Shetland Croft House Museum
Fitful Head
13 Old Scatness
Jarlshof
14
Sumburgh
Sumburgh Head
Sumburgh Roost
0
10 miles
0
15 km
TO FAIR ISLE
TO ABERDEEN

☎ 01595/695057 🌐 *www.shetland-museum.org.uk* 🎫 *Free* ⏲ *May–Sept., daily 10–1 and 2–5.*

Old Scatness

13 *3½ mi south of Voe.*

Fodor's Choice ★

Excavations at Old Scatness, managed by the Shetland Amenity Trust, have uncovered an Iron Age broch and village, with one building that still has a roof. A visitor center has interpretive displays, and guides are available to show you around. Living-history teams conduct craft demonstrations and storytelling in the wheelhouse and a reconstructed roundhouse. Call for hours. ✉ *Virkie, Dunrossness* ☎ *01595/694688* 🌐 *www.shetland-heritage.co.uk/amenitytrust* 🎫 *£2* ⏲ *Hrs vary.*

Jarlshof

14 *½ mi south of Virkie.*

Fodor's Choice ★

Jarlshof, a centuries-old site, includes the extensive remains of Norse buildings, as well as prehistoric wheelhouses and earth houses representing thousands of years of continuous settlement. The site also has a 17th-century laird's (landowner's) house built on the ruins of a medieval farmstead. ✉ *Sumburgh Head* ☎ *0131/668–8800* 🌐 *www.historic-scotland.gov.uk* 🎫 *£3* ⏲ *Apr.–Sept., daily 9:30–6.*

St. Ninian's Isle

15 *8 mi north of Sumburgh via A970 and B9122; turn left at Skelberry.*

It was on St. Ninian's Isle—actually a tombolo, a spit of sand that moors an island to the mainland—that archaeologists in the 1950s uncovered the St. Ninian treasure, a collection of 28 silver objects from the 8th century. The archaeologists were excavating the site of a 12th-century church when they happened upon the remains of an 8th-century chapel, a sword, a torque (neck collar), and bowls and spoons. This Celtic silver is now in the Museum of Scotland in Edinburgh, though good replicas are on view in the Shetland Museum in Lerwick. Though the silver has been removed, this is still a lovely, scenic spot with a sense of history.

Scalloway

16 *21 mi north of St. Ninian's Isle, 6 mi west of Lerwick.*

On the west coast of Mainland Island is Scalloway, which preceded Lerwick as capital of the islands and still has a very active harbor. During World War II, Scalloway was the port for the "Shetland Bus," a boat operation to and from Norway. The boats would carry British agents to Norway to perform acts of sabotage against Germany. On the return trips, the boats would carry escaped British prisoners of war back to Shetland. Look for the information board just off the main road (A970), which overlooks the settlement and its castle. **Scalloway Castle** was built in 1600 by Patrick Stewart, earl of Orkney, who coerced the locals to build it for him. He was executed in 1615 for his cruelty and misdeeds, and the castle was never used again. To enter the castle, you must retrieve the key from the shopkeeper at Shetland Woolen Company, or, on Sunday, from the host at the Royal Hotel. You may explore the castle to your heart's content; unsafe areas are fenced off. ✉ *On A970* ☎ *01466/793191 or 0131/668–8800* 🌐 *www.historic-scotland.gov.uk* 🎫 *Free* ⏲ *Daily.*

Shopping

The **Shetland Woollen Company** (✉ Castle St. ☎ 01595/880243), open from Monday to Saturday, 9:30 to 5, is one of many purveyors in Scalloway with a selection of Shetland knitwear.

Brae

17 *24 mi north of Scalloway.*

Brae is the home of Busta House, one of the best hotels on the island. Beyond Brae the main road meanders past **Mavis Grind,** a strip of land so narrow you can throw a stone—if you are strong—from the Atlantic, in one inlet, to the North Sea, in another.

off the beaten path

ESHA NESS AND RONAS HILL – For outstanding views of the rugged, forbidding cliffs around Esha Ness, drive north, then turn left onto the B9078. On the way, look for the sandstone stacks in the bay that resemble a Viking galley under sail. After viewing the cliffs at Esha Ness, and calling in at **Tangwick Haa Museum** (✉ off B9078, Tangwick ☎ 01806/503389), a former laird's house, return to join the A970 at Hillswick and follow an ancillary road from the head of Ura Firth. This road provides vistas of rounded, bare Ronas Hill, the highest hill in Shetland. Though only 1,468 feet high, it's noted for its arctic-alpine flora growing at low levels.

Where to Stay & Eat

★ £££ **Busta House.** Busta House dates in part from the 16th century and is surrounded by terraced grounds. Rooms are prettily furnished in pale colors and antique furniture; one room has a canopied, four-poster bed. The 16th-century Long Room is a delightful place to sample the hotel's selection of malt whiskies while sitting beside a peat fire. Choose between a four-course dinner in the restaurant (£££££), or an á la carte menu in the bar (££). Shetland salmon and lamb are usually available. *✉ Brae, ZE2 9QN ☎ 01806/522506 01806/522588 www.bustahouse.com 20 rooms Restaurant, bar, lounge, library, Internet; no a/c AE, DC, MC, V BP.*

Yell

11 mi northeast of Brae, 31 mi north of Lerwick via A970, A968, or B9076, and ferry from Toft.

There's not a lot to say about the blanket bog that cloaks two-thirds of the island of Yell, but the Old Haa building here is worth visiting, and you have to pass through Yell to get to Unst. To get here, catch the ferry
18 from Toft to Ulsta and take the B9081 east to **Burravoe.** The **Old Haa** (hall) of Burravoe, the oldest building on the island, is architecturally interesting. White and with crow-stepped gables, this is a typical example of an early 18th-century Shetland merchant's house. One of the displays in the upstairs museum tells the story of the wrecking of the German sail ship, the *Bohus,* in 1924. A copy of the ship's figurehead is displayed outside the Old Haa itself; the original is at the shipwreck site, overlooking Otterswick along the coast on the B9081. The Old Haa serves light meals with home-baked buns, cakes, and other goodies and also acts as a kind of unofficial information point. The staff is friendly and gives advice to sightseers. There's also a crafts shop on the premises. *✉ Burravoe ☎ 01957/722339 Free Late Apr.–Sept., Tues.–Thurs. and Sat. 10–4, Sun. 2–5.*

Unst

49 mi north of Lerwick via ferry from Gutcher.

The ferry (take the main A968 at Mid Yell to Gutcher) crosses the Bluemull Sound to Unst, the northernmost inhabited island in Scotland. On a long summer evening, views north to Muckle Flugga, with miles of landless water beyond, are incomparable. If you are a birdwatcher, head to the Hermaness and Keen of Hamar nature reserves.

19 **Muness Castle** (🌐 www.historic-scotland.gov.uk), Scotland's northernmost castle, was built just before the end of the 16th century. Admission is free. To get here from the A968, turn right onto the B9084. Just to the north of Muness Castle is the **Keen of Hamar National Nature Reserve,** with subarctic flora and arctic terns.

20 In the far north of Unst is **Haroldswick,** with its post office, proud of its status as the most northerly one, and heritage center. Also here is **Unst Boat Haven,** displaying a collection of traditional small fishing and sailing boats reflecting Shetland's maritime heritage. ☎ *01957/711528* 🎫 *£2* ⏲ *May–Sept., daily 2–5.*

★ **Hermaness National Nature Reserve,** a bleak moorland ending in rocky cliffs, is prime bird-watching territory. About half the world's population (6,000 pairs) of great skuas, called "bonxies" by locals, live here. These single-minded sky pirates attack anything that strays near their nest sites, including humans, so keep to the paths. Thousands of other seabirds, including more than 50,000 puffins, nest in spectacular profusion on the cliffs, about one hour's walk from the reserve entrance. But Hermaness is not just about birds—the flora includes the insect-eating butterwort and sundew, purple field gentians, orchids, and red campion. Grey seals gather in caves at the foot of the cliffs in fall, and offshore, dolphins and whales (including orcas) can be seen on calm days. The visitor center at the lighthouse has leaflets that describe a suggested walking tour. To get here from Haroldswick, follow the B9086 around the head of Burra Firth, a sea inlet. ✉ *Shore Station, Burrafirth* ☎ *01957/711278* 🎫 *Free* ⏲ *Reserve daily; visitor center mid-Apr.–mid-Sept., daily 9–5.*

A path in the Hermaness National Nature Reserve meanders across moorland and climbs up a gentle hill, from which you can see, to the north, a series of tilting offshore rocks; the largest of these sea-battered protrusions is **Muckle Flugga,** meaning "big, steep-sided island," on which stands a lighthouse. This is the northernmost point in Scotland—the sea rolls out on three sides, and no land lies beyond.

THE NORTHERN ISLES A TO Z

To research prices, get advice from other travelers, and book travel arrangements, visit www.fodors.com.

AIR TRAVEL

British Airways provides regular service to Lerwick (Shetland) and Kirkwall (Orkney) from Edinburgh, Glasgow, Aberdeen, and Inverness. Because of the isolation of Orkney and Shetland there's a network of interisland flights. Tourist information centers can provide details, or call Loganair for more information.

British Airways ☎ 08457/733377 🌐 www.britishairways.com. **Loganair** ☎ 08457/733377, 01856/872494 in Orkney 🌐 www.loganair.co.uk.

BOAT & FERRY TRAVEL

To get to Lerwick, Shetland, take the ferry from the port in Aberdeen. To reach Stromness, Orkney, take the ferry from the port in Scrabster. Contact Northlink Ferries for reservations. Northlink also runs longer sea voyages from Aberdeen to Kirkwall on Orkney.

As an alternative, you can take the ferry from John o'Groats to Burwick, Orkney, operated by John o'Groats Ferries, with up to four sailings daily May through September. Another alternative is the ferry from Gill's Bay, Caithness, to St. Margaret's Hope, Orkney, operated by Pentland Ferries, with three sailings a day in summer, two a day in winter.

Both Orkney and Shetland are part of a network of islands with interconnecting ferries that are heavily subsidized. Book ferry tickets in advance. In Shetland, for ferry information, contact the tourist information center or call Northlink Orkney and Shetland Ferries. If you want to get to Orkney from Shetland (or vice versa) you can do so by way of Northlink ferry between Lerwick and Kirkwall. In Orkney, for details of ferry services operated interisland, call Orkney Ferries.

John o'Groats Ferries ☎ 01955/611353 🌐 www.jogferry.co.uk. **Orkney Ferries** ☎ 01856/872044 🌐 www.orkneyferries.co.uk. **Northlink Orkney and Shetland Ferries** ☎ 01856/851144 📠 01856/851155 🌐 www.northlinkferries.co.uk. **Pentland Ferries** ☎ 01856/831226 📠 01856/831614 🌐 www.pentlandferries.co.uk.

BUS TRAVEL

Aberdeen and Thurso, one of the closest towns on the mainland to the Northern Isles, have two reliable bus links to and from each other and all over Scotland and the rest of Britain: Scottish Citylink and National Express. John o'Groats Ferries operates the Orkney Bus, a direct express coach from Inverness to Kirkwall (via ferry) that runs daily from May to early September.

The main bus services on Orkney are operated by Causeway Coaches and Orkney Coaches (Rapson's) and on Shetland, by Shalder Coaches and J. Leask.

Causeway Coaches ☎ 01856/831444 🌐 www.causewaycoachesorkney.co.uk. **John o'Groats Ferries** ☎ 01955/611353 🌐 www.jogferry.co.uk. **J. Leask** ☎ 01595/693162 🌐 www.leaskstravel.co.uk. **National Express** ☎ 08705/808080 🌐 www.nationalexpress.co.uk. **Orkney Coaches** ☎ 01856/870555 🌐 www.rapsons.co.uk. **Scottish Citylink** ☎ 08705/505050 🌐 www.citylink.co.uk. **Shalder Coaches** ☎ 01595/880217.

CAR RENTAL

You can take your car from Aberdeen by sea, but generally, for fewer than five days, it's cheaper to rent a car from one of Shetland's many car-rental agencies. Most rental companies are based in Lerwick, Shetland, and Kirkwall, Orkney.

Agencies **Bolts Car and Minibus Hire** ✉ 26 North Rd., Lerwick ☎ 01595/693636. **James D. Peace & Co.** ✉ Junction Rd., Kirkwall ☎ 01856/872866 🌐 www.orkneycarhire.co.uk. **Star Rent-a-Car** ✉ 22 Commercial Rd., Lerwick ☎ 01595/692075 🌐 www.starrentacar.co.uk. **W. R. Tullock** ✉ Terminal Building, Kirkwall Airport, Kirkwall ☎ 01856/875500 🌐 www.orkneycarrental.co.uk.

CAR TRAVEL

Because of its oil wealth, the roads on Shetland are in very good shape. Orkney has causeways connecting some of the islands, but in some cases using these roads will take you on fairly roundabout routes.

DISCOUNTS & DEALS

A joint entry ticket to all of Historic Scotland's Orkney sites is available from the sites themselves. The ticket lasts until you've seen all the sites and costs £12 (£11 in October and November).

EMERGENCIES

Dial ☎ 999 for the police, fire department, or an ambulance (no coins are needed for emergency calls from public phone booths).

Hospitals **Balfour Hospital** ✉ New Scapa Rd., Kirkwall, Orkney ☎ 01856/885400. **Gilbert Bain Hospital** ✉ South Rd., Lerwick, Shetland ☎ 01595/695678.

TOURS

Orkney Coaches (Rapson's) and Causeway Coaches run general tours as well as special-interest tours of Orkney. J. Leask arranges tours of Shetland. These companies can also tailor tours to your interests. Michael Hartley, an accredited tour guide in Orkney, runs Wildabout; phone for details on minibus tours that combine sightseeing of archaeological sites and the folklore, flora, and fauna of the islands. In Shetland several companies tour the spectacular Noss Bird Sanctuary, a national nature reserve, in summer, weather permitting. The tourist information center can provide details and take reservations.

Causeway Coaches ☎ 01856/831444 🌐 www.causewaycoachesorkney.co.uk.**J. Leask** ☎ 01595/693162. **Orkney Coaches** ☎ 01856/870555 🌐 www.rapsons.co.uk. **Wildabout** ☎ 01856/851011 🌐 www.orknet.co.uk/wildabout.

TRAIN TRAVEL

There are no trains on Orkney or Shetland, but you can take the train to Aberdeen or Thurso and then transfer to a ferry to get to the islands. For information contact National Rail. From Thurso a bus connects to Scrabster for Orkney.

National Rail ☎ 08457/484950 🌐 www.railtrack.co.uk.

VISITOR INFORMATION

The Orkney and Shetland tourist centers are open year-round.

Kirkwall, Orkney ✉ 6 Broad St., Kirkwall, Orkney KW15 1NX ☎ 01856/872856 🌐 www.visitorkney.com. **Lerwick, Shetland** ✉ Market Cross, Lerwick, Shetland ZE1 0LU ☎ 01595/693434 🌐 www.visitshetland.com. **Stromness, Orkney** ✉ Ferry Terminal Bldg. ☎ 01856/850716.

A GOLFER'S COUNTRY

11

FODOR'S CHOICE

Nairn, *on the Moray Coast*

Royal Dornoch, *in Dornoch Firth*

HIGHLY RECOMMENDED

Rosemount, Blairgowrie Golf Club, *in Perthshire*

Western Gailes, *on the Clyde Coast*

By John Hutchinson

Updated by Beth Ingpen

THERE ARE SOME 500 GOLF COURSES in Scotland and only 5 million residents, so the country has probably the highest ratio of courses to people anywhere in the world. If you're a golfer coming to Scotland, you'll probably want to play the "famous names" sometime in your career. Telling your friends in the clubhouse back home that you got a birdie at the Road Hole on the Old Course in St. Andrews, where Lyle, Faldo, and Jacklin have played, somehow conveys more prestige than an excellent round at a delightful but obscure course.

So, by all means, play the championship courses and impress your friends, but remember they *are* championship courses and therefore difficult; you may enjoy the game itself much more at a less challenging, albeit lesser known, course. Remember, too, that everyone else wants to play them, so booking can be a problem, particularly at peak times in summer. Book early, or if you're staying in a hotel attached to a course, get them to book for you.

Happily, golf has always had a peculiar classlessness in Scotland. It's a game for everyone, and for centuries Scottish towns and cities have maintained golf courses for the enjoyment of their citizens. The snobbishness and elitism of golf clubs in some parts of the world have few echoes here. Admittedly, there are a few clubs that have always been noted for their exclusive air, and newer golf courses are emerging as part of exclusive leisure complexes, but these are exceptions to the long tradition of recreation for all. Golf here is usually a democratic game, played by ordinary folk as well as the wealthy. Indeed, signs saying NO GOLF can be seen on grassy areas around the public housing projects in parts of Edinburgh and Glasgow; some children prefer a golf club and ball even to a soccer ball.

Where to Play

Golf courses are everywhere in Scotland except for in the far northern Highlands and some islands. Most courses welcome visitors with a minimum of formalities, and some at surprisingly low cost. Off-season, a few clubs still use the "honesty box," into which you drop your fees.

Just three pieces of advice, particularly for North Americans: 1) In Scotland the game is usually played fairly quickly, so don't dawdle if others are waiting; 2) caddy carts are hand-pulled carts for your clubs; driven golf carts are rarely available; and 3) when they say "rough," they really mean "rough."

Unless specified otherwise below, course playing hours are generally 9 AM to sundown, which in June can be as late as 10 PM. Note that some courses advertise the *SSS,* "standard scratch score," or average score, instead of par. For more information about regional courses, *see* Sports & the Outdoors *in* individual chapters. For a complete list of courses, contact local tourist offices.

The Stewartry

At the very southern border, the Stewartry is a delightful part of Scotland set in the rich farmlands around Dumfries, a golfing vacation area since Victorian times. There are also several fine 9-hole courses in the area.

Powfoot. A pleasant mix of links and parkland holes (9 of each) and views south over the Solway Firth to distract you make this lesser-known British Championship course a pleasure to play. ✉ *Powfoot Golf Club, Cummertrees, Annan* ☎ *01461/700276* *18 holes, 6,266 yards, SSS 71* *£26 per round, £33 per day* ⏲ *Weekdays and Sun. after 1.*

From windswept links with sea views and salty breezes to interior parklands colored with heather and birch to upland courses with mountain views that well and truly lure your eye away from the ball, Scotland fulfills a golfer's every fantasy. The following tour takes in some of the country's most famous historic courses and some lesser-known but equally challenging courses, both private and municipal.

If you have
2 days

If you are based in Glasgow and have two days to play, head for Ayshire and the Clyde Coast. (If you are starting from Edinburgh, skip to the five-day itinerary below.) You can drive down or fly into Prestwick Airport, 30 mi southwest of the city. Either way, you find yourself in the middle of a seamless progression of golf links, many of which have been played for over 100 years. If your handicap is low and your budget high, head straight for a round at the Old Prestwick Golf Course. The first Open Championship was held here in 1860. If time, light, and limbs allow, you can test your skills in the afternoon amidst the hills at Royal Troon, just south of the town of Troon. Just note that the middle six holes lay claim to some of the most taxing golf terrain in the world.

Less crowded and less expensive but no less difficult is Prestwick St. Nicholas, a walking course with seaward vistas and a cunningly landscaped eighth that has a sunken green and water hazards. The municipal course at Lochgreen (near Troon) has a challenging fifth befitting its illustrious neighbor. Beginners should try Seafield, a parkland-and-links course with a driving range and practice putting greens. Fullarton, a short upland-links course with small practice greens, is good for beginners and anyone else who wants to hone his or her shorter-game skills. ⇨ Chapter 2

If you have
5 days

With five days, you can play in Ayrshire *and* in Edinburgh and East Lothian. From Ayrshire, travel to Edinburgh via the A70. Near to the city, look for signs to the western suburb of Barnton, home of the Royal Burgess Golfing Society, founded in 1735. Play an afternoon round on the club's present parkland course, then take a walk on the club's former course, Bruntsfield Links, south of the city center—don't confuse this public park with another course also called Bruntsfield Links, outside Crammond in the Barnton area. The municipally owned, beautifully laid-out courses at Braids are less-expensive alternatives for afternoon play.

The next day, travel out to East Lothian on the A198 to discover another roll call of famous courses: Muirfield, Gullane, Musselburgh, and Dunbar. All these, and a dozen more, are links courses, but with a different feel from the Ayrshire courses you played earlier. Muirfield is home to probably the world's oldest golf club, the Honourable Company of Edinburgh Golfers, founded in 1744. Fees are steep, visitor access very limited, and a handicap certificate required. You will find a round much easier to book, and less damaging to your pocket, at North Berwick, which has stunning views of Bass Rock, the skerries, and the Firth of Forth; at Gullane No. 2 and No. 3, the former more challenging, the latter cheaper and shorter; and at Dunbar, established in 1794. ⇨ Chapter 1

If you have 8 days

After five days of playing near Glasgow and Edinburgh, you'll be ready to take on St. Andrews. From Edinburgh, take the A90/M90 over the Forth Road Bridge and into Fife, then take the A91 to the town of St. Andrews, golf's spiritual heartland. Here you will find golf-wear specialty stores, hotel rooms with views over The Scores, the British Golf Museum, golf schools, and locally made golf balls—and you haven't even picked up a club yet. And yes, you may be able to play a round on the celebrated Old Course (if you have the proper handicap certificate and you have booked months ahead), but there are also four other 18-hole courses and a 9-hole course in the St. Andrews Links Trust, the organization that operates and maintains the six courses and their facilities. After a round or two at St. Andrews, spend a day at one of Fife's coastal links, such as Leven (14 mi south of St. Andrews) and another at one of the uncrowded inland gems, like Ladybank (18 mi west of St. Andrews). ⇨ Chapter 4

If you have 10 days

Haven't had enough golf yet? On your way back to Prestwick, you can fit in an extra day of golf at one of the world's most famous golf resorts, Gleneagles, off the A9, about 40 mi west of St. Andrews. The hotel has three 18-hole courses and one 9-hole course as well as facilities for horseback riding and a spa. If Gleneagles is beyond your skill level or budget, travel on down to Callander, about 22 mi southwest of Auchterarder. This attractive, bustling town is home to a hilly, truly delightful course with mountain views and a few tricks up its sleeve, slipped in by designer Tom Morris. Prestwick, your starting point, is a two-hour drive south and southwest. ⇨ Chapter 5

Southerness. Mackenzie Ross designed this course, the first built in Scotland after World War II, in 1947. Southerness is a long course, played over extensive links with fine views southward over the Solway Firth. The greens are hard and fast, and the frequent winds make for some testing golf. ✉ *Southerness Golf Club, Southerness* ☎ *01387/880677* ✍ *Reservations essential* 🏌 *18 holes, 6,566 yards, par 69* 🎫 *Weekdays £38 per day; weekends £48 per day* ⏲ *Daily.*

Ayrshire & the Clyde Coast

An hour south of Glasgow, Ayrshire and the Clyde Coast have been a holiday area for Glaswegians for generations. Few golfers need an introduction to the names of Turnberry, Royal Troon, Prestwick, or Western Gailes—all challenging links courses along this coast. There are at least 20 other courses in the area within an hour's drive.

Girvan. This is an old, established course with play along a narrow coastal strip and a more lush inland section next to the Water of Girvan—a river that constitutes a particular hazard at the 15th, unless you are a big hitter. The course is scenic, with good views of Ailsa Craig and the Clyde Estuary. ✉ *40 Golf Course Rd., Girvan* ☎ *01465/714346* 🏌 *18 holes, 4,590 yards, par 64* 🎫 *Weekdays £13 per round, £21 per day; weekends £16.50 per round, £29 per day* ⏲ *Daily.*

Prestwick. Tom Morris was involved in designing this challenging Ayrshire coastal links course, which saw the birth of the British Open Championship in 1860. Prestwick has excellent, fast rail links with Glasgow. ✉ *2 Links Rd., Prestwick* ☎ *01292/477404* 🏌 *18 holes, 6,544 yards, par 71* 🎫 *Weekdays £90 per round, £130 per day; Sun. £105 per round* ⏲ *Sun.–Fri.*

Royal Troon. Of the two courses at Royal Troon, it's the Old Course—a traditional links course with superb sea views—that is used for the British Open Championship. You can buy a day ticket for one round on each course, a good value, as the ticket includes an excellent lunch. ✉ *Craigend Rd., Troon* ☎ *01292/311555* *Old Course: 18 holes, 7,107 yards, SSS 74. Portland Course: 18 holes, 6,289, yards, SSS 70* *£170 per day (one round on each course), lunch included* *Mon., Tues., and Thurs.*

Turnberry. The Ailsa Course at Turnberry is perhaps the most famous links course in Scotland. Right on the seashore, the course is open to the elements, and the 9th hole requires you to hit the ball over the open sea. The British Open was staged here in 1977, 1986, and 1994. A second course, the Kintyre, is more compact than the Ailsa, with tricky sloped greens. Five of the holes have sea views, the rest are more inland. ✉ *Turnberry Hotel, Golf Courses and Spa, Turnberry* ☎ *01655/331000* *Ailsa Course: 18 holes, 6,976 yards, SSS 72. Kintyre Course: 18 holes, 6,853 yards, SSS 72* *Ailsa Course: weekdays £105 per round for hotel guests, £130 per round for nonguests; weekends £105 per round for hotel guests, £175 per round for nonguests. Kintyre Course: £90 per round for hotel guests, £105 per round for nonguests, weekdays and weekends* *Daily.*

★ **Western Gailes.** Known as the finest natural links course in Scotland, Western Gailes is entirely nature-made, and the greens are kept in truly magnificent condition. This is the final qualifying course when the British Open is held at Troon or Turnberry. Tom Watson lists the par-5 sixth as one of his favorite holes. ✉ *Gailes, Irvine* ☎ *01294/311357* *18 holes, 6,700 yards, par 71* *Mon., Wed., Fri. £90 per round, £125 per day (lunch included); Sun. afternoon £90 per round* *Mon., Wed., Fri., and Sun. afternoon.*

Glasgow

Most of Glasgow's old golf clubs have moved out to the suburbs—you can tee off from at least 30 different courses less than an hour from the city center. And remember: in addition to these, all the Ayrshire courses are just down the road.

Douglas Park. North of the city near Milngavie (pronounced mul-*gai*), Douglas Park is a long, attractive course set among birch and pine trees with masses of rhododendrons blooming in early summer. The Campsie Fells form a pleasant backdrop. ✉ *Hillfoot, Bearsden* ☎ *0141/942–0985* *18 holes, 5,962 yards, par 69* *£23 per round, £31 per day* *Wed. and Thurs., by appointment only.*

Gailes. The Glasgow Golf Club originally played on Glasgow Green in the heart of the ancient city center, but as the pressure for space grew, it moved north to the leafy suburb of Bearsden, on the road to Loch Lomond. Killermont, the club's home course, is not open to visitor's, but you can play the club's other course at Gailes, near Irvine on the Firth of Clyde. The Glasgow Club's Tennant Cup, in June, is the oldest open amateur tournament in the world. ✉ *Gailes, near Irvine* ☎ *0141/942–2011* *18 holes, 6,537 yards, SSS 72* *Weekdays £45 per round, £60 per day; weekends £58 per round* *Weekdays 9:30–4:30, weekends after 2:30.*

East Lothian

The sand dunes that stretch eastward from Edinburgh along the southern shore of the Firth of Forth made an ideal location for some of the world's earliest golf courses. Muirfield is perhaps the most famous course in the area, but around it are more than a dozen others. All are links courses, many with views to the islands of the Firth of Forth and northward to Fife. If you weary of the East Lothian courses, try one of the nearly 30 courses within the city of Edinburgh, just 20 mi or so to the west.

Dunbar. This ancient golfing site by the sea was founded in 1794 and has a lighthouse at the ninth hole. It's a good choice for a typical east-coast links course in a seaside town but within easy reach of Edinburgh. ✉ *East Links, Dunbar* ☎ *01368/862086* ✍ *Reservations essential* *18 holes, 6,404 yards, par 71* *Mon.–Wed. and Fri. £37 per round, £50 per day; weekends £45 per round, £60 per day* ⏲ *Fri.–Wed. after 9:30.*

Muirfield. The championship course at Muirfield is one of the best known links courses in the world, so be prepared to pay the price of fame with expensive greens fees and severe limitations on when you can play. But it may be worth the expense and hassle to be able to walk in the footsteps of some of the greatest names in golf. A handicap certificate is required (18 or less for men, 24 or less for women). ✉ *Muirfield, Gullane* ☎ *01620/842123* ✍ *Reservations essential* *18 holes, 6,601 yards, par 70* *£100 per round, £130 per day* ⏲ *Visitors Tues. and Thurs., tee off between 8:30 and 9:50.*

Edinburgh

Scotland's capital has nearly 30 golf courses within its boundaries. Most are parkland courses, though along the shores of the Firth of Forth they take on the characteristics of traditional links. Some are used by private clubs and offer visitors limited access; others that belong to the city are more accessible and have much lower fees.

Barnton, Royal Burgess Golfing Society. Dating to 1735, this is one of the world's oldest golf clubs. Its members originally played on Bruntsfield Links; now they and their guests play on elegantly manicured parkland in the city's northwestern suburbs. It's a long course with fine greens. ✉ *181 Whitehouse Rd., Barnton* ☎ *0131/339–2075* ✍ *Reservations essential* *18 holes, 6,111 yards, par 68* *£45 per round, £55 per day* ⏲ *Weekdays.*

Braids. Braids (no connection with James Braid) is beautifully laid out over a rugged range of small hills in the southern suburbs. The views to the south and the Pentland Hills and north toward the Edinburgh skyline are worth a visit in themselves. The city built this course at the turn of the 20th century after urban development forced golfers out of the city center. The 9-hole Princes Course was completed in 2003. Reservations are recommended for weekend play. ✉ *The Braids, Braids Hill Approach* ☎ *0131/447–6666* *Braids: 18 holes, 5,865 yards, par 70. Princes: 9 holes* *Braids: weekdays £14 per round, weekends £16 per round; Princes: weekdays £7 per round, weekends £8 per round* ⏲ *Daily.*

Bruntsfield Links. The British Seniors and several other championship games are held at this Willie Park–designed 1898 course 3 mi west of the city. The course meanders among 155 acres of mature parkland and has fine views over the Firth of Forth to Fife. Bruntsfield takes its name from one of the oldest golf links in Scotland, in the center of Edinburgh—now just a 9-hole pitch-and-putt course—where the club used to play. ✉ *32 Barnton Ave., Davidson's Mains* ☎ *0131/336–1479* ✍ *Reservations essential* *18 holes, 6,407 yards, par 71* *Weekdays £42 per round, £60 per day; weekends £47 per round, £65 per day* ⏲ *Daily.*

Fife

Few would dispute the claim of St. Andrews to be the home of golf, holding as it does the Royal & Ancient, the organization that governs the sport worldwide. Golf has been played here since the game's inception, and to play in Fife is for most golfers a cherished ambition. St. Andrews itself has several full 18-hole courses besides the famous 15th-century Old Course. Along the north shores of the Firth of Forth is a string of ancient villages, each with its harbor, ancient red-roof buildings, and golf course. In all, there are about 30 courses in the area.

Ladybank. Fife is known for its coastal courses, but this one is an interesting inland contrast: although Ladybank, designed by Tom Morris in 1876, is laid out on fairly level ground, the fir woods, birches, and heathery rough give it a Highland flavor among the gentle Lowland fields. Qualifying rounds of the British Open are played here when the main championship is played at St. Andrews. ✉ *Annsmuir, Ladybank* ☎ *01337/830814* ✍ *Reservations essential* ⛳ *18 holes, 6,601 yards, par 71* 🎫 *Apr.–Oct., weekdays £40 per round, £50 per day; weekends £45 per round. Nov.–Mar., daily £12.50 per round* ⏲ *Daily.*

Leven. A fine Fife course used as a British Open qualifier, this one, a links course, feels like the more famous St. Andrews, with hummocky terrain and a tang of salt in the air. The 1st and 18th share the same fairway, and the 18th green has a creek running by it. ✉ *The Promenade, Leven* ☎ *01333/428859* ✍ *Reservations essential* ⛳ *18 holes, 6,427 yards, par 71* 🎫 *Weekdays £30 per round, £40 per day; Sun. £35 per round, £50 per day* ⏲ *Sun.–Fri.*

Perthshire

Perthshire has several attractive country courses developed specifically for visiting golfers. Gleneagles Hotel is, with its outstanding facilities, the most famous of these golf resorts. But several courses in the area, set on the edges of beautiful Highland scenery, will delight any golfer.

Callander. Callander was designed by Tom Morris in 1913 and has a scenic upland feel in a town well prepared for visitors. Pine and birch woods and hilly fairways afford fine views, especially toward Ben Ledi, and the tricky moorland layout demands accurate hitting off the tee. ✉ *Callander Golf Club, Aveland Rd., Callander* ☎ *01877/330090* ⛳ *18 holes, 4,410 yards, par 63* 🎫 *Weekdays £18 per round, £26 per day; weekends £26 per round, £31 per day* ⏲ *Daily.*

Killin. A scenic course, Killin is typically Highland, with a roaring river, woodland birdsong, and a backdrop of high green hills. There are a few surprises, including two blind shots to reach the green at the fourth. The attractive village of Killin has an almost alpine feel, especially in spring, when the hilltops may still be white. ✉ *Killin Golf Club, Aberfeldy Rd., Killin* ☎ *01567/820312* ⛳ *9 holes, 2,508 yards, par 65* 🎫 *£12 per round, £15 per day* ⏲ *Apr.–Oct., daily.*

★ **Rosemount, Blairgowrie Golf Club.** Well known to native golfers looking for a challenge, Rosemount's 18 (James Braid, 1934) are laid out on rolling land in the pine, birch, and fir woods, which bring a wild air to the scene. You may encounter a browsing roe deer if you stray too far. There are, however, wide fairways and at least some large greens. The club is open daily, but visitor play may be restricted depending on tournament and match schedules. If you can't manage a game on Rosemount itself, you can play on Lansdowne, another 18-hole course, or Wee, a 9-hole course. A handicap certificate is required to play here. ✉ *Golf Course Rd., Blairgowrie* ☎ *01250/873116* ⛳ *Rosemount: 18 holes, 6,590 yards, par 72. Lansdowne: 18 holes, 6,802 yards, par 72. Wee: 9 holes, 2,352 yards, par 32* 🎫 *Rosemount: £55 per round; Lansdowne: £40 per round, Wee: £20 per round. £75 per day (includes 1 round on Rose-*

mount and 1 on Lansdowne), £60 per day (includes 1 round on Lansdowne and 1 on Wee) ⏲ Daily.

Angus

East of Perthshire, north of the city of Dundee, lies a string of demanding courses along the shores of the North Sea and inland into the foothills of the Grampian Mountains. The most famous course in Angus is probably Carnoustie, one of several British Open Championship venues in Scotland. Golfers who excel in windy conditions particularly enjoy the sea breezes blowing eastward from the sea. Inland Edzell, Forfar, Brechin, and Kirriemuir all have courses nestling in the Strathmore farmlands.

Carnoustie. The venue for the British Open Championship in 1999, the extensive coastal links around Carnoustie have been played since at least 1527. Open winners here have included Armour, Hogan, Cotton, Player, and Watson. Carnoustie was also once a training ground for coaches, many of whom went to the United States. The choice municipal course here is full of historical snippets and local color, as well as being tough and interesting. ✉ *Links Parade, Carnoustie* ☎ *01241/853789* ✍ *Reservations essential* 🏌 *18 holes, 6,941 yards, par 75* 🎫 *May–Oct., £82 per round; Nov.–Apr., £41 per round* ⏲ *Weekdays 9–3:50, Sat. after 2, Sun. after 12:30.*

Aberdeenshire

Aberdeen, Scotland's third-largest city, is known for its sparkling granite buildings and amazing displays of roses each summer. Within the city, there are six courses, and to the north, as far as Fraserburgh and Peterhead, there are five others, including the popular Cruden Bay.

Balgownie, Royal Aberdeen Golf Club. This old club, founded in 1780, is the archetypal Scottish links course: long and testing over uneven ground, with the frequently added hazard of a sea breeze. Prickly gorse is inclined to close in and form an additional hurdle. The two courses are tucked behind the rough, grassy sand dunes, and there are surprisingly few views of the sea. One historical note: in 1783 this club originated the five-minute-search rule for a lost ball. A handicap certificate (the limit is 24) or letter of introduction is required. ✉ *Links Rd., Bridge of Don, Aberdeen* ☎ *01224/702571* ✍ *Reservations essential* 🏌 *Balgownie: 18 holes, 6,415 yards, par 70. Silverburn: 18 holes, 4,021 yards, SSS 61* 🎫 *Balgownie: weekdays £65 per round, £90 per day; weekends £75 per round, £120 per day. Silverburn: weekdays £32.50 per round, weekends £37.50 per round (no day rate)* ⏲ *Balgownie: tee off weekdays 10–11:30 and 2–3:30; weekends after 3:30. Silverburn: daily.*

Ballater. The mountains of Royal Deeside surround this course laid out along the sandy flats of the River Dee. Ideal for a relaxing round of golf, the course makes maximum use of the fine setting between river and woods. The club, originally opened in 1906, has a holiday atmosphere, and the shops and pleasant walks in nearby Ballater make this a good place for nongolfing partners. Reservations are advised. ✉ *Victoria Rd., Ballater* ☎ *013397/55567* 🏌 *18 holes, 6,112 yards, par 70* 🎫 *Weekdays £21 per round, £30 per day; weekends £25 per round, £35 per day* ⏲ *Daily.*

Cruden Bay. An east-coast Lowland course sheltered behind extensive sand hills, Cruden Bay offers a typical Scottish golf experience. Runnels and valleys, among other hazards, on the challenging fairways ensure plenty of excitement, and some of the holes are rated among the country's finest. Like Gleneagles and Turnberry, this course owes its origins to an association with the grand railway hotels that were built in

THE EVOLUTION OF "GOWF"

THE MATTER OF WHO INVENTED GOLF *has been long debated, but there's no doubt that its development into one of the most popular games in the world stems from Scotland.*

The first written reference to golf, variously spelled as "gowf" or "goff," was as long ago as 1457, when James II (1430–60) of Scotland declared that both golf and football (soccer) should be "utterly cryit doune and nocht usit" (publicly criticized and prohibited) because they were distracting his subjects from their archery practice. Mary, Queen of Scots (1542–87), it seems, was fond of golf. When in Edinburgh in 1567, she played on Leith Links and on Bruntsfield Links. When in Fife, she played at Falkland and at St. Andrews itself. Golf must surely rank as one of Scotland's earliest cultural exports. In 1603, when James VI (1566–1625) of Scotland also became James I of England, he moved his court to London. With him went his golf-loving friends, and they set up a course on Blackheath Common, then on the outskirts of London.

Golf clubs (i.e., organizations) first arose in the middle of the 18th century. Written evidence attests to the founding of the Honourable Company of Edinburgh Golfers, now residing at Muirfield, in 1744, and to the Royal & Ancient at St. Andrews, which began in 1754. From then on, clubs sprang up all over Scotland: Royal Aberdeen (1780), Crail Golfing Society (1786), Dunbar (1794), and the Royal Perth Golfing Society (1824). By the early 19th century, clubs had been set up in England, and the game was being carried all over the world by enthusiastic Scots. These golf missionaries spread their knowledge not only of the sport, but also of the courses. Large parts of the Scottish coast are natural golf courses; indeed, the origins of bunkers and the word links *(courses) are found in the sand dunes of Scotland's shores. In countries where such natural terrain didn't exist, courses had to be designed and created. Willie Park of Musselburgh (who laid out Sunningdale), James Braid, and C. K. Hutchison (whose crowning glory is at Gleneagles Hotel) are some of the best known of Scotland's golf-course architects.*

Many of the important changes in the design and construction of balls and clubs were pioneered by the players who lived and worked around the town courses and who made the balls and clubs themselves. The original balls, called featheries, *were leather bags stuffed with boiled feathers. Often they lasted only one round. When, in 1848, the gutta-percha ball, called a* guttie, *was introduced, there was considerable friction, particularly in St. Andrews, between the makers of the two rival types of ball. The gutta-percha proved superior and was in general use until the invention of the rubber-core ball in 1901. Clubs were traditionally made of wood: shafts were of ash, later hickory, and heads were of thorn or some other hardwood such as apple or pear. Heads were spliced, then bound to the shaft with twine. Players generally managed with far fewer clubs than today. About 1628 the marquis of Montrose, a golf enthusiast, had a set of clubs made for him in St. Andrews that illustrates the range of clubs used in Stuart times: "Bonker clubis, a irone club, and twa play clubs."*

Caddies—the word comes from the French cadet *(young boy) and was used to refer to anyone who ran messages—carried the players' clubs around, usually under the arm. Golf carts didn't come into fashion in Britain until the 1950s, and some people still considered them to be potentially injurious to the national health and moral fiber.*

The technology of golf may change, but its addictive qualities are timeless. Toward the end of the 18th century, an Edinburgh golfer named Alexander McKellar regularly played golf all day and refused to stop even when it grew dark. One night his wife carried his dinner and nightcap onto Bruntsfield Links, where he was playing, in an attempt to shame him into changing his ways. She failed.

And the addiction continues.

the heyday of steam. Unlike the other two, however, Cruden Bay's railway hotel and the railway itself have gone, but the course remains in fine shape. ✉ *Aulton Rd., Cruden Bay, Peterhead* ☎ *01779/812285* ✍ *Reservations essential* 🏌 *18 holes, 6,395 yards, par 70* 🎫 *Weekdays £55 per round, £75 per day; weekends £65 per round* ⏲ *Daily.*

Speyside

On the main A9 road an hour south of Inverness amid the Cairngorm Mountains, the valley of the River Spey is one of Scotland's most attractive all-year sports centers, with winter skiing and fine golf the rest of the year. The area's main courses are Newtonmore, Grantown-on-Spey, and Boat of Garten, all fine inland courses with wonderful views of the surrounding mountains and challenging golf provided by the springy turf and the heather.

Boat of Garten. This is possibly one of Scotland's greatest "undiscovered" courses. Boat of Garten, which dates to the late 19th century, was redesigned and extended by famous golf architect James Braid in 1932, and each of its 18 holes is individual: some cut through birch wood and heathery rough; most have long views to the Cairngorms and a strong Highland air. An unusual feature is the preserved steam railway that runs along part of the course. The occasional puffing locomotive can hardly be considered a hazard. ✉ *Boat of Garten village center* ☎ *01479/831282* ✍ *Reservations essential* 🏌 *18 holes, 5,967, yards, par 70* 🎫 *Weekdays £28 per round, £33 per day; weekends £33 per round, £38 per day* ⏲ *Daily.*

Moray Coast

No one can say that the Lowlands have a monopoly on Scotland's fine seaside golf courses. The Moray Coast, stretching eastward from Inverness, has some spectacular sand dunes that have been adapted to create stimulating and exciting links courses. The two courses at Nairn have long been known to golfers both famous and unknown. Charlie Chaplin regularly played here. But in addition there are a dozen courses looking out over the sea from Inverness as far along as Banff, Macduff, and Fraserburgh and several inland amid the fertile Moray farmland.

Banff, Duff House Royal Golf Club. Just moments away from the sea, this club combines a coastal course with a parkland setting. It lies only minutes from Banff center, within the parkland grounds of Duff House, a country-house art gallery in a William Adam–designed mansion. The club has inherited the ancient traditions of seaside play (golf records here go back to the 17th century). Mature trees and gentle slopes create a pleasant playing environment. ✉ *The Barnyards, Banff* ☎ *01261/812075* ✍ *Reservations essential* 🏌 *18 holes, 6,161 yards, par 70* 🎫 *Weekdays £20 per round, £26 per day; weekends £27 per round, £32 per day. Fees halved Nov.–Mar.* ⏲ *Daily.*

Fraserburgh. This northeast fishing town has extensive links and dunes that seem to have grown up around the course rather than the other way around. Be prepared for a hill climb and a tough finish. You can warm up on the extra 9 holes. ✉ *Philorth, Fraserburgh, at the eastern end of town* ☎ *01346/518287* 🏌 *18 holes, 6,200 yards, par 70* 🎫 *Weekdays £19 per round, £22 per day; weekends £25 per round, £30 per day* ⏲ *Daily.*

Lossiemouth, Moray Golf Club. Discover the mild airs of what's called the Moray Riviera, as Tom Morris did in 1889 when he was inspired by the lay of the natural links. There are two courses plus a 6-hole minicourse. There's lots of atmosphere here, with golfing memorabilia in the clubhouse, as well as the tale of the pre–World War I British prime minister

Asquith, who took a vacation in this out-of-the-way spot yet still managed to be attacked by a crowd of suffragettes at the 17th. All other hazards on these testing courses are entirely natural, with the 18th hole providing a memorable finish. ✉ *Stotfield Rd., Lossiemouth* ☎ *01343/813330* *Old Course: 18 holes, 6,617 yards, par 71. New Course: 18 holes, 6,004 yards, par 69* *Old Course: weekdays £40 per round, £55 per day; weekends £50 per round, £70 per day. New Course: weekdays £30 per round, £40 per day; weekends £35 per round, £45 per day. Joint ticket (1 round on each course) £50 weekdays, £60 weekends* *Daily.*

Fodor's Choice ★ **Nairn.** Well regarded in golfing circles, Nairn dates from 1887 and is the regular home of Scotland's Northern Open. Huge greens, aggressive gorse, a beach hazard for five of the holes, a steady prevailing wind, and distracting views across the Moray Firth to the northern hills make play here unforgettable. ✉ *Seabank Rd., Nairn* ☎ *01667/453208* *Reservations essential* *18 holes, 6,705 yards, par 72* *£70 per round* *Daily.*

Dornoch Firth

The east coast north of Inverness is deeply indented with firths (the word is linked to the Norwegian *fjord*) that border some excellent, relatively unknown golf courses. Knowledgeable golfers have been making the northern pilgrimage to these courses for well over 100 years. There are half a dozen enjoyable links courses around Dornoch and Strathpeffer, an inland Victorian golfing holiday center.

Fodor's Choice ★ **Royal Dornoch.** This course, laid out by Tom Morris in 1886 on a sort of coastal shelf behind the shore, has matured to become one of the world's finest. Its location in the north of Scotland, though less than an hour's drive from Inverness Airport, means it's far from overrun even in peak season. It may not have the fame of a Gleneagles or a St. Andrews, but Royal Dornoch is memorable. The little town of Dornoch, behind the course, is sleepy and timeless. A handicap certificate is required. The limits are 24 for men, 39 for women. ✉ *Golf Rd., Dornoch* ☎ *01862/810219* *Reservations essential* *18 holes, 6,514 yards, par 70* *Weekdays £66 per round; weekends £76 per round* *Daily.*

Argyll

The lochs and glens of Argyll in the west of Scotland have provided the scenic backdrop for family outings for generations. Wherever Scots take their holidays, golf courses are soon developed, so the string of courses north from the Mull of Kintyre all offer golf in a relaxed environment, with sea, beach, and hills not far away.

Machrihanish, by Campbeltown. Many enthusiasts discuss this course in hushed tones—it's a kind of out-of-the-way golfers' Shangri-la. It was laid out in 1876 by Tom Morris on the links around the sandy Machrihanish Bay. The drive off the first tee is across the beach to reach the green—an intimidating start to a memorable series of individual holes. If you're short on time, consider flying from Glasgow to nearby Campbeltown, the last town on the long peninsula of Kintyre. ✉ *Machrihanish, near Campbeltown* ☎ *01586/810277* *Reservations essential* *18 holes, 6,225 yards, par 70* *Weekdays and Sun. £30 per round, £50 per day; Sat. £40 per round, £60 per day* *Daily.*

UNDERSTANDING SCOTLAND

BEYOND THE TARTAN PLAID

ON SOME OLD RECORDINGS OF Scottish songs still in circulation, you may run across "Roamin' in the Gloamin' " or "I Love a Lassie" or one of the other comic ditties of Harry Lauder, a star of the music halls of the 1920s. With his garish kilt, short crooked walking stick, rich rolling *R*s, and *pawky* (cheerfully impudent) humor—chiefly based on the alleged meanness of the Scots—he impressed a Scottish character on the world. But his was, needless to say, a false impression and one the Scots have been trying to stamp out ever since.

How, then, do you characterize the Scots? Temperamentally, they're a mass of contradictions. They've been likened to a soft-boiled egg: a dour, hard shell, a mushy middle. Historically, fortitude and resilience have been their hallmarks, and in their makeup there are streaks of both resignation and ferocity warring with sentimentality and love of family. Very Scottish was the instant reaction of an elderly woman of Edinburgh 200 years ago, when news arrived of the defeat in Mysore, India, and of the Scottish soldiers being fettered in irons two by two: "God help the puir chiel that's chained tae oor Davie."

The Scots are in general suspicious of the go-getter, respecting success only when it has been a few hundred years in the making. But they're by no means plodders. This is the nation that built commerce throughout the British Empire, opened wild territories, and was responsible for much of humankind's scientific and technological advancement; a nation boastful about things it's not too good at and shamefacedly modest about genuine achievements. Consider the following extract from a handout about the Edinburgh School of Medicine: "If one excepts a few discoveries such as that of 'fixed air' by Black, of the diverse functions of the nerve-roots by Bell, of the anaesthetic properties of chloroform by Simpson, of the invention of certain powerful drugs by Christison, and of the importance of antiseptic procedures by Lister, the influence of Edinburgh medicine has been of a steady constructive rather than a revolutionary type."

Among things that strike most newcomers to Scotland are the generosity of the Scots; their obsession with respectability; their satisfaction with themselves and their desire to stay as they are; and, above all, their passionate love of Scotland. An obstinate refusal to go along with English ideas has led to accusations that the nation has a head-in-the-sand attitude toward progress. But the Scots have their own ideas of progress, and they jealously guard the institutions that remain unique to them. The return of a parliament to Scottish soil, albeit one with limited powers, has generated a surge of pride in national identity; the parliament is due to move into its own specially built premises at the foot of the Royal Mile in late 2004.

When it comes to education, Scotland has a proud record. The nation had four universities—St. Andrews, Aberdeen, Glasgow, and Edinburgh—when England had only two: Oxford and Cambridge. A phenomenon of Scottish social history is the *lad o' pairts* (lad from the countryside)—the poor child of a feckless father and a fiercely self-sacrificing mother, sternly tutored by the village *dominie* (schoolmaster) and turned loose at the age of 13 with so firm a base of learning that he rose to the top of his profession. The sacrifices that boys made as a matter of course to further their education are an old Scottish tradition. "Meal Monday," the midsemester holiday at a Scottish university, is a survivor of the long weekend that once enabled students to return to their distant homes—on foot—and replenish the sack of "meal" (oatmeal) that was their only sustenance.

Just as the Scots have their own traditions in education, so is their legal system distinct from England's. In England the police both investigate crime and prosecute suspects. In Scotland there's a public prosecutor directly responsible to the lord advocate (equivalent to England's attorney general), who is in turn accountable to parliament. For the most part, however, you'll notice few practical differences, except in terminology. The barrister in England becomes an advocate in Scotland. Law-office nameplates designate their occupants "s. s. c." (solicitor to the Supreme Court) or "w. s." (writer to the signet); cases for prosecution go before the "procurator fiscal" and are tried by the "sheriff" or "sheriff-substitute." The terms are different in England, and procedures are slightly different, too, for Scotland is one of the few countries that still bases its legal system on old Roman law. Crimes with picturesque names from ancient times remain on the statute book: *hamesucken,* for example, means assaulting a person in his home. In criminal cases Scotland adds to "guilty" and "not guilty" a third verdict: "not proven." This, say the cynics, signifies "We know you did it—but not enough evidence has been presented to prove it."

The Presbyterian Church of Scotland—the Kirk—is entirely independent of the Church of England. Until the 20th century it was a power in the land and did much to shape Scottish character. There are still those who can remember when the minister visited houses like an inquisitor and put members of the families through their catechism, punishing or reprimanding those who weren't word perfect. On Sunday morning the elders patrolled the streets, ordering people into church and rebuking those who sat at home in their gardens.

Religion in Scotland, as elsewhere, has lost much of its grip. But the Kirk remains influential in rural districts, where Kirk officials are pillars of local society. Ministers and their spouses are seen in all their somber glory in Edinburgh in springtime, when the General Assembly of the Kirk takes place, and for a week or more Scottish newspapers devote several column inches daily to the deliberations. The Episcopal Church of Scotland has bishops, as its name implies (unlike the Kirk, where the ministers are all equal), and a more colorful ritual. Considered genteel, Episcopalianism in Scotland has been described rather sourly by the Scottish novelist Lewis Grassie Gibbon as "more a matter of social status than theological conviction . . . a grateful bourgeois acknowledgment of anglicisation."

Of the various nonconformist offshoots of the established Kirk, the Free Kirk of Scotland is the largest. It remains faithful to the monolithic unity of its forefathers, adhering to the grim discipline that John Knox promoted long ago. The Free Kirk is strong in parts of the Outer Hebrides—Lewis, Harris, and North Uist. On Sunday in these areas no buses run, and all the shops are shut. Among the fishing communities, especially those of the northeast from Buckie to Peterhead, evangelical movements, such as the Close Brethren and Jehovah's Witnesses, have made impressive inroads.

Finally, a word is needed on the vexed subject of nomenclature. A "scotchman" is not a native of Scotland but a nautical device for "scotching," or clamping, a running rope. Though you may find that some of those who are more conservative refer to themselves as Scotchmen and consider themselves Scotch, most prefer Scot or Scotsman and call themselves Scottish or Scots. You may include the Scots in the broader term *British,* but they dislike the word *Brits,* and nothing infuriates them more than being called English. Nonetheless, there are a lot of Anglo-Scots, that is, people of Scottish birth who live in England or are the offspring of marriages between Scottish and English people. The term Anglo-Scots is not to be confused with Sassenachs, the Gaelic word for "Saxon," which is applied facetiously or disdainfully to all the English. But at the same time, English people who live in Scotland remain English to their dying day, and their children after them. Similarly, the designation of "North Britain" for Scotland, which was used after the Jacobite Uprising of 1745, has now gone. It survives only in the names of a few "North British" hotels. Scots feel it denies their national identity, and there are some who, on receiving a letter with "N. B." or "North Britain" in the address, will cross it out and return the envelope to the sender.

ROBERT BURNS, SCOTLAND'S ETERNAL LAUREATE

YOU WILL ENCOUNTER ROBERT BURNS everywhere in Scotland. His rakish dark eyes and bold features peer skeptically from portraits, monuments, and even biscuit tins; phrases from his poems pop up in advertising jingles and newspaper headlines and in the names of tea shops and bed-and-breakfasts.

He was born in the Kyle district of Ayrshire and the whole of Southwest Scotland is covered with places that claim an association with the great man: not just his homes—and there are plenty, since he was constantly on the move—but pubs where he drank, landscapes he praised, and graveyards where his lovers, his family, and his enemies are buried.

Burns has been called the "ploughman poet" and the "heaven-taught poet" as if he were some sort of simple peasant who was miraculously touched by genius. It's untrue, of course, because Burns, for his time, was a well-educated man, who knew his history and philosophy, could read music, and speak passable French. In fact, he may have been better educated than some of the aristocracy who lionized him when he visited Edinburgh. Burns was born into the family of a tenant farmer who, while nowhere near rich, employed servants and farmhands. And, while modern-day Burns Suppers come replete with kilts, tartan, and all the other accoutrements now associated with Scotland, Burns never, in his whole life, wore a kilt, or indeed, ever considered doing so. He was a Lowlander, and the kilt at that time was an exclusively Highland garment.

Ayrshire and Dumfriesshire are officially Burns country, from the thatched cottage in Alloway, near Ayr, where Burns was born in 1759, to Dumfries, where he was buried in St. Michael's churchyard in 1796 on the same day his youngest son was born. Tarbolton was the village where young Burns and his friends founded the Bachelor's Club, a debating society where the great issues of the day were discussed and dissected. After his father died he moved to Mauchline, where he fell in love with Margaret "Mary" Campbell, a dairy maid at the nearby mansion of Coilsfield (Burns's "Montgomery"). Campbell was the subject of some of Burns's finest love lyrics ("Ye banks and braes and streams around / The castle o' Montgomery! / Green be your woods, and fair your flowers, / Your waters never drumlie. / There Simmer first unfald her robes, / And there the langest tarry; / For there I took the last fareweel / O' my sweet Highland Mary"). The couple planned to emigrate to Jamaica together, but Mary took ill and died while preparations were still being made.

It was at Mossgiel Farm (not open to the public), that Burns ploughed the "Wee, sleekit, cowrin, tim'rous beastie" eulogized in "To a Mouse." Mauchline was where Burns and Jean Armour, the only true and constant love of his life, married and had their first home together. Its churchyard contains the graves of some of their children, Burns's friends, and his enemies, such as Willam Fisher, the Holy Willie of "Holy Willie's Prayer." Kilmarnock was where Burns's first book of poetry, *Poems Chiefly in the Scottish Dialect,* was printed in 1786. Ayr, Irvine, Kirkoswald, and many other Ayrshire towns also have some kind of connection to Burns, often of a purely imaginative provenance.

Even the Highlands claim Burns associations: "Wherever I wander, wherever I rove/The hills of the Highlands forever I love." Burns traveled there in 1787, following what was probably a fairly typical tourist's itinerary. He began in Stirling, where he visited the battlefield of Bannockburn, then he rode to Inverness, with side trips to Culloden Moor and to Cawdor. From there he went east along the Moray Firth, down to Peterhead, and along the coast to Aberdeen, Dundee, and Perth, where he took side trips to Scone Palace and Ossian's grave at Crieff. Burns also toured the Borders, crossing over into England at Coldstream.

Traveling through Scotland, you get the impression that Robert Burns is as important a poet as Shakespeare, Milton, or Keats or any of those English scribblers. Keats, in fact, was inspired by Burns's writing and even made a pilgrimage to Alloway to see where his hero was born.

Burns didn't just spring out of nowhere, of course. He was one of the many fruits of the Scottish Enlightenment, that glorious era of the 18th century when Scotland, seeking its own identity after being swallowed up in a political union with England, suddenly produced an astonishing crop of scientists, philosophers, and writers. Scotland's literary history up to that point boasted only the 15th century's so-called Scottish Chaucerians—William Dunbar and Robert Henryson—and Gavin Douglas, who translated the *Aeneid* into Scots (the dialect of the Lowlands) in 1513. The earliest lights of the 18th-century Scottish literary renaissance had to prove themselves by writing in English and hobnobbing in London, as did Edinburgh-born James Thomson, who published the first book of the immensely popular poem *The Seasons* in 1726, and James Boswell, whose *Journal of a Tour of the Hebrides,* documenting his travels with the sage Samuel Johnson, appeared in 1785. In midcentury two somewhat more homegrown talents, Allan Ramsay and Robert Fergusson, brought forth poetry written in a literary mixture of Scots and English. Meanwhile, Inverness-shire's James Macpherson published several volumes of Gaelic epic poems supposedly written by Ossian, the son of the ancient Scottish hero, Fingal, which Macpherson said he had simply translated into modern English. This turned into a scandal, however, when Macpherson, encouraged by his success, kept "discovering" more lost poems—whose authentic manuscripts he couldn't produce.

Although this hoax tarnished Scotland's reputation in London, Edinburgh was still a flourishing cultural capital in 1786, when the first edition of Robert Burns's poetry appeared. Intellectuals and wealthy patrons of the arts in Edinburgh were quick to seize upon this Ayrshire farmer's son, praising his portraits of rural Scotland and extolling the vigor and grace of his use of Scots dialect. To boot, Burns came equipped with good looks, a way with the ladies, dangerously radical political views, and a taste for hard liquor. Though not conventionally handsome, with his stocky build, thick features, and thin, dark hair, he managed to cut quite a figure at fashionable Edinburgh soirees between 1786 and 1788, after the phenomenal success of his first volume. Perhaps it helped that everyone, expecting to meet a clownish Ayrshire farmer with clods of mud still sticking to his boots, found instead a literate, intelligent fellow in genteel dark jacket, light-color waistcoat, and modestly ruffled lined shirt.

Yet while Edinburgh's elite pursued this new prodigy, Burns himself seemed uncomfortable with all the lionizing, asserting himself with forthright honesty that all too often bordered on rudeness. It was while he was in Edinburgh that Burns wrote one of his most famous poems, "To a Haggis." An earthy work, full of alliteration and working-class language, it was written not only to praise one of the staple fares of Scotland's peasantry, but also to satirize the habits of the Scottish aristocracy, who at the time was becoming further influenced by English and French habits, food, and speech. Haggis, a dish made from sheep's stomach, lamb's liver, oatmeal, and spices, traditionally is served on Burns Night. Burns himself became increasingly restless as his stay in Edinburgh dragged on (and his debts piled up and his love affairs grew more entangled). One senses in his letters a note of relief upon his return to Ayrshire and to the uncertain prospect of life as a farmer—and after the failure of his crops, as an excise collector in Dumfriesshire. Centuries later these are the images that live on: Burns riding about the countryside, singing to himself as he molded random bits of song into polished poems, or hunkering down with a congenial group of local wits at a country pub.

Neither of Scotland's other two great literary figures, Sir Walter Scott (1771–1832) or Robert Louis Stevenson (1850–94), have remained as firmly lodged in the hearts of their compatriots as Burns has. Scott, who celebrated Scotland in both poetry (*The Lady of the Last Minstrel, Marmion,* and *The Lady of the Lake*) and novels (*Ivanhoe, The Heart of Midlothian,* and *Waverly*), was enormously popular throughout the 19th cenury, and his career was longer and his output greater than Burns's. Stevenson, although born in Edinburgh, was never associated as closely with Scotland as Burns and Scott were, since frail health and a roaming spirit conspired to make him live abroad from the age of 23. Except for a handful of Scottish historical novels—*The Master of Ballantrae, Kidnapped,* and *Weir of Hermiston*—Stevenson's best known works (The *Strange Case of Dr. Jekyll and Mr. Hyde* and *Treasure Island*) are not even set in Scotland.

Robert Burns has never really faded from the general public's literary consciousness. Just about every song we associate with Scotland turns out to have lyrics by Burns: "My Love Is Like a Red, Red Rose," "Auld Lang Syne," "Flow Gently, Sweet Afton," "Green Grow the Rushes," "My Heart's in the Highlands," "Ye Banks and Braes." *Bartlett's Quotations* devotes several pages to Burns, listing such well-known phrases as "the best-laid schemes of mice and men," "man's inhumanity to man," "death's untimely frost," "a man's a man for all that," "nursing her wrath to keep it warm," and "nae man can tether time or tide."

The main barrier for modern readers may be the unfamiliar Scots dialect in Burns's poems. But if you read the verses out loud—the best way to enjoy those lilting stanzas anyway—many of the oddly spelled Scots words are perfectly easy to understand. After all, Burns was not writing in some kind of primitive, substandard rural slang. He was following a very specific literary style, following the precedent of Allan Ramsay and Robert Fergusson. Despite his rural upbringing Burns had enough education to write perfectly standard (and in some cases, extremely elegant) English, as shown by all his personal correspondence and a good number of his poems (though, tellingly, these are usually not his most successful verses). Burns himself, teetering precariously between social classes, probably shifted in conversation from correct English, which he would have spoken at dinner parties thrown by his wealthy Edinburgh patrons, to broad Scots dialect, which he would have used when he took his farm produce to market or set about wooing local peasant girls. (Scots was the everyday speech of Lowland Scotland, as opposed to the Highlands' Gaelic, which is a separate language with few connections to English). In his poems Burns inserted dialect where any good poet uses his or her most unusual vocabulary—as intensifying adjectives, line endings, and rhymes. The result is an extraordinarily effective poetic language, with a wide range of emotion and humor.

There are other reasons, apart from the quality of his verse, why Robert Burns has become enshrined as Scotland's national bard and why his birthday, January 25, is still celebrated with formal dinners (called Burns Suppers) around the globe. People who knew him wrote invariably of his personal magnetism—his dark, flashing eyes; his lively wit; his zest for living—and what has survived of his correspondence suggests he must have been one of those people you can't help liking. He also embodies something very near and dear to the Scottish national character: he had a common touch. He felt at home with the ordinary village life; loved bawdiness and roistering; and was deeply suspicious of authority, especially as it was invested in the Scottish kirk of the time, with all its dour piety. Instinctively, he was a hardy partisan of individual liberty, though his political convictions were inconsistent: he lauded the French Revolution and at the same time nursed a sentimental fondness for Scottish royalty, especially the romantic figure of Charles Edward Stuart. Burns was as capable a writer of achingly romantic love poetry as he was of bawdy verses about lust. And although poems such as "The Cotter's Saturday Night" mawkishly extol the virtues of humble poverty, Burns laments how hard it is to eke out a living in the poignant last stanza of "To A Mouse": "Still thou are blest, compar'd wi' me; / The present only toucheth thee, / But och! I backward cast me e'e, / On prospects drear! / An' forward, tho' I canna see, / I guess an' fear!"

There's no question that Burns enjoyed carousing—after all, this is the man who wrote, in "Scotch Drink": "O Whisky! soul o' plays and pranks! / Accept a bardie's gratefu' thanks! / When wanting thee, what tuneless cranks / Are my poor verses!" But he was probably only a social drinker; Burns's death was most likely a result of bacterial endocarditis brought on by rheumatic fever. He worsened his condition by seeking a cure at the Brow Well on the Solway Firth, where he immersed himself in cold, saline water. Within three weeks he was dead. Never really robust, he had been subject to periods of weakness ever since he was a teenager working long, hard days on his father's farm.

Another indelible part of the Burns myth is the image of him as a great womanizer; seducing well-born ladies, making peasant girls swoon, and scattering bastard bairns around the countryside. It's true that his first children with Jean Armour were born out of wedlock, and one of his finest poems is written to the child he fathered with Elizabeth Paton ("Welcome! my bonie, sweet, wee dochter, / Tho' ye come here a wee unsought for; / And tho' your comin' I hae fought for, / Baith kirk and queir; / Yet, by my faith, ye're no unwrought for; / Thast I shall swear!"). But Burns was no mere rake—his writing shows that he was usually romantically in love with whichever woman he was chasing, and he remained a loyal (if not entirely faithful) husband to Jean. She herself seemed resigned to his ardent nature, saying philosophically, "Our Robbie should ha' had twa wives."

By Holly Hughes.

Revised by James Gracie.

BOOKS & MOVIES

Books

Scotland has always had a love and respect for books and learning, for poetry and song. From the poems of Robert Burns, which reflect his Ayrshire roots, to the "bothy ballads" of the northeast, with which the farmhands entertained each other after a hard day's work, from Sir Walter Scott's Borders sagas to Mairi Hedderwick's Katie Morag children's stories set in the Western Isles—all share the strong visual thread of their own Scottish landscapes. Whether written 200 or 2 years ago, these books and poems have much to tell visitors about the character of Scotland's hugely varied countryside and of the resilient, soft-hearted, yet sometimes dour Scottish people. Wherever you intend to travel in Scotland, there are books to read to set the scene beforehand.

Edinburgh has inspired many writers. Muriel Spark's *The Prime of Miss Jean Brodie* was written in 1961 yet still has much to say about the importance of the city's private schools to the financial success and social life of Edinburgh's prim middle classes. Even today, attending one of the "right" schools oils the wheels in business. Children's author Aileen Paterson affectionately and amusingly highlights the importance of external factors such as a good school and material goods, sometimes at the expense of more worthwhile internal qualities (at its extreme, summed up in the apt expression "She's all fur coat and nae knickers"), in her Maisie series. The books, set in the "fur coat" Edinburgh suburb of Morningside tell the story of Maisie, a kitten sent to live with her grandmother in a typical Edinburgh tenement building. Maisie also visits many Scottish landmarks, such as the Royal Museum in Edinburgh and Loch Ness.

The darker side of Edinburgh appears in Ian Rankin's excellent Inspector Rebus crime thrillers. They cunningly contrast the architecture and wealth of Edinburgh's Old and New towns and the poverty of public housing occupants. Among his best works are *Let It Bleed, Mortal Causes,* and *Black and Blue*. Even harder-hitting is *Trainspotting,* by Irvine Welsh, with its depiction of disaffected Edinburgh youth and the drug scene in the city's public housing districts. Neither will impinge on the average visitor, however.

Glasgow, too, has its dark side, chronicled in William McIlvanney's Inspector Jack Laidlaw crime books. There are three: *Laidlaw, The Papers of Tony Veitch,* and *Strange Loyalties*. Perhaps his best known work, however, is *Docherty,* which won the Whitbread Prize in 1975 and is set in the fictional Ayrshire town of Graithnock (a thinly disguised Kilmarnock). It illustrates the deprivations and aspirations of the Scottish working class in the early 20th century.

The novels of Lewis Grassic Gibbon (pseudonym of James Leslie Mitchell, 1901–35) are set in the bleak farmlands of Kincardineshire, in an area known as the Howe of Mearns, south of Stonehaven, where he grew up. His trilogy *A Scots Quair* (*Sunset Song, Cloud Howe,* and *Grey Granite*) incorporates the rhythms and cadences of speech in the northeast, which you can still hear today. The unremitting harshness of farming life, described in *A Scots Quair,* is still to some extent valid today, despite the advent of modern machinery and farming practices: this is not the lush, warm countryside of southern England. Nonetheless, the spare beauty of the landscape—with its patchwork of fields rising to higher ground and a spectacular coastline with towering cliffs and white-sand beaches—rewards those who visit the area. While in this part of Scotland, visit Glamis Castle, mentioned in Shakespeare's *Macbeth,* and said to be the most haunted castle in Scotland. Or travel northwest to Cawdor, near Nairn, to visit beautiful Cawdor Castle, the supposed home of Macbeth, Thane of Cawdor. It has 600 years worth of furniture, paintings, and artifacts within its walls.

Another writer and poet whose work is intimately related to his environment is George Mackay Brown (1921–96), born in Stromness, Orkney. His work reflects Orkney's rich heritage of prehistoric sites, its farming and fishing communities, and its religious history. *Greenvoe* vividly describes life in an imaginary Orkney village; you may also want to read *Fishermen with Ploughs* or his other books of poems.

Brown was greatly influenced by the 13th-century *Orkneyinga Saga*, which tells of Magnus, Orkney's own saint, and the earls of Orkney. The glowing, reddish-stone St. Magnus Cathedral is still a center of worship in Kirkwall and well worth a visit for its warmly enclosed, ancient atmosphere and the carvings on its grave slabs. Also open to visitors are the ruins of Earl Patrick's Palace, in Kirkwall, and Earl's Palace at Birsay; both date from the 16th century, testifying to the continuing status and wealth of the earls of Orkney over the centuries.

Scotland's most famous poet and champion of the underdog was Robert Burns (1759–96), who found inspiration in the landscapes of his native Ayrshire in Southwest Scotland. His poems and songs will never be far away during your visit, and indeed he has been translated into more languages than any other poet writing in English, including Shakespeare. The Burns Heritage Trail takes you to Alloway, where you can visit his birthplace; to Auld Alloway Kirk, where Tam o'Shanter saw the witches; and to the Tam o'Shanter Experience, a tourist attraction that brings the poem to life. Burns Night (January 25) is still a fixture on the Scottish calendar, with readings of "To a Haggis" and "The Selkirk Grace" being the highlights.

For a taste of life in the Scottish Hebridean islands before you arrive, read Mairi Hedderwick's delightful Katie Morag stories, set on a Hebridean island. Children's stories they may be, but for insights into life on the islands—positive and negative—they are hard to equal. Many teenagers on the islands still dream of their eventual escape to Glasgow or Edinburgh, just as they did 50 or 100 years ago, and Katie Morag's day-to-day life perhaps shows why: the islands are not rich in dance clubs, sports and entertainment centers, fashion boutiques, or Internet cafés. But they are rich in community spirit, tradition and music, and beauty of land and seascape, all of which comes across vividly both in Mairi Hedderwick's text and in the superb, amusingly detailed illustrations. *Kaite Morag and the Big Boy Cousins* is a good title to start with.

Historical novels are a painless way to absorb some of Scotland's history. Mollie Hunter's work is geared toward teenagers; *Escape from Loch Leven* deals with Mary, Queen of Scots, and *The Ghosts of Glencoe* covers the infamous Glencoe massacre. Eric Linklater's *The Prince in the Heather* tells of Bonnie Prince Charlie's efforts to escape after the failure of the 1745 Jacobite rebellion. D. K. Broster's *The Flight of the Heron* and its sequel, *The Dark Mile,* deal with the changes to the clan system effected by the defeat of the Jacobites at Culloden in the mid-18th century. If you want your history fiction-free, try *Scotland: A New History* by Michael Lynch. Though he's one of the country's foremost historians, this is no dry read, and it takes you from Scotland's distant past right up until the beginning of the 1990s.

And then there are those quintessentially Scottish books that you are told to read (but few, even Scottish people, seem to get around to reading). The novels and narrative poems of Sir Walter Scott (1771–1832) don't seem very user-friendly these days, and with their lengthy introductions, melodramatic plots, overpowering wealth of historical detail, and stately language, they offer no instant gratification. But Scott not only tells a great story, he is historically accurate, and his settings among the hills and river valleys of southern Scotland are not so very different today: try reading *Rob Roy* or *The Lady of the Lake* when traveling in the Trossachs, or *Redgauntlet* if you're in Dumfries and Galloway.

Also a top storyteller was Robert Louis Stevenson (1850–1894), born in Edinburgh though destined to spend much of his life outside Scotland. Read *Kidnapped* and shiver amid the bleak expanse of Rannoch Moor. Then go and gaze across that very moor—its gray, brown, and watery wastes so accurately described by Stevenson—and imagine being a fugitive among its hummocks and pools.

The *Oxford Literary Guide to the British Isles,* edited by Dorothy Eagle and Hilary Carnell, *A Reader's Guide to Writers' Britain* by Sally Varlow, and *Scotland: A Literary Guide,* by Alan Bold, can direct you to other literary landscapes in addition to those mentioned above.

And what about essential reference books to take around with you as you explore Scotland? The series of guides to Scotland's regional architecture produced by the Rutland Press, the publishing wing of the RIAS (Royal Incorporation of Architects in Scotland), are well illustrated, easy to read, and compact enough to keep in the car glove compartment or a handbag. If you enjoy walking, the Official Guides produced for the West Highland Way, the Southern Upland Way, and the Speyside Way are invaluable, and can be purchased locally or before you arrive. There are also several walking guides available locally, including *Walk Loch Lomond and the Trossachs* and *Walk Perthshire.*

Movies

The quintessential "kilt movies" are *Rob Roy* (1995), with Liam Neeson and Jessica Lange—shot at and around Glen Nevis and Glencoe, the gardens of Drummond Castle, and Crichton Castle—and Mel Gibson's *Braveheart* (1995), the story of Scotland's first freedom fighter, Sir William Wallace (circa 1270–1305), which also uses the spectacular craggy scenery of Glen Nevis. Both films are great on atmosphere, not so hot on accurate historical detail, but give a fine preview of Scotland's varied scenery. *Highlander* (1986), with Christopher Lambert and Sean Connery, also uses the spectacular crags of Glencoe, along with the prototypical Scottish castle Eilean Donan—almost a visual cliché in Scottish terms. Mel Gibson's *Hamlet* (1990) was filmed at the far more dramatic ruins of cliff-top Dunnottar Castle, Stonehaven, on the coast south of Aberdeen.

The movie of the Scottish classic tale by Muriel Spark, *The Prime of Miss Jean Brodie* (1969), starring Maggie Smith, was filmed in several locations around Edinburgh (as well as in London). In stark contrast, *Trainspotting* (1996), starring Ewan McGregor and based on the book by Irvine Welsh, is a commentary on heroin addicts in a depressed Edinburgh housing scheme. *Small Faces* (1995), written and directed by Gillies MacKinnon, sketches a gritty picture of Glasgow and its gangland violence in the 1960s.

On a more off-beat (and upbeat) note, get hold of *Local Hero* (1983), with Burt Lancaster and Peter Riegert. Set in the northeast of Scotland but incorporating a west-coast white-sand beach, the film portrays the best of the east and the west coasts. In the movie the village of Pennan, an hour's drive north of Aberdeen, which huddles below spectacular cliffs, became Ferness, a village threatened by oil development. The village phone box (telephone booth), which played an important part in the film's story, has been carefully preserved. (And, yes, you can see the aurora borealis [the northern lights] from it—sometimes.)

For sheer enjoyment, try to see *Her Majesty, Mrs Brown* (1997), known in Scotland as *Mrs Brown,* and starring Dame Judi Dench and Billy Connolly. It tells the story of Queen Victoria and John Brown, her favorite gillie, and was filmed at locations in the Borders and the Highlands, with the Ardverikie Estate near Dalwhinnie standing in for the Balmoral policies.

For more information on movies filmed in Scotland, you can buy *The Pocket Scottish Movie Book* by Brian Pendreigh, or you can visit the Scotland the Movie Guide Web site (🌐 www.scotlandthemovieguide.com).

CHRONOLOGY

7000 BC Hunter & gatherers move north into Scotland after the last Ice Age recedes, leaving arrowheads and bone implements as testimony to their passing.

ca. 6000 BC First settlers arrive, bringing farming methods with them.

ca. 3000 BC Neolithic migration from Mediterranean: "chambered cairn" people in north (such as the Grey Cairns of Camster), "beaker people" in southeast.

ca. 300 BC Iron Age: infusion of Celtic peoples from the south and from Ireland; "Gallic forts" and "brochs" (towers) built.

AD 79–89 Julius Agricola (AD 40–93), Roman governor of Britain, invades Scotland; Scots tribes defeated at the battle of Mons Graupius (thought to be somewhere in the Grampians). Roman forts built at Inchtuthil and Ardoch.

142 Emperor Antoninus Pius (86–161) orders the defensive Antonine Wall built between the Firths of Forth and Clyde.

185 Antonine Wall abandoned.

400–500 Tribes of Celtic origin, including the Scotti, emigrate from Ireland to present day Argyllshire and establish the kingdom of Dalriada.

392 St. Ninian's (ca. 360–432) mission to Picts sets out from the first Christian chapel at Whitehorn.

400–843 Four kingdoms exist in Scotland: Dalriada (Argyllshire), the kingdom of the Picts (Aberdeenshire down to Fife and the Highlands excepting Argyllshire), Strathclyde (Southwest Scotland), and the Lothians (Edinburgh and the Borders).

563 Columba (ca. 521–97) establishes monastery at Iona.

843 Kenneth MacAlpin, king of Dalriada, unites with the Picts while remaining king. Thus the embryonic Kingdom of Scotland is born, with its capital at Scone.

780–1065 Scandinavian invasions; Hebrides remain Norse until 1263, Orkney and Shetland until 1472.

1018 Malcolm II (ca. 953–1034) brings the Lothians into the Kingdom of Scotland and (temporarily) repels the English.

1034 Duncan (d. 1040), king of Strathclyde, ascends the throne of Scotland and unification is complete.

1040 Duncan is slain by his rival, Macbeth (d. 1057), whose wife has a claim to the throne.

House of Canmore

1057 Malcolm III (ca. 1031–93), known as Canmore (Big Head), murders Macbeth and assumes the throne.

1093 Death of Malcolm's queen, St. Margaret (1046–93), who brought Roman Catholicism to Scotland.

1124–53 David I (ca. 1082–1153), *sair sanct* (sore saint), builds the abbeys of Jedburgh (1118), Kelso (1128), Melrose (1136), and Dryburgh (1150) and brings Norman culture to Scotland.

1290 Death of Alexander III, great great grandson of David I. The heir is his granddaughter, Margaret, Maid of Norway (1283–1290). She dies at sea on her way from Norway to claim the Scottish throne and marry the future Edward II (1284–1327), son of Edward I of England (1239–1307). The Scots naively ask Edward I, subsequently known as the Hammer of the Scots, to arbitrate between the remaining 13 claimants to the throne. Edward's choice, John Balliol (1249–1315), is known as Toom Tabard (Empty Coat).

1295 Under continued threat from England, Scotland signs its first treaty of the "auld alliance" with France. Wine trade flourishes.

1297 Revolutionary William Wallace (ca. 1270–1305), immortalized by Burns, leads the Scots against the English.

1305 Wallace captured by the English and executed.

1306–29 Reign of Robert the Bruce (1274–1329), later to become King Robert I. Defeats Edward II (1284–1327) at Bannockburn, 1314; Treaty of Northampton, 1328, recognizes Scottish sovereignty.

House of Stewart

1371 Robert II (1316–90), the first Stewart monarch and son of Robert the Bruce's daughter Marjorie and Walter the Steward, is crowned. Struggle (dramatized in Scott's novels) between the crown and the barony ensues for the next century, punctuated by sporadic warfare with England.

1411 University of St. Andrews founded.

1451 University of Glasgow founded.

1488–1513 Reign of James IV (1473–1513). The Renaissance reaches Scotland. The Golden Age of Scots poetry includes Robert Henryson (ca. 1425–1508), William Dunbar (ca. 1460–1530), Gavin Douglas (1474–1522), and the king himself.

1495 University of Aberdeen founded.

1507 Andrew Myllar and Walter Chapman set up first Scots printing press in Edinburgh.

1513 After invading England in support of the French, James IV is slain at Flodden.

1542 Henry VIII (1491–1547) defeats James V (1512–42) at Solway Moss; the dying James, hearing of the birth of his daughter, Mary, declares: "It came with a lass [Marjorie Bruce] and it will pass with a lass."

1542–67 Reign of Mary, Queen of Scots (1542–87). Romantic, Catholic, and with an excellent claim to the English throne, Mary proved to be no match for her barons, John Knox (1513–72), or her cousin Elizabeth I (1533–1603) of England.

1560 Mary returns to Scotland from France after the death of her husband, Francis II of France, at the same time that Catholicism is abolished in favor of Protestantism. The spelling "Stuart" adopted instead of "Stewart."

1565 Mary marries Lord Darnley (1545–67), a Catholic.

1567 Darnley is murdered at Kirk o' Field; Mary marries one of the conspirators, the earl of Bothwell (ca. 1535–78). Driven from Scotland, she appeals to Elizabeth, who imprisons her. Mary's son, James (1566–1625), is crowned James VI of Scotland.

1582 University of Edinburgh is founded.

1587 Elizabeth orders the execution of Mary.

1603 Elizabeth dies without issue; James VI is crowned James I of England. Parliaments remain separate for another century.

1638 National Covenant challenges Charles I's personal rule.

1639–41 Crisis. The Scots and then the English parliaments revolt against Charles I (1600–49).

1643 Solemn League and Covenant establishes Presbyterianism as the Church of Scotland (the Kirk). Civil War in England.

1649 Charles I beheaded. Oliver Cromwell (1599–1658) made Protector.

1650–52 Cromwell roots out Scots royalists.

1658 The first Edinburgh–London coach is established. The journey takes two weeks.

1660 Restoration of Charles II (1630–85). Episcopalianism reestablished in Scotland; Covenanters persecuted.

1688–89 Glorious Revolution; James VII and II (1633–1701; the first title is Scottish, the second English), a Catholic, deposed in favor of his daughter Mary (1662–94) and her husband, William of Orange (1650–1702). Supporters of James (known as Jacobites) defeated at Killiecrankie. Presbyterianism reestablished.

1692 Highlanders who were late in taking oath to William and Mary massacred at Glencoe.

1698–1700 Attempted Scottish colony at Darien fails. Many of the Scottish nobility face bankruptcy, and are therefore open to overtures from an English government anxious to unite the Scottish and English parliaments.

1707 Union of English and Scots parliaments under Queen Anne (1665–1714), the last Stuart monarch; deprived of French wine trade, Scots turn to whisky.

House of Hanover

1714 Queen Anne dies; George I (1660–1727) of Hanover, descended from a daughter of James VI and I, crowned.

1715 First Jacobite Rebellion. Earl of Mar (1675–1732) defeated.

1730–90 Scottish Enlightenment. The Edinburgh Medical School is the best in Europe; David Hume (1711–76) and Adam Smith (1723–90) redefine philosophy and economics. In the arts, Allan Ramsay the elder (1686–1758) and Robert Burns (1759–96) refine Scottish poetry; Allan Ramsay the younger (1713–84) and Henry Raeburn (1756–1823) rank among the finest painters of the era. Edinburgh's New Town, begun in the 1770s by the brothers Adam (Robert, 1728–92; brother James, 1730–94; father William 1689–1748), provides a fitting setting.

1745–46 Last Jacobite Rebellion. Bonnie Prince Charlie (1720–88), grandson of James VII and II, is defeated at Culloden and eventually escapes back to France; wearing of the kilt is forbidden until 1782. James Watt (1736–1819), born in Greenock, is granted a patent for his steam engine.

1771 Birth of Walter Scott (1771–1832), Romantic novelist.

1778 First cotton mill, at Rothesay.

1788 Death of Bonnie Prince Charlie in Rome.

1790 Forth and Clyde Canal opened.

1800–50 Highland Clearances: increased rents, and conversion of farms to sheep pasture lead to mass migration, sometimes forced, to North America and elsewhere. Meanwhile, the Lowlands industrialize; Catholic Irish immigrate to factories of Glasgow and the southwest.

1822 Visit of George IV to Scotland, the first British monarch to do so since Charles I. Sir Walter Scott orchestrates the visit, and almost single-handedly invents Scotland's national costume: the formal kilt, tartan plaid, and jacket.

1828 Execution of Burke, who, with his partner Hare, sold their murder victims to an Edinburgh anatomist, a lucrative trade. Hare was released after giving evidence against Burke.

1832 Parliamentary Reform Act expands the franchise, redistributes seats.

1837 Victoria (1819–1901) ascends to the British throne.

1842 Edinburgh–Glasgow railroad opened.

1846 Edinburgh–London railroad opened.

1848 Queen Victoria buys estate at Balmoral as her Scottish residence. Andrew Carnegie emigrates from Dunfermline to Pittsburgh.

1884–85 Gladstone's Reform Act establishes manhood suffrage. Office of Secretary for Scotland authorized.

1886 Scottish Home Rule Association founded.

1890 Forth Rail Bridge opened.

1901 Death of Queen Victoria.

House of Windsor

1928 Equal Franchise Act gives the vote to women. Scottish Office established as governmental department in Edinburgh. Scottish National Party founded.

1931 Depression hits industrialized Scotland severely.

1945 Two Scottish Nationalists elected to parliament.

1959 Finnart Oil Terminal, Chapelcross Nuclear Power Station, and Dounreay Fast Breeder Reactor opened.

1964 Forth Road Bridge opened.

1970 British Petroleum strikes oil in the North Sea; revives economy of northeast.

1973 Britain becomes a member of the European Economic Community (formerly known as the Common Market).

1974 Eleven Scottish Nationalists elected as members of parliament. Old counties reorganized and renamed as new regions and districts.

1979 Referendum on devolution—the creation of a separate Scotland: 33% for, 31% against; 36% don't vote.

1981 Europe's largest oil terminal opens at Sullom Voe, Shetland.

1992 Increasing attention focused on Scotland's dissatisfaction with rule from London. Poll shows 50% of Scots want independence.

1995 In the face of a Tory government that looks increasingly like a lame duck, and divided on the issue of Europe, Scotland continues to argue its own way forward. The Labour Party, if elected in the 1997 general election, promises a Scottish parliament but wants to keep Scotland within the United Kingdom; the Scottish National Party still wants independence and sees Labour's Scottish parliament as a stepping-stone to full autonomy.

1997 The Labour Party wins the general election in May. A referendum held in Scotland votes in favor of the establishment of a Scottish parliament (with restricted powers).

1999 Scotland elects its first parliament in 200 years. A coalition is formed between the Labour Party and the Liberal Democrats to run the country.

2000 Death of Scotland's first, and much respected, First Minister, Donald Dewar. Henry McLeish becomes First Minister.

2001 Henry McLeish resigns amid scandal. Jack McConnel becomes First Minister.

2002 The Millennium Link—the restoration of the canal link between Glasgow and Edinburgh—completed at a cost of £78 million. It includes the Falkirk Wheel, the world's only rotating boat lift.

INDEX

NOTES

NOTES

NOTES

NOTES

NOTES

NOTES

FODOR'S KEY TO THE GUIDES

America's guidebook leader publishes guides for every kind of traveler. Check out our many series and find your perfect match.

FODOR'S GOLD GUIDES

America's favorite travel-guide series offers the most detailed insider reviews of hotels, restaurants, and attractions in all price ranges, plus great background information, smart tips, and useful maps.

COMPASS AMERICAN GUIDES

Stunning guides from top local writers and photographers, with gorgeous photos, literary excerpts, and colorful anecdotes. A must-have for culture mavens, history buffs, and new residents.

FODOR'S CITYPACKS

Concise city coverage in a guide plus a foldout map. The right choice for urban travelers who want everything under one cover.

FODOR'S EXPLORING GUIDES

Hundreds of color photos bring your destination to life. Lively stories lend insight into the culture, history, and people.

FODOR'S TRAVEL HISTORIC AMERICA

For travelers who want to experience history firsthand, this series gives in-depth coverage of historic sights, plus nearby restaurants and hotels. Themes include the Thirteen Colonies, the Old West, and the Lewis and Clark Trail.

FODOR'S POCKET GUIDES

For travelers who need only the essentials. The best of Fodor's in pocket-size packages for just $9.95.

FODOR'S FLASHMAPS

Every resident's map guide, with 60 easy-to-follow maps of public transit, parks, museums, zip codes, and more.

FODOR'S CITYGUIDES

Sourcebooks for living in the city: thousands of in-the-know listings for restaurants, shops, sports, nightlife, and other city resources.

FODOR'S AROUND THE CITY WITH KIDS

Up to 68 great ideas for family days, recommended by resident parents. Perfect for exploring in your own backyard or on the road.

FODOR'S HOW TO GUIDES

Get tips from the pros on planning the perfect trip. Learn how to pack, fly hassle-free, plan a honeymoon or cruise, stay healthy on the road, and travel with your baby.

FODOR'S LANGUAGES FOR TRAVELERS

Practice the local language before you hit the road. Available in phrase books, cassette sets, and CD sets.

KAREN BROWN'S GUIDES

Engaging guides—many with easy-to-follow inn-to-inn itineraries—to the most charming inns and B&Bs in the U.S.A. and Europe.

BAEDEKER'S GUIDES

Comprehensive guides, trusted since 1829, packed with A–Z reviews and star ratings.

OTHER GREAT TITLES FROM FODOR'S

Baseball Vacations, The Complete Guide to the National Parks, Family Vacations, Golf Digest's Places to Play, Great American Drives of the East, Great American Drives of the West, Great American Vacations, Healthy Escapes, National Parks of the West, Skiing USA.

At bookstores everywhere. www.fodors.com/books